Newman after a Hundred Years

Newman after a Hundred Years

EDITED BY
IAN KER
AND
ALAN G. HILL

CLARENDON PRESS · OXFORD
1990

Oxford University Press, Walton Street, Oxford OX2 6DP
Oxford New York Toronto
Delhi Bombay Calcutta Madras Karachi
Petaling Jaya Singapore Hong Kong Tokyo
Nairobi Dar es Salaam Cape Town
Melbourne Auckland
and associated companies in
Berlin Ibadan

Oxford is a trade mark of Oxford University Press

Published in the United States
by Oxford University Press, New York

British Library Cataloguing in Publication Data
Newman after a hundred years.
1. England. Catholic Church. Newman, John Henry, 1801–1890
I. Ker, Ian II. Hill, Alan G. (Alan Geoffrey), 1931–
282.092
ISBN 0–19–812891–6

Library of Congress Cataloging in Publication Data
p. cm.
Newman after a hundred years / edited by Ian Ker and Alan G. Hill.
(Oxford University Press)
1. Newman, John Henry, 1801–1890—Criticism and interpretation.
I. Ker, Ian. II. Hill, Alan G.
PR5109.N218 1990
828'.809—dc20 90–30481
ISBN 0–19–812891–6

Set by Hope Services (Abingdon) Ltd
Printed and bound in
Great Britain by Biddles Ltd,
Guildford and King's Lynn

Preface and Acknowledgements

THE genius of John Henry Newman is now surely universally acknowledged, after all the misunderstandings of his lifetime and the controversies that followed his death in 1890. But the full range and scope of his achievements—literary, historical, educational, philosophical, theological—have still to be more fully appreciated.

In this centenary year, we have invited Newman scholars, as well as scholars of distinction in other fields who are not Newman specialists, to join together in a reappraisal of Newman's significance after a hundred years. No single collection of essays could encompass the entire range of Newman's 'imperial intellect'. But we have attempted to concentrate on breaking new ground in hitherto more or less unexplored areas of his writings, and on eliciting authoritative reassessments of some central aspects of his thought.

We are grateful to the Revd Richard Franklin for his advice, and Keith LaVon Dvorak, jun., for his assistance, in the preparation of this volume.

I.T.K.
A.G.H.

Contents

Notes on Contributors

JEROME H. BUCKLEY is Gurney Professor Emeritus of English Literature, Harvard University. His books include *The Victorian Temper* (1951), *Tennyson: The Growth of a Poet* (1960), *The Triumph of Time* (1966), and *The Turning Key: Autobiography and the Subjective Impulse since 1800* (1984).

HENRY CHADWICK is Master of Peterhouse, Cambridge. His books include *Early Christian Thought and the Classical Tradition* (1966), *The Early Church* (1967), *Boethius* (1981), *Augustine* (1986), and *Origen contra Celsum* (3rd edn., 1980).

A. O. J. COCKSHUT is All Souls (G. M. Young) Lecturer in nineteenth-century English Literature and Fellow of Hertford College, Oxford. His books include *The Unbelievers* (1964), *Truth to Life* (1974), and *The Art of Autobiography* (1984).

AVERY DULLES, SJ is the Laurence J. McGinley Professor of Religion and Society, Fordham University, New York. His books include *Models of the Church* (1974) and *Models of Revelation* (1983).

JOHN FINNIS is Professor of Law and Legal Philosophy and Fellow of University College, Oxford. He is the author of *Natural Law and Natural Rights* (1980), *Fundamentals of Ethics* (1983), and *Nuclear Deterrence, Morality and Realism*, with Joseph Boyle and Germain Grisez (1987).

ERIC GRIFFITHS is Lecturer in English and Fellow of Trinity College, Cambridge. He is the author of *The Printed Voice of Victorian Poetry* (1989).

COLIN GUNTON is Professor of Christian Doctrine, King's College, University of London. He is the author of *Becoming and Being: The Doctrine of God in Charles Hartshorne and Karl Barth* (1978), *Yesterday and Today: A Study of Continuities in Christology* (1983), *Enlightenment and Alienation: An Essay Towards a Trinitarian Theology* (1985), and *The Actuality of Atonement: A Study of Metaphor, Rationality and the Christian Tradition* (1989).

ALAN G. HILL is Professor of English Language and Literature, Royal Holloway and Bedford New College, University of London.

He is general editor of *The Letters of William and Dorothy Wordsworth*, 8 vols. (1967–), and principal contributor to the series. He has also edited Newman's *Loss and Gain: The Story of a Convert* (1986).

IAN KER formerly held the Endowed Chair in Theology and Philosophy, College of St Thomas, Minnesota, USA. He is the author of *John Henry Newman: A Biography* (1988), editor of the Oxford critical editions of Newman's *The Idea of a University* (1976) and *An Essay in Aid of a Grammar of Assent* (1985), and coeditor of *The Letters and Diaries of John Henry Newman*, vols. i–iv (1978–80).

NICHOLAS LASH is Norris-Hulse Professor of Divinity and Fellow of Clare Hall, Cambridge. His publications include *Newman on Development: The Search for an Explanation in History* (1975), *A Matter of Hope: A Theologian's Reflections on the Thought of Karl Marx* (1981), and *Easter in Ordinary: Reflections on Human Experience and the Knowledge of God* (1988).

HUGO MEYNELL is Professor of Religious Studies, University of Calgary. His books include *Freud, Marx and Morals* (1981), *The Intelligible Universe* (1982), and *The Nature of Aesthetic Value* (1986).

BASIL MITCHELL was formerly Nolloth Professor of the Philosophy of the Christian Religion, Oxford University. His publications include *The Justification of Religious Belief* (1973), *Law, Morality and Religion in a Secular Society* (1967), and *Morality: Religious and Secular* (1980).

EDWARD NORMAN was formerly Lecturer in Modern History and Dean of Peterhouse, Cambridge. His publications include *Church and Society in Modern England* (1976) and *The English Catholic Church in the Nineteenth Century* (1984).

GERALD O'COLLINS, SJ is Professor of Fundamental Theology, Gregorian University, Rome, where he is Dean of the theology faculty. His publications include *The Easter Jesus* (1973), *Fundamental Theology* (1981), *Interpreting Jesus* (1983), *Jesus Risen* (1987), and *Interpreting the Resurrection* (1989).

MARVIN R. O'CONNELL is Professor of History, University of Notre Dame, Indiana. His books include *Thomas Stapleton and the Counter Reformation* (1964), *The Oxford Conspirators: A History of the Oxford Reformation 1833–1845* (1969), *The Counter Reformation 1559–1610* (1974), and *John Ireland and the American Catholic Church* (1988).

J. M. Roberts was formerly Vice-Chancellor, University of Southampton and is now Warden of Merton College, Oxford. Among his publications are *The Mythology of the Secret Societies* (1972), *The Paris Commune seen from the Right* (1974), a *History of the World* (1976), *The French Revolution* (1978), and *The Triumph of the West* (1985).

Roger Sharrock is Emeritus Professor of English Language and Literature, King's College, University of London. He is the author of *Saints, Sinners and Comedians: The Novels of Graham Greene* (1984) and the editor of the Oxford edition of Bunyan's works.

Roderick Strange was Catholic Chaplain at Oxford University. He is the author of *Newman and the Gospel of Christ* (1981) and *The Catholic Faith* (1986).

Francis A. Sullivan, SJ is Professor of Theology, Gregorian University, Rome. He is the author of *The Christology of Theodore of Mopsuestia* (1956), *Charisms and Charismatic Renewal* (1982), *Magisterium; Teaching Authority in the Catholic Church* (1983), and *The Church We Believe In* (1989).

S. W. Sykes was formerly Regius Professor of Divinity and Fellow of St John's College, Cambridge, and is now Bishop of Ely. He is the author of *Friedrich Schleiermacher* (1971), *Christian Theology Today* (1971), *The Integrity of Anglicanism* (1978), and *The Identity of Christianity* (1984).

Rowan Williams is Lady Margaret Professor of Divinity and Canon of Christ Church, Oxford. He is the author of *The Wound of Knowledge: Christian Spirituality from the New Testament to St John of the Cross* (1979) and *Arius: Heresy and Tradition* (1987).

Abbreviations

NEWMAN collected his works in a uniform edition of 36 volumes. (1868–81). Until his death in 1890 he continued making minor textual changes in reprints of individual volumes in this edition, of which all the volumes from 1886 were published by Longmans, Green, and Co. of London. References are usually to volumes in the uniform edition published after 1890 by Longmans, which are distinguished from other editions by not including publication details in brackets after the title.

Apo.	*Apologia pro Vita Sua*, ed. Martin J. Svaglic (Oxford, 1967)
Ari.	*The Arians of the Fourth Century*
Ath. i, ii	*Select Treatises of St. Athanasius*, 2 vols.
AW	*John Henry Newman: Autobiographical Writings*, ed. Henry Tristram (London and New York, 1956)
Call.	*Callista: A Tale of the Third Century*
Campaign	*My Campaign in Ireland, Part I*, ed. W. Neville (privately printed, 1896)
CS	*Catholic Sermons of Cardinal Newman*, ed. at the Birmingham Oratory (London, 1957)
Cons.	*On Consulting the Faithful in Matters of Doctrine*, ed. John Coulson (London, 1961)
DA	*Discussions and Arguments on Various Subjects*
Dev.	*An Essay on the Development of Christian Doctrine*
Diff. i, ii	*Certain Difficulties felt by Anglicans in Catholic Teaching*, 2 vols.
Ess. i, ii	*Essays Critical and Historical*, 2 vols.
GA	*An Essay in Aid of a Grammar of Assent*, ed. I. T. Ker (Oxford, 1985)
HS i, ii, iii	*Historical Sketches*, 3 vols.
Idea	*The Idea of a University*, ed. I. T. Ker (Oxford, 1976)
Jfc.	*Lectures on the Doctrine of Justification*
KC	*Correspondence of John Henry Newman with John Keble and Others 1839–1845*, ed. at the Birmingham Oratory (London, 1917)
LD	*The Letters and Diaries of John Henry Newman*, ed. Charles Stephen Dessain *et al.*, vols. i–vi (Oxford, 1978–84), xi–xxii (London, 1961–72), xxiii–xxxi (Oxford, 1973–7)

LG	*Loss and Gain: The Story of a Convert*
Mir.	*Two Essays on Biblical and on Ecclesiastical Miracles*
Mix.	*Discourses addressed to Mixed Congregations*
Moz. i, ii	*Letters and Correspondence of John Henry Newman during his Life in the English Church*, ed. Anne Mozley, 2 vols. (London, 1891)
OS	*Sermons preached on Various Occasions*
PS i–viii	*Parochial and Plain Sermons*, 8 vols.
Phil. N. i, ii	*The Philosophical Notebook of John Henry Newman*, ed. Edward Sillem, 2 vols. (Louvain, 1969–70)
Pre. Pos.	*Lectures on the Present Position of Catholics in England*
SD	*Sermons bearing on Subjects of the Day*
SN	*Sermon Notes of John Henry Cardinal Newman 1849–1878*, ed. Fathers of the Birmingham Oratory (London, 1913)
TP i	*The Theological Papers of John Henry Newman on Faith and Certainty*, ed. Hugo M. de Achaval, SJ, and J. Derek Holmes (Oxford, 1976)
TP ii	*The Theological Papers of John Henry Newman on Biblical Inspiration and on Infallibility*, ed J. Derek Holmes (Oxford, 1979)
TT	*Tracts Theological and Ecclesiastical*
US	*Fifteen Sermons preached before the University of Oxford*
VM i, ii	*The Via Media of the Anglican Church*, 2 vols.
VV	*Verses on Various Occasions*
Ward i, ii	Wilfrid Ward, *The Life of John Henry Cardinal Newman*, 2 vols. (London, 1912)

1

Newman the Satirist

IAN KER

A comparison of the latest edition of *The Oxford Companion to English Literature* with its predecessor shows little change in the received view of Newman's literary standing. The *Apologia*, which is the only book that both entries praise as a work of literature, is no longer called 'a literary masterpiece', but the new entry does draw attention not merely to its 'sincerity' but also to its 'formidable powers of argument'. *Loss and Gain* received a bare mention in 1967, but in 1985 it is acknowledged to be a 'vivid portrait', distinguished for its 'satiric wit'. However, this small advance in appreciation of Newman as a writer is offset by the fact that the later entry completely ignores *Lectures on the Present Position of Catholics in England*, which at least in the earlier edition was noted for being 'fiercely contemptuous'. On the other hand, there is no longer any attempt to highlight the verse, the only work in the previous entry, apart from the *Apologia*, that was judged to be of any literary significance. Yet it still receives honorific mention, while the *Tamworth Reading Room* and *Difficulties of Anglicans*, not to mention the letters, simply do not exist as far as either *Oxford Companion* is concerned. The continued reference to the verse, which by any reckoning must surely be deemed to belong to the category of 'minor' poetry, taken together with the absence of any awareness of works, which at least from the literary point of view must be counted among Newman's finest writings, shows clearly enough that the real nature of Newman's originality and greatness as a writer is still generally unrecognized. The only omission that would possibly cause some general surprise is the lack of any acknowledgement of the stylist and the rhetorician, not to mention the eloquence of the preacher.[1]

[1] *The Oxford Companion to English Literature*, ed. Sir Paul Harvey, rev. D. Eagle (4th edn., Oxford, 1967), 577; op. cit., ed. M. Drabble (5th edn., Oxford, 1985), 694–5.

To say that to all intents and purposes Newman is known as the author of a moving religious autobiography and some eloquent lectures on the idea of a university, would be a reasonable account of his current literary reputation. It is true that the growth of Victorian studies in recent times has led to some excellent critical studies of particular aspects of Newman, such as his rhetoric and prose style[2] and his development of the form of the religious novel.[3] A new surge of interest in the genre of autobiography has also produced some fresh evaluations of the *Apologia*.[4] But it can hardly be denied that Newman has been better served, if one may make the distinction, by the scholars than the critics: there is no criticism that can compare with A. Dwight Culler's illuminating educational biography[5] or David J. DeLaura's seminal work on Newman's literary influence.[6] The one outstanding partial exception remains Geoffrey Tillotson's brilliant but brief attempt to establish Newman's literary genius.[7] And even that essay fails, I think, to focus sufficiently on Newman's true originality as a writer, although it admirably emphasizes such qualities as the personal tone of voice, the concreteness, the imagery, and the vivid clarity.[8]

Tillotson rightly stresses the 'occasional' nature of most of Newman's writings, but he fails, it seems to me, to understand

[2] Especially by John Holloway in his critique of the rhetorical techniques in *The Victorian Sage: Studies in Argument* (London, 1953), 158–201. There are also some perceptive stylistic points in W. E. Houghton, *The Art of Newman's Apologia* (New Haven, Conn., 1945), 50–7.

[3] See *Loss and Gain: The Story of a Convert*, ed. A. G. Hill (Oxford, 1986), pp. vii–xix.

[4] See esp. A. O. J. Cockshut, *The Art of Autobiography in 19th and 20th Century England* (New Haven, Conn., and London, 1984), 209–14; L. H. Peterson, 'Newman's *Apologia Pro Vita Sua*: The Dilemma of the Catholic Autobiographer', in ead., *Victorian Autobiography: The Tradition of Self-Interpretation* (New Haven, Conn., and London, 1986), 93–211.

[5] A. D. Culler, *The Imperial Intellect: A Study of Newman's Educational Ideal* (New Haven, Conn., and London, 1955). I say 'biography' advisedly because the latter part of the study, which is a rather confused critique of Newman's educational theory, compares badly with the earlier factual account of his life as a student and teacher.

[6] D. J. Delaura, *Hebrew and Hellene in Victorian England: Newman, Arnold, and Pater* (Austin, Tex., and London, 1969).

[7] G. Tillotson, 'Newman the Writer', in G. and K. Tillotson, *Mid-Victorian Studies* (London, 1965), 239–58, a revised version of the Introduction to his Reynard Library selection *Newman: Prose and Poetry* (London, 1957), 7–25.

[8] It is indicative that Tillotson's literary selection from the works contains nothing from *Present Position of Catholics*.

why, in an important sense, they had to arise out of particular occasions. He suggests that Newman preferred to write under 'the psychological or social condition of having an occasion that could be agreed to be public enough to allow him not to seem obtrusive'.[9] But however true that may be, there was surely a much more important reason of a strictly literary nature. Newman's brother F. W. Newman tells us, in one of the more detached and reliable parts of his hostile little posthumous memoir, that his brother learned his skills as a controversialist from Cicero and that he could have been an 'eminent' barrister, adding that as a writer he always had to have 'a thesis to attack or defend'.[10] This is a testimony which is supported by the internal evidence of the writings.

Newman's success as an undergraduate in winning a scholarship at Trinity College, Oxford, led him for a short time to give up his cherished desire to take holy orders and instead to entertain ambitions of a more secular nature, with the result that in November 1819 he became a member of Lincoln's Inn with a view to a career at the Bar (as his father wanted). He had already advocated the formation of a university debating-society in a letter he wrote for a short-lived periodical called *The Undergraduate*, which he and his friend J. W. Bowden began in February 1819.[11] Five years later, as a fellow of Oriel, he wrote a lengthy essay on Cicero for the *Encyclopaedia Metropolitana*, in which he said not only that the Roman orator was the most interesting and attractive figure of classical antiquity, self-revealed as he was in his letters, but also that he was 'the greatest master of composition that the world has seen'. When we think of Newman's own rhetorical art, we may surely detect more than a hint of influence in this assessment of Cicero's forensic powers: 'He accounts for everything so naturally, makes trivial circumstances tell so happily, so adroitly converts apparent objections into confirmations of his argument, connects independent facts with such ease and plausibility, that it becomes impossible to entertain a question on the truth of his statement.'[12] In fact, we

[9] Tillotson, 'Newman the Writer', pp. 242, 249.

[10] F. W. Newman, *Contributions chiefly to the Early History of the Late Cardinal Newman* (2nd edn., London, 1891), 44.

[11] *LO* i. 63–4.

[12] *HS* i. 297, 293.

have Newman's own personal acknowledgement of the unique influence of Cicero:

As to patterns for imitation, the only master of style I have ever had (which is strange considering the differences of the languages) is Cicero. I think I owe a great deal to him, and as far as I know to no one else. His great mastery of Latin is shown especially in his clearness.[13]

But it is not so 'strange' if we think not just of the extraordinary luminosity of Newman's style, but also, more importantly, of Francis Newman's illuminating point that his brother 'always needed a thesis to attack or defend'. For what Newman found in Cicero was a literature of argument and controversy. Newman did not, like Cicero, compose speeches but he wrote typically to advocate or prosecute, or both at the same time. Thus it is something of a paradox that the most famous of his writings, the *Apologia*, is so unlike his other works, since, with the exception of the last chapter, documentary history (albeit, to a considerable extent, of controversy) replaces the usual cut and thrust of debate, with the result that its limpid prose is quite unique in the works. But even the *Apologia*, of course, was written because its author felt he had been placed in the dock by Kingsley and was required to defend his integrity before public opinion against his assailant's charges. Almost the only one of his books which he himself noted was not occasional in its origin was the *Grammar of Assent*, and no doubt the absence of the usual explicitly controversial element in its genesis accounts for its strikingly untypical and unreadable beginning.

The fact that Newman, then, was essentially an occasional writer is surely inseparable from the fact that he was 'a controversialist of superb gifts, perhaps the most remarkable in the history of English letters'.[14] For his most distinctive strength as a writer depended on the kind of what Newman called 'external stimulus' ('I fancy I write better when I am led to write by what comes in my way')[15] that controversy provided. Given the close connection between controversy and satire, it is hardly surprising that in his essay on Cicero, Newman emphasized the Roman orator's use of 'raillery' and 'irony'.[16] It is to this aspect of

[13] *LD* xxiv. 242.

[14] J. M. Cameron, *John Henry Newman* (London, 1956), 7.

[15] *LD* xxi. 69, 178.

[16] *HS* i. 294.

Newman's own writing that I want to turn now, as I believe that first and foremost he was not only a great controversialist but also one of the great satirical writers in the English language.

In February 1864 R. H. Hutton the literary critic wrote a two-part review of the pamphlet Newman had published containing his correspondence with Charles Kingsley. It appeared in the *Spectator*, of which Hutton was the literary editor, under the title 'Father Newman's Sarcasm'. The article claimed that Newman was 'not only one of the greatest of English writers, but, perhaps, the very greatest master of delicate and polished sarcasm in the English language'.[17] Hutton, who was not a Catholic, but who was one of the leading Victorian literary critics, was the first critic to write seriously about Newman as a writer. As we have seen, he was also almost the last. Hutton not only had a clear perception of Newman's distinctive literary genius, but his insight into Newman's mind enabled him to write one of the first and best biographical studies of Newman after his death.

In this book Hutton again wrote of Newman's 'keen and searching irony', but asserted that it did not manifest itself until he was fifty. According to Hutton, 'It was not indeed till after he became a Roman Catholic that Dr. Newman's literary genius showed itself adequately in his prose writings.'[18] Before that, he argued, not only was he too absorbed in the Oxford Movement, but he was constrained and inhibited by the peculiar difficulty of being a Tractarian in the Church of England. Now it is true that Newman's satirical humour blossomed and flowered in his Catholic period, but it is quite wrong to suggest that it was not present, and powerfully present, in his Anglican period. There certainly was a development, but then that was part of a general maturing of his intellectual and literary powers. And although the confidence and relief that undoubtedly followed the conversion of 1845 did lead to a new exuberance of satire, in fact very much the same kind of ebb and flow of humour can be traced in his later as in his earlier life. Hutton's line was followed by Wilfrid Ward, who even wrote, 'His powers of irony had never been displayed at all in his Oxford days.' This astonishing statement is to be found in the otherwise penetrating and perceptive discussion

[17] Cit. in *LD* xxi. 61 n. 2.

[18] R. H. Hutton, *Cardinal Newman* (2nd edn., London, 1891), 11.

of Newman in his *Last Lectures.*[19] Ward, as his *Life* shows, had a deep and sympathetic understanding of Newman's mind as conservative but open to development, traditional yet progressive —as well as of his profound intellectual consistency and integrity notwithstanding his acute sensitivity to and sympathy for different points of view. But his sad and solemn biography presents a warped view of the man, one of whose most striking characteristics was an enormous and exuberant sense of humour. At one point Ward actually asserts that the Tractarian dislike of 'literary display' meant that Newman was 'always' so 'reserved' in his letters, 'breaking out only occasionally and accidentally, almost in spite of himself, into raciness', that 'humour, wit, and sarcasm . . . hardly ever appear'—an assertion which surely has a good claim to be considered the most absurdly false thing ever to have been said about Newman![20]

In spite of Ward's claim that the 'earlier writings' show no 'trace' of the 'fantastic imagination' and the 'keen sense of humour' of *Lectures on the Present Position of Catholics in England* (1851)[21]—which is indeed surely Newman's satirical masterpiece—the exact date of the début of the satirical controversialist can in fact be pinpointed nearly twenty years earlier to the time of the remarkable and momentous tour of the Mediterranean during 1832 and 1833.

In the middle of March 1833, while they were in Rome, Newman and Hurrell Froude heard from Keble about the publication of Thomas Arnold's *Principles of Church Reform*, which argued for religious comprehensiveness as the only way of avoiding the disaster of the disestablishment of the Church of England. The news of Arnold's 'very comprehensive' plan provoked Newman into penning his first really caustic piece of writing:

> If I understand it right, all sects (the Church inclusive) are to hold their meetings in the Parish Church—though not at the same hour of course. He excludes Quakers and Roman Catholics—yet even with this exclusion surely there will be too many sects in some places for one day? . . . If I might propose an amendment, I should say, pass an Act to oblige some persuasions to *change* the Sunday—if you have two Sundays in the week, it is plain you could easily accommodate any

[19] Ward, *Last Lectures* (London, 1918), 109.
[20] Ward, ii. 316. [21] Ward, *Last Lectures*, p. 116.

probable number of sects. . . . Nor would this interfere with the Jews' worship (which of course is to be in the Church)—they are too few to take up a whole day. Luckily the Mohammedan holiday is already on a Friday; so there will be no difficulty of arrangement in that quarter.[22]

Of course, this was not the first time Newman had written either sharply and critically or amusingly and humorously, but it is the first example of the two coming together in the form of satirical humour. There were indeed two periods in Newman's life, both as an Anglican and as a Catholic, when the controversialist was practically forced into silence, but there is no doubt that it was the crisis of relations between Church and State after the Reform Bill that first stimulated the creative talent that would eventually produce the *Tamworth Reading Room*, the satirical masterpiece of his Anglican period. A month later he sharpened the cutting edge of his new weapon in a passage of even more gleeful irony at Arnold's expense:

he is said to exclude the Jews, Roman Catholics, and Quakers from the Churches—this seems to me illiberal. The only objection I can fancy is the want of time in one day for these in addition to those already admitted to participation in the Churches—I am aware the Quakers remain an indefinite period at one sitting—and it would not do to keep the Sandemonians or the Socinians waiting—there must be a punctuality, if all are to be accommodated. Yet I think the difficulty might be met by forcing the Evangelicals to keep their Sunday on the Saturday . . . The Jews could take Saturday too—and the Roman Catholics would come in for Sunday in place of the Evangelicals. The Mahometan Feast being Friday would not interfere.—Or on the whole, since it is immaterial on what day the Christian festival is kept, the whole week might be divided among the various denominations of Christians.—I have another plan, which I hold to be altogether original and is the firstfruits of my late conversion and runs Dr A hard. It is to allot the 24 Colleges and Halls of Oxford among the various denominations . . . I would allow of exchanges or conversions.[23]

The scornful aside—'and it would not do to keep the Sandemonians or the Socinians waiting'—is arguably the first example of Newman's colloquial tone of voice being put to the kind of sarcastic use that would one day be perfected in the duel with Kingsley. Even if Dr Arnold's book did not have the ecclesiastical

[22] *LD* iii. 257–8.
[23] *LD* iii. 298.

effect its author intended, it deserves a footnote in literary history for the way in which it triggered off Newman's first real attempt at satire.

It is important to notice that the satirical animadversions on Arnold involve the implicit objection: if religious comprehensiveness is the ideal and dogmatic differences unimportant, then is it not inconsistent to exclude Quakers, Roman Catholics, and Jews—not to mention Mohammedans? Arnold, of course, does want to draw the line—but does not consistency exclude any such attempt at exclusion? Rhetoric and satire effectively come together: one of the most efficacious ways of winning an argument is to show that one's opponent is inconsistent, but it is also one of the best ways of showing that his point of view is not only wrong but also absurd. In a letter of 13 June 1844 Newman prophesied to Keble that Arnold's posthumously published *Remains* would have little '*effect*'—for 'there is so little *consistency* in his intellectual basis'.[24] Different things provoke the laughter of contempt in different satirists, and it is remarkable how pervasively the theme of inconsistency runs through Newman's satirical writings. Nothing else seems to inspire so much amused contempt in him as the absence or lack of consistency. And given Newman's relentlessly logical mind, such a satirical vision is surely not inappropriate. As an indication of the measure of his preoccupation with the subject, it is worth noting how it even entered into a discussion of the nature of holiness, when Newman offered this novel and unexpected definition of a saint—'I have ever made consistency the mark of a Saint'.[25] This is not the place to explore the extraordinary concern with the 'real' and the 'unreal' which Newman evinces in his writings, but the definition is not so surprising when we appreciate that for Newman being consistent or inconsistent is tantamount to being real or unreal.

Newman is funniest as a satirist when he is exposing the incongruous, in the sense of the inconsistent. When, for example, he warns the American Episcopalians against becoming 'inconsistent and unreal', he singles out the interior of their churches for special censure, because 'pews, carpets, cushions, and fine speaking are not developments of the Apostolical Succession':

[24] *KC* 321.
[25] *LD* xi. 191.

Dispense with your props and kneelers; learn to go down on the floor. What has possessed you and us to choose square boxes to pray in, while we despise Simeon upon his pillar? Why squeeze and huddle together as you neither do, nor would dream of doing, at a dinner-table or in a drawing-room? Let the visible be a type of the invisible. You have dispensed with the clerk, you are spared the royal arms; but still who would ever recognize in a large double cube, with bare walls, wide windows, high pulpit, capacious reading-desk, galleries projecting, and altar obscured, an outward emblem of the heavenly Jerusalem, the fount of grace, the resort of Angels?[26]

Writing on 'The Protestant Idea of Antichrist' he points out with a certain relish that the 'private life' of Thomas Newton, who was the 'main source' for the English tradition, hardly inspired confidence. True, there was no doubting his 'kindness of heart and amiableness',

but a man so idolatrous of comfort, so liquorish of preferment, whose most fervent aspiration apparently was that he might ride in a carriage and sleep on down, whose keenest sorrow that he could not get a second appointment without relinquishing the first, who cast a regretful look back upon his dinner while he was at supper, and anticipated his morning chocolate in his evening muffins, who will say that this is the man, not merely to unchurch, but to smite, to ban, to wither the whole of Christendom for many centuries, and the greater part of it even in his own day . . .

This superb jibe is followed by the sarcastic admission, 'Who would not rather be found even with Whitfield and Wesley, than with ecclesiastics whose life is literary ease at the best, whose highest flights attain but to Downing Street or the levee?' The anti-Popery tradition is absurd if only because of its own manifest inconsistency—

how men, thinking that the Pope is the Beast of the Apocalypse, can endure the sight of any of his servants . . . or can sit with them in the same Council or Parliament, or can do business with them, buy and sell, trade and traffic, or can gaze upon and admire the architecture of churches built by Antichrist, or make much of his pictures,—or how they can read any book of his servants . . . all this is to us inexplicable.[27]

[26] *Ess.* i. 350–1.
[27] *Ess.* ii. 138–40, 148–9.

The traditional Protestant insistence on Scripture as the sole authority for faith is also gleefully satirized for its inherent inconsistency:

'We [Protestants] uphold the pure unmutilated Scripture; the Bible, and the Bible only, is the religion of Protestants; the Bible and our own sense of the Bible. We claim a sort of parliamentary privilege to interpret laws in our own way, and not to suffer an appeal to any court beyond ourselves. We know, and we view it with consternation, that all Antiquity runs counter to our interpretation; and therefore, alas, the Church was corrupt from *very* early times indeed. But mind, we hold all this in a truly Catholic spirit, not in bigotry. We allow in others the right of private judgment, and confess that we, as others, are fallible men. We confess facts are against us; we do but claim the liberty of theorizing in spite of them. Far be it from us to say that we are certainly right; we only say that the whole early Church was certainly wrong. We do not impose our belief on any one; we only say that those who take the contrary side are Papists, firebrands, persecutors, madmen, zealots, bigots, and an insult to the nineteenth century.'[28]

Newman seizes on Protestant opposition to those who abandon Protestantism for another kind of religion as the proof that the principle of 'private judgement' is itself self-contradictory. Did it not prove that 'this great people is not such a conscientious supporter of the sacred right of Private Judgement as a good Protestant would desire'? He enjoys satirizing the glaring inconsistency in an exuberantly comic passage:

Is it not sheer wantonness and cruelty in Baptist, Independent, Irvingite, Wesleyan, Establishment-man, Jumper, and Mormonite, to delight in trampling on and crushing these manifestations of their own pure and precious charter, instead of dutifully and reverently exalting, at Bethel, or at Dan, each instance of it, as it occurs, to the gaze of its professing votaries? If a staunch Protestant's daughter turns Roman, and betakes herself to a convent, why does he not exult in the occurrence? Why does he not give a public breakfast, or hold a meeting, or erect a memorial, or write a pamphlet in honour of her, and of the great undying principle she has so gloriously vindicated? Why is he in this base, disloyal style muttering about priests, and Jesuits, and the horrors of nunneries, in solution of the phenomenon, when he has the fair and ample form of Private Judgment rising before his eyes, and pleading with him . . . All this would lead us to suspect that the doctrine of

[28] *HS* i. 420–1.

private judgment, in its simplicity, purity, and integrity,—private judgment, all private judgment, and nothing but private judgment,—is held by very few persons indeed; and that the great mass of the population are either stark unbelievers in it, or deplorably dark about it; and that even the minority who are in a manner faithful to it, have glossed and corrupted the true sense of it by a miserably faulty reading, and hold, not the right of private judgment, but the private right of judgment; in other words, their own private right, and no one else's.[29]

Professor Owen Chadwick has written that as an Anglican Newman 'slaughtered the Roman Catholic Church with scorn and satire'.[30] The observation seems plausible enough, even self-evident. But in fact neither the works he published nor the private letters he wrote as an Anglican support the point. For what is so interesting and noteworthy about all that he said as an Anglican about the Roman Catholic Church—and he said some very rude and scathing things—is the almost total absence of any satire in all his various critical comments and strictures. Indeed, there appears to be only one place where Newman allows himself anything approaching ridicule or satire, and that is a passage (which he quotes in the *Apologia*) in his 1840 article on the 'Catholicity of the Anglican Church', which was a desperate attempt to shore up the theory of the *via media* against the article by Wiseman in the *Dublin Review* on the relevance of the Donatist controversy to the Anglican position, which had given him such a shock. The passage I have in mind is actually only a single sentence which occurs at the end of an attack on Roman Catholicism.

When we go into foreign countries, we see superstitions in the Roman Church which shock us; when we read history, we find its spirit of intrigue so rife, so widely spread, that 'jesuitism' has become a by-word; when we look round us at home, we see it associated everywhere with the low democracy, pandering to the spirit of rebellion . . . We see it attempting to gain converts among us, by unreal representations of its doctrines . . . We see its agents smiling and nodding and ducking to attract attention, as gipsies make up to truant boys, holding out tales for the nursery, and pretty pictures, and gold gingerbread, and physic concealed in jam, and sugar-plums for good children.

The satirical dig at the end is quite exceptional, but the word 'unreal' prepares us for the apologetic, explanatory sentence that

[29] *Ess.* ii. 339–41.

[30] O. Chadwick, *Newman* (Oxford, 1983), 63.

follows: 'Who can but feel shame when the religion of Ximenes, Borromeo, and Pascal is so overlaid?'[31] In other words, for once the Roman Catholic Church is satirized because for once she is seen as inconsistent, and therefore unreal, and therefore ridiculous. Normally, while Newman was a Tractarian, confident in the *via media*, there was never any doubt as to the Church of Rome's *consistency*, whatever else could be urged against her. Criticism and invective were in order, but not satire because there was nothing ridiculous about a Church so massively, even objectionably, not to say alarmingly, consistent. It is not surprising that the slight satirical sally here is not very funny. The point is in fact made explicitly by Newman himself when in *Present Position of Catholics* he supports the saying 'that ridicule is the test of truth' by commenting: 'Methodism is ridiculous, so is Puritanism; it is not so with the Catholic religion; it may be, and is, maligned and defamed; ridiculed it cannot be. It is too real . . . to have aught to fear from the most brilliant efforts of the satirist or the wit.'[32]

From the literary point of view alone, the most important of Newman's Anglican writings is the *Tamworth Reading Room*, which consists of a series of letters published in *The Times* in February 1841, attacking a distinctly utilitarian speech delivered by Sir Robert Peel at the opening of a new library and reading-room at Tamworth. It is also the one sustained work of satire that Newman wrote as an Anglican. He begins by noting that the address would have come more consistently from a Whig politician like Lord Brougham at the founding of the secular London University than from a distinguished Tory statesman. For it is a 'remarkable example of self-sacrifice', he observes sarcastically, how Peel has become 'the disciple of his political foe'. But the Brougham philosophy which Peel has adopted is not itself wholly consistent. Certainly the idea that knowledge can totally replace religion as a basis for morality would be perfectly consistent with the philosophy of Jeremy Bentham, to whom the objection that 'To know is one thing, to do is another' is easily met by the answer that 'the knowledge which carries virtue along with it, is the knowledge how to take care of number one', for 'Useful Knowledge is that which tends to make us more useful to ourselves;—a most definite and intelligible

[31] *Ess.* ii. 71–2.
[32] *Pre. Pos.*, p. 393.

account of the matter, and needing no explanation'. But then the utilitarian philosopher 'had not a spark of poetry in him', while, by contrast, 'there is much of high aspiration, generous sentiment, and impassioned feeling in the tone of Lord Brougham and Sir Robert'. It is their 'lofty enthusiasm' which makes their substitution of knowledge for religious faith so incongruous and absurd. How, for instance, does a knowledge of science have a morally uplifting effect? 'Can the process be analyzed and drawn out, or does it act like a dose or a charm which comes into general use empirically?' In fact, 'great teachers of morals' like Brougham and Peel are engaged in 'the incessant search after stimulants and sedatives, by which unruly nature may . . . be kept in order', for just as Peel 'makes no pretence of subduing the giant nature, in which we were born, of smiting the loins of the domestic enemies of our peace, of overthrowing passion and fortifying reason', so too Lord Brougham

frankly offers us a philosophy of expedients: he shows us how to live by medicine. Digestive pills half an hour before dinner, and a posset at bedtime at the best; and at the worst, dram-drinking and opium,—the very remedy against broken hearts, or remorse of conscience, which is in request among the many, in gin-palaces *not* intellectual.

The alleged connection between knowledge and morality is as inconsistent with the language used to describe it, as the proposed remedy is incommensurate with the malady: 'who was ever consoled in real trouble by the small beer of literature or science?' Or when, Newman asks sarcastically, 'was a choleric temperament ever brought under by a scientific King Canute planting his professor's chair before the rising waves?' The colloquial tone of voice only adds to the sense of the outrageously incongruous: 'Such is this new art of living, offered to the labouring classes,—we will say, for instance, in a severe winter, snow on the ground, glass falling, bread rising, coal at 20d. the cwt., and no work.' It is doubtful if Newman ever wrote anything more searingly sarcastic than this:

that the mind is changed by a discovery, or saved by a diversion, and can thus be amused into immortality,—that grief, anger, cowardice, self-conceit, pride, or passion, can be subdued by an examination of shells or grasses, or inhaling of gases, or chipping of rocks, or calculating the longitude, is the veriest of pretences which sophist or mountebank ever professed to a gaping auditory. If virtue be a mastery over the mind, if its end be action, if its perfection be inward order, harmony, and peace, we must seek it in graver and holier places than in Libraries and Reading-rooms.

Again, it is worth noting that there is no attempt to ridicule or satirize the arch-utilitarian Jeremy Bentham. There is nothing unreal or inconsistent about that 'stern realist', whose 'system has nothing ideal about it' and who 'limits his realism to things which he can see, hear, taste, touch, and handle'. His philosophy is *real*, whatever else it may be. But what could be more unreal than to imagine that knowledge ever 'healed a wounded heart' or 'changed a sinful one'?[33] In the *Apologia* Newman describes how he 'came to the conclusion that there was no medium, in true philosophy, between Atheism and Catholicity, and that a perfectly consistent mind . . . must embrace either the one or the other'.[34] It is because he regarded both atheists and Roman Catholics as completely consistent on their own premisses that they are beyond the reach of his satire; for ridicule cannot touch the real. Lord Brougham, on the other hand, who 'understands that something more is necessary for men's happiness than self-love' and that 'man has affections and aspirations which Bentham does not take account of', but who also dimisses Christianity as 'dogmatism', is less consistent: 'Human nature wants recasting, but Lord Brougham is all for tinkering it.' Sir Robert Peel is confident that scientific study will lead to religious faith; but, if we 'lay any great stress upon it as the basis of personal Christianity, or attempt to make man moral and religious by Libraries and Museums, let us in consistency take chemists for our cooks, and mineralogists for our masons'. No, 'Let Benthamism reign, if men have no aspirations; but do not tell them to be romantic, and then solace them with glory; do not attempt by philosophy what once was done by religion.' Finally, Newman cannot resist ridiculing one curiously illiberal inconsistency in the actual project of the Tamworth Reading Room: why does it only admit '*virtuous* women' as members?

A very emphatic silence is maintained about women not virtuous. What does this mean? Does it mean to exclude them, while bad *men* are admitted? Is this accident, or design, sinister and insidious, against a

[33] *DA*, pp. 285, 262–4, 266–70. [34] *Apo.*, pp. 179–80.

portion of the community? What has virtue to do with a Reading-room? It is to *make* its members virtuous . . .

Alas, that 'bigotry should have left the mark of its hoof' on the liberal philosophy of the Tamworth Reading Room—'Sir Robert Peel is bound in consistency to attempt its obliteration.'[35]

Newman's novel *Loss and Gain*, the first of his Roman Catholic works, opens his most creative period as a satirist. Running through the novel is a strong, often comic, sense of reality and unreality. The issue for the hero Charles Reding becomes not so much which is the *true* religion, but which is the *real* religion. The doctrinal comprehensiveness of the Church of England is seen to be not a source of strength but fatal to its reality, for two contradictory points of view cannot 'both be real'. In the face of Broad Anglicanism, it is no longer a question of satirizing inconsistencies, but of satirizing inconsistency itself as an ideal.

'Our Church,' he [Mr Vincent] said, 'admitted of great liberty of thought within her pale. Even our greatest divines differed from each other in many respects; nay, Bishop Taylor differed from himself. It was a great principle in the English Church. Her true children agree to differ. In truth, there is that robust, masculine, noble independence in the English mind, which refuses to be tied down to artificial shapes, but is like, I will say, some great and beautiful production of nature—a tree, which is rich in foliage and fantastic in limb, no sickly denizen of the hothouse, or helpless dependent of the garden wall, but in careless magnificence sheds its fruits upon the free earth, for the bird of the air and the beast of the field, and all sorts of cattle, to eat thereof and rejoice.'

There is a hilarious scene towards the end of the novel in a religious bookshop at Bath when the hero comes across a former Oxford friend, not a Broad Anglican but an Anglo-Catholic who had once idealized clerical celibacy, although he is now a clergyman engaged to be married. His pretty bride cannot remember the name of a book she wanted. Can it be 'The Catholic Parsonage'? or 'Modified Celibacy'? No, it is 'Abbeys and Abbots'—' "I want to get some hints for improving the rectory windows when we get home; and our church wants, you know, a porch for the poor people." '[36] In a later letter Newman insisted that his satire was directed against the same 'unreality and inconsistency of

[35] *DA*, pp. 277, 281–2, 292, 295–6. [36] *LG*, pp. 34, 84–5, 351.

conduct' which he had laughed at as an Anglican.[37] But the doctrinal inconsistencies which he had come to see in the Anglo-Catholic position and which are touched on in the course of the novel he would satirize in the first of his two major satirical works.

Lectures on certain Difficulties felt by Anglicans in submitting to the Catholic Church were delivered in 1850, following the celebrated judgement in the Gorham case which led to many conversions to Rome. As in *Loss and Gain*, the contrast between the real and the unreal is central to Newman's argument, and is the source of much of the humour. Anglo-Catholics 'dream' that the Church of England is part of the Catholic Church, when in fact it is nothing more than a State Protestant Church.

If, indeed, we dress it up in an ideal form, as if it were something real . . . as if it were in deed and not only in name a Church, then indeed we may feel interest in it, and reverence towards it, and affection for it, as men have fallen in love with pictures, or knights in romance do battle for high dames whom they have never seen. Thus it is that students of the Fathers, antiquaries, and poets, begin by assuming that the body to which they belong is that of which they read in times past, and then proceed to decorate it with that majesty and beauty of which history tells, or which their genius creates.

Gentle irony gives way to a rather more brutal sarcasm as the real identity of the Anglican Church is revealed:

and, as in fairy tales, the magic castle vanishes when the spell is broken, and nothing is seen but the wild heath, the barren rock, and the forlorn sheep-walk, so is it with us as regards the Church of England, when we look in amazement on that we thought so unearthly, and find so commonplace or worthless.

As usual in Newman, the idea of consistency and inconsistency is closely involved in that of reality and unreality. Thus it is 'an intellectual absurdity'

that such as you, my brethren, should consider Christianity given from heaven once for all, should protest against private judgment, should profess to transmit what you have received, and yet from diligent study of the Fathers, from your thorough knowledge of St. Basil and St. Chrysostom, from living, as you say, in the atmosphere of Antiquity,

[37] *LD* xv. 399.

that you should come forth into open day with your new edition of the Catholic faith, different from that held in any existing body of Christians anywhere . . . and then, withal, should be as positive about its truth in every part, as if the voice of mankind were with you instead of being against you.

It is no less absurd than arrogant to profess to 'have a mission to teach the National Church, which is to teach the British empire, which is to teach the world'. Nor is it consistent to provide a defence for the Church 'which she has no dream of appropriating', to 'innovate on her professions of doctrine' and then 'bid us love her for your innovations', to 'cling to her for what she denounces', and 'almost anathematize us for taking a step which you would please her best by taking also'. The 'theories' on which the Oxford Movement was based 'claimed to represent the theological and the ecclesiastical teaching of the Fathers; and the Fathers, when interrogated, did but pronounce them to be the offspring of eclecticism, and the exponent of a State Church'. Anglo-Catholic theologians had appealed to the authority of the Fathers:

there they found a haven of rest; thence they looked out upon the troubled surge of human opinion and upon the crazy vessels which were labouring, without chart or compass, upon it. Judge then of their dismay, when, according to the Arabian tale, on their striking their anchors into the supposed soil, lighting their fires on it, and fixing in it the poles of their tents, suddenly their island began to move, to heave, to splash, to frisk to and fro, to dive, and at last to swim away, spouting out inhospitable jets of water upon the credulous mariners who had made it their home.[38]

For the most part, the irony of *Difficulties of Anglicans* is gentle enough; it is, after all, addressed to former associates and friends and directed against a form of religion in which Newman had himself once believed and of which he was the principal architect. Very different is the much more aggressive sarcasm of *Present Position of Catholics*, where Newman takes on the virulently hostile anti-popery tradition of English Protestantism, which had been inflamed by the restoration of the Catholic hierarchy. It certainly contains the best of his satirical writing. But its literary claims go further. In 1872 Newman remarked, 'I have ever considered it my best written book.'[39] In other words,

[38] *Diff.* i. 4–6, 157–8, 161, 386, 150.

[39] *LD* xxvi. 115.

from a specifically literary point of view, he regarded it as a more important book than either the *Apologia* or *The Idea of a University*. However, not only has the book been generally ignored by writers on Newman, but it can surely claim to be one of the most underrated works in the English language.

Newman takes particular pleasure in showing up the inconsistencies of Protestant prejudice. Anti-Catholicism itself rests on '*tradition* immemorial, unauthenticated *tradition*'—whereas it is precisely the Catholic insistence on tradition as well as Scripture which it objects to! But in fact, because the 'anti-Catholic Tradition' is the most effective weapon the Established Church has, its special duty is 'to preserve it from rust and decay, to keep it bright and keen, and ready for action on any emergency or peril'. Or, to change the image, the 'Establishment is the Keeper in ordinary of those national types and blocks from which Popery is ever to be printed off'. Some facts are useful for nurturing the tradition, so it is not surprising that 'preachers and declaimers' have 'now a weary while been longing, and panting, and praying for some good fat scandal, one, only just one . . . to batten upon and revel in'. The prejudiced Protestant is the child of the tradition, 'and, like a man who has been for a long while in one position, he is cramped and disabled, and has a difficulty and pain . . . in stretching his limbs, straightening them, and moving them freely'.

The book contains some of the most startling and vivid imagery to be found anywhere in the works, and Newman is quite happy to turn the images that have stained the Protestant imagination against Protestantism itself. Thus it is no benighted Catholic country but Protestant England which, 'as far as religion is concerned, really must be called one large convent, or rather workhouse; the old pictures hang on the walls; the world-wide Church is chalked up on every side as a wivern or a griffin; no pure gleam of light finds its way in or from without; the thick atmosphere refracts and distorts such straggling rays as gain admittance'. Again, it is 'familiar to an Englishman to wonder at and to pity the recluse and the devotee who surround themselves with a high enclosure, and shut out what is on the other side of it; but was there ever such an instance of self-sufficient, dense, and religious bigotry, as that which rises up and walls in the minds of our fellow-countrymen from all knowledge of one of the most remarkable phenomena which the world has seen?' In an 'inquisitive age, when the Alps are crested, and seas fathomed, and mines ransacked, and sands sifted, and rocks cracked into specimens, and beasts caught and catalogued, as little is known by Englishmen of the religious sentiments, the religious usages, the religious motives, the religious ideas of two hundred millions of Christians poured to and fro, among them and around them, as if, I will not say, they were Tartars or Patagonians, but as if they inhabited the moon'. And so the English Protestant who despises the enclosed monk or nun is shown to be as 'enclosed' himself, while, in spite of his vaunted knowledge of the world, he is wholly ignorant of the Catholics about whom he has so much to say.

Analogies also reveal inconsistencies. The so-called 'omnipotence' of the Virgin Mary is no more to be taken literally than the 'Omnipotence of Parliament'. Just as the notice 'Ring the Bell' presupposes 'if you have business within', so indulgences presuppose but do not convey absolution. Protestants emphasize the value of freedom of thought, 'but towards us they do not dream of practising it'. The Reformers had used their 'private judgment' against the Church—but 'There was enough of private judgment in the world, they thought, when they had done with it themselves. So they forcibly shut-to the door which they had opened, and imposed on the populations they had reformed an artificial tradition of their own, instead of the liberty of inquiry and disputation'. Protestantism vehemently rejects the very notion of infallibility, but in practice regards as infallible its own objections to Catholicism. Protestants disapprove of images in Catholic churches, and yet they are quite happy to burn the Pope in effigy—but 'How is it childish to honour an image, if it is not childish to dishonour it?' Toleration is the particular boast of Protestants, but they love persecuting Catholics. It is true that the Catholic Church does not recognize the absolute right to religious freedom that Protestantism does—but are Protestants to 'bring their own inconsistency as the excuse for their crime' of atrocities at least as bloody as any perpetrated by Catholics? Certainly the Protestant readiness to do so is hardly consistent with the view that Catholicism 'is so irrational that it will fall to pieces of itself'. Again, since honesty is one of the boasted virtues of Englishmen, it is paradoxical that it is by 'wholesale, retail, systematic, unscrupulous lying . . . that the many rivulets are made to flow for the feeding the great Protestant Tradition'.[40]

Present Position of Catholics is a neglected masterpiece; and yet it should surely rank among the classics of English satire. The same may be said of Newman himself: far from being counted among the great satirical writers in the language, his genius as a satirist continues to be unacknowledged. It is this aspect of his writings which more than any other calls out for recognition in any reappraisal of his achievement.

[40] *Pre. Pos.*, pp. 45, 74–5, 139, 178, 43–5, 55, 180, 219, 275, 126.

2

Originality and Realism in Newman's Novels

ALAN G. HILL

'Newman a *novelist*?' One can imagine the chorus of disbelief that at one time would have greeted such a claim. Literary critics find it hard to accept that one whose priorities were ordered so differently from their own could treat the genre *seriously*, while churchmen have naturally sought his larger achievement elsewhere. In the cultural divide which Newman himself predicted in *The Idea of a University*, a unified response to his varied achievements as a writer becomes increasingly difficult. And yet the originality of both his novels, and his sustained engagement with the form over many years, are now surely less in doubt. In his approach to the novel, as in so much else, he was ahead of his time.

Newman was destined by outlook and circumstances to take up the form just as the parameters of nineteenth-century realism were beginning to emerge. His openness to the passing shows of the world was indeed part of his empiricist inheritance, and it showed itself as soon as he began to respond to his Oxford surroundings. He even had ambitions as a periodical commentator on University life, in the manner of the *Spectator*. Long before he thought of writing a novel himself, his letters reveal the novelist's penchant for graphic and humorous description and a sense of style that moved with ease between the colloquial and the elevated; and he was naturally attracted to the rising new form which had come of age in Scott's historical romances.

But as a poet himself, and a child of the Romantic movement, Newman was inspired most of all by other poets. As he wrote in his early essay on Aristotle's *Poetics*,

> With Christians, a poetical view of things is a duty,—we are bid to colour all things with hues of faith, to see a Divine meaning in every event, and a superhuman tendency.[1]

[1] *Ess.* i. 23. The essay originally appeared in the *London Review* for 1829.

His imagination was haunted by a sense of mystery and romance. Like Aeschylus, he marked the ironies in human affairs and the inscrutable purposes of Providence, and he was captivated by the metrical tales of his own day, Southey's in particular. Their quests and journeys, their relentless movement through time, and their vision of the life of dedication and faith, seemed to offer a foretaste of his own spiritual pilgrimage. His first narrative *St. Bartholomew's Eve*, a collaboration with J. W. Bowden, was predictably a verse tale after Sir Walter Scott. But he was quick to assimilate other Romantic influences as well, when they echoed his own intuitions, and Wordsworth and Byron in their separate ways urged the need for individual decision and commitment in the face of 'the unimaginable touch of Time'.

All these influences mingled with the *Poetics*, his beloved Terence, and Shakespeare's guiding presence within the scenic art of Jane Austen and Scott, to shape Newman's sense of dramatic narrative. Together, they suggested a novel more suited to the ideals of the younger generation than the fashionable society fiction of the day, and a more dynamic role for the hero. Novel-reading, he implied in an early Tractarian sermon,[2] must not become a form of self-indulgence or escapism, which had no practical effect on behaviour. The novelist must confront the real challenges of life and carry the reader with him. Autobiography and fiction were now to come together within the purlieu of the realistic novel, where the aspirations of the individual are tested in the rough and tumble of the real world. The first hint of this in Newman occurs perhaps in his confessional letters from the Mediterranean in 1833, which blend poetic self-searching and vivid documentary within a single journey of discovery through pagan and Christian landscapes; and had he completed his first novel in 1835, as planned,[3] he would have shown how far he had preceded Dickens and Thackeray along the path of early Victorian realism. But the moment for a popular treatment of the Anglican *via media*, either in a 'period' or a university setting, passed him by: and fortunately, as it turned out. The drama of his own life had to develop fully towards crisis and resolution before it could

[2] 'The Danger of Accomplishments', *PS* ii. 371.

[3] See R. H. Froude's letter to Newman, 6 Aug. 1835 (*LD* v. 118), from which it is clear that Newman had the plot worked out in his own mind.

be transformed through a 'representative' hero into a fictional paradigm of the age. He had to know himself first.

But in the meantime the potential of the novel could be explored in the work of others. Jane Austen, hitherto a firm favourite in the family circle, began to pall. 'There is a want of *body* to the story of *Emma*,' he complained. 'The action is frittered away in over-little things.' She also lacked 'romance' and idealism. 'What vile creatures her parsons are!'[4] Scott's plots (he thought) had not always been properly developed, and now that novelist's neutral stance in matters of belief was also coming under scrutiny. Newman recognized greater commitment among his followers, praising *I promessi sposi* for its truth to 'Nature' and 'depth of religious feeling'.[5] As Bagehot noted later on, the passion for intellectual and religious enquiry was one of the strongest impulses of this period, and could not be omitted from any true delineation of it.[6]

Newman also made his début as a fiction reviewer for the *British Critic* with a devastating exposé of *Geraldine: A Tale of Conscience*,[7] one of those 'silly novels by lady novelists' which George Eliot was to ridicule in the *Westminster Review*. It was 'an attempt at a tale which is left unravelled.' There was 'little incident and no ending', and the heroine's psychology and her final submission to Rome were equally improbable:

> Surely there is something most unbecoming in youth and beauty and fashion and the rest of it being represented as mounted aloft on a library stair, and labouring under the weight of books which she was to make subservient to the settlement of her religious sentiments. . . . And there is something quite ludicrous in fancying that truth could be attained by such child's play.

Religious certitude, he implies, develops in testing situations, not libraries, and (a recurrent theme) the human mind must have elbow-room to grow by natural stages towards it:

> The human intellect needs some play, as it may be called, and Providence has mercifully consulted this peculiarity, whether we call it a weakness

[4] *LD* vi. 16.

[5] *LD* vi. 150.

[6] See Bagehot, *Collected Works*, ed. N. St John Stevas (London, 1965–), ii. 67–8.

[7] *British Critics*, 24 (1838), 61–82: not reprinted subsequently. The author of the anonymous novel (London, 1837) published under the initials E. C. A. was Eleanor C. Agnew, a Roman Catholic convert.

or not. He has given us an innocent outlet for its busy and restless activity. We might have been told peremptorily not to let our minds expatiate at all beyond what is positively revealed; but we are not so told; and the consequence of forbidding what God has not forbidden, will be like stopping a safety-valve. The mind obstructed in its lawful avenues of thought, will be under the strong temptation to employ itself on subjects where thought *is* precluded, the sacred and fundamental articles of faith. The irritation of the reason being denied its natural course, will strike inwards, and fall upon vital parts. . .

The argument was not without its hidden ironies, as Newman strove to defend the Anglican *via media*. He could not have foreseen that, some ten years later, he would have to justify his own conversion in *Loss and Gain*. But he was already suggesting how such a venture of faith might be made more credible.

But above all at this time, he was trying to promote novel-writing within his own circle. 'It is so very desirable', he told his sister Jemima, 'that you should, if possible, all pull together.'[8] Their tales could undermine the efforts of Evangelicals like Mrs Sherwood by showing principles in action and realized in credible characters, thereby instilling a higher ethos altogether. Under his direction, Maria Giberne's *Little Mary* was abridged and reshaped, and published by Rivington's in 1841 with a Preface by Newman himself.[9] According to his sister Harriett, the story had been 'transformed' by his 'magic touch'. Harriett's own talents were also given every encouragement, and Newman's influence can be traced in *The Fairy Bower* and more markedly in *Louisa*, an imitation of Jane Austen and her only adult novel. True to his Aristotelian principles, Newman was quick to note weaknesses of structure or development: 'I have been reading your *Louisa* with great satisfaction. The only fault is in its shortness, else it would be perfect . . . it does not fill the eye of the mind or the just expectation of the reader.'[10] Did it go far enough in developing towards an appropriate denouement that would bring out the significance of the whole?

[8] *LD* v. 387–88.

[9] *Newman Family Letters*, ed. D. Mozley (London, 1962), 94–5. I am grateful to Professor Kathleen Tillotson for further information on this point. Newman's Preface is unrecorded by V. F. Blehl, *John Henry Newman: A Bibliographical Catalogue of His Writings* (Charlottesville, Va., 1978), and a copy of the book has not been traced.

[10] *Newman Family Letters*, ed. D. Mozley, p. 120.

Any further engagement with the novel, however, ended with Newman's retirement to Littlemore and the weakening of family ties as his conversion became more likely. Until that event, he had no secure viewpoint; and afterwards he had to await a fresh opportunity for writing. Only after his own discovery of the truth and reversal of fortune (in the worldly sense, at any rate) could he bring a truly *human* response to issues that might otherwise have seemed sectarian or remote, and strike the final balance of 'loss and gain'. The phrase itself recurs throughout his writings, but he may have been reminded of it by lines from Wordsworth's *Excursion* included in his sister-in-law Anne's anthology *Days and Seasons; Or Church Poetry for the Year*, and published just before his conversion:

> O blest seclusion! when the mind admits
> The law of duty; and can therefore move
> Through each vicissitude of loss and gain,
> Linked in entire complacence with her choice[11]

Meanwhile, new literary stars were in the ascendant (the family had been 'ensnared' by *Nicholas Nickleby*), and there were fresh sources of inspiration to reckon with. Dickens had already shown in *Pickwick* how Newman might turn his own satirical bent against Evangelical targets, and now, as his hopes for the High-Church movement were finally extinguished, its faddishness and gentility were being exposed by Thackeray in the pages of *Punch*.[12] *The Book of Snobs*, published in volume form (1848) the same year as *Loss and Gain*, gave more earnest attention to the same issues, and acclimatized a new term in the English language. As Newman began at last to write his first novel in Rome in the summer of 1847, when the early parts of *Dombey* and *Vanity Fair* were appearing in London, he instinctively aligned himself with those who were exploring new settings and character-types and extending the linguistic range and expressiveness of fiction. The English novel was not exempt from the far-reaching changes that were overtaking every facet of national life in the age of the Railway Kings and the Chartists.

[11] Wordsworth, *Excursion*, iv. 1035–8.

[12] See 'Lines upon my Sister's Portrait by the Lord Southdown' and 'The Diary of C. Jeames de la Pluche, Esq., with his Letters', *Ballads and Contributions to Punch 1842–50* (Oxford, 1908), 35–7, 355–437.

A general appreciation of *Loss and Gain* and its Tractarian background has been given elsewhere,[13] and need not be repeated here. But the realism of its idiom and setting, and the complex treatment of the hero, deserve more extended discussion. Newman was (it will be recalled) 'answering' an anonymous work entitled *From Oxford to Rome: And how it fared with some who lately made the Journey*, which accused the Roman Catholic converts of 1845, Newman included, of backsliding. He confronted the challenge, not by detailed refutation, but by writing a much more lively and entertaining novel which showed how an individual mind of the time might arrive at religious certitude in the trials and tribulations of university life. He substituted a dramatic picture for abstract argument.

The success of his riposte turned on showing that the converts were not bizarre adherents of some foreign creed, but more truly 'English' than their opponents and with better credentials to speak as Oxford men. His 'answer', he claimed in the Advertisement to the sixth edition (1874), was 'drawn up with a stricter regard to truth and probability and with at least some personal knowledge of Oxford'. It was also couched in real English. The turgidities of *From Oxford to Rome*, which had been overlooked by Gladstone in an unguarded moment,[14] were an affront to Newman's sense of style and could not be ignored:

> Especially was he desirous of dissipating the fog of pomposity and solemn pretence, which the writer had thrown around the personages introduced into it, by showing, as in a specimen, that those who were smitten with love of the Catholic Church, were nevertheless as able to write common-sense prose as other men.

'Common-sense prose' is perhaps an inadequate description for the resourcefulness and gusto of Newman's colloquial style, but it does at least emphasize the down-to-earth realism of the whole exercise.

In his own novel, the Oxford setting is as up to date and factually accurate as the extension of the railway from Didcot can make it. The characters speak in the idiom of their time and place, their discussions are natural and uncontrived, and the

[13] *Loss and Gain: The Story of a Convert*, ed. A. G. Hill (Oxford, 1986).

[14] *Quarterly Review*, 81 (1847), 131–66: 'it has just claims to notice for its qualities as a work of art'.

voice of the narrator, unquestionably an Oxford man himself, is flexible enough to alternate the light-hearted with the serious and allow for the free play of humour and irony over the developing action. Writing from a distance, Newman could look back on Oxford as a complete world in itself. Its sights and sounds flowed back to him like echoes from a past which he had apparently put behind him for ever.

Loss and Gain creates an idyllic picture of unreformed Oxford from the inside—its landscapes and lifestyle, and the 'feel' of the place at different seasons of the year, matching the hero's mood in the manner of *Jane Eyre* (1847)—though Newman cannot have seen Charlotte Brontë's novel before he began writing his own. The university was largely unexplored territory for the novelist,[15] as the 'documentary' digressions on staircase life and Oxford bores (to take just two examples) suggest. But it is a refined picture. There is no sign of the cruder side of university life hinted at in 'Cuthbert Bede's' *Adventures of Mr. Verdant Green* (1853) or Thomas Hughes's *Tom Brown at Oxford* (1861). Newman uses the private language and slang of the place to create the sense of a very special community with its own customs, institutions, and ethos. Normal Oxford terminology apart (freshmen, bachelors, masters, dons, scouts, bulldogs, the Schools, the House, the Clarendon, the Long, the Latin Verse, etc.), he deliberately uses unfamiliar colloquialisms to define his speakers and their milieu. Though largely unrecorded in the *Oxford English Dictionary* (not to mention Eric Partridge's *Dictionary of Slang*), *Loss and Gain* seems to mark the first appearance in fiction—and in some cases, anywhere—of a whole range of Oxford words, including the following:

pp. 8, 124 *lecture* (audience or class attending a lecture), cf. *in lecture*, p. 26, and an *Article lecture* (a class on the Thirty-Nine Articles), pp. 129, 138, 219, 232, 252;

p. 8 *a beaver walk* (a walk in mufti or non-academic dress), cf. *in beaver*, p. 89;

pp. 9, 100 *the pokers* (bedels who carry the mace before the Vice-Chancellor;

[15] *Loss and Gain* is probably the first example of a novel devoted entirely to a university setting. J. G. Lockhart's *Reginald Dalton* (London, 1823) is only partly set in Oxford.

p. 18 *the Pro* (the Pro-proctor);
p. 28 *lionesses* (lady visitors);
pp. 33, 76 *plucked in the schools* (failed in the examination schools);
p. 67 *shutting his oak* (outer door of college rooms);
p. 73 *crammed in Greek plays*;
p. 76 *smalls* (Responsions or 'Littlego');
p. 79 *dinner paper* (menu);
p. 115 *battel paper* (account);
p. 230 *a rowing set*;
p. 235 *Mr. Vice* (Vice-Principal, normally used of the Vice-Chancellor);
p. 355 *aeger dinners* (dinners delivered to rooms of sick members of college).

Newman makes one or two concessions to the uninitiated by way of explanation (' "I was kept here by these confounded smalls." "Your *Responsiones*", answered the tutor in a tone of rebuke.'); otherwise, he deliberately exploits the 'in' language of Oxford to establish the reality of his picture and his own authority as a commentator on it. Occasionally he risks obscurity. Or is he addressing his work primarily to his old Tractarian friends?

To be an occasional writer like Newman meant responding to the world of contingent events or 'facts', intervening at a particular moment in the process and detecting the providential purpose behind the veil of sense. His portrait of Oxford had to be true to the ever-changing details of his own life there.

This is a place of fashions [says Mr Malcolm]; there have been many fashions in my time. The greater part of the residents, that is, the boys, change once in three years; the fellows and tutors, perhaps in half a dozen; and every generation has its own fashion. There is no principle of stability in Oxford (p. 30)

If Newman did not stick to the exact particulars of place and time, would not his accuracy in more fundamental matters be called into question? Perhaps the most extraordinary example of this in the novel is the casual (and unexplained) reference (p. 87) to the *Dio-astro-doxon* and its exhibition near Folly Bridge. Unknown as it is to the *Oxford English Dictionary*, this turns out to be a giant illuminated orrery which an itinerant lecturer named Lloyd regularly demonstrated in Oxford during Newman's undergraduate years at Oriel by way of illustration to a course of lectures on astronomy, the mysterious processes of which had always fascinated Newman. The apparatus was almost as ephemeral as the form of entertainment it provided and was soon forgotten, but not before it had inspired a poem on 'The Terrestrial Year: On her Progress thro' the Signs of the Zodiac', by Scott's friend Anna Seward, the 'Swan of Lichfield', and made this fleeting appearance in *Loss and Gain*.[16] Why did Newman dwell on such bizarre curiosities, if it was not that his fiction had to be continuous with real life in all its richness of specification?

Within this authentic Oxford setting, the dialogues dramatize the workings of Charles Reding's mind as step by step he pursues his quest for certainty, and finds his destined home in the Catholic Church. 'It is impossible to stop the growth of the mind.' The other characters, comic and serious, represent the various options open to him, but are not intended to be living portraits of contemporaries. All are themselves developing, in different directions. 'We are in the time of life to change', says Charles, 'we have changed already, and shall change still.' No one has the monopoly of wisdom, and the truth emerges through different speakers who press the argument forward in an ideal tutorial (or Platonic) situation. Each has his own idiom and tone of voice. No reader could mistake Sheffield, a rationalist with a dislike of 'fudge' and 'shams', for Fairborn the Evangelical, or Bateman and White with their spate of ecclesiological jargon, or Vincent, the non-party man, a superb verbal performer in the Dickensian mould, who affects a trendy scientific vocabulary. Newman can mimic the tones of all of them, with devastating effect.

The tone of debate is remarkably relaxed and colloquial by the standards of contemporary controversy. It bristles with new words and up-to-date usages which are distributed between the narrator, the hero (who has by far the most), and the undergraduate characters. Only Willis, whose religious vocation takes him out of the world, has very few, and to his urgent voice is given the most elevated passage of rhetoric in the novel, the well-known panegyric on the Mass. The older generation, and dons

[16] See *Poetical Works of Anna Seward*, ed. W. Scott, iii (Edinburgh, 1810), 319. I am grateful to Mr F. R. Maddison and Mr A. V. Simcock of the Museum of the History of Science, Oxford, for information about Lloyd and his activities. See also H. C. King, *Geared to the Stars* (Bristol and Toronto, 1978), 314–15.

like Carlton, the Keble-like exponent of the *via media*, and Campbell, the dependable Anglican rector who marries Charles's sister, speak more formally as befits their seniority. The unusual contemporaneity of Newman's language can be tested from the French and Italian translations of *Loss and Gain*, which appeared around 1855. Both translators were stumped by much of the university slang, and toned down many of the colloquialisms listed below, thereby losing their unique flavour. In some cases they miss Newman's meaning altogether.[17]

Only a full analysis of the text, and more research into the usages current at the time, could bring out the linguistic uniqueness of *Loss and Gain*. What follows is a random sample of words and usages which would deserve fuller investigation, some of them more or less current in the colloquial language of the time, others rare or unrecorded for so early a date:

p. 8 *donnish*. First recorded here, according to *OED*. Cf. *donnishness* in Newman's *Letters* (1835).
p. 8 '*regular prose* and unreal' (dull). Newman's usage, also in *Letters* (1840).
p. 9 'the most approved Oxford *bandbox-cut* of trimness'. Cf. Thackeray (1844), 'spick and span bandbox churches'.
p. 9 'University dresses are great *fudge*' (nonsense). Cf. p. 22, '*fudge* and humbug', p. 416, *fudge*!
p. 10 'a pompous and *up-and-down* tone'. Also in Byron (1812).
pp. 16, 19, 163 *viewy* (holding views). First recorded here, but the context implies current Oxford usage.
p. 24 *ungentlemanlikness*. Newman's word, unrecorded elsewhere.
pp. 32, 219 *a new broom* (fig.). *OED* cites 1621, then Dickens, *Little Dorrit* (1855).
p. 35 'professed to be *aesthetic*' (appreciating beauty). Earliest quotations in *OED* are Darwin (1871) and W. S. Gilbert (1880). The context here implies that the term was already current in Oxford.

[17] The translator of the French edition was L'Abbé Segondy of Montpellier, and his preface is dated Nov. 1855. Segondy sent Newman an inscribed copy of the second edition of *Perte et gain* (Paris, 1859), and Newman also received the Italian edition of *Perdita e guadagno* (Milan, 1857) from its anonymous translator. Both volumes are in the Birmingham Oratory Library. The two translators were very conscious of the versatility of Newman's text and the difficulty of their task.

p. 38 'who thought it *a bore*'. *OED* cites 1807 and Whately (1831).
p. 53 'a good kind-hearted old *fogie*'. Early 19th-cent. Scots usage, before Thackeray, *Book of Snobs* (1848).
p. 53 'an *awful* evangelical'. Cf. p. 176, 'their images are *awful*', and p. 180, 'affected me *awfully*'. Slang of the 1830s and 1840s, perhaps American in origin.
p. 59 'the Duke's *a queer hand*'. 19th-cent. colloquial.
p. 68 'straight *macadamised* roads'. *OED* cites 1827.
p. 72 *philosophism*. *OED* cites Coleridge (1799), Carlyle (1843), and *Loss and Gain*. Also in Newman's *Letters* (1829).
p. 76 'The conversation, or rather *mono-polylogue*, as some great performer calls it'. Term associated with the actor Charles Mathews, from 1824.
p. 77 'I am rather *choice* in my tea' (fastidious). Obs. (e.g. Jeremy Taylor), or possibly Berks., dialect?
p. 79 'it is not my *habitat* out of term-time'. Scientific term, here (and in Newman's *Letters*) used more generally of 'dwelling place' and pre-dating *OED* reference to Lowell (1854).
p. 83 'Our great divines . . . were so *racy*' (vigorous writers). *OED* cites Dryden, then Charlotte Brontë (1849), and Miss Mitford (1852).
p. 89 'Where did you find that *get-off*?' Unrecorded as noun.
p. 93 'its low *nunting* table' (ungainly). Northampton dialect, rare; appropriate for the Redings's Midland domicile. Did Newman hear the word at the Mozleys?
p. 97 'She calls a bonnet '*a sweet*' one year'. Apparently unrecorded.
p. 97 which makes her '*a perfect fright* the next'. 19th-cent. colloquial, as in *Don Juan*.
p. 117 'a . . . *nice-looking* fellow'. *OED* cites Jane Austen (1807) and Dickens, *Oliver Twist* (1838).
p. 117 'What's *the upshot*? Obs. (16th-cent.), but colloquial from *c.* 1830. Also in *Callista*.
p. 118 'But the Catholic Church isn't St. Paul, *I guess*'. Americanism, cited as such from Byron and Scott onwards.
p. 125 *a toss-up* (an even chance). *OED* cites Malkin (1809) and Dickens, *Martin Chuzzlewit* (1844).
p. 163 'He gave us capital *feeds*' (meals). Colloquial from *c.*1830, originally used for horses.

p. 164 'the *animus* of party'. *OED* cites Thackeray (1840).
p. 170 'whose wife, what is called *did* for his lodgers'. First recorded here.
p. 171 'we were *sporting* . . . a great paradox'. Colloquial from late 18th cent.
p. 171 'I mean *pretty much* what he says'. *OED* cites Hughes, *Tom Brown at Oxford* (1861).
p. 176 'he would make trial himself, and he has *caught it*'. *OED* cites Marryat (1835) and Mrs Gaskell (1848).
p. 180 'sugar should not be a *substantive* ingredient in tea but *an adjective*'. Unrecorded in this combination.
p. 183 'by the *rail*'. (railway). Cf. p. 362, 'our rail'. *OED* cites Sydney Smith (1843).
p. 189 'some *ultra-book* or other' (extreme). Unrecorded. Cf. p. 278, *Ultra-Protestants*; a word of the 1840s.
p. 200 '*a make-up* for sin' (compensation). Rare—first reference in *OED* is 1859.
p. 212 'some impudent non-protectionist'. Unrecorded. *OED* cites *Protectionist*, 1844.
p. 215 'the theology or *no-theology* of the day'. Unrecorded.
p. 225 'helpless and *do-nothing*' (adj.). *OED* cites Washington Irving (1832) and Carlyle, *Chartism* (1839). Also in Newman's *Letters*.
p. 230 'a large proportion of *snobs*'. The new sense propagated by Thackeray in the 1840s in his papers in *Punch*, and in the *Book of Snobs*. Also in *Callista*.
p. 231 'a system of *espionage*' (fig.). Rare.
p. 233 'a *kill-or-cure* remedy'. Unrecorded as adj. until Jowett (1875).
p. 240 *jesuitries*. *OED* cites Coleridge, and Carlyle, *French Revolution* (1837).
pp. 243, 252 *to get up* (learn). *OED* cites Dean Alford (1828).
p. 251 'You have no notion how *strong* the old Principal was' (vehement).
p. 256 'my *uncongeniality* . . . with things as they are'. *OED* cites 1805, then Dickens, *Dombey and Son* (1847–8).
p. 261 'I've *make a hash of it*' (fig.). Apparently Newman's own usage, as in his *Letters* (1833).
p. 271 '*trotted out* for the amusement of the ladies'. *OED* cites Lytton (1838), and Thackeray, *Book of Snobs*.

p. 305 'They are *in a fix*' (tight corner). Americanism—*OED* cites Marryat (1839).
p. 308 *an Anglo-Catholic*. The noun here pre-dates Charlotte Brontë, *Shirley* (1849), the *OED* example. Also in Newman's *Essays Critical and Historical* (1840).
p. 308 'so positive, so *knock-me-down*'. *OED* cites 1760, then *Loss and Gain*.
p. 310 'determined *to make a field-day* of it' (fig.). *OED* cites Thackeray, *Book of Snobs*.
p. 313 *armistice* (fig.). *OED* cites 1841 only.
p. 320 '*to oh-oh* it' (cast doubt on). Apparently Hurrell Froude's usage (1833), here used by Willis.
p. 325 'one ought to be up to their *dodges*'. Colloquial in 1840s, e.g. Thackeray, *Pendennis* (1849). Also in *Callista*.
p. 329 '*shaky*, in your adherence to Romanism' (unsettled). *OED* cites Lytton (1853).
p. 330 'he's *a brick, a regular brick*'. Originally, perhaps university slang: Steerforth's word in Dickens, *David Copperfield* (1849–50).
p. 335 *untenableness*. *OED* cites G. S. Faber (1833) and Lewes (1846).
p. 341 'I have exhausted it, I have *drunk it out*'. Obs., in Scott.
pp. 353, 403 '*all-momentous* errand'. Unrecorded.
p. 356 'He chose a bedroom . . . *inducting himself* into it' (fig.). In Dickens, *Barnaby Rudge* (1840).
p. 376 'a *first class* of the Great Western' (carriage). *OED* cites 1846 for the adj.
p. 390 'we have given up *Tongue*' (prophesying). Unrecorded—Irvingite or Pentecostalist usage?
p. 418 'You must have your *hobby*' (hobby-horse). Obs., Scott's word, also in *Callista* and *Letters* (1863).
p. 426 'one vast instrument or *Panharmonicon*' (mechanical musical instrument). *OED* cites *Loss and Gain*.

One final example will serve to emphasize Newman's idiosyncratic idiom. At the end of chapter 15 of part II, the dialogue on the merits and shortcomings of Romanism is brought to an abrupt end by a remark of Bateman's, which (Newman says) 'put a corona on the discussion' for the rest of dinner (p. 281). What does he mean? Surely that Bateman put a *stopper* on the discussion, not a *crown* (whatever that might mean)? The *Oxford English Dictionary* is unhelpful; the translators make no sense of the passage, and the word presents an insoluble puzzle while it is spelt in Newman's way. On the assumption, however, that he meant *coroner*, an intriguing possibility is opened up at once; for according to Partridge, *coroner* was a slang term used around 1870 for 'a heavy fall', i.e. an abrupt end likely to lead to an inquest. Was Newman drawing here on a long-standing colloquialism that had never surfaced in the written language—misspelling the word, and confusing his readers, because he had always *heard* it and never seen it in print? The solution is attractive; but whatever the explanation, the fact remains that his penchant for racy language clearly led him into trouble on at least one occasion.

Newman's racy expression is matched by the psychological realism he brings to Charles Reding's mental life, and the wider ties of sympathy and duty which bind him to his family and friends. But this does not preclude some mystification at the expense of the reader.[18] How could it be otherwise when Newman had occupied such a prominent place on the Oxford scene *in propria persona*?

Though he put a lot of himself into the psychological and emotional life of his hero, the novel is not really autobiographical. Reding is not Newman's *alter ego*, but a typical undergraduate of the younger generation and at a different stage of development from Newman in 1840. But Newman could hardly leave himself out altogether from a picture of university life that purported to be factually accurate; and he gets round the difficulty by adopting the persona of 'Smith', a shadowy clerical *éminence* 'who never speaks decidedly in difficult questions', and who is reputedly 'a sceptic at bottom'. With such self-mockery Newman contrives to acknowledge the shakiness of his previous Anglican stance. As the novel progresses, 'Smith's' sermons at St Mary's become allegedly 'injudicious', a change of allegiance is on the cards, and after the wave of conversions in 1845, 'Smith' seems to drop out of the novel altogether.

But does he? When Reding joins the London train after his poignant farewell to Oxford, one of the most graphic and moving scenes in the novel, he falls in with a Roman Catholic priest,

[18] This mystification extended to Newman's extraordinarily involved account of the novel in his 'Answer in Detail to Mr. Kingsley's Accusations', *Apo.*, pp. 422–3.

whose face seems vaguely familiar to him. Though he cannot identify his companion, the encounter is crucial in settling any remaining doubts he has about the true religion. Who is this mysterious stranger who makes such a powerful impression on Reding? He is carefully visualized, and bears a curious resemblance to Newman himself at this period, 'passing or past the middle age', worn-looking, and easily taken for a Frenchman (which Reding mistakes him for at first): clearly a convert who has sadly put Oxford behind him and is anxious for news of his Alma Mater. Is this not perhaps intended to be a self-portrait of Newman himself, alias Smith, now home and dry in the Catholic Church and suffering for his convictions? If Reding embodies vital aspects of Newman's former Anglican self, the stranger surely represents his present and future role as a newly ordained Catholic priest, soon to return as an alien in his own land and only to enjoy the distant spires of Oxford from the railway line (as he was poignantly to recall in retrospect in the *Apologia*). Whatever Newman meant by this enigmatic culmination however, he surely succeeds in combining mirror-images of past and future, loss and gain, in a final unflinching moment of truth.

The freshness and subtlety of *Loss and Gain* were largely lost on its early readers who divided, for and against, on predictably denominational lines. The *Athenaeum* found it 'flippant and farcical', the *Rambler* 'life-like'; and Wiseman, while noting 'the raciness and thorough English' of the language, questioned whether the work was really a novel at all.[19] From the Broad Church side, Sara Coleridge (perhaps with the Gothic scene of the flagellant before the Cross in mind) found it utterly repugnant:

> It is clever—but, as I think, very unworthy. The style is excellent—the dialogue runs well—and there is a good deal of humour in the sketches of character. Still it is in many respects—as most readers feel—an *odious* book in point of feeling—and in argument nothing at all. What will Newman sink to as a reasoner? Is there a lower depth to which he can yet fall?[20]

[19] Wiseman, *Dublin Review*, 24 (1848), 218–26.

[20] MS letter of *c.*18 July 1848 to Mrs Derwent Coleridge (University of Texas MSS).

Frederick Oakeley sprang to Newman's defence a few years later, but to little avail.[21] The treatment of the psychology of belief, here and in *Callista*, had to await fuller elucidation in the *Grammar of Assent* (1870), and his modest, but not unimportant, role in the development of the nineteenth-century novel could only be appreciated much later when the masterpieces of Victorian fiction began to appear. It was left to an ex-Unitarian admirer, R. H. Hutton, to confess to the author that *Loss and Gain* had marked in some sense 'an era' in his life.[22] But he, more than any other critic of the time, had recognized the importance of the novel as a neutral forum for dramatizing moral and religious issues at a time when the official Churches were beginning to lose their authority.

Perhaps the initial mistake was to treat the novel as didactic, or prescriptive. Newman could hardly avoid having designs on his readers, but his overriding purpose was to defend the converts of 1845, not to lay down the law for others. In fact, the novel is remarkably genial and magnanimous. Faith is a 'venture' which some will embark on when confronted with the 'right' arguments or circumstances, and others, equally sincerely, will not. All his characters have free will, and they will fulfil their destinies, come what may. The ways of Providence are in the last resort inexplicable. Only the cranks and charlatans who invade the hero's peace and quiet at the end, like a farcical procession of 'tempters', are laughed off the scene before he is ready for the final service of Benediction at the close. Those who read the book with the attention it deserves will find that Newman's instincts as a novelist are entirely at one with his deepest-held religious convictions.

The secret of his success in *Loss and Gain*—as in *Callista*—lay in bringing quite new perspectives to time-honoured formulas. Reding finds his true identity through suffering, like a tragic hero, and every step in his progress is dogged by hidden ironies. Yet the school of experience is not without its compensations. In the rural interludes of family life which punctuate the more feverish round of parties and discussions at Oxford, the keynote is struck early on by reminiscences of *As You Like It*. 'Sweet are the uses of adversity' would be a not inappropriate motto for

[21] F. Oakeley, *Personal Reminiscences of the Oxford Movement with Illustrations from Dr. Newman's 'Loss and Gain'* (London, 1855).

[22] *LD* xxi. 60. See also R. H. Hutton, *Cardinal Newman* (London, 1891), 194–7.

Loss and Gain and its picture of 'this working-day world', as it became much later on for George Eliot's sense of life's lessons.

As a reflection of Newman's career so far, before it moved into a new phase, *Loss and Gain* was a *tour de force* that could not be repeated. His second novel *Callista* (1856) is very different in tone and substance, more exploratory in its handling of some of Newman's later concerns, and though 'a tale of the third century' intended, apparently, as a dark parable for his own time, although there is little or no hint of this in his original proposal to Burns the publisher.

What I should like, would be to bring out the ἦθος of the heathen from St. Paul's day down to St. Gregory, when under the process, or in sight of the phenomenon, of conversion; what conversion *was* in those times, what the position of the Christian in that world of sin, what the sophistries of philosophy viewed as realities influencing men.[23]

The original germ lay dormant in his mind for years, awaiting the right moment for development. Preliminary sketches of the Juba sections were completed before he left Rome in 1848, but laid aside on his return to more pressing duties in Birmingham, and then Dublin, and they were only followed up years later when other writers had provided a pretext for a contribution of his own. Whether he was deliberately 'answering' Charles Kingsley's *Hypatia* (1853),[24] or merely responding on his own terms to Wiseman's request for a sequel to *Fabiola* (1854), the final result was a highly individual work that offers unique insights into Newman's own personality. No other of his works creates such a vivid picture of Christian commitment and its overriding claims on the individual, or embodies such a nightmarish vision of unregenerate Man. As a cautionary tale for the modern world 'from a Catholic point of view', *Callista* is, to say the least, disconcerting, and in ways that Newman may barely have been aware of himself.

In previous romances about the early Church on Scott's model, like Lockhart's *Valerius* or Sismondi's *Julia Severa*,[25] the

[23] *LD* xiii. 69.

[24] See S. Dorman, '*Hypatia and Callista*: The Initial Skirmish between Kingsley and Newman', *Nineteenth Century Fiction*, 34 (1979), 173–93, which brings out the fundamental differences between the two writers.

[25] J. G. Lockhart, *Valerius* (Edinburgh, 1821); L. S. de Sismondi, *Julia Severa* (Paris and London, 1822). Newman had read both. He may also have known

marriage of hero and heroine, following the timely conversion of the non-Christian partner, had resolved the conflict of allegiances and set the seal on their withdrawal from public view into unstrenuous domesticity. In Newman's eyes, however, the priorities were quite different. The Christian must put faith and duty before every other claim on his loyalty, even at the price of martyrdom. There could be no compromise with pagan ideals, though they were decked out in all the colours of ancient civilization and philosophy. The Christian Agellius, urged on by his uncle Jucundus, a wordly-wise old pagan, seeks the hand of the Greek image-painter Callista in what looks like a typical courtship situation from Roman comedy. But the drama takes an unexpected turn in perhaps the most extraordinary rejection scene in the English novel, as Callista recognizes the confusion of motives which, to her dismay, he has fallen into, and which lowers him in her eyes. It marks the beginning of her own quest for the truth, and both eventually find their true destinies apart, as martyrs. Like the two lovers in Southey's *Thalaba*, 'the most sublime of English poems',[26] they are only reunited after death. Callista's venture of faith, the central theme of the novel which engaged Newman's sympathies at the deepest level, is not a sudden turn-about, but a gradual development which fulfils the needs of every side of her personality. But how was he to envisage circumstances of time and place appropriate to such a private and intimate process? As his proposal to Burns concluded:

> I don't think I could do it from history. I despair of finding facts enough—as if an imaginary tale could alone embody the conclusions to which existing facts *lead*.

What would be the natural 'facts' in this case, where success depended on balancing the 'inner' life of the individual with the historical world of pagan Rome, and choice of period and setting was all-important?

Callista is deliberately set outside mainstream history in an ordinary provincial city in proconsular North Africa before and during the Christian persecutions under Decius. All over the Roman Empire there were prosperous backwaters like Sicca:

Chateaubriand's *Les Martyrs ou le triomphe de la religion chrétienne* (Paris, 1809; English trans. 1812).

[26] *LD* xiii. 449.

'their historical distinction was that they were ordinary', as Sir Mortimer Wheeler once remarked. It offered Newman therefore an ideal focus for depicting the natural history of provincial life at this obscure period, and what he called 'the feelings and mutual relations of Christians and heathens'. The novel is neither a costume piece nor an antiquarian reconstruction of the life and times of Cyprian of Carthage. It is the *spirit* of the pagan Empire, embodied in its legal and religious forms and usages, which count for most in Newman's presentation of the 'facts'. Otherwise, the work is almost entirely fiction. The shadowy historical personages merge easily into their background; the celebration of Roman might at Jucundus' banquet serves only to bring out the momentous choices facing individuals; and Agellius' own dilemma is comically pointed up in his uncle's interminable discussion of Roman marriage customs. Newman did a good deal of research on what he called the 'locale' of the novel,[27] but his own memories of Sicily were just as useful in helping him to visualize a historical landscape which seems reassuringly familiar in his homely 'rural' vocabulary. Sicca presents a smiling face to the world. But the natural setting is at odds with the horrifying practices that go on there—more like, perhaps, a glimpse into Conrad's 'heart of darkness' than the cosy paganism of other novelists and genre painters of the Victorian period.

'How is this vast, this solid establishment of error, this incubus of many thousand years, ever to have an end?' asks Agellius at the beginning of the novel. The extraordinary chain of events in *Callista* suggests the nature of Newman's answer, as he shows the mysteries of the divine dispensation in action, in the lives of communities and individuals. When the novel opens, the people of Sicca, pagans and Christians alike, are sunk in worldliness. As Juba taunts his brother in a characteristically colloquial outburst:

> I despise you . . . you have not the pluck to be a Christian. Be consistent and fizz upon a stake; but you're not made of that stuff. . . . I despise you, and the whole kit of you. . . . You are all of you as fond of the world, as set upon gain, as chary of reputation, as ambitious of power, as the jolly old heathen, who, you say, is going the way of the pit. (p. 35)

[27] See *LD* xiv. 343. The MS of the novel, and Newman's working notes on the geography, Roman administration, and religions of proconsular Africa, are preserved at the Birmingham Oratory.

But retribution comes inexorably with the invasion of the locusts, 'an instrument of divine power', and one disaster follows another in a seemingly endless chain of calamities. Famine and disease are followed by a popular uprising in which the rioters attack the Christians, and then persecutors in turn become victims and the grim catalogue of violence and carnage is only brought to a halt by the brutal efficiency of the Roman soldiery. And yet by some mysterious process, the lives of those caught up in these almost sensational events are transformed and redirected. Deliverance, as always with Newman, is the work of individuals, not groups. Agellius' unsuccessful suit to Callista starts her on her journey from shadows into realities (the words Charles Reding uses about his own quest in Newman's previous novel[28]), and Agellius is recalled to his own true purpose, the revival of the Church at Sicca. The followers of the old order are unable, or unwilling, to change: 'better stay where I am,' says the sceptical Arnobius, 'I may go further, and gain a loss for my pains'. Jucundus will continue to trade in false images, and Polemo to believe that Rome is 'the last, the perfect state of human society'. But unwittingly, they all promote the purposes they seek to frustrate. Even Juba, bewitched and driven crazy by his mother in one of the most sensational scenes in the novel, has his part to play in the ironic pattern of events. The reader is left with Newman's wonderment at 'this mystery of life',

> Where good and ill, together blent,
> Wage an undying strife, (p. 379)

a theme to which he was to return memorably at the climax of the *Apologia*.

Callista is remarkable for its great descriptive set pieces, its grasp of Terentian scenic method for dramatic confrontations and contrasts, and above all, perhaps, for its psychological realism. Where else in a novel of this date could be found a subtler or more economically worded piece of Jamesian interior analysis than the following?

> She might, indeed, have been able afterwards, on looking back, to say many things of herself; and she would have recognised that while she was continually differing from herself, in that she was changing, yet it

[28] An echo of the words which Newman eventually had engraved on his memorial at Rednal: 'Ex umbris et imaginibus in veritatem'.

was not a change which involved contrariety, but one which expanded itself in (as it were) concentric circles, and only fulfilled, as time went on, the promise of its beginning. Every day, as it came, was, so to say, the child of the preceding, the parent of that which followed; and the end to which she tended could not get beyond the aim with which she set out. Yet, had she been asked, at the time of which we speak, where was her principle and her consistency, what was her logic, or whether she acted on reason, or on impulse, or on feeling, or in fancy, or in passion, she would have been reduced to silence. What did she know about herself, but that, to her surprise, the more she thought over what she heard of Christianity, the more she was drawn to it, and the more it approved itself to her whole soul, and the more it seemed to respond to all her needs and aspirations, and the more intimate was her presentiment that it was true? (pp. 291–2)

Less obvious, perhaps, but equally striking for Newman's day, is the bluntness with which he brings out the seamier 'facts' of pagan life, urged on, no doubt, by lurid details in the early Christian Fathers. The fate of the Christian children in the riot, for example, who are to become either temple prostitutes or eunuch priests, is openly implied, without any deference to Victorian proprieties:

The whole five were carried off in triumph; it was the greatest success of the day. There was some hesitation how to dispose of them; at last the girls were handed over to the priestesses of Astarte, and the boys to the loathsome votaries of Cybele. (pp. 194–5)[29]

And while Callista finds her true love on the rack, her brother Aristo, frustrated in his efforts to secure her release, is shown seeking solace among the prostitutes at the Thermae. Juba's catchy little song ('The little black moor is the chap for me') is another instance of this down-to-earth quality in Newman. Unlike Callista's Byronic complaint 'Where are the Islands of the Blest?', it was omitted from his *Verses on Various Occasions* (1867),[30] and is little known today. Yet in its colloquial, jaunty ballad rhythms it looks back to some of Newman's earliest experiments in verse, and forward to the devils' chorus in *Gerontius*.

[29] I am grateful to Mr Simon Pembroke for help in elucidating this passage, which probably draws on Eusebius or Athanasius.

[30] It was reprinted in *The Poems of John Henry Newman*, ed. F. Chapman (London, [1913]), 342–4, along with Callista's other song 'I wander by that River's Brink', which was also omitted from *Verses on Various Occasions*.

No further opportunities for novel-writing came Newman's way after *Callista*. But he remained a keen and discriminating reader of fiction for the rest of his life (Trollope was a special favourite), and he continued to revise his two novels and ponder their significance for himself and his readers, as every new edition was called for.[31] His practice of the novel at an important juncture in its history had helped him to find his own bearings, opening up some of the larger preoccupations of his career and widening the range and expressiveness of his prose writing. The two works that achieved all this and, in addition, carried such mysterious intimations of the author's own personality, cannot be treated simply as by-products of his other concerns. Newman was doubtless conscious of this himself when he gave them an honoured place among his collected works.

[31] *Loss and Gain* and *Callista* both went through at least nine English editions in Newman's lifetime.

3

Newman's Poetry

ROGER SHARROCK

Newman's poems form a subsidiary and comparatively small part of his total work. The title of *Verses on Various Occasions* (1868), the volume in which they were first collected, seems an adequate acknowledgement of the manner in which for the most part they are attached to passing moods and to particular events. Even his most substantial poetic work *The Dream of Gerontius* was occasioned by an illness which led him to contemplate the onset of death. Yet, after all, most of the great prose works of Newman, the *Apologia* and *The Idea of a University* among them, were in the same way connected with particular occasions. The poems share with the prose the quality of presenting the encounter of a powerful mind with individual problems, personal or public, so that the treatment of reality and God is never abstract but arises freshly out of actual incidents and the demands of certain moments in the life of an intellectual man of action. For this reason, and because his verse is, after a fashion, less considered, less serious than his prose, an enquirer into this neglected branch of his work may at least hope to uncover some inadvertent betrayals of the hidden springs of his mental life. It is of the nature of autobiography that we should not look for these in the *Apologia*; honesty as the world sees it is a seamless garment of integrity and is not inclined to inner revelation or self-betrayal. Newman wrote his poems more loosely than his prose, partly in deference to the Romantic doctrine of spontaneity, partly in accordance with the contemporary view of verse as every educated man's plaything. So it is in the poems that we might be able to trace, as it were, the dream-work of his imagination upon the contents of his thought. This essay may show whether the hope is to be fulfilled.

There are two kinds of difficulty which stand between today's reader and Newman. I think they apply to Christian as well as to non-Christian readers, though perhaps to the former rather differently and rather less acutely. The first difficulty applies to his works in general; the second is a special problem associated with the poems.

The first obstacle is that created by Newman's opposition to liberalism, and still more by its nature and passion. For it is the sheer passion of dogmatic adherence which cuts Newman off from our own age. Even in a period when, in the *Spectator* and elsewhere, a variety of intellectual conservatism is moderately fashionable, his stance of *Athanasius contra mundum* teaches us that, at least in England, liberalism has won the battle of intellectual manners. It was to the age of Basil and Athanasius that he felt instinctively drawn. 'I had fierce thoughts against the Liberals', he writes at the period of the bill for the suppression of the Irish sees. His fierceness is that of the Newman who said, after reading the *Despatches* of the Duke of Wellington, 'It makes one burn to have been a soldier'. An aspect of fierceness is that terrifying Oxford aloofness or coldness he shows at times,[1] as in his rejection of Mgr. Talbot's invitation to preach in Rome ('Birmingham people have souls; and I have neither taste nor talent for the sort of work which you cut out for me. And I beg to decline your offer.') Certainly this uncompromising quality is also to be found in other Victorian figures, like Gladstone; it was an age which saw moral and spiritual issues in black and white, and that marks the difference from our relativism and eirenicism, even when the issues seem to be still with us, or to come round again. The recent controversy on authority in the Church of England, both preceding and following the *Crockford's* Preface (1987), echoed, but with how muffled a sound, the old Tractarian debates.

This distancing of Newman is thus a matter of personal and period style, but it is reinforced by more material factors. One of these is the narrowness of range of his interest in the thought and literature of his own day; all that new growth of speculative philosophy and historical method in Germany, of which Matthew Arnold was so much aware, was totally occluded from his gaze. The interesting attempt by some recent writers to place Newman as the successor of Coleridge and a vital participator in a 'common tradition' linking *Aids to Reflection* with modern theology, is

[1] 'I think I am very cold and reserved to people, but I cannot ever realize to myself that anyone loves me.' *LD* vi. 119.

relevant here. There are important parallels between the two; but to claim Newman for a tradition of seeing like Coleridge the essential unity of the religious and the literary symbol is to ignore the hard dogmatism of his mental style and its resistance to synthesis. He speaks sharply of Coleridge 'looking at the Church, sacraments, doctrines &c., rather as symbols of a philosophy than as truths—as the mere accidental types of principles'.[2] In the light of this remark we can imagine what he would have made of Coleridge's highly metaphysical rendering of the Trinity into an ingeniously balanced pattern of ideas.

The sceptical thread running through all his thought is the most effective means we have to align Newman on the interpretative horizon of the modern reader. The common tradition here can be followed from Pascal's wager through Newman to twentieth-century converts like T. S. Eliot and Graham Greene. They are united with Newman in their realistic and practical acceptance of orthodoxy: 'If the Church would be vigorous and influential it must be decided and plainspoken in its doctrine.'[3] They are linked by their imaginative and practical recognition of the 'vast aboriginal calamity' under which mankind labours. But in Newman's case this recognition which saw beyond the confidence of a century of progress did not result in the production of imaginative work, as it did for Baudelaire, Eliot, and Greene. *Loss and Gain* and *Callista* are far removed from *The Waste Land* and *The Power and the Glory*; *Callista* even might be said to resemble the saint's life read by the mother to her little boy in *The Power and the Glory*. *Loss and Gain* is an elegy over a certain moment of Oxford culture and to say that is to accept the gulf that time has fixed.

The other obstacle, which especially applies to the poetry, is more immediate and palpable, less a matter of taste. It shows in the stiltedness of diction and the commonplace and unexciting movement of most of the lyric metres. Like many minor writers of the second quarter of the century, the period following after the great Romantics, Newman is content to behave in verse as if nothing had happened and to make do with a late eighteenth-century vocabulary and phraseology. If he is at times Wordsworthian, he is mildly Wordsworthian.

[2] *LD* v. 225.
[3] *Ari.*, p. 147.

There is a spirit ranging through
  The earth, the stream, the air;
Ten thousand shapes, garbs ever new,
  That restless One doth wear;
In colour, scent, and taste, and sound
  The energy of life is found.

The logical upshot of this poem 'Nature and Art' is the superiority of the former to the latter; it is a doubtful position for a poet of talent. The poet goes to 'Where iron rule, stern precedent | Mistreat the graceful day', presumably to his new office as tutorial fellow of Oriel; the conflict is finally resolved since he will carry memories of his rural retreat into his new life, 'an Ulcombe of the heart'. This may seem a too easy resolution to finish a poem, but what is really significant here is the glimpse of a strain in Newman which consistently rejects the active business of life in favour of an inner spiritual quietness. It is thus with a great effort, and as it were against nature, that he sets himself to the campaigning of the Oxford Movement. Newman must surely have been influenced by Keble's lectures in the chair of poetry; and Keble is at his most interesting and suggestive when he outlines an intimate kinship between poetry and religion:

since it is clear, or at least a probable hypothesis, that in the highest of all interests, on which alone depends the final happiness of the race of man, poetry was providentially destined to prepare the way for Revealed Truth itself, and to guide and shape men's minds for reception of still nobler teaching, it is consistent to see the same principle at work in what I may call less important departments of its influence.[4]

But his expression of the idea is usually more tepid than this, and it is further diluted by a tendency to view poetry as a form of relief for overcharged feelings, a palliative for violent emotions anaesthetizing in its function:

Let us therefore deem the glorious art of Poetry a kind of medicine divinely bestowed upon man: which gives healing relief to secret mental emotion, yet without detriment to modest reserve: and, while giving scope to enthusiasm, yet rules it with order and due control[5]

[4] J. Keble, *Lectures on Poetry*, trans. E. K. Francis, 2 vols. (Oxford, 1912), ii. 481. Cf. G. Battiscombe, *John Keble: A Study in Limitations* (1963), 139–44.

[5] Keble, *Lectures on Poetry*, i. 22.

This is far removed from the lofty conception of the relation of the poet and the Christian believer set out by Wordsworth in the Preface in 1815 which Keble must have known: there it is the dynamic power of poetry over the human spirit which associates it with sacramental religion.[6]

As G. B. Tennyson has noted, in many of his short lyrics Newman leans more to a Wordsworthian programme than to that of Keble. He claims a more active and less merely therapeutic role for poetry.[7] The greater number of these poems were included in *Lyra Apostolica* (1836) where they greatly outnumber those of Keble, Isaac Williams, and the other contributors. In that volume they sketch out a militant programme for the new Tractarian movement. In the best of these poems Newman sounds a different kind of Wordsworthian note, the rallying trumpet-call of the sonnets on national liberty and independence. 'Progress of Unbelief' is a comment on that national apostasy denounced by Keble in the sermon which is usually taken as inaugurating the Oxford Movement.

> Truth after truth, of various scent and hue,
> Fades, and in fading stirs the angels' grief.

In 'Protestantism' it is prophesied that a personified Wrath from heaven will make to suffer the Church which has betrayed the charge of the Holy Spirit. The mark of this crusade, which was to result in the Tracts and twelve years' disruption in the Church of England, is its dedicated severity; the poem 'Zeal and Love' declares that charity is only reached after 'Hatred of sin, and Zeal, and Fear', and then it must appear as a form of self-denial. The dedication is a highly personal one: it is the psychological history of the disciplining of a sensitive spirit to a cause, rather than mere advocacy, that gives these poems their interest and intensity. The sense of calling is anticipated in an early poem to his brother Francis, 'To F. W. N.' (1826). But it is most present in the large group of poems written on his Mediterranean tour with Hurrell Froude in 1832–3. If these are read as a group, a kind of progression in resoluteness may be traced. Sometimes the tone is one of intimate personal confession as in 'Sensitiveness',

6 Wordsworth, *Poetical Works*, ed. E. De Selincourt, ii (Oxford, 1944), 412–13.

7 G. B. Tennyson, *Victorian Devotional Poetry: The Tractarian Mode* (Cambridge, Mass., 1981), 115–33.

where he condemns his own gentle and shrinking personality for hindering him from speaking out on previous occasions; now all will be different, uncompromising: 'Such dread of sin was indolence'. A number of poems salute major figures of the Old Testament, Isaac, Moses, Melchisedek, Joseph, and Jeremiah, but always with a sense of immediate empathy and kinship which enables Newman to greet them almost as collaborators in the present struggle. There follow poems in the same vein on St Paul; again the concern is personal and immediate. Paul is of aid to the exile brooding on the crisis in England because he can teach how the claims of zeal and patience may be reconciled; and the passionate wish for association with the saint,

> I dream'd that, with a passionate complaint
> I wish'd me born amid God's deeds of might:

is answered with superb assurance when a voice proclaims, 'St Paul is at thy side.'

This assured voice speaks with most eloquence in 'The Pillar of the Cloud', Newman's most famous short poem. Its reputation has inevitably caused it to be included in hymn books. But the determination it expresses is too personal and introspective to make it suitable for congregational use. The best characteristics of Newman's religious lyrics are here, simplicity, intense feeling, but also an authoritative firmness which leaves no doubt that he knows the way he is going: the mode of address to God is presumably an optative but it has a commanding imperative ring about it. The second stanza, 'I was not ever thus . . .' was condemned outright by one writer on Newman's literary work as constituting a complete departure from the initial thought to which a return is only made in the third and final stanza.[8] However, any difficulty is removed if this poem is read as one among the whole series of the Sicilian voyage, a crucial stage in the unified account of the progress and disciplining of an individual soul for the great contest in store for it (as with the faults overcome which are recounted in 'Sensitiveness'). At any point in the progress the subject can look backwards or forwards to earlier or later stages. It is all part of a complex ascetic exercise, the preparation of a spiritual Achilles for that moment when he

[8] J. J. Reilly, *Newman as a Man of Letters* (New York, 1925), 112.

shall re-enter on the scene and be able to say, 'You shall know the difference now that I am back.'[9]

The delicate yet resolved spirit that endures this discipline is, to begin with, strangely remote from the life with which it now must grapple:

> Then what this world to thee, my heart?
> Its gifts nor feed thee nor can bless.
> Thou hast no owner's part
> In all its fleetingness.
>
> The flame, the storm, the quaking ground,
> Earth's joy, earth's terror, nought is thine;
> Thou must but hear the sound
> Of the still voice divine.

Even when the spirit can aspire to see itself as one of 'a chosen few', a company of saints, with his fellows he is marked off from the world, living a secret life shut away from the noise of history:

> Hid are the saints of God—
> Uncertified by high angelic sign;
> Nor raiment soft nor empire's golden rod
> Marks them divine.
> Theirs but the unbought air, earth's parent sod,
> And the sun's smile benign;—
> Christ rears his throne within the secret heart,
> From the haughty world apart.

This sense of the uniqueness and separateness of the individual soul owes something to Newman's early Calvinist training; but it is a feature that remains part of him. 'Substance and Shadow' is a sonnet embodying his rejection of the 'mechanical philosophy' of the last age, still current in the ideas and programmes of the utilitarians. The octave dwells on the folly of creating idols out of the limited evidence of sense-experience, but it is in the sestet, which carries a more decisive turn of thought than is usual in Newman's sonnets, that the real emphasis of the argument lies:

> Know thy dread gift,—a creature, yet a cause:
> Each mind is its own centre, and it draws
> Home to itself, and moulds in its thought's span
> All outward things.

[9] A free adaptation of *Iliad*, xviii. 125.

It is in moments like this when the rhetoric of his poetry plays around the core of his deepest thought that the imperatives and assertions which constitute the grammar of these poems are at their most powerful: they have the weight of solemn personal directives in a diary of the soul. The chastening scepticism of Newman which rejects 'viewiness' and abstraction is not so much a scepticism about human knowledge conceived in terms of the capability of a single Cartesian mind as an acceptance that real knowledge must be filtered through a myriad individual perceptions.[10]

It has been suggested that Newman's contribution to *Lyra Apostolica* can best be appreciated when read as parts of an integrated whole, a record of faith and self-discipline written on his memorable tour, on the voyage out, in the Adriatic, in Malta and Sicily, or becalmed in the Strait of Bonifacio; when incorporated into *Lyra Apostolica* they appeared suitably enough in the later editions of that work on pages designed like those of a devotional book with red and black lines and Gothic type for headings. But one cannot help but be dismayed by signs of the low esteem in which Newman held the art of poetry; in receiving and adapting Keble's aesthetic, which associated poetry with religion, it is as if while he was prepared to accept a Church speaking through poetry, in liturgy and symbol, he was not ready to elevate poetry in a corresponding manner; he only adhered to a half of the high Romantic compact. If he does not shrink from the claims of the aesthetic he certainly rations them. In 'The Pilgrim' he positively vows not to indulge in natural beauty, turning his face away from the loved scenes of the Devon countryside. He passes through the scenery of the Dart as one who 'durst not love' it and who keeps his vow of non-attachment inviolate, 'prizing his pilgrim-lot'. There is evidence that he viewed the writing of verse as a form of relaxation; though he revised in later editions there is no parallel to the artistic care he lavished on the prose works. A letter of 1833 suggests that the dress of verse might be a fitting receptacle for ideas for which the writer might not desire to claim full responsibility.[11] The steady flow of poems on the Mediterranean journey

[10] 'But in truth, though a given evidence does not vary in force, the antecedent probability attending it does vary without limit, according to the temper of the mind surveying it.' *US*, p. 193.

[11] *LD* iii. 236.

may have been partly due to an effort to relieve the tedium of a long voyage. But once Newman got into the vein there is no doubt that a serious part of his mind became engaged by the contemplation of a distant England under the sway of liberalism; nor that the ensuing series gained a momentum of its own and developed into a minor *Apologia*, a review of the writer's spiritual fitness together with his weaknesses and his aspirations.

What remains bewildering is the width of the gap between the conventional rhetoric of most of these poems and the exceptional mind behind them. Newman's poetic practice is at odds with his eloquent exposition in *The Idea of a University* of the essential unity of personal thought and a personal language in the greatest writers.[12] The passage looks back to the Romantic concept of the unified imagination; but it also anticipates structuralist and post-structuralist concern with the primacy of the forms of language in the literary work. Indeed it might be said that Newman's analysis of literary language takes into account the actual discourse of an individual's *parole* while Saussure, having made the distinction between *parole* and *langue*, concentrated solely on the synchronic language of the latter and the distinction of its signs. Newman insists on the element of distinguishable personality by which *parole* is informed. If there is so little cultivation of a personal idiom in his verse it may be due to humility. At its best the verse rises above conventional diction into a sturdy neutral plainness. This is marked in some of the sonnets, in the straightforward meditation of 'Angelic Guidance', the plain assertion of 'Substance and Shadow'; it is of course there in the powerfully reiterated 'Lead thou me on' of 'The Pillar of the Cloud'. In many poems what looks at first like a logical progression can be seen more exactly as a movement associated with the technique of meditative prayer. Thus in the two stanzas of 'The Power of Prayer', there is in the first the statement that any faithful soul may obtain grace for itself by prayer; by a natural association there follows in the second stanza the thought that the prayer of the truly heavenward mind is for the relief of others, for 'gifts on the world to shower', and that this is far harder to obtain. The alternating shorter lines create a halting, slowed down rhythm imitative of the slow progression of the habit of prayer.

[12] *Idea*, pp. 211–45.

Brevity, a biblical plainness, a sort of businesslike spirituality, guide these poems of the voyage, and a few later ones such as 'The Two Worlds'. As Meriol Trevor has said, they are 'stark as bits of stone in a field';[13] but their kind of objective strength, so different from the gently flowing rill of Keble's verse, has not often been remarked because it is presented without any ostentation and restrained by natural speech forms.

Newman's metrical practice is on the whole unremarkable, though varied and capable, ranging through common metre, ballad stanza, the sonnet, and various other stanzas. There are however exceptions in two poems of much more interest which he describes as 'tragic choruses': 'The Elements' and 'Judaism'. In these, clearly looking towards the choruses of Aeschylus and Sophocles, Newman does catch at a Greek austerity and gnomic concentration in tune with his own verse habits. The choric model enhances his disciplined plainness; at the same time he avails himself, if somewhat sparingly, of the freer movement of Greek choric verse:

> Man is permitted much
>   To scan and learn
>   In Nature's frame;
> Till he well-nigh can tame
> Brute mischiefs and can touch
> Invisible things, and turn
> All warring ills to purposes of good.
> Thus, as a god below,
> He can control,
> And harmonize, what seems amiss to flow
> As sever'd from the whole
> And dimly understood.
>
> But o'er the elements
>   One hand alone
>   One hand has sway.
> What influence day by day
> In straiter belt prevents
> The impious Ocean, thrown
> Alternate o'er the ever-sounding shore?
> Or who has eye to trace
> How the Plague came?

[13] M. Trevor, *Newman: The Pillar of the Cloud* (London, 1962), 112.

Forerun the doublings of the Tempest's race?
Or the Air's weight and flame
On a set scale explore?

In these verses Newman, speaking in the accents of natural religion, achieves an effective compromise with an Aeschylean spirit of *σωφροσὺνη*: man must know his own feebleness, since he is 'Encompass'd all his hours by fearfullest powers | Inflexible to him'; the conclusion is that God holds the keys 'of either home', this world and that to come. The second stanza is crucial for our reading today since it creates a strong doubt whether this sort of humanist criticism of scientific claims is not now after a century and a half wholly outmoded. What exactly does he mean by 'the Air's weight and flame'? There had been quantitative investigation of the elements in the atmosphere by Dalton and Gay-Lussac within his own lifetime. The ignorance on one side of the division of the two cultures seems blatantly obvious here: only thirty years later Pasteur, with his germ theory of disease, was to establish 'how the Plague came'. If he had said in this stanza that even in an advanced stage of human science and technology the ravages of infectious disease and tempest might not be entirely resisted, he would still be persuasive. But his abrupt rejection here of the very possibility of further human knowledge is unwarranted dogmatism; it is on a par with his claim elsewhere that theology and the Bible furnish a knowledge as exact as that of physical science. The story of the Ark must simply be accepted as a truth of revelation.[14] It is curious to find Newman underwriting the literalism of Arnold's contestant Bishop Colenso. His more judicious voice speaks elsewhere in *The Idea of a University* when he prefers to dwell on the harmlessly neutral role of the special sciences in the eye of faith.

The experimental choric verse of 'The Elements' may be compared to that of Arnold in *The Strayed Reveller* and a few other poems. Arnold too was aspiring to an objective voice and recalling the integral steadiness of Sophocles; however his free verse has a looser movement than Newman's lines because of his study of the same form in Goethe and Heine. To invoke Arnold is to notice a more fundamental difference of point of view on the history of human culture. Within the frame of his perennial

[14] *Idea*, p. 73.

humanism Arnold can find room for the fact of nineteenth-century scientific progress.[15]

When he collected his poems in 1868 Newman wrote to R. H. Hutton:

> If I had my way I should give myself up to verse-making; it is nearly the only kind of composition which is not a trouble to me, but I have never had time. As to my prose volumes, I have scarcely written any one without an external stimulus.

Yet the two great poetic efforts of his life were each associated with external pressures. Behind the group of lyrics written on the Mediterranean journey was the intense nervous stimulus of convalescence from his dangerous fever in Sicily; and over all those poems hung the challenge of the religious crisis at home. Thirty years later he wrote *The Dream of Gerontius* with great rapidity in January and February 1865. He had lately emerged from the strains of the controversy with Kingsley and *Apologia pro Vita Sua* had been published in the previous year. He had at that time a vivid sense of impending death. This took the form of a particular concern about sudden paralysis. It is as if he contemplated the attack on the vital powers which would most threaten his intense and all-absorbing sense of identity.[16] The period of the Kingsley controversy came at the end of the saddest and most frustrating year of Newman's life. The Achilli libel suit, the *Rambler* affair, and the opposition of Manning, all conspired to make him feel neglected and useless. Then the reception of the *Apologia* brought relief and exhilaration. Thus there were external factors at work in both his chief poetic epochs. At each time his sensitive spirit was oriented outwards to public debate; at each time he was convalescent from sickness and under the threat of death. The short poems and the longer dramatic one each communicate a sense of the precious uniqueness of the individual soul and the corresponding weight of its moral responsibility.

[15] Arnold was to write that there was 'really no question between Professor Huxley and me as to whether knowing the great results of the modern scientific study of nature is not required as part of our culture'. See P. Honan, *Matthew Arnold: A Life* (London, 1981), 415–16.

[16] 'Paralysis has this of awfulness, that it is so sudden. I have asked medical men, and they have been unable to assign any necessary premonitory symptom; nay, the very vigorousness and self-possession (as they seem) of mind and body, which ought to argue health, are often the proper precursors of an attack.' *LD* xxi. 364.

The composition of *The Dream of Gerontius* took about three weeks. Newman records, 'I wrote on till it was finished on small bits of paper, and I could no more write anything else by willing it than I could fly.'[17] The poem was published in the Jesuit periodical *The Month* in the April and May issues of 1865. Its immediate popularity with a readership far wider than the Roman Catholic public again links it with the literary activity of 1833. Gordon at Khartoum read and reread his underlined copy of *Gerontius* which after his death came into Newman's hands. 'The Pillar of the Cloud' likewise exerted a universal appeal.

English poetry in the mid-century schooled itself to contemplate the last things. There was *In Memoriam* and Philip John Bailey's *Festus*. In the use of blank verse for the psychological analysis of exceptional mental states Newman, surprisingly, recalls the Browning of *Paracelsus*. The poem begins at the moment before death. Consciousness of identity brings as its corollary fear of the destruction of that identity:

> I can no more; for now it comes again,
> That sense of ruin, which is worse than pain,
> That masterful negation and collapse
> Of all that makes me man; as though I bent
> Over the dizzy brink
> Of some sheer infinite descent;
> Or worse, as though
> Down, down for ever I was falling through
> The solid framework of created things,
> And needs must sink and sink
> Into the vast abyss.

The whole work is an extraordinary feat. Colourless, pure, austere, it exhibits more daring in its metrical and sound effects than most of Newman's verse. The lines given to the Assistants at the moment of Gerontius's death have a calypso dip and lilt about them.

> Rescue him, O Lord, in this his evil hour,
> As of old so many by Thy gracious power: (Amen)
> Enoch and Elias from the common doom; (Amen)
> Noe from the waters in a saving home; (Amen)
> Abraham from th' abounding guilt of Heathenesse; (Amen)
> Job from all his multiform and fell distress; (Amen)

[17] *LD* xxii. 72.

Isaac, when his father's knife was raised to slay; (Amen)
Lot from burning Sodom on its judgment-day; (Amen)
Moses from the land of bondage and despair; (Amen)
Daniel from the hungry lions in their lair; (Amen)

From the first it was apparent that the work invited a musical setting. The personal meditation of the soul is firmly supported in a liturgical framework: the priest utters the prayers for the dying by the bedside, 'Proficiscere, anima Christiana, de hoc mundo', and later the Angelic choirs chant hymns of praise. But the first hymn, 'Firmly I believe and truly', a concise summary of the dogma of the Incarnation, is spoken by Gerontius, the English lines merging into the Latin Office hymn:

Sanctus fortis, Sanctus Deus,
De profundis oro te,
Miserere, Judex meus,
Mortis in discrimine.

Most extraordinary, here and elsewhere, is the absence of any false note, the avoidance of all sentimentality or local indulgence which might come to be dated. There are few long Victorian poems which do not at some point date themselves in this way or invite untoward mirth. The part of *Gerontius* which contemporary and later critics have been least happy about is the speeches assigned to the Demons immediately after Gerontius's death. These have an animal vulgarity: the Demons jeer at human intellectual pretentions, at 'the mind bold and independent, the purpose free', and at the saint who is a stinking bag of bones before his death; Gerontius cannot see them but hears their scoffing which breaks out in jerky dissonant lines. Critics of their dissonance are essentially making a protest against indecorum. But to demand more dignity and a better tune for the devil is a Romantic, Byronic illusion. Marlowe in the comic parts of *Faustus* and C. S. Lewis in *The Screwtape Letters* have demonstrated that the demonic is a burlesque activity mimicking and playing upon human weaknesses. The Demons are ridiculous and disgusting even when they are presenting the most deadly temptation—the thought that the saint, like Eliot's Becket, may be doing the right thing for the wrong reason.

Gerontius awakens to the first moments of death and the company of his good Angel. There is imagination of a state beyond temporal understanding which is yet necessarily rendered by analogy with experience in time; the levels of experience are finely discriminated in tentative questions.

> Hitherto
> All has been darkness since I left the earth;
> Shall I remain thus sight-bereft all through
> My penance-time? If so, how comes it then
> That I have hearing still, and taste, and touch,
> Yet not a glimmer of that princely sense
> Which binds ideas in one and makes them live?

This discrimination, and the subsequent halt, in extreme adoration and fear, at a point short of the presence of God, are far more strangely moving than any attempt to paint a paradise in words. The difficult idea that the soul, freed from the controlling framework of time and space, has its own thought as a mode of organization is conveyed by the Angel in a luminous scholastic statement, free from jargon:

> Nor touch, nor taste, nor hearing has thou now;
> Thou livest in a world of signs and types,
> The presentation of most holy truths,
> Living and strong, which now encompass thee.
> A disembodied soul, thou hast by right
> No converse with aught else beside thyself;
> But, lest so stern a solitude should load
> And break thy being, in mercy are vouchsafed
> Some lower measures of perception,
> Which seems to thee, as though through channels brought,
> Through ear, or nerves, or palate, which are gone.
> And thou art wrapp'd and swathed around in dreams,
> Dreams that are true, yet enigmatical;
> For the belongings of thy present state,
> Save through such symbols, come not home to thee.

The soul now lives 'in a world of signs and types', wrapped round by dreams which are truth-telling. It is a world familiar to literary critics of the last generation, the realm of the poetic symbol in which meaning and sensuous effect are perfectly joined; the dream or 'sign' is the concrete universal adumbrated by Kant and Hegel and defined by W. K. Wimsatt. Yet, as has been noted earlier, in the prose writings Newman is ambivalent in his attitude towards the Romantic unifying symbol and distrustful of the speculative philosophy of Coleridge who detected such symbols both in works of the secular poetic imagination and in the Bible, and therefore proceeded to view the reception of divine truth as another exercise of the synthetic imagination. If there is a paradox here it may be resolved by attempting to take the perspective of the soul on the threshold of the beatific vision. Beyond the frontiers of life the nature of theological orthodoxy and its defence can be seen as purely instrumental. Truth is now mediated directly but it must still be spoken of in that language of concrete particulars which the soul has heard on earth.

The feeling, the passion for holiness, is not poured out loosely, but conforms to the measured edifice of belief which sustains the ascent of the soul. The five choirs of Angelicals present in their hymns this tiered structure in which theological truth has become pure fact: successively they sing the Incarnation, Man, the Fall, and the Redemption. The fusion of intense feeling, doctrinal precision, and metrical control is assured (perhaps especially in the fifth hymn).

As the soul prepares for the vision of God before entering purgatory it listens to the choirs of Angelicals. Between the songs of the second and third choirs the soul responds with a metaphor which alludes, gently and remotely, to the Romantic tradition of natural religion which is now superseded by revealed truth:

> The sound is like the rushing of the wind—
> The summer wind—among the lofty pines;
> Swelling and dying, echoing round about,
> Now here, now distant, wild and beautiful;
> While, scatter'd from the branches it has stirr'd,
> Descend ecstatic odours.

There are many instances of the Romantic poets employing the image of the Aeolian harp stirred by the wind to render inspiration, natural genius, and the working of the creative imagination. Keats likens the words of Thea to the fallen Saturn to this natural magic:

> As when upon a trancèd summer night,
> Forests, branch-charmèd by the earnest stars,
> Dream, and so dream all night, without a noise,
> Save from one gradual solitary gust,

Swelling upon the silence; dying off;
As if the ebbing air had but one wave.[18]

Here there is no harp, only the natural magic of trees in the wind. Coleridge in *The Aeolian Harp* traces out the full image of a harp designed to catch the wind and indulges in the speculation whether 'all of animated nature' may be a vehicle for divinity in this manner. The image of the breathing life of the wind as adapted by Newman has archaic origins in most Indo-European languages. It has always been able to function in either direction of the naturalism/supernaturalism polarity. In Greek the word *πνεῦμα* served for both 'breath' and 'spirit', and the usage is similar in Hebrew. What is brought into play is a fundamental semantic resource for describing life, physical or spiritual. The life of being is everything in the House of Judgment now described. The Angel has already informed Gerontius that 'a million-million-millionth part' of a moment could not suffice to describe the minuteness of the interval between death and the soul's recognition of its new state; in keeping with this rejection of any scheme based on human time, and in line with Newman's austere refusal of metaphor, the House of Judgment is wholly immaterial; it is composed of living Being:

The very pavement is made up of life.

Symbol of a sort has allowed Gerontius to communicate in this state because, though as a disembodied soul

thou hast by right
No converse with aught else beside thyself

such a sublime solipsism would impose too stern a solitude 'and break thy being'.[19]

With all its simplicity and restraint the measured account of fundamental Christian belief in the hymns might seem too much a mere balancing of the books if there were not in this world where the categories are living being a living dynamic act on the part of Gerontius. This comes in the rush of sympathy by which he enters completely into Christ's sacrifice and sufferings:

[18] Keats, *The Fall of Hyperion*, xi. 372–7.

[19] One is reminded of those early moods of Wordsworth when he wished to kick his foot against a stone to assure himself of his identity.

Thou wilt be sick with love, and yearn for Him,
And feel as though thou couldst but pity Him.

This act leads on naturally to the soul's prostrating itself at the feet of the Saviour. The pain of purgatory is embraced both necessarily and voluntarily. It is to be remarked here how, in spite of a few phrases like 'sick with love', 'scorch'd and shrivell'd', the language absolutely abstains from that ecstatic Counter-Reformation rhetoric in which other Catholic poets, Crashaw for instance, have indulged themselves. This avoidance of the local, of the narrowly cultural, might have freed the poem for infinity at the expense of ultimate human impoverishment. Is not Newman throwing aside every device by which language lives and has its being? Is he not likely to fail in thus reducing time and space and material richness to a pale Platonic Form of Forms? The form of his heaven cannot even permit him to dwell much on the human side of Christ's nature, vital for the soul though that link is in the total scene. It is only a partial answer to say that much is accomplished by grace and sweetness of diction and by the tact which steers deftly between mild archaism and natural word order. The formal problem is that of depicting a state where depiction is ruled out beforehand; in which there are no points of reference except one, God, who cannot be approached directly. By skirting these impossibilities Newman clears a space in this ecstatic world which is a true standing outside of all recognizable experience. He has abstained from the effort to evoke paradise by any more charged and colourful imagery; but he does succeed in finding a substitute for the suspension of temporal succession in the eternal state. Fallen human nerves demand a point to look forward to beyond whatever is the present stage of things; thought is unimaginable that is not entangled with hope or fear or expectation. The total freedom of heaven from linear time and the riddenness of space in the world is unimaginable. So Newman's poem allows the strangeness of its vision to be mediated to the reader by certain points of expectation which have been retained. There is a before and after for the soul's vision of God; then there is the expectation of purgatory. When the Angel commits the soul to purgatory at the end it is a stage, or a series of stages, and thus the graspable notion of a period of probation, an ascesis, familiar from the saint's period of probation on earth, is retained.

The poem begins as a kind of personal commentary on the Office for the Dead; it ends in a similar manner by returning to its biblical and liturgical sources. The Angel's last speech, committing the soul to a 'night of trial' which will be brief, is preceded by a prose version of Psalm 90. It is a measure of Newman's achievement and its assured serenity that it can mingle its rhythms unostentatiously with biblical texts. The serenity is not impersonal and there is a sense in which *The Dream of Gerontius* completes the *Apologia*. It follows on from it chronologically in Newman's writing career, but it also embodies the completion of this particular Christian soul's journey— from the particularity of Oxford and Birmingham to this purely spiritual ascent.

And yet in the process Gerontius has become a simpler, less subtle man than Newman. There is a sense in which no literary work can be described as finished or enjoying a full existence until it has achieved perfect understanding and possession by a public: it must come to terms with its society. This was accomplished for *The Dream of Gerontius* in and after 1900 when Elgar's musical setting brought the work into the minds of English concert audiences as a satisfying amalgam of aesthetic and religious emotion. To be liable to this the austerity of the text had left certain points of entry; there are, for instance, the warm tenderness of the lines following on 'Take me away and in the lowest deep | There let me be . . .'. The frontier of the personality of Gerontius as thrown out by Newman had to be extended to permit a more typical, a more identifiable man; but the potentiality for this extension had to be there in the first place, in the seed of that individuality generalized by death which the text proclaims:

Look here: I imagine Gerontius to be a man like us, not a priest or a saint but a *sinner*, a repentant one of course but still no end of a *worldly* man in his life, and now brought to book. Therefore I've not filled *his* part with church tunes and rubbish, but a good, healthy, full-blooded romantic, remembered worldliness, so to speak. It is, I imagine, much more difficult to tear one's self away from a well-to-do world than from a cloister.[20]

[20] Edward Elgar, letter to A. J. Jaeger (1900) quoted in Basil Maine, *Elgar: His Life and Works* (London, 1932), 104. Cf. J. Northrop Moore, *Edward Elgar: A Creative Life* (Oxford, 1984), 284–337, for a fuller account of the genesis and development of the oratorio.

4

Newman: The Foolishness of Preaching

ERIC GRIFFITHS

To call these sermons eloquent would be no word for them[1]

All preachers must at times fear what Newman at least once feared. Preaching in the University Church at Oxford on Romans 13: 11—'Now it is high time to wake out of sleep'—he told his congregation: 'there is great reason for fearing that very many of you are not wide awake'.[2] Accustomed as he was to public speaking, he felt the vocational nervousness of someone who takes it upon himself to address an assembled company: the fidgeted worry 'I hope I'm not boring you' which runs through much of what we say and particularly races under our words when we are, for some formal reason, appointed to speak.

Yet this is not the heart of Newman's anxiety. It is an Advent sermon, and so any specific Oxonian sleepiness finds a liturgical place in that season's customary urging of mankind to awake. He had reasons enough to know that *he* was not boring them; the Church of Saint Mary the Virgin on Sunday afternoons was regularly full and attentively hushed. Of course, he had not read the thrilled reminiscences which members of his congregation (Matthew Arnold, R. W. Church, J. A. Froude, William Lockhart, James Mozley, J. C. Shairp amongst others[3]) later published but he can hardly not have noticed several hundred people gazing at him as if he were an angel, however little heed he paid to such rapture. This thronged concentration on Newman could itself be a torpor just in its fervour, as appears from Doyle's slackly

[1] J. C. Shairp, *Studies in Poetry and Philosophy* (1868; 4th edn., London, 1886), 249.

[2] *PS* i. 59.

[3] A selection from these accounts may be found in R. D. Middleton's 'The Vicar of St Mary's' in G. Wheeler (ed.), *Newman Centenary Essays* (London, 1945); further anecdotal references are given below.

phrased enthusiasm for Newman's 'mesmeric influence'.[4] The preacher as hypnotist, theatrical charmer—this role is far from Newman's ambitions, far from the type of homiletic perfection as that is exemplified in Christ: 'Christ gives us counsel; as is proper for God, he speaks without constraining us.'[5] The cult of Newman might have shown that it was God who was boring the congregation.

A more general issue arises here than the trickiness of dealing with a fan club when the fans are supposed to be devout. Newman had an acute suspicion of the workings of imagination in the religious life, of those who 'mix up the Holy Word of God with their own idle imaginings'.[6] Hence his liking for the 'Breviary Devotions' of the Roman Office because 'They are for the whole year, varying day by day more or less. This again I like much; it keeps up attention and rouses the imagination towards the course of the Christian year, without exciting it'.[7] He specially mistrusts the power of imagination to doll up religious life and deliver it over as a toy for the delectation of a consumer who then 'appreciates' it rather than being judged by it. The sermons persistently warn against religious allure: 'Men admire religion, while they can gaze on it as a picture. They think it lovely in books'; 'Many a man likes to be religious in graceful language'; 'I am much opposed to certain *religious* novels . . . they lead men to cultivate the religious affections separate from religious practice'; 'It is beautiful in a picture to wash the disciples' feet; but the sands of the real desert have no lustre in them to compensate for the servile nature of the occupation.'[8] The danger of whetting a taste for religion is that, once aroused, it leads people to consider religion as a matter of taste: they adopt 'the notion that, when they retire from the business of their temporal calling, then they may (in a quiet, unexceptionable way of course) consult their own tastes and likings'.[9] Even the pious delight of his undergraduate audience, their very interest in him, might turn out in a parodic reversal of his hopes and intention to be complicit with that liberalism and doctrinal indifferentism against which he preached

[4] F. Doyle, *Reminiscences*, quoted in R. W. Church, *The Oxford Movement: Twelve Years 1833–1845* (1891; 3rd edn., London, 1892), 143.

[5] St Irenaeus, Epideixis 55, quoted in S. Tugwell, *The Way of the Preacher* (London, 1979), 7.

[6] *PS* i. 58.

[7] *LD* vi. 47.

[8] *PS* i. 162; *PS* i. 270; *PS* ii. 373–4.

[9] *PS* vii. 87.

but *to* which he had also to address his words. The appetite for religious eloquence as a cultural spice guaranteed nothing about the faith of the community which consumed it. England in the 1830s was evidently Laodicea, 'neither cold nor hot' (Rev. 3: 15), but it would do no good to supply the lukewarm with stimulants for then they would blow hot and cold, exchanging their stable tepidity for fluctuations equally without consequence.

Sermons were business in Newman's England, though not very big business. Rivington's catalogue alone for 1880 lists fifty-five separate volumes which they had in print that year. When Newman began to arrange the publication of his parochial sermons, he showed at once a canny sense of the market and a refusal to exploit it or accommodate its demands, as, for instance, in his preference for publication in octavo rather than a handier size: 'the duodecimo form is used, I believe, for the sake of reading in the pulpit. Now I have no wish to be spouted over the kingdom.'[10] Not only did he not wish to irrigate the barrenness of his fellow clerics, he also almost never availed himself of the practice of delivering other people's sermons, a practice which had been quite normal for more than a century; he records the rare exceptions in his diary, when, a month after the death of Hurrell Froude, he 'read one of dear H.F.'s sermon[s] (on his birthday) being the first not my own I ever read in my life'.[11] He tells Robert Wilberforce in 1828 that 'I have before now felt in my own mind the distress you speak of about the right mode of preaching—at one time . . . so sorely that I thought I must have given up my curacy, nay have left the Church'; he points out to S. L. Pope the horns of a satanic dilemma:

As to Town-preacherships, they seem to me dangerous to the holder, as corrupting the minister into the orator. . . . One out of many dilemmas in which a London-preacher finds himself, is the following—let *him withstand* the popular love of novelty and desire of excitement, he must preach (what will be called) *dully* and if so, he will *empty his chapel*—let him try to keep his congregation together, he will be pampering their bad tempers and habits.[12]

[10] *LD* iv. 146.

[11] *LD* v. 267; Newman again read sermons by Hurrell Froude on 3 Apr. 1836 and 10 July 1836. These are the only instances I know of his reading someone else's compositions from the pulpit.

[12] *LD* ii. 84, 337–8.

This mistrust of the oratorical continued in his Oratorian life. Preaching on St Philip Neri, he was at pains to make clear that 'Philip had no vocation, and little affection, for the pulpit: he was jealous of what the world calls eloquence . . . he discoursed and conversed rather than preached'.[13] It seems likely, then, that Newman would have been pleased by the recollection of the Birmingham Fathers that 'His manner of speaking was the same in the pulpit as on ordinary occasions; in fact, he was not preaching but conversing'.[14]

His first two heads of advice in his notes on writing sermons turn on an opposition between earnestness and eloquence such as he often stressed in the sermons themselves: '1. A man should be in earnest, by which I mean he should write not for the sake of writing, but to bring out his thoughts. 2. He should never aim at being eloquent.'[15] After his conversion, he ceased to record that he had preached on a particular day, so that on the celebrated occasion of his sermon on 'The Pope and Revolution', during which it was noted, as a rare gesture from the usually immobile Newman, that he stamped his foot when describing the followers of Victor Emmanuel as 'a force of sacrilegious robbers', his diary entry reads simply 'Service for the Pope Palmer went Fr Suffield came', as if he had said nothing, done nothing.[16]

These are anecdotal instances of something his auditors caught in his voice again and again: 'self was altogether repressed'; 'his mind was so *objective* that his own subjectivity was well-nigh forgotten'; the contrast between 'the humble pleading way in which he spoke his own words, and the reverence with which he read' quotations from Scripture 'made every sermon a sermon on the objectivity of Revealed Truth'.[17] However much scholars have emphasized Newman's subjective cast of mind and the pressure of autobiographical material into his ecclesiological or theological reflection, the testimony of those who heard him preach a sermon, in which responsibility to doctrinal orthodoxy meets the manifestation of individual temperament, is to the contrary. It is not true, as a recent book on the *Parochial and*

[13] *OS*, p. 237. [14] *SN*, p. vii. [15] Quoted in Ward, ii. 335.

[16] Ibid. i. 520 records the stamping; the relevant passage of the sermon is in *OS* 289; the diary entry for 7 Oct. 1866 is reprinted in *LD* xxii. 296.

[17] H. Liddon, *Life of Edward Bouverie Pusey*, 2 vols. (1893–7), ii. 375; W. Lockhart, *Cardinal Newman: Reminiscences of Fifty Years Since* (London, 1891), 23; *SN*, p. xii.

Plain Sermons claims, that 'Nei sermoni parrochiali Newman parla molto di sé' ('In his parochial sermons Newman talks a lot about himself').[18] What is truly startling and distinctive in his sermons is the absence of the pronoun 'I'. It appears in 'The Parting of Friends', for instance, only in biblical quotations and through the formulaic phrase 'my brethren'; in this sermon, delivered on the most piercing occasion in his life to that time, Newman appears as 'one' and 'he'.[19] He advised S. L. Pope: 'in one place, you speak of *yourself* in your sermon. This I think should be omitted.'[20]

He was not ever thus. Though he almost never spoke of himself when preaching, he thought much about what he had said and how he had said it. In 1874 he remembered a fit of self-concern over his performance in his first university sermon: 'I lay on my sofa writhing at the thought what a fool I had made of myself.'[21] The diaries for his first years as an Anglican minister meticulously detail the composition and delivery of sermons, specially noting his worry that his voice was weak and his treatment of that complaint with medicinal glasses of wine and a few eggs.[22] Such worries show a proper concern for those others who, as well as himself, would hear him preach. The regime he adopted for composition in this period is exhausting even to contemplate; he wrote two sermons a week every week for about fifteen months, usually preparing the first between Tuesday and Thursday, the second on Friday and Saturday. Almost nothing interrupted this flood of homilies, as a poignant diary entry for 1 October 1824 reveals: 'saw my dear Father for the last time—began sermon Eph v, 14'.[23] That text in the King James Version reads: 'Wherefore he saith, Awake thou that sleepest, and arise from the dead, and Christ shall give thee light.' One senses, even this early in his ministry, how swift and instinctive was Newman's transformation of the contingencies of his life into the pattern

[18] P. Udini, *Il messaggio di J. H. Newman nei sermoni parochiali* (Vicenza, 1981), 113.

[19] This sermon, Newman's last as an Anglican, is reprinted in *Sermons bearing on Subjects of the Day*. Newman's references to himself are in the last paragraph, *SD*, p. 409.

[20] *LD* iv. 325.

[21] *AW*, p. 168.

[22] See e.g. diary entries for 25 July 1824, 8 Aug. 1824, 15 Aug. 1824, in *LD* i. 180, 183, 185.

[23] *LD* i. 193.

of liturgy and doctrine, something radically different from the familiar anecdotalism of the preacher—'As I was on my way here today . . .'—in which experiences merely more or less nattily illustrate a text. Newman's life was impregnated by Scripture. Around 1825 this drilling rhythm of comment and exhortation slows down; it becomes more frequent for him to mention a guest preacher at St Clement's; he also begins to repeat sermons from the stock he has built up. He settles to composing one sermon a week from 1828 until the beginning of the Oxford Movement in 1833, after which, for a year or so, he draws on his reserves, until early in 1835 he resumes the practice of writing a new sermon each week. While he devoted himself with painful intensity to these labours of edification, he also looked askance at himself, examined the motives and effect of his busyness: 'These advantages of composing sermons are greatly counterbalanced by the empty vanity of mind, to which they have given rise. Many gownsmen frequent the Church—several of our College sometimes go, and all this puffs me up.'[24]

Newman works through relentless application to the task of preaching and moments when his industry crumbles in his hands, when he both feels unworthy to perform the task and also wonders whether it is worth doing, even when done as well as he does it, for preaching draws the preacher cruelly into self-content just while it flatters his audience with temporary convictions that they are religiously alive and awake whereas they are mostly subjects of a homiletic galvanism. Perhaps such thoughts belong only to that depression which often results from overwork. It says a lot for his patience and determination that he persevered through them. To some it will seem that what actuates him is at least as much an inescapable obsession, a persistence comparable to neurotic hand-washing, as a fidelity which commands respect. Whether these two kinds of description are really in competition with each other, and, if they are, which of them should be awarded the victory, will not be decided here. But Newman did not suffer his doubts alone. He participates in what Geoffrey Hill has called 'that obsessive self-critical . . . monologue in which eloquence and guilt are intertwined'.[25] Newman's case

[24] *AW*, p. 205, diary for 21 Feb. 1825.

[25] G. Hill, 'Poetry as "Menace" and "Atonement"', in id., *The Lords of Limit* (London, 1984), 3–4.

doesn't quite fit these terms because a sermon is not exactly a monologue and because Hill refers to works of literature whereas sermons are not exactly 'literature', at least not in the sense people usually mean by that word nowadays (though the current sense does not establish itself as predominant until about the middle of the nineteenth century).

Still, there is a fellowship in being gravelled by one's task between the man of letters and the man of the cloth. Hill suggests that the 'appropriate epigraph' for the literary strain he identifies would be 'one abrupt entry in Coleridge's 1796 Notebook: "Poetry—excites us to artificial feelings—makes us callous to real ones."'[26] Newman might have said: 'Preaching—excites us to artificial feelings—makes us callous to real ones.' In fact, he did say that, though not in so many words. Of religious literature:

> the art of composing, which is a chief accomplishment, has in itself a tendency to make us artificial and insincere. For to be ever attending to the fitness and propriety of our words, is (or at least there is the risk of its being) a kind of acting; and knowing what can be said on both sides of a subject, is a main step towards thinking the one side as good as the other.

Or again, strikingly:

> Literature is almost in its essence unreal; for it is the exhibition of thought disjoined from practice.[27]

For all their vehemence, these remarks are shifty. Does Newman propose that we should never attend to the fitness and propriety of our words?—that would be imprudent. Or that we should do so only now and again? And, if the latter, *when* should we do so? Knowing what can be said on both sides of a subject is as good a safeguard against going wrong (because to know what can be said is to know where precisely the sides are and so to know on the edges of which precipices we move) as it is an inducement to think it makes no difference which way we go. And what does 'almost in its essence unreal' mean? The notion of an almost essential attribute is slippery to the grasp, as is the idea of something which essentially is almost unreal.

Particularly, it is strange to say that 'Literature . . . is the exhibition of thought disjoined from practice', for an exhibition is

[26] Ibid. 4.

[27] *PS* ii. 374, and *PS* v. 42.

a practical matter; it may be more or less thoughtfully or decently mounted, it might be closed by the authorities. Composition, considering the fitness and propriety of words, is 'a kind of acting', according to Newman; he probably means that it is a kind of theatrical performance or histrionicism. His phrase would be more true if it recognized that even acting is a kind of action which may be at times the one thing needful for practical authenticity (as when, in mid-sermon, a preacher loses personal confidence in what he is saying or why he is saying it but carries on regardless; you may call him an old stager but the stagey thing, the self-regarding thing, to do in those circumstances would be to break off the homily and entertain the congregation to his individual difficulties). Just because 'Literature' is an exhibition, it is not 'disjoined from practice', because composition is a 'kind of acting' it is also a form of action. Newman knew this well, which is why he could say that 'humility which is a great Christian virtue has a place in literary composition'.[28] This could not be so if all exhibitions were merely showy and no acting ever an action.

Saying where humility can be found in Newman's homiletic composition involves subjecting some of his sermons to that kind of literary criticism known as 'close reading'. This might seem askew from what Newman would have desired or even sanctioned. It involves looking at and listening to details of expression in a way which could be at odds with his abhorrence of self-regard, an act of impertinence (or worse). Yet the discipline of minute verbal attention may sometimes have the advantage of rousing the imagination, without exciting it. The attention which starts at words does not end on them, for 'Precious doctrines are strung, like jewels, upon slender threads'.[29] This is actually at once a theological and a literary-critical truth: 'such creatures as we are, there is the most close and remarkable connexion between small observances and the permanence of our chief habits and practices'.[30] The same is true of small observations.

One way of coping with Laodiceans, their appetite for both verbal flights of fancied piety and a life in fact of earthly quiet, was to incorporate their ordinary language of backsliding, shuffling-off, and 'moderation' into the sermon. Where the audience sat back, expecting silver eloquence, they heard instead their own

[28] Ward, ii. 335. [29] *PS* ii. 76. [30] *PS* i, 252.

shoddy. Newman expertly mimics the concessives and reservations with which people hedge their bets on God, wagering with Pascal, maybe, but playing the field as well: 'How often do we hear them say that a man must do so and so, unless he would be singular and absurd; that he must not be too strict, or indulge high-flown notions of virtue, which may be good to talk about, but are not fit for this world!'; 'though truth and religion are certainly all-commanding and all-important, yet still the world could not go on, public business would be at a stand, political parties would be unable to act . . . if religion refused at all times to give way ever so little'; 'they argue that it is our duty to solace ourselves here (in moderation, of course) with the goods of this life,— . . . that the world is, on the whole, very well disposed towards religion,—that we should avoid enthusiasm,—that we should not be over serious'; 'They maintain that it is impossible that religion should really be so strict according to God's design. They condemn the notion as over-strained and morose. They profess to admire and take pleasure in religion as a whole, but think it should not be needlessly pressed in details, or, as they express it, carried too far.'[31] The mumbled litany of 'up to a point', 'on the whole', 'in a measure' runs through the sermons, as if his words included within themselves, found an imaginative place for, the moral acoustic of double-talk in which they sounded quite as much as they rang in the actual place of their first utterance, in the Gothic stillness of the church of St Mary the Virgin. Half-hearted devotion is a favourite topic for pulpit exhortations but if we compare Newman's handling of the subject with, say, Wesley's or Wiseman's,[32] it becomes apparent that the dictional acquaintance of a Newman sermon with the language and attitudes it repudiates is much more intimate and needling. Not that he confined himself to such feints at the language of the world. He also brings phrases from that language uncomfortably face to face with the graver tones of scriptural denunciation, as when he warns that a man's concern to provide for his family may mutate into something less respectable: 'A man may live from week to week in the fever of a decent covetousness, to

[31] *PS* ii. 337, *PS* iv. 10; *PS* i. 319; *PS* iv. 13.

[32] See Wesley's 'The Almost Christian' in Robert Nye (ed.), *The English Sermon*, iii (Manchester, 1976), 36–43, or Wiseman's 'On the Love of the World', in id., *Sermons on Moral Subjects* (Dublin, 1864), 1–17.

which he gives some more specious name', where the direct conflict of 'decent' with 'covetousness' lexically enacts what it is to try to serve two masters ('decent' does not appear in Cruden's *Concordance* . . .). Similarly, dictional hybrids of the worldly and the biblical in this passage unerringly touch on the strange growths which stem from a grafting of religious approbation on to economic drive: 'Money is a sort of creation, and gives the acquirer, even more than the possessor, an imagination of his own power; and tends to make him idolize self.'[33]

St Augustine felt and resisted the temptation of music: 'Sed cavendum est ne divinis gravibusque sententiis, dum additur numerus, pondus detrahatur' ('But we must take care that we do not lessen the weight of sacred and solemn remarks by giving them cadences').[34] The sentence is itself cadenced by the chiastic arrangement of nouns and passive verbs. Given the many witnesses to the musicality of Newman's style, he might seem to have ignored Augustine's caveat, but there are elements in his compositions which show him markedly and audibly avoiding symmetry and cadence. Merely to lack shapeliness is the common condition of speech; the lack alone would not challenge a judgement that sermons ought to display ornamental graces. Such a challenge can be made only by showing oneself capable of eloquence and then abstaining from it. The appetite for rhetorical delicacies is seriously tantalized; the congregation must recognize the perils inherent in its own desires, rebuke itself, understand and overcome its own leanings and weakness. As in the following passage:

> St. Paul, and the Apostles, and all Christ's ministers after them, are of one nature with other men. They have to go through what other men go through. They suffer pain, sorrow, bereavement, anxiety, desolateness, privations; and they have need, as other men, of patience, cheerfulness, faith, hope, contentment, resignation, firmness, to bear all that comes on them well. But even more than other men are they called on to bear the opposition of the world.[35]

The common humanity of Christ's ministers and their excellence both appear in the syntactic contours of the extract. The second

[33] *PS* iii. 338; *PS* ii. 355.
[34] Augustine, *De doctrina christiana*, IV. XX. 41.
[35] *PS* viii. 148–9.

sentence patiently explains the slightly recondite 'of our nature', condescending from the term of theological art to the language of 'other men', that keynote phrase which is sounded in each of the sentences quoted. Newman changes his prose in the third sentence with its catalogue of tribulations and their answering virtues. 'Answering' very exactly, because each element of the list of ills is matched in order with the response it requires: 'patience' to bear 'pain', 'cheerfulness' even in 'sorrow', 'faith' in eternal life during a 'bereavement', 'hope' to find an issue from 'anxiety', 'contentment' to face spiritual 'desolateness', 'resignation' to inevitable physical 'privations'. Then he breaks the symmetry he has arranged, for there is still a virtue more though distresses have ceased: 'firmness'. That extra word, which sends the cadence awry, actually crowns the thought; such 'firmness' is the apostolic virtue of unswerving commitment in a world of half hearts. This small moment is extremely characteristic of its author; the passionate crowding of thoughts in the weary list of adversities turns out to be a balanced meditation on virtue and circumstance when the point-by-point correspondence of the second catalogue to the first is heard but the meditation does not settle into a schema, it thrusts beyond a settled pattern with a further effort of the voice towards 'firmness', and it is this capacity for yet a further effort which changes the apostles from 'other men' to 'even more than other men', though their special capacity is to be more sorely tried.[36]

Another glamour which the preacher must put by is described by Humbert of Romans in his great treatise *On the Formation of Preachers*:

> There are others who work hard to find a lot to say, multiplying the sections of their sermons or using too many distinctions or producing long lists of authorities or strings of arguments or illustrations; or they look for lots of different words all meaning the same thing, or they repeat the same ideas over and over again, or they produce interminable prothemes or expound a single word in all kinds of different senses. All of these are serious faults in a sermon.[37]

[36] Cf. amongst many other similar moments *PS* vi. 40, passage beginning 'Does it not stand to reason' or *PS* vii. 180, passage beginning 'To be dead to sin'.

[37] I quote from Simon Tugwell's translation in *Early Dominicans: Selected Writings* (Ramsey, NJ, and London, 1982), 205–6. I am grateful to Richard Finn, *OP*, for drawing my attention to this work.

Newman almost never quotes anything but the Bible in his Anglican sermons (the Catholic sermons mention the Fathers and saints, but not often); in this he is distinct from Keble, and especially from Pusey whose sermons are tissues of patristic references. Newman shows particular aptitude in finding fluent sequences of terms which are never mere ricochets off each other; the gradations of his rhetorical progressions allow and demand time for thought rather than condensing temporal series into an instantaneously graspable, diagrammatic coherence. For example, this passage on those who have turned from God to the world only to be disappointed in it:

> They are led to say, with St. Peter, 'Lord, to whom *shall* we go?' for they have tried the world, and it fails them; they have trusted it, and it deceives them; they have leant upon it, and it pierces them through; they have sought it for indulgence, and it has scourged them for their penance.[38]

He carefully abstains from saying what is the place of sin in the dispensation of providence by the ambiguity of 'They are led' and he patterns even the most sinful, the most aberrantly contingent, life on a Scriptural frame, as he so often does, when he makes the world-weary ask their question '*with* St. Peter' (my emphasis)—there is an implicit wealth of comprehension in that small 'with', a marriage of his human sympathies and his faith such as he also showed in thinking so soon after his father died of St Paul's Letter to the Ephesians. Consider the pairings which follow: tried/fails; trusted/deceives; leant upon it/pierces them through; sought it for indulgence/has scourged them for their penance. The turns from preterite to present tense may look at first like repeated homiletic versions of the 'before/after' pictures in advertisements for miracle diets, but they are more humanely various than that. The opening pair hints at the way a sinner imagines that it is he who judges or examines the world, takes it 'on trial', as it were, when he 'tries' it, but actually the world is the examiner for it 'fails' him, lets him down but also finds him wanting just as he has wanted it; 'trusted' picks up alliteratively from 'tried' but the relation imagined has become more intimate —he desires the world as a lover or a friend but it 'deceives' him in a double sense, 'cheats on' him as well as misleading him.

[38] *PS* iv. 186.

After these distresses the sinner looks to the world for support but the world is like an alpenstock upside-down—it has a spike where the handle should be, lean on it and it pierces. (The diction and order of the prose are deeply and subduedly biblical: 'leant' and 'pierces' come from Isaiah 36: 6, where the prophet speaks of trust 'in the staff of this broken reed, on Egypt'. That 'reed' then prompts 'scourged' because a reed appears in Mark 15: 19 in the account of the scourging of Christ.) The last pairing rapidly but gravely puns on 'indulgence': the world should supply materials for gratification ('indulgence') and also a remission of penalties ('indulgence') but it can offer only that scourging penance which must precede indulgence (in one sense) and which follows indulgence (in another sense). The activity of mind within these stable syntactical patterns is exceptional in its unshowy insight, its agile tenderness. The writing is full of care, a care that is simultaneously an ethical compassion and a meticulous concern for literary propriety.

Or take this reflection on the Eucharist:

> Christ then took our nature, when He would redeem it; He redeemed it by making it suffer in His own Person; He purified it, by making it pure in His own Person. He first sanctified it in Himself, made it righteous, made it acceptable to God, submitted it to an expiatory passion, and then He imparted it to us. He took it, consecrated it, broke it, and said, 'Take, and divide it among yourselves.'[39]

Newman rarely expounded doctrine on the sacraments in his Anglican sermons (with the exception of the immediately and inescapably controversial matter of infant baptism) and even this passage of theological genius figures in a discourse on 'Christian Sympathy' rather than in what would at that time in the Anglican Church have been a polemical contribution to debate about the real presence and the sacrificial nature of the Mass. His theological mastery shines in the quietness with which it is delivered. Newman makes his parallel between the Incarnation, the course of Christ's actuality in mankind, and the words of the Anglican communion service as he knew it—'who in the same night that he was betrayed, took Bread; and, when he had given thanks, he brake it, and gave it to his disciples, saying, "Take . . ."'—so fleetingly, in such measured but undeliberated words, and with

[39] *PS* v. 117–18.

so complete and unsignalled a symmetry, that it might almost not be noticed. That is a triumph of understanding, an act of intellectual friendship with doctrine so entire that, like a friend's kindness, it is often only in retrospect that it is noticed, registered, and given its due. His words tell why the Mass is a sacrifice which reconciles mankind to God and mankind to itself as, through Christ's passional life, passional in His birth as in His death, mankind receives its nature again from Him. Newman says this in the simplicity of the move 'took . . . took . . . and said, "Take . . ." '. Unlike Humbert of Romans's faulty preacher who scrabbles about for many words which all turn out to mean the same old thing, Newman's one, unsearched-for, negligibly plain word 'take', means several things and each of them anew.

He advised himself on one aspect of the ethics of a preacher's style when he cautioned his hearers against fluency of religious utterance:

> It is easy to make professions, easy to say fine things in speech or in writing, easy to astonish men with truths which they do not know, and sentiments which rise above human nature. 'But thou, O servant of God, flee these things, and follow after righteousness, godliness, faith, love, patience, meekness.' Let not your words run on; force every one of them into action as it goes[40]

'Let not your words run on': this is a motto for that calling to account of wordly eloquence, that creation of a halting speech in whose lowlinesses, avoidances of evidently clinching cadences, Newman found a place for humility in literary composition.

Stopping his words was one of his most remarked idiosyncrasies as a preacher:

> The delivery had a peculiarity which it took a new hearer some time to get over. Each separate sentence, or at least each short paragraph, was spoken rapidly, but with great clearness of intonation; and then at its close there was a pause, lasting for nearly half a minute; then another rapidly but clearly spoken sentence, followed by another pause.[41]

Froude recalled the effect of one such pause:

> Newman described closely some of the incidents of our Lord's passion; he then paused. For a few moments there was a breathless silence. Then, in a low, clear voice, of which the faintest vibration was audible

[40] *PS* i. 70–1.

[41] Shairp, *Studies in Poetry and Philosophy*, p. 247.

in the farthest corner of St. Mary's, he said, 'Now, I bid you recollect that He to whom these things were done was Almighty God.' It was as if an electric stroke had gone through the church, as if every person present understood for the first time the meaning of what he had all his life been saying. I suppose it was an epoch in the mental history of more than one of my Oxford contemporaries.[42]

The Birmingham Oratorians' recollection chimes with the agnostic historian's, though they heard Newman's pauses in a way that suggests his delivery had become, during his Catholic years, more marked by liturgical observance; they note a distinction between his reading of the Epistle and of the Gospel:

His manner of reading the Gospel was different. There were of course the pauses required to mark off the purely narrative portions from the words of different speakers, accompanied by some slight changes in the voice. But the marked thing, which cannot be described, was the increased reverence in the reader's voice which culminated when he came to the words of our Saviour. Before and after these there was a kind of hush. A most wonderful thing about it all was the complete elimination of the personality of the reader.[43]

Printed texts being what they are, we have some of Newman's words but none of his silences, though we know that these silences were 'a stillness that speaks'.[44] We can attempt with some hesitation to give one of these silences a life again.

It cannot be the case, as Shairp unclearly claims, that Newman took a pause of nearly thirty seconds after each sentence (a sermon such as 'Faith and Obedience' which he preached on his own birthday in 1830 would, by this measure, have had more than five hours of silences, if the printed text represents even roughly what he said). The printed sermons are, anyway, revised versions of what was on various occasions spoken. Allowing for the unreliability of evidences hereabouts, something yet speaks in the stillness between paragraphs of Newman's sermon 'Waiting for Christ'. This eschatological meditation fully weighs the historical variety of expectations about the end of the world; its profundity lives just in its marking of time and times within eschatology. I quote at length because it is a passage about lengths. He begins in the mind of early Christians:

[42] J. A. Froude, *Short Studies on Great Subjects*, 4 vols. (1882; 1894), iv. 286.
[43] *SN*, pp. xi–xii.
[44] *PS* vi. 103.

when once Christ had come, as the Son over His own house, and with His perfect Gospel, nothing remained but to gather in His saints. No higher Priest could come,—no truer doctrine. The Light and Life of men had appeared and had suffered, and had risen again; and nothing more was left to do. Earth had had its most solemn event, and seen its most august sight; and therefore it was the last time. And hence, though time intervene between Christ's first and second coming, it is not *recognized* (as I may say) in the Gospel scheme, but is, as it were, an accident. For so it was, that up to Christ's coming in the flesh, the course of things ran straight towards that end, nearing it by every step; but now, under the Gospel, that course has (if I may so speak) altered its direction, as regards His second coming, and runs, not towards the end, but along it, and on the brink of it; and is at all times equally near that great event, which, did it run towards, it would at once run into. Christ, then, is ever at our doors; as near eighteen hundred years ago as now, and not nearer now than then; and not nearer when He comes than now. When He says that He will come soon, 'soon' is not a word of time, but of natural order. This present state of things, 'the present distress' as St. Paul calls it, is ever *close upon* the next world, and resolves itself into it. As when a man is given over, he may die at any moment, yet lingers; as an implement of war may at any moment explode, and must at some time; as we listen for a clock to strike, and at length it surprises us; as a crumbling arch hangs, we know not how, and is not safe to pass under; so creeps on this feeble weary world, and one day, before we know where we are, it will end.

And here I may observe in passing, on the light thus thrown upon the doctrine, that Christ is the sole Priest under the Gospel, or that the Apostles ever sit on twelve thrones, judging the twelve tribes of Israel, or that Christ is with them always, even unto the end of the moon, and in the stars[45]

Appropriately for a passasge which marks time and senses of time, the control of tenses is accurate and exquisite; the certain finality of time in the early Church sounds in the pluperfects, a tense of absolute achievedness—'had come . . . had appeared . . . had suffered . . . had risen . . . had had'—which then develops (I use the word with Newman's full emphasis) through the perfect of 'has . . . altered' into that instant but permanent simple present which is the condition of the Church nowadays, at once measurably uncertain of the date when this world will end yet assured of now living that end—'runs . . . is at all times . . . is ever . . . is

[45] *PS* vi. 240–2.

ever *close upon*'. As the tense develops, so too does the sense of the word 'end'. 'Up to Christ's coming in the flesh, the course of things ran straight towards that end, nearing it by every step': here, 'end' is a purpose, and that purpose a birth; an event is to occur at a point in time and in space, so that it is possible to speak of 'nearing' and of steps. The 'end' of which he goes on to speak is not a point but a path, something we move 'along' and which is at all times 'equally near'; this 'end' is not only an event but the condition in which all events now occur, a revaluation of what it is for things to happen and of the medium in which they happen. Such a notion of eschatological reality as both impending and immanent is familiar to theologians but the subdued,[46] translucent eloquence Newman lends it in this sermon is rare. As he accounts for time, he controls it and submits to it in the pacing of his words. The last sentence of the first paragraph I quote unusually and elaborately suspends its main clause over four extended similes; it is a picture of waiting as well as a syntactic exercise in patience. (Note also the Shakespearean allusion, as apt as it is undemonstrative: 'so creeps on this feeble weary world, and one day' comes from Macbeth's evacuated sense of a time which lacks meaning because it lacks anything but more of itself to wait for: 'To-morrow, and to-morrow, and to-morrow, | Creeps in this petty pace from day to day'.) The whole composition moves to the word 'end' which ends the paragraph, but it moves *along* that word rather than approaches it, for the end is foreseen and foreheard, is the condition of the eloquence it closes, even though it still comes as a surprise because it comes at last, for the first time in this passage, as a verb rather than a noun, and also because the ending of the paragraph comes so casually, on so off-key a cadence, it catches us, like the last days, 'before we know where we are'. After that 'end', I imagine one of Newman's electric silences which is then broken upon by a wholly new, and dry, tone of voice: 'And here I may observe in passing . . .'.[47] He possibly did not intend the pun of

[46] 'Subdued' is perhaps Newman's favourite word for right Christian conduct of eloquence as of life: see e.g. *PS* iv. 239; *PS* v. 339; *PS* vii. 21. Other cognates are 'calm', 'collected' (of which Pusey was also fond), and 'practical'.

[47] This imagining of pause, and the weight I give it, may be called 'speculative'; I have no evidence that Newman paused here in delivering the sermon. Cf. Proust's imagination of pause in St Luke's Gospel, in 'Journées de lecture' (1919) repr. in *Contre Sainte-Beuve*, ed. P. Clarac and Y. Sandre (Paris, 1971), 193–4.

'in passing', felicitous though it is in this context of transience and finality. But something like the effect that pun would have had occurs in the transition made when his voice rises again out of the pause after 'end', a voice urbanely persistent, making observations for all the world as if the world had not ended. The shape of tone in the sermon lives itself through that transformed time of which he speaks, a time ended, ending, and unending; the formality of printed paragraphs in the text of the passage faintly suggests the drama of pause in his utterance of that moment, a pause which is both an abyss and, as he has composed it, a bridge across the gap he makes in eloquence.

Newman said that God 'has made history to be doctrine'.[48] The life of Christ does not *illustrate* a pre-existent conceptual truth as the death of Socrates might illustrate the universal proposition that all men are mortal. Our Lord's conception and birth are not an example of the Incarnation, they are the Incarnation; his death and resurrection are not instances but the actuality of the Atonement. This may be one reason why the Greeks in their search for 'wisdom' found the preaching of Christ crucified 'foolishness' (1 Cor. 1: 23); the impulse to articulate general truths, to sift the essential from the contingent, as that impulse appeared 'wisdom' to St Paul's Greeks, had to be disappointed when brought only to the foot of the Cross and shown that brutally particular incident as the Christian reply to the questions of philosophy (it did not seem to be an 'answer', let alone a 'solution'). Something kin to such bringing and showing of complex fact in the face, or in the teeth, of an urge for systematic exposition stands at the centre of Newman's preaching when he encounters the Greeks of his day—principally, it seemed to him, Evangelical Protestants. The 'fashion of the day' in preaching consisted, on the one hand, in an inflated, gratifyingly fervid emotionalism and, on the other, in a shrinking of scriptural narrative into vignettes more or less convenient as accompanying the exposition of narrowly sectarian tenets. The contemporary preacher, Newman claims,

> assume[s] that there is some one end of his ministerial labours, such as to be ascertainable by him, some one revealed object of God's dealings with man in the Gospel. Then, perhaps, he arbitrarily assigns this end

[48] *PS* ii. 227.

to be the salvation of the world, or the conversion of sinners. Next he measures all the Scripture doctrines by their respective sensible tendency to effect this end. He goes on to discard or degrade this or that sacred truth as superfluous in consequence, or of inferior importance; and throws the stress of his teaching upon one or other, which he pronounces to contain in it the essence of the Gospel, and on which he rests all others which he retains. Lastly, he reconstructs the language of theology to suit his (so-called) improved views of Scripture doctrine.[49]

Newman deplores such homiletic practices not because they are philosophical but because they are insufficiently so; they inadequately grasp what the system of Scripture is, and at the same time mangle the proper operation of philosophy. Just because such expositors have not the patience to understand the gradualness of revelation, in both Scripture and the tradition of the Church, because (so to speak) they refuse the contingencies of Christianity, they never taste its essence; they ignore its history, and therefore they do not even approach its mysteriousness. In contradistinction to this 'instant truth' exposition of the faith, Newman tried to restore in his preaching the coinherence of 'history' and 'doctrine' which he found in Scripture.

One consequence of his attempt must be that the space and time of his own teaching in the sermons needs attending to—not only by placing it in a contemporary setting of argument and ideas, nor only by retelling the valuable anecdotes that have been left us of his manner in the pulpit, but by that more intimate attention to the physique of what is said which is part of the task of literary criticism. For literary criticism is a specialism of the contingency in utterances, their colours, accent, and transience. If Newman stressed the incarnational nature of Scripture, of all Christian thinking, as I believe he did, and was right to do so, as I believe he was, then to restore, as best we can, the body of the speaker to printed words is to do at least what they ask and need, and may be to do more than that because 'The human body is the best picture of the human soul'.[50] By the body of an utterance, I mean just its locatedness in time and place, its essential contingencies. These physical facts of discourse make their appearance

[49] *PS* ii. 259–60. See also the vivid account of Satan as a systematizer of the Gospels in *PS* i. 310–11, and the attack on Evangelical reductivism in *PS* ii. 168–70.

[50] Wittgenstein, *Philosophical Investigations*, trans. G. E. M. Anscombe (1953; 3rd end., London, 1967), 178.

variously, as when Newman supplies a stage-direction to a passage from the Bible. He invokes the voice, the attitude, of the speaker: St John writes, 'The Word was made flesh, and dwelt among us'; Newman hears him speaking 'briefly and simply . . . as if fearing he should fail in fitting reverence'. Similarly: 'again, when S. John says with such deep feeling, and such beautiful calmness, and such deep meditation,—he says, "Dearly beloved, we are now the sons of God, and it hath not yet appeared what we shall be." '[51] The most extraordinary of such dramatic hearings comes when Newman listens to our Lord in the Garden of Gethsemane:

Lastly, when He was actually betrayed by him, 'Friend, wherefore art thou come?' 'Judas' (He addresses him by name), 'betrayest thou the Son of man with a kiss?' I am not attempting to reconcile His divine foreknowledge with this special and prolonged anxiety, this personal feeling towards Judas; but wish you only to dwell upon the latter, in order to observe what is given us by the revelation of Almighty God in the Gospels, viz., an acquaintance with His providential regard for *individuals*, making His sun to rise on the evil as well as on the good.[52]

From the small detail that our Lord calls on Judas by name, Newman moves through a theological perplexity to a doctrinal truth, and the whole move of his thought, its awareness of difficulty as well as its winning to a revealed providence, stems from and centres in the hearing of 'this special and prolonged anxiety, this personal feeling towards Judas' in the saying of that name then, the located utterance of our Lord's meaning.

Or take something that can be heard in Newman's own voice. I have mentioned how the syntax of the sermons allows for time, for the gradualness of revelation. He places the truths of faith as much as he times them, and he does so, aptly, by what Christopher Ricks has called in a different context the 'humbly essential medium' of the preposition.[53] A late Anglican sermon traces an implication of the real presence (which Newman was so delighted by in its full, physical proximity after his conversion):

[51] *PS* ii. 32: *Two Sermons Preached in the Church of S. Aloysius, Oxford* (Oxford, 1880), 14.

[52] *PS* iii. 122.

[53] 'William Wordsworth 2: "A sinking inward into ourselves from thought to thought" ', in C. Ricks, *The Force of Poetry* (Oxford, 1984), 120.

He has shown to us, that to come to Him for life is a literal bodily action; not a mere figure, not a mere movement of the heart towards Him, but an action of the visible limbs; not a mere secret faith, but a coming to church, a passing on along the aisle to His holy table, a kneeling down there before Him, and a receiving of the gift of eternal life in the form of bread and wine.[54]

The literally spatial prepositions—'coming to church . . . passing on along the aisle to His holy table, a kneeling down there'—deeply animate with their sense of sacramental locality those relations which seem more figurative, such as 'shown to us . . . come to Him . . . before Him . . . eternal life in the form of bread and wine'. The style might be said to be transubstantive in its informing of the accidents of both physical motion and linguistic ambiguity with an essential significance. Even when not so profoundly eucharistic, Newman's sense of place passes lightly between abstract concept and real space and time, a lightness which incarnates his dwelling at once in two worlds which seem much of the time remote from each other, as when he notes:

There is no reason except our own wilful corruption, that we are not by this time walking in the steps of St. Paul or St. John, and following them as they followed Christ. What a thought is this! Do not cast it from you, my brethren, but take it to your homes, and may God give you grace to profit by it![55]

'Walking in the steps of St. Paul or St. John' might come to no more than a cliché did not Newman turn it into truly pedestrian language when he urges his congregation to take the thought to their homes. They will walk home; they can walk home in those steps if they will. And, in fact, the walk home from church, as the walk from home to church, constantly springs to his mind when he preaches, as he calls to the lives into which his words must enter if they are to be more than a performance. Englishmen's homes are their castles, from which they make occasional sorties to church, and so 'they are sure to say we carry things too far when we carry them home to themselves',[56] as he puts it with his characteristic, quietly sad sense that these paradoxes of the remote

[54] *PS* vii. 149.

[55] *PS* i. 82.

[56] *PS* iv. 300. For other instances of Newman's rich and various play with 'home', cf. *PS* i. 270; *PS* ii. 288; *PS* v. 226. The extreme importance of the word for him continues in his Catholic life; see *SN*, p. 207 and the beautiful record of his return to Edgbaston after receiving the cardinal's hat, in Ward, ii. 471.

and the homely are not something he has ingeniously contrived himself. The ingenuity is wholly other.

A preacher must always be somewhere in particular when he preaches, and should speak as if he were. To recognize this is not to practise doctrinal trimming nor to espouse the aggrandized trimming sometimes known as 'relativism'. It is simply to speak as Newman does when he speaks of, and in, Adam's fallen state:

> And in this unrighteous state he has remained, viewed in himself, ever since; knowing the Law, but not doing it; admiring, not loving; assenting, not following; not utterly without the Law, yet not with it; with the Law not within him, but before him,—not any longer in his heart, as the pillar of a cloud, which was a gracious token and a guide to the Israelites, but departing from him, and moving away, and taking up its place, as it were over against him, and confronting him as an enemy, accuser, and avenger.[57]

The dismaying stagger of prepositions—'not utterly without . . . yet not with . . . with the Law not within'—mimes Adam's disorientation, his intermittent clutch at a moral harmony which recedes from him as he reaches towards it, moving from 'within' to 'before' to 'away' to 'over against him'. Yet this is a true mime, not an act of mimicry, because Newman's words themselves speak out of the condition they represent; the created stumbles of the passage belong to anybody's effort to comprehend the moral opacity of his fallen state as they do to imagining Adam: 'Chose étonnante cependant que le mystère le plus éloigné de notre connaissance qui est celui de la transmission du péché soit une chose sans laquelle nous ne pouvons avoir aucune connaissance de nous-même.' ('Yet how startling it is that the mystery most remote from our understanding—the mystery of our inheritance of Adam's sin—should be that very thing without which we can have absolutely no understanding of ourselves.')[58] So, when Newman describes our current state of self-bafflement, he does so with a similar intensity of charge in his prepositions as in the passage on Adam:

> We are in the dark about ourselves. When we act, we are groping in the dark, and may meet with a fall any moment. Here and there, perhaps, we see a little; or, in our attempts to influence and move our minds, we

[57] *PS* v. 146.

[58] Pascal, *Pensées*, ed. L. Layuma (1670; Paris, 1962), 74–5.

are making experiments (as it were) with some delicate and dangerous instrument, which works we do not know how, and may produce unexpected and disastrous effects. The management of our hearts is quite above us. Under these circumstances it becomes our comfort to look up to God. 'Thou, God, seest me!' Such was the consolation of the forlorn Hagar in the wilderness.[59]

The very ambiguity of relational words, which stands for the bewilderment of our relations to ourselves, such that we may be 'in' the dark as if the dark were a place like the wilderness Hagar finds herself 'in', such that the dark may be 'about ourselves' as if it were an encircling gloom or we may ourselves be in that dark about ourselves as when we say 'I don't know what to think about this'—this very ambiguity yields, by miracle, the intimation of the needed release through a grave pun: 'The management of our hearts is quite above us. Under these circumstances, it becomes our comfort to look up to God.' 'Above . . . under . . . up': the sequence is so casual as to be almost tacit, but it compacts both the common predicament and an orthodox hope. As Newman said, again hinging his conviction on an essentially humble word:

Such is the conduct of insincere men in difficulty. Perhaps their difficulty may be a real one; but in this they differ from the sincere:—the latter seek God *in* their difficulty, feeling that He only who imposes it can remove it; but insincere men do not like to go to God; and to them the difficulty is only so much gain, for it gives them an apparent reason, a sort of excuse, for not going by God's rule, but for deciding in their own way.[60]

It is not that being sincere implies freedom from sin; the sincere man too may be a sinner, but to seek God *in* the difficulty of sin is to begin to find a way out of both sin and insincerity.

A principal difficulty *in* which Newman sought God while preaching was the difficulty of reconciling 'apparently opposite declarations of Christ and His Prophets and Apostles'.[61] Given his dislike of picking and choosing scriptural texts in order to fabricate a sectarian homogeneity, he was bound to acknowledge the strain for thought in the narrated diversity of Gospel utterances such as the injunctions both not to hide one's light under a

[59] *PS* i. 173. [60] *PS* v. 233.
[61] *PS* i. 98. Cf. similar questions at *PS* i. 152; *PS* iv. 312; *PS* vi. 120, to name but a few.

bushel and not to give alms or pray ostentatiously (e.g. Matt. 5: 16 and 6: 1–6): 'How are these commands to be reconciled? how are we at once to *profess* ourselves Christians, and yet hide our Christian words, deeds, and self-denials?'[62] Some of these variant admonitions were to be accounted for in terms of the differing 'tempers and likings'[63] of those to whom they were addressed, but more than the contingencies of interlocution was involved in the deep, initial appearance that portions of Scripture are at odds with each other. It is not just separate passages which don't at once cohere; even within single sayings, Newman discovers an amplitude of divine significance which exceeds what the human mind can immediately recognize as self-consistent. And this is of the essence of divine speech as we receive it:

> In truth, if we may say it with reverence, the All-wise, All-knowing God cannot speak without meaning many things at once. He sees the end from the beginning; He understands the numberless connexions and relations of all things one with another. Every word of His is full of instruction, looking many ways; and though it is not often given us to attempt lightly to imagine them, yet, as far as they are told us, and as far as we may reasonably infer them, we must thankfully accept them. Look at Christ's words, and this same character of them will strike you; whatever He says is fruitful in meaning, and refers to many things.[64]

It is, then, not the preacher's only task to elicit a meaning from a text but rather to show the fruitfulness of the saying he expounds, though the task is not undertaken lightly nor ever all at once completed. In declining to straighten out or tidy up scriptural utterances, the preacher does not fail to give his hearers the comfort, warning, or guidance they need because human nature has in it a capacity for emotional ambivalence which responds to the quickening fecundity of God's words. Thus, our Lord's remarks at the time of his Ascension, which speak both of rejoicing and fasting, involve 'an apparent contradiction, such as attends the putting any high feeling into human language . . . they were to joy because Christ was come, and yet weep because He was away; that is, to have a feeling so refined, so strange and new, that nothing could be said of it, but that it combined in one all that was sweet and soothing in contrary human feelings, as commonly experienced'[65] but, in practice, we can experience

[62] *PS* i. 152.
[63] See e.g. *PS* i. 113.
[64] *PS* i. 272.
[65] *PS* v. 26.

such mingled states, hard as we find it to articulate them: 'We are two or three selves at once, in the wonderful structure of our minds, and can weep while we smile, and labour while we meditate.'[66] (It might be suggested, though Newman does not say so much, that just this inherent, generative meaningfulness in Scripture makes it so adapted to the 'concrete being' of its hearers, so lasting and piercing in its influence when heard, beyond what writings more conformed to 'paper logic' could achieve.)

God's word gives not a key to the meaning of life but life itself and requires a life in return:

> The Eternal Wisdom of God did not utter His voice that we might at once catch up His words in an irreverent manner, think we understand them at a glance, and pass them over. But His word endureth for ever; it has a depth of meaning suited to all times and places, and hardly and painfully to be understood in any. They, who think they enter into it easily, may be quite sure they do not enter into it at all.[67]

For Newman, interpretation and exposition of Scripture go on essentially in practice and demand the practical virtues, in particular the virtue of patience which might, in this context, be defined as the ability to take God's words in God's good time. Newman's dilemmas in the ethics of preaching were akin to some of the self-doubts of Romantic poets, and the way he meets difficulties of understanding and makes them central to the right conduct of the intellect in matters of faith bears a relation to Keats's celebration of the poetic virtue he called '*Negative Capability*, that is when man is capable of being in uncertainties, Mysteries, doubts, without any irritable reaching after fact & reason'.[68]

Compare, in their sterner tone, Newman's words to those who are perplexed about the question whether intercessory prayer detracts from the completeness of Christ's redemptive sacrifice:

> I say *perplexed*, for I will not contemplate the case of those, though there are such, who, when the text of Scripture seems to them to be at variance with itself, and one portion to diverge from another, will not allow themselves to be perplexed, will not suspend their minds and

[66] *PS* iv. 147. Cf. *PS* v. 66: 'How joy and fear can be reconciled, words cannot show. Act and deed alone can show how.'

[67] *PS* i. 28.

[68] Letter to George and Tom Keats, 21, 27(?) Dec. 1817, in *The Letters of John Keats 1814–1821*, ed. H. E. Rollins, 2 vols. (Cambridge Mass., 1958), i. 193.

humbly wait for light, will not believe that the Divine Scheme is larger and deeper than their own capacities, but boldly wrest into a factitious agreement what is already harmonious in God's infinite counsels, though not to them. I speak to perplexed persons[69]

It is a sign how lively Newman's reverence was that, much later in life, when trying to explain to a Catholic congregation why the disciples were slow to understand that Christ would be crucified, he should have ascribed their obtuseness to just such a selective wresting of Scripture. Doing so, he shows a more human understanding than Keats does in his youthful enthusiasm for the intellectual abstemiousness of poets. For a moment, Keats makes it sound as if negative capability or perplexity could become a consistent rule of life, perhaps even should become such a rule. While insisting on caution as a mark of religious fear and obedience, Newman is also prepared to admit the passionate attachment that presses to conclusions, for the zeal which blinded the disciples to what was written is only another form of that protective love which led Peter to strike off the high priest's servant's ear. None the less, he knows where they went wrong:

They took parts of Scripture which pleased their fancy, in the first place, and utterly put out of their minds such as went contrary to these. It is quite certain that the Prophet Isaias and other prophets speak of our Lord, then to come, as a conqueror. . . . It is also true that Scripture elsewhere speaks of the Messias otherwise. He is spoken of as rejected of men, as a leper, as an outcast, as persecuted, as spat upon and pierced and slain. But these passages they put away from them. They did not let them produce their legitimate effects upon their hearts. They heard them with the ear and not with the head, and so it was all one as if they had not been written; to them they were not written.[70]

Selective reading and preaching of Scripture shrinks the interims in which texts come to mean in relation to each other. That is, it tries to make of the texts primarily a single and simultaneous consistency, whereas the meaningfulness of Scripture lives in the times between sayings, the timing of our Lord's words being as necessary for their sense as his spatio-temporal uniqueness as a man is a necessary condition of his Incarnation. His sayings are incarnationally spoken, and what they speak is his Incarnation,

[69] *PS* iii. 358.
[70] *CS*, pp. 57–8.

the incidence of truth in times. In this sense, selective preaching fails to grant the liturgical place of understanding. Sermons (which we may take as a type of interpretative activity with regard to Scripture) occur within the composed rhythm of gradualness, within that system *of unfolding*, which is the Church's year. In the Tridentine rite, readings from the Gospel were always prefaced with the traditional phrase 'In illo tempore' ('At that time'). Great preaching, such as Newman's, also carries on its face, in its breath, an 'in illo tempore'; it acknowledges its own location in a larger span which, though it cannot all be said at once, any more than a whole liturgical year can occur on one day, is perpetually invoked as the setting for what at a particular time is being said.

Liturgical preaching is also lyrical. Not that it consists in the effusion of personal feelings but in the conscious and integral measure of what at present urges itself on speech against what has been and will later be spoken. A lyric poet who bewails or sings 'hey nonny' does not imagine, or encourage us to imagine, that this is all there is to be said; his intelligence resides in the calibration of the moment of song with that which is just now unsung. Liturgy is lyricism directed to and by God. And so, though not a sacramental act, preaching like Newman's sets as its aim a sacramental understanding:

> Thus the thought of what Christ is, must not obliterate from the mind the thought of what He was; and faith is always sorrowing with Him while it rejoices. And the same union of opposite thoughts is impressed on us in Holy Communion, in which we see Christ's death and resurrection together, at one and the same time[71]

Particular sermons, however, will rarely encompass, and should probably not attempt, such wholeness. This, at least, is the view Newman expressed in a letter to Samuel Wilberforce:

> I think good part of our difference in the *idea* of a Sermon, lies in this—that you think of it as much more of a totum and rotundum than I do. It seems to me abundant, to bring out one point—and to speak my mind I think that other subjects introduced have a tendency to defeat this. You will say, 'What? are we to leave a different *impression* from that of Scripture?' no—not on the *whole*. No one, who *habitually* hears me, ought to have any other than the whole Scripture impression—but any one who reads only certain 26, and much more only one or other of

[71] *PS* iv. 324.

them, *must*. I lay it down as a fundamental Canon, that a Sermon to be effective must be imperfect. A second sermon will correct it. . . . I feel this as a vital principle—viz till we consent to follow Scripture in abandoning *completeness* in our Sermons, we do nothing *accurately*.[72]

In this necessary imperfection and incompleteness lie both the fidelity and the foolishness of preaching—its foolishness in that what the preacher says will be lacking, partial, in known need of correction (it is his love for the revelation to which he ministers which demands that he not conceal the element of stammering, of the premature and tentative, in what he says), its fidelity in that he speaks, as the Apostles spoke, as a placed individual and cannot say everything at one time (it is his love for his hearers which compels him to speak even though he is always not exactly ready to speak).

Preaching, in so far as it is a foolishness, would be opposed to philosophy, if philosophy is the love of wisdom; these lyrical, these liturgical utterances look very little like the reflective completeness of philosophy's self-image. St Ambrose may have had this opposition in mind when he wrote, 'Non in dialectica complacuit Deo salvum facere populum suum' ('It is not by logic that it has pleased God to bring about the salvation of his people'),[73] the words which Newman chose as epigraph to *An Essay in Aid of a Grammar of Assent*. St Ambrose was probably alluding to St Paul's First Letter to the Corinthians; his 'complacuit Deo salvum facere populum suum' pre-echoes the Vulgate: 'Nam quia in Dei sapientia non cognovit mundus per sapientiam Deum: placuit Deo per stultitiam praedicationis salvos facere credentes.' ('For seeing that in the wisdom of God, the world, by wisdom, knew not God, it pleased God, by the foolishness of preaching, to save them that believe.') (1 Cor. 1: 21.) Yet the lyricism of preaching must form part of practical wisdom, for the preacher must know his time and place—it is from that knowledge his lyricism begins—and practical wisdom is not alien to philosophy. We might think of preaching and philosophy as two prisms which refract the light of revelation into different spectra, each in its way colourful, edifying, and inadequate. It is Newman's distinction to have tried to align these prisms with regard to each other so that the dispersed colours one produces

[72] *LD* v. 38.

[73] Ambrose, *De Fide ad Gratianum Augustum*, I. v. 42.

should be, as it were, reintegrated into white light by the other. He tried this because

True faith is what may be called colourless, like air or water; it is but the medium through which the soul sees Christ; and the soul as little really rests upon it and contemplates it, as the eye can see the air. When, then, men are bent on holding it (as it were) in their hands, curiously inspecting, analyzing, and so aiming at it, they are obliged to colour and thicken it, that it may be seen and touched. That is, they substitute for it something or other, a feeling, notion, sentiment, conviction, or act of reason, which they may hang over and doat upon. They rather aim at experiences (as they are called) within them, than at Him that is without them.[74]

To the extent that he succeeded, his sermons gained humility, that colourless, self-forgetful eloquence which is a distinctive Christian virtue in literary composition. That he continued to make the attempt over sixty-three years of preaching between 23 June 1824 and 1 December 1888, gives his sermons also the patience of a saint.

[74] 'On Preaching the Gospel', *Jfc.*, p. 336.

5

Newman's Autobiography

JEROME H. BUCKLEY

In the opening pages of his *Apologia pro Vita Sua* Newman recalls his 'childish imaginations', especially his mistrust of material things and his all-sustaining reliance on 'the thought of two and two only absolute and luminously self-evident beings, myself and my Creator'.[1] Towards the end, early in the last chapter, he reaffirms the same subjective certainty, his conviction that the reality of God, taken as a first premiss, is the one support and guarantee of his own individual existence. But now as an adult he can no longer so readily dismiss the material universe, which in all its godlessness encroaches upon him, confusing his very being. 'If I looked into a mirror, and did not see my face,' he explains, 'I should have the sort of feeling which actually comes upon me, when I look into this living busy world, and see no reflexion of its Creator.' His faith now in both God and self must take mature cognizance of all the pain and error that seems to give the lie to his abiding intuition:

To consider the world in its length and breadth, its various history, the many races of man, their starts, their fortunes, their mutual alienation, their conflicts; and then their ways, habits, governments, forms of worship; their enterprises, their aimless courses, their random achievements and acquirements, the impotent conclusion of long-standing facts, the tokens so faint and broken of a superintending design, the blind evolution of what turn out to be great powers or truths, the progress of things, as if from unreasoning elements, not towards final causes, the greatness and littleness of man, his far-reaching aims, his short duration, the curtain hung over his futurity, the disappointments of life, the defeat of good, the success of evil, physical pain, mental

[1] *Apo.*, p. 118. The 1865 *Apologia* revises the more polemical pamphlets which appeared in 1864, separately and then in book-form; in the process all direct reference to Charles Kingsley, who instigated the controversy, is omitted. Martin J. Svaglic's excellent modern edition (Oxford, 1967) supplies much bibliographical data and other related materials.

anguish, the prevalence and intensity of sin, the pervading idolatries, the corruptions, the dreary hopeless irreligion, that condition of the whole race, so fearfully yet exactly described in the Apostle's words, 'having no hope and without God in the world,'—all this is a vision to dizzy and appal; and inflicts upon the mind the sense of a profound mystery, which is absolutely beyond human solution.[2]

Here, in one great periodic sentence, the *Apologia* reaches its passionate climax. Here Newman addresses the total human condition in timeless terms, far beyond the initial need for a reply to Charles Kingsley's ill-considered attack and even beyond the dogmatic particulars of this own final religious position. At the same time the argument, though it now transcends a specific self-defence, expresses Newman's essential *raison d'être*, the very quality of his luminous selfhood. In its context the unflinching contemplation of the aggregate human tragedy is the product of the earned assurance of a complex individuality which has defined itself throughout a highly personal narrative.

The *Apologia* differs in nearly every basic assumption from John Stuart Mill's essay *On Liberty*, which appeared several years earlier. Yet, in one respect at least, these two landmarks of Victorian prose may be viewed as religious and secular counterparts. Each is a strong statement of personal faith and values. Each demands, with an intensity yet a high degree of disinterest, an understanding of the principles and attitudes that sanctioned and guided a dedicated way of life, Mill's on the one hand, Newman's on the other. Mill's eloquent description of the intellectual nonconformity of Jesus and Socrates and the tragic consequences in both instances makes an implicit plea for his own individual freedom of thought and expression. Newman's appalled vision of the world's sin is set in the perspective of his dependence on the greater reality of God.

Mill's high argument, however, descends eventually to a pragmatic, or narrowly utilitarian, level. In the last section of his essay 'Applications', intended to test the theory, the idea of liberty, hitherto pertinent to any culture, begins to subserve the local claims of economic liberalism and the specific practices of a contentious nineteenth-century *laissez-faire*. And the *Apologia*

[2] *Apo.*, p. 217.

likewise, I believe, in the pages immediately following its climactic survey of the world, drops sharply to the level and tone of partisan topical debate as it seeks to defend or rationalize some of the dogmas and usages of the Catholic Church that had been most frequently subject to Anglican censure, not only Kingsley's but Newman's own in his years as Oxford Tractarian.

In so moving in its last chapter away from self-history, the *Apologia* undergoes a sudden shift in strategy and genre.[3] It becomes for some forty pages an 'apology' in the usual generic sense of that term—that is, an exercise in interested advocacy defending a system or creed, rather than a single life, from attack or neglect, a treatise like Richard Watson's once popular *Apology for Christianity* or the Renaissance anti-Lutheran *Apology for the Truth of Catholic Faith and Dogma* by the militant Archbishop of Gonza.[4] In its first four chapters the *Apologia* is developed not as an aggressive apology of this sort but as a review of one man's religious positions, where the polemical mode of the original pamphlet exchange with Kingsley yields to a patient self-explanation in which the detractor has no apparent part and even his name disappears. Newman, none the less, in writing of himself, cannot have forgotten Kingsley's charge that his attitudes and conduct were characteristic of the Catholic priesthood generally in evasiveness and duplicity. The *Apologia* long before its ending has sufficiently demonstrated its author's personal regard for truth and candour and his sincere will to confront the choices he has elected. Yet it is understandable that Newman, taking on the role of apologist in his last pages, should have wished to rebut the larger allegation. Still the extended defence, however commendable the motivation, may strike Catholic and non-Catholic readers alike as somewhat less than adequate, an effort to accept practices that deserve or demand, as the case may be, an ampler, clearer, and more objective exposition than a personal testimony should be expected to offer.

It is scarcely a persuasive defence of belief in the Immaculate Conception to argue that the doctrine, though long ago opposed

[3] The difference in tone of ch. 5 may be accounted for in part by the fact that the argument, or 'apology', has been adapted from the pamphlet 'General Answer to Mr. Kingsley', which closed the original controversy.

[4] R. Watson's *Apology for Christianity* first appeared in 1776; the Archbishop of Gonza's *Apologia pro veritate Catholicae et apostolicae fidei ac doctrinae* in 1520.

by St Bernard of Clairvaux and St Thomas Aquinas, would have been readily acceptable to both these eminent schoolmen, had they been able to foresee its gradual redefinition over centuries of dispute until its official adoption as an article of faith in 1854.[5]

Nor does the practice of European casuistry receive cogent support from evidence that Milton, Johnson, and other English Protestant worthies thought it sometimes permissible to tell a lie.[6] But what may be still more questionable is the notion that the authority of the Church often may and indeed should reach beyond the religious sphere into secular areas of literature and science. Newman declares past censorship of books 'mainly in the right', since even true new ideas must not be circulated at the wrong time. For the moment he seems to be answering Mill rather than Kingsley when he suggests that the original thinker who advances his radical thought prematurely may be not 'a bold champion for the truth and a martyr to free opinion' (as *On Liberty* would have assumed) but rather 'just one of those persons whom the competent authority ought to silence', even 'though the case may not fall within that subject-matter in which that authority is infallible, or the formal conditions of the exercise of that gift may be wanting.'[7] Since, the argument continues, it may be 'imprudent to bring [some ideas] before the public at all',[8] the Church has the right and duty to guard against subversive opinion of all kinds and in particular to suppress, at least temporarily, scientific theories which seem to threaten its doctrines. Newman is not an obscurantist, and he is manifestly uncomfortable in his support of an 'expediency' which involves the deliberate withholding of fact and hypothesis until the general public is ready to receive a disturbing disclosure.[9] But we could wish him more cautious in placing restrictions on the free flow of ideas. The views he propounds or seems to justify as apologist remain as contentious as Mill's applications and require for any real defence a more closely reasoned debate willing to ponder strong counter-arguments.

Fortunately the *Apologia* returns in its last page to its dominant personal mode, now expressed in a moving coda to Newman's friends and supporters at the Birmingham Oratory. Many of the

[5] See *Apo.*, p. 229.
[6] See *Apo.*, p. 245.
[7] *Apo.*, p. 232.
[8] *Apo.*, p. 235.
[9] *Cf. Apo.*, pp. 241, 242, and Newman's note 'The Economy', *Apo.*, pp. 299–301.

Victorian reviewers of the book were dissatisfied with the tone and logic of the general apology,[10] but most readers properly recognized the polemics as a minor element in a record memorable for its power as personal statement, a compelling achievement in spiritual autobiography. And it is as such, I submit, rather than as an excursion into apologetics, that it has achieved its enduring appeal.

In his Preface to the *Apologia* Newman announces that he is setting out not to expound Catholic doctrine but to be 'simply personal and historical', to explain himself and his 'opinions and actions'. But the prospect of self-revelation, though necessary, is, he declares, thoroughly distasteful to him:

> It is not at all pleasant for me to be egotistical; nor to be criticized for being so. It is not pleasant to reveal to high and low, young and old, what has gone on within me from my early years. It is not pleasant to be giving to every shallow or flippant disputant the advantage over me of knowing my most private thoughts, I might even say the intercourse between myself and my Maker.[11]

The subjective impulse, nevertheless, operating on a less public level, was strong in Newman all his life, and he had been a perpetual self-recorder almost from the beginning. The publishing of an autobiography in 1864 was a new departure, an act probably not intended at all before the necessity of answering Kingsley's attack. But the writing down of his private thoughts and emotions was a familiar, indeed habitual, practice long before

[10] James Fitzjames Stephen in a long trenchant review respects Newman's honesty but assails his logic (*Fraser's*, 70 (1864), 265–303). G. R. Gleig (*Blackwood's Edinburgh Magazine*, 96 (1864), 292–308) believes that Newman has ably defended himself against Kingsley's 'ridiculous' attack but has been misled in his apology for Catholic dogmatism. Samuel Wilberforce praises the self-history but finds 'the dogmatic portion of the work . . . poor and tame' (*Quarterly Review*, 111 (1864), 528–73). For a modern survey of the reviews, see V. F. Blehl, SJ, 'Early Criticism of the *Apologia*' in id. and F. X. Connolly (eds.), *Newman's Apologia: A Classic Reconsidered* (New York, 1964), 47–63; Blehl concludes, 'Those who conceded that Newman's sincerity had been vindicated generally did not agree with his doctrinal views.' English Catholics of the far right, however, were unimpressed by both the defence and the apology; Henry (later Cardinal) Manning in particular 'did not like the last chapter' or the popularity Newman gained as a 'minimiser' of Roman Catholic doctrine: see E. Kelly, SJ, 'The *Apologia* and the Ultramontanes' in Blehl and Connolly (eds.), *Newman's Apologia*, pp. 26–46.

[11] Preface, *Apo.*, p. 14.

the *Apologia* and for many years afterwards. Newman wrote thousands of letters throughout his long career, often quite intimate and confiding, many of which he copied out for his own reference or else reclaimed from his correspondents; and he kept diaries and journals from his early youth onwards, notes he filed away with descriptive labels, yet frequently reviewed and often rewrote.[12]

In his middle and later life he may have preserved such materials so that his future biographers might have reliable primary sources to draw upon. But his autobiographical writings in several sorts must also have served a more immediate need. Many indeed date from a period when he could not have been assured that there would ever actually be the occasion for a definitive biography. Self-expression preceded self-explanation.

From the beginning we find a self-conscious search for an appropriate personal idiom. His first journals, as Newman himself comments, were 'composed': 'I seldom write without an eye to style, and since my taste was bad, my style was bad. I wrote in style, as another might write in verse, or sing instead of speaking, or dance instead of walking.'[13] But the artifice of style, however mannered it may have been, afforded the youth a disguise and protection, a distinct embodiment of an as yet amorphous selfhood. And by the time of the *Apologia* the stylist had become a great prose master, one whose control of language itself could help focus and objectify a personal image. Yet even then, Newman perceived, the clearest self-depiction in the most carefully weighed phrases must remain only a partial self-portrait drawn from fading memory and always insufficient self-knowledge. 'For who', he asked, 'can know himself, and the multitude of subtle influences which act upon him? And who can recollect, at the distance of twenty-five years, all that he once knew about his thoughts and deeds . . .?'[14]

Newman always insisted that a judicious selection of letters must necessarily be the most useful and succinct form of biography (and also presumably of autobiography), and in writing the

[12] In his edition *John Henry Newman: Autobiographical Writings* Henry Tristram brings together with helpful introductions many materials previously unpublished or published only in part, especially 'The Autobiographical Memoir', 'My Illness in Sicily', and 'Journals', all of which I draw upon below.

[13] *AW*, p. 149.

[14] *Apo.*, p. 90.

Apologia he drew heavily and effectively on his own dated and often annotated correspondence, which he considered the best record of his state of mind at any given past period. But most of his personal letters are inevitably more discreet than his colloquies with himself in his private journals, and often less revealing than his more oblique self-expressions in poetry and fiction.

Many of the pieces in Newman's *Verses on Various Occasions*,[15] assigned to the time and place of composition, may be read as fragments of autobiography, even when ostensibly concerned with general rather than personal themes. The early riddle 'Snapdragon', for instance, attests the writer's own love of Oxford in the flower's resolve to cling forever to the reverend walls:

> May it be! then well might I
> In College cloister live and die.

A late dialogue, 'The Married and the Single', argues the conflicting claims of marriage and celibacy, though the debate breaks off before the latter receives the defence Newman would clearly have wished. Elsewhere the poet sees his own love of retrospect in the happy disposition he assigns to St Gregory Nazianzen,

> According thee the lot thou lovedst best,
> To muse upon the past,—to serve, yet be at rest.

And in a song for the stoical St Philip Neri he berates himself for fretful tongue, complaining, and nervous irritation:

> I'm ashamed of myself, of my tears and my tongue,
> So easily fretted, so often unstrung;
> Mad at trifles, to which a chance moment gives birth,
> Complaining of heaven, and complaining of earth.

The largest group of short poems dates from the Mediterranean travels of 1833. One of these, 'Fair Words', describes verbal insincerity or misuse of language as 'A sin against the light', a phrase echoed in the *Apologia* in the account of Newman's illness in Sicily: 'I repeated, "I shall not die, for I have not sinned against light". . . . I have never been able quite to make out what I meant.'[16] Several of the travel poems confess to a stubborn self-will. 'Moses' makes an explicit equation between the patriarch who 'lost Canaan by self-will' and the troubled speaker, who

[15] *VV*, pp. 23, 202, 152, 313, 88, 91, 121, 156, 323.

[16] *Apo.*, p. 43.

presumably is Newman himself. 'A Blight' regrets the wilfulness of the poet's youth, the memory of which has brought him 'Fear, and self-hate, and vain remorseful stings'. And the familiar hymn 'The Pillar of the Cloud' ('Lead, Kindly Light'), in origin the most intensely personal of these lyrics, avows contritely: 'I loved to choose and see my path. . . . Pride ruled my will: remember not past years.' Even the longest of the poems in *Verses*, *The Dream of Gerontius*, written shortly after the *Apologia*, may have a strong subjective significance as a sort of extrapolated autobiography arising from a keen sense of advancing age, ill health, and the imagined imminence of death, twenty-five years before the event.[17]

The novel *Loss and Gain* retraces the decisive transition in Newman's life under thin fictional guise. Charles Reding the hero, a young Oxford man at the time of the Tractarians, moves —with slow deliberation and a great reluctance to offend his mother or desert his friends—from a staunch Anglicanism to a convinced Catholicism. Unlike Newman, Charles comes of a clergyman's family and has attended Eton rather than a smaller school at Ealing, but the differences and substitutions are relatively few and minor. Charles shares Newman's tastes and values; he plays the fiddle, enjoys garrulous rambles with a friend in the countryside, dislikes dancing and the general frivolity of his worldly peers, steadily ponders religious questions, and early dedicates himself to a celibate life. Newman regards his surrogate with detachment as well as sympathy, describing him in terms that recall the trenchant self-analysis of his own private journals; Charles is said to be 'naturally timid and retiring, over-sensitive, and, though lively and cheerful, yet not without a tinge of melancholy in his character, which sometimes degenerated into mawkishness'. Charles's eventual 'gain' is the dogmatic faith he requires; his 'loss' is the academic life of Oxford. Near the end of the narrative, Charles sadly recalls a night some years earlier when, taken to a university tower to observe the stars, he looked 'down into the deep, gaslit, dark-shadowed quadrangles', in the secret hope that he might one day take up permanent residence in one of the sheltering colleges. But now with his conversion to

[17] See E. E. Kelly, '"The Dream of Gerontius": An Appended Finale to the *Apologia*?' in J. D. Bastable (ed.), *Newman and Gladstone: Centennial Essays* (Dublin, 1978), 305–19.

Catholicism, his Oxford experience is forever closed to him, and he is henceforth 'a stranger where he had hoped to have had a home'.[18]

If his tone suggests that Newman is speaking of himself when he describes Charles's attachment to the academic world, we have direct evidence that he is in fact doing so. His late 'Autobiographical Memoir' quotes the tower passage at length[19] as representing his own desire and sentiment. Intended to supplement the *Apologia* as a personal record of the Oxford years, this 'Memoir' has something of the obliquity of *Loss and Gain*, for it, too, is written in the third person—the author–protagonist now calling himself 'Mr Newman'. Yet it is far less restrained than the *Apologia* in divulging precise details of character and event. 'Mr Newman' is depicted as a silent sober young man, confident of his abilities, very much aware of college politics and rivalries, but always sensitive, reticent, and withdrawn ('solitary' is the recurrent epithet). He compares himself once again to the snapdragon of his riddle and repeats his desire to cling like the flower to the cloister walls. He is severely disappointed at his failure to win highest honours at Trinity, but he considers his standing no proper 'measure of his intellectual merits',[20] for he knows himself to be 'more advanced in the studies necessary to Oxford than the run of youths even two years beyond him in age'.[21] He is accordingly delighted by his election a year and a half later to an Oriel fellowship. He vividly remembers hearing the good news, his persistence in playing the violin when the befuddled messenger first arrives with a summons from the provost, his mad proud dash through a crowd of bowing tradesmen to his reception by the fellows, his extravagance in ordering the bells to be rung from three Trinity towers, and his lasting elation: 'As to Mr Newman he ever felt this twelfth of April, 1822 to be the turning point of his life, and of all days most memorable.'[22]

The journals—in the first person—record less happy days, times of introspection and self-rebuke, especially successive birthdays, each the occasion for earnest retrospect over the past year. As a self-conscious young man, Newman again and again upbraids himself for vanity and deceit, as if he were the errant Rousseau: 'Wherever I go, I think people are looking at me and

[18] *LG*, pp. 6, 207. [19] *AW*, pp. 49–50. [20] *AW*, pp. 49.
[21] *AW*, pp. 39. [22] *AW*, pp. 63.

thinking of me. . . . Again, I am a great liar, a mean liar . . . from pride, lest I should confess myself wrong. . . . I am still very vain, cold in prayer, proud, ill tempered, insincere, implacable.' In a calmer mood he notes thankfully that God has helped him 'to wrestle with [his] solitary thoughts, and to drive from [him] the devilish imaginations of [his] superiority of intellect'. Years later, just before his ordination in Rome, he finds himself, 'querulous, timid, lazy, suspicious; I crawl along the ground; feeble, downcast and despondent',[23] caluminated by his old allies and mistrusted by the present Catholic hierarchy. No indictment brought against him, certainly not Kingsley's, could have been sharper than his private self-reproach, his endless fascination with what he called the 'inconsistency' of his own character.

The most considerable of Newman's early autobiographical fragments and the one bearing most significantly on the *Apologia* is 'My Illness in Sicily', in which he recalls in clinical detail a true crisis, both physical and psychological.[24] Writing at intervals from 1834 to 1840, Newman here re-presents to himself his suffering and distress, the specific symptoms of a life-threatening fever, the self-reproach for a stubborn will, and the sense that God was fighting against him, but also the ineluctable confidence that he would recover since he had not 'sinned against light'. He lingers awhile over each painful circumstance, as if he recognizes the illness and its after-effects as a kind of death and rebirth, a dying into a new life. Then abruptly he turns upon himself bitterly to question his motive in setting down so harrowing a recapitulation of his misery:

> The thought keeps pressing on me, while I write this, what am I writing it for? For myself, I may look at it once or twice in my whole life, and what sympathy is there in *my* looking at it? Whom have I, whom can I have, who would take interest in it?

Only a wife, he decides, could feel affectionate concern for his narrative, but that source of sympathy is denied him, committed as he is to a celibate life. The need for shared understanding grows hard to bear, until suddenly comes a revulsion of sentiment. The account ends on a note of annoyance, self-pity, and perhaps a dash of irony. The writer remembers his refusing to give his blue cloak to his servant Gennaro when paying him off in Palermo and

[23] *AW*, pp. 189, 193–4, 196, 246.

[24] *AW*, pp. 126, 137, 138.

his keeping it close to him ever since through many vicissitudes almost, he seems to suggest, as a substitute wife. 'I have it still,' he concludes. 'I have brought it up here to Littlemore, & on some cold nights I have had it on my bed. I have so few things to sympathize with me, that I take to clokes.'

As eventually published (in full, not till 1956), 'My Illness in Sicily' covers eighteen printed pages. The *Apologia* describes the same experience in ten terse sentences. The record now makes no mention of the blue cloak or of any other object of Gennaro's acquisitiveness; it is tense, understated, devoid of self-pity, an appropriate climax at the end of a predominantly factual first chapter, placed there, we may assume, with a sense of its symbolic importance. Newman now knows his purpose in writing and his likely audience. One striking divergence from the longer narrative suggests the gain in sharpness of impact: the sick man's expressed will to live, 'I thought God had some work for me,' has been replaced by a more resolute statement, 'I have a work to do in England.'[25] Though reduced to less than two paragraphs, the Sicilian passage still records a dramatic crisis ending one phase of Newman's career and carrying him on to another, 'the start'—within a few weeks of his return to Oxford—'of the religious movement of 1833',[26] which publicly established his name and prominence.

Even so, at the beginning of chapter 2, Newman characteristically demurs. As if fearful that he might be accused of overplaying the Sicilian episode, he warns his readers, 'in spite of the foregoing pages', not to expect a 'romantic story'. None the less, his narrative, as it continues, retains its own sense of drama, less physical now and more intellectual, but self-conscious always and astonished at the personal consequence of ideas developed with emotion.

The *Apologia* is the most narrowly focused of major English autobiographies. It proceeds by deliberate and drastic exclusion of all that Newman considers irrelevant to his purpose.[27] It has

[25] Cf. *AW*, pp. 122, and *Apo.*, p. 43.

[26] *Apo.*, p. 43.

[27] On the limited subject-matter of the *Apologia*, see W. Houghton, *The Art of Newman's Apologia* (New Haven, Conn., 1945), 89–91, 99, and C. F. Harrold, *John Henry Newman* (New York, 1945), 310, and *Apologia*, ed. Harrold (New York, 1947), ed.'s introd., pp. xi–xiii.

very little to say of such relations as usually fascinate other autobiographers, virtually nothing of family background, growing up, or schooling. It affords no notion of Newman's interest in music and poetry, his delight in landscape, his success as a preacher, or his concern with a liberal education. It provides for few nostalgic digressions or chatty asides. The title of its first four chapters, 'History of My Religious Opinions' (each time with successive dates), clearly indicates the direction of the narrative. Much of the subject-matter so limited and selected remains abstruse and difficult. Many of the theological references now require annotation, and most of the Oxford factions of the time, the fervid debates on the provenance of dogma, the disciplinary disputes within the Anglican and Catholic hierarchies seem long since remote and scarcely pertinent to the modern reader. Yet the tenor and method of the argument and, above all, the intensity of the narrator himself compel our attention even when the precise circumstances no longer so fully engage it.

In its close concentration on a personal religious history, the *Apologia* has been related to the genre of the conversion-narrative as established by John Bunyan in *Grace Abounding* and perpetuated largely by the Dissenters and Methodists of the eighteenth century who followed his example.[28] But it differs sharply from autobiographical confessions of this sort, which typically set out to record, with great hortatory zeal, the conviction of sin, deliverance by grace, and sudden redeeming change of heart. The only source of the kind acknowledged in the *Apologia* is *The Force of Truth* (1779) by Thomas Scott of Aston Sanford, a writer, said Newman, 'to whom (humanly speaking) I almost owe my soul'.[29] And that text itself in its quiet moderation stands quite apart from the other, more 'enthusiastic' contributions to the genre.[30] In Scott Newman found an affinity of devout temperament rather than a lasting theological influence. Indeed his sincere admiration did not preclude an early questioning of

[28] See L. Peterson, *Victorian Autobiography* (New Haven, Conn., 1986), 93–119, arguing that Newman belongs partly in the Bunyan tradition but as a Catholic is reluctant to accept a Protestant genre. I am not persuaded that Newman in writing the *Apologia* is suffering 'a generic crisis' (p. 108).

[29] *Apo*., p. 18.

[30] Scott denies that his work 'can reasonably be condemned as enthusiasm'; T. Scott, *The Force of Truth: An Authentic Narrative* (Boston, Mass., 1854), 174 ('enthusiasm' here in the 18th-cent. sense as 'fanaticism').

Scott's notions of election and predestination.[31] Scott anticipates both Newman's worried awareness of his intellectual distinction and also the candour of his self-appraisals. He admits 'a proud conceit of [his] abilities', charges himself with being 'a vain-glorious candidate for human applause', and fears that his past sermons may have been merely a 'smooth palatable mixture of law and gospel, . . . flattering pride and prejudice, and soothing the conscience'. He foreshadows Newman's habit of weighing one argument against another, checking and wavering, rationalizing and reviewing his commitments. The deliberation with which he shifts ground must have appealed to Newman's regard for a necessary and reasonable caution; Scott's movement over a three-year period towards Evangelical tenets is comparable, at least in distrust of precipitant action, to Newman's four-year-long final break with Anglicanism. And the rationale of gradualism that Scott provides reveals a sensitivity, very like Newman's, to the attitude of his friends and associates: 'When a person suddenly changes his religious opinions for others very different from them, it is no inconsiderable evidence of a changeable and fickle disposition. . . . So long, deliberately, and step by step I examined the premises before I finally proceeded to draw my conclusion.'[32]

In the *Apologia* Newman like Scott is intent on presenting an orderly development, a consistent evolution with no sudden or 'fickle' reversals. The single 'epiphany' (if indeed it can be rightly so called) is an intellectual illumination prepared for by extensive reading and reflection, rather than a sudden overwhelming change of heart or direction; Newman's response to the words of St Augustine, by which 'the theory of the *Via Media* was absolutely pulverized',[33] simply confirms his steadily growing dissatisfaction with the Anglican position. Near the beginning of his first chapter he insists on the logic even of his anomalous early belief in an order of angels operative in human affairs, a credence, he admits, that some readers may take as evidence of imagination rather than sound judgement: 'I am not setting myself up as a pattern of good sense or of anything else: I am but giving a history of my

[31] Newman questions Scott as early as 1825: 'I have taken many doctrines almost on trust from Scott &c and on serious examination hardly find them confirmed by Scripture" (*AW*, p. 204).

[32] Scott, *Force of Truth*, quoted in order: pp. 26, 139, 59, 149, 152.

[33] *Apo.*, p. 111.

opinions, and that, with the view of showing that I have come by them through intelligible processes of thought and honest external means.'[34] His fear somewhat later that the Sicilian episode may have struck his audience as unduly 'romantic' similarly suggests his reluctance to displace a patient exposition of ideas and sentiments with an account of rapid action or sudden conversion. Yet the Mediterranean narrative, apart from its intrinsic significance, does serve a typological purpose in the larger, slower design of the *Apologia* as a whole; it provides a basis in fact for the recurrent shaping metaphors of illness and recovery, troubled journey and home-coming, that extend the brief experience abroad over a much longer period of gradual growth and change.

The traveller 'aching to get home' from Sicily is thinking less of his 'mother's house', to which he first returns, than of his intellectual 'home', the Oxford where his early religious opinions have met both confirmation and serious challenge and where his new 'work' is shortly to begin. The first chapter of the *Apologia* has introduced members of the academic family who have been sources of mixed support, affection, and tension. Newman is generous in his remembrance of his elders and mentors Edward Hawkins and Richard Whately, despite their eventual anger at his Catholic sympathies. He is almost worshipful in his regard for the gentle, conservative John Keble, who welcomed him to the fellowship of Oriel. And he depicts the zealous Hurrell Froude as his closest friend and confidant in terms far warmer than he could ever have bestowed on his own brother Francis Newman. Oxford, here and as it is remembered at the beginning of chapter 3, has been truly 'my own home, to which I was bound by so many strong and tender ties',[35] the place of self-discovery, refuge, and return, and the point of reluctant final departure.

The central part of the *Apologia* concerns Newman's rôle as a principal Tractarian from 1833 to 1841. For much of this time, despite his honoured place in the community, he half-suspects that he must one day leave his Oxford home; he perceives, at first but dimly, 'that my mind had not found its ultimate rest and that in some sense or other I was on journey'.[36] At the outset the journey is animated by a singular euphoria, 'that exuberant and joyous energy with which I had returned from abroad, and

[34] *Apo.*, p. 39. [35] *Apo.*, p. 90. [36] *Apo.*, p. 112.

which I never had before or since'. The course of the 'movement' seems clearly charted: 'I felt as on board a vessel, which first gets under weigh, and then the deck is cleared out, and luggage and live stock stowed away into their proper receptacles.'[37] In his eagerness to have other men accompany him 'step by step, as far as they would go' (the journey is now by land), his conduct becomes 'a mixture . . . of fierceness and sport', an arrogance in affirming dogmatic views and a Socratic irony in forcing opponents 'to the brink of some intellectual absurdity'.[38] But by the writing and stormy reception of Tract Ninety he is often 'in a state of moral sickness'[39] and no longer so certain of the valid claims of Anglican orthodoxy or of his own direction. 'How was I', he asks, 'any more to have absolute confidence in myself? how was I to have confidence in my present confidence?'[40]

At all stages of his journey the autobiographer strives carefully to document (with personal letters and explications of his Tractarian positions) his changing states of mind and spiritual health. From 1841 to 1845, the period covered in his fourth chapter, he describes himself, clearly recalling his illness in Sicily, as on the death-bed of his Anglicanism, 'a tedious decline with seasons of rallying and seasons of falling back'.[41] His future course is now apparent to him, but his progress cannot be hurried by argument or persuasion. 'All the logic in the world', he insists, 'would not have made me move faster towards Rome than I did; as well might you say that I have arrived at the end of my journey, because I see the village church before me, as venture to assert that the miles, over which my soul had to pass before it got to Rome, could be annihilated, even though I had been in possession of some far clearer view than I then had, that Rome was my ultimate destination.'[42] He is dismayed now by those who observe—some with unkind satisfaction—his many months of indecision as to how or when he will continue his journey, and he complains, in defiant self-pity, 'Why will you not let me die in peace? Wounded brutes creep into some hole to die in, and no one grudges it them. Let me alone, I shall not trouble you long.'[43] Disturbing, too, are the more patient ones who are eager to follow his action as soon as he is ready to

[37] *Apo.*, pp. 49–50.
[38] *Apo.*, p. 51.
[39] *Apo.*, p. 69.
[40] *Apo.*, p. 88.
[41] *Apo.*, p. 137.
[42] *Apo.*, pp. 155–6.
[43] *Apo.*, p. 158.

proceed. But, if he once led others, he is determined now to decide for himself alone, to move forward only with full personal commitment: 'I wished to go to my Lord by myself, and in my own way, or rather His way. I had neither wish, nor, I may say, thought of taking a number with me.'[44] When at last he has persuaded himself that there can be no medium for him 'between Atheism and Catholicity', he prepares to leave Oxford and his much loved home forever, the command of the Psalmist ringing in his ears, 'Forget thine own people and thy father's house.' And his leaving, he notes, is 'like going on the open sea'.[45] His reception into the Roman Church, 'like coming into port after a rough sea',[46] completes the journey and brings the personal part of the *Apologia* to its conclusion. The last chapter begins with a statement of that ending: 'From the time that I became a Catholic, of course I have no further history of my religious opinions to narrate.' What then remains is essentially 'apology' rather than autobiography.

The *Apologia* both records and creates a personality. In the several years before its composition Newman, as his journal testifies,[47] had been frequently disheartened, tormented by neurotic fancies, oppressed by a sense of failure, lonely, long since alienated from his Anglican friends and still mistrusted by many of his fellow-Catholics. His labours as educator in Ireland, he felt, had come to nothing; his brief experience as editor of the *Rambler* had been cruelly frustrating; and his recent essays seemed to him altogether ineffectual. 'What I wrote as a Protestant', he was convinced, 'has had far greater power, force, meaning, success, than my Catholic works.' Or again, 'The consequence is, that, so far from being thought engaged in any good work, I am simply discouraged and regarded suspiciously by the governing powers as doing an actual harm.'

But the *Apologia* projected a more positive and redeeming self-image. From the angry necessity of answering Kingsley's charges of evasion and dishonesty came a new measure of self-esteem, a poise in the adducing of contrary evidence, and an

[44] *Apo.*, p. 198.

[45] *Apo.*, pp. 179, 212; Newman hears the words of the Psalmist in Latin: 'Obliviscere populum tuum et domum patris tui'.

[46] *Apo.*, p. 214.

[47] See *AW*, pp. 251, 253, 259.

invigorating release, as the narrative advanced, in the sure command of a self-assertive language. The review of his life in the sharpened focus of his religious opinions provided Newman with the sense of consistency and continuity he required to reassume a purposeful role in the Church and in society.

This new confidence emerges gradually from the text. The first chapter of the self-history presents a withdrawn bookish youth, for a time 'not quite at home' among the Oriel fellows and gently rebuked by the provost for being too solitary, but then coming 'out of [his] shell' as vicar of St Mary's, where he quite literally found a persuasive voice and public presence. The second gives him a dominant place in the Oxford Movement. Though reluctant to 'take the lead of a party' and content instead to be no more than 'a leading author of a school',[48] he soon realizes that, in spite of himself, many regard him as virtual leader of the Tractarians. He sees clearly that the cause demands more than what 'a board of safe, sound, sensible men'[49] could offer it, that it can succeed only by dint of extraordinary personal vigour. And he perceives that his own most effective writing represents, as it must, 'the antagonist principle of personality',[50] the readiness to speak out boldly, provocatively, with engaged force. In it he achieves an unfamiliar self-expression, a manner marked by the 'fierceness and sport' of strong dogmatic conviction and sometimes by heady overstatement. As an active personality, intent with others on inaugurating 'a second reformation', he now experiences, 'in a human point of view, the happiest time of [his] life'.[51] The appearance of the fierce Tract Ninety', of course, ends the period of contentment, but not the resolute individuality.

Chapter 3 carries the energy of the remembered 'fierce' assertiveness over to the actual narrating of its sequel in the years of unrest and painful decision. Newman deals again in emphatic superlatives as he approaches the description of his break with Oxford and Anglicanism. The recalling of the past, as he now must review it, becomes 'a cruel operation, the ripping up of old griefs', which requires an unprecedented courage: 'I have done various bold things in my life: this is the boldest: and, were I not sure I should after all succeed in my object, it would be madness to

48 *Apo.*, p. 62.
49 *Apo.*, p. 47.
50 *Apo.*, p. 47
51 *Apo.*, p. 76.

set about it.'[52] The certainty that the surgery can be accomplished depends on the accrued stamina of the patient. Newman in the present gains reassurance from his recollection of his past strength, the forceful expression of personality twenty to thirty years earlier. Returning now to his self-history he relies more and more on letters, cited with precise dates as a chronology of his last years as an Anglican and as certified evidence of the reasonableness of his pauses and advances on his religious journey. Gradually as he nears his conversion in 1845, past and present come together, and the protagonist and narrator become one assured personality, the man who can declare his unwavering faith in God and selfhood, despite the world's monstrous negations.

The generally favourable reception of the *Apologia* by readers of various religious persuasions—or of none at all—did more than reinforce the self-image that Newman had established in shaping his autobiography. It actually changed his future public life and prospects, in so far as it reaffirmed his reputation as a spiritual leader, deserving an increased consideration within the Catholic Church and a renewed respect outside it, and so prepared the way for a more alert recognition of the work he had yet to do in England. The *Apologia*, he said, had been 'marvellously blest' in achieving its purpose, and he could at last rejoice that Kingsley had compelled him to write it.[53]

[52] *Apo.*, p. 91.

[53] *AW*, p. 260, and Harrold, *Newman*, p. 308, where Harrold quotes Newman's letter at the time of Kingsley's death (13 Feb. 1875) recognizing Kingsley as a providential 'instrument' in providing the occasion and the necessity of the *Apologia*.

6

The Literary and Historical Significance of the *Present Position of Catholics*

A. O. J. COCKSHUT

> Have we any right to take it strange, if, in this English land, the spring-time of the Church should turn out to be an English spring, an uncertain, anxious time of hope and fear, of joy and suffering,—of bright promises and budding hopes, yet withal, of keen blasts, and cold showers, and sudden storms?

> The lion rends his prey, and gives no reason for doing so; but man cannot persecute without assigning to himself a reason for his act; he must settle it with his conscience[1]

A gap of twenty years is awkward for historical retrospect. We are in a better position now to judge the Suez Crisis or Indian Independence than we were ten or twenty years ago. But the Parisian student troubles of 1968 seem blurred, neither far nor near, neither historical nor contemporary.

In 1850, when Pius IX restored the English hierarchy, and talk of 'papal aggression' began, and in 1851, when Newman gave the lectures which became his book on the *Present Position of Catholics* public opinion was in just this half-formed state about the Catholic Emancipation of 1829. There was a feeling, wide-spread though by no means universal, that the measure had been inevitable, and was now irreversible, just as it was hard for any but incurable romantics to imagine the reinstatement of the Corn Laws after 1846. Many who were unfriendly to Catholicism, or even bitterly opposed, agreed with Macaulay that it had been a progressive measure, and therefore immune to serious criticism. Yet both traditional Protestants, and the battered successors of the Oxford Movement could be excused for wondering whether

[1] Sources for the epigraphs are 'The Second Spring', *OS*, pp. 179–80; and *Pre. Pos.*, p. 225, respectively.

after all it had not been the source of some of their bitterest troubles and lasting regrets. For what had followed? Rapid Irish immigration and numerous conversions had combined to rebuild the strength of Rome in England. A Tory prime minister had proposed, in the Maynooth grant, to 'put Rome on the rates'. Men of the choicest English education were writing Catholic books, proclaiming Protestantism to be absurd, and Anglo-Catholicism an illogical half-measure. Not since the 1680s had Protestant England felt so threatened. As Newman was to hint, 'papal aggression' could be seen as a milder recurrence of the hysteria of the 'Popish Plot' of that time; and, although milder, it was at the same time shriller and more despairing. Everyone knew that, in the nineteenth century, opinion was lord. You could no longer put down Catholicism by royal proclamation.

In another way, the crisis of 1851 pointed forward. It proved to be the last great explosion of anti-Catholic feeling in mainland Britain, which united popular agitation with the sentiments of the educated classes. Later outbursts were to be transient and local. But here the movement was led by *The Times*, a newspaper capable of influencing, or as some said, dictating law and public policy, as it showed again a few years later, when it campaigned for war with Russia. During the months of anti-Catholic excitement, a remarkable harmony prevailed between different classes. As in a patriotic war, people felt proud to be English; the man in the street felt that the prime minister (the son of a duke) was expressing his own sentiments. Both gloried in a shared sense of insular superiority to the world. But, as it proved to be, so it was at the time obscurely felt to be, the last occasion of its kind.

The next generation would see the founding of the Metaphysical Society, in which Archbishop Manning and Father Dalgairns dined amicably with Anglicans and unbelievers, and afterwards debated fundamental questions. Newman could have been a member had he wished. Events inconceivable in the 1840s became commonplace. I select two as emblematic: in 1878 Newman became an honorary fellow of Trinity, Oxford, and in 1880, Lord Ripon, a convert to Catholicism, became governor-general of India.

We cannot be surprised that Rome was surprised by the outburst of 1850. Papal policy had been marked by a desire to conciliate England, especially because of the rapid growth of

Catholicism in British territories overseas that had begun in the time of Gregory XVI (1831–46). Informally consulted, the Government had expressed indifference about the restoration of the hierarchy. The pope must have felt rather like a man who greets his neighbour with the remark that it's a fine day and is accused of uttering a deadly insult. The change from vicars apostolic to territorial bishops was a technical matter that the supposedly shrewd, practical English might be expected to ignore. The startling suddeness of the whole affair was well illustrated by the extraordinary reversal of opinion in the chief instigator, Lord John Russell himself. He had been all for conciliation over Maynooth, quoting from the *Georgics* about the rusting of the forgotten armour of the civil war and the bones of warriors found by the farmer.[2] In the same pacific temper, he had proposed a committee to consider the removal of the prohibition of residence for members of religious orders (retained in the act of 1829), and had maintained that 'severe penalties ought not to be threatened, which no person and no Government can venture to execute'.[3] Ironically he thus became the unconscious prophet of the ineffectiveness of the Ecclesiastical Titles Bill, which his own agitation helped to pass. It had a large majority in the Commons; the penalties it laid down against the bishops were never enforced; it was repealed in 1871 at the time of the disestablishment of the Anglican Church in Ireland.

Indeed, no one expected to see Russell's finger on the trigger. With hindsight, though, we can see that Russell and Wiseman were incompatible characters, destined to misunderstand each other. Russell was touchy, vain, and changeable, as if compensating for being a younger son of low stature. (*Punch* often dwelt on his smallness, and once portrayed him as a street urchin running away after chalking 'No Popery' on Wiseman's door.) He was at least as anxious to attack Puseyism as Catholicism itself. His letter to the Bishop of Durham is interesting not only for its crafty political intent, but also for its implied statement of what the respectable considered the inviolable Protestant tradition to be:

> There is a danger, however, which alarms me much more than any aggression of a foreign Sovereign.

[2] Virgil: *Georgics*, i. 492–7.

[3] A. Barrister, *Political Opinions of Lord John Russell* (London, 1850).

Clergymen of our own Church, who have subscribed the Thirty-nine Articles, and acknowledged in explicit terms the Queen's supremacy, have been the most forward in leading their flocks, 'step by step to the very verge of the precipice.' The honour paid to saints, the claim of infallibility of the Church, the superstitious use of the sign of the cross, the muttering of the liturgy . . . the recommendation of auricular confession, and the administration of penance and absolution . . .[4]

Probably he had never looked into the Prayer Book, in which several of the beliefs and practices he complains of are enjoined.

Of Wiseman, his vicar-general Dr Whitty once said: 'In many respects he remained a child all his life.'[5] He was more unlike the hereditary portion of his flock than many of the Oxford converts were. Born in Spain of Irish parents, he had spent most of his adult life in Rome, first as vice-rector, then as rector of the English College. His time at Ushaw in the north of England, and the distinguished English influence of Lingard had perhaps been less formative than Roman architecture and Roman theological schools. He was flamboyant, excitable, unsystematic, and struck some people as being un-English, or even downright vulgar. He had a strong sense of the majestic influence of the Catholic Church on the history of many centuries. He was extremely learned; but his learning, based on the study of oriental languages, did not much overlap with that of the English intellectual élite. His letter from the Flaminian Gate was an error of tact and judgement. Yet his second production[6] was shrewd in its appeal to English fair play; and his confidence that Protestant England's bark would prove worse than its bite was well-founded. In a country where not even *The Times*, and certainly no politician wished to alienate the Dissenters, he chose his ground well when he said:

The Royal Supremacy is no more admitted by the Scotch Kirk, by Baptists, Methodists, Independents, Presbyterians, Unitarians, and other Dissenters, than by the Catholics.[7]

The first question any reader of *Present Position of Catholics* is likely to ask is, 'Did Newman exaggerate?' Anyone who immerses

[4] *The Times*, 7 Nov. 1850.

[5] Quoted in E. R. Norman, *Anti-Catholicism in Victorian England* (London, 1968), 56.

[6] Wiseman, *An Appeal to the Reason and Good Feeling of the English People* (London, 1850).

[7] Ibid. 10.

himself for a week in the relevant books, pamphlets, sermons, leading articles, and episcopal charges may well reply, 'No, he understated.' Things he omitted were often more wild and poisonous than what he included. He did not dwell, for instance, on a dangerously inflammatory use of Scripture, where Catholics were cast in the role of Jonah; as if their acceptance as citizens brought down on the whole nation the anger of God. A sermon at Walthamstow on 5 November 1850 (two days before Russell's letter in *The Times*) proclaimed that all recent disasters, especially the cholera, were the manifest judgement of God in his anger against the Emancipation of 1829. A new edition in 1854 of a work Newman did quote, put the point more plainly and ominously than before: 'Since the Reformation we have enjoyed many special national blessings; so since the Revolution of 1829 we have suffered many natural disasters.'[8] The writer is typical of a whole school of authors in assuming that any conduct, reprehensible in Scripture—the lust of Jezebel or the cruelty of Nero—must refer prophetically to popery; and he proves to his own satisfaction that the number 666 means the pope himself, a point which Newman neatly parodied by showing that similar reasoning could make it refer to Queen Victoria.[9]

A new edition of *Maria Monk*, originally published in New York in 1836, appeared in 1851; and the strong pornographic appeal, which Newman's extracts well illustrated, still proved fascinating. Doctrines that the most ill-instructed Catholic would recognize as heretical (such as that priests are incapable of sin) were presented as standard teaching in convents. Even the footnotes might minister to a febrile excitement. For instance:

> Read that well-authenticated Narrative entitled 'Horrors of the Nunnery' in Nos 2 and 3 of the *Anti-Popish Reviewer* or *Protestant Lamp for the Christian Churchman* . . . only one penny each number.[10]

But the historical distortions imposed by writers of education are in a way more striking, because more sincere and more easily refuted. Thus, in a lengthy historical survey, which insouciantly turns Bossuet's argument on its head, one writer had maintained in 1838 that Catholics have no agreed standard of faith or bond

[8] T. Stephen, *Spirit of the Church of Rome* (1854; 3rd edn., London, 1854), p. v.
[9] *Pre. Pos.*, p. 35.
[10] *Maria Monk* (1836; new edn., London, 1851), 26 n.

of union, while all the Protestant sects have the same creed: 'The harmony of these declarations of belief is truly surprising and constitutes an extraordinary event in the history of man.'[11] And with magnificent effrontery he asserts that popery was never embraced by more than a fifth of Christendom,[12] while another maintains that the Russian Church is more numerous than the Roman.[13]

Catherine Sinclair, whose book *Popish Legends on Bible Truths* was published after Newman's, was by no means a member of what Hensley Henson would later call 'the Protestant underworld' but a lady of education, praised by respectable reviewers. She regards the legend of Pope Joan as proved, confuses infallibility with impeccability[14] (this is a standard error repeated from one book to another), calls St Vincent de Paul a 'fradulent gamester',[15] but has a surprise in store when she calls St John Chrysostom a Protestant, since he had a reverence for Scripture, of which, as is well known, no Catholic is capable.[16] Self-contradictions abound. She thinks poverty holy, but reproaches the Church for the poverty of Ireland and Italy. She castigates Catholicism as the religion of the rich, but then appeals to England's prosperity as a mark of God's favour.[17] A long book which certainly inclines to be tedious is illumined by a pure shaft of unconscious humour when she says that Judas was the only person in Scripture who confessed to a priest.[18]

Two general points are noticeable in a whole group of books of which *Popish Legends* may serve as a fair example. The current state of England can be proclaimed as uniquely blessed if the context deals with its defiant Protestant traditions; but it can suddenly become miserable and accursed if the issue is Catholic Emancipation, or conversions to Rome or the Oxford Movement. Then authors who express the loftiest scorn for Popish legends show themselves childishly credulous of scandals learnt by hearsay, baseless historical myths, and wild tales of depravity. Thus one author recounts as certain truth that Pope Joan (who actually never existed) gave birth to a child between St Clement's Church

[11] S. Edgar, *Variations of Popery* (2nd edn., London, 1838), 4.
[12] Ibid. 41.
[13] Stephen, *Church of Rome*, p. 38.
[14] C. Sinclair, *Popish Legends on Bible Truths* (London, 1852), p. lii.
[15] Ibid. p. vi.
[16] Ibid. p. xiv.
[17] Ibid. p. xlvii.
[18] Ibid. 213.

in Rome and the amphitheatre, when being led in procession to be crowned with the papal tiara.[19] One is often led to wonder whether the contradictions, the studied ignorance of even the outline of history, or the credulity would have been shown in the discussion of any other topic.

But the versions of history offered, even though the general drift of hatred and prejudice may not vary, often differ strikingly in their details. Newman said: 'They drop a thousand years from the world's chronicle.'[20] But this record is easily exceeded by J. M. Cramp, a learned Doctor of Divinity. For him, the popish Antichrist was plainly visible at the time of the accession of Constantine.[21] So much so that 'intelligent, scriptural piety was scarcely known, wrapt in the rocks and fastnesses which concealed the chosen few who had not received the mark of the beast'.[22] Here, and in many other writers, the proliferation of animal metaphors, sometimes interspersed with assertions that human beings, if Catholic, actually are not more than animals, is a disturbing feature. Thus Cramp moves in a few pages of a long book chronologically arranged from the end of the third century to the sixteenth. But in T. Stephen's *Spirit of the Church of Rome*, Pope Gregory the Great, three centuries later, was still a good Protestant. Had its implications been considered, this would have been found an inconvenient view, entailing the consequence that the high Marian doctrines of the Councils of Ephesus and Calchedon were sound Protestantism. But perhaps the author never thought of this, but simply couldn't bear that the man who sent St Augustine to convert England could have been a 'papist', even if he undeniably was a pope.

In turning to the subject of moral blame, a term whose studied understatement will appear, we must bear in mind Newman's words: 'they wish us to be what they believe us to be . . . they delight to look at us, and to believe that we are the veriest reptiles and vermin'.[23]

Maria Monk was no doubt exceptional in being a deliberate liar, who had the fruitful literary idea of describing a brothel in detail and then saying it was a convent. But most of the

[19] Stephen, *Church of Rome*, p. 38.

[20] *Pre. Pos.*, p. 43.

[21] J. M. Cramp, *Text-Book of Popery* (3rd edn., London, 1851). One of many anti-Catholic books reissued in or about 1851.

[22] Ibid. 13.

[23] *Pre. Pos.*, p. 263.

denunciations impress by their sincerity, tinged, as Newman implies, by wishful thinking. Catherine Sinclair, who strikes me as perfectly honest, quotes with approval in her novel *Beatrice* a judgement that the life of an Italian is 'little more than an animal one', that of 'an ape endowed with speech'; and she goes on: 'Thus it is with all nations or individuals, whose misfortune it is to fall under the . . . Papal tyranny.'[24] This was published in 1852, after Newman's book, and a third edition was called for as late as 1879. In the last quotation, the word 'individuals' is especially striking. It must have been easy for many Englishmen to believe the worst of far countries they had never seen, or of Ireland about whose misgovernment they might feel guilty. But, however familiar we may be with the human tendency to self-deception, we may still feel surprise that a whole class of readers could accept that men of brilliant intellectual attainments like Wiseman and Newman were no more than apes.

Catherine Sinclair goes on to express outrage that popish sisters are to be allowed to minister to British troops at Varna,[25] to assert that 'the Papists consider it a crime to marry, as well as to read the Bible',[26] and to repeat the accusations (dealt with by Newman in connection with another author) of money payments to condone sin, and of idolatry of images.[27] After this, we may take the invention of female Jesuits as mere high-spirited good humour, note with amusement that the same men (if they are priests) are found to be both brutally ignorant and preternaturally subtle, and without surprise that the grasping Irish landlord happens to be a Catholic. But the special interest of the work is found in the skilful way she mingles two separate streams of literary tradition, different, or even incompatible, in every respect except their anti-Catholicism. One—that of serious, if highly censorious theological controversy—was already three centuries old; the other, that of the Gothic novel, went back only to the eighteenth century.

An instance of the first is: '[There is] no evidence that St Catherine of Siena ever existed, and it would certainly be better for her that she was never born.'[28] (It would be hard to think of a saint more certainly attested by secular history.) And as an

[24] C. Sinclair, *Beatrice* (London, 1852), p. xiv.
[25] Ibid. p. xxvii. [26] Ibid. 42. [27] Ibid. 49.
[28] Ibid. 383.

example of the second there is the story, recounted as a fact, that a Spanish lady caused her brothers to crucify her on the door of the drawing-room, after which they inherited her fortune.[29] The confessional is habitually treated in this 'Gothic' spirit; the other tradition appears when we are told that Catholics never worship God but only Mary, blasphemously prefer Friday to Sunday, and hate the Bible. In the case of books published after Newman's, one is often struck by their close conformity to the types he describes.

Newman's amusing account of the way in which conversions to the Catholic Church are treated by the prejudiced man is well reflected in an article in the weighty Tory journal the *Quarterly Review*, which speaks of 'two or three dozen contemptible apostasies' which have made an unnecessary sensation.[30] Some writers maintain that all the converts are eccentric scholars, crazed with overmuch learning, while others think that they are mainly to be found among silly, enthusiastic young ladies. Newman's sly account of the presumption that conversions were temporary, and followed soon by the return of the wanderers, proved prophetic of widespread reports over many years, that he had returned or was about to return to the Church of England.

We must presume that had Lord John Russell, or a *Times* leader-writer, or an Anglican bishop happened to read *Maria Monk*, they would have done so either with distaste or with amusement. Nevertheless the strange salient point about the uproar is the merging of responsible opinion and established respectability in the half-illiterate Protestant underworld. *The Times* wrote that the restoration of the hierarchy was 'one of the grossest acts of folly and impertinence which the Court of Rome has ventured to commit since the Crown and people of England threw off its yoke'.[31] And one of Newman's choicest examples of the libel about selling the right to sin was taken from *The Times*.[32] The Lord Chancellor, at the Lord Mayor's banquet said to applause (quoting Shakespeare): 'Under our feet we'll stamp thy Cardinal's hat.' An Anglican clergyman denounced auricular confession thus: 'Transportation should not satisfy me, for that would merely transfer the evil from one part of the world to

[29] Ibid. 64. [30] *Quarterly Review*, 88 (1851), 566.
[31] *The Times*, 14 Oct. 1850.
[32] *Pre. Pos.*, pp. 109–10.

another. Capital punishment alone would satisfy.'[33] Perhaps he had not read the Prayer Book any more than Lord John Russell had.

The charges of Anglican prelates which provided Newman with one of the most brilliant passages he ever wrote, dwelt mainly on a few simple themes, and followed a single pattern, whether this is due to imitation or to simple like-mindedness. The typical one thanks correspondents, clerical or lay, for the hot anger of their letter of protest, asserts two doctrines, the sufficiency of Scripture and the Royal Supremacy (prudently avoiding any suggestion as to ways of reconciling them), indulges in a little vituperation against Rome, and perhaps even more fiercely, against the Oxford Movement, and asserts the writer's pride in being English, and his confidence in the legislature of his country. Above all, the absolute religious authority of Queen Victoria is their theme; never was the episcopal office more gracefully merged in that of the courtier. The Oxford Movement had by then had a considerable effect in some parishes. It had had none on the bishops, except to irritate and alarm them. In 1830 they had been complacent Erastians; in 1850 they were anxious Erastians.[34]

II

Newman thought *Present Position of Catholics* his best-written book,[35] and it was probably the most enjoyable to write. All his other major works involved him in grave difficulties, intellectual or emotional, or both. The *Essay on the Development of Christian Doctrine* was the painful tracing of a labyrinth of personal experience, leading to his conversion. *Difficulties of Anglicans* placed him on a tightrope, where a false step could land him on one side in tactlessly antagonizing his old associates of the Oxford Movement, and on the other in the fruitless minimizing of important differences. It required the skills of private correspondence to be used publicly. The *Apologia* was written with incredible speed, resulting in severe fatigue, and under the lash of

[33] For these and other instances see W. Ward, *W. G. Ward and the Catholic Revival* (London, 1893), 2–3.

[34] See various authors, *The Roman Catholic Question*. (London 1851), sec. 7, p. 12 (Abp. of Canterbury); sec. 7, p. 13 (Abp. of York); sec. 8, p. 9 (Bp. of Lichfield); sec. 4, pp. 11–13 (Dean of Bristol); and many others.

[35] *Ward*, i. 264

a gratuitous insult. A *Grammar of Assent*, the only one that was not, in some sense, occasional, was the most difficult of all, and the one in writing which he had the greatest fear of failure. In contrast *Present Position of Catholics* was the release of many tensions, and the unchaining of literary gifts, comic, satirical and grotesque, which the discipline of his life seldom allowed a free run. It had an unpleasant sequel in the Achilli trial, as the evidence used for a charge of libel came from its text; but this was in the unknown future as he wrote. It is a happy book about an unhappy situation. Though brilliant, it has no need of abstruse learning. He could let himself go.

He may not have been aware that the book was indirectly affected by his long Fabian avoidance of battle against his growing conviction between 1839 and 1843 that the Protestant history and style of the Anglican Church was, after all, a correct image of its abiding nature. He over-compensates a little, minimizing the High Church strain in Anglican history as much as he had once over-estimated it. Here he constantly uses the word 'Protestant' as if it was an actual title of the Church (which in America it is). Still, the word is inexact, failing to distinguish the Establishment from the Dissenters.

And yet, inexact as it is, it was shrewdly chosen. For his tactical aim was to separate the high Protestant tradition of the ruling groups, the universities, and the organs of serious opinion from the underworld in which they seemed for the time to have merged themselves. He wished to shame educated readers out of an alliance with ignorant and vulgar associates. Thus he contrasted the immense popularity of the unspeakable *Maria Monk* with the comparative indifference shown to the sober, truthful indictment of Blanco White, a man he had known himself.[36] He quoted his old friend Archbishop Whately, who had declared that Jews and Mahometans should be protected by law from mockery and insult, and then pointed to the glaring anomaly of the refusal of this protection to Catholics:

> I appeal to the last fifth of November, when jeers against the Blessed Sacrament were chalked up in the Metropolis with impunity, under the very shadow of the Court, and before the eyes of the Home Office and the Police.[37]

[36] *Pre. Pos.*, pp. 174–5. [37] Ibid. 202–5.

He shamed his readers as English gentlemen for conniving at cowardly attacks on women and schoolgirls.[38] He cited fair-minded opponents like J. Martineau in the *Westminster Review*,[39] and he made extensive use of the common literary tradition, quoting Walter Scott and others. He sowed seeds of doubt, and perhaps in some, of remorse, by historical parallels, of which the murderous slanders of Titus Oates were the most arresting. It is hard to gauge the effectiveness of all this, but as *The Times* had taken a lead in the agitation, it must have been gratifying to read its leader on the Achilli verdict, in which a jury decided that Newman had libelled an apostate priest with no reputation to lose:

> We consider that a great blow has been given to the administration of justice in this country, and that Roman Catholics will henceforth have only too good reasons for asserting that there is no justice for them in cases tending to arouse the Protestant feelings of judges and juries.[40]

As a work of literature, the book is unusual in combining so many different genres. It is fiery and tender, analytical and rhetorical, bitter, comic, and solemn. At different times it is as calmly reasonable as Hume, as fiercely contemptuous as Swift, as funny as Dickens. It contains history, philosophy, psychology, persuasive argument, ridicule, and unbridled fantasy. Yet it has a single theme, a continuous thread of argument, and a strict policy of excluding the irrelevant. Newman's sense of classic form was always strong; he always defined the chosen limit of his subject. But here, much more than in his other books, classic form took the strain of incongruous materials.

One lecture ends with a challenge to the traditions of England:

> It is by wholesale, retail, systematic, unscrupulous lying . . . that the many rivulets are made to flow for the feeding of the great Protestant tradition . . .[41]

Another ends with a calm assurance of religious comfort:

> Truth is eternal; it is great, and will prevail. The end is the proof of Brothers of the Oratory, surely we shall succeed, because 'they say all manner of evil against us falsely for his Name's sake'.[42]

38 *Pre. Pos.*, p. 205–6.
39 Ibid. 331–2.
40 *The Times*, 26 June 1852.
41 *Pre. Pos.*, p. 126.
42 Ibid. 176.

The book certainly has its weaknesses. Among them we may note a tendency, carried over from his High Anglican days, to underrate the strength and public influence of Dissenters. More strangely—and it would be hard to explain this—he attributed the English literary tradition an exclusively Protestant character which it does not possess. He knows nothing of the glories of the fourteenth century; and he much undervalues the Catholic contribution to later literature. A sixteenth-century historian might be inclined to fault him for ascribing to politicians and churchmen, improvising under the pressure of events, a single Machiavellian line of policy. The history of the United States must throw doubt on his contention that Protestantism withers when unsupported by a State establishment. Perhaps, too, he gave a handle to opponents by an over-eager acceptance of dubious accounts of miracles.

But a weakness that might well have been expected in such a work is not found. There is no disharmony between polemical journalism and calm general reflection. The unifying power of the writer's personality and thought melts down intractable materials at great heat until they become parts of a perceived unity. This is another feature that may remind us of Swift.

It is a little surprising that one of his most effective weapons should be the *tu quoque*. Since two wrongs do not make a right, this is often a weak mode of argument. But it becomes a strong one, if the contest is about principles not practice, and if opponents can be shown to be reasoning on principles they have already denounced as absurd. Even more, if they are seen to be acting on a principle which is a debased travesty of the one they assail. Thus the assertion that leave to sin had been traded for money in Brussels had been shown to be based on mere mistake, fostered by ignorance of a foreign language. A detailed refutation had been provided. But:

> The exposure happened in March and April; but Protestantism is infallible and the judgement of its doctors is irreversible; accordingly, in the following June the newspaper . . . thought it necessary to show that the Tradition was not injured by the blow; so out came the Tradition again . . . not at all the worse for the accident. 'It is the practice,' the writer pronounces *ex cathedra*, 'as our readers are aware in Roman Catholic countries, to post up a list of all the crimes to which human frailty can

be tempted, placing opposite to them the exact sum of money for which their perpetration will be indulged.'[43]

Newman's artful use here of technical terms in theology does not portend, as might be expected, a criticism of Anglican bishops or Acts of Parliament. In place of the expert processes of the Catholic system, Protestant England proudly places the rootless authority of the anonymous leader-writer, who can commit libels with impunity. The implicit appeal is to the tradition of the English gentleman, who withdraws if he makes an accusation that cannot be sustained, and apologizes if he has used weak evidence. In the next decade Charles Kingsley, a clergyman, a 'gentleman by law', a courtier and friend of the sovereign, corruptly appointed to a high academic position, was to illustrate Newman's point with uncanny accuracy, refusing to withdraw an accusation proved to be false.

In one of the most brilliant passages, Newman is able to turn the *tu quoque* into glorious farce. This is the Russian section, where venerable maxims of constitutional law are interpreted without regard to the tradition of technical legal language. The effect is gained by combining what might be a dry technical discussion with a vivid sketch of a Protestant meeting in a state of feverish excitement:

> The gallant speaker then delivered the following passage from Blackstone's volume in a very distinct and articulate whisper . . . the OMNIPOTENCE of Parliament! No one can conceive the thrilling effect of these words; they were heard all over the immense assemblage; every man turned pale; a dead silence followed.[44]

The choice of Blackstone's *Commentaries* is a master stroke. It is a work that conjures up an image of rank upon rank of judges finding precedents for safe, obstructive, unimaginative, and indubitably Protestant decisions, the subject of the sparkling satire employed a few years later by Dickens in *Bleak House*. Behind the fun is a serious point. The uninstructed will always go wrong if they interpret technical language by common sense. Why treat this as obvious in the case of English law, and as sinister in the case of Roman theology? In no other work of Newman would such a body of thought have been clothed in such exuberant fantasy.

[43] *Pre. Pos.*, p. 118. [44] Ibid. 33.

The book is unusual for him too in being organized round visual images, which are not merely metaphors but symbols of clusters of ideas, events, and arguments. The most important are the bells, which represent episcopal charges about 'papal aggression'; the gaping crowd peering into the foundations of the Birmingham building; the dishonoured statue of William III, and the Benediction in a London chapel. All are linked by illustrating the multiple guises and operations of prejudice. They do not merely show forth what they represent; they *absorb* it. Just as, for many, it would now be impossible to call to mind the politics of the reign of George I without picturing little men dancing on tightropes, so episcopal charges of 1850–1 will evoke wildly swinging bells in human form:

A movement is in birth which has no natural crisis or resolution. Spontaneously the bells of the steeples begin to sound. Not by an act of volition, but by a sort of mechanical impulse, bishop and dean, archdeacon and canon, rector and curate, one after another, each on his high tower, off they set, swinging and booming, tolling and chiming, with nervous intenseness, and thickening emotion, and deepening volume, the old ding-dong which has scared town and country this weary time; tolling and chiming away, jingling and clamouring and ringing the changes on their poor half-dozen notes, all about 'the Popish aggression', 'insolent and insidious', 'insidious and insolent', 'insolent and atrocious', 'atrocious and insolent', 'atrocious, insolent and ungrateful', 'ungrateful, insolent and atrocious', 'foul and offensive', 'pestilent and horrid', 'subtle and unholy', 'audacious and revolting', 'contemptible and shameless', 'malignant', 'frightful', 'mad', 'meretricious',—bobs (I think the ringers call them), bobs and bobs-royal and triple-bob majors, and grandsires,—to the extent of their compass and the full ring of their metal, in honour of Queen Bess, and to the confusion of the Holy Father and the Princes of the Church.[45]

Similarly we retain the picture of a bemused crowd gazing at the foundations of the Birmingham Oratory, and conjuring up underground chambers of torture, until perhaps:

fifty years hence, if some sudden frenzy of the hour roused anti-Catholic jealousy still lingering in the town, a mob might have swarmed upon our innocent building to rescue certain legs of mutton and pats of butter from imprisonment, and hold an inquest over a dozen packing-cases,

[45] Ibid. 76–7.

some old hampers, a knife-board, and a range of empty blacking bottles.[46]

The image of the statue of King William contains an argument that if Protestants are entitled to reverence visible signs of secular loyalties, they cannot deny Catholics a similar right with holy objects. There is a telling climax, which may have touched on the raw those Protestants who sincerely felt devotion to the person of Christ. He noted how often the pronouns 'he' and 'him' had been applied to the inanimate statue, and:

Protestants would be horrified, had I used 'he' and 'him' of a crucifix . . . did I but honour my living Lord as they their dead king.[47]

In the account of the rite of Benediction given by the 'Protestant Scripture Reader', Newman was able to offer an even more telling contrast than that between the dead king and the living Lord. The contrast here is immediately present in the image. On the one hand, the peaceful, consoling worship of the Church; on the other the angry, brooding spirit of the unbidden visitor, muddling everything, misinterpreting everything, storing up lies and half-truths for his pamphlet. It is very funny; but behind it lies an unspoken question to his educated reader: 'Are you proud of the associates you have chosen?'[48]

Round the leading images are organized minor and local ones, like the wasp that is surprised at not flying through a window-pane,[49] or hunt-the-slipper.[50] They are humdrum, and produce an effect of gentle domestic mockery. Some suggest childishness, and insinuate the query, 'Why cannot Protestant England grow up?'

Behind the irony, the stern satire, the fantastic humour, the analysis of historical and logical error, lies, paradoxically and hearteningly, confidence in his fellow-countrymen felt by a patriot who, thirteen years later, was to appeal to English fairness, when attacked at his most sensitive point—his reputation for truthfulness. That appeal was to be abundantly successful. Perhaps already in 1851 he obscurely felt that the long reign of prejudice was ending. He had found the English narrow, ignorant, impulsive, but not cruel or vindictive. He embodied this view of

[46] *Pre. Pos.*, p. 125.
[47] Ibid. 180–1.
[48] Ibid. 253–61.
[49] Ibid. 240–1.
[50] Ibid. 388.

his countrymen too in an image which was to prove strangely prophetic:

I will say a bold thing—but I am not at all sure that . . . the Pope himself, however he might be abused behind his back, would not be received with cheers and run after by admiring crowds, if he visited this country . . . winning favour, attracting hearts, when he showed himself in real flesh and blood[51]

[51] Ibid. 61.

7

Newman as a Letter-Writer

ALAN G. HILL AND IAN KER

1. Themes and Models

Alan G. Hill

Letter-writing always held a high place in Newman's scale of priorities. It was not for him a marginal or leisure-time activity but an integral part of his mission, and he devoted all his powers of mind and genius for human understanding and sympathy to it. The collected edition of his letters, therefore, adds a quite new dimension to the record of his life and work 'after a hundred years'. For where else but in these unstudied day-by-day exchanges can we hope to trace the inner dynamics of his spiritual development, or the secret of the spell he cast over his followers? As he himself wrote in 1863, echoing a remark of Southey's in his *Life of Cowper*:

> The true life of a man is in his letters. Not only for the interest of a biography, but for arriving at the inside of things, the publication of letters is the true method. Biographers varnish, they assign motives, they conjecture feelings . . . but contemporary letters are facts.[1]

Newman's faith in the letter as an empirical 'fact' in a world of fleeting appearances stands in marked contrast to the unease which Wordsworth had felt (in spite of evidence to the contrary in Mason's *Life of Gray*) that the 'casual effusions' of literary men had been given far too much prominence in the modern world, as the controversies about Coleridge and Lamb, not to mention the earlier case of Robert Burns, had proved. But Newman's confidence was decisively vindicated during the controversy with Charles Kingsley. The writing of the *Apologia* would have been impossible without the letters which document and corroborate the argument at every stage.

[1] *LD* xx. 443 and n. The quotation is from the first draft of the letter.

Newman's commitment to the 'occasional' as an inescapable part of the human condition found its appropriate form in the Ciceronian letter. Its restrained warmth, and the colloquial familiarity and candour of its procedures, did not preclude discussion of the serious issues that were never far from Newman's thoughts, while discouraging the pleasantries and indiscretions that are often thought indispensable for a successful correspondence. He writes with the ease of private conversation, and often in a markedly colloquial idiom, but weighing his words carefully. 'I do not object to be called to account for any words of mine, however privately and casually spoken,' he wrote in 1833 at the start of the Oxford Movement,[2] and this overwhelming sense of responsibility *sub specie aeternitatis* pervades his letters, Anglican and Catholic, till the end of his days, whatever the occasion or his relationship with his correspondent. His faith in 'the warm affections and charities of the human heart, of which correspondence is both the stimulant and the expression',[3] was absolute. He had none of George Eliot's distrust of what she called 'the uncertain process of letter-writing'.[4]

In the more elegant and settled society of eighteenth-century England, Horace Walpole and Thomas Gray had chosen the Ciceronian model for their polished and witty exchanges of mutual sympathy with their friends, but Newman's affinities with Cicero run much deeper and they must have been obvious to himself from the beginning. They had in common a love of study and a remarkable capacity for friendships. But both of them were reluctantly drawn from books and friends into the maelstrom of public events, the one in the last fateful days of the Roman republic, the other during the political and religious crises of 1828–33, the almost apocalyptic manifestation (as it seemed at the time) of the 'liberalism' which it became Newman's life-work to oppose; and their letters, like those of Erasmus, embody their individual recipes for the good life in an insecure and changing world. All the major concerns of the fellow of Oriel, the oratorian, and the cardinal, take shape for the first time in his letters and are given a human face and significance for the individual recipient (or the reader):

[2] *LD* iv. 105.

[3] *LD* xx. 442.

[4] *The George Eliot Letters*, ed. G. S. Haight (Oxford, 1954–6), ii. 254.

We all look at things with our own eyes—and invest the whole face of nature with colors of our own.—Each mind pursues its own course and is actuated in that course by ten thousand indescribable incommunicable feelings and imaginings. It would be comparatively easy to enumerate the various external impulses which determine the capricious motions of a floating feather or web, and to express in an algebraical formula the line it describes—so mysterious are the paths of thought. . . . Necessary as it is, that we should all hold the same truths (as we would be saved) still each of us holds them in his own way . . .[5]

In his early sermons, and in the letters (with their accompanying poems) which he sent home to family and friends from his momentous voyage to the Mediterranean before the opening of the Oxford Movement, Newman had already given abundant signs of rare qualities of imagination and human feeling. His brilliant 'documentary' writing,[6] for example, so rare in novels of that date, would alone mark him off as 'a special correspondent for posterity', in Bagehot's phrase; and his journey through Sicily, so different in its inner meaning from other Romantic and Victorian travelogues like Ruskin's, is transformed in his imagination into a quest for spiritual enlightenment, in which his own salvation is ultimately in the balance, and passing scenes and events are less significant for themselves than as affording 'types' and analogies of profounder spiritual truths. But thereafter his growing mastery of literary effect was largely put to the service of his religious and controversial aims, though throughout his life it always found a natural and immediate channel in his correspondence. 'You want an outlet for your mind and heart, which are running over, where there is no call for their riches,' protested Blanco White in 1828, urging him to write for the *London Review*. 'Tell the world at large what you feel and think.'[7]

But literary distinction in the ordinary sense of the term Newman neither admired nor sought at any time in his career. Personal influence—for which letters were the perfect medium—could do more than publications to build up the life of faith in others; for men live on after their time, not in written records, but in the unwritten memories of a 'school of pupils' who trace their 'moral parentage' to them. 'I shall turn philosopher—rail at the world at large and be content with a few friends who know

[5] *LD* ii. 60. [6] See *LD* iii. 133. [7] *LD* ii. 105.

me.'[8] And so Newman's letters bear witness above all to the growth and flowering of friendships over the years, and the confidence and sense of purpose they inspired. 'Whenever I think of you', Newman writes to Blanco White, 'your name is connected in my mind with so many grand and beautiful visions, that I quite wonder how it is that having known you so short a time I seem so at home with you.'[9] The personal efforts of like-minded individuals were all-important:

> No great work was done by a system—whereas systems rise out of individual exertions. . . . The very faults of an individual excite attention —he loses, but his cause (if good, and he powerful minded) gains—this is the way of things, we promote truth by a self sacrifice.[10]

Newman saw no reason to modify this stance (with its poignant relevance to his own predicaments) after his conversion, as his later correspondence reveals. If many letters demonstrate his rare qualities of leadership, and the influence he exercised over his disciples within and outside the Roman Church, many more embody in a more intimate way the pastoral concern of his sermons, but extended far beyond his own immediate circle. What C. S. Dessain called the 'apostolate' of the letter[11] was a primary concern of Newman's into extreme old age, and he would have utterly repudiated the dismissive view of Southey (himself an accomplished letter-writer) that

> Letter-writing is a favourite amusement with the young; as men grow older they find less leisure for it, and as they cease to want employment for idle hours, their inclination for it ceases also.[12]

In the same way he would have shunned the egotism or ennui of the younger T. S. Eliot in his plea to Conrad Aiken (to take a more recent example):

> I hope you will write soon and tell me about yourself. I think one's letters ought to be about oneself (I live up to this theory!)—what else is there to talk about? Letters should be indiscretions—otherwise they are simply official bulletins.[13]

[8] *LD* ii. 255.

[9] *LD* ii. 80.

[10] *LD* iv. 308.

[11] *LD* xi. 17.

[12] *A Selection from the Letters of Robert Southey*, ed. J. W. Warter, ii (London, 1856), 51.

[13] *The Letters of T. S. Eliot*, ed. V. Eliot (London, 1988–), i. 75.

Newman's letters bear abundant witness to his steadiness and inner consistency of purpose at every stage of his long and arduous spiritual pilgrimage, and the way in which he was guided step by step in his vocation by immediate circumstances—in his family circle for example. In his early letters to his younger brother Charles, who was drifting away from Christianity into unbelief, Newman was already, years before the Tractarian movement, cutting his teeth on problems that were to preoccupy him more and more in the years of the *Oxford University Sermons* on the relations of faith and reason, and much later in the *Grammar of Assent*, as he momentarily anticipates his mature thinking about Christian evidences and the nature of personal belief and commitment. Other letters, from the Tractarian period and earlier, reflect the argument of his Tract Seventy-Three 'On the Introduction of Rationalistic Principles into Revealed Religion' and look forward to his defence of the dogmatic principle in his *biglietto* speech at Rome in 1879 and his last essays and letters as a cardinal. Taken as a whole, Newman's correspondence demonstrates that when he made his momentous change of allegiance in 1845, he did not change in very much else.

Even more than other Victorians, Newman was a compulsive hoarder of letters. They enabled him to relive his past and find his bearings in a changing world. He drew on Hurrell Froude's letters for the controversial edition of Froude's *Remains* in 1838: 'I feared at first', he writes to Keble, 'they would be too personal as regards *others*, but then I began to think that, if they could be given, they would be next best to talking with him'.[14] And he cannot have been unaware of Carlyle's effective use of correspondence in his *Life of John Sterling* (1851) for clarifying the career of that casualty of early Victorian uncertainties. But he does not seem fully to have appreciated the use to which his own letters might be put for defending his own record until the misunderstandings and disappointments of his life as a Catholic—over the Dublin University, the London Oratory, and the *Rambler* affair—brought it more forcibly home to him in the years before his controversy with Kingsley, and he felt the need to take stock of his life, which (it seemed) might be drawing to a premature close.

[14] *LD* vi. 96.

To what different kinds of work should one give oneself [he writes to his bishop in 1857], if one knew that life was to be continued for one, two, or three years, or on the other hand for 20! Such is the trial of a person at my age—I may be entering on a long course of years, or closing my reckoning.[15]

The power of the letter, when combined with other personal forms of writing, to give the fullest possible revelation of the character and ethos of the author, is the theme of Newman's Introduction to his 'Life of St. Chrysostom', first published in the *Rambler* in 1859, and later incorporated into his *Historical Sketches*. It is surely one of the most engaging and revealing short pieces he ever wrote. The traditional saint's life, he maintains, is a poor substitute for 'that kind of literature which more than any other represents the abundance of the heart, which more than any other approaches to conversation', of which the supreme exemplar is Cicero.[16] It is through their letters, above all, that the early Christian Fathers are intimately known to us; and so complete have Newman's ties of sympathy and imagination with them become by this time that in describing their letters he might almost be outlining the scope and interest of his own as well.

These letters are of very various characters, compared one with another: a large portion of them were intended simply for the parties to whom they are addressed; a large portion consist of brief answers to questions asked of the writer, or a few words of good counsel or spiritual exhortation, disclosing his character either by the topic selected, or his mode of dealing with it. Many are doctrinal; great numbers, again, are strictly ecclesiastical . . . Many are historical and biographical . . . some narrate public transactions, and how the writer felt towards them, or why he took part in them. . . . Instead of writing formal doctrinal treatises they write controversy; and their controversy, again, is correspondence.[17]

And then, very characteristically, he turns from their miscellaneous content, so close to the 'facts' of everyday experience, to the writers' broader purposes:

The line of their discussion traverses a region rich and interesting, and opens on those who follow them in it, a succession of instructive views as to the aims, the difficulties, the disappointments, under which they journeyed on heavenward, their care of the brethren, their anxieties

[15] *LD* xvii. 534. [16] *HS* ii. 221. [17] *HS* ii. 222–3.

about contemporary teachers of error. . . . They wrote for the occasion, and seldom on a carefully digested plan.[18]

No better account could be given of Newman's own letters than this. In his organic metaphor, the multifarious concerns of the Fathers grow together into what he calls 'an unstudied self-manifestation', which impresses the reader with 'the idea of moral unity, identity, growth, continuity, personality'.

When a Saint converses with me, I am conscious of one active principle of thought, one individual character, flowing on and into the various matters which he discusses, and the different transactions in which he mixes. It is what no memorials can reach, however skilfully elaborated . . . Why cannot art rival the lily or the rose? Because the colours of the flower are developed and blended by the force of an inward life . . .[19]

It is an extraordinary and quite unconscious anticipation of the effect which Newman's own letters when taken as a whole, as they now can be for the first time, will have on a reader today.

Newman's letters are intrinsically interesting for their subject-matter, but more so for their intimate revelation of Newman himself, so much fuller than Tennyson's picture of himself in his letters, for example; so different in tone and refinement from the pungent self-analysis and idiosyncracies of Carlyle or the obliquities of Coleridge. Here is Newman as he really was, in all his 'naturalness' (to adopt Dean Church's word)—the grandeur, the humour, the pathos, the conflicts and the inner serenity, the care for the smallest details of everyday life as well as the largest issues of eternity—but restrained from self-display by the principle of reserve and a classical sense of propriety and form.

2. *The Varied Voices*

Ian Ker

Apart from its obvious biographical and historical interest, Newman's vast correspondence is important for two reasons. First, it complements and supplements Newman's thought in many revealing ways. Second, it adds appreciably to our estimate of Newman's standing as a writer. Interesting and illuminating as the letters of Dickens and George Eliot are, for example, they do not alter their authors' literary standing: even

[18] *HS* ii. 223. [19] *HS* ii. 227.

if no correspondence survived at all, we should not think any the less of either novelist as a writer. The letters of George Eliot certainly add to our understanding of her intellectual life, but their literary merit is negligible; Dickens's energy in letter-writing was characteristically prodigious, but again, although his letters are fully consonant with the genius of the novelist, they do not increase our perception of his literary greatness. It is different with Newman: his letters not only enhance his position as one of the great writers of non-fiction prose, but they also constitute a uniquely rich and varied contribution to the epistolary genre in the English language. His letters indeed are as truly integral to his *œuvre* as are the letters of Cicero.

There are a number of different voices in the letters. Apart from the fact that Newman never wrote impersonal letters but always wrote directly and personally to each of his correspondents, his range of subject and tone is extensive. The sheer variety can only be hinted at here.

One of the earliest letters Newman ever wrote, when he was aged eleven, reveals two of his most salient characteristics as a writer, his exuberance and his wit:

> Dear Aunt,
>
> The joyful 21 again approaches when our books are closed according to delightful custom, and when I hope for the additional pleasure of seeing you all well and happy at home.
>
> Already in imagination I pay my respects to the mince Pies, Turkies, and the other good things of Christmas.
>
> In the meantime the Notches on my wooden Calendar diminish apace, but not so the duty and affection with which I am,
>
> Dear Aunt, Your's ever John H. Newman.[20]

An interest in food is common to boys, and there is a well-known letter that Newman wrote to his father about his first impressions of Trinity College, Oxford, where he took up residence at the precocious age of sixteen, in which he gives a delightful description of his first dinner in hall:

> At dinner I was much entertained with the novelty of the thing. First, flesh and fowl, beautiful salmon, haunches of mutton, lamb etc and fine, very fine (to my taste) strong beer, served up on old pewter plates, and mis-shapen earthenware jars. Tell Mama there are gooseberry,

[20] *LD* i. 9–10.

rasberry, and apricot pies. And in all this the joint did not go round, but there was such a profusion that scarcely two ate of the same joint. Neither do they sit according to their ranks, but as they happen to come in.[21]

This is the first of many marvellous descriptive letters, of which it is typical. Even in this early letter there is no attempt to evoke the atmosphere of the scene in general terms; instead, the atmosphere and the scene, as Newman experienced them, are realized through the sharply observed concrete details. In another description of one of those early dinners in hall, this time in vacation, his sense of solitariness is again conveyed not through any rendering of his feelings or mood but through his precise reporting of the occasion as he heard and saw it:

The other day I had a nice dinner set before me of veal cutlets and peas, so much to myself that I could hear the noise I made in chewing through the empty hall; till at length one came in, and sat opposite to me, but I had not been introduced to him, and he could not speak to me. Consequently we preserved an amicable silence, and conversed with our teeth . . .

The best of the dinner now is that half a dozen servants wait behind me and watch me.[22]

The same close observation is to be found in Newman's travel letters. Although there is little 'picture-painting', when Newman does try his hand at it he is extremely effective. Here, for example, is a remarkably sensuous description of the Devonshire countryside:

What strikes me most is the strange richness of every thing. The rocks blush into every variety of colour—the trees and fields are emeralds, and the cottages are rubies. A beetle I picked up at Torquay was as green and gold as the stone it lay on, and a squirrel which ran up a tree here just now was not a pale reddish brown . . . but a bright brown red. Nay, my very hands and fingers look rosy, like Homer's Aurora, and I have been gazing on them with astonishment . . . The exuberance of the grass and the foliage is oppressive, as if one had not room to breathe, though this is a fancy . . . The scents are extremely fine, so very delicate, yet so powerful, and the colours of the flowers as if they were all shot with white. The sweet peas especially have the complexion of a beautiful face—they trail up the wall, mixed with myrtles, as creepers[.] As to the

[21] *LD* i. 35. [22] *LD* i. 40.

sunset, the Dartmoor heights look purple, and the sky close upon a clear orange. When I turn back to think of Southampton Water and the Isle of Wight, they seem by contrast to be drawn in india-ink or pencil.[23]

Or again, on his voyage to the Mediterranean at the end of 1832, he reveals a wonderful sensitivity to colour when he describes how, as the weather grew brighter, the sea 'now became of a rich indigo colour, and the wind freshening was tipped with the most striking white edges, which breaking in foam turned into momentary rainbows', until evening when 'the sea brightened to a glowing purple inclined to lilac—the sun set in a car of gold and was succeeded by a sky first pale orange, then gradually heightening to a dusky red'.[24]

But more characteristic of Newman than this sort of purple passage is the kind of description where, like in his account of the solitary dinner in hall, he uses a close attention to detail for ironic or comic purposes, as in his account of the ship's preparations prior to departure from Falmouth:

It was most amusing to see the stores arrive. Fowls, Ducks, Turkeys, all alive and squatted down under legs of beef, hampers, and vegetables. One unfortunate Duck got away, and a chase ensued—I should have liked to have let him off, but the poor fool did not know how to use his fortune—and instead of making for the shore, kept quacking with absurd vehemence close to us—he was not caught for a considerable time, as he ducked and fluttered away, whenever the men got near him.[25]

Newman's letters on business matters often show an almost obsessive attention to practical detail, but this preoccupation with the concrete particular is essential to the extraordinary effect of some of the best descriptive writing in the letters. The following account of sea-sickness, for example, is not only funny and a remarkable anticipation of Dickens's descriptive style, but marvellously real:

the worst of seasickness is the sympathy which all things on board have with the illness, as if they were seasick too. First all the chairs, tables, much more the things on them are moving, moving, up and down, up and down—swing, swing—a tumbler turns over, knife and fork run down, wine is spilt—swing, swing. In this condition you go on talking

[23] *LD* ii. 342–3. [24] *LD* iii. 129. [25] *LD* iii. 130–1.

and eating, as fast as you can, hiding your misery, which is provoking[ly] thrust upon you by every motion of the furniture which surrounds you. At length you are seized with sickness, up you get, swing, swing, you cannot move a step—you knock yourself against the table—run smack against the side of the cabin—you *cannot* make the door, the only point you want—you get into your berth at last, but the door will not shut—bang, bang, you slam your fingers. At last things go right with you and down you lie. You are much better, but now a new misery begins, the noise of the bulkheads (i.e. the wooden partitions thro' the vessel). This is not heard on deck—in the cabin it is considerable—but when you lie down, you are in a perfect millhouse. All sorts of noises tenfold increased by the gale; creaking, clattering, shivering, and dashing. And then your bed is seasick too—up and down—swinging without exaggeration as high and as fast (to your feelings) as a swing in a fair . . .[26]

It is not simply that Newman uses a conversational style in his letters, but he reproduces the actual sound and tone of the speaking voice with all its cadences and stresses, often for a highly dramatic effect as here, where the voice of the speaker, far from being disembodied, is heard as it rises and falls with the roll of the ship. Once again, Newman does not dwell on how he felt, but he makes the reader feel how he felt by realizing in the rhythm of his prose the movement of the ship and the sea-sick stomachs of the passengers in it. As one modern critic has written, 'he has no rival as a recorder of experience that is in the act of being experienced'.[27]

If Newman could describe the physical fluctuations of sea-travel, he also knew how to convey a very different kind of sickness of heart and its emotional fluctuations, as can be seen in the letter that follows, one of many concerned with the recollection of the past. It describes how he revisited Alton in Hampshire, where his father had been forced to undertake (unsuccessfully in the event) the management of a brewery after the London bank in which he was a partner had failed. When he approached the place associated with the family's financial ruin, 'he felt quite sick at heart'.

There was something so mysterious too in seeing old sights, half re-collecting them, and doubting. It is like seeing the ghosts of friends . . .

[26] *LD* iii. 159.

[27] G. Tillotson, 'Newman: Thought and Action', in G. and K. Tillotson, *Mid-Victorian Studies* (London, 1965), 260.

it seemed to me so very strange, that every thing was in its place after so long a time . . . it was as fearful as if I was standing on the grave of some one I knew, and saw him gradually recover life and rise again. Quite a lifetime seems to divide me from the time I was here. I wished myself away from the pain of it. And then the excitement caused a re-action, and I got quite insensible and callous—and then again got disgusted with myself, and thought I had made a great fool of myself in coming here at all, and wondered what I should do with myself, now that I was here.[28]

The careful notation of feelings is a familiar feature of the letters and is another aspect of the realism which produced the subtle explorations of our mental processes in the *Oxford University Sermons* and the *Grammar of Assent.*

The letters of the late 1830s show a new, bold use of imagery which pre-dates its appearance in the published writings. This, together with the insistent sound of the speaker's voice, can, for example, combine to create a letter of considerable verve on an apparently unpromising subject—the difficulty of writing!

I write—I write again—I write a third time, in the course of six months—then I take the third—I literally fill the paper with corrections so that another person could not read it—I then write it out fair for the printer—I put it by—I take it up—I begin to correct again—it will not do—alterations multiply—pages are re-written—little lines sneak in and crawl about—the whole page is disfigured—I write again. I cannot count how many times this process goes on.—I can but compare the whole business to a very homely undertaking . . . washing a sponge of the sea gravel and sea smell. Well—as many fresh *waters* have I taken to my book.[29]

As the Tractarian movement progressed and prospered, so the attacks on Newman increased: one happy result, from a literary point of view, was the development of a new kind of letter displaying an exuberant panache not seen before. The gloating fascination with which Newman pursues his metaphor in the following letter again anticipates the type of gleefully grotesque imagery he would develop much later in the satirical writings of his Catholic period:

There is a great fat lie, a lie to the back bone, and in all its component parts, and in its soul and body, inside and out, in all sides of it, and in its

[28] *LD* iv. 332. [29] *LD* vi. 193.

very origin, in the Record [newspaper]. . . . It has no element of truth in it—it is born of a lie—its father and mother are lies and all its ancestry—and to complete it, it is about me.[30]

Again, far from decreasing, the humour of the letters seems to increase in exuberance as Tractarianism entered a more critical phase. The new Romanizing tendency which alarmed Newman so much had no adverse effect on his sense of comedy, rather the opposite. One extreme adherent of the movement, who had taken his place in the pulpit at St Mary's, was inspired to 'preach a Sermon, not simply on Angels, but on his one subject for which he has a monomania, of fasting, nay and say it was a good thing, whereas Angels feasted on festivals, to make the brute creation fast on fast days. . . . May he . . . have a fasting horse the next time he goes steeple chasing.'[31] The same eccentric don 'once at a breakfast table after long silence turned round to a nice and pretty young lady who was next to him and said with his peculiar smile that he thought it not worse to burn a man for heresy than to hang him for sheepstealing'.[32] Newman's retirement to Littlemore after his resignation from St Mary's aroused a great deal of unfriendly gossip which he did not relish, but the notoriety of the quasi-monastic cottages there had its funny side, which he was not slow to appreciate, as is shown in this account of one visitor, who, the community suspected, had been tempted to use their retreat as a convenient hotel for visiting Oxford—that is, until he heard about its reputation, whereupon he became

so mystified and terrified about this place, which I suppose he thought before to be some sort of rural villa, that, when he at length reached us, he was as grave and solemn as an old cat, and we could make nothing of him. I thought marriage had spoiled him. He looked thin too, and yellow, and was full of fidget. The shock his nerves had experienced went further still—for he was sick all night, and had not a wink of sleep. Next Morning he went to Oxford, and contrived to breathe more freely—and in no long time took up his abode in Christ Church—and soon became as lively and chirping as usual, and his face lost all its gibbous effect and swelled into a gleaming glistening full moon.—So

[30] *LD* vi. 352.
[31] To J. W. Bowden, 4 Nov. 1839. The text of letters not published in *LD* is taken from the original or copy in the collection at the Birmingham Oratory.
[32] To T. Mozley, 21 Feb. 1843.

you see we have our fun, without practising any tricks upon him. His *imagination* did it for us.

In another letter to his Aunt Elizabeth, who was becoming increasingly anxious about her famous nephew's part in the movement, Newman dwells again on the comic element in a situation that was soon to end in tragedy. Pusey had been suspended from preaching in June 1843; but although this was the first serious official action taken by the university authorities against the Tractarians, Newman tried to divert his worried elderly relation with the story of the Devonshire farmer who

had heard Dr. Pusey very much abused, and had believed and joined in the abuse. At last he was undeceived and being a generous fellow, and not knowing how else to relieve the painful feeling of remorse which came upon him, being just then about to send up a bull to Derby to stand for the prize, he gave it the name of Dr Pusey—and as such I believe it has been entered in the books, perhaps in the report, of the British Agricultural and Farming Society. . . . You see how Puseyism is spreading. It has reached our very cattle. Here is the first Puseyite bull. Our domestic animals will be the next victims. Homer talks of the plague falling first on mules and dogs, then on man. This has observed a reverse order; except that I think Heads of Houses will catch it last. We shall have Puseyite lapdogs and kittens—butcher's meat and grocery will come next—till at last we shall be unable to pay a morning call, or put our candle out at night without Puseyism.[33]

Another example of Newman's ability to write not just humorously but comically in the midst of great personal anguish is his account of his return from London not long after the death of his oldest friend John Bowden, and only a year before his own long-delayed secession from the Church of England. He had caught the early morning train to Oxford. 'Three persons were in the parallel carriage, and they began talking at the pitch of their voice in the dark, forgetting that walls had ears.' One of them reported to his travelling companions that 'the soundest divine in the Church' had told him,

'Depend on it, Newman, Newman (very loud) is a jesuit, a jesuit.' Somehow I could not help interfearing . . . So I put my head through the cross window which separates the carriages and said (in the dark) 'Gentlemen, please don't speak so loud, for persons are here whom you

[33] To Mrs E. Newman, 2 Aug. 1842 and 28 July 1843.

would not like to speak before.' On which there was a deep silence—but in a while the conversation was resumed in a lower pitch.[34]

This is an instance not just of the kind of ironic description in which Newman so excelled, but also of his power of delineating a dramatic scene. And it reminds us that he was a novelist of no mean powers. Usually, of course, the dramatis personae were known to each other—but not always, as in this description of his stay at Abbotsford, the house built by Sir Walter Scott, where the passages were so narrow that

I could shake hands with the nursery maids in the rooms opposite me, without leaving my own room—and sometimes of a morning or evening in going down stairs, seeing nothing, I hear a step approaching, and am obliged to stand still where I am, for fear of consequences, and then a little light figure shoots past me on the right or left . . . Once there was an awful moral stoppage, neither daring to move.[35]

Sometimes an introduction may have been made, but knowledge of the other actor or actors did not go further, as at Carlow in Ireland when Newman was trying to drum up support for the new Catholic University of Ireland and after dinner

went to sleep—and was awakened from a refreshing repose by his next neighbour on the right shouting in his ear, 'Gentlemen, Dr N. is about to explain to you the plan he proposes for establishing the new University,' an announcement, which the said Dr N. does aver most solemnly took him utterly by surprise, and he cannot think what he could have said in his sleep which could have been understood to mean something so utterly foreign to his intentions and his habits.[36]

On the same tour he visited a convent school, where he described how he found assembled seventy young ladies,

all dressed in blue, with medals on, some blue, some green, some red; and how he found he had to make them a speech, and how he puzzled and fussed himself what on earth he should say impromptu to a parcel of school girls—and how in his distress he *did* make what he considered his best speech—and how, when it was ended, the Mother School-mistress did not know he had made it, or even begun it, and still asked for his speech. And how he would not, because he could not make a second speech; and how, to make it up, he asked for a holiday for the

[34] To Mrs J. W. Bowden, 8 Oct. 1844.
[35] *LD* xv. 247.
[36] *LD* xvi. 52.

girls, and how the Mother Schoolmistress flatly refused him, by reason (as he verily believes) because she would not recognise and accept his speech, and wanted another, and thought she had dressed up her girls for nothing—and how he nevertheless drank her rasberry's vinegar, which much resembles a nun's anger, being a sweet acid[37]

Sometimes Newman, not content with a merely historic account, makes an encounter vividly present to his correspondent by attempting to render the actual sound of the other person's voice. As we saw in the letter about sea-sickness, rapidity and repetition in the Dickensian vein are two essential ingredients in his re-creation of a scene, even where no one is actually speaking as in the letter on the difficulty of writing or in this general description of the 'vile' Italian 'practice of spitting':

They spit everywhere—they spit on the kneeling boards—they encourage it, and as if for amusement go on every ten seconds. . . . They spit over the floors of their rooms—their floors are filthy principally with dust —if you drop your coat or stocking in undressing, it is far worse than if you dropped them in the street. . . . I could have fancied they liked spit . . . except that I saw a neighbour in the caffee spit by mistake on his coat, and I had great satisfaction in seeing the pains he was at to get rid of it.[38]

But the device is put to wonderfully authentic and funny effect in this representation of the diplomacy of a high Vatican official who visited the Oratory:

I was a great man—no denying it—a great writer—good style—good strong logic—my style went very easily into Italian—it was a classical style. Of course I had my enemies—they are in England or Englishmen —but all Catholics, to speak as a whole, were my friends. He did not speak from flattery—no—he always spoke his mind, even to the Pope . . . There were things in what I had written which he did not like . . . about a people's religion being a corrupt religion—But perhaps this vehemence of writing could not be helped. I had very good friends. Fr St John was a good friend of mine, very—and a great gentleman. Cardinal Cullen was a good friend, yes—a very good friend . . . I ought to send persons from time to time to explain things . . . I ought to go to Rome myself. I would rejoice the Holy Father—I ought to be a bishop, archbishop—yes, yes—I ought, I ought—yes, a very good bishop—it *is* your line, it *is*, it *is*—it was no good my saying it was not.

[37] *LD* xvi. 53.

[38] *LD* xi. 259.

I ought to take the part of the Pope. 'We have *very* few friends' he said—'very few'—he spoke in a very grave earnest mournful tone . . .[39]

Not all Newman's renderings of dramatic or unusual encounters are humorous. At times they can be extremely moving, like the poignant but precisely described reunion with Keble and Pusey:

Keble was at the door, he did not know me, or I him. How mysterious that first sight of friends is! for when I came to contemplate him, it was the old face and manner, but the first effect and impression was different. His wife had been taken ill again in the night, and at the first moment he, I *think*, and *certainly* I, wished myself away. Then he said, Have you missed my letters? meaning Pusey is here, and I wrote to stop you coming. He said I must go and prepare Pusey. He did so, and then took me into the room. I went in rapidly, and it is strange how action overcomes pain. Pusey, as being passive, was evidently shrinking back into the corner of the room—as I should have done if he had rushed in upon me. He could not help contemplating the look of me narrowly and long—Ah, I thought, you are thinking how old I am grown and I see myself in you—though you, I do think, are more altered than I am. Indeed, the alteration in him shocked me . . . it pained and grieved me. I should have known him any where—his face is not changed, but it is as if you looked at him through a prodigious magnifier. I recollect him short and small—with a round head—smallish features—flaxen curly hair—huddled up together from his shoulders downward—and walking fast. This was as a young man—but comparing him even when last I saw him, when he was slow in his motions and staid in his figure, still there is a wonderful change. His head and his features are half as large again—his chest is very broad—and he has, I think, a paunch—His voice is the same—with my eyes shut, I should not have been sensible of any lapse of time. As we three sat together at one table, I had as painful thoughts as I ever recollect, though it was a pain, not acute, but heavy. There were three old men, who had worked together vigorously in their prime. This is what they have come to—poor human nature—after 20 years they meet together round a table, but without a common cause, or free outspoken thoughts—but, though kind yet subdued, and antagonistic in their mode of speaking, and all of them with broken prospects.[40]

Like the development in imagery, so the emergence of Newman's satirical powers is seen first in the letters. The two splendid satirical animadversions he penned in March and April 1833 on

[39] *LD* xxiii. 318–19. [40] *LD* xxii. 52.

Dr Thomas Arnold's plans to make the Church of England more theologically comprehensive are noted elsewhere in this volume.[41] But the best satire in the letters belongs not surprisingly to the time of Newman's finest satirical writings, the 'honeymoon' period of his life as a Catholic. These were the early years of the Oratory, and there is, for example, a hilarious letter about an unfortunate Irish priest who was hesitating about joining:

> his notion is that he is sent to the poor, that is to the Irish poor, that is to those who are in gross sin, that is to those who have in them the materials of saints, that is not to those who are going on to perfection, that is not to the many for he is not strong enough, that is to London, that is to Lord or Lady that.[42]

Then there was the Anglican clergyman who had called Newman's whole public life 'one unmitigated lie', and who elicited the following letter from Newman to a newspaper:

> He has professed to quote two passages from me, in support of his charge. He does so in the received Protestant fashion on such occasions; for he has *cut off the beginning* of the first sentence of the former of the two; and he has *cut out the middle* of the latter.[43]

As well as being a satirist of considerable powers, Newman was also of course a formidable controversialist. And it is no surprise that some of his most memorable letters were written in the heat of controversy. Take, for example, these lines written to the editor of a provincial newspaper which had published a report from a correspondent alleging that the famous so-called 'clerical pervert' was now a sceptic living in Paris:

> In an age of light, where in the world has the unfortunate man been living? Of what select circle is he the oracle? What bad luck has seduced him into print? What has ailed him to take up a position so false, that the Law might come down upon him, and every Englishman must cry shame upon him?

Has any English writer ever written more bitingly or more blisteringly? Continuing and increasing rumours in the early 1860s that Newman had left or was about to leave the Roman Catholic Church finally induced him to write his famous or notorious letter to the *Globe* newspaper:

41 *LD* xiii. 190–1. 42 *LD* xiv. 331. 43 *LD* xx. 208–9.

I do hereby profess *ex animo*, with an absolute internal assent and consent, that Protestantism is the dreariest of possible religions; that the thought of the Anglican service makes me shiver, and the thought of the Thirty-nine Articles makes me shudder. Return to the Church of England! no; 'the net is broken, and we are delivered.' I should be a consummate fool (to use a mild term) if in my old age I left 'the Land flowing with milk and honey' for the city of confusion and the house of bondage.[44]

Regardless of whether the outburst was justified or not (Newman thought it was), writing like this surely raises the art of controversy on to an altogether new literary level. As we have seen, Newman's developments and experiments as a writer often appear in his letters before his published writings. Such letters as these certainly prepare the way for his greatest duel, as a controversialist, the contest with Charles Kingsley.

When Newman first read the original offending passage in Kingsley's review in *Macmillan's Magazine*, he immediately wrote to the publisher:

I should not dream of expostulating with the writer of such a passage, nor with the editor who could insert it without appending evidence in proof of its allegations. Nor do I want any reparation from either of them. I neither complain of them for their act, nor should I thank them if they reversed it. Nor do I even write to you with any desire of troubling you to send me an answer. I do but wish to draw the attention of yourselves, as gentlemen, to a grave and gratuitous slander, with which I feel confident you will be sorry to find associated a name so eminent as yours.[45]

This coolly poised protest was followed by a much more vehement letter in reply to a response from the publisher explaining that he had never dreamed a Catholic would take offence at Kingsley's charge. It includes one of the most superbly indignant passages in all Newman's controversial writings, including a brilliant analogy that recalls the most devastating satire of *Lectures on the Present Position of Catholics in England*:

I, on my side, have long thought, even before I was a Catholic, that the Protestant system, as such, leads to a lax observance of the rule of purity; Protestants think that the Catholic system, as such, leads to a lax observance of the rule of truth. I am very sorry that they should

[44] *LD* xx. 216. [45] *LD* xx. 571–2.

think so, but I cannot help it; I lament their mistake, but I bear it as I may. If Mr. Kingsley had said no more than this, I should not have felt it necessary to criticize such an ordinary remark. But, as I should be committing a crime, heaping dirt upon my soul, and storing up for myself remorse and confusion of face at a future day, if I applied my abstract belief of the latent sensuality of Protestantism, on a priori reasoning, to individuals, to living persons, to authors and men of name, and said (not to make disrespectful allusion to the living) that Bishop Van Mildert, or the Rev. Dr. Spry, or Dean Milner, or the Rev. Charles Simeon 'informs us that chastity for its own sake need not be, and on the whole ought not to be, a virtue with the Anglican clergy,' and then, when challenged for the proof, said, '*Vide* Van Mildert's Bampton Lectures and Simeon's Skeleton Sermons *passim*;' and, as I should only make the matter still worse, if I pointed to flagrant instances of paradoxical divines or of bad clergymen among Protestants . . . and so, in like manner, for a writer, when he is criticizing definite historical facts of the sixteenth century, which stand or fall on their own merits, to go out of his way to have a fling at an unpopular name, living but 'down,' and boldly to say . . . of *me*, 'Father Newman *informs* us that Truth for its own sake *need not be*, *and on the whole ought not to be*, a virtue with the Roman clergy,' and to be thus brilliant and antithetical (save the mark!) in the very cause of Truth, is a proceeding of so special a character as to lead me to exclaim, after the pattern of the celebrated saying, 'O Truth, how many lies are told in thy name!'[46]

Just as the sneer is an essential weapon in the armoury of the satirist, so too the snub is the stock-in-trade of the controversialist. Urged by his former patron Cardinal Wiseman, from whom he was now estranged, to visit Father Faber on his death-bed, Newman sent this solemn, stately snub:

> I thank your Eminence for the feeling which dictated your Eminence's letter.
>
> I am perfectly aware of the hopeless state in which Fr Faber lies.
>
> Your Eminence will be glad to know that Fr Faber has already been informed by me, not only of my wish to see him, but of the precise time when I hope to have that sad satisfaction[47]

It is surely the most superb snub Newman ever penned, notwithstanding the letter to Mgr. Talbot turning down his invitation to preach in Rome, which contains the famous rebuke: 'However, Birmingham people have souls; and I have neither taste nor

[46] *LD* xxi. 13–14. [47] *LD* xx. 494.

talent for the sort of work, which you cut out for me: and I beg to decline your offer.'[48]

Newman has often been criticized for being over-sensitive, but it would seem frequently nearer the mark to charge him with hardness or intransigence than with taking offence. Thus, for example, he could write about Faber with an apparently complete absence of any emotion, but with a devastating frankness:

I never have been so intimate with Fr Faber from any *personal* tie, as to make it strange that I have no personal trust in him now. He was never one of my intimate friends—not at Littlemore—not at Rome. On my return from Rome the Cardinal made him and his people Oratorians. I took them as a duty, and made them my friends. In process of time they swarmed. In the interval I found that there was that in Fr Faber, with all his good qualities and talents, which made it impossible to trust him. I did not even tell my own people here of this.[49]

The marvellous image 'they swarmed' says everything. But the reticence here is not simply a diplomatic or literary device: the great realist thought he had seen through Faber in such a way as to make wounded feelings redundant. And so he remarks elsewhere of Faber with a total lack of emotion but with brutal candour, 'With many shining, many winning qualities, he has no heart.'[50]

There are many voices in Newman's letters, and if the tone can be harsh, it can also be soft, even melting. Not long after his letter to the *Globe* disavowing all sympathy with the Church of England, he replied movingly to a letter from Keble after a silence of seventeen years:

Never have I doubted for one moment your affection for me—never have I been hurt at your silence. I interpreted it easily—it was not the silence of men, nor the forgetfulness of men, who can recollect about me and talk about me enough, when there is something to be said to my disparagement. You are always with me a thought of reverence and love—and there is nothing I love better than you, and Isaac [Williams] and Copeland and many others I could name, except Him whom I ought to love best of all and supremely. May He Himself, who is the over abundant compensation for all losses, give me His own Presence—and then I shall want nothing and desiderate nothing—but none *but*

48 *LD* xxi. 167. 49 *LD* xix. 113. 50 *LD* xix. 446.

He, *can* make up for the losses of those old familiar faces which haunt me continually.[51]

There was a strongly 'masculine' side to Newman's character, but there was also a keenly 'feminine' side which shows in many other affectionate, tender letters. His correspondence in those early days of the Oratory is full of energy and exuberance, but it includes a little gem of a letter or rather note to a novice, bewailing the reserve and shyness which hindered his relations with other members of the community:

> It is strange to write to you a note about nothing; but such is my fate just now and for some time, that, since I have nothing to say to you, I must either be silent or unseasonable.
>
> Many is the time I have stood over the fire at breakfast or looked at you at Recreation, hunting for something to talk about.[52]

During the later years of his life there are many sad letters mourning the deaths of friends. When one old friend died, he cried out at the

> heavy, sudden, unexpected blow—I shall not see him now, till I cross the stream which he has crossed. How dense is our ignorance of the future, a darkness which can be felt, and the keenest consequence and token of the Fall. Till we remind ourselves of what we are,—in a state of punishment,—such surprises make us impatient, and almost angry, alas![53]

The advent of spring now brought mixed feelings:

> it is too intense in its nature, to be unaccompanied with pain, I may say, great pain . . . now especially as life is waning, and friends dropping away, the extreme beauty of the ever-recurring triumphant spring seems to have something of young mockery in it, till one recollects that that beauty is an image and a promise of something more sweet and more lasting than itself.[54]

Where the 'feminine' and the 'masculine' Newman are at one is in his complete realism; and just as his toughness is without bitterness and self-pity, so the pathos of letters like these totally lacks any sentimentality. Comforting the mother-in-law of a young bride who had died after childbirth, he wrote:

[51] *LD* xx. 503.
[52] *LD* xiii. 32.
[53] *LD* xxiv. 56.
[54] *LD* xxviii. 55.

This I have observed, that such dreadful blows do issue in great blessings, and when we look back upon them years afterwards, we see what mercy there is in them, and learn with all our hearts to kiss the scourge . . . which has made our hearts bleed. This is after the wound is healed, but oh! how long it will be in healing.[55]

He preferred cruel to cosy comfort in the face of painfully inexplicable suffering, once remarking that those whom God 'singularly and specially loves, He pursues with His blows, sometimes on one and the same wound, till perhaps they are tempted to cry out for mercy'.[56]

The man who judged people by whether they were 'real' or 'unreal', the preacher who sought above all to bring before his congregation the real person of the Christ of the Gospels, the philosopher who contrasted 'real' with 'notional' knowledge, the theologian who eschewed unreal theories that did not accord with historical facts—the same man was also the letter-writer whose many voices are all attempts to do justice to the reality of each situation as it confronted him and as he tried to realize it for his correspondent.

[55] *LD* xxviii. 235–6. [56] *LD* xxxi. 53–4*.

8

Newman's Social and Political Thinking

EDWARD NORMAN

What was wrong with human society, Newman persistently contended, was spiritual and moral rather than social or political: what he sought to achieve for men was some kind of intimation of their own liability to mistake the transient for the permanent in their understanding of human affairs. Where others saw intellectual certainties embodied in the structures of the state or society, he recognized only shades of meaning being misrepresented as totalities—'No idea or principle of political society includes in its operation all conceivable good, or excludes all evil.'[1] Thus in Newman's own priorities the institutional arrangements for the world received a fairly lowly position, for he was addressing himself to antecedent matters of gravity. 'It has never been my line to take up political or social questions', he explained towards the end of his life, 'unless they came close to me as matters of personal duty.'[2] And indeed he did not. But the reasons why Newman observed this rule of life, and the explanations of his political reticence, disclose some extraordinary and penetrating insights into just those areas of human concern which others had made the foundations of their activism.

The apparatus of political organization, and, as Newman supposed, most political ideals, derived from natural truth. He was insistent on the priority of revelation, however. God was known to men through his presence in the created order of things: he was encountered universally, and the primitive moral systems of human societies were indications that God's purposes for men could be perceived and acted upon. Similarly with primitive religion. Intimations of the divine presented themselves to people in every diversity of life, and the religious systems of the world were authentic but latent expressions of God's

[1] *DA*, p. 354. [2] *LD* xxx. 209.

purposes for mankind. Natural truth was adequate for furnishing the pointers to moral order and for spiritual consciousness. Its latter-day evidences were the widespread benevolence of political intentions in the nineteenth-century world of Newman's immediate observation, and the supposition, particularly attractive to contemporaneous intellectual opinion, that all religious phenomena were in some sense equally valid. Newman did not quarrel with the foundations laid for human experience in natural truth: they were factually present, and he was forever insistent on the sovereignty of concrete evidence. 'We are in a world of facts', he wrote, 'and we use them; for there is nothing else to use.'[3] This was, in social terms, the world of mere morality—men were capable of organizing a scheme of values and of achieving a moral culture to which they attached a superstructure of higher ideals. Yet Newman's urgent concern was not with behaviour but with belief. Men left in the realm of mere morality attained certain rather low-level social states, which often had the external appearance of considerable sophistication and advance; they were, nevertheless, still left as creatures of the earth, earthy. God had made men to share in the progressive unfolding of the divine scheme; what really mattered was not the relatively easily attainable social norms, but actual transcendence. Revealed truth offered men this. It was conceivable to men only because natural knowledge already prepared the moulds of experience and the preliminaries of authentic spirituality. In Christianity, Newman argued, the universal creator particularized himself, made himself known for what he was, a person, and then converted men's latent knowledge into the proper materials of salvation. The Incarnation, that is to say, not only confirmed that the language and images men had always used to disclose the existence of the divine were in themselves correct, but wrought, in addition, and most supremely, the active work of redemption. Revealed truth could thereafter be seen to have grown out of natural truth but was in every way superior to it. Precisely because it required men's active participation in the work of redemption, however, it needed also to be continually expressed in a unique vocabulary of holiness and to be perpetually identified and categorized by an authoritative body of teaching—expressed in an authoritative

[3] *GA*, p. 223.

and appropriate body. That was the Church of Christ. 'There can be no combination on the basis of truth without an organ of truth,' Newman wrote; 'If Christianity is both social and dogmatic, and intended for all ages, it must humanly speaking have an infallible expounder.'[4] This was the very hallmark of revealed knowledge. There were, of course, all kinds of complications in the actual process of determining what was authentic truth and what was a corruption, and some of Newman's most distinguished writing was concerned with expounding a method by which this could be approached; yet the central issue was plain enough. Revealed truth is dogma: it derives from God in the flesh and is known through the continuation of his mysterious presence in the form of his followers in the world. Natural truth is a first step. Revealed truth and the means by which it is conveyed to men are inseparable. Natural truth becomes fragmented and atomistic, and men develop individual cultures based upon their territorial and other perceptions of implicit knowledge. 'And the whole tenor of Scripture from beginning to end is to this effect,' Newman insisted;

> the matter of revelation is not a mere collection of truths, not a philosophical view, not a religious sentiment or spirit, not a special morality—poured out upon mankind as a stream might pour itself into the sea, mixing with the world's thought, modifying, purifying, invigorating it—but an authoritative teaching, which bears witness to itself and keeps itself together as one, in contrast to the assemblage of opinions on all sides of it, and speaks to all men, as being ever and everywhere one and the same.[5]

Above all, for the present purpose, Newman noticed that the world of political organization, however ultimate the claims to pedigree made by its own enthusiasts, was derived from the order of natural truth. The structures of society, too, though reflecting the widely diffused moral sense of mankind, were derived from the same place. But what was wrong with men, Newman insisted again, was not social or even moral: it was spiritual. In his own development Newman observed how easily men slide from the priority of the one to the seeming authority of the other. 'The truth is', he reflected on his early years in Oxford, 'I was beginning to prefer intellectual excellence to

[4] *Dev.*, p. 90. [5] *GA*, p. 250.

moral'.[6] And by 'moral' he did not mean the mere morality of the natural order but the moral sense which spirituality requires to give content to revealed truth in the world of our ordinary experience.

With such a view of things—with the priority of calling back a race which was always mistaking natural truth for full revelation—it is not surprising that Newman was largely unconcerned with the political. He recognized social duty and saw the obvious importance of political organization; but he regarded the basis and conduct of political society as matters easily determined and as, anyway, not specifically the subject of revealed truth—whose importance to men was being tragically ignored, the real purposes and destiny of human life being accordingly represented in material and moral enthusiasms much smaller than themselves. He ruefully observed that the Christianity of the day was quite happy in identifying itself with its less-precise and less-active predecessor. 'They lay much stress on works of Natural Theology, and think that all religion is contained in these,' he wrote, 'whereas, in truth, there is no greater fallacy than to suppose such works to be in themselves in any sense religious at all.'[7] Thus, too, in a larger projection the entire realm of the political. By becoming preoccupied with the lower concerns of organizing society in the world, men lose sight of the purposes of redemption: politics was a necessary but hazardous undertaking, not the exclusive and ultimate work which it was represented as being by men. 'They think they have reason for concluding, they think they see', Newman wrote, 'that this world is the world for which they are to labour, and to which they are to devote their faculties.' It was to mistake a fragment for the totality—'And therefore they persist in denying that they must live for the next world.'[8] Politicians, Newman believed, expended their virtues in 'tinkering' with humanity; whereas in reality 'Human nature wants recasting.'[9] Time and time again he came back to this urgency of the primary fact of revelation.

Newman also noticed—it is a central theme in all his writing—that men never cease to contrive substitutes for spirituality. Many of the political virtues of his day were among the substitutes which his contemporaries promoted, and this, too, helps to

[6] *Apo.*, p. 26. [7] *PS* i. 317. [8] *SD*, p. 82.
[9] *DA*, p. 277.

explain Newman's reluctance to espouse social and political causes. The immediate allure of moral sense was the first and most obvious case which worried Newman: men clothed their preoccupation with material resources, and dressed the management of society in moral attributes, and mistook the result for 'higher' authority. Newman recognized that virtually anything can be represented in the language of morality, but that men were still left at the levels of ordinary natural truth—and expressed in markedly relative terms as well. Thus he condemned 'the heresy, as it may be called' of 'the substitution of a moral sense or taste for conscience'.[10] In every age, he supposed, there existed what could be identified as 'a religion of the world'; it 'so far imitates the one true religion, as to deceive the unstable and the unwary'.[11] In the world of the nineteenth century it took the form of benevolence—the decency and compassion in human dealings, much in evidence in natural morality, which helped to describe civilized men, but which left them, nevertheless, without the insights and additional obligations of revealed truth. Contemporary 'religion', Newman noticed, 'has taken the brighter side of the Gospel—its tidings of comfort, its precepts of love; all darker, deeper views of man's condition and prospects being comparatively forgotten'. The result was that men satisfied themelves with the occupation of a lower ground and mistook it for the higher: 'As the reason is cultivated, the taste formed, the affections and sentiments refined, a general decency and grace will of course spread over the face of society, quite independently of the influence of Revelation.'[12] Genuine promptings of conscience are then over-laid, for it is 'superseded in the minds of men by the so-called moral sense, which is regarded merely as the love of the beautiful; partly by the rule of expediency, which is forthwith substituted for it in the details of conduct'. Thus 'religion' becomes 'pleasant and easy, benevolence is its chief virtue; intolerance, bigotry, excess of zeal, are the first sins'. In words, therefore, both exact and prophetic, Newman described the emptying of the content of authentic religion and its replacement by its own predecessor—mere moral sense and general benevolence. These characteristics, furthermore (though he did not anywhere spell this out so precisely), were readily incorporated

[10] *Idea*, p. 166. [11] *PS* i. 309. [12] *PS* i. 311.

into the public aspirations of political society, and enabled political morality to replace spiritual insights as the vehicle of men's pursuit of meaning. The secularization of the public mind—for it amounted to no less—was thus accomplished without any realization of a radical, or any, departure from the traditions and images of received religion. 'Consider', Newman warned, 'whether such a state of refinement as I have attempted to describe, is not that to which men might be brought, quite independent of religion, by the mere influence of education and civilization.'[13] In his well-known assault upon the principles of liberalism as applied to religion Newman gave significance to the resulting confusion: men of the new enlightenment would judge religious expressions and organizations, not in the light of their proximity to revelation, but in terms of their sympathy for contemporaneous models of social progress, and all those which passed the test would be regarded as of equal value. Here the implications were directly political. 'Take any of the plans and systems now in fashion,' he observed; 'plans for the well-being of the poor, or of the young, or of the community at large; you will find, so far from being built on religion, religion is actually in the way, it is an incumbrance.' He was thinking, clearly, of issues of his day where denominational insistences on religious difference—the proper application of dogma—complicated political action in the sphere of social administration: issues like education and the provision of institutional welfare. 'The advocates and promoters of these plans confess that they do not know what to do with religion; their plans work very well but for religion; religion suggests difficulties which cannot be got over.'[14] The goal of universal benevolence, Newman believed, was actually unworthy of a people called by God to share in the higher purposes of creation. It was too elementary in its demands; too material in its objectives. Writers and reformers of his own day who insisted that 'the good of mankind is the ultimate end' of human society were simply wrong.[15] It was to evaluate men as little advanced upon the beasts; their highest aspirations, their veiled perception of spirituality, their distant vision of the aspiring pinnacles of higher truth, all subordinated to mere concern with material distribution. He was so wearied by the false priority of existing

[13] *PS* i. 313. [14] *SD*, p. 107. [15] *US*, p. 106.

impulsions to benevolence, as he saw it, that he once even explained that 'moral' was 'a word which I avoid, as having a very vague meaning'.[16] What was made to serve so universal an objective as the general good of mankind, that is to say, thereby lost its content and its utility as an actual guide to those with some insight into the ambiguities and frailties of human nature.

In the world of education, also, Newman recognized a comparable process at work. Here, too, the implications had unavoidable political resonances, since he lived through the decades which saw the first collectivist advances in the sphere of education. His chief interest was in higher education, and the process which he observed was the replacement of theological science by other sciences. The background was the Government's essay in secular education: the Irish Queen's Colleges of 1845. 'If you drop any science out of the circle of knowledge, you cannot keep its place vacant for it; that science is forgotten; the other sciences close up, or, in other words, they exceed their proper bounds, and intrude where they have no right.'[17] The result was the 'perversion' of those other sciences—the perversion of knowledge.[18] In addition there was a modern tendency to substitute knowledge itself for virtue, and again Newman hammered away at the false categories of understanding which resulted. 'Knowledge is one thing, virtue is another; good sense is not conscience, refinement is not humility, nor is largeness and justness of view faith,' he insisted; 'Philosophy, however enlightened, however profound, gives no command over the passions, no influential motives, no vivifying principles.'[19] Nor was this in the literal sense an academic observation. Newman realized that the language of political morality in his day was crucially related to these substitutes for authentic religious attributes. His particular attack was made upon the Radical Lord Brougham and the Conservative leader Sir Robert Peel—both of whom, though with some variations of emphasis and subject-matter, had acclaimed 'useful knowledge' and benevolence of intention as the goals of social progress. Brougham simply lumped together, into his 'new Pantheon', all 'human beings who agreed in nothing but in their humanity and in their love of knowledge'.[20] The interior lives of men may be hidden from

[16] *GA*, p. 206. [17] *Idea*, pp. 73–4. [18] Ibid. 77.
[19] Ibid. 110. [20] *DA*, pp. 288–9.

casual observation, but they make up the real definition of a person's being; they are what endures, and it caused Newman immense spiritual pain to see the progressive enlightenment of his own day cast them to one side in the pursuit of benevolence and information. 'After all,' he noticed, 'man is *not* a reasoning animal; he is a seeing, feeling, contemplating, active animal.'[21] Peel, who had gone down to Tamworth in the innocent supposition that the opening of a reading-room for the emergent political classes would enhance their moral as well as their intellectual standing, was unhesitatingly condemned for a species of theological indifferentism. Newman simply denied that there was any correlation between intellectual and moral excellence—let alone spirituality. In an almost classic offering of nineteenth-century liberal benevolence, Peel aspired to lay aside 'party feeling' in religious matters in the interests of social and moral advance. Newman's response was precise; what Peel had suggested was actually 'irreligious'. No wonder Newman was sceptical of political enthusiasms: in the Tamworth Reading-Room he beheld the face of the anti-dogmatic principle, seen in the circumstances of political culture. 'Christianity is faith, faith implies a doctrine, a doctrine propositions, propositions yes or no, yes or no differences', he explained; 'Differences, then, are the natural attendants on Christianity, and you cannot have Christianity and not have differences.'[22] He lived in another world from the one inhabited by the liberal enthusiasts for humanity—and what was wrong with them, in Newman's view, was not their intentions but their faulty view of the spiritual nature and limited moral capacity of men. But those enthusiasts constituted a general category, found, to his great sadness, as thickly distributed within the leadership of the Church as within the State. His scepticism about political solutions to the ills of human society was in very large measure at variance with the most dynamic political impulses of the nineteenth century. He accordingly rejected 'a state of society such as ours, in which authority, prescription, tradition, habit, moral instinct, and the divine influences go for nothing, in which patience of thought, and depth and consistency of view, are scorned as subtle and scholastic, in which free discussion and fallible judgment are prized as the birthright of each individual.'[23]

[21] *DA*, p. 294. [22] *DA*, p. 284. [23] *Idea*, pp. 46–7.

Men who had ordered their spiritual being according to wrong priorities, or who ignored its promptings and capacities altogether, were unfitted even to act upon truth when they encountered it. He was able to refer to 'an opinion being abstractly true, and yet the person who holds it wrong in his mode of holding it'.[24] Modern liberal society was being constructed without reference to the spiritual nature of men. It was, in effect, a reversion to the lower ground of natural truth, and was all the worse for the ignorance of authentic spirituality which its advocates displayed in the very act of discarding spiritual culture. 'Instead of raising the world by faith to the level of a regenerate son of God, they debase themselves to the world and its ordinances.'[25]

Newman did not regard these evidences of the substitution of the material for the spiritual, of the reversion to the natural from the revealed, an isolated phenomena, thrown up by social adjustments in his day, but as more fundamental signs that the whole order, ecclesiastical and political, was sliding into a human culture antipathetic to men's actual status as spiritual creatures. The pervasiveness of these errors, as he believed them to be, in the emergent liberal state, and in the political discourse which sustained it, inevitably reinforced his disposition to avoid discussion of public issues. The conveyances of political information themselves—the magazines and papers of the day—were tainted, and Newman saw a link between unsound religion and the 'cultivated mind, which recreates itself in the varieties of literature and knowledge, and is interested in the ever-accumulating discoveries of science, and the ever-fresh accessions of information, political or otherwise'. 'Hence excitements are eagerly sought out', he observed; 'New objects in religion, new systems and plans, new doctrines, new preachers, are necessary to satisfy that craving which the so-called spread of knowledge has created.'[26] The age looked not to seats of learning, as once it did, but to the world of journalism for its discussion of truth—but the practitioners there, in Newman's estimation, 'give no better guarantee for the philosophical truth of their principles than their popularity at the moment, and their happy conformity in ethical character to the age which admires them'.[27] Men, deprived of true spiritual consciousness, were seeking the satisfaction of their need for

[24] *US*, p. 100.
[25] *SD*, p. 106.
[26] *PS* i. 313.
[27] *Idea*, p. 15.

personal and moral significance, that is to say, in an obsessive concern with current affairs. There are clearly modern resonances to Newman's observations. So are there with his belief that 'accomplishments'—the love of music and of art—though qualities desirable and proper in themselves, are less than satisfactory when made the occasions of a substitute for spirituality, the means by which half-secularized men could achieve a kind of contrived and simulated spiritual uplift. Poetry and music, he thought, were given to 'exciting emotions without insuring correspondent practice, and so destroying the connexion between feeling and acting'.[28] They thus cultivated a vicarious sense of involvement with higher destiny without actually obliging the devotee to do anything in the real world. Christian service to the world, Newman taught, was genuinely activist, and was not likely to be inspired by the literary, information-obsessed, and cultured preoccupations which appeared to describe the motivations of the politicians and churchmen of the day. 'In most books Christian conduct is made grand, elevated, and splendid; so that any one, who only knows of true religion from books, is sure to be offended at religion when he actually comes upon it, from the roughness and humbleness of his duties, and his necessary deficiencies in doing them,' Newman wrote, thus connecting this vicarious quality of social concern with the theme of mere benevolence. 'It is beautiful in a picture to wash the disciples' feet; but the sands of the real desert have no lustre in them to compensate for the servile nature of the occupation.'[29] Newman was, in effect, pointing to the educated classes of his day, who wrote a great deal about social good works, but who actually liked organizing those who were going to have to do them.

In his attitude to the world, as in some other things, Newman was an Augustinian rather than a Thomist. It was his emphasis upon original sin, not an adhesion to traditional society, which laid the foundations of his disposition to political conservatism. The early Toryism of his first years in Oxford had been absorbed from the Anglican ethos: the company in which he found himself articulated political principles to defend institutions which were under attack. Liberal reformers sought to change the Church, to broaden the basis of the state in ways which made its capacity to

[28] *PS* ii. 373, see also *Idea*, p. 77.
[29] *PS* i. 374.

govern the Church doubtful, and to open up the university itself to progressive influences thought to be hazardous for the survival of its traditional links with religion. Later Newman came to recognize that only institutions directed by revealed truth—by the Church itself, in fact—were effective as guardians of traditional values. The world itself was given over to evil: he quoted St John's words that 'the world lieth in evil'.[30] It may, indeed, be in one age somewhat better or somewhat worse than in another, 'but it is in substance always the same.' He meant 'that the whole visible course of things, nations, empires, states, polities, professions, trades, society, pursuits of all kinds' were, though not formally evil in themselves, soaked in the evil of the world and were 'the instrument of evil'; they are 'the progeny of sinful Adam', and all of them, 'every thing in the world' was 'alien from God',[31] It was an orthodox view. Government was provided for mankind as part of the divine dispensation; it helped to save men from their corruption through the provision of that order in which men could lead the moral life. Government, therefore, was part of the natural order, and did not belong to revelation. Newman's conservatism was established in this belief, and in his rejection of the modern tendency to require of government the kind of authority which alone belongs to the realm of revealed truth. This was a tendency reinforced, he noticed, by the false confidence of liberal ideas and empty claims to personal enlightenment: 'The warnings contained in the historical Scriptures, concerning the original baseness and corruption of the heart, are, in the course of time, neglected; or, rather, those very representations are adduced as a proof how much better the world now is than it was once; how much more enlightened, refined, intellectual manly.'[32] Men were as they had always been, and a society which existed in anticipation of essential improvements was self-deluded.

Yet Newman's disbelief in the virtues of traditional society was an important and primary aspect of his general scepticism about political capabilities. It came, indeed, as an accompaniment of one of his most celebrated intellectual convictions: the dynamism of historical processes, the development of ideas. Newman did not hanker after the social norms and structures of

[30] *SD*, p. 104. [31] *SD*, p. 105. [32] *US*, p. 103.

the past quite simply because he recognized that they had never, despite appearances, been stable. Though not particularly widely read in historical evidences (except for the early history of the Church), and though exceedingly far in intellectual style from contemporary understandings of the study of history, Newman had grasped the essential truth, as he saw it, of historical relativism. His resulting scepticism about the permanence of human institutions and the ideas which sustained them was bound to have political implications. An *Oxford University Sermon* on 'The Theory of Developments in Religious Doctrine' in 1843, and the *Essay on Development* of 1845, were concerned to show how revealed truth, precisely because of its universal application, may take centuries to disclose its fullness. His purpose, as is well-known, was to furnish authority for dogmas defined in later periods of the Church's existence for which there was scant evidence in the Scriptures, yet 'which had been all along the secret life of millions of faithful souls'.[33] The nature of his examination of this phenomenon, however, laid out a description of the interrelations of ideas and moral structures, of religion and culture, which revealed a condition of permanent change and flux. Revealed truth had its own guide and expositor in the processes of history: the authority of the Church. Natural truth, again, was nevertheless dynamically involved with historical changes and was not static. Natural truth keeps recurring throughout history, the same in substance despite variations of form. Although Newman did not explicitly discuss political experiences in the light of the mutation of ideas and cultures it is quite plain that he regarded them as belonging to the natural order; and their capabilities as respositories of lasting values were seen by him, by implication, as limited. Nevertheless, political thought unquestionably promoted 'ideas', and these must be regarded as among the ideas whose relationship with the religious ones born of revelation was important in the general formation of truth. 'The idea never was that throve and lasted, yet, like mathematical truth, incorporated nothing from external sources,' Newman wrote; 'development is a process of incorporation'. For 'doctrines and views which relate to man are not placed in a void, but in the crowded world, and make way for

[33] *US*, p. 323.

themselves by interpenetration, and develope by absorption'.[34] The standpoint of the individual, furthermore, is never adequate, and 'no mind, however large, however penetrating, can directly and fully by one act understand any one truth, however simple'.[35] Although Newman recognized the importance of *all* ideas in the processes of history, and saw also the hopelessness of an isolated response in a texture of change which was alive with the conflict of values held by groups, he did insist on the unique ability of revealed truth to sustain itself upon the external criterion of its divine origin. The absence of the same, or a comparable, facility for natural truth, of the realm of the political, therefore, not surprisingly assisted Newman's existing inclination to regard its claims to authentic insights into the position of humanity with reserve. Newman, quite simply, acclaimed the fact and permanence of change as a security for religious truth but a disadvantage for political truth. Political and social structures were transient; only the structures of ecclesiastical authority, the guardians of dogmatic formulations, were lasting. 'A great idea', he contended, 'enters upon strange territory; points of controversy alter their bearing; parties rise and fall around it; dangers and hopes appear in all new relations; and old principles reappear under new forms'. The idea survives if it has authentic value: 'it changes with them in order to remain the same'. Newman's commitment to the process was emphatic: 'In a higher world it is otherwise, but here below to live is to change, and to be perfect is to have changed often.'[36] There was a practical lesson: 'Wrap not yourself round in the associations of years past.'[37] Newman's conservatism was certainly not derived from the after-glow of the old world, like the Toryism of his contemporaries. It represented the deepest understanding of a mind fully conscious of the relative nature of men's claims to truth, and sceptical of the ability of political society to fulfil the requirements of those who looked to political mechanisms as the effective vehicle of permanent truths about men and society. Nor did Newman content himself with the latency of this notion. 'Do not be satisfied with the state in which you find yourselves,' he told the Christians of his day; 'do not be satisfied with nature; be satisfied only with grace.'[38] The changes he saw as characteristic of the historical processes had

[34] *Dev.*, p. 186.
[35] *GA*, p. 101.
[36] *Dev.*, p. 40.
[37] *Dev.*, p. 443.
[38] *SD*, p. 110.

not drawn themselves to a halt on the liberal plateau of the nineteenth century. Change was real and unavoidable. Newman's vision of the instability of political ideas, and consequently of institutions and social forms, was in many ways more radical than that of the liberals around him.

Although Newman gave a lifetime to opposing the influence of liberalism in religion—to attacking 'the anti-dogmatic principle and its developments'[39]—his political sensibilities were not untouched by a practical acceptance, if not of the values, at least of the actual arrangements which political liberals in his day promoted. He also saw the need to act without consensus, since there would never be agreement among men about things that really matter: 'If we assume nothing but what has universal reception, the field of our possible discussions will suffer much contraction.'[40] In the real world of affairs he noticed how ideas penetrated educated opinion and the political classes by degrees, 'changes in society are, by a providential appointment, commonly preceded and facilitated by the setting in of a certain current in men's thoughts and feelings in that direction towards which a change is to be made'.[41] Again: 'great truths, practical or ethical, float on the surface of society, admitted by all, valued by few', he observed, 'until changed circumstances, accident, or the continued pressure of their advocates, force them upon its attention'. He cited the agitation for the abolition of the slave-trade in evidence, with its 'tracts and speeches innumerable'.[42] Newman's general acceptance of the legitimacy both of change as such and of these kinds of presentations of ideas as the means by which they were effected, placed him very much nearer to the heart of the nineteenth-century dynamics of political society than he might at first have appeared to be. It was a very English scheme of things, too, and a further reminder, if one was needed, of just how English Newman's general outlook was.

There was a thorough empiricism about Newman's attitude to public issues. He operated through facts and through what was to hand; what served the most effective purpose in the prosecution of an idea. This he called 'an economy' when pursued in theological investigations: 'we sometimes use a definition or a formula, not as exact, but as being sufficient for our purpose, for

[39] *Apo.*, p. 54.
[40] *GA*, p. 83.
[41] *Dev.*, p. 211.
[42] *GA*, p. 56.

working out certain conclusions, for a practical approximation, the error being small, till a certain point is reached'.[43] He rarely discussed the structures of political society, forms of government, or social theory; but when he did so it was with modes of expression which indicated how suffused his mind was with the general empiricism of the English political tradition. This was particularly clear in his consideration of Church and State, a key issue in the relationship of attrition between the liberal State and surviving religious confessionalism. He was as a young man an ardent supporter of the traditional establishment of religion. His reasons, however, were untouched by the quasi-mystical and organic concepts which other practitioners of ideas on the question espoused—men like Coleridge, Maurice, and Gladstone. Newman supported the establishment of religion for practical reasons: because 'all revolutions are awful things'; because the upper classes would otherwise be left without religion; because parliamentary control guaranteed that doctrine would not be changed; because the clergy were spared the voluntary system of endowments.[44] Fifty years after these considerations were offered, Newman reflected on the organic notion of the State having a 'conscience', and he indeed then claimed an admiration for the idea—but regarded it as quite impractical. For the facts of social and ideological pluralism were against it. During the century, he then noticed, 'first one class of the community, then another, has awakened up to thought and opinion'.[45] The resulting diversity could not be blown away; it was there, and public men had to take account of it. 'The State ought to have a conscience,' he continued; 'but what if it happen to have half-a-dozen, or a score, or a hundred, in religious matters, each different from each?' In practical terms, again, he noticed that the consequence of the rise of social pluralism was the disintegration of 'the whole theory of Toryism', the scheme which had defended confessional Oxford and preserved the Church of England in the possession of its public privileges. That theory 'came to pieces and went the way of all flesh'.[46] In Newman's case the transition to a pragmatic acceptance of liberal pluralism in the State had been facilitated by the parliamentary use of its Erastian control over the Church to further a series of, as he supposed, insensitive and

[43] *GA*, p. 37.
[44] *LD* ii. 130.
[45] *Diff*. ii. 267.
[46] Ibid.

even sacrilegious reforms. In later life he was a candid supporter of the separation of Church and State, on, once more, quite empirical grounds. The Church of Rome alone in his day, as he understood it, seemed to be free of State control; elsewhere, as within English Protestantism and the Orthodox churches of the East, religion was subject to government and suffered accordingly, as government developed in ways and for purposes which had no necessary connexion with Christianity. '"I spoke of Thy testimonies", says the Psalmist, "even before kings, and I was not ashamed"', Newman quoted; 'This verse, I think Dr. Arnold used to say, rose up in judgment against the Anglican Church, in spite of its real excellences.'[47] Acceptance of the notion of a free Church in a free State was something of a badge of liberalism within nineteenth-century Catholicism, and in Newman's always unclear affinity with the Liberal Catholics' various positions this must be considered something of a pointer. So must the encouragement he gave, as in the *Rambler*, to lay Catholic journalism, and to the place of the laity in the ultimate composition of the *magisterium* of the Church. But Newman was never really a Liberal Catholic himself. His empiricism in political outlook was too small a part of his general make-up to be weighted that significantly, and it was, anyway, an expression of English resignation from ideology in the political sphere rather than a theory of politics as such.

When Newman came to suggest that the temporal sovereignty of the papacy in Italy was an encumbrance, rather than a guarantee of papal independence from the political forces of the area, it was not because he approved of the political claims of the pope's subjects but because he thought those claims could not in practice be resisted—'who can force a Sovereign on a people which deliberately rejects him?' There may be success for a while, through force of arms; 'but at length the people, if they persist, will get their way'.[48] Newman certainly had no belief in the theories of popular sovereignty: 'No one can dislike the democratic principle more than I do.'[49] That was not, of course, a particularly unusual opinion for its day (the 1870s), since most members of the English liberal intelligentsia were opposed to the idea of deriving values through the counting of heads, whatever

[47] *LD* ii. 197. [48] *OS*, p. 293. [49] *Diff*. ii. 268.

their preparedness to admit a progressively expanding section of safely educated opinion to the franchise. Nor was Newman's lifelong distaste for 'those wretched Socialists'[50] at all unusual, for like most of his class he regarded socialism as a direct threat to order. Yet he did have a real respect for the moral integrity of ordinary people which amounted to a kind of 'democratic' impulse. Though their overt opinions on matters of public debate were often the fruits of ignorance, their basic instinct for truth remained intact. Newman's depiction of what he called the 'illative' sense, laid out in the *Grammar of Assent*, was intended to provide a framework of explanation about the capability of the uneducated and simple to embrace religious certitude about ideas which they could not have expressed in conventional intellectual categories, or with any satisfactory coherence. Newman's high doctrine of 'conscience', furthermore, carried similar implications, for conscience was not merely collected memories from the earliest norms of childhood: it was the 'Divine Law', resident in each soul; and though it 'may suffer refraction in passing into the intellectual medium of each, it is not thereby so affected as to lose its character of being the Divine Law'. This idea, like the 'illative' sense, gave an interior dignity to each person, however unaccomplished or intellectually deficient he might be. The conscience was objectively true, 'as an Angel walking on the earth would be no citizen or dependant of the civil power'.[51] Newman's disbelief in democracy was a characteristic of his pragmatic opposition to ignorance in charge of public affairs; it did not derive from any disbelief in the basic value of each person or the inherent dignity of each as a bearer of God's purpose. He shared, of course, many of the social assumptions of his class. Education, especially, illustrated this: Newman's own work in this area—and, it needs to be remembered, it covered most of his life—was restricted to governing groups in society. The Oratory was explicitly intended to undertake educational training for the upper classes; the Catholic University of Dublin was directed towards the ideal of a gentleman's education, for all its practical emphasis on professional vocations. Yet this kind of bias was only a minor feature of Newman's concern with education. It was an external appearance, an acceptance of the

[50] Moz. ii. 268 (Feb. 1840). [51] *Diff*. ii. 247–8.

social materials to hand. What most preoccupied him in his educational endeavours was not to do with social class at all, but with the office of religion as the foundation of knowledge. Where Christianity 'has been laid as the first stone, and acknowledged as the governing spirit, it will take up into itself, assimilate, and give character to literature and science'.[52] All learning that had ultimate utility was, in Newman's perspective, available to the humblest of men, for it derived from simple men who loved God: 'this world of thought is the expansion of a few words uttered, as if casually, by the fishermen of Galilee'.[53]

In the scattered places where he discussed forms of government Newman was, again, pragmatic, and also showed how dependent he was on essentially English terms of reference. The State, he argued, had two main elements, power and liberty—'for without power there is no protection, and without liberty there is nothing to protect'.[54] Government was the seat of power, and the Constitution was the seat of liberty; the 'State' and the 'Nation' were also to be distinguished, the first being an agency of organized political power, the second the source of its energy and authority. In terms of actual polity, Newman favoured 'delegation'. By this he did not mean the older, early nineteenth-century idea, favoured by Radicals, that representatives in the legislature were 'delegates' of the people and mandated for closely defined purposes, but the commission of power for a certain specified time to individuals who were charged with political responsibilities and were later, on the expiracy of their period in office, to be accountable for their acts. 'There are great advantages to a system like this,' he wrote; 'it is the mode of bringing out great men, and of working great measures.'[55] Hence the advantage of the English political arrangements, which clearly corresponded to this model: 'I thought it was a received theory of our Reformed Constitution that Members of Parliament were representatives, and in some sort delegates of their constituents, and that the strength of each interest was shown, and the course of the nation determined, by the divisions in the House of Commons.'[56] Newman's long life extended across decades which also saw considerable changes in the theory and practice of the Constitution in England, and in this sort of observation he

[52] *DA*, p. 274.
[53] *US*, p. 317.
[54] *DA*, pp. 317–8.
[55] *DA*, pp. 322–3.
[56] *Diff*. ii. 184.

shows how it was still possible to regard the representative system as operating around defined 'interests' while at the same time it was becoming responsive to a more widely conceived electorate. In opposition to 'delegation' Newman placed 'participation'. Here the people 'would leave nothing to its rulers, but has itself, or by its immediate instruments, a concurrent part in everything that is done'. This described his understanding of democracy, and he accordingly disapproved of it: 'instead of making a venture for the transcendent, it keeps fast by safe mediocrity';[57] and, in another place: 'living movements do not come of committees'.[58] In classic fashion, he also contended for a balance of powers, and for the conventional nineteenth-century belief in limitations on the competence of government. 'Those political institutions are the best which subtract as little as possible from a people's natural independence as the price of their protection', he wrote; 'The stronger you make the Ruler, the more he can do for you, *but* the more he also can do against you'.[59] The best government was the one which governed least: this doctrine of a people's 'natural independence' was classical nineteenth-century liberalism. He wanted a weak State and a strong nation. Like any Manchester Radical he praised the political virtues of private enterprise, for 'of private enterprise I have been speaking all along', he noted at the end of a description of limited government.[60] The strength of a society and its influence derives from the free energy of its people, 'strong in the strength of its multitudinous enterprise, which gives to its Government a position in the world, which that Government could not claim for itself by any prowess or device of its own'.[61] For the people of England were 'a power in themselves', quite 'independently of political arrangements'; government 'is their natural foe', and although 'they cannot do without it altogether' they will nevertheless 'have of it as little as they can'.[62] Newman's English nationalism, which flickered dimly in his theological presuppositions too, as the ecclesiastical authorities in Rome sometimes noticed, was well represented in his ideas on government. 'England is, in a political and national point of view, the best country to live in in the world,' he declared: 'nowhere else

[57] *DA*, p. 323.
[58] *Apo.*, p. 46.
[59] *DA*, p. 325.
[60] *DA*, p. 336.
[61] *DA*, p. 338.
[62] *DA*, p. 341.

surely can you have so much your own way.'[63] Newman was careful in his attitude to reform, however, to avoid setting limits or guidelines, but 'a limit there is', he believed, 'and things must remain in substance what they are, or "Old England" will cease to be'.[64] Thomas Hughes himself could not have tempered his views on government with a more robust expression of traditional concepts of English liberty. Newman warned against 'dangerous innovations', and reminded the generation to whom he addressed himself that 'we cannot in this world have all things as we should like to have them'.[65] This blend of liberalism and conservatism was quite widely distributed within the political classes by Newman's day. In his discussion of government he had little to say that was especially original, and nothing that was at all outside the conventional areas of public debate. He had no intention of producing a scheme of systematic thought on political questions.[66] The same could be said for his fleeting considerations of economic circumstance. And why should it be otherwise? Newman thought and wrote for other reasons; his was the world of transcendence, not of the immediate and the passing. Thus in his consideration of riches he was unconcerned with the justice or otherwise of existing distribution, and regarded the matter from the perspective of spiritual integrity. He believed the very possession of riches constituted a danger to the possessor, for they so easily produced yet another occasion of the substitution of a shadow for the spiritual reality. Wealth becomes 'a substitute in our hearts for that One Object to which our supreme devotion is due'. Riches corrupt: 'They are present; God is unseen';[67] their hazard is in 'the carnal security to which they lead'.[68] Similarly the science of political economy, though proper in itself as 'the science of wealth'—'for it is no sin to make money'—could easily offer 'the occasions of sin'.[69] As a branch of knowledge it was concerned with the rules of gaining and disposing of wealth, but that was as far as the political economist should go: 'he has no right to determine that wealth is at any rate to be sought, or that it is the way to be virtuous and the price of happiness', for that was 'to pass the bounds of his

[63] *DA*, p. 353. [64] *DA*, p. 354. [65] *DA*, p. 360.
[66] T. Kenny, *The Political Thought of John Henry Newman* (London, 1957), 144.
[67] *PS* ii. 347.
[68] *PS* ii. 349. [69] *Idea*, p. 83.

science'.[70] As usual, Newman's prior concern was with the spiritual and moral state of the individual.

In a world progressively given over to the representation of moral values in material terms, and to the substitution of immediate goals in place of eternal ones—even in its most earnest attempts at benevolence and altruism—Newman never departed from his witness to the sovereignty of authentic religion. The sickness of human society was spiritual; his preoccupation was with the error in men's hearts rather than with the circumstances of their material lives. His priorities were, accordingly, not in correspondence with those of the world which has succeeded his. Newman would not have been surprised. He recognized society as in a steady state of corruption, and supposed each age capable of its own versions. His confidence derived from the victory of the Church over the world, by 'the novel expedient of sanctity and suffering'.[71]

[70] Ibid. 84.

[71] *GA*, p. 293.

9

Politics and Prophecy
Newman and Lamennais

MARVIN R. O'CONNELL

'I am going to review Lamennais' work in October,' Newman told Frederic Rogers in the summer of 1837. 'It is *most curious*.'[1] The book to which Newman referred was Lamennais's *Affaires de Rome: des maux de l'Église et de la société*, published the year before, and, as he promised, his essay appeared in the October 1837 number of the *British Critic*.[2] This was the only occasion on which the paths of these two monumental figures crossed, or perhaps it would be more accurate to say the only instance in which one of them paid any formal attention to the other. Newman after 1837 did indeed comment now and then upon Lamennais's career, but only privately and in the most casual manner, and there is no evidence that he ever read another line of the Frenchman's florid prose. Lamennais for his part appears to have been scarcely aware of Newman's existence.[3]

One gets a feeling almost of disappointment that this should have been so, that these two should never have met and never have jousted intellectually with one another, except for a single review-essay of thirty pages. They had much in common, at least superficially. Both were clerics who led religious movements of great consequence at approximately the same time. Both were marvels of literary industry. Both proved to be exceptionally attractive masters, drawing to themselves the deep loyalty and affection of talented disciples, toward whom each responded with a love that was strongly possessive.[4] Both had had a youthful

[1] *LD* vi. 89.

[2] [Newman], review article 'Affairs of Rome', *British Critic*, 22 (1837), 261–83; repr. as 'The Fall of de la Mennais', *Ess*. i. 102–36.

[3] For instance Newman is not mentioned in *Correspondance générale de Félicité de Lamennais*, ed. L. le Guillon, 9 vols. (Paris, 1971–81), nor in C. Boutard, *Lamennais: sa vie et ses doctrines*, 3 vols. (Paris, 1913).

[4] E. Lecanuet, *Montalembert*, 3 vols. (Paris, 1900–2), i. 130. For Newman's relations with his disciples see M. R. O'Connell, *The Oxford Conspirators* (New York, 1969), 226–8.

conversion experience which gave shape to the rest of their lives. And both eventually built their systems upon that foundation so typical of nineteenth-century thought, a theory of development.

In fact, however, these last two similarities were mostly illusory. Lamennais's conversion (in 1804, when he was twenty-two) possessed a social and naturalistic texture sharply antipathetic to the stark individualism of Newman's experience, twelve years later, which left its recipient at 'rest in the thought of two and two only supreme and luminously self-evident beings, myself and my Creator'.[5] Likewise, Newman's slowly maturing and carefully circumscribed views of the development of doctrine were a far cry from Lamennais's ideas about mankind's ineluctable march toward political liberty and social equality. In his single recorded allusion to the Oxford Movement—in 1844, only a year after Newman preached his celebrated *Oxford University Sermon*, 'The Theory of Developments in Religious Doctrine'[6]—Lamennais complained that the Tractarians 'dealt with . . . questions too *theologically*, . . . that they ought to be treated upon *wider*, . . . *rational* principles'.[7] By that date, to be sure, Lamennais had severed all connection with institutional religion and could hardly have been expected to display any sympathy for the kind of ecclesial problem Newman and his friends were confronting. But then Lamennais had never been a religious thinker in any conventional sense; for him Christianity's relevance lay in its political and social implications, in its unique power to deliver humanity from the twin demons of tyranny and anarchy. And what he may have meant in 1844 or earlier by 'rational' as opposed to 'theological' principles, remains obscured by his peculiar epistemology, with its emphasis upon a *sensus communis* as the sole guide to understanding a confused primitive revelation.[8] Lord Acton, explaining many years later why 'it is a mistake to connect Lamennais with . . . Newman', pointed to Lamennais's 'theory of the common sense, the theory that we can be certain of truth only by the agreement of mankind. . . . When he said *quod semper, quod ubique, quod ab omnibus*, he was not thinking of

[5] *Apo.*, pp. 17–18, 54.

[6] *US*, pp. 312–51.

[7] In a conversation with Christopher Wordsworth. See W. G. Roe, *Lamennais and England* (Oxford, 1966), 92.

[8] Best expressed in F. R. de Lamennais, *Essai sur l'indifférence en matière de la religion*, in *Œuvres complètes*, 12 vols. (Paris, 1836–7), ii. 121–8.

the Christian Church, but of Christianity as old as the creation.'[9]

Other, more tangential, circumstances also tended to diminish the likelihood of any connection. Lamennais, the elder by a generation, was already a famous man, at least within Parisian intellectual circles, before Newman's career had even begun. Newman was the flower of reformed Oxford, the product of the Oriel common-room, the model of the self-disciplined tutor and don, the university man to his fingertips. Lamennais, by contrast, was virtually an autodidact who in his youth, as Saint-Beuve said, had read voraciously anything and everything and who seldom troubled himself with consistency or intellectual restraint.[10] Neither spoke the other's language nor wrote it with any facility.[11] Newman never indulged in foreign travel if he could help it,[12] while Lamennais during his lifetime spent only a few months in England—he prudently left Paris during Napoleon's 'Hundred Days' in 1815—and even during that brief span most of his associations were with French émigrés.[13] Their respective physical insularity moreover was matched during the mid-1830s by each man's almost obsessive concern with what he conceived to be his own special mission: for Newman, the preservation of the English Church from the snares of modernity; for Lamennais, the preparation of the French Church for the glories of modernity.

Wilfred Ward was hardly correct when he asserted that Newman during these years took a lively interest in French ecclesiastical affairs. True enough, 'he had been in close correspondence with a French Abbé, M. Jager' during 1835 and 1836.[14] But the published exchanges between them had had to do with the large theological questions involved in the relationship of Scripture to tradition, and not at all with France as such. For

[9] Lord Acton, *The History of Freedom and other Essays* (1895; London, 1922), 593.

[10] [C. A. Sainte-Beuve], 'Lamennais', *Revue des deux mondes*, 1 Feb. 1832, pp. 3–4. 'No one possessed to the same degree Lamennais' faculty for forgetting', says Lecanuet, *Montalembert*, i. 131.

[11] Newman welcomed a visit from a former contemporary at Trinity because the latter could help in the Jager controversy (see below) 'by exercising your talent of translating into French'. *LD* v. 86.

[12] 'I never will leave England again', Newman wrote after his return from Sicily. Nearly thirty years later he added this notation: 'N.B. I have fulfilled this anticipation up to this day. May 3. 1862.' *LD* iv. 31–2.

[13] Boutard, *Lamennais*, i. 99–114.

[14] Ward, i. 314–15.

Newman *l'affaire* Jager was hardly more than an opportunity to 'get some experience in . . . controversy and the Romanist mode of arguing', and, characteristically, he prepared for it by reading not Bossuet but venerable Anglican divines like Laud and Stillingfleet.[15] Nor did he attempt to hide his contempt for his foreign opponent, this 'chattering French Abbé who says three words where one would do', this 'most ignorant of men and the most inconsequent of reasoners', from whom 'I do not for an instant expect . . . fair play'.[16] Lamennais had no loftier views of—and hardly any more acquaintance with—England and the English Church. He despised what he called the Protestant gloom and the extreme Gallicanism he discerned within the Anglican communion. Though he met occasionally individual Englishmen whom he liked well enough, he disdained English society as 'un système d'impostures', producing 'conspirations générales contre la vérité'. To exchange six months in France for twenty years anywhere else, he once observed, was a bad bargain.[17]

In 1829 Lamennais caused a sensation in Paris when he declared himself an open enemy of the Bourbon monarchy and an adherent of democracy. This apparent volte-face by one long labelled as an ardent royalist should not, however, have surprised those who had listened to Lamennais or had read his books and articles over the preceding twenty years.[18] The position he now espoused represented a change in tactics, not in strategy. The mennasian philosophy had always been fundamentally a kind of religious populism. The *égalité* proposed by the Revolution had failed, in Lamennais's view, because it had not been Christian in its inspiration, had not, that is, been the kind of equality expounded in the pages of the gospel. Intruding into the revolutionary process had been that ultimate wickedness, the individualism of

[15] *LD* iv. 347; *LD* iv. 360.

[16] *LD* v. 133; *LD* v. 100; *LD* v. 132. For the controversy see L. Allen, *John Henry Newman and the Abbé Jager* (London, 1975), and H. Tristram, 'In the Lists with the Abbé Jager', in id. (ed), *John Henry Newman: Centenary Essays* (Westminster, Md., 1945), 201–22. Tristram supplies a biographical sketch of Jean-Nicolas Jager (1790–1868).

[17] Lamennais to La Comtesse de Senfft, 24 Apr. 1826, *Correspondence*, ed. le Guillon, iii. 189–91; to Berryer, 18 Nov. 1825, ibid. 115–16; to La Baronne Cottu, 29 Sept. 1833, ibid. v. 489.

[18] Lamennais's first book *Réflexions sur l'état de l'Église en France pendant le xviiie siècle et sur la situation actuelle*, was published in 1808.

Voltaire and the Enlightenment. 'Une liberté vague' was all that remained of the Declaration of the Rights of Man and the Citizen, because the French people were now enslaved by the tyrannical centralization imposed by Napoleon and maintained by the restored Bourbons.[19] The villains of this piece, however, had not been the kings but the bourgeoisie and the aristocracy, the élites who, forty years after the storming of the Bastille, still controlled the system, still exploited the masses. As for the Gallican Church, it had played the tart's role, for, despoiled and persecuted by the Revolution, it had then settled for peace at the price of selling itself to the state by the terms of the Concordat of 1801. Lamennais had indeed persisted as long as he could in defining the king in the classic mould of the popular leader who protects the people from the depredations of barons and businessmen and bishops. But in the end Charles X had proved too frail a reed to lean upon.

Lamennais did not deny that the people needed guidance. Obedience to proper authority was for him an iron law of nature, for without it came that anarchy which was not less destructive than tyranny. The king, compromised by the vested interests around him, had failed in his mission of leadership, and so the king had to go. Another authority figure was available, however, one more venerable and sacred than all the kings and parliaments combined. The future, Lamennais proclaimed—*l'avenir*—belonged to the people and to the pope. Royal populism had given way to papal populism.

The Bourbons were expelled from France by the revolution of July 1830, and a few months later Lamennais launched his celebrated journal *L'Avenir*. Over the next year this paper, with the slogan 'Dieu et la liberté' boldly set on its masthead, put forward a vast programme of social and political reform.[20] At the heart of it lay the conviction of Lamennais and his collaborators—dedicated Catholics all—that the Church had to assume the lead in bringing into reality a brave new world, and that it could never do so so long as it languished in the smothering embrace of the regime. The Monarchy of July had changed nothing, had surrendered not a jot or tittle of government control over the Church. The whole ecclesiastical apparatus continued to be

[19] *L'Avenir*, 28 June 1831.

[20] See e.g. *L'Avenir*, 17 Oct. 1830, 10 Jan. 1831, 7 Mar. 1831.

maintained by politicians who were open unbelievers and by tax monies paid by a largely hostile public. Priests were salaried servants of the state and despised as such. And the Gallican bishops, all élitists and many Voltairian individualists, still lived in the eighteenth century, still pined for the good old days of Louis XIV, unaware, Lamennais said, 'that everything around us has changed. Ideas have taken and incessantly continue to take new directions. Institutions, law, morals, opinions—nothing is the same as what our fathers knew.'[21]

L'Avenir's demand for the separation of Church and State—'We are being paid by our enemies, by those who think us hypocrites or imbeciles, and who believe that our lives can be held ransom by their money'[22]—aroused fierce opposition from the established leadership within France, ecclesiastical no less than political. But the editors soldiered on for thirteen months, confident that their trust in a higher power had not been misplaced. Hymns of praise for the papacy echoed continuously through the journal's pages, and the basic argument was, like a refrain, repeated again and again. The Church, which in earlier times had freed the slaves and given dignity to the serfs, had a similar task before it now, a task no other institution could achieve. The vicar of Christ, in the tradition of Gregory VII, Innocent III, and the other great medieval popes, had to place himself at the head of the masses, and thereby lead society to a better day.

> Soon a calm and powerful voice, spoken by a shepherd in Rome, at the foot of the cross, will give the signal that the world is in store for its final regeneration. . . . The peoples will open their eyes and recognize each other as brothers, because they will have a common father.[23]

Then in November 1831, beset by *L'Avenir*'s legal and financial difficulties, Lamennais suspended publication. He determined to go on pilgrimage to Rome and thus put to the lie the taunt of his enemies that the pope, silent until now, was in fact opposed to his views. He spent four dismal months in the eternal city, and discovered that his enemies were right.[24]

[21] F. R. Lamennais, *Des progrès de la Révolution et de la guerre contre l'Église* (Paris, 1829), 251–4.

[22] *L'Avenir*, 15 Nov. 1830.

[23] Ibid., 22 Dec. 1830.

[24] For a summary see M. R. O'Connell, 'Montalembert at Mechlin: A Reprise of 1830', *Journal of Church and State*, 26 (1984), 526–32.

These were the 'affairs of Rome' that Newman read about in the summer of 1837 and found so 'curious'. Not that some of the ideas in Lamennais's account were altogether foreign to him. Indeed, during that pivotal year for Lamennais, 1829, Newman too had begun to ponder the problems involved in the union of Church and State.

The occasion was the famous Oxford by-election in which Robert Peel, Home Secretary and Leader of the House of Commons in the Duke of Wellington's ministry, failed to keep his seat as Member of Parliament for the university.[25] Peel and the Tory Party—of which he was the luminary—had long opposed the granting of full civil rights to Roman Catholics. But agitation in Ireland had grown so threatening by the beginning of 1829 that Wellington and Peel reversed their position and announced their intention to introduce a Catholic relief bill when Parliament next assembled. Before that, however, it was incumbent upon Peel to seek the approval of his constituents who presumably had voted for him as an opponent rather than a supporter of Catholic emancipation. The poll took place during the last three days of February, and Peel was defeated by a majority of 146.

Newman, fellow and tutor of Oriel College, was very active in the Oxford campaign against Peel.[26] He claimed to have 'no opinion about the Catholic Question' as such, 'but still, its passing is one of the signs of the times, of the encroachment of Philosophism and Indifferentism in the Church'.[27] And he took great satisfaction in the university's repudiation of one who was so ready to abide by 'the signs of the times':

> We have achieved a glorious Victory [he told his mother the day after the election]. It is the first public event I have been concerned in, and I thank God from my heart both for my cause and its success. We have proved the independence of the Church and of Oxford. So rarely is either of the two in opposition to Government that not once in fifty years can independent principle be shown; yet in these times, when its existence has been generally doubted, the moral power we shall gain by it cannot be overestimated.[28]

[25] N. Gash, *Mr. Secretary Peel* (London, 1969), 561–4.
[26] See the diary entries in *LD* ii. 124–5.
[27] *LD* ii. 120.
[28] *LD* ii. 125.

The assertion of 'independent principle' represented by the defeat of Peel continued to occupy Newman's thoughts. He wrote two weeks later,

> All parties seem to acknowledge that the stream of opinion is setting against the Church. I do believe it will ultimately be separated from the State, and at this prospect I look with apprehension, 1. because all revolutions are awful things, and the effect of this revolution is unknown. 2 because the upper classes will be left religionless. 3 because there will not be that security for sound doctrine without change which is given by an Act of Parliament. 4 because the Clergy will be thrown on their Congregations for voluntary contributions.

Such sentiments had little in common with those of Lamennais, who, practically at this very moment, had shifted his long-standing policy and called for a separation of Church and State in France. But Newman's further musings on the subject exhibited a curiously mennasian character. For though of course he knew nothing at all at this date about Lamennais, Newman seemed to be groping toward the same notion of a *sensus communis* which underpinned Lamennais's conviction of the inevitability of democracy and the consequent need to separate Church from State. Newman continued:

> Listen to my theory. As each individual has certain instincts of right and wrong antecedently to reasoning, . . . so, I think, has the world of men collectively. God gave them truths in His miraculous revelations and other truths in the unsophisticated infancy of nations, scarcely less necessary and divine. These are transmitted as 'the wisdom of our ancestors', through men, . . . on, from age to age, not the less truths because many of the generations through which they are transmitted are unable to prove them.[29]

Catholic emancipation duly received assent from a reluctant king in 1829, and four years later the recently reformed House of Commons declared its intention to begin to put to rights that most glaring of anomalies, the Protestant Church of Ireland. The debate leading to the suppression of ten Irish sees and the diversion of their revenues was in its last stages when, on Sunday 14 July 1833, John Keble, fellow of Oriel College and Professor of Poetry in the University of Oxford, preached a sermon which, in its published form, he titled 'National Apostasy'. 'I

[29] *LD* ii. 129–30.

have ever considered and kept the day', Newman said in the *Apologia*, 'as the start of the religious movement of 1833.'

The Oxford Movement did indeed have for its proximate cause this crisis in the relations between Church and State. However much Anglicans might quarrel among themselves about doctrinal matters, they had to agree that their ecclesiastical system rested upon its episcopal character. The Irish Church bill was an attack upon the bishops and therefore upon the very heart of Anglicanism. That the assault should have been launched by a Parliament into which had intruded dissenters and Roman Catholics moved the usually gentle Keble to the deepest rage, and he was quickly joined in those feelings by many churchmen who might on other grounds have differed profoundly with him. But the most effective of his allies in the cause were two of his colleagues at Oriel who were at the same time his most intimate friends, Newman and Richard Hurrell Froude.

The story of those hectic months in the summer of 1833—the meetings, the outraged sermons and manifestos, the gathering of monster petitions, and, most significantly, the beginning of the series of publications that came to be known collectively as *The Tracts for the Times*—has often been told.[30] Suffice it here to observe that Froude adopted the hardest line of all those who participated in the first stages of the movement. 'I have now made up my sage mind', he said, 'that the country is too bad to deserve an established church.'[31] Such outspokenness was characteristic of Froude. More relevant to present purposes is the fact that among the early Tractarians only he had some acquaintance with France and with the views of Lamennais.

One must take care not to make too much of this circumstance.[32] Froude's knowledge of the French language was not very secure, and he did not travel in France until after *L'Avenir* had ceased publication. Nevertheless, he had read some issues of that journal and had found its message intriguing. In May 1833 he wrote:

[30] See O'Connell, *Oxford Conspirators*, pp. 123–60.

[31] R. H. Froude, *Remains of the Reverend Richard Hurrell Froude, M.A., Fellow of Oriel College, Oxford*, ed. J. H. Newman and John Keble, 2 vols. (London, 1838), i. 246.

[32] As C. Dawson clearly does, in *The Spirit of the Oxford Movement* (London, 1933), 59–65.

There is now in France a High Church Party who are Republicans, and wish for universal suffrage, on the ground that in proportion as the franchise falls lower, the influence of the Church makes itself more felt; at present its limits about coincide with those of the infidel faction. Don't be surprised if one of these days . . . [we turn] Radicals on similar grounds.[33]

There were other echoes of Lamennais in an article Froude published in the *British Magazine* in July 1833. Here he argued that the ecclesiastical situations in England and France were unhappily similar, that in both countries the Church was oppressed by a government unrepresentative of the faithful, and that the English bishops would do well to repudiate all monetary support from the State.[34]

Newman during those exciting days was more circumspect than his friend, but he was by no means disposed to ignore the possibilities of invoking the French model. In August he proposed to Froude a series of articles to which both of them would contribute; he described first his own part of the work, and then said: 'And I want you to write a chapter on France—or at least to supply an account of Le Mennais [*sic*] system.'[35] Nothing came of this idea,[36] but Newman continued to ponder whether the Church of England could any longer afford to depend upon the State. He told Rogers:

I confess, Tory as I still am, historically and theoretically, I begin to be a Radical practically. . . . [T]he most natural and becoming state of things is for the aristocratical power to be the upholder of the Church; yet I cannot deny the plain fact that in most ages the latter has been based on a popular power. It was so in its rise, in the days of Ambrose and in the days of Becket, and it will be so again. . . . The state has *deserted* us and we cannot help ourselves.[37]

It may be appropriate, he said to another friend, 'that the Monarchy and the Aristocracy should be our secular instrument of influence—but if these powers will not, "lo! we turn to the people." . . . Surely it is time to "flee to the mountains," to take

[33] Froude, *Remains*, i. 311–12. [34] Ibid. 193–7. [35] *LD* iv. 32.

[36] Except 'Home Thoughts Abroad', a draft of which Newman enclosed for Froude's perusal (see preceding note). This piece was eventually published in the *British Magazine*, 20 (1836) and reprinted under the title 'How to Accomplish It' in *DA*, pp. 1–43.

[37] *LD* iv. 35.

any means of safety that offers itself,' perhaps even to become 'long-headed, unfeeling, unflinching radicals'.[38]

The radical stance, however, was not one with which Newman could long be comfortable, and by November he had drawn back. 'I have left off being anti-aristocratical,' he told Froude. 'I do not feel the time is come.'[39] One reason was no doubt the strong and quite unexpected support the Oxford Tractarians were receiving from all quarters of the country and from most parties in the Church.[40] But more fundamental was Newman's conviction—so like him and so unlike Lamennais—that God's providential designs cannot be hurried, and therefore 'I am against all measures *on our part* tending to the separation of Church and State, such as putting the bishops out of Parliament.'[41] Though one cannot ignore 'the tyrannical encroachments of the civil power at various eras', or 'the deliberate impiety of the French Revolution', or 'the present apparent breaking up of Ecclesiastical Polity everywhere, . . . let it be remembered, that when our Lord seems at greatest distance from His Church, then He is even at the doors'.[42]

By 1837, when Newman was reading Lamennais, the standing of both men had changed significantly. Newman was approaching the height of his influence within the Church of England. His books and articles, his sermons at St Mary's, the widespread success of the Tractarian movement he managed (the eminent Dr Pusey had become a recruit), all contributed to an aura which was summed up in a saying repeated only half-facetiously by many an Oxford undergraduate: 'Credo in Newmanum'. He was still confident that the Catholic *via media* he preached was a safe path between the doctrinal distortions of Protestant dissent and the practical corruptions of the Roman system. The threats and alarums of the summer of 1833 had receded, and with them much of the immediate anxiety about the Church's relation to the State. Froude's persuasive voice was heard no longer, on this

[38] *LD* iv. 44. The allusions in inverted commas are to Acts and to Matthew and Luke.

[39] *LD* iv. 90.

[40] See e.g. the instances in the letter cited in the preceding note, and in *LD* iv. 118–19.

[41] *LD* iv. 35. Emphasis added.

[42] [J. H. Newman], Tract Thirty-One (25 Apr. 1834), 2–4.

or any other subject, but even Froude, before his untimely death early in 1836, had moderated his position and had contented himself with an oblique warning to the Erastians: 'Firmly as we may be resolved at present, from the dictates of a sober and contented spirit, not to commence changes, . . . yet when changes are commenced, . . . it may . . . be the duty of Churchmen, in mere self-defence, to . . . protest against their . . . oppressed condition.'[43]

Lamennais, by contrast, had seen all his hopes dashed, first, by the pope's refusal to endorse the programme of *L'Avenir*, and then by two papal briefs positively condemning his views.[44] At first he formally submitted to the pope's sentence, retired to a retreat in Brittany, and made no attempt to resume publication of his journal. But silence could mask his deep bitterness only for a while, and little by little he withdrew from all priestly functions and finally from all Christian practice. His poignant *Paroles d'un croyant*, which appeared in 1834, was at once a *cri de cœur* and a declaration to the world that Lamennais professed faith now only in 'humanity'. His young Catholic disciples sadly left him, to be replaced, however, by others more attuned to his new creed, like the novelist George Sand to whom he sent a copy of *Affaires de Rome*.[45]

It may well have been that Newman's attention was drawn to that book by Nicholas Wiseman, then emerging as the leading Roman Catholic spokesman in England. Wiseman had written an article in which he contrasted the swift excision of the unorthodox Lamennais from the Catholic body with the inability of the Church of England to remove from high office a divine with heretical views—or at least a divine whom Wiseman knew the Tractarians considered heretical.[46] If indeed Newman had been thus prompted, reviewing *Affaires de Rome* provided him with a splendid opportunity to offer a contrast of his own, between an

[43] [R. H. Froude], Tract Fifty-Nine, (25 Apr. 1834). 8.

[44] The two papal encyclicals 'Mirari vos' (1832) and 'Singulari nos' (1834) were bound into later editions of *Affaires de Rome*.

[45] Sand to Lamennais, n.d. (late Nov. 1836), in *Correspondance*, ed. le Guillon, vii. 605.

[46] N. Wiseman, 'Dr. Hampden', *Dublin Review*, 1 (1836), 250–65. Roe, *Lamennais*, p. 108, says categorically that Wiseman's article prompted Newman to read *Affaires de Rome*, but the evidence does not seem conclusive. For R. D. Hampden and the Tractarians, see O'Connell, *Oxford Conspirators*, pp. 191–206.

essentially capricious system of authority and one based upon the teachings of the Fathers of the ancient Church. It also allowed him a chance to demonstrate his matchless talent for getting into the mind of another author and not only treating him fairly but stating his arguments more clearly than the other author had done himself. In this latter respect, no book needed more to have order imposed upon it than did the emotional, rhetorical, sometimes scarcely coherent *Affaires de Rome*.[47]

Newman succeeded in piecing together the story Lamennais was trying to tell, the story of Gallican wickedness carried forward by Napoleon and the restored Bourbons, and of the compliant French bishops who, 'according to M. de la Mennais, [committed] the Church to a position essentially schismatical, and thereby ruinous to its highest interests'. *L'Avenir* was founded to promote 'a purer ecclesiastical system than the existing one'. Lamennais 'desired [the Church] to throw herself upon the onward course of democracy, and to lead a revolutionary movement, which in her first stages she had created'. Central to this policy was the enhancement of the position of the pope. 'Rome is, in this point of view, the guardian and security of the religious liberties of the whole world, being a court of final appeal between the Church and the local civil government.' Of course, as Newman shrewdly observed, Lamennais had already before 1830 taken 'the Pope's side against the Gallicanism of the Bourbons (yet without any intention whatever of exalting thereby the Pope as [he] found him, but of imposing on him duties)'.

But the ill-fated sojourn in Rome in 1832 revealed to Lamennais that, far from recognizing its duties,

> 'the centre of unity' itself, . . . having been bribed long ago in common with its dependencies, has not yet been called upon to part with its portion of the 'consideration'. . . . Hence M. de la Mennais has no hopes for Christendom while the Pope is a temporal prince. . . . He considers the See of St. Peter as the . . . fulcrum by which he is to move the world; and he finds it removed from the rock on which it was originally built, and based upon the low and marshy ground which lies beside it.

Gregory VII, after much tribulation, triumphed over his powerful

[47] What follows is taken from 'Fall of de la Mennais', *Ess.* i. 102–36. See above, n. 2.

secular enemies by rallying popular support. His successors have 'condescended to take part in the intrigues of the Italian states as mere temporal princes. . . . The temporal splendour of the Popedom has been the ruin of its spiritual Empire'.

With this fundamental statement of fact Newman had no quarrel. Lamennais was right in saying that 'the Latin Church rose to power, not by the favour of princes, but of people;' despite its aristocratic trappings, it had always found 'the true basis of its power [in] the multitude'. Indeed Lamennais has been 'the confessor' of this truth, 'and, as far as a man can be in these times, the martyr'. Nor could the ascetic in Newman refrain from approving Lamennais's insistence upon the need for austerity in a papacy whose mission was the exercise of a worldwide spiritual principality: 'If, as our author considers, a universal empire is an object to be desired, the fashions of the world, the pomp of a temporal court, wordly alliances and engagements, wealth, rank, and ease, certainly must be set aside.' It was Lamennais's misfortune to have found the pope little disposed to listen to abstract arguments glorifying *le peuple mystique* and pleas to separate Church from State, when his own unruly subjects and the realities of Great-Power politics posed so immediate a threat to him. What the Austrians were up to in the Romagna, and the French at Ancona, and what the Russians meant by their offer to intervene to keep order in the Papal States—'Such', Newman observed sarcastically, 'were the matters which occupied the mind of the Supreme Pontiff during the visit of de la Mennais'.

Newman's sympathy for Lamennais's plight did not, however, go so far as to embrace the latter's first principles. It was not only that Lamennais, 'like Jeroboam, cannot bear to wait God's time' for change, or that, 'in a word, he is thoroughly political in his views and feelings'. 'The elementary error of M. de la Mennais, an error fruitful in many others and which betokens him the true disciple of the Gregories and Innocents of past times' was his failure 'to recognize, nay to contemplate the idea, that rebellion is a sin'. Newman shrank in horror from the notion of 'the divine people', and wondered whether it was anything more than a new version of the serpent's promise to Eve, 'Ye shall be as gods.' Lamennais blamed 'the excesses, tumults, and waywardness' of the 'masses' on their rulers. Newman called them simply the sinfulness of the many.

We almost could fancy [Lamennais] held that the multitude of men were at bottom actually good Christians. . . . Hence he is able to draw close to the democratical party, in that very point in which they most resemble antichrist; and by a strange combination takes for the motto of his *L'Avenir*, 'Dieu et la Liberté.'

Such an absurd and perverse doctrine, Newman continued, indicated that Lamennais 'is a believer in the general and constant advance of the species, on the whole, in knowledge and virtue,' in which unscriptural view he but represented the 'feeling' and 'the teaching of his own Church'. Lamennais insisted upon a 'society [that] rejects her old institutions [and] the ideas which animated them, before reason was raised to a more enlarged notion of right', and so it was natural for him to exaggerate the function of the papacy and to expect the pope to become a partner in the process of revolution. Newman was quite prepared to admit that the Roman See had had at one time a providential, though ill-defined, role to play in the economy of salvation: 'As [God] is now effecting great good in the world by the British power, in spite of its great religious errors, so surely He may, in a dark age also, be represented by a light short of the brightest and purest.' But Lamennais, with his irrepressible itch for novelty, has suffered his tragic 'fall', because he identified his views of social revolution with the papacy's claims to be a continuing source of divine enlightenment.

They who look at Antiquity as supplying the rule of faith, do not believe in the possibility of any substantial increase in religious knowledge; but the Romantist believes in a standing organ of Revelation, like the series of Jewish prophets, unfolding from time to time fresh and fresh truths from the abyss of the divine counsels.

In the end Lamennais, who, 'in spite of his contempt for Protestantism, likes his private judgment', had to confront in his own conscience the choice every thinking Roman Catholic had to confront: Must the pope be *believed* in all things or merely *obeyed*? The irony was that the editors of *L'Avenir* had elevated democratic institutions to the level of revealed truth, and when the pope forbade them to say so and, more than that, asserted the opposite to be the case, Lamennais—but not his associates—protested that they had been debating mere politics all along. He thus placed himself in an impossible position in which he could neither believe nor obey, as a reading of *Affaires de Rome* made abundantly clear. Newman found much to admire in Lamennais but also much to regard with apprehension.

He is a powerful, original, and instructive writer; but there is just that ill-flavour in his doctrine which, in spite of all that is excellent in it, reminds one that it is drugged and unwholesome; and the conviction of his makes one tremble lest the same spirit, which would lead him to throw off civil authority, may urge him under disappointment to deny the authority of Religion itself.

Newman's uneasy feeling about Lamennais's eventual fate proved to be prophetic.[48] There is no evidence, however, that he gave the matter any further thought before 1871 when the review article '*Affaires de Rome*' was reprinted under its new title.[49] Much had transpired during that long interval. Lamennais had died (1854), unreconciled to the communion he had tried zealously to serve, albeit on his own terms. Newman himself had become a Catholic and had had to wrestle with some of those problems of conscience and authority which had bedevilled Lamennais.

The volume of *Essays* containing 'The Fall of de la Mennais' was published in October 1871. Among those who read it then was Matthew Arnold, who wrote to Newman at the end of November and, among other pertinent observations, remarked that 'though the R. Catholic Church may in fact have been anti-democratic in modern times on the continent, there seems nothing in her nature [as there is in that of the Church of England] to make her so'. Newman replied a few days later.

I agree with what you say about the Anglican and Catholic Churches relatively to democratic ideas. It was one of Hurrell Froude's main views that the Church must alter her position in the political world—and, when he heard of la Mennais, he took up his views with great eagerness. I have said the same in the beginning of the Church of the Fathers—'I shall offend many men when I say, we must look to the people' etc etc. I said this apropos of St Ambrose, and based my view upon the Fathers. Froude had seized upon it from the intuitive apprehension he had of what was coming, and what was fitting. We both hated the notion of rebellion—and thought that the Church must bide

[48] Newman appended to the reprint in *Essays*, i. 137–42, an account of Lamennais's alienation from the Church, taken from Montalembert's *Life* of Lacordaire.

[49] Except perhaps when commenting on an article about Lamennais during his brief tenure as editor of the *Rambler*. See *LD*, xix. 106.

her time. . . . It often happens that those who will not bide their time, fail, not because they are not substantially right, but because they are thus impatient. I used to say Montanus, Tertullian, Novatian, etc were instances in point, their ideas were eventually carried out—Perhaps la Mennais will be a true prophet after all.[50]

[50] *LD* xxv. 440–2.

10

The Idea of a University revisited

J. M. ROBERTS

Newman once said that he would be concerned were he supposed to have 'got up' his opinions for the occasion.[1] Yet that is now what I seem to have done. I first read *The Idea of a University* many years ago, but without excitement and, as I discovered on rereading it more recently, in a misleadingly incomplete version. For the rest, apart from the *Apologia* and some pages of the *Essay on the Development of Christian Doctrine* it was a matter of scraps and impressions, picked up almost by osmosis, materials casually and injudiciously acquired. That seemed a pretty narrow, rickety causeway across which to approach *The Idea of a University* for a third time. On the other hand, when I reread the *Idea* I had been serving as a head of a university, in an exciting, but also harassing and distracting, time. Its glare might, I thought, throw some new light on Newman's judgement about priorities and principles. Obviously, one would not look to a book written over a century ago for practical guidance in an entirely different world. But could that different world reflect back a light which would reveal proportions and forms in the *Idea* which we might have overlooked? That question prompted what follows.

Talking about Newman's assumptions demands great care. Notoriously, he is a subtle writer, supremely conscious of his utterance. He is a great technician of qualifications, partial releases, and let-out clauses. He often holds a much less entrenched, unyielding position than at first appears. Much we might expect him to say remains specifically unsaid; much which seems to follow from what he does say turns out, on closer

[1] *Idea*, p. 21. I refer throughout to the edition by Ker, a grouping of the 'Discourses' and 'Lectures and Essays' which Newman himself revised and published in 1873, with appendices from other writings. Ker's introduction and notes provide a firm guide to textual, bibliographical, and historical points, and I have consulted hardly any other secondary material.

examination, to be no necessary inference. What is more, he is a master architect of argument, building complex and solid foundations for his conclusions. Subordinate elements in his structure have their own value and importance, as well as contributing to the larger design. This gives him room—for instance—to appreciate and to value justly the partial, incomplete, imperfect good. He reminds us, if only at times by implication and indirection, that the imperfect is a derogation from the perfect, not merely something to be preferred to the absolutely bad. So, he can accept that there may exist a university which is not the best that could be hoped for, but which none the less has in it something good in itself, considered within its proper limits, something serviceable to higher goals which it could not of itself attain. Most of us would agree. Moreover, he thinks that education and knowledge, even if they do not have as a necessary consequence a good moral outcome, may still have a contingent tendency in that direction.[2] He could admire an Oxford he remembered for its 'heathen code of ethics', producing men who were, *inter alia*, 'able to domineer over Catholics',[3] because it could also boast a limited but still valuable success in training the mind, preparing it for knowledge. That in some cases this could also encompass moral improvement is the proposition that leads Newman through a long argument about the essential insufficiency of important values (honour, self-respect, etc.) to the ironical conclusion of his celebrated (not to say notorious) 'almost' a definition of a gentleman.[4]

Newman's style of thought and exposition, then, makes it harder than we might guess to disagree with him a priori. It may be disconcerting to some, but while Newman would reject (and might even be repelled by) much about a modern university, his premisses do not oblige him to reject it all in principle. Historically speaking, of course, the paradox is unreal: he could hardly have predicted or envisaged much (perhaps most) of what goes on in a university today. The study of hotel management, or computation, as the basis for a degree course would be, we may reasonably

[2] The point is made in *Idea*, p. 161, though the lack of any *necessary* coherence between intellectual cultivation, even when it leads to moral goodness, and religious virtue is emphasized with reference to the awful example of Julian the Apostate (ibid. 165–9).

[3] Ibid. 129–30.

[4] Ibid. 179–80, and see Ker's note to p. 616.

believe, inconceivable to Newman, unlikely ever to have occurred to him, even in fancy. Nevertheless, though he might be incredulous and might recoil fastidiously, he acknowledges that virtually any matter might be the point of departure for education. A traditional academic subject—theology, for instance—could be both a means of liberal education and a training.[5] Not all modern innovations, therefore, must be repugnant to him. Since the Open University does not dispense with tutorial relationships, even 'distance teaching' might fall in principle within the bounds of acceptability for Newman. His near-silence on women seems to pose greater difficulty. Taking, as he does, the current practice of his age for granted, he is sure the university has no place for them.[6] But the exclusion of women from universities is not prescribed and there is no point in pursing our lips about it. Newman's argument may embrace silently, and in principle, what he may not much like in practice. True, his language leaves practical questions in our minds. Universities now do (and often must) provide for the education of women. Yet all that Newman could offer them seems to be an extension of arrangements designed for men. So, in this and many other matters great gaps open between Newman's assumptions and our own, and that must limit his helpfulness, even if his views are not systematically irrelevant to our problems.

The huge contrast between Newman's university world and ours, between that in which he wrote, and that in which he will now be read, is in fact a good starting-point. His was narrow, even for his day. His pages say nothing of the variety of such institutions as the universities of the young United States, or those (ancient and modern) of Scotland, or, say, the Free University of Brussels founded in 1834 (perhaps its anticlerical and masonic roots explain that), or the Friedrichs-Wilhelms-Universität of Berlin whose foundation in 1810 launched the hugely influential ideas of Humboldt. He wrote consciously with challenges from 'godless' London and 'godless' institutions proposed for Ireland in mind; otherwise, a nod or two to

[5] Ibid. 101, where the antithesis between autonomous, liberal pursuits, and utilitarian application is also somewhat surprisingly illustrated by the examples of fox-hunting and horse-racing (though the latter only in ancient Greece, it seems).

[6] 'A university has . . . some traits of human nature more prominently developed than others . . . It is composed of men not women': ibid. 336.

Louvain apart, Newman remains very English in his insular disregard of what went on abroad. Except for an abridged English translation of Huber's book,[7] he seems unaware of what foreigners found remarkable in English universities (and Huber wrote only about Oxford and Cambridge, even if his English editor added brief notes on Durham and London). Newman thought in terms of a university sure of its limited goals, small in numbers, collegiate and tutorial in its working, virtually without public funding or any but external and legal relations with public authority, and comprehensive in its intellectual scope. He takes for granted, that is to say, a university which exists nowhere in the world today. In so far as it once had any actuality, and that is not much, it is to be sought in the Oxford of his youth.

Oxford had then been slowly confronting new problems. They were in the end to yield only to political coercion. The university and the colleges were truly autonomous. They still enjoyed wide public esteem and showed great self-confidence. What a falling-off is here! One private university apart, British universities are nowadays centralized in direct dependence on public money. They are therefore poked and prodded in certain directions by public authorities. Though often ineffective, this is uncomfortable. There is a widespread feeling that something is wrong. Many people believe that it could quickly be put right by more money, but this is too simple. Even if money might help, some of us remain uneasy. We recall that although there are more graduates of British universities alive than ever, public sympathy for the universities was hard to discern when the 1980s brought reduction in their budgets. Clearly, our universities have failed to awake respect for learning and the intellectual life among our countrymen. This should not have been surprising: we do not know what part the universities should or can play in our national culture. Nor do their obvious weaknesses and preoccupations seem likely to be very responsive to Newmanesque prescriptions, whether of remedies or palliatives.

The contrast between what Newman wants to talk about and our preoccupations is condensed in the key-word of his title—the *Idea*. Almost the last thing British universities seek is a single idea. Newman's reduction of 'the bare idea'[8] of a university to a

[7] V. A. Huber, *The English Universities*, ed. F. W. Newman (London, 1843).

[8] Newman's phrase, *Idea*, p. 114.

single function cannot make sense to them. They are rooted in philosophical and intellectual incoherence. They are cluttered up with doctrinal and practical accretions, and are expected and usually willing to do much more than provide intellectual training. Unsurprisingly, they have not sought to identify a single voice to speak for them. Clinging to 'autonomy' and with no articulated philosophy to which their individual purposes could be related, British universities have not sought a spokesman. The pragmatically constructed, historically conditioned system of which they are part met needs as they arose, and they arose, for a long time, only slowly and in a context which made their management and piecemeal satisfaction relatively easy. British society itself is deeply antipathetic to change and this suited the piecemeal style. As a result, modern British universities cannot put forward the sort of integral argument which characterizes the *Idea* because they do not embody such an argument and have never sought to do so. Central simplicities are hard to come by.

Worse still, obscurity surrounds the nature, role, and purpose of British higher education as a whole. Newman did not need to consider other parts of 'tertiary' education, but there is now a whole spectrum of institutions in it with little in common except their sequential place: they come in when schooling is done. While specific tasks remain hard to define within this spectrum, it is hard to decide how and to what extent universities should be supported, influenced, regulated. We do not know, or do not agree, whether (for example) we should expect higher education to be reserved for few, many, or very many; what part vocational and what part general education should have in it; how it should be shared between universities and other institutions, how it should be spread over the student's life—or many other things. Division in the ranks has surfaced in the last ten years as different universities responded differently to shortages of money, questions about social utility, and proposals for change. There has been alarm over status (always a telling symptom of decadence).[9] To

[9] e.g. over the aspirations of non-university institutions. The Robbins report of 1963 was one of the most influential documents in shaping the terms of discussion of British higher education in this century. Interestingly, its authors, in this as in much else so sensible, felt they had to remind dons that 'much of the work done in certain technical colleges and colleges for the education and training of teachers has risen to university or near university level' (*Higher Education: Report of the Committee*, Cmnd. 2154 (1963), 4).

make matters more difficult still, we have had to face challenging questions in the context of the democratic politics of a nation conditioned to seeing universities in unsympathetic ways.

Yet we have often gone on trying to talk (as Newman naturally did) as if universities were of their nature special in status and function and were all engaged in the same task. This is hypocritical. Sheer scale and actual practice make that clear. Even if we have not yet universities so large as some abroad, not even the smallest non-collegiate British university, I suspect, could now realize Newman's vision of pastoral care.[10] Scale implies a vast range of activities and a huge variety of clients. With that goes the impossibility of single-mindedness. Universities have major commitments to research (not always linked to education), maintain nurseries and crèches, provide sports-grounds and changing-rooms, encourage the arts by direct expenditure (as well as by the indirect stimulus and suggestion of study), run shops and cultivate gardens, as well as many other things. We are in practice utterly remote from the academic world taken for granted by Newman, even if we seem sometimes to hanker after ideas similar to his.

So much for Europe's off-shore islands. But the university is now a worldwide institution. Five years after Newman delivered his 'Discourses', the first three Indian universities were founded by the government. Twenty years before that academic debate about India had already called in question much that is fundamental to the *Idea*. Should the British government set up curricula drawn from western civilization, or from the native? What was to be done with religion in a non-Christian continent? Was the purpose of new institutions to make Indian Indians, or Westernized Indians? (Or, for that matter, Bengali, Sikh, Buddhist, Gujarati, or any of dozens of other culturally distinct kinds of Indian)? Was it to provide trained manpower for the ambitions (we might call them development programmes) of British enlightened despotism? Or was it to cultivate the individual? Similar questions have been asked many times since. Now, worldwide, the word 'university' is applied to institutions European in origin, yet which have very varied aspirations and goals. All that they have in common are their recognizably European institutional origins.

[10] Our last major reconsideration of higher educational provision emphatically did not endorse an extension of tutorial teaching (ibid. 187).

Black, brown, and yellow alike, the children of animistic, Hindu, Confucian, and many other cultures, wear mortarboards, put on robes which indicate 'degrees', accept a professional classification into 'doctors', 'masters', and 'bachelors', put in authority 'chancellors', 'vice-chancellors', 'rectors', and 'deans', and much, much else, all because medieval European clergymen once did such things. Yet such procedures blur huge and essential differences. Acclimatization and adaptation, whether benign or malign, change the working and nature of transplanted institutions. Curricula are evolved which reflect local demand and specialized needs.

Newman himself saw clearly that any university must be rooted in a particular society. He could acknowledge what his own vision of a university for Catholic Ireland owed to Protestant England. But he did not envisage the implications of a wide geographical spread of the European university tradition, often in forms remote from the vision held by its founders or implanters. We cannot ignore them. They come home to vice-chancellors every day in practical judgements about overseas students or research activity. We now take, in fact, a very nominalist view of the university (or the universities) of the modern world.[11] We face huge differences of scale, both between countries, and between universities varying in numerical size by orders of hundreds to one. We confront functional diversity and no more than a tiny number of subjects which most of them believe they must teach. One way of putting the problem which results (though a pretty heavy-footed one) might be to say that we who make our lives in the university nowadays have to come to terms with its contingency. Our universities are rooted in particular cultures, dependent on particular contexts, which are cultures often changing quite fast. Greater diversity raises questions of values. Those no longer sure about our own western culture's unquestionable standing will certainly be wary of views like Newman's.[12] Steadily, the cultural relativism of

[11] A confused nomenclature does not make thinking about universities easier, and is itself a symptom of uncertainty. For a simple brief introduction to the problem even within a few countries, see H. Tonkin and J. Edwards, 'Role of the University in America and Europe: Similarities and Differences', *CRE-Information*, 77 (Geneva, 1987), 119–33.

[12] See *Idea*, p. 213, for his very traditional view. China he sees, at best, as a 'huge, stationary, unattractive, morose civilization'.

'developed' societies erodes still further the plausibility of seeing a university as an essential, continuing reality or, indeed, as an intellectual system. It is harder to identify any common tasks of universities and therefore to assess the legitimacy of what is being asked of them.

As an Aristotelian, Newman could seek the university's nature in a teleology. But that may mean his idea of a university is non-transferable. Rooted in a particular culture and particular assumptions, it cannot be utilized elsewhere. If so, at most it can only awake a very diminished resonance in our increasingly cosmopolitan and global culture. Newman had a very different, much more coherent, world in mind. We discover, in reading him, that he does not merely accept, but positively delights in a rhetoric rooted in the old universal ideal of the university linked to a particular view of the European Middle Ages. In that ideal (or, better, myth), some non-historical selection has already ironed out differences arising from circumstance. The sharpness of personal motives and the actual interests which founded and shaped medieval universities are easily lost to sight in summary statements of such ideals and concepts. Yet the idealization was a reality for Newman. It did not make him insensible to his own age; explicitly, he wrote for contemporaries. However unconfidently (and, though in ignorance, I sometimes wonder whether Newman was in action ever so unconfident as he sometimes asserts), he accepted the task of founding a national university for Ireland, serving particular Irish purposes and designed to meet Irish circumstances. But it is clear that so much, however sincerely and enthusiastically undertaken, was strictly accidental: what he had in mind to do was to actualize a model which was in principle of universal application. The *Idea* is more than a mere promotional tract. It is not just about reassuring the uneasy and recruiting support for a new institution.[13]

All this helps to explain why Newman (in effect) often turns out to be asking us to take for granted much that we cannot. Take the intellectual life *per se*; its value was self-evident to him

[13] Yet Newman was very conscious of the immediate context of his writing. 'It has been the fortune of the author throughout life, that the Volumes which he has published have grown for the most part out of the duties which lay upon him, or out of the circumstances of the moment' (ibid. 207). But Ker tells us, too, that his text was deliberately revised with an eye to an audience outside Ireland.

and hardly needed justification or defence. Yet, in all 'developed' countries the prevailing culture is now in some measure hostile to the life of the mind: scholarly values no longer exact an automatic deference except (paradoxically) in conservative, sometimes backward, societies. There, they are often associated with élites enjoying power and prestige. The respect which universities retain in them seems to derive from their control over access to instruction and qualification, and from their association with the manipulation of Nature and the creation of wealth—from their connection, that is, with various forms of power. Nor can we now take it for granted that the intellectual—far less academic—life is self-evidently justifiable or admirable in the eyes of modern youth anywhere. Yet Newman believes that what he terms knowledge, which is what successful education communicates, produces, or inculcates, is an end in itself, serving no other end, except accidentally. Many of us agree; perhaps most of us do when we feel threatened and we sometimes say so. Yet, it is now impossible to pretend that knowledge for its own sake explains everything that universities actually do, or what we think they should do. Much that goes on in a modern university is consciously a means to useful ends, whether external or internal. Moreover, it is highly unlikely that most students—or even a substantial minority—would recognize the pursuit of knowledge for its own sake as the reason for attending a university. They have careers in mind, as have had their prececessors in centuries past. Jude thought 'Christminster' a city of light where the tree of knowledge grew, but he also thought he might become a bishop if he went there. Universities have always been ready, and some were founded and shaped, to provide for such hopes.

This brings us to utility. There can be few topics now more talked about in higher education and Newman himself says much about it. Characteristically, he is less clear-cut than one might think at first sight. It may only be a wish to provide a rhetorical stimulus that led him in his *Office and Work of Universities* (1856) to entitle one chapter 'Supply and demand: The Schoolman', and to depict in it students flocking to the great medieval teachers and centres of learning because of their competitive pull (an image, incidentally, which some of those who persist in the defence of subjects and establishments without regard to demand for places and denounce schemes for increasing the students' freedom of choice might ponder). But he also remarked, apparently without disapproval, that his age sought 'that the True and Serviceable as well as the Beautiful should be the aims of the academic intellect and the business of the University'.[14] Further, 'though the useful is not always good, the good is always useful' and at the highest level the case for an indissoluble connection of utility and knowledge is axiomatic: 'a cultivated intellect, because it is a good in itself, brings with it a power and a grace to every work and occupation which it undertakes, and enables us to be more useful, and to a greater number'.[15] What is more, he recognizes that certain studies may bring benefits to very large numbers of people. Of Bacon (whom he takes more than once as the archetypal figure in this matter) he says that 'his is simply a Method whereby bodily discomforts and temporal wants are to be most effectually removed from the greatest number; and already, before it has shown any signs of exhaustion, the gifts of nature, in their most artificial shapes and luxurious provision and diversity, from all quarters of the earth, are, it is undeniable, by its means brought even to our doors, and we rejoice in them'.[16]

Yet, all this goes little way with him. He is suspicious of those who argue 'that where there has been a great outlay, they have a right to expect a return in kind' and for whom utility has become a watchword.[17] Newman rejects any forcing of utility upon the university. He criticizes would-be reforms on this ground. He argues that utility should not be allowed to encroach upon the essential domain of the university, liberal education. Increased well-being will not do as a definition of the aim of university teaching (any more than will the task of making men better). 'A University, taken in its bare idea . . . contemplates neither moral impression nor mechanical production'.[18] The 'Baconian Philosophy', he says, by using the physical sciences in the service of man, 'does thereby transfer them from the order of Liberal Pursuits to, I do not say the inferior, but the distinct class of the Useful.'[19] This is a long way from the realities of modern

[14] *HS* iii. 81. [15] See *Idea*, pp. 143–6. [16] Ibid. 109.

[17] Ibid. 135, and, on the moral insufficiency even of liberal education, an earlier passage (ibid. 110): 'its direct business is not to steel the soul against temptation or to console it in affliction, any more than to set the loom in motion, or to direct the steam carriage'.

[18] Ibid. 114. [19] Ibid. 101.

universities urged by society to give greater attention to the social utility of their 'outputs'. We cannot look to him for help amid the confusion of our own wishes and those of the 'consumers' off-campus.

Though Newman is careful to distinguish the good that liberal education may do even in the absence of religion, religion seems to creep in when he speaks of what ought to be. Clearly, even ostentatiously, his advocacy proceeds from a special religious standpoint and his argument is always set in the context of religion. It is not Catholicism which is at issue, though. Newman even says that most of what he says implies no antecedent religious principles, and that 'common sense' will recognize it[20] (which seems a little overstated). It is not a question of Catholic religion, but of religion itself. Newman sees systematic insufficiency in a university whose own practice, be it never so free from viciousness, yet is not completed by the presence and influence of religion. Like many in his age, he believed that if a man has all things save that, then those things are worth nothing. Like any human institution, his university had to have, to develop its full value, the tincture of religion. Certain practical consequences must follow: there ought to be some institutionalization of religion in the university. Few would now say that. Religion no longer has an unquestioned relevance. The very consciousness of its importance, and that it requires consideration and even debate, has now ebbed. Its conflict with science, so instantly and ominously in the background of the lives of most Victorian intellectuals, no longer seems urgent or exciting even to dons. Yet Newman held that only religion could provide a proper framework for the student whose life, directed merely by his studies, will otherwise surely tend to paganism and sin, just because he is a man (or, as we might now have to say in order to be wholly intelligible, because he or she is a person).

Again and again, it appears, Newman's assumptions reveal themselves to be so different from ours, the background against which he writes is so utterly remote from our own, the universities of his day are so unlike ours either in their business or their ethos, that we cannot expect him to speak to our specific needs. He confronted nothing like the intellectual and structural chaos

[20] Ibid. 22.

which any *Idea* of a modern university would have to take into account. We can question his title. It is also relevant that our own society is not merely actually different from Newman's but radically different in one particularly important respect. Its civilization is committed, whether consciously or unconsciously, to the likelihood of continuing, often fundamental change, while he, on the other hand, takes for granted a solid, firmly based culture. He recognizes there may, indeed will, be change, but it is not of the essence of his view of the world and it implies no possible transformation of his intellectual universe. Though he lived in a world where historic change was startlingly, growingly evident, he does not seem much troubled by it.[21] He stands on rock. He had grown up in the after-glow of the French Revolution. Yet for all the destruction and the turbulence it brought to the world of the young Newman, for all its fecundity, for all the mythological impact it could demonstrate as late as 1848 (to look no later than the conception of our text), he and (I guess) most of his contemporaries and intellectual peers still lived in a society believing in or looking for unchanging values. Even if his age was one of revolutionary potential, the immense weight of the past imposed a time-lag between radical speculation and the changes it provoked in the day-to-day working of society; what sociologists call 'behavioural norms' long remained pretty much intact, however challenged. Even if George Eliot's powerful conscience was already on the prowl when he wrote, he and his generation had certainties for which we can only crave.

When we move from assumptions to working arrangements the gulf looks wider still. Take Newman's view that a central task of the university is to provide a comprehensive account of knowledge. Once again, we must beware of his caveat.[22] Yet in practice,

[21] Sometimes he spoke almost admiringly of it: 'what largeness . . . of view, what intrepidity, vigour and resolution are implied in the Reform Bill, in the emancipation of the Blacks, in the finance changes, in the Useful Knowledge movement, the organisation of the True Kirk, in the introduction of the penny postage, and in the railroads! This is an age, if not of great men, at least of great works': *University Sketches*, ed Tierney, p. 55.

[22] It appears in the appendix to the 1852 'Discourses' (*Idea*, p. 440); 'though I have spoken of a University as a place for cultivating all knowledge, yet this does not imply that in matter of fact a particular University might not be deficient in this or that branch . . . but only that all branches of knowledge were presupposed or implied, and none omitted on principle'. This is a slippery notion. On what kind of principle? It is arguable that a university ought not to support a subject when others

what he wants is impossible. The professional philosophers would discuss better than I the proposition that in order to have possession of truth at all, we must have the whole truth, but it seems at first sight implausible and on reflection unacceptable except as a tautology: that the whole truth is the whole truth. Partial knowledge often suffices; I need not have much technical knowledge in order to make elementary corrections to faulty machines. We are also sure that on much more abstract and theoretical matters, it is not necessary to know everything in order to know something. We can know that some things are not true, while knowing little else. We can correctly assess our duty, without fully comprehending why. Perhaps Newman acknowledges this indirectly in his comments on the major branches of study as partial, incomplete representations of the truth.[23]

Yet why should a university even aspire to teach every subject? Is it true that any subject can only be taught in the context of all the others? For most students it is impossible fully to understand and make one subject their own: to understand its interconnections with all others is unimaginable. Here, Newman's special concern and arguments for theology especially seem unconvincing.[24] That a university should teach all knowledge and that it is impossible to teach anything 'thoroughly' unless all other subjects are 'taken into account' (whatever those phrases mean) are premisses already contested; another of his arguments (that theology has a special regulating role among other disciplines) we can reject as unproven. All that is left is the argument that if theology is not taught, its intellectual province will be usurped by other disciplines. This may indicate a real danger, but one not unique to theology. What is more, at least in a rich western country, any subject or science is likely to be taught and studied *somewhere*; if one university cannot provide it, another will. If a single university cannot deliver the comprehensive view of knowledge Newman wants, certainly the whole system can. Why, then, should any single university not deliberately exclude some subjects?

Newman's view of the range of subjects which a single university should offer its students has to be, in fact, at once more

are more important to it, and some hierarchies of importance seem to be acceptable to Newman. And at what point do you call a halt to a university's expansion if resources are available?

[23] Ibid. 50.

[24] Ibid. 91–2.

actually varied and more practically restricted than we can accept, even allowing his caveats and our own.[25] This in part reflects the reality of educational development since his day; a huge proliferation of subjects by natural division and specialization is now an insurmountable barrier to the synoptic view. We are hard-pressed to say that any individual subject is essential to a university (though I recall at one moment searching my mind at senate and expressing the view that perhaps mathematics was the only one; Mrs Thatcher is said to believe that physics and chemistry are). Moreover, there is a certain core of integrative vision in Newman's idea which we cannot easily accept, because its implications would impose a retreat upon us: we should have to give up so much that we take for granted a university—some university, somewhere—should do. His criticisms of London University make this clear, especially if we remember what he had said when Macaulay defended it in 1826. Newman said:

> Such writers do not rise to the very idea of a University. They consider it a sort of bazaar or pantechnicon, in which wares of all kinds are heaped together in stalls independent of each other . . . whereas, if we would rightly deem of it, a University is the home, it is the mansion-house, of the goodly family of the Sciences, sisters all, and sisterly in their mutual dispositions[26]

The conscious rhetoric of this passage, its building of metaphor on metaphor, testify to his strong feeling. Even if (as I think we must) we reject his principle as insufficient and impractical, what he says poses a searching question, for if we do not locate the identity of a university in the unity of an intellectual system, then we must locate it somewhere else. Where?

One function Newman gives the university is the maintenance of intellectual discipline. He is much preoccupied with what we might term academic demarcation disputes. Indeed, he sets out a view of the university at one point which makes its ordering, delimiting role almost paramount. He says that the university

> professes to assign to each study, . . . its own proper place and its just boundaries; to define the rights, to establish the mutual relations, and to effect the intercommunion of one and all; to keep in check the ambitious and encroaching, and to succour and maintain those which

[25] See *Idea*, 440, for his reservation (one of practice, not of principle).
[26] Ibid. 421.

from time to time are succumbing under the more popular and more fortunately circumstanced, to keep the peace between them all . . .[27]

Given the remoteness of this from actuality, it would be easy to pass over it with a smile (his picture of an imaginary senate prompted my only other actual outbreak of spontaneous hilarity while reading the *Idea*).[28] It is also easy to react in a peremptory way; whatever difficulties vice-chancellors may face in the form of over-mighty heads of department competing for resources at the expense of the less well-placed subjects, we do not see them as philosophical umpires. Yet Newman's concern was very real. Why? Reasonably, as an Aristotelian he believed that immoderate growth is monstrous. But that is not all. The answer may lie at more than one level, or in more than one place. First, Newman's intellectual world is essentially hierarchical. There are higher and lower studies. Some sustain the primary task of education, and others normally have the secondary commission of training in specialized skills. Take but degree away, and you are deprived of the fundamental articulation of a proper course of studies. Not only discord but confusion follows. We should not be surprised if someone who takes such a general view sees a need for an authority to arbitrate uncertainties and to correct divagation from right order. We, on the other hand, do not find it easy (except ceremonially) to let a hierarchical view of knowledge shape the actual organization and structure of a university. Nor is categorization easy. A subject which one university sees as an arts subject finds its niche elsewhere among the social or even the natural sciences. As for esteem and status, whatever may be the unacknowledged reality, it would indeed be a rash vice-chancellor who commited himself publicly to a view that one subject was innately superior to another. A wise one would be cautious in making any such judgement at all.

[27] Ibid. 369. This passage (and the famous phrase about 'an imperial intellect'), one of Newman's most sustained and eloquent exercises in definition, comes not in any of the nine 'Discourses', but in a lecture written specially for the school of science.

[28] 'Professors are like the ministers of various political powers . . . They represent their respective sciences, and attend to the private interests of those sciences respectively; and, should dispute arise . . . they are the persons to talk over and arrange it, without risk of extravagant pretensions on any side, of angry collision, or of popular commotion. A liberal philosophy becomes the habit of minds thus exercised; a breadth and spaciousness of thought, in which lines, seemingly parallel, may converge at leisure, and principles, recognized as incommensurable, may be safety antagonistic'. Ibid. 371. The last sentence is somewhat ambiguous, but the drift is clear.

In the second place, Newman is also particularly concerned about the evil effects of an uncontrolled advance of knowledge. Unregulated work in the arts (he tells us) leads to 'corruption' of revealed truth; the evil consequence in science is its 'exclusion'.[29] Nor does he see the inductive method characteristic of science as an appropriate instrument for all investigations. Protestantism, Newman tells us, has followed the scientists in applying the inductive method to Holy Scripture (more exactly, he might have said that some Protestants had).[30] It is therefore desirable that an authoritative demarcation between the natural sciences and (in this case) theology is enforced. But we cannot follow him, because we accept, implicitly, a freely competitive view of the way in which subjects are expounded. We think it is up to, say, theology, or philosophy, to defend its own boundaries in practice and by what means it wishes, and the same is true of physics or biology.

A third ground for Newman's enthusiasm for the university's regulative role was undoubtedly his wish to combat the exclusion of theology altogether. In the first half of the nineteenth century such exclusion had, broadly speaking, two roots. One may be termed ideological: theology was seen as in principle unnecessary or undesirable (University College London). The other was pragmatic and political: how could one teach it without arousing the whirlwinds of sectarian animosity (the Irish experiments of Peel)? Nowadays, the issue has been blurred by the appearance of departments of religion and religious studies, but practical questions sometimes force it to the fore. Now whatever precise meaning is given to the world 'theology', many more people in his day than ours (non-Catholics among them) would have shared with Newman a belief in the pre-eminence among studies of something with that name. That has now gone. So, I understand, is general agreement, even among its practitioners, such as he took for granted, that theology provides access to knowledge. Yet we are told in the *Idea* that it is intellectually necessary for theology to be taught in a university, because comprehensiveness in the sciences it professes is a necessary characteristic of a true university and theology is a science like any other. Were he alive today, Newman would no doubt have opposed the decision of

[29] *Idea*, 187.
[30] Ibid. 191.

one English university in 1980 to wind up its department and end honours teaching in theology, but his grounds for doing so now seem beside the point; no one then denied that theology was a legitimate subject for university teaching, but neither did its defenders claim that a university could not be a university without it. If deduction from Newman's axioms leads to conclusions that institutions without theology are not universities, we can only reply that we prefer ostensive definition. Obviously, to point to what we do is not an argument in itself against an argument about what we ought to do but it reveals assumptions and possibilities, and the tide is not running Newman's way.

Authoritative demarcation is also difficult because of the way academic minds work. Nowadays, intellectual advance often takes place 'between' subjects, 'at the borders', or 'interface', of areas previously independent of one another. These tired metaphors describe, in the context of traditional and long-accepted divisions of intellectual activity, excursions into what has hitherto been seen as someone else's territory—or, at least as unclaimed no man's land. Furthermore, there is nowadays much borrowing or importation of ways of thinking and techniques from one subject to another. In short, the way much intellectual advance proceeds is by everything getting a little more mixed up with other things than was once the case. I do not see how the task of demarcation which Newman gives the university could easily be carried out without unacceptably impeding or hindering this process. Nor can a university always be impartial; it has an interest of its own, distinct from that of its parts, which must at times be defended at the cost of particular studies. This is not merely a question of money. The interest of the university (as opposed to that of any of its parts) may well be served by fostering an activity not easily defended on grounds of cost, at the expense of other activities. There may well be some things it should not do, moreover, even if all academic departments were to advocate them. To realize capital assets to protect jobs by selling books from its libraries, for instance, might well send signals about the university's attitude towards donors and benefactors which would not serve its interest. Again, a university may well find it desirable to act very positively, whatever the theoretical relationship of the subjects concerned and the inconvenience to some individuals, by reorganizing activities. No university can always act distinterestedly towards its constituent academic units.

One contentious area where disagreement (about expenditure, for example) often arises touches on Newman's central obsession: education. True, he saw even this, the university's only indispensable task, as ultimately insufficient, because merely temporal, when viewed in the widest context. Yet education is, he believes, a sufficient definition of that task if we only consider the limits of what a university *can* do *qua* university. About this he is specific. In spite of his book's title, Newman has set out not a view of the university, but a view of university education. The nine 'Discourses' are about *university teaching*, and that means liberal education.

Newman seeks the cultivation of the individual mind rather than a social effect. He hopes that social utility (as well as utility for the individual) will follow from the cultivation of the mind by liberal education, but social utility is not the goal, but a by-product. In so far as he believes education has effects upon society, it is through individuals. 'If . . . a practical end must be assigned to a University course', he says, 'I say that it is that of training good members of society'. He goes on to spell this out:

> A University training is the great ordinary means to a great but ordinary end; it aims at raising the intellectual tone of society, at cultivating the public mind, at purifying the national taste, at supplying true principles to popular enthusiasm and fixed aims to popular aspirations, at giving enlargement and sobriety to the ideas of the age, and facilitating the exercise of political power, and refining the intercourse of private life.[31]

Even for Newman, this comes in an especially eloquent passage, carefully composed, with a succession of thoughtful and pondered instances. Yet it provides for the influencing of society only in one way: through the formation of more individuals well equipped for life. Of the deployment of university teaching (or research) with the aim of shaping society in any more direct way, he does not speak. Nor is it a question of training individuals for specific qualifications. Newman's education is essentially preparatory, laying the foundations for specialized study and providing an approach to it through breadth of vision and

[31] *Idea*, 154.

understanding. The mind is to be given a capacity to undertake further study, and a training of its critical faculty. But education has also a larger aim. Newman produces several formulations of what it might lead to. The most concise sets it out as that 'real cultivation of the mind' which will produce 'the intellect . . . properly trained and formed to have a connected view or grasp of things'.[32] It has been suggested that what we are really being told about is the 'ability to think' but the language seems sometimes to go somewhat beyond that,[33] though we should not fall into the error of seeing him as an advocate (far less a prophet) of dogmatic 'system', intending to bring everyone to the acceptance of a similar framework for their thought.

We may ask of Newman, who is to be educated? Both the emphasis of his own argument and our historical knowledge of the assumptions of his age point to the same conclusion: very few. They are all men and Newman hopes they will be Christian gentlemen, but it seems that he would be content with gentlemen *tout court*, given that it is all most universities will be able to provide. Not only in its restricted members, but in its restricted sympathy, this seems unimaginative. Our society's need of educational provision is something Newman could not be expected to envisage, but that can hardly mean simply that more should now have access to Newman's ideal. We need not question Newman's sincerity in believing that in the end individuals must be changed if the world is to be changed. But is that the whole story? At least some of those who speak of 'relevance' in university study think otherwise. More deeply, some of us might wish a university to uphold and embody certain cultural standards and ideals, because it is an institution well fitted to uphold and embody them on our behalf. We would expect the university's choices of the subjects it promotes, and the content of its courses, to reflect and respect (though not exclusively) what the Robbins report termed 'the transmission of a common culture and common standards of citizenship'.[34] We have already touched on the difficulty of asserting the claims of intellect in our society; some of us think that one of our main tasks is just to communicate to most people a sense that academic and intellectual activity matters at all.

[32] Ibid. 11. [33] Ibid., p. lvii. [34] Robbins report, p. 7.

So far, no doubt, so good: Newman would be with us. But we have to go only a little further to come once again into conflict with actual circumstances which make it impossible to look to Newman for advice. He is, for example, penetrating in his comments on the need to contest by education the tendency to superficiality, viewiness, ill-considered judgement shown in what he terms the 'literary world'.[35] We might make very similar observations, even more forcefully, about the 'media world', or the 'chattering classes'. But whereas Newman regrets that intellectual and cultural 'authority' has shifted from the universities to another agency, he can feel hopeful that the distinct position of the universities will make it possible for some of them to recover it. It is almost a religious version of the vision of an F. R. Leavis. But it is now inconceivable that an independent and over-reaching cultural authority can rest in our universities. They are now so completely a part of a democratic, post-literate, materialist society such as Newman can hardly have dreamt of, that we cannot imagine them standing back from the society in which they are so closely involved, so as to exercise a distinct cultural role. After all, they produce most of the *bien-pensants* of the media.

I again recall the Robbins report. Besides the pursuit of knowledge for its own sake, it spoke of three other functions of higher education: instruction in skills, the creation of cultivated men and women, and the advancement of learning. Newman endorses the second. He would specifically exclude from the objects of education the first. Given that we have elsewhere observed the clear, firm boundary he draws along the frontiers of utility and 'training' (and, it may be noted, Robbins was frank about instruction in skills as a means of grappling with 'pressing problems'), he thus leaves out much that can now be seen as part of a university's task, even if, looking at what is actually done in some universities, we may sometimes feel that they cast the net too far. We may also find Newman too peremptory over the advancement of learning by research. He is very blunt and exclusive: 'if its object were scientific and philosophical discovery, I do not see why a University should have students'.[36] Now it is true that in some countries—France, for instance—research

[35] *Idea*, pp. 13–15.
[36] Ibid. 5.

has usually been segregated outside the universities in special institutions. Our own institutionalizing of higher education, though (at least at one time), reflected the belief that research should not only always be part of the university's work, but should be carried on in no other institution of higher education: the poor polytechnics ought not to be allowed to do any, it once appeared. As often happens, history has arranged otherwise; such dogmatism was, none the less, evidence of the inseparable part research is believed to play in the life of a university.

Other grounds for misgiving arise over his positive attitudes. One is the educational priority given to what Newman calls literature, and we usually term the humanities, or the arts subjects. It is not that he has any vulgar, donnish, empire-building in mind when he allows them predominating weight in education. He had himself studied more mathematics than most British undergraduates nowadays will have done and acknowledged the educational potential of the natural sciences and, we may remark, professional subjects, law and medicine.[37] Newman regarded any academic subject as a potentially valuable educational instrument. The examples he offers us of tutorial technique show this; so do his views on theological training.[38] Nevertheless, he has a rooted primary confidence in the humanities and believes them to be the indispensable part of education. 'Literature' was still for him, the main instrument conveying a knowledge of man.

Many of us can no longer agree. This is not just a matter of saying the sciences have arrived, but let us start there. There is, at first sight, small place for them in Newman's view of university education. True, he formally recognizes them. Nor should we object that he nowhere shows any real sense of what the pursuit of science might mean in material and political terms.[39] He did not envisage the cloud-capped towers of modern science

[37] A. D. Culler tells us (*The Imperial Intellect: A Study of Newman's Educational Ideal* (New Haven Conn., 1955), 159) that although Newman established an independent school of sciences at Dublin, with a dean and three professors, it never had any students.

[38] For the first, *Idea*, pp. 281–4; for the second, ed.'s introd., ibid., pp. lix–lx. See also the app., ibid. 440–4; 'all branches of knowledge are subject matter of University Education'.

[39] Though, says Culler (*Imperial Intellect*, p. 226), his practice at Dublin was better than the 'Discourses' might lead us to expect.

departments, the vast suction with which scientific research draws to it a flood of money, the arrogance of some science professors, but how could he? What he might have done was to make us feel that the potential for intellectual training which the sciences afford is every whit as great as that of the humanities, and might be pursued in just as single-minded a way. He might have shown more awareness of an educational instrument whose usefulness went beyond the purely intellectual, a method which was more than mere gymnastic. Yet he could not do that.

> The simple question to be considered is, how best to strengthen, refine, and enrich the intellectual powers; the perusal of the poets, historians, and philosophers of Greece and Rome will accomplish this purpose, as long experience has shown; but that the study of the experimental sciences will do the like, is proved to us as yet by no experience whatever.[40]

His judgement is reserved, but the reserve is confident.

Setting aside the knowledge of God (which he believes a university must impart or else accept that it is educationally incomplete), Newman divided the university's educational task into the study of the knowledge of nature, which has to be approached through the sciences, and the study of the knowledge of man, which he calls literature. That sounds alright, but in so far as he ever discusses the sciences as specific educational disciplines, the impression with which we are left is that they are useful as a training of rigorous thought through the exercise of the inductive method. He does not conceive that physics may exercise the imagination as profoundly as philosophy (and much more than some styles of philosophy) or literature, or that engineering, a complex of applied and experimental sciences, can be a broadening and humanizing discipline when imaginatively taught. From recollection, flexibility of mind, resourcefulness, a willingness to envisage new approaches, and a sympathetic curiosity about what might be instructive in other disciplines—all of them desirable qualities of an educated mind—are often more evident in science than in arts departments, and rarely less. Moreover, although all subjects are educationally valuable when taught at the highest level of inspiration and skill, few subjects are taught like that most of the time. Yet even at its most

[40] *Idea*, pp. 221–2.

humdrum, the teaching of science has an irreducible specificity and rigour which is less and less to be found in arts subjects, where 'education' at a humdrum level too often consists of the assimilation of a conventional jargon and the parroting of slick judgements.

Presumably, Newman would be pleased that the humanities are still so strongly entrenched in our universities. Many of us are. Yet we also sometimes feel uneasiness about the actual preponderance of the humanities in education. 'Uneasiness' is an ambiguous, or perhaps indefinite, word and does not exhaust the matter. Nevertheless, we live long after the Indian summer of that ascendancy of liberal education at Oxford on which, for all its imperfections in his eyes, Newman based his case. The humanities have now spawned strange offspring. The centre of the old notion of the humanities, surely, was that they provided access to classical models. They showed what was excellent. The implication was that the models could be imitated or used as touchstones for the testing of style, morals, beauty, rigorousness of thought, and many other things. This view has long been abandoned. At their best, the humanities still require knowledge, clear thought, and linguistic skill. But they have now expanded their thematic scope to include virtually any subject which cannot be anchored by its method in the notion of 'science', and the subject-matter of some of them is trivial, if we seek normative guides. Some have turned into mere exercises in form. Even their practitioners show uneasiness about them. The desire of those in the 'social sciences' to distinguish their interests from the humanities by that term, and the wish of some in the humanities to appropriate the word 'science' to their own disciplines seems to me to show a loss of nerve, and one often justified.

Of course the defence of the humanities is still possible and desirable. That defence can even, reasonably, include a utilitarian component. The humanities, properly taught, can still prepare the mind for deployment in the practical world by inculcating such qualities as attention to detail, careful scrutiny of words, rigorousness in argument, an ability to sense and identify relations, and so on. Though learning clutters up prose more than used to be the case, good classicists, linguists, or historians still find themselves, at the end of their studies, well furnished with skills any perceptive employer should prize. The humanities are neither obsolete, nor useless. But there are arguments to be put against their inherited prestige. Tentatively, it is worth considering whether, in some versions, they may not have actually become non-educational as Newman could not have envisaged, through their fostering of subjective response and self-realization as primary goals.[41] We may be in danger of going down a blind alley in indulging the old cult of the humanities. It may reasonably be urged that society needs something different. Society is more than a collectivity of solitudes, and many will ask more from educational institutions than the encouragement of obsessive individualism. Of course, what the humanities may now shelter is not what Newman wanted. But he had his religion to keep him sanely recognizing what was due to heaven and to society: the maintenance of faith, the restraint of sensuality, and the elevation of self-discipline and respect for true principles. Unsurprisingly, he saw no difficulty in reconciling this with a humane education, for when he experienced it in Oxford, that education had as yet made few concessions to the Romantic ideal. In our day, it has made many.

The gap between Newman's operational prescriptions and the instruments we have available to us is even striking at humbler levels. He objected to the 'bazaar' view of the university not only because it was, he believed, indiscriminate and unsystematic in its choice of subjects for study, but because it instructed by lecture—as do most universities. Newman, though, believed in the tutorial system—not necessarily in the sense of the one-to-one academic exercise, but as a relationship between two people which permeated the student's life, and ensured a specific, sensitive response to his needs by an observant, dutiful tutor. The importance he attached to this can be seen in his care to keep the appointment of tutors in his own hands.[42] Without the moral 'attraction' of tutor and pupil, he tells us elsewhere, 'a University is alive only in name' and 'an academical system without the personal influences of teachers upon pupils, is an arctic winter'.[43] We must believe that such a method is possible: Newman was

[41] See the comments of L. Trilling, on 'The Uncertain Future of the Humanistic Educational Ideal' (*American Scholar*, 44, (1975), 52–67). He there draws attention to our culture's tendency towards a degenerate, or at least uncontrollable and subjective, romanticism, which the humanistic ideal seems powerless to correct.

[42] Ker cites *LD* xiv. 383 and xv. 85.

[43] *HS* iii. 48–9, 74.

drawing upon his own experience. It is, too, a method of which a version, eroded in practice, but, at its best, intact in principle, some of us have glimpsed, though without the religious component Newman believed in. It is now hardly to be found anywhere. Individual tutorial guidance to the numbers now passing through our universities is only possible where it has special financial protection. But suppose the money be found, many (most?) university teachers no longer want to exercise such moral and pedagogic guidance which Newman cherished. He presupposes, too, the collegiate system, or a fair imitation of it and stresses that students should live in small communities under tutorial guidance and not as isolated individuals in student lodgings as in continental Europe (or even, presumably, in the comfortable, but lightly supervised halls of residence provided by generous tax-payers for the British student élite). Perhaps an Oxford man may be allowed to say that Newman's preoccupation, understandable though it may be, with his old university is here a disabling force. Sometimes it seems as if all that Newman is advocating in the *Idea* is a purer, braced, idealized Oxford, one rising to the heights of which, in his vision, she was capable. Assuredly, it is a vision of great attraction and charm. Nowhere is Newman more suasive and seductive in his hints of what he means by having faith in the individual and allowing elbow room for education, than in putting them against that background. We might benefit from this not by trying to imitate Oxford, though, but by allowing it to stimulate our imagination, relating Newman's vision to our own university experience in other ways.[44]

Whatever sensitivity to local and temporary needs Newman showed, it does not seem unfair to say that his title itself now suggests a view of university education which is so specific as to be ultimately cramping. It is difficult now to accept the truths he believed universal and the proposals he thought of universal efficacy. Rather, his book is now more interesting as biographical evidence, as an expression of a moment of intellectual strain, a

[44] Our educational rulers seem prejudiced against such institutions as the small, residential liberal arts colleges or the Junior and Community colleges of the US (though I suspect that a few of our more enlightened teacher-training colleges have from time to time played something of their role). Such institutions could provide us with much of what Newman seeks and—as in the US—could also be linked to the university system by providing graduates for graduate work while not necessarily carrying out such work themselves.

document of his confrontation with the institutional and social reality of Catholicism in operation in an area he believed he knew much about, education. In fact, what he knew was pretty restricted; he knew Oxford, and when he fell back on it for guidance the best help he could draw on was the old liberal Aristotelian education. This was ironical. He had in the end quarrelled with it at Oxford. But it looked much better from Dublin.

Yet some say that Newman has been influential, and that his influence shows his continuing relevance. True, in the nearest thing we have had to organized public debate over the universities in recent years, the *Idea* was invoked even in the House of Commons.[45] His book, then, is known to be 'a Good Thing'. But has it been *read* by those who make crucial decisions? It is not easy to demonstrate, but I fear it has not, and regret that. Nor am I convinced that much of Newman's doctrine can be shown to have been absorbed into our educational thinking (though that does not disappoint me). We might ask (since 'influence' is a vague word) influence on whom? Or on what? Perhaps there has been confusion over appearances. The Oxford model has undoubtedly been influential (though often unacknowledged) in, for example, our system's commitment to the residential idea and its continual lip-service to the ideal of forming the whole man or woman.[46] Like much else in that system, both are coherent with Newman's ideal. But even if we think Newman would have approved of them, we can hardly believe he did much to shape such institutions; entrenched assumptions and practicality mattered more. Though he said 'a metropolis is not the place for a number of resident youths',[47] that is not why new British universities were sited in or near

[45] The Chairman of the Committee of Vice-Chancellors and Principals spoke on 9 July 1985 of Newman being much quoted recently and in the House of Commons four days earlier, Sir Keith Joseph, the minister charged with educational policy, spoke of Newman's 'vision which we can still universally admire and to which I adhere'. True, he said 'admire' and not 'endorse' and said nothing else about what it was he adhered to, so perhaps this was only window-dressing.

[46] The residential system is, of course, also practised in some establishments abroad, notably the French École Normale Supérieure (an eminently 'metropolitan' institution) and its female equivalent, and attempts have been made with varying success to apply the residential system elsewhere (e.g. Yale). But motivation for such arrangements is usually very different from Newman's.

[47] Quoted from *Idea*, ed.'s introd. p. xxviii.

country towns in the 1960s; the availability of cheap land was more important. We may well be saddled with a still very restrictive, inflexible, hierarchical, status-obsessed, socially narrow university system, and if so, it is sad, but that Newman might approve does not make him responsible for it. Far less ought we to blame him because the 1960s turned out to have some sad consequences. The possibilities of success along the *bien-pensant* lines of British academic publicists were destroyed by behaviour on the part of teachers and students which Newman would have condemned, whatever the superficial similarity of some fashionable ideas of the era to his own. We should not trust the rhetoric of his admirers.[48]

As I reread the *Idea* it seemed to me that its doctrines were narrow, exaggerated, and likely to be sterile as sources of institutional reform. There is danger in all argument (such as his) which postulates a special, unique role for an educational institution; universities, like schools, are social creations and should remain responsive to society. They all too often harden into conservatism and an approach such as Newman's reinforces this tendency (and, of course, is in his case linked to a very static view of society). If Newman were to be shown to have exercised practical influence, it is not something I should wish to celebrate, but to deplore. But on these matters I am prepared to listen to those better instructed than I. When we turn to the record, though, we should remember that the writings now brought together in the *Idea* were frequently reprinted, often with careful modifications, during Newman's lifetime. Yet there is little sign that much notice was taken of them. They were not even reviewed, it seems, except by Catholic journals.[49] As for Oxford's own memories of Newman, they were memories of a man: of a master-preacher in St Mary's, or of a great apostate, or of an austere, saintly teacher. What he advocated was indeed one pole

[48] Ker quotes (ibid., ed.'s introd., p.v.), J. M. Cameron's comment that 'modern thinking on university education is a series of footnotes to Newman's lectures and essays', but I hope only as a particular perception which he does not share. The same commentator has also said that the *Idea* is 'the most influential (I suppose) book yet written on university education' (J. M. Cameron, *On the Idea of a University* (Toronto, 1978), p. xi, see also p. 8). Perhaps, but I nowhere find the case proven.

[49] Ker speaks in his introduction (*Idea*, p. xxviii) of the 'almost total failure of the writings . . . to attract any serious attention or interest in their own time'.

of subsequent debate at Oxford (though not in the form which Newman believed it might have, but one much inferior, and perhaps unavoidably so). This was because Newman shared with very different men (Jowett, for example) a central idea about the university's institutional end: that its primary concern was education. From that blazed up much else: the locking of horns of tutors and professors, the rhetorical slighting of 'research', the idealization of the all-rounder as the characteristic product. But Newman should not be held responsible. Vested interest, social assumptions, inertia, and the self-generating biliousness of donnish controversy are sufficient explanations; we need not assume that people read his books. The inertia accumulated in the historic structures of Oxford and their serviceability to the great Victorian and imperial ideals is enough to explain both the success of a long rearguard action against other notions of the university and the nineteenth-century renewal of the unique influence of Oxford in our university system.

Newman has always been more read by intellectuals and academic publicists, than by those building or running universities (and even that can be exaggerated; citation is not a good measure of influence, thought it is, often, a good measure of the wish to acknowledge influence, and that says something about the wider issue).[50] But this does not mean that he may not indirectly have had a bad effect on the way we tend to debate university policy. People may not have read him, but they had heard of his title, and it suggested an essential university, almost a Platonic Idea of one, of which all actual universities would be but feeble examples, and to whose unity of being and purpose all should aspire. So, although his ideas were not applied consciously, he helped to shape in a general way the terms of future argument. His title thrust into the debate a large presumption that the university *should* have a single and an overriding purpose.

Given such reservations, what is there then left to admire in Newman? I have sometimes found myself thinking there was in fact not much point in reading the *Idea* except as a work of literature and a document in the history of ideas. Newman

[50] In the mass of English writing on universities between 1940 and 1960, only W. Moberley's book, *The Crisis in the University* (London, 1949) appears to me to make much use of Newman and that is because of the author's special concern about Christianity and theology in the universities.

operates at a level very remote from that of the wheelhorse vice-chancellor and the average don. It is probable that his idea of the university is non-utilizable in a morally disintegrated, pluralistic world. The cultivation of a satisfactory personal metaphysic such as he presupposes is now very difficult and perhaps an impossibility for most of us. Vast dislocations and needs impose themselves as educational priorities, brooking, because of our social and political arrangements, no delay—what can be the point of even considering the applicability of Newman's ideas to them? It is surely not enough to reply that he has written a masterpiece, true though that is. The status of a masterpiece is no longer thought to justify a prior claim upon attention. And even if it is not a waste of time to read him, it could be a mistake to debate (so to speak) with him. There are not, after all, many new ideas in his book, even if there are striking formulations of old ones. It is founded on luxurious premisses—about the possibility of encompassing universal knowledge in a single institution, about priorities and practical possibilities—which we can no longer accept. What is left?

There is an answer which I find sufficient. Newman is worth reading because he is the persuasive, inspiring advocate of an often wholesome and therefore sometimes useful mythology. He might well have hated that formulation; it carries no necessary connotation of truthfulness. Yet in the *Idea* he presents a vision with which those of us who are concerned with education should from time to time try to refresh ourselves, more especially at a time when the 'the incapacity to embody high ideals in great institutions is general'.[51] It is easy, moreover, to see that much which Newman says is coherent with much of what is usually regarded as the universities' best practice. It is not difficult to agree that education is more than instruction or training and that, if not solely, it must focus primarily on the individual. It reveals something about ourselves. This is how it comes to transform lives: by revealing his or her potential to the person undergoing it. If much education is the acquisition of an identity there is clearly a place for many means and instruments to play a

[51] J. Coulson, 'Newman's Idea of an Open University and its Consequences today', in J. D. Bastable (ed.), *Newman and Gladstone: Centennial Essays* (Dublin, 1978), 232.

part in it and the personal example Newman prized is certainly one, though one cannot institutionalize it.

One conclusion should be that we should not waste our time in trying to force new meaning upon or rewrite him as we cast about for nostrums applicable to our needs. We do not need to make him fit. We should, rather, praise him for turning our attention to certain topics, rather than for providing us with helpful formulas. Like many visions, Newman's can inspire, stimulate, and it can check. He can sometimes reanimate us to defend values now under threat. It is helpful to recall that an educated man is not a man who knows certain things, but a man whose mind has been formed in a certain way and who can take up a certain stance when confronted with new experience. It can also remind us of neglected detail; we have never needed more in this country Newman's emphasis on the importance in education of writing and of good language.

Reflection on the actual book as a whole though, when not under its immediate spell, seems to me to point to two rather unexciting conclusions. One is that it is no longer possible to write a book with such a title. If it carries implications of comprehensiveness or essentiality, *The Idea of a University* is no longer conceivable. No general doctrine of universities is possible. The idea of a particular university still is, for any specific university can have a goal and perhaps should. From this follows the other conclusion, that we must expect actual universities to contribute to the common good in different ways and different degree. That surely could be agreed easily, even by Newman himself.

11

Newman as a Philosopher

BASIL MITCHELL

Newman's importance as a philosopher is only now beginning to be acknowledged. Because the centre of his philosophical concern is theological he does not figure in the canon of British empiricism whose practitioners in the last hundred years have been predominantly hostile or indifferent to religious belief. Yet the fact that Newman was nevertheless firmly rooted in the empiricist tradition of Locke and Hume separated him from those idealist philosophers who, in Britain and the continent of Europe, continued to discuss religious themes in a philosophical vocabulary very different from Newman's. Although himself deeply influenced by the Romantic concern with the interior life and with historical development, he did not share the tendency, apparent in Schleiermacher and Matthew Arnold, to interpret the dogmatic assertions of Christianity as expressions merely of emotion, imagination, or will. Until quite recently he seemed simply irrelevant to the dominant concerns of either philosophers or theologians.

I

More than any other single philosopher, Newman engaged with Locke who, in book IV of the *Essay concerning Human Understanding* had insisted on the primacy of reason in religion. This involves:

> the not entertaining any proposition with greater assurance than the proofs it is built upon will warrant. Whatsoever credit or authority we give to any proposition more than it receives from the principles and proofs it supports itself on, is owing to our inclinations that way, and is so far a derogation from the love of truth as such; which, as it can receive no evidence from our passions or interests, so it should receive no tincture from them.[1]

[1] Locke, *An Essay concerning Human Understanding*, IV. xix. 1.

Locke's careful and sympathetic attempt to delimit the spheres of reason and revelation, while leaving the final judgement with reason, was felt by Newman to be profoundly unsatisfactory, albeit never to be dismissed out of hand. But this entire aspect of Locke's thought was of no interest to later empiricists who, under the influence of Berkeley and Hume, regarded it as a piece of outmoded and ill-assimilated rationalism. In that empiricist tradition, as it developed through Mill and Russell, Newman could only be regarded as engaging with an adversary who was no longer worth fighting on behalf of a 'reasonable faith' which was no longer defensible.

The Lockian scheme was simple and straightforward. That there is a God is a 'truth according to reason' provable by a combination of the cosmological and the teleological arguments. The existence of God is postulated to explain the fact that there is a world at all, together with the fact that it displays intelligible order. The God thus proved reveals to us further truths which human reason could not have established unaided, 'truths above reason'—that God is three persons, that there is a life to come—and the authority of this revelation is warranted by signs or 'evidences', in the shape of prophecy and miracles, which must convince any reasonable person. Faith, then, is belief founded 'on the credit of the proposer': God has spoken and men have reason to believe that he has spoken. The position is succinctly stated by Tillotson in a passage which Newman quoted in sermon XIII:

> 'Nothing ought to be received as a divine doctrine and revelation, *without good evidence* that it is so: that is, without some *argument* sufficient to *satisfy* a prudent and considerate man'.[2]

Newman's dissatisfaction with this scheme was primarily religious. From this standpoint it had three major defects:

1. It was excessively cerebral. Faith, on this account, was the outcome of an intellectual argument and, so long as the argument was apprehended and accepted, it was sufficient. It need not engross the entire personality.
2. By placing so much emphasis upon the satisfactory completion of a process of reasoning it effectively restricted

[2] *US*, p. 260.

faith to those who were intellectually capable of following the argument. It left no room for the simple believer.

3. The person to whom the argument was addressed was conceived of as an isolated individual. He belonged to no community and stood in no tradition. This was Christianity without the Church.

But Newman had at least two further criticisms of a more philosophical kind:

4. The account of the reasoning involved in the approach to faith was in itself inadequate. It represented an abstract conception of what reasoning ought to be like and bore no relation to the way in which concrete individuals actually think. 'He [Locke] consults his own ideal of how the mind ought to act, instead of interrogating human nature as an existing thing, or as it is found in the world'.[3]
5. As soon as attention is directed to the actual convictions of existing people and the way they are arrived at, it becomes apparent that they are not, and could not be, based solely upon the evidence available to the individual at any given time. The religious beliefs of most people, even the most devout and reflective, if limited to what could be based on such evidence, would have to be dismissed as having been formed upon somewhat weak grounds.

These criticisms of the Lockian pattern reinforced one another in Newman's mind in such a way as to generate an alternative scheme. If faith was not merely cerebral it must be connected with a man's whole character and, if this was so, the way in which different individuals viewed the evidence would profoundly affect the interpretation each put upon it. Arguments which appeared weak, when abstractly considered in terms of evidence that could readily be produced to any inquirer, could be strong when taken in conjunction with antecedent assumptions, themselves imbued with the character of the individual believer. Moreover, any such believer derives many, if not all, of his antecedent assumptions from some tradition of thought and practice whose history precedes him and whose present intellectual and imaginative resources far exceed his own. His character is largely formed by it. Because the simple believer can draw upon the tradition and identify

[3] *GA*, p. 109.

himself with it, his faith is not rendered inadequate by his admitted inability to provide a rational defence of it upon demand.

Newman developed these ideas initially in his *Oxford University Sermons* which represent for the most part a prolonged wrestling with the problem of the relationship between faith and reason as it had been forced upon him by the conflict between the two traditions to which he himself was heir—the Lockian tradition in philosophy and the Catholic renewal in the Church of England. The development of Newman's thought in this period exemplified in itself the kind of intellectual process that he was in the course of analysing and illuminating in the sermons. It is important to recognize in this connection that, although at this time Oxford was far from being a leading academic centre on a European scale, it fostered, partly because of its very parochialism, an intense spiritual and intellectual life. If Oxford was, in international terms, a backwater, it was one into which living streams from the past continued to flow. In philosophy the study of Plato and Aristotle (particularly the latter) complemented that of Locke, Berkeley, Hume, and Butler and in theology the thought of the patristic period was increasingly cultivated. Newman was able to draw upon these resources freely, and the task of reconciling these divergent traditions was of direct existential importance to him.

II

Newman's response to Locke was not to reject the claims of reason as such but to demand a much more subtle appreciation of the way reason works, not only in relation to religious truth but also in respect of all matters of serious importance. 'I shall attempt to show that Faith is not the only exercise of Reason, which, when critically examined, would be called unreasonable, and yet is not so.'[4] Newman undertook to show that reason in matters of religion did not operate differently from the way it worked in history, philosophy, or morality. Hence both in the *Oxford University Sermons* and, later, in the *Grammar of Assent* he extended his concern to the whole range of human inquiry. This means that, if Newman's thought is of philosophical interest today, that interest is not confined to theology and the philosophy

[4] *US*, p. 209.

of religion. It will be the contention of this essay that Newman identifies problems in epistemology which have only recently been recognized and offers the outlines of a solution to them.

Three themes in particular are to be found in Newman's treatment of reason:

1. Much of our reasoning is tacit and informal. It cannot be expressed in syllogistic form (for Newman the only form available to logic) but involves the continuous exercise of personal judgement operating upon a range of disparate considerations. 'It is the cumulation of probabilities, independent of each other, arising out of the nature and circumstances of the particular case which is under review; probabilities too fine to avail separately, too subtle and circuitous to be convertible into syllogisms, too numerous and various for such conversion, even were they convertible.'[5]

2. Most arguments upon matters of any substance are cumulative in form. They involve taking account of a range of considerations, none of which alone suffices to generate the required conclusion, but which together converge upon it. Newman has no difficulty in providing illustration of this informal and cumulative process of reasoning from everyday life:

> Let a person only call to mind the clear impression he has about matters of every day's occurrence, that this man is bent on a certain object, or that that man was displeased, or another suspicious; or that that one is happy, and another unhappy; and how much depends in such impressions on manner, voice, accent, words offered, silence instead of words, and all the many subtle symptoms which are felt by the mind, but cannot be contemplated; and let him consider how very poor an account he is able to give of his impression, if he avows it, and is called upon to justify it. This, indeed, is meant by what is called moral proof, in opposition to legal.[6]

3. There is no bar to the possibility of arguments of this type achieving certainty. The various considerations to which appeal is made may co-operate so effectively as to put a particular conclusion beyond reasonable doubt.

The effectiveness of Newman's account of reasoning as a contribution to Christian apologetics is apparent enough. The

[5] *GA*, p. 187. [6] *US*, p. 274.

hostile critic of theism is likely to proceed, in the manner of David Hume, by attacking the different elements in the Christian case piecemeal. The traditional proofs of the existence of God, he argues, do not succeed in demonstrating their conclusion and, so long as they are construed deductively, cannot reinforce each other. As a modern Humean, Professor A. G. N. Flew has expressed it epigrammatically, ten leaky buckets do not hold more water than one leaky bucket. Should the Christian apologist abandon the attempt to prove God's existence deductively, and endeavour instead to construct an inductive case, the critic retorts that the resulting argument is not very strong and that, moreover, in so far as it succeeds, it only shows that God's existence is more or less probable. But a probable God is no God, so that the conclusion of any such argument is inadequate as a basis for Christian faith. To this critique it is possible, following Newman, to reply that the very diverse arguments for the existence of God, although no single one of them is decisive in itself, nevertheless converge in such a way as to put the conclusion beyond all reasonable doubt. Christian belief is more like a many stranded rope than like ten leaky buckets. Newman, by drawing suitable analogies, has no difficulty in showing that in innumerable non-theological contexts, informal cumulative arguments can and do lead to conclusions that are certain.[7]

Newman, however, in attempting to show that Christian belief was capable of achieving certainty in this way was to face the charge that, although in principle an informal, cumulative argument may issue in conclusions which are certain, it manifestly fails to do so in the case of religion. An uncommitted and impartial mind must find the rational case based upon 'the evidences of Christianity' somewhat weak.

There are various possible responses to this line of attack.

1. One is simply to meet the challenge head on and to claim that, properly considered, the inductive argument for Christian theism is strong enough to yield the desired conclusion.

2. Another is to concede that the case is merely a probable

[7] Newman explains that 'I use probable as opposed to demonstrative, not to certainty' (*LD*, xi. 293, quoted by W. R. Fey, *Faith and Doubt* (Shepherdstown, 1976) 42). That probable i.e. inductive arguments may issue in certainty had been maintained by Reid against Locke, but the case is elaborated by Newman with much greater subtlety and wealth of illustration.

one, but to claim that it is, nevertheless, sufficient for its purpose. For its purpose is not to achieve speculative certainty, but rather to warrant practical confidence in the conclusion. There is need, on this showing, for a 'leap of faith', by which the transition is made between a given degree of speculative probability and the whole-hearted commitment of faith. This had been Butler's view and was to be classically developed by William James. There were certain choices in life that were, in James's words, 'lively, forced and momentous', and it was proper, indeed obligatory, to go beyond the available evidence and commit oneself to a decision. Newman gives expression to this view with great eloquence:

> We are so constituted, that if we insist upon being as sure as is conceivable, in every step of our course, we must be content to creep along the ground, and can never soar. If we are intended for great ends, we are called to great hazards; and, whereas we are given absolute certainty in nothing, we must in all things choose between doubt and inactivity.[8]

Newman later glossed this passage with a note which abated the force of 'absolute certainty in nothing', but he also later admitted that 'left to myself, I should be very much tempted to adopt Butler's view and understand credibility as probability upon which it is safe to act'.[9] Whether or not he actually at any time embraced this view, he clearly acknowledged it as an arguable position.

3. A further option is to concede the inadequacy of argument for Christian belief in so far as it is based on 'the evidence', but to insist that any such argument is inevitably incomplete, because no account has been taken of the antecedent assumptions which the particular reasoner brings to the evidence. This was the route which Newman chiefly chose to explore and it constitutes both the most original and the most problematic theme in his philosophy.

It was, as we have seen, a key element of Newman's strategy in confronting his empiricist opponents to insist on broadening the debate. Their attack on characteristic features of religious reasoning can to some extent be turned if he can show that features thought to be objectionable in the religious case are to

[8] *US*, p. 215.

[9] *LD*, xv. 456, quoted in Fey, *Faith and Doubt*, p. 51.

be found equally in non-religious cases. He thus constructs an *ad hominem* argument against Hume.

'As Faith may be viewed as opposed to Reason, in the popular sense of the latter word, it must not be overlooked that Unbelief is opposed to Reason also. Unbelief indeed considers itself especially rational, or critical of evidence; but it criticizes the evidence of Religion, only because it does not like it, and really goes upon presumptions and prejudices as much as Faith does, only presumptions of an opposite nature. . . . It considers a religious system so improbable, that it will not listen to the evidence of it.[10]

And it is a point in favour of Newman's emphasis upon antecedent assumptions that they are, on the face of it, found equally not only in debates about religion, but also in relation to our moral, political, and metaphysical convictions. He had noticed that disagreements on such matters commonly left the disputants passing one another in the dark. The experience was one which was felt with peculiar poignancy by the more sensitive minds of the nineteenth century and expressed most movingly and memorably by Matthew Arnold in *Dover Beach*:

> And we are here as on a darkling plain,
> Swept with confused clamour of struggle and flight,
> Where ignorant armies clash by night.

Newman, strikingly, employs the same analogy at the end of the tenth of his *Oxford University Sermons*: 'it is a sort of night battle, where each fights for himself, and friend and foe stand together'.[11]

III

Since it cannot be said that the experience is any rarer in our own time—it is only that we have come to take it for granted—Newman's analysis of it has a continuing relevance. Indeed it would be true to say that he had a sharper awareness of the problem it raises than any other philosopher up to the present day, with the possible exception of Wittgenstein. The question we are bound to ask is whether Newman is able to suggest a way of resolving the problem. The difficulty, evidently, is that the more persuasively we account for the fundamental disagreements

[10] *US*, p. 230. [11] *US*, p. 201.

about matters of importance that we actually encounter, in terms of antecedent assumptions, divergent traditions, and so on, the more impossible it seems to become to envisage any rational means of resolving the disagreements and reconciling the contending parties. The debate is commonly conceived to lie between those who claim that there are basic principles of rationality common to all the disputants and who are, therefore, hard put to it to account for the intensity of the experienced disagreements; and those who ascribe the latter to the coexistence of variant conceptual schemes which are ultimately incommensurable—and who are, therefore, unable to suggest how the disagreements might be resolved.

Newman's treatment of this issue illustrates the informal and unsystematic character of his thought. He constantly recurs to the theme, varying his terminology and applying it, apparently, to rather different things. It is as if he is trying to get a wide terrain into clear focus, directing his lens now in one direction, now in another, without at any stage piecing the results together in any single coherent picture.

What is common to his treatment of 'antecedent probabilities', 'presumptions', 'first principles' is that they are taken to predispose the mind to interpret and assess the evidence before it in a particular way, as it might not be interpreted and assessed by some other mind, operating with other assumptions. There is an implicit distinction between 'the evidence' or 'the evidences' which are, for the time-being at least, not in dispute and are readily available to any unprejudiced mind, and certain attitudes, approaches, traits of character, etc. which are brought to the evidence by the mind of the inquirer. What are these?

Sometimes they seem to be nothing more than certain propositions which are taken for granted for the time being by a particular person and lead him to interpret the evidence in a certain way. Thus there may be evidence that a healing miracle has occurred. Prayers have been said, hands laid on, and the invalid is cured of an ailment that has hitherto resisted medical treatment, the cure being inexplicable in terms of the current state of medical science. All this is 'the evidence' which is not in dispute. Confronted by this evidence Hume will argue that the incident, although inexplicable at present, will eventually turn out to be explicable in terms of a more adequate understanding of scientific laws than we at present possess. Where the evidence is provided by historical documents and the testimony is correspondingly weaker, he will insist that it is more reasonable to discount it and to deny the occurrence of a miracle than to accept that something has happened contrary to all observation and experience. He operates with entirely naturalistic assumptions. A devout Catholic, however, who believes that there is a loving and omnipotent God and that he can and does intervene in the historical process in answer to prayer, will take the evidence as showing that here was a genuine instance of such divine intervention. (Newman studied Hume's *Discourse on Miracles* closely and this is the sort of case he had very much in mind.)

In the case of such a disagreement the effect of uncovering the antecedent assumptions of the Humean and the Catholic would naturally be to broaden the area of debate. The question at issue now becomes not whether the evidence suffices to prove a miracle, but whether Christian theism as a total system of belief is or is not better grounded than Hume's naturalism. Nothing so far said implies that such a question could not be rationally decided.

Among antecedent assumptions also figure what may be called certain 'principles of rationality'. Rational inquiry cannot proceed without them and they themselves are incapable of proof. They are such principles as that our senses can be trusted (for the most part); that our memories are in general reliable, that the testimony of others is to be accepted unless it can be successfully challenged. We depend, similarly, on the general fidelity of our reasoning powers. Hence, as Newman puts it, we find ourselves in a 'state in which we must assume something to prove anything, and can gain nothing without a venture'.[12] That there are such principles is attested by the fact that we cannot deny them without at the same time presupposing them. By this token they have universal validity and do not simply reflect the temper of a particular mind. Only a determined sceptic would resist them and Newman is not attempting to rebut scepticism.

More controversially, Newman allows that the presence of certain needs or desires in one person rather than another may properly influence the interpretation of evidence. Having remarked that the practice of physical science not infrequently leads to

[12] *US*, p. 215.

atheism, he goes on: 'the practical safeguard against Atheism in the case of scientific inquirers is the inward need and desire, the inward experience of that Power, existing in the mind before and independently of their examination of His material world'.[13]

On the face of it this is a mere sanctioning of wishful thinking. Why should my desiring something to be the case or my feeling a need for it to be the case make it at all more likely for it to be the case? Whatever may be the answer to this question, it is worth noticing that Newman is once again reflecting a characteristically nineteenth-century concern, as voiced in Coleridge's cry:

> Evidences of Christianity: I am weary of the word. Make a man feel the want of it: rouse him, if you can, to the self-knowledge of his need of it.[14]

Both Newman and Coleridge show an awareness, conspicuously absent in Locke, of the relationship between reason and emotion. If there is a saving truth it cannot be discovered by those who are indifferent to it; they will not be alert to clues which, as Newman is always insisting, are often tenuous and subtle. Reason, as commonly understood, is too blunt an instrument:

> when we come to what is called Evidence, or, in popular language, exercises of Reason, prejudices and mental peculiarities are excluded from the discussion; we descend to grounds common to all; certain scientific rules and fixed standards for weighing testimony, and examining facts, are received. Nothing can be urged, or made to tell, but what all feel, all comprehend, all can put into words; current language becomes the measure of thought; only such conclusions may be drawn as can produce their reasons; only such reasons are in point as can be exhibited in simple propositions; the multiform and intricate assemblage of considerations, which really lead to judgement and action, must be attenuated or mutilated into a major and a minor premise.[15]

This is most readily seen in our judgements of people. We are not likely to understand and appreciate the motives of an individual person unless we are interested in him enough to enter into his world of thought and feeling in all its subtlety and complexity. Studied neutrality, and the language that goes with it, is not adequate to the task.

[13] *US*, p. 194.
[14] Coleridge, *Aids to Reflection* (London, 1825), 397.
[15] *US*, p. 229.

In the theological case Newman is perhaps going further than this example warrants. He believes that there is a saving truth, ignorance of which impoverishes and eventually destroys our lives. There is nothing we can need more than to know it and, in a Christian understanding of human nature, we must be presumed to want it. If, then, only the love of God can fulfil our nature, we need to be assured of the love of God, to be convinced that there is a God and that he is loving, in order to be satisfied. To be indifferent to the outcome of the inquiry is to be fatally inhibited from its pursuit. As to the risk of distortion through the influence of antecedent wishes, the presence of a wish works both ways. If I am in a storm at sea and desperately wish to see a well-known landmark, it is true that I am more likely to think I see it when I do not; but it is also true that I am more likely to detect it when it is there but hard to see. The question is which risk is the more worth running, that of hallucination through intense concern or of perceptual failure through indifference.

When Newman says 'On irreligious men evidences are thrown away' he nevertheless lays himself open to the charge of begging all the important questions from the start. It is, apparently, impossible to preach except to the converted. Yet this is clearly not his intention, as is sufficiently evidenced by his care in examining the rational foundations of belief.

Newman's meaning can, perhaps, best be seen by comparison with Aristotle's treatment of the relation between moral discernment and moral character, which doubtless influenced him. 'We become just men by doing just acts.'[16] Children must be taught to act justly and to seek justice before they are able to understand what justice is and why particular just acts are just. Someone who had been brought up with no experience of acting justly and had no inclination to act justly would not, through having had no bias imparted to him, be better placed than others to understand the nature of justice but would wholly lack the means of doing so. This consideration goes some way to mitigate the paradox of Newman's contention:

> since probabilities have no definite ascertained value, and are reducible to no scientific standard, what are such to each individual, depends on his moral temperament. A good and a bad man will think very different things probable.[17]

[16] Aristotle, *Nicomachean Ethics*, 1103^{b}1.

[17] *US*, p. 191.

More generally, Newman sometimes speaks of the importance for a proper reading of the evidence of a certain 'temper of mind':

> But in truth, though a given evidence does not vary in force, the antecedent probability attending it does vary without limit, according to the temper of the mind surveying it.[18]

By this he seems to mean something other than the acceptance of certain presuppositions that could, if necessary, be stated, but are taken for granted in the present inquiry; also something other than the 'needs and desires' we have just been discussing. These latter pertain to human nature in general, whereas the 'temper of mind' is a more individual thing (although of course individuals may resemble one another in temper of mind). Newman can be taken, in the first instance, to be simply noting, as a matter of observation, that people differ in the way they approach a given subject matter and often differ systematically. These differences do, observably, affect their assessment of evidence and the conclusions drawn from it. The phenomenon is, perhaps, most clearly recognizable in the thinking of judges, because it is always subject to uniform constraints which allow individual differences to become apparent. Different judges have before them the same admitted evidence and the same law as set out in statute or embodied in precedent. Judges are obliged to put aside their personal preferences and administer the law of the land. Yet they often interpret the law differently, and the judgements of a particular judge can be seen over time to exhibit a coherent 'philosophy' which stamps them as the product of an individual judicial mind. Newman's expression 'a certain temper of mind' is peculiarly appropriate to the judicial career of, in our own time, Lord Denning. Denning's approach to the law assumes that the law should not only make sense, but make good sense, and together with this conviction goes a certain adventurousness and a discernible impatience with more cautious and conservative minds.

That, as a matter of observation, people's reading of evidence is affected by their temper of mind in this way is undeniable, but whether this is, as Newman seems to believe, a desirable circumstance or rather, as many would think, a more or less unavoidable

[18] *US*, p. 193.

human weakness, remains to be decided. Newman seems to be maintaining that some tempers of mind are wrong, without implying that only one temper of mind is right. His view seems to be that there is an irreducibly personal colouring to people's convictions on serious matters and that, within limits, this variety is desirable.

There are occasions when Newman seems to include among antecedent assumptions certain kinds of experience without which particular types of evidence cannot be understood. In a passage already quoted he speaks of 'the inward need and desire, the inward experience of that Power, existing in the mind'. Similarly he refers to 'that instinctive apprehension of the Omnipresence of God and His unwearied and minute Providence which holiness and love create within us', without which 'the evidence of Christianity does not perform an office which was never intended for it,—*viz* that of recommending itself as well as the Revelation'.[19]

Newman does not, as a rule, make explicit use of what has become known as 'the Argument from Religious Experience'. He retains too much of the eighteenth-century suspicion of 'enthusiasm'. Yet he does attach importance to an underlying awareness of God which is not based on inference and gives life to 'evidences' which would otherwise be ineffective to awaken faith.

IV

Any attempt to assess Newman's contribution to philosophy must address two questions: to what extent did he identify genuine and important problems; and to what extent did he succeed in resolving them? As we saw earlier, for much of the period that has elapsed since his death it must have seemed that his predominant concerns were simply irrelevant to the development of philosophy. Philosophy of religion was itself increasingly peripheral to the interests of professional philosophers and, within the philosophy of religion, the central question was taken to be that of the meaning of theological utterances. The outstanding challenge to the whole theological enterprise was taken to consist in the problematic character of theological claims as

[19] *US*, p. 214.

judged by the standards of scientific thought. Whether these were articulated crudely in terms of verifiability or in more sophisticated ways, it was generally taken for granted that theology could not satisfy them. Hence the task for the Christian apologist was either to show how religious utterances could be factually meaningful in spite of their non-scientific character; or to give an alternative account of their meaning which would not put them in competition with science at all. The running was made, for the most part, by the second of these two strategies, and a tradition developed among theologians from Kant by way of Schleiermacher and Kierkegaard to Bultmann and his successors in which it was regarded as a fundamental mistake to interpret theological doctrines as involving any attempt to describe or explain the way things are. The entire realm of fact belonged to the sciences; to religion belonged the sphere of emotion, imagination, and existential choice. Hence the task for defenders of religious faith was to establish its credentials as a valid aspect of human experience in a culture in which science was accepted as the dominant influence upon our way of understanding the world. To thinkers preoccupied with this range of problems Newman had nothing to say.

What more than anything else has altered the situation and restored Newman to decisive relevance are developments in the philosophy of science, which have, for the first time in the modern era, cast doubt upon the credentials of science itself as an avenue to truth. 'The difficulty', writes Alvin Plantinga, 'concerns the adequacy of the canons of justification implicit in science and ordinary linguistic practice—what reason is there to suppose that they guide us towards the truth?'[20] Philosophers of science have argued, with some plausibility, that modern physics represents an intellectual tradition with its own internal standards of rationality, which are different from though not demonstrably superior to, those of Newton—or, indeed, of Aristotle. The claim that modern physics is more coherent and comprehensive than its predecessors and, therefore, approximates more closely to the truth, is one that can, no doubt, reasonably be urged, but this claim does not any longer enjoy its earlier non-controversial status. Scientists who wish to vindicate their capacity to discover

[20] In an unpublished lecture.

the intelligible but unseen structure of the physical world can no longer simply take it for granted, but are required to make out a case. Hence the paradigm instance of factual knowledge, by comparison with which the claims of religion were thought to be problematic, can no longer be made to serve this purpose. Yet, of course, scientists do unhesitatingly rely upon the validity of scientific method and so do all westernly educated people. It is a mark of 'modernity' so to do. Their situation is, thus, curiously analogous to that in which Newman found himself as he struggled to analyse the nature of reason and its relation to Christian faith.

That these problems have arisen in connection with natural science has forced people to take them seriously, because there is not, in this case, the simple expedient available of taking refuge in some alternative system of knowledge supposed to be altogether untouched by these problems, such as science had appeared to provide to earlier philosophers and theologians when faced with difficulties about religious faith. But, of course, the issues raised in this debate between realism and anti-realism, rationalism and anti-rationalism, are not confined to the realm of the sciences. If it is at least arguable that Newtonian science represents an intellectual tradition having its own internal standards of meaning and truth which are strictly incommensurable with those of Einsteinian science, with the apparent implication that no rational choice can be made between them; so that neither can claim to represent, or even approximate to, the truth about things, the same charge must lie *a fortiori* against rival schools of psychology, history, literary criticism, philosophy, theology. And in so far as these problems can be resolved in relation to natural science, the possibility must be taken seriously that they can be resolved in relation to these other disciplines also. What is at issue with regard to all of them is whether their status can be established as rational disciplines capable of achieving truth.

V

But this, as we have seen, is precisely Newman's central concern. He was convinced that the Christian faith is true. Hence he was not tempted by Matthew Arnold's conception of religion as 'morality touched with emotion'. He was convinced also of its rationality and retained all the Lockian distrust of 'enthusiasm'.

But it was apparent to him that Christian faith was not rational as rationality was commonly understood by philosophers in the tradition of Locke. It was necessary, therefore, for him to explore other conceptions of rationality and, in so doing, to attend carefully to the ways in which men actually reason, especially when dealing with substantial questions of great complexity. It was essential to this enterprise to venture beyond the confines of religious thought and to consider how, for instance, men think in assessing one another's motives or developing a historical argument. He noticed that, even when people agree as to the evidence, their treatment of it is influenced by presuppositions of various kinds, some of them virtually universal, some deriving from a particular tradition in which they stand, some reflecting their own peculiar temper of mind. He was, therefore, highly sensitive to the considerations which have tempted so many modern minds to relativism—to such an extent, indeed, that some of his own pronouncements sound distinctly relativist, as in the words that terminate his tenth university sermon: 'When men understand each other's meaning, they see, for the most part, that controversy is either superfluous or hopeless'.[21]

'Examine your deepest convictions', Newman seems to be saying, 'and you will find that it is in these, philosophically suspect, ways that you actually arrive at them. You cannot in fact proceed otherwise. Why, then, should you be persuaded by philosophers to find fault with them?' This strain in Newman's thought anticipates Wittgenstein: there is no appeal from our actual practices, whether in thinking or acting, to any ideal, would-be neutral, standard of rationality.

But, in so far as Newman does resemble Wittgenstein, his account raises the same problems as notoriously attend Wittgenstein's. Utterances are to be understood in relation to the appropriate 'language-game' and 'language-games' relate to 'forms of life' which alone make them intelligible. But how, in that case, can any kind of rational choice be made between forms of life? Newman's language is different but we are similarly led to ask how, on his account, Christian faith can be rational if, as he seems to be maintaining, it is necessary to have had one's moral and intellectual being shaped by Christianity before one

[21] *US*, p. 201.

can understand and appreciate the rational case for Christian belief. Would not a Moslem or a Marxist, similarly shaped by his 'form of life', be equally entitled to claim truth for his beliefs?

Newman's thought can be described as 'dialectical' in the straightforward sense that his emphasis at any time depends upon who it is that he is arguing with at that time. Most of the time (especially in the university sermons) he is arguing with Whately and his other Oriel colleagues who champion the claims of reason as understood by Locke. Sometimes (less often) he is facing the other way and confronting those who think of faith as a basic commitment which is independent of reason, either because we enjoy a kind of direct awareness of God or because we can rely unquestioningly on scripture or some other religious authority. Comparatively rarely does he attempt to systematize the conclusions of these separate dialogues. Yet it seems clear that, on balance, Newman does want to admit the need for proofs, although it is the necessary qualifications of this admission that he is most anxious to stress:

> Nothing need be detracted from the use of the Evidences on this score; much less can any sober mind run into the wild notion that actually no proof at all is implied in the maintenance, or may be exacted for the profession of Christianity. I would only maintain that proof need not be the subject of analysis, or take a methodical form, or be complete and symmetrical, in the believing mind; and that probability is its life.[22]

Newman then is, undoubtedly, a rationalist of some kind, albeit one who is sensitive to the many different ways in which rationality can be manifested. But, if so, he is inescapably exposed to the question we formulated earlier. Has he not given so much weight to the role of antecedent assumptions in all their rich variety as to render it impossible, even in principle, to adjudicate between the claims of rival traditions?

Locke, as we have seen, does not have this problem. He maintains (1) that the claims of revelation need to be supported by reasons; (2) that reasons are in fact available of a kind that can be stated and should satisfy any reasonable mind. On consideration, however, (2) turns out to be ambiguous. Does it mean that the individual ought not to believe (i.e. is not justified in believing) unless he or she can produce reasons; or that reasons must be

[22] *US*, pp. 199–200.

available within the tradition? Newman is clear in his answer to the first of these alternatives. It is not, in his view, necessary that the individual believer should be able to produce reasons—otherwise all 'simple believers' would be ruled out. And he has no difficulty in showing that, in other spheres than that of religion, we naturally, and surely justifiably, rely on authority or common sense for most of our opinions. He is less clear on the second alternative (partly because he does not always distinguish it from the first). There would seem to be two possible answers:

1. There must be reasons available within the tradition, although there is no need, and perhaps, no possibility, that individual believers should be able to cite them, let alone articulate them, on demand.
2. There need not be reasons even within the tradition, if 'reasons' means considerations, however subtle and various, which are relied upon to *justify* the central claims of the tradition.

As a rationalist Newman seems to be committed to the first of these answers, and it is at this point that he makes contact with contemporary debates in the philosophy of religion.

VI

The Lockian position (very much more thoroughly worked out) has been developed by R. G. Swinburne in his book *The Existence of God*. Swinburne holds that faith requires to be supported by evidence and that the evidence is provided by a range of considerations—that there is a world, that it displays intelligible order, that there is consciousness, that many people claim to be aware of the presence of God—which are best explained by the hypothesis that there is a personal creator. This position is opposed by, among others, Plantinga, who claims to detect in Swinburne's account the error of 'foundationalism'. For the 'foundationalist' it is rational for someone to accept a proposition only if the proposition itself is self-evident or incorrigible or evident to the senses, or if it is supported by other such propositions, which are 'properly basic' for him. Plantinga rejects foundationalism and defends the right of the Christian believer to hold belief in God as 'properly basic'. This does not, he insists, make him a fideist because he is maintaining that it is, precisely, *rational* to take God's existence as properly basic.

Plantinga's thesis has undergone substantial recensions since it was first put forward and is now markedly closer to Newman's, and indeed to Swinburne's, than it originally was. Thus the error of foundationalism now consists in holding that one's 'noetic structure' requires to be based upon *propositions* that are foundational. There is no objection to beliefs that are properly basic resting on *grounds* that are not propositional and Plantinga admits that belief in God characteristically rests on such grounds as a sense of the presence of God, conscience experienced as the voice of God, the feeling of the Holy Spirit at work in our lives, and so on. Taken together with the testimony of others to similar experiences all this provides warrant for reading the evidence available to us in a theistic way, and the Christian believer is entitled so to read it unless this whole scheme of thought can be successfully challenged.

How this process might operate is well shown in the argument from conscience, which both Newman and Plantinga employ. Plantinga sketches an argument to the effect that the strong sense of the objectivity of right and wrong which many of us have cannot be accounted for by any naturalistic theory of human nature, but can only be explained in terms of God as creator and legislator. Newman explores the route from conscience to God rather more exhaustively but in a way that should approve itself to Plantinga. We experience conscience as exerting an authority which we cannot identify with any element in our own nature. Moreover the deliverances of conscience evoke in us emotions of fear and reverence which only a person can properly inspire. So we are right to conclude, according to Newman, that through our conscience we know God. Do we, then, know God in conscience directly or by inference? Newman is inclined, I think, to regard these as false alternatives; it is not, simply, a matter of direct awareness, because it requires thought to tell us what it is that we are aware of; it is not, simply, a matter of inference, because that implies that the conclusion that there is a God remains abstract and impersonal.

The ultimate question, with Newman as with Plantinga, is how to avoid the charge of circularity or arbitrariness. The greater the sensitivity of both thinkers to the informality of the cumulative arguments we habitually employ, and the role of personal judgement in evaluating them, influenced as this is bound to be by the individual's personal cast of mind and the tradition in which he stands, the greater the plausibility of the objection that the body of evidence to which appeal is made only gives support to the system of belief in favour of which it is adduced to the extent that it is interpreted in terms of that system, for it is this which supplies the presumptions or antecedent probabilities whose importance is constantly emphasized.

Newman and Plantinga both seek to mitigate the severity of the problem by insisting that God has created in us certain tendencies or dispositions to believe, which will make themselves felt in our actual beliefs so long as the latter are not diluted or distorted by sin. This is, in effect, a theistic version of Hume's appeal to nature as a remedy for scepticism. As an element in a theistic world view it has its place; but it manifestly begs the question against any opponent who sees no reason to believe in God. Of what use is it to claim that God has instilled in us a natural tendency to hear his voice in the dictates of conscience, if we do not believe in God and if our conscience, formed by a different cultural tradition, does not issue categorical commands which inspire in us the emotions of fear and reverence?

Part of the answer, no doubt, to this objection is that some of Newman's antecedent probabilities are in fact neutral as between systems of belief. No system of belief can maintain itself without relying on memory, testimony or the senses. Similarly, as Newman was continually insisting, there are innumerable facts of a kind that are not in dispute between the parties to any given debate, and which are often such as to be at least as certain as any evidence that might be brought against them. Not everything can be doubted all the time. But, as he was well aware, such neutrality is not always available. It is, indeed, one of his main contentions that there is no secure and substantial standpoint which an individual can occupy from which he can adjudicate as a neutral arbiter between contending convictions. Were there, *per impossibile*, such a situation, the individual occupying it would be capable of only notional assent and would, indeed, because lacking an identifiable character, scarcely be recognizable as a human being.

VII

One possibility remains. It is that a rational resolution of disputes between rival traditions does not depend upon the availability of such a neutral standpoint. Both Newman and Plantinga concede that antecedent presumptions may need revision in the light of fresh experience or hostile theories. This requires that the experiences should be genuine and the theories well founded. Whether they are so may sometimes be immediately obvious; their relevance may just not have been noticed. But more often their credentials will need to be critically examined. Thus Newman's account of conscience is incompatible with Freud's and must find some answer to the Freudian claim that the categorical demands of conscience originate with the commands of a human father and need no other explanation. Freud's views, for their part, take for granted a background of scientific determinism and metaphysical materialism. In Newman's terms these constitute Freud's antecedent assumptions. And the contrast between these assumptions and Newman's provides, at first sight, a clear case in which 'when men understand each other's meaning, they see, for the most part, that controversy is either superfluous or hopeless'. But Newman's own account of reasoning shows how, nevertheless, progress can be made, in principle at least, towards a resolution of the dispute. When, by an effort of sympathetic imagination, each participant in the debate has come to understand the other's position in all its complexity, it is possible to consider how well each position is able to accommodate the strengths of the other and to remedy its own weaknesses. Freud, notoriously, has difficulty in accounting for the capacity of conscience to criticize prevailing standards, and Newman is somewhat unconvincing in his treatment of the underdeveloped or corrupt conscience. Newman's Freudian critic will generally not, if pressed, be prepared to sanction a conscience inured to racial prejudice; and Newman must admit that the sort of conscience he appeals to is developed in some cultural traditions and not in others. Newman can, however, make this admission consistently with his principles, for he has all along insisted upon the role of a sound tradition in forming consciences. In his overall account of reasoning he has the resources to recognize and remedy his inadequacies. Freud's system is less flexible and can meet criticism only by submitting to substantial revision of its original mechanistic assumptions.

But does not this example serve only to intensify the problem? Newman appeals to conscience as a witness to God's existence, but only consciences formed in a certain tradition will provide the support he needs. Is he not, then, arguing in a circle? In replying to this challenge Newman is entitled to employ his customary tactic of inviting us to consider analogous cases outside the religious, or in this case, the ethical field. There is, after all, nothing controversial in the claim that innate sensitivity and rigorous training are required for the discovery and recognition of certain truths, whether in relation to quantum mechanics or the poetry of T. S. Eliot. If, in such cases, there is a truth of the matter, not everyone will be equipped to grasp it. It does not follow from this admission that there is no truth of the matter and no rational means of assessing it. To be sure, there might be independent grounds for supposing that in some areas, for example the interpretation of poetry or the appreciation of music, what we call 'the truth' has no objective validity, but is the expression merely of the creative judgement of individuals or groups. In that case we could study the psychological or sociological factors which lead them to judge in just the way they do. But, in the absence or insufficiency of such grounds, the fact that there are certain pre-conditions for the exercise of literary or musical discrimination does not favour a subjectivist analysis. It is only if the evidence is approached with subjectivist assumptions in the first instance that it appears to do so.

This is the case even where the individual's 'temper of mind' is among the factors which influence judgement. It may call for a certain 'temper of mind' which not everyone has, which may, indeed, be extremely rare, for particular insights to be achieved, which are then for the first time available for others to take over. Consider the genius of an Augustine or a Rousseau. What is needed in these others is the imagination to comprehend what they could not have discovered, and the capacity to recognize how the fresh insights thus achieved render the existing pattern of knowledge more intelligible and more coherent.

It is an essential feature of Newman's account, that, although principles of rationality are involved in reasoning, they do not completely exhaust its resources, for it may always be necessary to modify them or weigh them against one another; and for this no rules are available. Yet the total outcome can reasonably be judged successful or unsuccessful. As he says of the mind, in one of his boldest similes:

and thus it makes progress not unlike a clamberer on a steep cliff, who, by quick eye, prompt hand, and firm foot, ascends how he knows not himself, by personal endowments and by practice, rather than by rule, leaving no track behind him, and unable to teach another. It is not too much to say that the stepping by which great geniuses scale the mountains of truth is as unsafe and precarious to men in general, as the ascent of a skilful mountaineer up a literal crag. It is a way which they alone can take; and its justification lies in their success.[23]

[23] *US*, p. 257.

12

Newman's Vindication of Faith in the *Grammar of Assent*

HUGO MEYNELL

The *Grammar of Assent* is arguably Newman's most solid intellectual achievement, but it has been prone to a surprisingly wide range of interpretations, and both the bearing and the soundness of its basic contentions and arguments have been very differently assessed. Of the many questions liable to strike serious readers of the work, two are perhaps outstanding. (1) Does Newman's account of the business of human reasoning in general hit it off? (2) If so, does reasoning as Newman conceives it really lead to the conclusions which he supposes that it does?[1]

Newman is especially at pains to defend the claim of the ordinary non-intellectual believer to have a reasonable faith—this is the point of his famous example of the factory girl.[2] It is easy to jump to the conclusion that he can only do this at the cost of a dismissive attitude to all reasoning that is really worth the name.[3] If Newman's factory girl is reasonable in her faith, it might be protested, what would it be for anyone to be unreasonable about anything? In effect, Newman attempts to meet this point by representing the faith of simple believers as having a kind of implicit and not-spelled-out rationality about it. One might ask, apropos of the factory girl, 'for such unreflective persons, isn't any stupid dogmatism as good as another?' But Newman maintains that there is a kind of implicit grasp of intellectual and moral appropriateness of their faith in the multitude of ordinary believers, which *could* be spelled out, but in fact generally is *not*. For example, it rings true to their moral sensibility, it influences their conduct in general for the better,

[1] I shall try to provide reasons for dissenting from Jay Newman's conclusion that 'most of the major theses in the *Grammar* are false, and most of its major arguments are unsound' (Jay Newman, *The Mental Philosophy of John Henry Newman* (Waterloo, 1986), 196).

[2] *GA*, p. 202.

[3] Jay Newman, *Mental Philosophy*, *passim*.

and it persistently brings strength and consolation in times of stress or trouble.[4] The same considerations would of course apply to other forms of faith and belief than Roman Catholic Christianity. However, Newman makes clear enough, and supports at length with argument, his view that such considerations, in the case of other religions and denominations, would tend to confirm only what they have in common with Roman Catholic Christianity; and that a wider consideration of evidence, and a deeper seeking and finding of reasons would tend to disconfirm them so far as they differed from it.

On the nature of sound judgement in general, Newman wants to say that such judgement characteristically occurs on the basis of an accumulation of confirmations such as cannot be reduced to rule. Evidence converges on a judgement, he maintains, rather as a regular polygon tends towards the form of a circle, the more the number of its sides is increased, without ever quite attaining it. One is reminded of William Whewell's view that sound judgement in science is a matter of 'consilience of inductions'.[5]

> It is by the strength, variety, or multiplicity of premisses, which are only probable, not by invincible syllogisms,—by objections overcome, by adverse theories neutralized, by difficulties clearing up, by exceptions proving the rule, by unlooked-for correlations found for received truths, by suspense and delay in the process issuing in triumphant reactions,—by all these ways, and by many others, it is that the practised and experienced mind is able to make a sure divination.[6]

To illustrate his point, Newman provides quite detailed analyses, culled from the works of contemporary authorities, of actual processes of reason applied in science to establish the rotation of the earth, and in law to arrive at the truth in criminal prosecutions.[7] The point of all his examples is 'to illustrate the intellectual

[4] *GA*, p. 139.

[5] By way of explanation of Whewell's notion, Stephen Jay Gould wrote recently: 'We must see if a set of results so diverse that no one had ever considered their potential coordination might jump together as the varied products of a single process. Thus plate tectonics can explain magnetic stripes on the sea floor, the rise and later erosion of the Appalachians, the earthquakes of Lisbon and San Francisco, the eruption of Mount St. Helens, the presence of large flightless ground birds only on continents once united as Gondwanaland, and the discovery of fossil coal in Antarctica' (Gould, 'Darwinism Defined: The Difference between Fact and Theory', *Discover* 8/1 (1987), 70).

[6] *GA*, p. 208.

[7] *GA*, pp. 206, 212.

process by which we pass from conditional inference to unconditional assent'.[8] The kind of reasoning involved is exemplified both by ordinary human beings and by persons of genius, by 'those who know nothing of intellectual aids and rules, and those who care nothing for them'.[9] In some extreme cases, a person may not only be unable precisely to articulate the process by which she proceeds from evidence to conclusion, but may not be capable of stating what the evidence is. A countryman who is a successful weather prophet may not be able to supply the reasons for his predictions, or he may even give the wrong reasons. 'His mind does not proceed step by step, but he feels all at once and together the force of various combined phenomena, though he is not conscious of them.' In a similar manner, doctors of medicine may excel in diagnosis, without being able to defend their diagnoses to their medical peers.[10]

Newman suggests that our usual processes of reasoning about matters of fact are related to logical rules rather as poetry is to the canons of literary criticism; however applicable these may be to poetry, as he says, no one ever became a poet by following them.[11] Opinions differ on whether, and if so how far, Newman underestimated logic.[12] This is a dispute into which I do not care to be drawn. Suffice it to say, that Newman *does* assign a place to logic in confirming truth and detecting falsehood; but denies that it does play, or even can or ought to play, the dominant role in the business of getting to know about things.[13] Thus far at least it is difficult to disagree with him. It is by now notorious that the business of excogitating theories and hypotheses in any area of inquiry is a matter which cannot be reduced to logic; and just the same applies to the matching of such hypotheses with phenomena supposed to corroborate or to falsify them.[14] Yet for all that, logic does vastly facilitate the process of coming to know. Both these points are perfectly consistent with what

[8] *GA*, p. 213.
[9] *GA*, p. 214.
[10] *GA*, p. 214.
[11] *GA*, p. 214.
[12] Cf. Jay Newman, *Mental Philosophy*, pp. 136–8. This author cites Johannes Artz for the opinion that Newman does not undervalue logically formulated proof, N. D. O'Donoghue for the view that he does.
[13] See *GA*, pp. 181–5.
[14] Sir Karl Popper has been especially at pains to stress the first point in his work; Thomas Kuhn and Paul Feyerabend the second. See K. Popper, *Objective Knowledge* (Oxford, 1972); I. Lakatos and A. Musgrave (eds.), *Criticism and the Growth of Knowledge* (Cambridge, 1970).

Newman has to say about the subject. Newman has been taken to task for failing to take into account the first stirrings of modern non-Aristotelian logic, which had taken place before he wrote the *Grammar of Assent*.[15] This reproach may be justified; but I do not think that it greatly affects Newman's case. It is surely highly questionable whether the problems of 'induction', of the rational move from evidence to judgement with which Newman is concerned, are dealt with by the new logic any more satisfactorily than by the old.

When it comes to religion, Newman approvingly cites the great Anglican apologist Joseph Butler, to the effect that the same kind of cumulative argument as that already described in science and law may justly afford us certainty about the Christian revelation, where we find 'the same absence of demonstration of the thesis, the same cumulating and converging indications of it, the same indirectness in the proof . . ., the same recognition nevertheless that the conclusion is not only probable, but true'.[16] Butler does admit that there is one factor to be taken into account in religious matters which hardly applies in, say, astronomy; the moral state of the inquirers. They must be 'as much in earnest about religion, as about their temporal affairs'.[17] This is a consideration which weighs heavily with Newman, who evinces a distaste for commendations of religion which do not appeal to the subject's conscience.[18] The objection might be made that such appeals to moral sensibility are themselves a concession to irrationalism; but I think that this would be a mistake, as may be shown by many examples outside the realm of religion. If I happen to dislike a person, or hold a grudge against her, I may overstress the evidence that she is a cheat or a liar, and tend to brush aside such evidence as seems to impugn the claim. A man who has got away with dishonesty or cruelty may similarly have substantial motives for underplaying, both to himself and to others, such evidence as there may be which favours theism or Christianity. Few persons are so virtuous as unequivocally to *want*, say, the doctrine of the Last Judgement to be true.

But in general, Newman wants to stress the continuity between the kind of reasoning suitable in religious matters and that which applies to science and to ordinary life. One might sum up his

[15] Jay Newman, *Mental Philosophy*, p. 137.
[16] *GA*, p. 207. [17] *GA*, p. 207. [18] *GA*, p. 273.

fundamental point as to the effect that one ought to be content, in religion as elsewhere, with a convergence of many little confirmations, interlocking and mutually supporting, none by any means indisputable in itself, but properly carrying conviction in aggregate. If one withholds assent from some religious doctrine on the ground that, while confirmed by a multitude of interlocking data, it is not susceptible of strict demonstration, by what right does one not withhold it from such universally accepted opinions as the truth of the heliocentric cosmology, and (Newman's own favourite example) that Great Britain is an island?

So much for Newman's account of what it is to have adequate grounds for one's judgements; how does he think it should be applied to the case of Catholic Christianity? Very roughly and summarily, he maintains that there is a kind of religious and moral sensibility almost universal among humankind, for all that it may atrophy through being neglected or overlaid, which makes us aware of God as creator and judge, and leads us to expect some more detailed revelation of God's nature and purposes for us. Christianity fulfils the requirements of such an expected revelation as no other religion does, and when consistently and thoroughly thought through issues in the special doctrines of Roman Catholicism.

Newman reminds the reader of the weight he places on Aristotle's point, 'that a special preparation of mind is required for each separate department of inquiry and discussion (excepting, of course, that of abstract science)'.[19] Thus his review of Christianity is meant to appeal to 'those only whose minds are properly prepared for it';[20] he does not purport to establish its truth to, for example, a cynical worldling who has no sense of sin. Arguments of a strictly abstract nature, like those presented by William Paley in his *Evidences of Christianity*, are slick and clever; but as for Newman himself, 'I say plainly I do not care to overcome' the reason of others 'without touching their hearts. I wish to deal, not with controversialists, but with inquirers.'[21] There are certain fundamental moral principles, as Newman sees it, which are witnessed to by the general religious sense of humankind, as we find it manifested in the pagan religions. For

[19] *GA*, p. 266. [20] *GA*, p. 267. [21] *GA*, p. 273.

all the corruption evident in these, they have reverenced purity even if they have not practised it, 'hospitality has been a sacred duty, and dishonesty and injustice have been under a ban . . . I take our natural sense of right and wrong as the standard for determining the characteristics of Natural Religion.' And this provides us with a criterion by which any purported revelation of God may be tested—it could not contradict our basic moral sense.[22] Closely connected to our sense of right and wrong is our expectation or fear of divine retribution for bad conduct.[23] For all that the office of punishment has not been committed to human beings at large, imperfect and guilty as they are, even in our own case it is not wrong to harbour 'anger and indignation against cruelty and injustice', or 'desire that the false, the ungrateful, and the depraved should meet with punishment'. We may even say that 'retributive justice is the very attribute under which God is primarily brought before us in the teachings of our natural conscience'.[24] One of the most important effects of natural religion is the anticipation which it creates that a revelation will be given. 'Those who know nothing of the wounds of the soul, are not led to deal with the question . . .; but when our attention is roused, then, the more steadily we dwell upon it, the more probable does it seem that a revelation has been or will be given to us.' This conviction is founded on our sense of the goodness of God on the one hand, and of our extreme need on the other.[25] Some would take this as 'almost a proof, without direct evidence, of the divinity of a religion claiming to be true, supposing its history and doctrine are free from positive objection, and there be no rival religion with plausible claims of its own'.[26]

Newman concludes that 'there is only one religion in the world which tends to fulfil the aspirations, needs, and foreshadowings of natural faith and devotion'. He anticipates the objection that, having been educated in Christianity, he merely judges it in the light of its own principles. On the contrary, he insists, he has deliberately taken his idea of what a revelation ought to be from

[22] *GA*, p. 269.

[23] There is a poignant expression of this in *King Lear*, III. vii. The servant of the Duke of Cornwall has just witnessed the blinding of the Duke of Gloucester at the hands of his master; and exclaims: 'I'll never care what wickedness I do | If this man comes to good.'

[24] *GA*, p. 270. [25] *GA*, p. 272. [26] *GA*, p. 272.

actual non-Christian religions; and the ethical conceptions on which it is based derive largely from heathen moralists. And Christianity alone 'has a definite message addressed to all mankind'. Islam appears to have brought into the world no new doctrine whatever, except that of its own divine origin; 'and the character of its teaching is too exact a reflection of the race, time, place, and climate in which it arose, to admit of its becoming universal'. This last point applies, so far as Newman knows, to the religions of the Far East as well; and he is not aware of any definite messsage from God to humanity which they convey and protect.[27] Christianity, on the other hand, is characterized by such a message, and is found among all nations, in all climates, in every rank of society, and under every degree of civilization.[28]

It is important to note the distinction between what Newman calls 'natural religion' and what has traditionally been called 'natural theology'. 'Natural religion', as Newman describes it, is supposed to be present in persons of all cultural backgrounds and levels of intellectual attainment. A sense of right and wrong, which is so universal among human beings as properly to be called 'natural', places before our imagination the idea of an almighty judge who will ultimately bring us all to account. 'Natural theology' is a much more specialized affair; it involves the rational examination of arguments for and against the existence of something like the God worshipped by many of the traditional religions, and an investigation of what can be known of such a being, given that its existence can be established. 'Natural theology' and 'natural religion' in this sense have little in common, other than that they may each be regarded as a basis for the attempt to convince someone that she ought to espouse, or ought not to abandon, some form of theistic religious faith.

Newman's attitude to natural theology seems to me ambiguous, and not always self-consistent. At times he appears to imply that it is a legitimate activity, but not one with which he is personally concerned, or for which he feels that he has an aptitude. On other occasions—for example in his comments on the work of Paley[29]—he seems to be claiming that it is an improper activity for the religious apologist, as making no appeal to the moral

[27] *GA*, pp. 276–7.
[28] *GA*, p. 277.
[29] Cf. *GA*, pp. 273–5.

conscience. But whatever Newman's own views on the matter, it seems to me that the following points have to be made. Newman is surely quite right, that one very important condition that any alleged divine revelation must meet, is that it should confirm and enhance our natural moral sense. People have justified appalling moral enormities by appeal to revelation; and the sufficient answer to such justifications should be that God cannot command what is evil, and that we possess some natural apprehension, however overlaid by passion, ideology, and self-deception, of the nature of such evil and of its difference from good. However, someone might well admit that our moral conscience very naturally, in many minds at least, promotes the conviction that there is an almighty judge who will requite every human person in accordance with her or his works; without in the least implying that reflection on our moral conscience and its nature *justifies* belief that such a being exists. Thus the questions of natural theology cannot be avoided by religious apologetics. Confronted by what Newman calls natural religion, the exponent of natural theology has to ask whether it is really legitimate to read our moral consciences in this way on to the origin of worlds and the destiny of humankind. Could it not be that our moral conscience has no deeper basis than the instinct for co-operation which the human race has evolved in the struggle for survival? It may be that careful reflection will justify one in answering this question in the negative; but at least it ought not to be brushed aside. Even if natural religion does and should take the moral conscience for granted, natural theology may not do so.

Thus whatever Newman's views on the matter, it appears to me that there is an important place for a natural theology which does not necessarily appeal to the moral conscience, but simply to evidence and valid argument, in establishing the grounds for religious faith—that is, it must be reiterated, in establishing not merely why people *do* have religious faith, but to what extent they have *legitimate reasons* for having it. I may add that what applies to Newman's argument from natural religion applies in my view to all so-called 'moral arguments' for the existence of God and other religious doctrines. At best, such arguments prove only what one might call the existential relevance of religious faith, its importance for human life; it may well be maintained, for example, that it is a moral tragedy if happiness is not in the long run at least roughly proportionate to desert, which it is certainly not if the present life only is taken into account.[30] But this is a very different thing from establishing the *truth* of such doctrines. I conclude that, so far as Newman was disposed to deny the propriety of arguments for theism or for other religious doctrines which bypass the moral conscience, he was wrong to do so.

In what he has to say about 'certitude', Newman has been charged with confusions very like those in his treatment of this last point. In particular, he does not seem to make a sufficient distinction between what Jay Newman has called the 'phenomenological' and the 'epistemological' issues involved.[31] Newman certainly devotes a good deal of attention to the phenomenology of certitude, its 'taste in the head', so to say—on what it feels like to be certain, or the experience of becoming certain where one had previously doubted, or that of arriving at a judgement which seems certain on the basis of a cluster of considerations each of which in itself feels uncertain. But we do use 'certitude' and its cognate terms not only with reference to opinions of which we or others feel certain, but also of those where we imply that we have a right to be so, because they are true, and we have adequate evidence for their truth; this is the 'epistemological' sense. It may well be maintained that Newman often shifts illegitimately between one sense of 'certitude' and the other, and even that this vitiates the entire argument of the *Grammar of Assent*.

Newman does associate certitude with our ability to give reasons for what we believe. Many things, as he says, we take for granted without thinking about them, as, for example, that Britain was once invaded by Julius Caesar, and (in Newman's time) that it had colonies and an empire all over the earth. But if the need arose, we would not find it in the least difficult to give reasons for them. Some would change their assent to a number of propositions if they put it on an argumentative footing; for example, some believers in Christianity might renounce their faith as a result of subjecting it to examination. But this is just to admit that 'there is an assent which is not a virtual certitude, and is lost

[30] This roughly is the basis of Kant's 'moral' argument for the existence of God and the immortality of the soul.

[31] Jay Newman (*Mental Philosophy*, p. 27) says that, due among other things to neglect of this distinction, Newman's discussion of certitude is 'riddled with confusion'.

in the attempt to make it certitude'.[32] To the claim that Catholic doctrines are certitudes, it might be objected that they are by no means universally accepted. But this is not really a sound objection. Each one of us is gaining from moment to moment by sense-experience certitudes which no one shares. (For example, I am certain, without a shadow of doubt, as I write the first draft of this sentence, that there is an empty white jar, marked 'Biscuits' in red capital letters, within two feet of me; but I am sure that no one else knows this.) Again, the certitudes of the sciences are none the less so for being known (at least in Newman's time) only in some countries of the world, and only by members of the educated classes in those countries. It may properly be said to be a certitude that the earth rolls round the sun, however many people there may be who believe that it is supported by an elephant with a tortoise under it.[33]

But the real difficulty, it may be said, when it comes to religion, lies 'not in the variety of religions, but in the contradiction, conflict, and change of religious certitude'.[34] (Learned persons, unless indeed they go insane, are not liable to change their assent to the proposition that Julius Caesar invaded Britain or that the earth rolls round the sun; but the same hardly applies in the case of the existence of God or the divinity of Christ.) 'Those who have been the most certain in their (religious) beliefs are sometimes found to lose them, Catholics as well as others; and then to take up new beliefs, perhaps contrary ones, of which they become as certain as if they had never been certain of the old.' How can this be consistent with the indefectibility which Newman insists is characteristic of certitude, properly speaking?

Now there are different assents and kinds of assent which are characteristic of religion.[35] When we hear that a person has changed her religious position, it is worth asking what there is in common between the old religious position and the new. The next thing to ask is, whether she has ever made very much of doctrines other than those which are common to her new creed and her old.[36] Let us suppose there are three Protestants, one of whom becomes a Roman Catholic, the second a Unitarian, the third an atheist. The first, we will suppose, holds the divinity of Christ as a certitude. This makes him welcome and feel the

[32] *GA*, p. 140. [33] *GA*, p. 198. [34] *GA*, p. 198.
[35] *GA*, pp. 158–9. [36] *GA*, p. 160.

appropriateness of the doctrines that Christ is really present in the Eucharist, and that Mary is the mother of God; so ultimately he renounces his Protestantism, and makes his submission to the Roman Catholic Church. The second holds as certitudes the traditional Protestant doctrines that Scripture is the sole rule of faith, and a person's private judgement the sole rule for its interpretation. He finds that the Nicene and Athanasian Creeds cannot be inferred from the statements of Scripture as a matter of strict logic, and he thus concludes that they are due to a corruption of God's word by human traditions; so the only thing he can do is to profess what he takes to be primitive Christianity and become a Unitarian.[37] The third begins with the assumption, 'cherished in the depths of his nature', that priesthood amounts to a corruption of the Gospel's simplicity. He would protest in traditional Protestant fashion against the sacrifice of the Mass; but soon he would be led to give up the notion (dear to Protestants themselves) of regeneration through baptism, and the efficaciousness of sacraments in general. His next point of difficulty might be whether dogmas did not infringe on Christian liberty as seriously as sacraments. Then he would be led to ask, of what use is the religious teacher, and why should anyone stand between the individual and his God? After a while, it will strike him that the apostles have that question to answer just as much as the clergy of his own denomination. So he becomes a deist and remains one for a while. But soon it occurs to him, that the moral law remains in his heart, whether there be a God or no; and that to invoke God is unnecessary, since the moral law carries its own authority. Further, looking at the world about him, he sees no evidence that there is a God, so he duly embraces atheism.[38]

Now the world will say, that in these three cases old certitudes were lost, and new were gained; but it is not so: each of the three men started with just one certitude, as he would himself have professed, had he examined himself narrowly; and he carried it out and carried it with him into a new system of belief.[39]

[37] Newman means by 'Protestantism' the position where one accepts, in the manner of Luther or Calvin or Karl Barth, the crucial formulations on the Trinity and the divinity of Christ of the Councils of Nicaea and Chalcedon as true expressions of the faith whose ultimate norm is Scripture.

[38] *GA*, pp. 160–1.

[39] *GA*, p. 161.

To take a slightly different case, suppose a person becomes converted to Catholicism through general admiration of it, and disgust with Protestantism. After a while he renounces his new faith, and returns to his old. One may conjecture that the reason might be that 'he has never believed in the Church's infallibility; in her doctrinal truth he has believed, but in her infallibility, no'. He has confessed, at the time of his reception, that he believes all that the Church teaches; but he understood this principle to bear only on the doctrines the Church taught at that time, not on whatever she would teach. So, something like the promulgation of the doctrine of the Immaculate Conception[40] makes him renounce his new faith; it was more than he had bargained for. 'Thus he never had the indispensable and elementary faith of a Catholic, and was simply no subject for reception into the fold of the Church.'[41]

I agree with Jay Newman that there are profound ambiguities and even confusions in Newman's conception of certitude;[42] and that his failure sharply to distinguish phenomenological and epistemological questions is what is largely responsible for this. Yet, as I shall try to show, the confusions seem to affect curiously little the central thrust of his argument. A judgement or 'assent' seems to be a certitude for Newman in one or more of the following circumstances: (1) when it is true; (2) when some people feel certitude (in the phenomenological sense) about it; (3) when it can be supported by evidence and argument; (4) when further adducing of evidence and argument tends further to confirm it; (5) when it is indefectible; (6) when it remains stable through one or more rather fundamental changes in one's other judgements or assents. Let us, following Newman's own usage in his *Essay on the Development of Christian Doctrine*, call a 'certitude' in sense (6) a 'principle'.[43] Newman's description, both in the *Essay* and in the *Grammar*, of how a single principle or set of principles can remain stable over a radical change in doctrinal beliefs, or even over a series of such changes, is surely one of the most interesting features of his thought. The central

[40] This in fact took place in 1854, some nine years after Newman's reception into the Catholic Church, and some fourteen years before the publication of the *Grammar*.
[41] *GA*, pp. 161–2.
[42] Jay Newman, *Mental Philosophy*, p. 27.
[43] *Dev.*, pp. 178–82.

argument of the *Essay*, which brought Newman into the Roman Catholic Church, was that there is no consistent principle of development or legitimate change applicable to primitive Christianity which will yield the special features characteristic of Anglicanism (like assent to the Athanasian Creed and acceptance of the institution of episcopacy) without not also issuing in those special features of Roman Catholicism to which Anglicans object (like the institution of the papacy and the creed of Pope Pius V).[44] The conclusion of the argument can be generalized into Newman's notorious claim, which I believe is still to be taken very seriously, that Catholicism and atheism are in the last analysis the only two religious positions which can be made fully self-consistent.[45]

On Newman's own admission, the Catholic faith is not unequivocally a certitude in sense (5), as persons often cease to be Catholics; but it is so according to him in senses (1) to (4)—it is true, many people feel subjectively certain of it, and sustained argument and assessment of evidence tend more and more strongly to corroborate it. A Protestant or atheist would presumably concede that it was a certitude in senses (2) and (3)—some people unquestionably feel certain of it, and a certain number of arguments may be martialled in its defence. However, she would deny that it was a certitude in senses (1) or (4); according to her it is not true, and the adducing of evidence and arguments in a sufficiently unrestricted way will therefore tend to show that it is not true. Newman's examples of scientific and historical certitudes —that the earth rolls round the sun, and that Julius Caesar invaded Britain—are so in all six senses; they are true, people are sure of them, they are supportable by evidence and argument, they tend to become ever more so over the lapse of time, they are (virtually) never given up, and they remain stable through fundamental changes of opinion and attitude (for example, in other scientific and historical beliefs, and conceptions of scientific and historical method).

Newman's discussion of the three ex-Protestants, and the role of one central religious certitude in the changes of religious opinion on the part of each, seems really only to be concerned with certitude in sense (6). There is surely no reason, in spite of

[44] *Dev*, pp. 11–13. [45] *GA*, pp. 318–22.

what Newman seems to imply, why such certitudes should be indefectible, certitudes in sense (5). Why should not the Unitarian and atheist in Newman's second and third examples come to examine and reject the one stable principle which underlay all their previous changes in religious affiliation, and become Catholics after all? Or why should not the Catholic, perhaps appalled by some previously overlooked events and actions in the history of his church, come to doubt the conviction of the divinity of Christ which had led him from Protestantism to Catholicism, and become a Unitarian or an atheist? And on Newman's own showing, the certitudes which led to Unitarianism and atheism in these cases were not such in senses (1) or (4); that Scripture interpreted by private judgement is the sole rule of faith, or that priesthood involves a corruption of the Gospel's primitive simplicity, are on Newman's account neither true, nor such that they tend to be confirmed by sustained argument and adducing of evidence.

If there are so many confusions and ambiguities in Newman's discussion of certitude, what, if anything, is to be learned from it? Shorn of its ambiguities, Newman's central claim appears to amount to this. There are a number of religious doctrines which are apt to be held tenaciously and with conviction (and are thus certitudes in sense (2)), and which tend to remain unchanged through one or more alterations in a single person's religious allegiance (certitudes in sense (6)). Some of these tend to lead to Catholicism from other forms of Christian belief; others in the opposite direction, from Catholicism towards other forms of Christian belief and ultimately to atheism. Those which lead towards Catholicism tend to be confirmed more and more as they are subjected to critical scrutiny (they are certitudes in sense (4)), which gives us good reason to hold that they and Catholicism are true (certitudes in sense (1)), and hence ought to be indefectible in the sense of not ever given up. On the other hand, those certitudes (in senses (2) and (6)) which tend to lead away from Catholicism towards unbelief when their implications are followed through, are liable also to be falsified by critical scrutiny, and so not to be true. If they happen never to be given up by a particular individual, then they ought to be.

This position may be unsound, but it is not obviously so; and Newman's attempts to establish it, in the *Essay on Development* and the *Grammar of Assent* and elsewhere, are still worthy of careful attention.

The following conclusions may be suggested as a result of this discussion. (1) Newman's account of the grounds of sound judgement is impressive, and supported by some modern writing on the subject; though his points are obscured by his tendency to confuse phenomenological and epistemological considerations. (2) He is correct that corroboration by the natural conscience is a crucial test for any claimant to the status of divine revelation; though wrong so far as he thinks that arguments for religion which make no direct[46] appeal to the moral conscience are in all circumstances inappropriate.[47] (3) His argument to the effect that Roman Catholicism is the only completely self-consistent form of Christianity is still to be taken very seriously.

[46] It is sometimes forgotten that every argument advanced as sound makes at least an indirect appeal to the moral conscience; accepting the conclusions of a sound argument is something that one has a moral obligation to do.

[47] Newman is very perfunctory in his dismissal of the great rivals of Christianity (Islam, the Far Eastern religions) as claimants to definitive revelation (*GA*, pp. 276–7). But it does not immediately follow that a version of his argument could not be set out which was based on a more serious consideration of their claims. Thus R. C. Zaehner contended that Christianity notably fulfils the requirements both of 'prophetic' and of 'mystical' religion, and uniquely meets the 'hunger for an incarnate God' which seems so persistent a feature of human religious consciousness. See R. C. Zaehner, *Concordant Discord* (Oxford, 1970), 440–3.

13

Newman's *Arians* and the Question of Method in Doctrinal History

ROWAN WILLIAMS

I

It is a nice irony that the young Newman should have been accused of 'Arianizing' by Whately;[1] but, as he tells us in the *Apologia*, he was at first cool towards the language of post-Nicene theology, not at all enthusiastic for the idiom of the Athanasian Creed, and disposed to prefer ante-Nicene authorities.[2] He was, in other words, prepared to give some weight to the witness of antiquity, but unhappy with its more systematized forms. His sense of the legitimacy and necessity of doctrinal definition seems to have developed actually *in* the process of endeavouring to write Church history; and the various comments in *The Arians of the Fourth Century* directed against those who are lukewarm about dogmatic definition[3]—while granting the religious seriousness of their motivation—are the direct fruit of the experience of writing the book, and, in some degree, addressed to the Newman of 1827. What I shall be proposing in these pages is that Newman, in writing the *Arians*, is making the kind of *methodological* advance that will, on the one hand, make the writing of doctrinal history a more serious and scientific discipline, and, on the other, render theologically suspect any attempt to treat as normative the theological ethos and idiom of an earlier age. In leaving behind the doctrinal antiquarianism of his own earlier days, Newman begins the critique of traditional Anglican apologetic that will culminate in the *Essay on Development*; but he also looks forward to a yet more troubled era in doctrinal studies, in which we still wrestle with the question of how we are to affirm dogmatic confessions which are indissolubly

[1] *Apo*, p. 25.

[2] *Apo*, p. 25.

[3] See e.g. *Ari.* (London, 1833), 147–65, cf. pp. 195–7. All references are to the first edition.

bound to historical contingency. The *Arians*, in fact, opens something of a Pandora's box—though it also offers a few hints which might help to break the deadlock threatening an excessively historicized dogmatics.

At the beginning of the 1830s, Newman had some correspondence with Hugh James Rose, one of the editors of the projected Library of Anglo-Catholic Theology to be published by Rivington of London, about a possible study of the Thirty-Nine Articles; and the genesis of the *Arians* can be found in a letter of 9 March 1831, from Rose to Newman, suggesting that a history of the councils might be a desirable preliminary to any work on the Articles.[4] Newman replied on 28 March that he was 'well disposed' to this idea,[5] and by June 1831 had begun work in earnest on the background to the Council of Nicaea. His journal for 22 June reports that he had begun to 'see [his] way' in reading some of the standard narrative accounts.[6] Gibbon is mentioned here, as we might expect, and also the history of Arianism by Louis Maimbourg, a seventeenth-century French Jesuit;[7] but Newman also records in this entry his work on that classic of Anglican patristic learning, Bishop Bull's *Defensio*.[8] Bull was to be both an inspiration and a caution for Newman. The Advertisement which prefaces the *Arians* pays generous tribute to Bull, and, in the *Apologia*, Newman claims for Bull the credit of forcing him to take Christian antiquity with greater theological seriousness.[9] However, he also remarks in a letter to Samuel Rickards, written in the early days of working on the *Arians*,[10] that 'standard Divines' like Bull, Waterland, Petavius, and Baronius 'are magnificent fellows, but they are Antiquarians or Doctrinists, not Ecclesiastical Historians'; and this unease is further clarified in a passage from the *Essay on Development*, where Newman criticizes Bull's account of pre-Nicene theology because it 'begins with a presumption' (i.e. that the Creed of Nicaea contains no

[4] *LD* ii. 321. [5] *LD* ii. 321. [6] *LD* ii. 338.

[7] L. Maimbourg, *Histoire de l'Arianisme depuis sa naissance jusqu'à sa fin; avec l'origine et le progrès de l'hérésie des Sociniens* (Paris, 1673). This is a lively but uncritical narrative, referring to no secondary sources, offering no analysis of Arian origins, and strongly pro-Constantinian. Newman recalled using the work in later life when Maimbourg's Gallican tendencies had attracted some attention in the years after Vatican I; see LD xxvii. 268.

[8] Bull, *Defensio Fidei Nicaenae* (London, 1685).

[9] *Apo*, p. 36. [10] *LD* ii. 371.

theological novelty), and so distorts the material under review.[11] Although Newman in 1845 is already in these words passing critical judgement on some aspects of his own earlier work, he also recognized that he had made and continued to make some sort of attempt to go beyond the 'standard Divines'. The *Essay* claimed to be following the strict historical method of a Gibbon or a Mosheim,[12] and there is a letter of December 1830,[13] in which Newman insists on the necessity of writing ecclesiastical history 'from the original sources' rather than 'standard authorities'; he later annotated this to record that 'My "Arians" was the result of this application'. Bull might be a crucial source of insight into the 'interiority' of patristic thought, but he was not to be Newman's model.

Indeed, the manifest difficulty Newman experienced in the composition of the *Arians* has a lot to do with the lack of a single model for his enterprise. The great anthologists and epitomizers of doctrinal history, as we have seen, are unsatisfactory in his eyes; and he professes 'a very low opinion' of more straightforward narrative historians like Mosheim and Gibbon—however much, as the *Essay* suggests, he respected their *methods*.[14] The source of his dissatisfaction is articulated with great clarity in a letter to Rose of August 1831,[15] explaining his reluctance to begin the proposed history of the councils simply by expounding the formulas of the Creed of Nicaea: 'What light would be thrown on the Nicene Confession *merely* by explaining it article by article? to understand it, it must be prefaced by a sketch of the rise of the Arian heresy, the words introduced by Arius, his perversions of the hitherto orthodox terms, the necessity of new and clearer tests etc.'[16] Newman is, in fact, proposing that the history of theological concepts and vocabulary is a proper and necessary task for the historian, and so putting a question against Bull and the tradition he represents; but, equally importantly, he

[11] *Dev.* (London, 1845), p. 158; the comment is repeated in slightly stronger form in the 1878 edition. See N. Lash, *Newman on Development* (London, 1975), 21–3, for some pertinent comments.

[12] *Dev.* (1845), pp. 182–202 discusses historical method; most of this material was omitted in the 1878 edition, but 'the autonomy' of the historical method was still defended; Lash, *Newman on Development*, pp. 21–2.

[13] *LD* ii. 307.

[14] *LD* ii. 371; Cave and 'Tillement' (for Tillemont) are also criticized (they are 'highly respectable, but biographers').

[15] *LD* ii. 352–3.

[16] *LD* ii. 352.

is proposing that all this is no less a necessary task for the *theologian*. An historian like Mosheim (of whom more later) regards the intellectual history of the Church as a fundamentally secular affair, since true doctrine is found in Scripture, and what follows is at best unnecessary refinements and at worst corruptions. *A fortiori* with Gibbon, for whom doctrinal history is just a dramatic instance of those 'follies'—if not crimes—of humankind which are the historian's natural business. Newman, in contrast, assumes that the serious study of the shifts and adjustments of Christian language ('the necessity of new and clearer tests etc') uncovers something that the theologian ignores at his or her peril. Without a *theological* Church history, we shall not be competent or sensitive theologians; and such a Church history is what Newman is trying to define and execute.

The exact theological significance of doctrinal history is hinted at, once again, in those pages of the *Apologia* dealing with the composition of the *Arians*. Newman explains that 'What principally attracted [him] in the ante-Nicene period was the great church of Alexandria',[17] because of its espousal of a particular account of religious language. The utterances of mature faith, so far from being exhaustive descriptions of the divine reality, in fact presage more than they can articulate. There is a 'sacramental' dimension to theological vocabulary, an element of anticipation of further understanding and fruition—in the terms of classical hermeneutics, an 'anagogical', not merely allegorical, character. Newman observes that, to a mind nurtured on Butler's *Analogy* and Keble's *Christian Year*, the Alexandrian ethos was bound to be in this respect congenial.[18] And it is the exposition and defence of this general approach to religious language which occupies some of the most important pages of the *Arians*, and which were to occasion most controversy and suspicion among its first readers.

Newman embarks upon his chapter dealing with 'The Church of Alexandria'[19] by elaborating the distinction between 'exoteric' and 'esoteric' teaching in Christian practice. The former is what is

[17] *Apo*, p. 36.

[18] *Apo*, p. 37.

[19] *Ari.*, pp. 43–110. R. C. Selby, *The Principle of Reserve in the Writings of John Henry Cardinal Newman* (Oxford, 1975) has a very useful discussion of Newman's attitude to 'reserve' and 'economy' in the period before 1837, but lacks any full treatment of *Arians*.

appropriate for apologetic, characterized by 'caution and reserve',[20] dealing with 'natural religion' and the moral law: in sharp contrast to the Evangelical summons to penitence directed at the ungodly, appealing to remorse and gratitude, the primary presentation of the gospel to the unbeliever in the New Testament and in the primitive Church makes no emotional appeal to the doctrine of the Atonement, but assumes a light of conscience and natural piety already given.[21] Only to those committed to preparation for baptism is the doctrinal schema as such set forth—and even then only by degrees; and only at a late stage of catechesis is Scripture fully opened to the convert or would-be convert, in the context of developing doctrinal proficiency.[22] Newman alludes, in justification of all this, to distinctions drawn in Hebrews and 1 Corinthians between teaching suitable for those new in faith and teaching fitted for the mature,[23] as also to the method professed by Clement in the *Stromateis*,[24] and the catechetical practice of Theodoret, Cyril of Jerusalem, and others in the post-Nicene period.[25] The allegorical interpretation of Scripture, in the wide sense defined by Newman here ('admubrating greater truths under the image of lesser, implying the consequence or the basis of doctrines in their correlatives'[26]), fits neatly into the overall view. 'Allegory' is not a heathen importation, but rooted in 'the operation of a general principle of our nature',[27] the desire to speak of overwhelmingly significant vision in terms that somehow articulate the way in which it informs other perceptions—that is, to speak in figure and metaphor, lest the scope of the vision be narrowed. And such figure and metaphor become in turn part of a canonical vocabulary for another generation, equally afraid of using trivial or inadequate terms. 'No prophet ends his subject: his brethren after him renew, enlarge, transfigure or reconstruct it.'[28] Hence the obscurity of much of Scripture in point of detail: any specific passage in it is liable to be 'unfinished'. Allegorical exegesis thus puts a kind of warning notice over

[20] *Ari.*, p. 47.

[21] *Ari.*, pp. 50–2. Selby, *Principle of Reserve*, pp. 13–21, notes the influence upon Newman in this area of Provost Hawkins's sermon on 'Unauthoritative Tradition' (referred to in *Ari.*, p. 55), and J. B. Sumner's *Apostolical Preaching considered in an Examination of St Paul's Epistles* (London, 1815).

[22] *Ari.*, pp. 55–7. [23] *Ari.*, pp. 47–8. [24] *Ari.*, pp. 53–4.

[25] *Ari.*, pp. 48–50, 52–3.

[26] *Ari.*, p. 62. [27] *Ari.*, p. 63. [28] *Ari.*, p. 64.

Scripture to guard against hasty reading and to pre-empt its use in basic apologetic controversy or exposition as if it were an open book. To read allegorically is to acknowledge that God's revelation itself employs the same pedagogy as the skilled catechist, 'trying the earnestness and patience of enquirers, discriminating between the proud and the humble, and conveying instruction to believers, and that in the most permanently impressive manner, without the world's catching its meaning'.[29] Scripture and catechesis alike warn the neophyte that doctrinal understanding must go hand in hand with the development of Christian character: there is no 'short path from the false to the true knowledge'.[30] For all the possibilities of error and abuse in allegorism,[31] its importance abides as a means of uniting the language of theology with the essentially *progressive* nature of Christian discipleship—faith as a *παιδεία*, a process of being shaped by the truth over time.

Another way of expressing the main point here is to say that theological language never exists in a vacuum: its character is determined by *who* is being addressed and *when*. Thus Newman goes on from his discussion of 'exoteric' teaching and allegory, the whole of the *disciplina arcani*, as he terms it, to the question of 'economy' in religious utterance, 'setting [the truth] out to advantage'.[32] This is the method of fundamental apologetics in the ante-Nicene period: for the purposes of argument, the apologist does not simply begin from some neutral and purportedly timeless account of natural religion and morality, but takes up the terms and idiom in which they are spoken of in the intellectual world of the period, 'indulging the existing fashions to which [contemporary] literature was subjected'.[33] Once again, theology is linked with a *παιδεία*: with children, we shape their ideas 'according to the analogy of those to which we mean ultimately to bring them'.[34] To tell a blind man 'that scarlet was like the sound of a trumpet' is 'economical' in a similar sense: this is what can *truly* be said within the constraint of *these* circumstances,[35] and this is how—once again—Scripture itself works, by saying what can be comprehended under forms that point towards what is yet unknown, 'greater truths untold'; just

[29] *Ari.*, pp. 65–6.
[30] *Ari.*, p. 48.
[31] *Ari.*, pp. 69–72.
[32] *Ari.*, p. 72.
[33] *Ari.*, p. 75.
[34] *Ari.*, p. 80.
[35] *Ari.*, p. 80.

as the sense of general moral law and perhaps even 'the phenomena of the external world' are, in the divine *o'ικονομία*, symbols of a truth they do not in fact contain, but to which they open the way.[36] The regularity of the moral world is an illusion divorced from God, as is the substantiality of the external world, the existence of real and independent objects (Newman makes a brief but bold excursion into Berkeleianism, a taste of philosophical things to come in his intellectual career): but the historical nemesis of vice and the contingent organization of sense-experience into more or less unified percepts dispose us to the recognition of an intelligible and purposive reality beyond our minds; and so does God lead us to confession of his active existence, and to belief in reward and punishment beyond this life.[37]

It is, then, not surprising that the language of ante-Nicene theological utterance may be ambiguous and incomplete from the standpoint of developed orthodoxy. Theology manifestly does not begin with statements of systematic clarity, but—on the foregoing analysis—with metaphor and 'economy'. Newman's chapter on early Trinitarian language[38] describes how each formulation, even the hallowed word 'Son' for the Second Person, and each figure of Scripture is in itself inadequate and calls for some counterbalancing concept or image. Until crises arise, systemization is unnecessary: 'But false doctrine forces us to analyze our own notions in order to exclude it'.[39] The post-Nicene analysis of pre-Nicene divines is like the work of 'grammarians and critics' on a work of literature, and inevitably does less than justice to the material; but it is a necessity, 'lest, while praying without watching, we lose all'.[40] As Newman has observed earlier, in his chapter on creeds, 'the very sacredness and refinement' of early doctrinal statement[41] weakens it in the

[36] *Ari.*, pp. 82–5.

[37] It is worth comparing these pages with Butler's *Analogy*, chs. 2 and 3 of pt. I and ch. 4 of pt. II. This latter ('Of Christianity, considered as a Scheme or Constitution, imperfectly comprehended') offers some very interesting parallels to Newman's argument here, comparing the imperfect evidences of a consistent 'scheme' in the natural order with the evidences of Christianity, and pointing to the necessity of means of instruction extending over time in both cases. On Newman and Butler, see O. Chadwick, *From Bossuet to Newman* (Cambridge, 1957), 83–95—though Chadwick's discussion addresses a slightly different issue.

[38] *Ari.*, pp. 171–195.

[39] *Ari.*, p. 180.

[40] *Ari.*, p. 216.

[41] *Ari.*, p. 146.

face of assault; theologians were obliged to overcome their proper reluctance to subject matters of faith to debate and investigation.[42] It has been a necessary but real evil for the Church: 'Now, we allow ourselves publicly to canvass the most solemn truths in a careless or fiercely argumentative way'.[43] But the intellectual crisis must be met, at whatever cost; and the words of Scripture alone, or the words of Scripture combined with the unsystematic reflections of disciplined piety, cannot satisfy.[44] And so we move into the novel and risky business of refining terms, excluding or qualifying what was once acceptable, even baptizing, by clarification, what once was suspect (as with the '*ομοούσιον* itself).[45] We move towards a 'technical' language, superseding the innocent variety of earlier days.[46]

Newman's early admiration for the ante-Nicenes is still very much in evidence here; the advance of dogma is something almost tragic, a poignant ideological puberty. Only when inappropriate questions are put to the ante-Nicenes can they be made to appear heterodox: 'The reader, trying a rhetorical description by too rigid a rule, would attempt to elicit sense by imputing a heresy'.[47] But their probity must in due course be vindicated by a purification of their vocabulary. Newman comes close to a *Verfallstheorie* of dogmatic language, the notion of formulation itself being a kind of betrayal of some richer truth; but it is a necessary fall, a *felix culpa*, given that the Church lives in a history of change, contingency, and human sinfulness, and that the gospel must be preached in a variety of contexts. However, there is an obvious haziness of focus in all this discussion. Newman brackets together three rather different things, and the justification of one easily slips into being the eludication of another. There is first the *disciplina arcani*, the pedagogy of God (in nature and Scripture) and the Church (in catechesis), which leads human beings at a human pace into the greater mysteries; there is 'economy', the adaptation of theological language to circumstances, in apologetics above all; and there is the proper license of a pre-systematic age. The difficulty in Newman's presentation is that these three work on rather different presuppositions. The 'license' of ante-Nicene theology certainly suggests that the theologians of that era did not possess anything like a complete *conceptual* grasp of the

[42] *Ari.*, pp. 156–7. [43] *Ari.*, p. 150. [44] *Ari.*, pp. 158–65.
[45] *Ari.*, pp. 196–7, 203–7. [46] *Ari.*, p. 197. [47] *Ari.*, p. 216.

matters they discussed, whereas pedagogy and 'economy' assume a knowledge possessed but not fully communicated. In other words, Newman is still reluctant to commit himself to the idea that the ante-Nicene divines might not have recognized Nicene doctrine at once as identical with their own teaching; but his presentation moves discernibly in this direction. His general point about the character of God's *παιδεία* and the nature of theological language as adumbrating more than it can say is not explicitly applied to the actual *minds* of theologians, only to their methods of instruction and communication. But a crack has opened in the confident assertion that doctrine does not change, even if only in the recognition that its idiom changes.

II

Newman's readers were not slow to seize upon the implications of this. Rivington, the proposed publisher, particularly through the agency of Rose and his fellow-editor Archdeacon W. R. Lyall, expressed deepening concern about the way the book was taking shape, throughout the main period of its composition. The original idea of a single history of the councils had by June 1831[48] been modified into a first volume on the Greek councils, up to the time of the Monothelite controversy, though the hope of completing the larger project had obviously not been abandoned.[49] Newman's letter to Rose of 24 August 1831, already quoted, proposes a first volume along the lines indicated in June, but the declaration of intent to examine the background of Nicaea already points to a rather different sort of book. In the hope of making the work not too inaccessible, Newman here offers[50] to reserve most of the detailed argument for appendices. The writing was going forward—under great pressure[51]—in the summer of 1832, and in July Newman, evidently feeling he was in danger of losing his grip on the shape of the argument, asked for some detailed advice from Rose.[52] The publishers proved to be unhappy with the plan to provide a detailed commentary in the traditional style

[48] Journal for 22 June 1831, *LD* ii. 338.

[49] *LD* ii. 340.

[50] *LD* ii. 353.

[51] See the journal for 29 June 1832, *LD* iii. 60, glossed by Newman: 'The last days of my working upon the Arians, I was tried wonderfully—continually on the point of fainting away—quite worn out'. The same is recorded in *LD* xv. 183. It is still 'my first volume' (i.e. of the series on the councils) in the journal for 18 June, *LD* iii. 58.

[52] *LD* iii. 65–6.

on the creed; and Rose suggested (perhaps responding to Newman's earlier plan of reserving detail until a late stage in the book) that what appeared in the current draft as a 'Recapitulation' should be recast as an introduction.[53] Anyone reading the book was obviously going to need some help in orientation. But Newman—like other authors who have worked under pressure—found the prospect of major reconstruction more than he could contemplate.[54] Worse was to come, however. By 16 August Rose had complained that certain pages on Trinitarian doctrine were impenetrably difficult, and Newman replied with an offer to revise them, and a clarification for Rose of what he was trying to say—a passage of great theological interest in its own right.[55] But between August and October came the most serious criticisms from both Rose and Lyall, and the eventual decision not to include the *Arians* in the Library of Anglo-Catholic Theology.

On 21 October Rose forwarded to Newman the letter he had received from Lyall.[56] The editors had already decided to delay publication, and various 'dangers' in the book had been mentioned—almost certainly, in view of later evidence, connected with the treatment of the *disciplina arcani*.[57] Lyall had been the more critical. By the time of his letter to Rose, it had become clear that the *Arians* would not be accepted for the Library of Anglo-Catholic Theology, partly because it was thought to provide insufficient elementary exposition.[58] Lyall's objections, however, concentrated on the heart of Newman's concern, and show very clearly why the book could be seen by orthodox Anglicans as novel and dangerous. To Rose, Lyall had written that 'a "secret tradition" is no tradition at all' for Protestants;[59] and in a letter directly to Newman,[60] the archdeacon elaborates his criticism. Newman, it seems, had taken some offence at Lyall's attack, and the latter reassures him that the ground of his objection is not the

[53] *LD* iii. 74.

[54] *LD* iii. 74.

[55] *LD* iii. 78. Newman observes that it is 'as difficult to conceive God one Person as Three. . : . The Personality of God, in our *notion* of Personality, is a mystery'. In those scriptural images which in fact specify what it is for God to be personal—where his anger or repentance is spoken of, for instance—we grant the principle of economy. 'The whole [of the doctrine of God's personal character] is an economy.'

[56] Sent on 19 Oct. 1831, *LD* iii. 104–5.

[57] Various letters of Aug. and Sept. 1832, *LD* iii. 82, 84, 94, 97 mention some difficulties.

[58] Mentioned in *LD* iii. 103–4.

[59] *LD* iii. 105.

[60] *LD* iii. 112–13.

handling of the material, which he allows to be skilful and scholarly, but the actual subject (Rivington had by now, it should be noted, agreed to publish the book independently of the Theological Library, so that Rose and Lyall no longer had to 'own' it). Lyall sees, rightly, that the theory of doctrinal history being set out in the discussions of 'economy', the *disciplina*, and so on, is a major departure from the apologetics style of Bull and others. Newman opens the door to scepticism about the true apostolicity of certain doctrines, and Lyall is concerned that, without assurance of apostolicity and continuity of belief, these doctrines will lack authority. If the ante-Nicenes had not spoken *openly* (in some sense) about Incarnation and Atonement, 'it would be difficult not to believe that they had not interpreted Scripture as we do—a supposition that would be almost fatal to the doctrines as it seems to me'.[61]

Lyall has discerned that Newman's general drift is towards admitting that there *is* a change in how Scripture is read and interpreted—not only in the life of the Christian who is being led through to a fuller understanding, but in the history of the Church itself. Once grant that not everything is openly professed by ante-Nicene writers, even if the substance of what is believed is the same as that of the Nicene faith, and the appeal to a unanimous voice of the 'undivided Church' is significantly weakened: there is no era in Christian history that does not itself have a *history* of thought and vocabulary. And if this is so, the debate with Rome becomes a far more complex and troubling affair. Lyall, in short, has correctly seen the spectre of the *Essay on Development* behind Newman's tortuous and sometimes confused pages on the *disciplina arcani*.

The Arians of the Fourth Century was finally published on 5 November 1833. Newman was agreeably surprised at the sympathetic tone of some early reviews and reactions; but where there was criticism, it was focused once more on the question of the *disciplina*.[62] Bishop John Kaye of Norwich had sent some detailed criticisms to Rose, and in January 1834 we find Newman assembling notes for a full reply (though it does not appear ever to have been completed or sent to Kaye).[63] Newman believed he

[61] *LD* iii. 113.
[62] *LD* iv. 156 n. 1, on the review in the *British Magazine*, 5 (1834), 67–8.
[63] *LD* iv. 169 n. 1, for Newman's notes and memorandum on 10 and 11 Jan.

could adequately answer Kaye, but the notes suggest some degree of defensive awkwardness. Of course the *disciplina* in the primitive Church was not a rule but a 'principle and feeling'; only in the fourth century is there an identifiable systematic discipline of catechesis. In a letter composed around 26 January (but never sent), responding to some favourable comments on this subject from Thomas Falconer,[64] Newman repeats in almost the same words the points noted earlier in the month, adding that the nature of this 'discretionary rule' in pre-Nicene Christianity makes it impossible to write its history. This is not very satisfactory; and it is not surprising to find Newman admitting in two letters of mid-January[65] that any future edition of the book would have to contain some expansion and clarification of the remarks on the *disciplina*.[66] G. S. Faber's two volumes on *The Apostolicity of Trinitarianism*, published in 1832, but not read by Newman until 1834, seemed to offer support,[67] but the whole question seems to have ceased to engage Newman's interest as an *historical* issue—though the underlying question about the historical character of doctrine comes more and more clearly into focus.

It is also worth noting that Nicholas Wiseman in Rome (who had met Newman there in 1833) took an interest in the *Arians*. Thomas Dyke Acland wrote to Newman from Rome in May 1834,[68] commenting enthusiastically on the discussion of the *disciplina*, and rightly seeing it as essentially to do with the nature of religious language (like some more recent commentators, he is reminded of Coleridge[69]). He adds that Wiseman has suggested to him that Newman look at Möhler's work on Athanasius.[70] Newman was as ignorant of German as most of his Oxford contemporaries, but was provided by J. W. Bowden with

[64] *LD* iv. 179.

[65] *LD* iv. 174; *LD* iv. 177.

[66] Despite the many revisions which Newman claims this section had already undergone in draft (*LD* iv. 159).

[67] *LD* iv. 190.

[68] *LD* iv. 256–7.

[69] See esp. J. Coulson, 'Newman on the Church. His Final View, Its Origins and Influence', in id. and A. M. Allchin (eds.), *The Rediscovery of Newman: An Oxford Symposium* (London, 1967), 123–43, esp. pp. 125–9, and Allchin's essay on Coleridge and symbol, 'The Theological Vision of the Oxford Movement', in Coulson and Allchin (eds.), op. cit., pp. 50–75, esp. pp. 57 and 70 n. 1. For a fuller discussion of the whole background to this question, see Coulson's major work, *Newman and the Common Tradition: A Study in the Language of Church and Society* (Oxford, 1970).

[70] J. A. Möhler, *Athanasius der Grosse und die Kirche seiner Zeit* (Mainz, 1827).

a list of the contents of Möhler's book;[71] his appetite was sufficiently whetted for him to consider making a serious beginning with German,[72] but no more about Möhler appears. It is a tantalizing moment, given the evident convergence of interest between these two great students of the Athanasian age.[73] Wiseman himself was able to turn his reading of the *Arians* to good effect in his lectures of 1835 and 1836 on *The Principal Doctrines and Practices of the Catholic Church*. The first lecture has an account[74] of primitive Christian apologetic which runs strikingly close to what Newman says about 'economy'; but the closest contact is in the fifth lecture, where Wiseman treats of the *disciplina arcani*[75] and quotes from page 149 of the *Arians*[76] to establish the point that Scripture is not in and of itself an adequate norm for teaching. The authoritative catechesis of the Church is, rather, the norm according to which Scripture is read; and this, Wiseman claims, confirms his earlier argument (in the fourth lecture) to the infallibility of the Church as a teaching organ.[77] Newman might claim, writing to Manning in September 1836,[78] that 'Dr Wiseman will do us no harm at all', and his treatment of the lectures in the *British Critic*[79] assumed that Wiseman's skilful critique of Protestant biblicism was something that could be helpful in the reawakening of the Church of England to Catholicity. But Wiseman's simple opposition between infallible Scripture and the *present* reality of

[71] *LD* iv. 302–3. He also asks here for a digest of the contents of certain chapters.

[72] *LD* iv. 320.

[73] On Newman and Möhler, see Chadwick, *From Bossuet to Newman*, pp. 111–19, and Lash, *Newman on Development*, pp. 90–4 (on styles of anti-rationalist exegesis shared by the two writers), esp. the references to de Lubac, *The Sources of Revelation* (New York, 1969), esp. p. 62. There is a fuller discussion in H. Gissen, *Glaubenseinheit und Lehrentwicklung bei Johann Adam Möhler* (Göttingen, 1971), 262–75; and cf. W. Kasper, *Die Lehre von der Tradition in der Römischen Schule* (Freiburg, 1962). B. M. G. Reardon, *From Coleridge to Gore: A Century of Religious Thought in Britain* (London, 1971), notes that Newman mentions Möhler's *Symbolik* of 1832 in the introduction to the *Essay on Development*, but that there is no evidence of his having used or even read it.

[74] *Principal Doctrines and Practices of the Catholic Church* (London, 1836), i. 13–14.

[75] Ibid. 134–5.

[76] Ibid. 137–8. Newman's attention was drawn to this by J. E. Tyler in a letter of 3 Mar. 1836, *LD* v. 252.

[77] Futher parallels may be traced in what is said in the second lecture about Scripture, in the third about the insufficiency of Scripture as a sole *regula fidei*, and in the fifth, which appeals, like Newman, to the nature of the preaching recorded in Scripture itself.

[78] *LD* v. 349.

[79] *British Critic*, 20 (1836), 373–403.

an infallible teaching authority dissolves the traditional Anglican appeal to a normative period of interpretation in the past. As Newman was to discover, arguments like this were not safe weapons in an Anglican arsenal.

III

The *Arians* is an unsatisfactory book, as the older Newman fully acknowledged.[80] In practice, Newman assumes that the ante-Nicene period is a golden age of theological utterance that is both free (unsystematic) and carefully reverent, while allowing, indeed insisting upon, the iron necessity of closer formulation as circumstances change. His heart is still with much of the classical Anglican apologetic that he is undermining. He is on the verge of admitting that doctrine—not merely doctrinal idiom—changes, but is still sufficiently part of the tradition of Bull to believe that ante-Nicene faith needed only a minimal definition of form and vocabulary to require no further refinement.[81] Thus there is a real tension running through the book: historical pressure, historical conditioning, is given due weight, but it is still assumed that doctrinal *content* is fixed (Justin Martyr would have understood the 'ὁμοούσιον immediately), and that the pressure for dogmatic exactitude is somehow less immediate in the post-patristic period—though the Church's liberty and authority in teaching, free from the dominance of the state, is another major theme in the book's later pages,[82] an index of the most pressing practical concerns of Newman and his circle in the 1830s.

None the less, the important step has been taken: doctrine, even if only in its outward expression, does have a *history*. And if

[80] See e.g. *LD* xxiii. 46, xxv. 197, xxviii. 172, xxx. 105 (the book is 'inexact in thought and incorrect in language'). Newman refused to make more than minor changes in the later editions, though he made a number of significant small changes for the 1876 printing, mostly to do with derogatory references to the Roman Catholic Church.

[81] 'At the stage of the *Arians*, Newman's attention was not focused on the increase of doctrine. He merely saw another way of expressing the object of faith. That object itself remained identical and invariable . . . His idea of the faith is therefore, at this time, a static one' (Louis Allen, introducing his edition of the correspondence between Newman and Jager, *John Henry Newman and the Abbé Jager: A Controversy on Scripture and Tradition 1834–1836* (Oxford, 1975) 13).

[82] Esp. *Ari.*, p. 422; see the remarks in R. Williams, *Arius: Heresy and Tradition* (London, 1987), 5–6.

Newman is reacting on the one hand to the dogmatic homogenizing of early theology by the tradition of credal exposition, he is also reacting against the idea that variation and unclarity in doctrinal language are simply the result of the corruption of a single primitive truth by alien accretions. There are at least three different targets here. Seventeenth- and eighteenth-century Unitarianism had evolved a sophisticated 'primitivist' apologetic, for which Trinitarian doctrine was the evil effect of 'Platonizing' notions: Joseph Biddle[83] and Joseph Priestley[84] are two of the more prominent espousers of this case in England, though Servetus[85] had already pointed the finger at Plato in the first half of the sixteenth century. Platonism—very loosely defined, as Bishop Bull complained[86]—is the source of a doctrine of multiple divine hypostases, which clouds the scriptural simplicity of the confession of one sole creator. The apologists are regarded as specially culpable in corrupting the apostolic faith, and Nicaea is seen as the triumph of Platonizing mythology. But alongside this Unitarian suspicion of Platonism we find a second kind of story told, with much the same theme, but a wholly different end, by Petavius in his highly controversial studies of ante-Nicene Trinitarian doctrine in the seventeenth century.[87] The general tone of Petavius's discussion is anti-philosophical, chilly towards scholasticism and speculation; and, in the patristic era, idle and dangerous speculation is primarily associated with Platonism. For Petavius, the problem is not that Platonism teaches a multiplicity of divine hypostases but that it teaches a multiplicity of *hierarchically ordered* hypostases, with a cosmic intelligence acting as mediator between the true God and the universe.[88] Ante-Nicene theology is widely infected with this, and we must recognize that

[83]See J. Biddle, *A Confession of Faith touching the Holy Trinity, according to the Scriptures* (London, 1648).

[84] See esp. J. Priestley, *An History of the Corruptions of Christianity* (Birmingham, 1782).

[85] Servetus, *De Trinitatis erroribus libri septem* (The Hague, 1531). The anti-Platonic strand in Unitarian thought is well discussed in the so-far unpublished 1988 Jordan Lectures by J. Z. Smith, 'On the Comparison of Christianity with the Religions of Late Antiquity', to which I am much indebted.

[86] Bull, *Works on the Trinity* (Oxford, 1855), iii. 270 (I owe this reference to Prof. Smith).

[87] The second volume of Petavius's *Dogmata theologica* (1644) deals with the Trinity.

[88] Petavius *De Trinitate* (1644), I. i. 1–2.

its vocabulary, if not indeed its substantive content, falls short of ecclesiastical probity.[89]

Petavius is sometimes seen as a forerunner of Newman, as an early exponent of a theory of doctrinal development; but this must be treated with some caution. For one thing, Petavius works with a fairly clear model of primitive clarity and orthodoxy distorted by borrowing from alien sources; while, as the foregoing pages have sought to show, Newman's general theory of religious language and of the perception of faith assumes that the primary moment of theological and confessional insight is 'dark with excess of light', and so in need of gradual articulation in a process that has some elements of trial and error. It is hard to reconcile what Newman says with anything like a straightforward propositional theory of revelation. Furthermore, Petavius, partly in reaction to the charge that he had delivered too many hostages to a Socinian fortune,[90] seems to have attempted to distinguish between the accidental reverential 'economies' of orthodox pre-Nicene writers[91] and the errors of a Tertullian or an Origen—between incomplete statements of right belief and material heresy.[92] This is not very successful in Petavius's own terms, and it is, once again, pretty distant from Newman's concern to allow orthodox intention to practically all the major ante-Nicenes (and we may remember too that Newman, like Bull, accepts that *some* elements of subordinationist language are inevitable in a properly personalist Trinitarian theology[93]). In other words, Newman fully shares Bull's conviction about pre-Nicene orthodoxy, and is suspicious of the motives of 'Romanists' (Petavius is obviously in mind) who emphasize the unclarity of early doctrinal statement so as to draw out more plainly the need for an institution with authority to define dogma.[94] Nor, as we have seen, is Newman at all disposed to see the non-Christian philosophy of late antiquity as a corrupting influence: once again, in contrast to Petavius, he

[89] Bks III to VI of *De Trinitate* contain most of Petavius's sharpest judgements on the ante-Nicene period.

[90] See P. Galtier, 'Petavius', in the *Dictionnaire de théologie catholique*, vol. xii/1, cols. 1313–37, col. 1328 on early objections. Galtier's work is an excellent introduction to Petavius's achievement and the reactions to it.

[91] Petavius, *De Trinitate* III. i; cf. also 'praef. 3.5', quoted in *Ari.*, p. 79.

[92] Galtier, 'Petavius', *Dictionnaire*, XII. i. 1330–2.

[93] *Ari.*, pp. 178–83; cf. p. 171, on the definition of persons, in connection with n. 55 above.

[94] *Ari.*, p. 44.

has a consistent general theory of natural religion which allows a positive place to the searchings of the Greeks; and here are faint echoes not so much of Bull as of Cudworth.[95]

Mention of Cudworth brings us to the third great target of Newman's theology of doctrinal history, and perhaps the most formidable: Johann Lorenz von Mosheim (1694/5–1755),[96] the doyen of German Protestant church historians. The notes in the *Arians*, as well as Newman's letters and papers, testify abundantly to his reading of Mosheim—not only his major textbook on the pre-Constantinian Church,[97] but also his annotated Latin translation of Cudworth and his dissertations on the content and background of the Cambridge Platonist's thought.[98] Mosheim's starting-point is more overtly biblicist than Petavius's; and the corruptions wrought by late antique thought are more to do with exegesis than anything else. For Mosheim, early Christianity faces two fundamental philosophical traditions, the 'Eclectic' and the 'Oriental';[99] the latter, with its systematic dualism, is the major source of Gnostic error, the former (though it has elements of 'Orientalism') is distinguished by a sacramentalist, 'mystical' approach to knowledge through speculation and symbol, and so leads to an allegorization of Scripture which licenses the production of doctrinal novelty.[100] 'Eclecticism' pretends to be Platonism, but in fact mixes Plato with Pythagorean, Stoic, and 'Oriental' doctrines. Its roots are in Egypt, especially Alexandria, and, although Potamo is presented in doxographic tradition as its source, Philo is more important in the development of a mystical, hierophantic approach to sacred texts,[101] and the growth of mystagogy and the *disciplina arcani* in Christianity.[102] Allegory

[95] Esp. Cudworth, *The True Intellectual System of the Universe* (London, 1678).

[96] The best summary of Mosheim's career and work can be found in N. Bonwetsch's article in the *Realencyklopädie für Protestantische Theologie und Kirche* xiii (1903), 502–6.

[97] J. L. von Mosheim, *Commentarii de rebus Christianorum ante Constantinum Magnum* (Helmstadt, 1753).

[98] id., *Systema intellectuale huius universi seu de veris naturae rerum originibus* (Jena, 1733).

[99] id., *Commentarii*, pp. 25–33.

[100] Ibid. 629–58, esp. p. 632.

[101] Ibid. 25, 26, 303–10, 630–3. The role of Philo is far more strongly emphasized in *Commentarii* than in Mosheim's earlier *Institutiones historiae Christianae majores: Saeculum primum* (Helmstadt, 1739).

[102] id., *Commentarii*, pp. 303–10.

blurs the boundary between the power of the revealing Word of God and the speculations of human beings: 'divinis libris per immoderatum philosophiae amorem vis afferebatur'.[103] Human invention corrupts revelation, and 'Eclectic' philosophy encourages the free pursuit of truth through speculation[104] instead of obedience to the 'simplicity' of true faith.[105]

Mosheim's hostility to philosophy,[106] more particularly to what he dubs 'Eclecticism' (and we should call Middle-and Neo-Platonism), is matched by his suspicion of Alexandria as the source of such corruption: 'ex Aegypto cuncta fere mala profecta'.[107] From Philo through Ammonius to Origen, the intellectual climate of Alexandria nurtures error, culminating in the superstitions of monasticism and so-called mystical theology.[108] It is against this background that we must read Newman's impassioned defence of the Alexandrian Church; if Catholic historians like Petavius have one set of motives for impugning the orthodoxy of a Clement or an Origen, Protestants like Mosheim have another —the desire to exalt Scripture above the subtleties of human learning and tradition.[109] Newman thus sets out to vindicate Alexandria in as thoroughgoing a way as possible. Far more than Unitarian apologetic or Petavius's criticisms, it is Mosheim's picture of Alexandrian Christianity which conditions the polemical emphasis of the early chapters of the *Arians*. Newman picks up the term 'Eclecticism' from Mosheim's *Commentarii* and devotes a section[110] to 'the Eclectic Sect', designed to show that it is for the most part an heretical aberration from Christianity rather than a malign influence upon it: the Arian heresy is not the fruit of disordered philosophical speculation, though such speculation may be drawn upon for support at a later stage of the heresy's

[103] Ibid. 298.

[104] Mosheim, *Institutiones*, trans. A. Maclain as *An Ecclesiastical History Antient and Modern from the Birth of Christ to the Beginning of the Present Century* (1758), 212 (only the first volume appeared of Mosheim's original project, so that there is only one volume of the translation).

[105] Ibid. 142.

[106] Mosheim, *Commentarii*, p. 272: philosophy's influence is 'haud exiguum detrimentum'.

[107] Ibid. 299; cf. Maimbourg's *Histoire*, p. 39: 'Alexandrie, où la liberté de parler et d'agir avec insolence esté excessivé.

[108] Mosheim, *Commentarii*, pp. 310–19.

[109] This is what *Ari.*, p. 44 seems to imply.

[110] Mosheim, *Commentarii*, pp. 111–27.

evolution.[111] Like Cave[112] and Cudworth,[113] Newman also distinguishes between Plato's 'Trinitarianism' and the hierarchical systems of post-Plotinian cosmogony—a distinction with which Mosheim's commentaries on Cudworth had expressed some dissatisfaction, as tending towards an unduly benign attitude to philosophy. Indeed, Mosheim's accounts of 'Eclecticism' seem in part designed to minimize the influence of Plato on Christian doctrine by stressing the closer connections between Christianity and later Platonism.

For Newman, genuine Platonism is no source for Arianism, but a *praeparatio evangelica*; and the decadent Platonism of the 'Eclectics' is likewise not a source but a belated ally. There is therefore no ground for a blanket condemnation of philosophy as such. Whence then the Arian error? As is well known, Newman's conviction is that the root of the trouble lies in Antioch and in the Jewish influences prevailing in Christianity there.[114] It is this section of his work that is most vulnerable on scholarly grounds; his account of the Antiochene mentality, both in the 1833 edition and in the later revision (with its appendix on 'The Syrian School of Theology'[115]), is heavily distorted by polemical interest, and tends to project back into the pre-Nicene period many of the features properly belonging to the post-Nicene exegetical school of Antioch. These pages are also the most distasteful to the twentieth-century reader because of their uncritical repetition of certain features of patristic polemic against the Jews:[116] Newman is in this no worse an offender than most of his contemporaries, but that does not make these lines easier to read. However, the salient point for our present purpose is that Newman is attempting a kind of palinode of Mosheim: the biblicism and historicism of Antioch, with its 'Judaic' commitment to the literal sense of Scripture, is the true source of heresy, encouraging just such a 'humanitarian' (i.e. psilanthropist) Christology as Mosheim rightly associates with the 'Eclectics'.[117] It is this convergence

[111] Ibid. 124, cf. p. 111 on the lack of real connection between Platonism and Arianism.

[112] Both in Cave's *Scriptorum ecclesiasticorum historia literaria*, 2 vols. (London, 1688, 1698), and in his more popular *Ecclesiastici: Or the History of the Lives, Acts, Death and Writings of the most Eminent Fathers of the Church* (London, 1683).

[113] Cudworth, *True Intellectual System*.

[114] *Ari.*, pp. 1–27.

[115] *Ari.*, pp. 403–15 (1874 edn.).

[116] e.g. *Ari.*, pp. 20–1.

[117] Mosheim, *Commentarii*, pp. 293–4.

which later helps to pave the way for the alliance between Arianism and 'Eclecticism'.[118] And the allegory regarded by Mosheim as the source of corruption becomes the pivotal principle of sound and reverent theology, because it insists upon that reverence before *mystery* so despised by Judaizers and eclectics alike.[119] Newman meets Mosheim head-on: the German scholar castigates allegory as the source of doctrinal novelty, the fellow of Oriel defends it as the necessary expression of the crucial element of personal and spiritual παιδεία in Christian doctrine that alone can ward off rationalizing, minimalizing tendencies. And to defend allegory, and with it the Church that most consistently fostered it, it is necessary to create a rival source of error to which the ills of the early Church may be ascribed: hence the somewhat mythologized 'Antioch' of these early sections.

A reading of Mosheim thus illuminates both the weaknesses and the strengths of the *Arians*. It explains the eagerness to settle blame for Arianism upon Antioch, and the consistently positive attitude to Alexandria and to a good deal of classical philosophy. It also demonstrates (even more clearly than the contrast with Petavius) how far Newman is from a simplistic theory of primitive doctrinal purity sullied by alien influences: the problem of 'Judaizing' literalism is not so much one of foreign corruptions stealing in as of Christian theology itself failing to grow into the fulness that is its inheritance. As we have noted already, the 'fall' of theology is its necessary wrestling with the constraints of scientific formulation, not a historical decline; and the price of this fall is not heresy (quite the contrary) but the erosion of proper reticence and reverence, the licence given to self-indulgent or sophistical disputation—something about which Newman felt deeply in the context of his own day.[120] These are the risks of history, as much for the individual as for the community. And, while Newman may indeed still be within that theological frame of reference that assumes a more or less complete continuity in

[118] *Ari.*, p. 124. [119] *Ari.*, p. 124.

[120] His concern evoked warm response from the great Oxford patrologist William Bright, as late as 1883, when Bright reviewed Gwatkin's *Studies in Arianism* in the *Church Quarterly Review*, 16 (July 1883), 375–402, and compared Gwatkin's lack of reverential discretion unfavourably with the tone of *Arians*. When Newman wrote to express his appreciation of Bright's generosity, Bright replied on 20 Aug. 1883 that *Arians* 'lay, years ago, at the foundation of my earliest studies of that period'; *LD* xxx. 240 nn. 1 (for the reference to the review of Gwatkin) and 2 (for Bright's letter).

content between diverse stages in doctrinal history, his refusal to identify a single moment or epoch as *fully* crystallizing that content already suggests that the continuity or identity of belief can only appear *in* the interaction of the diverse articulations of belief through history that arise in response to various specific movements or crises. That is to say that, ultimately, the *unity* of Christian theology is not capable of being articulated in abstraction from the particularities of its history; that only in engagement with the labours of the past out of a keen sense of the pressures of the present can we begin to discriminate as to what is centrally and intelligibly an abiding feature of Christian identity. Only in the activity of conversation do we find what the depths and what the limits are of our common language, what it is that holds us together as sharers in one world.

Newman, then, not only opens up the possibility (which the *Arians* itself certainly does not realize) of a doctrinal history that is not hampered by polemical interest (even if it retains a strong theological investment) or by the search for an Edenic clarity and purity of belief; he hints that a sound dogmatic theology depends on honest doctrinal history, if it is to avoid distorting simplifications. But this still leaves us with some of the problems of the 1830s and 1840s. If we accept that there is no single point of authoritative reference in doctrinal history, are we not left (as Archdeacon Lyall feared) with the options of relativism, for which doctrinal commitment can only be arbitrary, or a rather positivistic reliance on some contemporary teaching authority? Perhaps we should bear in mind that Newman's own decision to join the Roman Catholic Church was not simply a decision for the latter of these options, but more a decision against what he had come to see as the archaeologism of Anglican doctrine, its historically (and geographically) *static* character, its absolutizing of the local, both in time (the first four centuries) and place. Hence the famous analogies in the *Apologia* between Anglicans on the one hand, and Arians, Donatists, and Eutychians on the other. It is not part of this essay's purpose to assess the fairness of these judgements; the point is that Newman's conversion is his identification of a Christian communion in which it seemed possible to take doctrinal history seriously. His answer to Lyall's dilemma (and Wiseman's exploitation of it) is, in the *Essay on Development*, to lay down a 'grammar' of authentic historical continuity—a solution based neither on some primitive norm nor on a contemporary absolute authority, but consisting in a set of guidelines by which we may test whether we really are still speaking the same language as our historical partners in conversation and forebears in faith. It is a characteristically pragmatic resolution.

However, it is perhaps not the only trajectory that might be traced from the *Arians*. The *Essay* proposes guidelines independent of the actual interpretative encounter with the Christian past, a set of formal criteria for distinguishing authentic development from corruption; but, as has often been remarked, this assumes that there is an identifiable central process in doctrinal history which can be 'read' in terms of steady organic growth according to fairly objective criteria. It does not leave much room for asking whether a particular development, necessary or at least intelligible at one stage of the story, might not legitimately be criticized at another. Newman shows, for instance, how the theology of merit developed out of specific refinements in the theology of baptism, from understandable and perhaps laudable motives; but how might one answer the obstinate Reformation contention that this development has so burgeoned as to obscure other more focal matters? how set about constructing an 'ecology' of doctrinal evolution?

The *Arians* itself does not presuppose quite such confidence in doctrinal evolution overall. Its author is, as we have seen, disposed to regard new and systematic formulation as a necessary evil, rather than simply a natural developmental moment. Only acute crisis justifies innovations that can be claimed as authoritative, and what constitutes an 'acute' crisis is not easy to specify in the abstract. But the *Arians* might be read as suggesting, in its general tenor, that crisis comes when the natural plurality, imprecision, and figurative character of primary theological reflection are thought to license the absolutizing and refining of one particular element in this complex to the detriment of the whole. In other words, crisis is precisely the upsetting of a 'doctrinal ecology'—a variety of theological discourse wide enough to communicate the full and disorienting significance of the generative theological experience, in which 'the mind . . . is prompted to give utterance to its feelings in a figurative style; for ordinary words will not convey the admiration, not literal words the reverence which possesses it'.[121] Doctrinal definition is, in this perspective, itself a response to narrowing over-definition. And this, of course, suggests that it is itself open to potential critique in the name of a better sense of doctrinal ecology; so that the history of doctrine has the paradoxical character of a repeated effort of definition designed to counter the ill effects of definition itself—rather like the way in which a good poet will struggle to find a fixed form of words that will decisively avoid narrowing and lifeless fixtures or closures of meaning. Perhaps the test of a 'sound' doctrinal definition is its capacity to generate new metaphors and the new questionings that go with them.

This is to go well beyond Newman, and, indeed, the scope of this paper. But it may be appropriate to end with this reminder that one of the things which gives the *Arians* its originality as a historical essay is that its discussions are set in the context of a general thesis about religious language and about the historical and mobile character of human perception in general. What Bright called[122] the 'awe and tenderness' of Newman's religious idiom was not merely a rhetorical gloss, but the key to a new critical seriousness about the history of doctrine, which continues to pose both awkward and constructive questions to Anglican and Roman Catholic theology alike.

121 *Ari.*, p. 63.
122 Bright, review of Gwatkin, *Studies in Arianism*, quoted in *LD* xxx. 240 n. 1.

14

The *Lectures on Justification*

HENRY CHADWICK

Newman's *Lectures on (the Doctrine of) Justification*[1] is a book that deserves to be ranked at least on a par with any of his more widely read writings on theology. In the twentieth century perhaps the book is comparatively seldom read, certainly less than the *Apologia* or the *Grammar of Assent* or *The Idea of a University* or the letters and diaries. In Newman's time one cannot say that the topic was in the forefront of discussion. There was a widespread feeling that the debate belonged almost entirely to the past of the sixteenth century; that in a topic of amazing intricacy relatively few people really understood what anyone was saying; indeed perhaps it was a dispute merely about words and polemical slogans, not religious realities, and could be neglected by Christians seriously engaged in the battle of the mind against the rising tide of secularist thinking. The eighteenth-century Enlightenment had showed little interest in the problem, which was then regarded as an exhausted debate, productive of schisms and bloodshed in religious wars, and at all times likely to become enveloped in an arid scholasticism. The desiccated disputes of the Lutherans and then the Calvinists during the second half of the sixteenth century,[2] the fiercely negative language of, for example, the Westminster Confession of Faith, chapter 11, the divisiveness of the too

[1] The title in the first and second editions (1838, 1840) lacked the bracketed words. The copies of the first and third editions at the Birmingham Oratory have corrections in Newman's hand. The fourth and fifth editions appeared in 1886 and 1890. A French translation by E. Robillard and M. Labelle has a valuable introduction and notes by Robillard (Montreal, 1980).

[2] For the Lutherans there is a reliable guide in R. D. Preus, *The Theology of Post-Reformation Lutheranism*, 2 vols. (St Louis and London, 1970–2). For a brief survey of the main Calvinist writers, see E. Bizer's introduction to his edition of H. Heppe, *Die Dogmatik der evangelisch-reformierten Kirche* (Neukirchen, 1958). The 1934 edition of Heppe's book appeared in an illegal but useful translation by G. T. Thomson (London, 1950); the first German edition is of 1861. There is useful matter in A. E. McGrath, *Iustitia Dei*, ii (Cambridge, 1986).

charitably entitled Formula of Concord, helped to generate a quest either for cool-headed rationality or for warm-hearted pietism, both alternatives being free of dogmatic wrangles about revealed theology in areas where truth was hard to grasp.

Nevertheless, devout people in the eighteenth century had not entirely pushed the matter on to the shelf. The Evangelical revival, especially where it was rooted in a soil prepared by the fertilizer of Calvinism, stimulated a special interest in justification by faith alone, because for the Evangelicals this doctrine was understood to be making the inner feelings a matter of primary consequence. Religion for them was no affair of external rites like sacraments but exclusively of the individual heart; it was not located in respected charitable activities, not in attendance at church services, not in prayers whether private or corporate, but in the individual's continual consciousness of utter depravity before God and exclusive dependence on the imputing to the believer of Christ's righteousness, in which the believer in no sense shared. So at least Newman was brought to believe when, in consequence of his Evangelical conversion in adolescence, he came under the momentous influence of Calvinist Evangelical preachers and writers, such as Thomas Scott (1747–1821) or William Romaine (1714–95).

In the spring of 1837 Newman gave lectures on justification in Adam de Brome's chapel at St Mary's, Oxford. The impulse to propose this subject came from a controversial brush with the vehemently Protestant *Christian Observer*. Newman had been thinking about the subject, off and on, for a full decade past, and had done considerable reading in the principal Reformation divines on the subject. Cassander's Catholic *Consultatio*, written in 1564 (published 1577), was read and evidently found congenial. Newman had carefully studied Chemnitz, Chamier, Gerhard, and naturally the main Anglican writers—Hooker, Field, Davenant (a Calvinist in whom Newman found much to admire),[3] and Bull.

[3] J. Davenant, *Praelectiones de duobus in theologia controversis capitibus* (Cambridge, 1631), 220–641, translated by J. Allport (London, 1844) under the title *Treatise on Justification*, is both rigid and inconsistent. He refused to make any separation between justifying faith and hope or love, and insisted that good works are necessary for the justified and a 'moving cause' (but not a 'necessary cause') of salvation. The coherence of his language was immediately questioned by W. Forbes, *Considerationes modestae et pacificae*, i (posthumously published in 1658, reissued with translation in 1850 in the Library of Anglo-Catholic Theology). Much in Davenant is remarkably close to Trent, despite his strong Calvinism.

The third book of Calvin's *Institutes* was also much pondered, and the cautious, conciliatory statements of Melanchthon. But in the delivered lectures and in the published book, with the exception of various appendices, Newman was anxious to make the central issues utterly clear to his hearers and readers. Accordingly, he avoided the elaborate technicalities with which the subject was commonly beset. Deliberately he adopted a style falling between lectures and sermons. In consequence, some parts of the text provide masterly and detached analysis, while other parts are like the parochial sermons in being in some degree rhetorical and homiletic. He wished to be understood by ordinary persons, clerical and lay alike. Although the book was not composed as a systematic or academic treatise, the work commanded the deep respect of weighty experts. The German historian J. J. Döllinger particularly admired it. Alfred Plummer's conversations with him report that he 'always spoke of Newman's *Justification* as the greatest masterpiece of theology that England had produced in a hundred years'.[4] As is commonly the case with Newman's writings, the prose is never so brilliant or the argument so acute as when he is stating the position of those with whom he makes no secret of disagreeing.

For Newman's *Justification* is a highly polemical work, and its main argument is directed against the beliefs which he himself had held as an Evangelical. At the age of thirty-six he had come to feel it essential to tackle the very citadel of the 'popular Protestantism,' the outworks of which he had already assaulted in the *Prophetical Office*. Without a treatment in some depth of the issue of justification, his statement of the *via media* must be gravely incomplete. The Evangelicals were legatees of the pietist convictions of Germans like P. J. Spener (1635–1705), inheritors of the tenaciously held opinion that the failure to grasp the doctrine of justification by faith alone lay at the heart of the Catholic distortion of the gospel of forgiveness and grace which was to them the very glory of the Reformation, thereby making the sixteenth Christian century age an age of sacredness as no century other than the first could be. Some of the less theologically minded Evangelicals liked to speak of the doctrine as 'the simple gospel'. The maze-like tortuousness and intricacy of the big

[4] R. Boudens (ed.), *Conversations with Dr. Döllinger* (Louvain, 1985), 254.

books on the subject (including Spener's which is a fat and formidable work to read)[5] generally passed them by.

In the seventeenth century, Bishop George Bull had begun his *Harmonia Apostolica* (in which he set out to reconcile St Paul and St James, fitting Pauline doctrine into a framework taken from St James rather than the other way round), by making the sharp observation of the doctrine of justification that 'theology does not afford an article more hard to be understood'. It is, he remarked, an article of faith of the greatest consequence; yet sadly the subject is full of 'minute distinctions' and 'ingenious devices', wrapped in 'clouds and thick darkness'. Newman certainly owed more than a little to Bull's *Harmonia* and to his vindications of that book against critics. But, significantly perhaps, his references to Bull are not numerous; nor does he much invoke Jeremy Taylor. Such writers were explicitly unsympathetic to Calvinism. Bull once turns on one of his critics with the sharp words that he is 'greatly given to the theology of Geneva'. Bull looks back on a time when 'things had got to such a state that it was scarcely lawful to interpret either the decrees of our Church [i.e. of England] or even the Scriptures themselves otherwise than according to the standard of Calvin's Institutes'. He concludes that 'every age has its own flood of opinions to which if anyone oppose himself he is either carried along by it or overwhelmed'.[6] Although Bull and especially Taylor certainly anticipated parts of Newman's positions, quotations from anti-Calvinists could not have served Newman's pastoral purpose. He could win more support by appealing to Hooker or especially Davenant or Melanchthon. Taylor had been suspected of too much sympathy for Rome in his lifetime, and had had to produce his *Dissuasive* to reassure; Calvinists disliked his recasting of the doctrine of original sin.

Accordingly, Newman's footnotes mainly refer to firmly

[5] P. J. Spener, *Die evangelische Glaubensgerechtigkeit von J. Brevings vergeblichen Angriffen also gerettet, dass nechst gründlicher Beantwortung alles in dessen so genandten Glaubensstreits Anfang und Ende enthaltenen die heilsame Lehr von der Rechtfertigung des Menschen vor Gott erwiesen wird* (Frankfurt, 1684). The book runs to nearly 1500 pages. I have used the Wolfenbüttel copy of this rare volume, which is also in the British Library. The reprint of Spener's writings (Hildesheim, Olms, 1979–) has not yet included this massive work. The Evangelical background to Newman is well studied by T. L. Sheridan, *Newman on Justification* (Staten Island, NY, 1967).

[6] Bull, *Apologia pro Harmonia*, VII. vii (Opera Latina; London, 1721), p. 668; trans. in Library of Anglo-Catholic Theology (Oxford, 1843), pp. 308–9).

Protestant authors, especially when he can find in them (as was not difficult) propositions that cohered with his main contention, namely that those who stand for imputed righteousness and those who stand for imparted righteousness are ultimately talking about one and the same thing.[7] Moreover (and here Newman's thesis became distinctive) believers are justified not by faith (Protestantism) nor by renewal (Catholicism), but by the indwelling Christ in the soul, 'God's presence and his very self and essence all divine'.

Newman wrote his book during 1837 and the first weeks of 1838, and found the subject one of extreme difficulty. The constant revision and rewriting were on such a scale that substantial sections were yet further reformulated at the proof stage.[8] 'Nothing I have done has given me such anxious thought and so much time and labour', he wrote to Mrs Thomas Mozley on 9 January 1838.[9] The main body of the lectures was already in proof before he even began to compose the necessarily technical (but crucial and to the theologian absorbing) appendix on 'the formal cause' of justification. So he wrote to Mrs John Mozley on 29 January.[10] Newman found himself taken by surprise at the difficulty. The subject had been in his thoughts 'years and years before a scientific treatment of either Church Authority or the Arian Question could be'.[11] 'What has taken me so much time is first the adjustment of the ideas into a system, next their adjustment in the Lectures, and thirdly and not the least the avoiding all technicalities and all but the simplest and broadest reasonings.' Because of the sheer difficulty of the subject, Newman feared that his book could be found 'hard and laboured to read'.[12]

[7] Melanchthon's *Apology for the Confession of Augsburg* (1531) grants this point, ii. 40: 'Because to be justified signifies that the wicked are made righteous through regeneration, it signifies also that they are pronounced or reputed as righteous. For the Scripture uses both these ways of speaking.' Also iii. 40: 'It is generally admitted that justification signifies not only the beginning of renovation, but the reconciliation by which we are afterwards accepted.' McGrath's judgement (*Iustitia Dei*, ii. 126) is that the historical Luther (not Newman's caricature) occupied a position remarkably close to Newman's.

[8] Newman used to say that he had rewritten the text fourteen times (14 Dec. 1869, *LD* xxix. 309). The experience of its composition was painful to a degree (*LD* xx. 169). Some Protestants came to suggest that Newman raised subtle and bewildering questions to drive the distressed to Roman infallibility; so an anonymous note in the *Christian Observer* (1854), 483).

[9] *LD* vi. 186.

[10] *LD* vi. 193.

[11] *LD* vi. 212.

[12] *LD* vi. 199.

The last proof was finally returned to the printer on 21 March 1838, and by the first week of April the book was in the shops. A few days after the last proofs were returned to press, Newman first acquired a copy, in French translation (for the German was beyond his powers), of Möhler's momentous *Symbolik*, the most eloquent and well-formulated restatement of Catholic doctrine published in the first half of the nineteenth century.[13] It is a surprising fact that his *Justification* owed nothing to Möhler, for they shared many things in common, despite the fact that in 1837–8 Newman's heart and mind were resolutely Anglican.

As copies became available to him, Newman particularly despatched complimentary copies of the book to at least two significantly interested parties. One was the rector of Winwick in south Lancashire, J. J. Hornby, who in 1834 had edited the *Remains* of the Irish Anglican layman Alexander Knox. One chapter in the first volume printed an essay by Knox on justification, which caused some stir. Knox interpreted Article XI of the Thirty-Nine Articles in a way strikingly akin to that of Bishop Bull. In Knox's understanding that Article certainly excluded individual merit from being a cause of personal justification and also certainly asserted 'imputation'; what it did not affirm was that such a 'reputative' justification is wholly independent of a prior root of righteousness implanted in the soul by God. Justification, in short, is not purely forensic without moral content.

The second principal recipient of an author's copy was George Stanley Faber (1773–1854), Master of Sherburn hospital, Durham, and at one time, as a young man (1795–1803), a fellow of Lincoln College, Oxford.[14] Faber was typical of his times in

[13] *LD* vi. 221. J. A. Möhler's *Symbolik* first appeared at Mainz in 1832. The fifth edition appeared in English translation by J. B. Robertson (London, 1843). The book was immediately attacked by his Protestant colleague at Tübingen, F. C. Baur, to whom Möhler made the rejoinder *Neue Untersuchungen der Gegensätze zwischen der Katholiken und Protestanten, eine Verteidigung meiner Symbolik* . . . (Mainz, 1834). This had a second edition in 1835. The exchanges are a battle of giants.

[14] G. S. Faber's writings included: *A Dissertation on the Prophecies that have been fulfilled, are now fulfilling or will hereafter be fulfilled relative to the Great Period of 1260 Years* (1807: 3rd edn., London, 1808); *Remarks on the Pyramid of Cephrenes lately opened by Mr Belzoni* (London, 1819); *A General and Connected View of the Prophecies relating to the Conversion, Restoration . . . of the Houses of Judah and Israel* (1808; 2nd edn., London, 1809). *The Predicted Downfall of the Turkish Power: The Preparation for the Return of the Ten Tribes* (London, 1853)—evidently two works of vast historical importance for the genesis of Zionism; *The Primitive Doctrine of Election* (1836; 2nd edn., London, 1842).

being an Evangelical clergyman fascinated by the discovery of the inner chambers of the Pyramids. He published work in which he searched the prophecies of the Apocalypse for the secret signs of Antichrist. He believed that Negro people have black skin because of the transmitted penalty of the sixth plague of Egypt in Exodus. He had written a widely used study of predestination, liked by Calvinistic Evangelicals, from whom he dissented by his contemptuous rejection of unrestricted private judgement. He felt confident that the sense of the Scriptures is perspicuous, and the individual must submit, not make up his own mind about the meaning. Faber was provoked by Hornby's publication of Knox's essays and letters, and shortly before Newman lectured wrote an attempted rebuttal of the dangerously papistical doctrines propagated by Bishop Bull and Alexander Knox. He was attacking two Anglican authors with whose writing on the subject Newman felt the deepest affinity. Newman accordingly sent him an early copy of his lectures, with a courteous letter. Faber's reply was also courteous, but reserved his position; he was reading the book amid the hubbub of London and needed to retreat to the quiet of the countryside to digest Newman's argument as it deserved.[15]

In the second edition of his book of 1839 G. S. Faber inserted a sharply hostile appendix about Newman's book. He complained both that he found Newman 'painfully difficult, if not absolutely impossible, of comprehension', and that the book's 'ingenuity of mystification would seduce incautious admirers into all the grossness of Tridentism'. For Newman 'mixes up together wholesome food and rank poison, the sound doctrine of the Church of England and the pernicious dogmas of the Church of Rome'.[16] After Newman had become a Roman Catholic in 1845, Faber put into print that he believed Newman to have been a secret Romanist for a full decade before being finally received.

[15] *LD* vi. 229–33. Faber's letter to Newman of 12 Apr. 1838 assured him that he read with disgust and contempt the attacks on Newman: 'You and I may not always agree; but I think I can insure you from any such attacks, so far as I am concerned.' The outcome was otherwise. The adverse reaction of Samuel Wilberforce to Newman's thesis is studied by D. Newsome, 'Justification and Sanctification: Newman and the Evangelicals', *Journal of Theological Studies*, NS 15 (1964), 32–53.

[16] G. S. Faber, *The Primitive Doctrine of Justification investigated relatively to the Definitions of the Church of Rome and the Church of England* (2nd edn., 1839), 409, 427.

Faber's nephew F. A. Faber, an Anglican clergyman, thought the charge unfortunate, and sought to mediate between Newman and his uncle. Newman included his letter to the nephew of 6 December 1849 in his *Apologia*, chapter 4.[17] Stanley Faber at first withdrew the accusation that Newman was for ten years saying what he did not actually think, but in 1851 renewed it with a peculiarly hurtful letter to Newman, advising him to bear with resignation the consequences of being a Roman Catholic priest who, as it was understood, would 'always lie for the good of his Church'.[18] Newman sent the letter straight back to him.

Newman's *Justification* set out to distinguish his middle way in Anglicanism from popular Protestantism of the time (to which he gave the blanket title 'Lutheranism') and from the Roman Catholic doctrine defined at Trent in 1546–7. Newman cannot honestly be said to have known very much about Martin Luther or the history of the German Reformation.[19] He did not read German, and showed no sign of sharing Bishop Bull's remarkable enthusiasm for the Augsburg and Württemberg Confessions.[20] He had evidently given some study and thought to Luther's tract 'On the Liberty of a Christian'. His quotations from Luther also show that he knew the 1533 commentary on Galatians, of which a bowdlerized version in English had been produced by Elizabethan Puritans (omitting the more Catholic bits, and especially the acknowledgement that the Church of Rome retained the fundamentals of the faith). He drew more from Gerhard's seventeenth-century systematization of Lutheranism in the age after the Formula of Concord.[21] Newman was familiar

[17] *Apo*., p. 169.

[18] *LD* xiv. 333–4.

[19] Much of what Newman knew is likely to have come through J. Milner's *History of the Church of Christ*, revised by I. Milner (Cambridge, 1795–1909), where Luther dominates the account of the Reformation and is given a pietist face.

[20] Bull, *Examen Censurae*, XIII. vii (Opera Latina, p. 576; Library of Anglo-Catholic Theology, p. 149); id., *Apologia pro Harmonia*, VI. ii (Opera Latina, p. 576; Library of Anglo-Catholic Theology, p. 109); ibid. VII. xvi (Opera Latina, p. 673; Library of Anglo-Catholic Theology, p. 320).

[21] M. Chemnitz's *Examen Concilii Tridentini* (Frankfurt, 1566) had many editions. There is a translation by F. Kramer, 2 vols. (St Louis, 1971–8). Johann Gerhard (1582–1637), after Chemnitz the greatest systematic theologian among the Lutherans, wrote *Loci theologici*, 9 vols. (Jena, 1610–22) and *Confessio Catholica*, 4 vols. (Jena, 1633–7) in which he cites passages from Catholic theologians in support of Lutheran theses; cf. id., *Bellarminius orthodoxias testis* (Jena, 1630). Newman may have learned something from Gerhard's controversial method when he cited Calvinist authors and Melanchthon to show their coincidence with Tridentine propositions. But this

with Calvinism, both by virtue of his early education and through his reading of the *Institutes* and commentaries.

The reader of *Justification* quickly receives the deep impression that the middle way for Newman is nearer to Rome than to Wittenberg or Geneva. The popular Protestant conception of justification is treated as morally dangerous, ecclesially sectarian, and selective in its use of a handful of scriptural texts. The Catholic view, by contrast, is never dangerous, though indeed incomplete and defective. Moreover, it is grounded, as Newman demonstrates at length, upon far wider biblical foundations, was endorsed by Augustine's transformist doctrine of grace and the main line of tradition, and had the merit of simplicity in treating right conduct as being in God's sight a matter of the most profound import for salvation.

The Protestants, Newman bluntly declared, were in this question like the Arians who settled everything to their own satisfaction by appealing to a few texts, which were then erected into an all-embracing principle for interpreting everything else. Newman distanced himself from the then widely held view among Evangelicals (a view which Philip Melanchthon expressly disowned in his *Apology for the Augsburg Confession*)[22] that to speak of justification 'by faith alone' necessarily excludes any means of communicating grace through the dominical sacraments or apostolic ministers. His most penetrating critique, however, lies in his pinpointing of a central difficulty of embarrassing proportions for the Protestant Evangelicals, namely that, while asserting faith alone to be the sole instrument of justification, they find it impossible to offer any but the foggiest definition of what they mean by faith: they can say something only of what it is not, namely not a mere assent to belief in God, or to the gospel history, or even submission to due authority. They are anxious to assert that it is to be radically distinguished from any moral quality: repentance or love may be accidents, but love is a by-

controversial technique was common, as in Cochlaeus and in Flacius's *Catalogus Testium*, and is as old as the Chalcedonian Definition of AD 451 in its string of phrases drawn from Cyril of Alexandria, designed to protect the citizenship rights of the school of Antioch.

[22] *Apologia Confessionis Augustanae* (1531), ch. 4, sec. 73: 'by "faith alone" we exclude merit, not the word or sacraments as our opponents slanderously claim' ('Excludimus autem opinionem meriti, non excludimus verbum aut sacramenta, ut calumniantur adversarii').

product, not of faith's essence. From Gerhard, Newman cites the phrase that faith is a 'fiduciary apprehension', a feeling of trust and total dependence on the Redeemer for mercy. Into that trust no element of love may be intruding. Nevertheless, the Protestants very rightly say that justifying faith must be a lively faith, not a mere mental assent. Newman wants to bring them to acknowledge that if faith is to possess the vitality they attribute to it, it will not be evacuated of repentance, love, and openness to renewal under God's grace. Trust necessarily includes elements of hope and love.

If the point is conceded that a saving and justifying faith is not to be divorced from repentance, obedience, and renewal, another great Evangelical divorce collapses also, namely their grand dichotomy between deliverance from guilt and deliverance from sin. Because they have made so absolute a separation between justification and sanctification, they have set asunder forgiveness and renewal. In time and experience, to be forgiven by God is not utterly distinct from being renewed in inner character by the grace of Christ and the indwelling of the Holy Spirit.

Newman was in no doubt that the term justification is a judicial term, and that in theology it speaks of the divine declaration which is also in its essence both forgiveness and renewal. He found in Calvin's critique of the Tridentine Decree on Justification (January 1547)[23] the remarkable concession that justification and renewal are not temporally successive, but simultaneous. Was the question, then, whether renewal belongs to the substance of justification, or whether renewal is not more than an inseparable accident? The very question implies the answer that renewal belongs to the essence of justification. Therefore the act of justification is not merely a declaration about a past event or testimony of a present fact or an announcement of what will be at some future time (such as the Last Judgement), but a causative act which does not leave the recipient a believer as he was before. It is no great step from granting that justification and renewal are conjoined in time to saying that they are conjoined *in re*, and Calvin's critique of Trent is found to say that forgive-

[23] Calvin's *Antidote* is printed in Corpus Reformatorum, vol. xxxv = Calvin, vol. vii (Berlin, 1868), 365–506. English translation in *Tracts and Treatises in Defence of the Reformed Faith*, iii (Edinburgh, 1851), reprinted with notes by T. F. Torrance (Edinburgh, 1958).

ness and regeneration are two ways of speaking about the same thing. The Evangelical Protestants are not mistaken to speak of justification as 'external'; but it is not more external than a sacrament. The external word has as its content the inward grace. When we speak of justification as God's act, we may say that he 'imputes' Christ's righteousness to believers; when we consider our own condition in being accepted and made heirs of eternal life, we should say that we are thereby being made righteous. One ought not to say that when God justifies a believer, the only difference is not in the believer but in the way God thinks about him; that would set aside the truth that the justified are so from eternity in the predestinate purpose of God.

As we have seen, Newman's language about Luther at times looks superficial. He holds Luther immediately responsible for most of the excesses of Evangelical pietism. Luther

> found Christians in bondage to their works and observances; he released them by his doctrine of faith; and he left them in bondage to their feelings. He weaned them from seeking assurance of salvation in standing ordinances, at the cost of teaching them that a personal consciousness of it was promised to every one who believed. For outward signs of grace he substituted inward; for references towards the Church contemplation of self. And thus, whereas he himself held the proper efficacy of the Sacraments, he has led others to disbelieve it; whereas he preached against reliance on self, he introduced it in a more subtle shape; whereas he professed to make the written word all in all, he sacrificed it in its length and breadth to the doctrine which he had wrested from a few texts. (*Jfc.*, p. 340)

Newman's view of Luther particularly enraged Julius Charles Hare, archdeacon of Lewes (1795–1855) who was moved to write a *Vindication of Luther*, and to publish a charge to the clergy of the diocese of Chichester in which he launched a frontal attack on Tractarianism as leading irresistibly to Rome (an opinion of the movement which Newman the convert came to adopt early in the 1850s).[24] Perhaps Newman chose Luther

[24] J. C. Hare, *Vindication of Luther against his recent English Assailants* (2nd edn., 1855). His *Charges* to the clergy of his archdeaconry were reprinted in three volumes (Cambridge, 1856). The opinion that Tractarianism must logically lead to Rome was notoriously not held by Pusey, Keble, and J. B. Mozley. Y. Brilioth, *The Anglican Revival* (London, 1933), pointed out that many ex-Evangelical Tractarians were among those who became Roman Catholics; there were ex-Evangelicals who did not, of course.

for his target because relatively few English people knew much of his writings, whereas they knew Calvin much better. Calvin and Calvinist writers are almost always cited by Newman as witnesses, even if at times reluctant or even unconscious witnesses, to the truth for which he is contending. The radical Protestant tradition in England had never really felt comfortable with Luther. Admittedly, when they sang *Ein feste Burg* (if they did), they were unaware that its author had written the hymn as a battle-song against Satan's latest emissary in the form of Zwingli's Eucharistic doctrine in the year 1527. In his *Actes and Monuments* John Foxe had expressed deep admiration for Luther's stand against the Papacy and insight on the centrality of the doctrine of justification; but Foxe found Luther's intransigence for the real presence embarrassing, and explicable only on the hypothesis that this great hero had not fully realized the extent to which the rags of popery have to be discarded.[25] At the opposite end of the ecclesiastical spectrum, Bull and before him William Forbes, first bishop of Edinburgh in the 1630s, had regarded Luther as a great but distinctly over-excitable person, who had grossly exaggerated, and embarrassed his own sympathizers.[26] So in Anglican writing about the age of the Reformation neither low churchmen nor high churchmen had found very kind language to use about Luther. That may have made it easier for Newman to pick on him as the fount of the excesses to which he now deeply objected in the Church of England's hospitality to the Evangelicals.

Historically it is undeniable that antinomianism appeared within the Lutheran camp in the sixteenth century. Luther used language which was one-sided and which was taken to mean that our salvation depends so wholly on the imputed righteousness of Christ that we need not trouble to have, by grace working within us, any righteousness in our conduct and character. He was taken to mean that by the divine decree of election the end is wholly determined in advance, and some people drew the inference that we do not need to bother too much about the means. Moreover, Luther and Melanchthon had defined justifying faith as confident

[25] Foxe, *Actes and Monuments*, ed. Pratt (London, 1853), iv. 259–322; Zwinglian anger with Luther at iv. 316–18.

[26] Bull, *Harmonia Apostolica* (1669), I. iii. 3, defended in his *Examen Censurae*, X. i. W. Forbes, *Considerationes modestae et pacificae*, I. iv. 1 *init.* ((4th edn. with English trans., Oxford, 1850), i. 300).

trust, *fiducia*. That was heard to mean that one is justified if one is unhesitatingly sure about it, and the subjective certitude is a criterion of being in a state of grace before God. Conservative critics soon observed that this doctrine of faith as assurance was confusing faith with one of its consequences. The problem was to draw the line between confidence resting on the mercy and promises of God and mere human presumption. The thirteenth canon of the Council of Trent on justification (session VI) attempted a *via media* on the subject, but was then widely understood to have censured the notion that the believer was entitled to have any kind of confidence at all.

The debates at Trent in 1546[27] show that the bishops and theologians present were haunted by the two difficulties of assurance and imputation. Several voices spoke for the doctrine that, while believers are indeed made just by 'inherent' or imparted righteousness in the gradual process of sanctification as the Holy Spirit pours the love of God into their hearts, nevertheless 'on account of the uncertainty of the righteousness of our own deeds and the danger of vainglory, it is safer to rest our whole confidence exclusively upon the mercy and loving-kindness of God'.[28] At Trent the most eloquent advocate of this position was Seripando, the General of the Augustinians, and perhaps one of the relatively small group of theologians at Trent not bewildered by the complexity of the problems raised by the issue of justification.[29] In the event Seripando was not able to persuade the Council to endorse his understanding of the matter. On 8 November 1546 Seripando sent an agonized note to the legate Cervini, regretting the failure in understanding manifested by the third draft of the decree, produced by someone so terrified of falling into the Lutheran heresey that he fell into error at the opposite extreme.[30] Seripando wished the council to acknowledge the validity of 'imputed' righteousness; the term had been used by St Paul, and should not be left in the

[27] *Concilium Tridentinum*, v, ed. S. Ehses (Freiburg im Breisgau, 1911).

[28] Bellarmine, *De Justificatione*, 5, 7 ((editio prima romana, 1840), iv. 886).

[29] One bishop at Trent who found the subject bewildering uttered a heartfelt plea for simplicity: *Concilium Tridentinum*, v. 428, 27. I have summarized Seripando's role at Trent in the Turvey Abbey journal *One in Christ* (1984), 191–225. The classic monograph on Seripando is H. Jedin, *Girolamo Seripando* (Würtzburg, 1937; repr. 1984).

[30] *Concilium Tridentinum*, v. 663 n.

triumphant possession of the Lutherans. The failing on the Lutheran side was primarily in their insufficient or even non-existent stress on inherent or imparted righteousness. Imperfect it must be if it is ours, even though the good works are done in God by the indwelling power of the Spirit. But Seripando could not accept, as Newman could not, the notion that justification can mean a declaring of something to be the case when it is certainly not so and is not in the future going to be so.

Seripando's view of imputed and inherent righteousness coincided precisely with that of Richard Hooker who wrote: 'We participate Christ partly by imputation, as when those things which he did and suffered for us are imputed unto us for righteousness; partly by habitual and real infusion, as when grace is inwardly bestowed while we are on earth, and afterwards more fully both our souls and bodies made like unto his in glory'.[31] In the *Discourse of Justification*, in which Hooker sought to ward off anxieties that he was not a sound Protestant, Hooker similarly insisted that because of the imperfection of inherent righteousness (in so far as that is truly ours, by God's grace), we need to rely on Christ's righteousness imputed to us by the divine act of justification. Hooker saw that it must be a mistake to make the divine act of justification to consist exclusively in remission and divorced from the renewal which that makes possible. Hooker's friend Richard Field's treatise of 1606 *Of the Church*[32] agreed with him. Newman found support for the doctrine in the pages of John Davenant (1631). Such language offered an easy bridge to the terminology of the Council of Trent, which affirmed the ground of salvation to be the death and merits of Christ, and handled with great caution the merits which by grace God confers on the justified man. One should not say that the moral value of a righteous life is in no sense the believer's because the gift of grace is seen in it. Nor may one say that the justified person, whose good works are done by the grace of God and the merit of Christ, does not merit increase of grace.[33] But nothing is said about merit of condignity or entitlement. What is clear from Trent's statements on justification is the

[31] R. Hooker, *Laws of Ecclesiastic Polity*, v, lxvi. 11 (ed. Keble (7th edn., Oxford, 1888), 254).

[32] Richard Field, *Of the Church*, III, xi. app. ((Cambridge, 1849), ii. 268–343).

[33] Sessio VI, can. 32 (*Concilium Tridentinum*, v. 799).

rejection of the notion that inherent or imparted righteousness has nothing to do with salvation.

The Protestant reaction to Trent on justification was (sadly) largely one of distrust. Writing to Cranmer in 1548 Melanchthon voiced the belief that the decree of Trent was crafty and ambiguous.[34] Chemnitz similarly expressed the view that canon 32, with its explicit declaration that by Christ's merits the justified come to have merits, was disingenuous.[35] In the nineteenth century the austere Calvinist James Buchanan[36] dismisses Trent on justification as quite unrepresentative of authentic Catholicism, 'vague and general', altogether 'less explicit and offensive' than the reality, too moderate and indeed remarkably close to Luther except for the muddle confounding justification and sanctification. It was irritating to find it so good.

The strict Calvinist doctrine is found in a classical formulation in the Westminster Confession of 1644, chapter 11, with a wealth of detailed precision and anti-Catholic sharpness strikingly absent from the Thirty-Nine Articles, whose inadequacies (or 'mingling of the Gospel with Popery') the far more Protestant Confession was intended to remedy and rectify. It is characteristic that where the Articles simply repeat the medieval canonists' claim that England has the privilege of being outside papal jurisdiction, the confession requires one to say that the pope is ex officio Antichrist. In the doctrine of justification, the crux of the Calvinist position lies in the denial that the divine act of acquittal takes into account any moral consequences in causing renewal in the penitent sinner's heart and mind. In the strongest possible sense of the word it is 'unconditional'. To this interpretation of justification it is cardinal that, because of the total destruction of God's image in fallen humanity, there is no spark or seed or latent capacity for righteousness in the sinner, whose sins have robbed him of free choice and even impaired his

[34] Melanchthon's letter to Cranmer, about Jan. 1548, is epistula 4142 in *Corpus Reformatorum*, vi (Berlin, 1839), 801: 'Synodus Tridentia veteratoria decreta fecit ut ambigue dictis tueatur suos errores. Hanc sophisticam procul ab ecclesia abesse oportuit.' Melanchthon goes on to deplore no less the Protestant wrangle about predestination.

[35] Chemnitz, *Examen Concilii Tridentini*, I. x. 4 (ed. E. Preuss (Berlin, 1861), 212–16).

[36] J. Buchanan, *The Doctrine of Justification* (Edinburgh, 1867), 126–7.

powers of clear rational judgement. There is no potentiality that can have significance for the divine acquittal.

The principle was from time to time stated by Augustine of Hippo (it was part of the Platonic philosophical tradition) that no sin ever goes unpunished even if forgiven. To the Calvinists the punishment for sin is to be seen in the death suffered by Christ. That was for them a satisfaction of divine justice which demanded the appropriate penalty. Newman encountered a rigidly juridical statement of this doctrine of Atonement in the pages of Thomas Erskine (1780–1870), where the theme was fitted into a theology marked by liberal rationalism; Newman thought he eliminated mystery and turned the Atonement into a lawyer's Opinion.

There was of course a grave problem for the Calvinists in combining so strictly juridical a theory of Atonement with a doctrine of the inscrutable sovereignty of grace, infinitely transcending our finite notions of law and justice. We may reckon it no justice to punish the innocent and to acquit the guilty, which would be a mark of a corrupt judge. But God's justice is other than ours. Because he is the source of law, his grace is free to acquit.

Nothing, therefore, within the believer, past, present, or future, even if entirely the work of the Holy Spirit's indwelling presence, can be deemed relevant to the divine acceptance of the sinner. Even after faith and baptism, our best achievements are flawed by pride and egotism. Only a perfect righteousness, one therefore which is Christ's and external to the believer's inward state, can satisfy the requirements of divine holiness. On this view, the question presses how Christ's goodness, righteousness, and holiness, being wholly external, can come to the believer's heart and mind to be appropriated.

At this point the term imputation takes on a special significance, a metaphor from financial accounting being brought in to help with a difficulty in the juridical framework. 'Imputation' is not easy to pin down with precision. In Scripture the verb 'to impute' is applied in cases where a just and good person is reckoned as such, or where a wicked person is reckoned as such. It is not used of a transference of reward from the wicked to the just or from the just to the wicked. The theological doctrine of imputed righteousness, when complemented by the idea that human sinfulness is imputed to the Redeemer, seems to be responsible for the linguistic usage of English that impute is usually a synonym for accuse, and often for 'falsely accuse', or 'attribute faults or crimes unjustly'.

Scripture does not provide a text to say that 'Christ's righteousness is imputed to us'.

A further question needing elucidation is the nature and role of faith in justification. In Catholic theology the faith that responds to divine love in Christ is not divorced from the sacraments and is essentially bound up with repentance, obedience, and renewal. Such a faith includes but is evidently more than the assent of the mind, whether to the core of the gospel history or to belief in God and his providence. It is a submitting of the rebellious individual will to the judgement and love of God and to the forming, nurturing authority of the holy community in the Church, where the gospel is proclaimed in word and sacrament and is lived out in life.

For Augustine of Hippo the term justification signifies the entire act and process of change in the sinner at and consequent upon conversion. He distinguishes between the way of sanctification, in which believers are called to imitate the Lord, and the act whereby Christ justifies the ungodly, an act which only he could do and which is not for our imitation.[37] He contrasts the decisive moment of baptism giving remission of sins and the long daily process of renewal and growth under grace.[38] Believers live all their lives 'under pardon',[39] and 'in this life our righteousness consists more in the forgiveness of sins than in perfection of the virtues'.[40] The righteousness of saints is manifested by their awareness of their imperfection.[41] Augustine, however, does not happily use the term imputation. In one text[42] he expresses fear at the open door to laxity or antinomianism in the notion that after death the soul may rely on the imputing of Christ's righteousness to make up for any shortcomings. On the other extreme, he regarded it as Pelagian to confine the initial grace of justification exclusively to the remission of sins.

[37] Augustine, *De peccatorum meritis*, i. 18.
[38] Id., *De Trinitate*, xiv. 23.
[39] Id., *De Civitate Dei*, x. 22. [40] Ibid. xix. 27.
[41] Id., *Contra duas Epistulas Pelagianorum*, iii. 19.
[42] Id., *Contra Faustum Manichaeum*, xxxiii. 5.

All parties to the sixteenth-century debate agreed that faith is an indispensable means, an instrument or condition through which the Atonement is applied to the baptized believer so that justification is declared. Is justification by faith *alone*? St James said it is not so. St Paul does not say 'alone', but does affirm that justification is by faith and not by the merit of works. All parties therefore concurred in saying that justifying faith is a 'lively' faith, not any kind of faith such as bare mental assent in which will and feeling are irrelevant. The Protestants were in great difficulty in answering the question, What ingredient is it in faith which imparts liveliness or vitality to it? The apostle has a text in Galatians 5.6 on faith working by love, or formed by love. Luther's commentary on Galatians feared that on the exegesis of medieval schoolmen this text could be taken to mean that a man is justified by good works of love, or that there is unformed faith, as if a chaos prior to being given form by love. He denied that the passage had anything to do with justifying faith, except that it is the test of true faith that works of charity result from it, and that is its life; that is, it is not feigned. Newman asks whence faith can derive the indispensable vitality if there is no constituent element of repentance, love, and openness to renewal. And if justifying, saving faith must be allowed to include repentance and obedience, the grand dichotomy between deliverance from guilt and deliverance from sin ceases to look as if it might be faithful to one or two places in scripture. Moreover, to be forgiven by God is not in time or experience wholly distinct from being renewed by grace in the Holy Spirit. Calvary and Pentecost are not to be radically divorced. Justifying faith is no transitory or momentary act but the entry to a permanent state or 'habit' of the soul affecting the character.

Once it has been conceded that justification, as a declaration of acquittal, spills over into acceptance and renewal of the inner heart and mind, the disagreement between Catholic and Protestant about the effect of justification is reduced to minuscule proportions. Because on the Catholic view justification is the name for the total act and process, much more consequence is given to justification than on the Protestant interpretation. Nevertheless the Protestants read the Catholic position in a way of their own, as implying that one can never be certain of being forgiven; that while mortal sins after baptism can be absolved with the result that eternal punishment is averted, yet satisfaction to God and the Church has to be made in time both here and by purification hereafter; that it is because the Catholic must continually go in fear that the Eucharist must be more than a memorial sacrifice or feast but a 'repetition' or re-enactment of the one propitiatory sacrifice of Calvary, thereby restoring hope to the worshippers present. Lack of assurance lies at the root.

Newman sensitively interpreted the eucharistic sacrifice more correctly. He was aware that for Trent there is but one unrepeatable sacrifice on Calvary, yet that the offering of the Church is a true sacrifice. So 'the Father looking on us sees not us but Christ in us' (*Jfc.*, p. 161). The sentence quoted illustrates the way in which Newman coalesces what Christ does for his people with that which he does in them. If one asks how Newman came to hold the indwelling presence of Christ in the soul to belong to the essence of authentic justification, the answer cannot be simply that he found congenial language in Bull and Alexander Knox. In broad terms he agreed with Knox, though characteristically he commented that Knox could usefully have taken pains to use language in more direct conformity with the Anglican formularies, the Prayer Book, Articles, and Ordinal.[43] Newman himself is most careful to underpin his argument with citations from these historical documents of his Church. From his Evangelical years, he could not but be aware that while Calvinist Evangelicals liked to speak as if their position were supported by the Articles and the English liturgy, numerous Evangelicals were in fact embarrassed by the many strongly Catholic features of the Book of Common Prayer, such as the absolution prescribed in the Visitation of the Sick (pointedly contrasted by Newman with a deathbed scene in *The Dairyman's Daughter*, *Jfc.*, p. 330) or the traditional elements in the Eucharistic rite, such as the prayer that by this thanksgiving 'all thy whole Church' may be granted remission of sins and the benefits of the passion. Evangelicals at times hinted that they would welcome a liturgy and confession of faith which were 'more scriptural' and might suggest that it would be well if Roman Catholics could come to say the same. That the Book of Common Prayer embodied the apostolic

[43] *LD* vi. 228.

tradition was not the judgement of 'far gone Evangelicals, as they are called'.[44]

It would have been difficult for such far-gone Evangelicals to understand that the force which really drove Newman to his interpretation of justification was his Bible study. Father Stephen Dessain rightly stressed this point in the chapter which he contributed to *The Rediscovery of Newman*.[45] He printed a pencilled note found in Newman's personal copy of the *Lectures on the Doctrine of Justification.* It is worth repeating here:

> The object of my book is this—to show that Lutheranism is either a truism or a paradox; a truism if with Melanchthon it is made rational, a paradox if with Luther it is made substantive; Melanchthon differs scarcely more than in terms from the Catholic; Luther scarcely in sense from the Antinomian. My book then is of the nature of an Irenicon in the doctrine of which it treats.

The acknowledgement that Scripture was the primary influence that led Newman to recast the doctrine of justification in a way that distanced him from the 'popular Protestantism' of contemporary Evangelicalism does not mean that Newman had no other debts. Bull had, of course, done something for him on the rational and intellectual side. But if Bull's discussion of justification has a weakness, that lies in the relative absence of very deep religious feeling in his writing on the subject. Like Paley, for whom Newman felt no rapport at all, Bull saw things in a cool clear light and had thought deeply about the subject. But one does not rise up from his book, as one might from Newman's, moved by the passion of the intense quest for scriptural and religious truth here and now. In that respect Alexander Knox probably did more for Newman than did Bull.

But there is one Anglican theologian of the seventeenth century, little cited except in the appendix on the 'formal cause' of justification, whose affinities with Newman's position are evident and whose passionate religious feeling went hand in hand with a rare lucidity of mind and expression, namely Jeremy Taylor. His discourse on justification brings justification and

[44] *LD* vi. 275.

[45] S. Dessain, 'The Biblical Basis of Newman's Ecumenical Theology', in J. Coulson and A. M. Allchin (eds.), *The Rediscovery of Newman: An Oxford Symposium* (London, 1967), 100–22.

sanctification into the closest connexion. They are allowed to be distinct to the detached reflecting mind, but not in religious experience where they are two ways of speaking about one and the same thing. Newman clearly felt an answering chord within himself when he read Taylor's observation that a fully detailed understanding of every intricate point in the doctrine of justification can be highly perilous to the soul. The subject is so complex and so fascinating that the theologian runs the risk of losing his own soul in mastering the labyrinthine arguments. Above all, for Taylor the heart of Christian faith and life lay where it did for Newman, namely in the indwelling Christ in whom the believer participates through the sacraments.[46] Hence Newman's statement in the book of 1838, later corrected in a footnote as a departure from Roman Catholic understanding, that not only baptism but the eucharist must be understood as sacraments of justification, and indeed constitute the primary means of this great grace (*Jfc.*, pp. 152, 184, 187, 226).

Newman was aware that Protestant critics would dismissively say he had failed to distinguish justification from sanctification. That is what they soon were saying as if that settled all questions. He was bound to feel that they had not considered the matter deeply enough. The distinction for religious experience is largely academic. He also expected criticism from another quarter, in those who would decry his interpretation as a piece of 'mysticism', a pejorative term in the 1830s (*Jfc.*, p. 145). He was sensitive to the unsacramental mind-set of liberal Protestants who would think that a stress on sacraments, which belong to the world of sense as well as of mind, could encourage superstition, or would introduce 'a pantheistic spirit' into the gospel. Nothing could be less like pantheism than Newman's theology. He wished to rest on the apostle's noble words: 'I live, yet not I but Christ lives in me.'

[46] Newman stands much closer in sympathy to Augustine than does Jeremy Taylor, whom both would have found too inclined to Pelagianism. But the Eucharistic devotion of Taylor, his Catholic conception of the sacrifice of the Mass, and the coincident understandings of the verbal distinction and real identity between justification and sanctification, constitute a bond. Newman can hardly have failed to respond to Taylor's profoundly religious feeling. See now H. R. McAdoo, *The Eucharistic Theology of Jeremy Taylor* (Norwich, 1988), for a masterly examination of Taylor's remarkable qualities.

Newman's Protestant critics came to read his book as consciously preparing the ground for the conversion of 1845, reconciling the Thirty-Nine Articles with Trent (which on justification is not very difficult to do), attempting a 'concordism' that might open the way for an ecumenical reconciliation between Canterbury and Rome. If there was any element of that in Newman's mind in 1838, it lay in his subconscious. He dedicated the published lectures to Richard Bagot, the Bishop of Oxford, an act which could be understood not merely as aspiring to gain his support in any coming controversy but also as a declaration of Anglican allegiance. In the ensuing storms Bishop Bagot was coolly neutral, and was sadly felt by Newman to have done nothing to support him when critics were telling him to get out and go to Rome. The book of 1838 is wholly Anglican in content and temper. It is instructive, nevertheless, that when as a Roman Catholic he came to reissue this volume, together with his other Anglican works, he found relatively few places where he needed to alter the text or to add a warning footnote that he would not put it that way thirty-six years later. Like much else in Newman, the book is among the major muniments of the modern ecumenical movement.

15

Newman's Dialectic
Dogma and Reason in the Seventy-Third *Tract for the Times*

COLIN GUNTON

1. THE DIALECTIC

Like all thinkers, Newman is what he is by virtue of what he made of the influences that formed him. Two in particular appear to have given shape to his questions and answers. The first is—despite Newman's interest in Athanasius and his opponents—the dominating mind of the West, Augustine of Hippo. To Augustine must go much of the credit—if that be the word—for the unique combination of rationalism and authoritarianism which was long the mark of Western theology. The leaning towards authoritarianism derived from Augustine's experience, and is well expressed by Harnack. Augustine's encounter with Manichaeism, he holds, shook for ever his confidence in the rationality of Christian truth, so that he acquired a compensating tendency to fall back upon ecclesiastical authority:

> The thousand doubts excited by theology, and especially Christology, could only be allayed by the Church . . . *The Church guaranteed the truth of the faith, where the individual could not perceive it* . . . Openly he proclaimed it: I believe in many articles only on the Church's authority; nay, I believe in the Gospel itself merely on the same ground.[1]

Both the experience and its outcome have parallels in Newman so long afterwards, and it is a noticeable feature of the *Grammar of Assent* that, where argument fails, a last resort is appeal to the authority of the Church. 'That the Church is the infallible oracle of truth is the fundamental dogma of the Catholic religion'.[2]

[1] A. von Harnack, *History of Dogma*, v, trans. J. Millar (London, 1898), 80.
[2] *GA*, p. 102.

The other side of Augustine is to be found echoed in Newman also, and that is a relentless drive to prove, within the limits of Catholic authority, the truth or at least conceivability of the doctrines of the faith. The dialectic of faith and reason, of trust in authority and drive for understanding, that marked Augustine's thought became the pattern for Western theology until the Reformation and Enlightenment. And that takes us to a second formative influence on Newman. In the Enlightenment, the Western dialectic received a one-sided radicalization. For Locke, reason and revelation were indeed two sources of thought, but the latter became subordinate to the former, and its credibility was to be assessed entirely by the light of reason. In place of the authority of the infallible Church there was posited the authority—at least in principle—of infallible reason. Thus was formed the anti-dogmatic principle which Newman rightly repudiated as the enemy of Christianity.

From such a point of view, Newman's programme can be read as a return to Augustinianism: the *Grammar of Assent* to move behind Locke, the *Lectures on the Doctrine of Justification* to move behind Luther, in both cases back to Augustine. The result is that, as with Augustine, we meet the appeal to authority and the free use of argument side by side—again as in Augustine not always very well co-ordinated. An examination of Newman's encounter with Thomas Erskine of Linlathen and others in Tract Seventy-Three 'On the Introduction of Rationalistic Principles into Revealed Religion' will enable us to appreciate something of the shape the Augustinian dialectic of authority and reason, of acceptance and argument took in Newman's thinking.[3]

2. THE CRITIQUE OF RATIONALISM

The brilliance of Newman's 1835 *Tract for the Times* is that it pinpoints with great clarity the inner logic and weakness of his opponents' positions, and at the same time allows his own conception of dogma and revelation to come to the surface. Despite its brilliance, however, the Tract is only half successful because it fails to deal with the underlying strength of the position it is concerned to attack. It has been suggested that the reason for a

[3] 'On the Introduction of Rationalistic Principles into Revealed Religion', *Ess.* i. 30–101.

fundamental disagreement between two opposed positions may often be found in their sharing of a false premiss,[4] and there is something to be said for that being the case here, too. Although the objects of Newman's polemics were harbingers of the depressing reductionism which has come to full flower in the century since his death, there is also much reason to be dissatisfied with the rather dualistic Augustinian theology which continues to dominate his thought.

First, then, a critique of the rationalistic theologies of Newman's adversaries. His general objection to rationalism is that it wants to know too much and so dismisses too easily that which cannot be exhaustively known. In his polemics, as in some of the points made in the *Grammar of Assent*, it is possible to hear anticipations of the arguments of Michael Polanyi in this century against the Enlightenment's demand for totally explicit and formal systems of knowledge. According to Polanyi, all knowledge is personal, which is not to say unreal but rather a function of the way in which finite persons engage with the world.[5] He would agree with Newman that 'Rationalism is a certain abuse of Reason; that is, a use of it for purposes for which it never was intended, and is unfitted' (*Ess*. i. 31). Human knowledge, being human, may not claim too much. The trouble with the theological rationalists is that they do precisely this, at once trespassing on the domains of mystery and falsifying the Christian revelation.

On the face of it, the programme of Thomas Erskine of Linlathen was an admirable one. Erskine was in salutary reaction against the defence of the indefensible, in particular the rigid form that predestinarian Calvinist orthodoxy had taken in the centuries after Calvin. His disapproval of the acceptance of theological formulas for their own sake, especially when they bore no relation to salvation, was surely justified. Moreover, Erskine's theology, even on Newman's rather unsympathetic account, breathes a concern to humanize theology, to stress the grace made real in Christ against attempts to frighten into belief.

And yet Newman is justified in many of the charges he makes against both Erskine and Abbott. The burden of his complaint is

[4] R. W. Newell, *Objectivity, Empiricism and Truth* (London and New York, 1986), 37.

[5] M. Polanyi, *Personal Knowledge: Towards a Post-Critical Philosophy* (1958; 2nd edn., London, 1962).

that both of his opponents, and particularly the latter, evacuate the faith of essential content by their rationalistic treatment of the given dogmas of the tradition. What Newman means by the rationalizing of Christianity can be analysed into a number of features, the following salient among them. First, there is the tendency to anthropocentrism: 'Our private judgement is made everything to us,—is contemplated, recognized, and consulted as the arbiter of all questions, and as independent of everything external to us' (*Ess.* i. 34). Here Newman anticipates what has in recent years become a commonplace among those who see in the elevation of subjective judgement which began with Descartes and took particularly rigid form in Kant, the foe of a due assessment of human limits and fallibility.

Newman expresses the opposition to the deification of human individual judgement in rather one-sidedly theocentric form: 'The Rationalist makes himself his own centre, not his Maker; he does not go to God, but he implies that God must come to him' (*Ess.* i. 33–4). And yet even there he is not out of step with voices from other fields of human scientific and cultural activity who have in recent years been heard to insist that without a due appreciation of the place of authority, community, and tradition there can be no rational activity. Something must be *given* if anything at all is to be achieved. It is, furthermore, worth noting that Newman is not simply making a point about the essential limitedness of the human intellect. In other respects too he reveals anticipations of more recent concerns. That he could destroy his credit in high places with a work entitled *On Consulting the Faithful in Matters of Doctrine* is a measure of a genuine move to a churchly or communal rather than merely clerical conception of the nature of authority.

A second vice of rationalism is its tendency to hold that unless everything is known, then nothing can be. The 'all or nothing' conception of knowledge is particularly destructive of theology, and is another fruit of the Enlightenment's deification of human judgement. Newman observes acutely the effects of this aspect of the syndrome on Christianity's teaching. Not only is mystery discarded (*Ess.* i. 34), but revelation is explained away or forced prematurely into a system. 'It [Rationalism] considers faith to consist rather in the knowledge of a system or scheme, than of an agent . . .' (*Ess.* i. 39). It is not that Newman denies the systematic nature of Christian doctrine. Rather, he operates with what can be called a dialectic of system. Revelation does indeed belong to a 'vast system' (*Ess*. i. 42), but is not such as can be expressed by means of any particular system of words: there is a gulf between the reality and the words which would give that reality rational form. There is therefore a distinction to be drawn between rationalism and faith. 'Rationalism takes the words of Scripture as signs of Ideas; Faith, of Things or Realities.' (*Ess*. i. 35.) In other words, we may not encompass divine realities by our logic, even though they have their own (unknown) logic in the mystery of eternity.

A similar point is made against those who will not believe anything unless its truth be first demonstrated. According to Erskine, 'doctrines, it seems, are not true, if they are not explicable' (*Ess*. i. 60). One citation from Erskine's work, indeed, reveals him as a classic rationalist: '"I may understand many things which I do not believe; but I cannot believe anything which I do not understand, unless it be something addressed merely to my senses and not to my thinking faculty"' (*Ess*. i. 39). The implied view of knowledge as a function of the relation of clear and distinct ideas links Erskine with both Descartes and Locke, but Newman's reply takes us much further back. It was in similar terms that Athanasius chided the Arians for assuming that nothing could be true unless they understood it. It is clear that we meet here something more than a mere appeal to mystery. Underlying Newman's objections is a general point about the limits of human ability to penetrate the structures of reality and of human language fully to encompass that which it attempts to express.

Yet another feature of rationalism's drive to system is its tendency to reduce all Christian teaching to a single principle, and so deny the richness of its various doctrines. In traditional dogmatic Christianity there is a range of doctrines, each of which stands as a mystery in its own right. Newman gives a list of what he takes to be the essentials, beginning: 'the Holy Trinity; the incarnation of the Eternal Son; His atonement and merits; the Church as His medium and instrument . . .' (*Ess*. i. 45). To this he contrasts the 'popular theology of the day . . . that the Atonement is the chief doctrine of the Gospel' (*Ess*. i. 47). It is not that he denies the importance of the atonement; as we have seen, it is high on his list of *credenda*. It is rather that he opposes any tendency to reduce Christianity to that which is seen and experienced. The economy of salvation is only a part, and must be seen to have its basis in eternity. '[I]t is the triumph of Rationalism to level everything to the lowest and most tangible form . . .' (*Ess.* i. 89). Corresponding, accordingly, to the dialectic of system which we have already met there is for Newman a dialectic of time and eternity which is, as we shall see, the key to his conception of dogma. Time and eternity are distinct realms of being which may not be confused.

The third sin of rationalism is manifest in its tendency to reduce religion to morality or utility. Against such a practice, Newman urges the priority of truth, the need to accept the faith for its own sake. One may not conclude from the fact that Christianity has a bearing on character to the 'general proposition, that in a genuine Revelation *all* doctrines revealed must have a direct bearing upon the moral character enjoined by it' (*Ess.* i. 56). Newman suspects that some such reduction underlies Erskine's desire to concentrate on what we know of God's saving action in Christ, but is certain that it is operative in Abbott's more radical reduction: 'the virtue of the great sacrifice is, not expiation, atonement in God's sight, but the *moral effect* of Christ's death on those who believe in it' (*Ess.* i. 85). As Newman observes, and the claim has been plentifully verified since, in cases where utility is given preference over truth the theologian simply becomes the organ of the spirit of the age (*Ess.* i. 91). A Christianity dominated by thoughts of relevance only advertises its own irrelevance.

3. THE PROBLEMS

The strength of Newman's assault on rationalism is manifest. He has unerringly indicated the inadequacies in its assumptions about God, the human mind, and the nature of Christianity. And yet the Achilles' heel of his position is to be found in the very moments of truth in the positions he assaults, in their reasons for making the assertions that they do. Corresponding to each of the three charges against rationalism there are equivalent complaints to be made against Newman's reconstituted Augustinianism. First comes the matter of anthropocentrism. Why had Newman's opponents succumbed, apparently so easily, to a sub-Christian anthropocentrism? The simple, and only partly true, answer is that they had succumbed to the spirit of the age, to the Enlightenment's divinizing of human knowledge and power.

Yet it could also be argued that the Enlightenment itself was a partly justified protest, within the framework of the Augustinian tradition, against that tradition's tendency to subject everything temporal to what have come to be called the constraints of heteronomy. It was thus the assertion of the due rights of time against eternity, of human freedom against divine determinism. If at the same time there was a tendency to elevate humankind to a kind of surrogate divinity in place of the triune God, its moments of truth should still not be denied. Alongside the negative and secularizing protest of the modern movement, there was a positive concern, for human freedom and dignity had suffered at the hands of oppressive regimes which had been either those of the Church itself or had been supported by the Church. No glorification of the Middle Ages should have ignored the wars, tortures, and burnings that had been perpetrated in the name of the crucified. In such a context, a reassertion of the centrality of the human could be understood as a return to some of the values of the Incarnation, of the eternal Son's enfleshment.

There is little doubt that Erskine's theology is contaminated by a strong dose of anthropocentric rationalism. But it must be remembered that he was in justified revolt against a predestinarian Calvinism which, in its concern for the right of God to do exactly as he pleased, at times appeared to ignore the humanity of the Incarnation. Erskine contemplated the biblical teaching about salvation, and found it strongly oriented to human well-being. He was moved in the direction of a doctrine of universal salvation—as had been Paul before him in Romans 11: 32—because what he read spoke to him primarily of the love of God: of his gracious rather than gratuitous action towards his creation. No doubt he did tend to reduce the being of God to his historical manifestation, but he did at least take that manifestation into the heart of his theology. The stress on grace and love was a note which Newman himself might well have both heard and sounded somewhat more strongly.

The second feature of rationalism which Newman rightly observed and rejected was its tendency to be over-systematic. It is, however, also possible to evade the need to be systematic, and so to give the impression of mystery mongering, or of what could be called dogmatic positivism—a take-it-or-leave-it casting of the pearls of dogma before the swine of humanity. One of the reasons for the apparent disfavour into which Trinitarian belief has fallen of late—and it is the only good reason—is the impression it sometimes gives of being the product of airy, almost mathematical, speculation, divorced from the concrete presence of God to the world through Jesus and the Spirit. Some passages in Newman's writings reinforce the impression:

> the Catholic doctrine of the Trinity is a mere juxtaposition of separate truths, which to our minds involves inconsistency, when viewed together; nothing more being attempted by theologians, for nothing more is told us. (*Ess.* i. 52)

We shall return to the matter of the Trinity later, but it must be said that in the light of the history of dogma such an assertion is simply false, being justified neither by Augustine's tireless efforts to do what Newman says we may not ('reduce them [the truths] into an intelligible dependence on each other, or harmony with each other' (*Ess.* i. 53)), nor by the more straightforward and concrete treatments of the Cappadocian Fathers.

Another equally instructive example of Newman's refusal to face the challenge to be systematic is found at the heart of his disagreement with Erskine. The two contestants agree, as we have seen, that the doctrine of the Atonement is somewhere near the centre of the Christian dispensation. It is also clear that Paul, for example in Romans 3: 26, sees the cross as the place where both the forgiveness of God and the requirements of universal justice are realized. The Epistle to the Romans is therefore itself a demonstration of the nature of divine justice, and an invitation to further reflection upon it. Newman, however, appears to render illegitimate such further theological articulation. 'He [Erskine] considers, in common with many other writers of his general way of thinking, that in that most solemn and wonderful event, we have a Manifestation, not only of God's love, but of His justice.' (*Ess.* i. 65.) We can, to be sure, understand Newman's warning: certain 'how' questions are ruled quite out of court by the character of God's ways towards us, and indeed, 'some "depth" of God's counsels would have been acknowledged and accepted on *faith*' (*Ess.* i. 66). Yet by his insistence that it is too much to claim that we have in the Cross a manifestation of both love and justice, Newman would appear to rule out Paul, and certainly calls into question Anselm's classic articulation in the *Cur Deus Homo* of the inner rationality of God's saving action in Christ.

We come, third, to Newman's—again salutary—protest against the reduction of dogma to its moral relevance and utility. Here, too, he shows signs of lurching into the equal and opposite error of a complete divorce of dogma from life. Again referring to the doctrine of the Trinity, Newman asks: 'does not the notion of a Mystery lead to awe and wonder? And are these not moral impressions?' (*Ess.* i. 59.) Up to a point; but much depends upon the nature of the mystery, and a doctrine consisting in the 'mere juxtaposition of separate truths' seems scarcely to be adequate.

The nature of the case can be illustrated from the thought of one who was born two years after Newman said his farewell to Oxford. P. T. Forsyth was as pungent and insistent a critic as Newman of the rationalism which had, by his time, made even greater inroads into the Churches. With his insistence on the churchly nature of Christianity, there is little doubt that this Congregationalist from Aberdeen owed something to the Oxford Movement. Yet he showed a greater freedom than Newman in receiving from the 'opposition' a liberation from abstract dogmatism. A Trinitarian thinker, with a strongly Christocentric emphasis, Forsyth, like Erskine, saw that, to a degree, dogma needed to be moralized: to be filled out with concrete content by reference to the historic saving activity of God. Forsyth had his weaknesses, too, but he does at least show that the choice is not entirely between rationalism and positivist dogmatism. To be fair to Newman, that is not quite the way in which he presents the alternatives. But there is no doubt that his manner of writing brings him rather near.

4. SHARED PRESUPPOSITIONS

It is sometimes claimed that the divided churches of Christendom are for the most part right in what they affirm, wrong in what they deny. With Newman's assertions about the nature of Christian doctrine, the opposite could be argued to the case, in that he is acute in his criticisms of theological rationalism, but less convincing in what he wishes to put in its place. To understand the basis of his position, we must return to the question of the presuppositions he shares with his opponents. In this respect, something has already been said of the Western dialectic, shared by Newman, of time and eternity, reason and faith. Time and eternity tend, on his account, to be conceived as utterly distinct realms, the one treated by human reason, the other unknown, but accepted through revelation on faith and by authority.[6] His own expression of the matter leaves no doubt that such is the case: 'the Church Catholic has ever taught . . . that there are facts revealed to us, not of this world, not of time, but of eternity, and that absolutely and independently . . .' (*Ess*. i. 69). The impression is consequently given that what happens in time, including even the economy of salvation, remains in an utterly different order from eternity, from God himself, so that the two orders can be related only by appeal to authority. By implication, as we have seen, even such explorations of the rationality of faith as Anselm's are made to appear questionable.

It may be objected that Newman, in a kind of reflex emphasizing of the eternal and mysterious, exaggerates the *diastasis* between time and eternity because of the strength of his opposition to the rationalist's stress on reason and temporality. There is without doubt something in that. But that such a one-sidedness is characteristic of Newman's position as a whole is revealed by features of his thought which are not to be accounted for solely in terms of such a reaction. A brief examination of two instances of his treatment of central Christian dogmas will indicate something of the deep-seatedness of the gulf.

The first is one we have already met, the doctrine of the Trinity. In order to do more than repeat the allusions to his treatment of that subject in Tract Seventy-Three, we turn to what he makes of it in the *Grammar of Assent*. The argument of that work, it will be remembered, centres on the distinction between 'real'—by which is chiefly meant concerned with the concrete and particular—and 'notional' apprehension and assent

[6] There are some clear echoes of Locke to be heard in Newman here. '*Faith* . . . is the assent to any proposition, not thus made out by the deductions of reason, but upon the credit of the proposer, as coming from God in some extraordinary way of communication. This way of discovering truths to men we call *revelation*.' Locke, *An Essay concerning Human Understanding*, IV. xviii. 2.

—that of the abstract and theoretical. Newman illustrates the distinction by references to the doctrine of the Trinity. First, he affirms that the Catholic dogma of the Trinity is that 'this essential characteristic of His Nature (sc. as personal) is reiterated in three distinct ways or modes; so that the Almighty God . . . has Three Personalities . . . a Divine Three . . .'. As such, the dogma is 'notional', a revelation to be accepted on faith as the eternal truth of God.[7] It is notional as belonging to the eternal world, as, so to speak, coming down directly from heaven, and is therefore not the object of rational exploration. Rather, it takes logical form only 'as it is a number of propositions, taken one by one', so that it is not possible to assent rationally to the whole, 'because, though we can image the separate propositions, we cannot image them altogether'.[8] (That last sentence is itself a revealing and surprisingly rationalist conception of what it is to conceive and assent to a proposition.)

Second, and on the other hand, Newman argues that it can be shown that particular elements of the set of propositions that go to make up the dogma of the Trinity are 'really' apprehensible. 'That systematized whole is the object of notional assent, and its propositions, one by one, are the objects of real.'[9] In spelling out what he means by these objects of real apprehension, Newman appeals largely to the particularities of Scripture, to the economy of salvation. Thus in this work too there emerges the dialectic between time and eternity. It is not that Newman fails entirely to relate the two. His thought is far more subtle than to posit an absolute gulf between the two sides of his dialectic. Rather, his tendency is to make the relations between the two more opaque than need be: to use the concept of ecclesiastical authority as the means of crossing an otherwise unbridgeable epistemological divide.

The other illustration of Newman's problematic treatment of the relation of eternity and time is to be found in his Christology. One effect of the form the West's dialectic has taken is to be found in a recurring feature of much traditional Christology, in which such stress is placed on the divinity of Christ that his humanity, although asserted, appears to be overwhelmed and effectively to play no substantive part in the drama of salvation.

[7] *GA*, p. 85. [8] *GA*, p. 88. [9] *GA*, p. 91.

It is this which gives the moments of truth to the arguments of Newman's rationalist opponents, under whose impetus the 'quest of the historical Jesus' took place. It must be acknowledged that Newman's fundamental rejection of the shape the modernist quest took has been amply justified by history. 'Mr Abbott, starting with the earthly existence of our Lord, does but enlarge upon the doctrine that a man is God.' (*Ess.* i. 75.) A typical nineteenth-century Christology is indeed one of Jesus as a divinized man. Nevertheless, it must also be acknowledged that Newman's own Christology justifies suspicions that the traditional form of the doctrine endangers the teaching of the full humanity of the Saviour. In his rebuttals of Abbott, Newman uses many phrases which can be taken in an orthodox manner, but which do appear to make the humanity of Jesus a cipher, a passive instrument of the eternal Word: 'His personality is in His Godhead' (*Ess.* i. 86); 'The Son of God made flesh, though a man, is beyond comparison with other men; His person is not human . . .' (*Ess.* i. 87).

Thus it is that, while Newman rightly suspects his opponents of limiting revelation to its temporal manifestations, they could in their turn rightly suspect him of evading the implications of the historical events in which God makes himself known. The presupposition that the two share, accordingly, is that, because time and eternity are incompatible realms of being, a measure of choice is required between them. For the rationalist, the eternal may be known only as being in some way a function of temporal things; for the traditional Augustinian, eternity can be apprehended, if at all, only the other side of or outside of the temporal. Of Newman, as of Augustine, it must be asked whether his thought is truly incarnational, truly able to conceive God as involved in time and space, and consequently to conceive of time and space as patient of taking the shape of the eternal. One, apparently almost chance, statement of Newman's in his *Apologia* suggests that there is in this respect a real parallel between him and Augustine. Speaking of his 1838 pamphlet on the real presence, Newman comments: 'The fundamental idea is consonant to that to which I had been so long attached; it is the denial of the existence of space except as a subjective idea of our minds.'[10] If

[10] *Apo.*, p. 74.

we compare here Augustine's wondering in the *Confessions*,[11] 'whether it [time] is an extension of the mind itself', we shall find the weak spot of all Augustinian thought. If time and space are projections of our minds, rather than qualifications of the objective or real world, how may we affirm that the temporal and spatial Jesus of Nazareth is the real presence of God to the world? It is from such a point of view that rationalism and dogmatism appear to be but two sides of the one coin, the one opting for time and reason, the other for eternity and faith. Both tend to assume that it is finally necessary to come down on one side or other of the dialectical divide.

5. CONCLUSION

As the modernist fashion takes its course, Newman's protests against rationalism appear more and more justified. With the benefit of another century of debate, however, it is also apparent that the mere assertion of dogma is an inadequate response to the crisis. But such a consideration raises a question. Is it not anachronistic to criticize a theologian with such benefit of hindsight? Is Newman, a nineteenth-century Catholic, being belaboured with weapons forged in later disputes and partly with his assistance? There are undoubtedly elements of truth in the objection. But a question is thereby raised about Newman's place in the history of theology.

The fact is that Newman was not alone, nor was he the first to engage in intellectual struggle with the forces of the Enlightenment. A generation before, Samuel Taylor Coleridge had done work whose sympathetic appropriation would have enabled Newman to sharpen his perception of what was at stake. In the area of the relation of faith and reason, and in his elaboration of an approach to the Trinitarian basis of all thought and reality, Coleridge had engaged with the very topics which Newman was later to treat as if he were beginning anew. He early wrote Coleridge out of his life as 'a very original thinker, who, while he indulged a liberty of speculation, which no Christian can tolerate, and advocated conclusions which were often heathen rather than Christian, yet after all instilled a higher philosophy into inquiring

[11] Augustine, *Confessions*, xi. 26.

minds, than they had hitherto been accustomed to accept'.[12] Once again, we witness Newman's tendency to so strong an opposition to rationalism that the elements of truth in the modern protest against the past are ignored.

One major difference between Coleridge and Newman was in their assessment of the Reformation. Coleridge, for whom Luther was a major spiritual guide, was able to incorporate the thought of the Reformers into a broadly orthodox Anglican position. He was therefore able to take a more synoptic view of the influences that formed English Christianity, and a more balanced approach to the tradition as a whole. Some of the major influences upon Newman, on the other hand, saw in the Reformation simply another form of the modernist enemy. The outcome was that Newman was less able than Coleridge to take into his system the best elements of modernity. In that respect, it must be said that he represents a step backwards. In other respects, however, as we have seen, he was an acute observer of the fact that the modernist denial of tradition and dogma is finally a denial of Christianity, as well as the author of a move in the direction of a conception of personal knowledge whose development is the responsibility of later generations.

[12] *Apo.*, p. 94.

16

Newman and the Mystery of Christ

RODERICK STRANGE

I

It is not difficult nowadays to feel a sense of dissatisfaction with Newman's teaching on the humanity of Christ. While the divinity was affirmed on countless occasions, time and again what was said of his humanity seems to be qualified. David Newsome, preaching the Oriel Commemoration Sermon in 1986, was led to describe Newman's Christology as 'bordering on the Monophysite'.[1] Evidence for such a view can come readily to hand. In his sermon 'Christ, the Son of God made Man', for example, Newman declared:

> though He was in nature perfect man, He was not man in exactly the same sense in which any one of us is a man. Though man, He was not, strictly speaking, in the English sense of the word, *a* man; . . . We may not speak of Him as we speak of any individual man, acting from and governed by a human intelligence within Him, but He was God, acting not only as God, but now through the flesh also, when He would.[2]

Such words as these and others in a similar tone prompted Hilda Graef to remark upon Newman's tendency to emphasize Christ's divinity 'to such a degree as to make him almost unapproachable'.[3] In fact, the passage expresses within a sermon the Alexandrian approach which was the basis for all Newman's thinking on Christ and must not be understood as dismissive of the human nature, which is how it will seem to the untutored, modern eye. Something far more theologically sophisticated was being said. Nevertheless, once allowance has been made for these observations, a remark of Gabriel Daly's may be judged to have captured the position succinctly: 'Put in Newman's own later

[1] See D. Newsome, Commemoration Sermon, *Oriel Record* (1987), 17.
[2] *PS* vi. 62.
[3] H. Graef, *God and Myself* (London, 1968), 51–2.

terminology, his Christ is really divine and notionally human.' And he added: 'The problem is not Christ's "possessing a human nature"—a point which Newman always secures notionally—but his actually living, feeling, and thinking as a recognisably human being.' Shortly afterwards he concluded: 'it is hard to deny that Newman shared in the functional monophysitism of traditional orthodoxy'.[4] That criticism seems to articulate a consensus. All the same, there is something further to be said.

II

Taking a cue from Daly, the question revolves, first of all, around what makes someone a recognizably human being. The answer must involve weakness, limitation, insecurity, and ignorance. Such experiences are the stuff of the human condition day by day. But these aspects are plainly missing from Newman's account of Christ as man who did not evidently suffer our limitations, live with our insecurities, or wrestle with our ignorance. He appeared on the contrary always to have been in complete control. In one sermon Newman suggested that when the Son of God 'took into Himself a human soul, He assumed that over which He had absolute and sovereign command'. And he offered an analogy:

> As a man's thoughts and wishes are part of himself, and if he has due control of himself, he governs, as he will, those thoughts and wishes, in some parallel way it may be supposed that our Lord absolutely orders that human nature which He has made His. He acts through it—according to it, *when* it pleases Him and only when, not otherwise.[5]

This control is well illustrated in his sermon 'Tears of Christ at the Grave of Lazarus', which he preached on 12 April 1835.

Newman was trying to answer the question why Christ should have wept at all, when he knew he had the power to raise Lazarus. Why, he asked, 'should He act the part of those who sorrow for the dead?'[6] It is revealing that he never suggested that

[4] G. Daly, review of R. Strange, *Newman and the Gospel of Christ* (Oxford, 1981), in *Journal of Ecclesiastical History*, 35 (1984), 289–90.

[5] MS sermon no. 407, pp. 14–15. MS Sermons can be found in the Birmingham Oratory Archives.

[6] *PS* iii. 128.

he might have wept from sheer, simple, human grief; he speculated rather that it was from spontaneous tenderness, or from pity, or from the realization of the consequences for himself of raising Lazarus, his own arrest, passion, and crucifixion. And he remarked: 'Here was the Creator of the world at a scene of death, seeing the issue of His gracious handiwork. Would not He revert in thought to the hour of creation, when He went forth from the bosom of the Father to bring all things into existence?'[7] This reference to the clarity of Jesus's divine consciousness strikes a jarring note, for it seems to compromise the genuineness of his manhood. It is, moreover, noteworthy that earlier in the same sermon Newman had described Jesus as 'partially ignorant', a phrase he had also used the month before when preaching on 'The Humiliation of the Eternal Son'. These words, however, occurred only in the Anglican editions of the sermons; in the uniform edition, published in 1868, they had been changed, in one sermon to 'apparently ignorant' and in the other to 'seemingly ignorant'.[8]

These alterations can be explained. Newman attributed ignorance to Christ at first, because he believed it was the common view of the fourth-century Fathers of the Church. He changed after studying the Agnoetae, a sixth-century Monophysite sect which had taught that Christ's human soul was limited in every way like the rest of mankind's and as such was ignorant. Once he became aware of their condemnation, he adapted his own view. Besides his study of this sect, a further influence on his position was the Greek teaching that ignorance was of sin and therefore could never be affirmed of Christ. One of his Athanasian notes stated: 'It is the doctrine of the Church that Christ, as man, was perfect in knowledge from the first, as if ignorance were hardly separable from sin, and were the direct consequence or accompaniment of original sin'.[9] In a letter to Henry Wilberforce, six months after becoming a Catholic, he had declared starkly: 'There can be no doubt that such expressions as "growing in virtue and knowledge," are untrue and wrong—My own mistake was saying that our Lord was "all knowing as God, ignorant as

[7] *PS* iii. 134.

[8] Cf. *PS* iii. 129 with a different edition of *Parochial Sermons*, iii (3rd edn., London, 1840), 141, and *PS* iii. 167 with *Parochial Sermons*, iii. 184.

[9] *Ath*. ii. 169.

man." Almost all the Fathers of the fourth century, I believe, say the same—but the Church has since determined such doctrine to be heresy.'[10] The matter is summarized conveniently in another letter which he wrote, this time to his friend William Dodsworth on 21 March 1852. It even included a reference to his sermon on the 'Tears of Christ', for he observed that the fourth-century view of Christ's ignorance had so impressed him at one time, 'that I committed myself to it in a Sermon in my Third Volume'. Then he added, 'When I read more, I found the view was condemned (or the substance of it) in the case of the Agnoetae, *after* St Athanasius's day'. And a little later he continued:

I suppose the ground of the doctrine is this: —human nature, at the fall, received four wounds, of which ignorance is one. They are wounds, chiefly as being, not the *absence*, but the *privation* of gifts . . . Our Lord then as little took on Him the wound of ignorance, as He did of concupiscence—which is another of the four, nor may we assign it to Him. And directly we admit He was not like us in this point, then, since He had the fullness of the Spirit, non ad mensuram, I suppose it is natural to conclude He had whatever human nature was capable of receiving.[11]

Newman's denial of Christ's ignorance, therefore, followed from the view he came to hold that ignorance was of sin.[12] All the same, to supply an explanation does not necessarily answer the difficulty. It remains true that his understanding of Christ's humanity emerges at this point as so idealized as to lack reality. The charge levelled by Daly is upheld. But it would be a mistake to leave the matter there.

III

It is always important to bear in mind the context and the circumstances in which Newman wrote. This is not a case of special pleading, but a matter of perspective. Newman was an occasional writer. He was prompted by the needs of the day. Some of his contemporaries were liberals whose faith in the divinity of Christ was fading; others were evangelicals who

[10] *LD* xi. 135. [11] *LD* xv. 56–7.

[12] For a fuller account of Newman's teaching on Christ's knowledge and ignorance, see Strange, *Newman*, pp. 74–5.

cherished a sentimentalized view of the divine Lord. Newman wished to supply what was lacking in these positions. He had no desire to be original. He wanted to be orthodox and to meet the spiritual and intellectual needs of the day. He emphasized Christ's divinity because he judged that to be at risk. For that reason he turned to Athanasius and Cyril and the Alexandrian school, whom he found so congenial, to expound a Christology in which the divinity of Christ could never be in doubt. His humanity was not in doubt in any case.

Moreover, it would be wrong to imagine that Newman was truly careless of Christ's humanity. The acknowledged weakness of Alexandrian Christology was its failure at first even to affirm the presence of a human soul in Christ and later, when affirmed, its failure to allow it theological significance. Given Newman's devotion to the Alexandrian approach, it is all the more interesting to come across a pencilled note in one of his unpublished sermons which reads, 'Here insert about His sorrowing, fearing, etc.'. That was precisely the point which had been found wanting in Athanasius. What he inserted was probably similar to what he wrote at the beginning of his following sermon: 'That our Blessed Lord and Saviour took upon Him a human soul as well as a body is proved, if it be necessary to prove it, by His fearing, sorrowing, being in an agony, praying the cup might pass from Him, and feeling Himself forsaken by His Father'.[13] One of his later sermons presented the same teaching. It spoke of Christ's becoming perfect man 'with body and soul' and then went on: 'and as He took on Him a body of flesh and nerves, which admitted of wounds and death, and was capable of suffering, so did He take a soul, too, which was susceptible of that suffering, and moreover was susceptible of the pain and sorrow which are proper to a human soul'.[14] The fact that this teaching comes from his Catholic days, when his views were stricter, makes it all the more significant.

These words are to be found in that most remarkable of his *Discourses addressed to Mixed Congregations*, 'Mental Sufferings of our Lord in His Passion'. There Newman faced squarely the objection which people raise so often, namely that Jesus's holiness would compensate for his suffering and annihilate his

[13] MS sermon no. 408, p. 1. The pencilled note is in MS sermon no. 407, p. 7.
[14] *Mix.*, pp. 324–5.

shame. He gave the charge breadth: 'Again, you may say that He knew His sufferings would be short, and that their issue would be joyful, whereas uncertainty of the future is the keenest element of human distress; but He could not have anxiety, for He was not in suspense; nor despondency or despair, for He never was deserted.' And he added scriptural texts to support this view and expressed in part his own agreement with the case. Newman's Christ is most of all the Johannine Christ: he is the master of events; he governed his own mind entirely. But 'He drew back, at the proper moment, the bolts and fastenings, and opened the gates, and the floods fell right upon His soul in all their fulness'. Newman's Christ acts deliberately, but he also decides to make himself the victim, completely helpless, so that 'it is nothing to the purpose to say that He would be supported under His trial by the consciousness of innocence and the anticipation of triumph; for His trial consisted in the withdrawal, as of other causes of consolation, so of that very consciousness and anticipation'.[15] For Newman 'pain is to be measured by the power of realising it', so the Christ suffered 'indefinitely more', for 'God was the sufferer'.[16] The tone of this sermon has prompted one modern author to observe that 'Newman's Christology, for all its adamantine Athanasian orthodoxy, had more of the Epistle to the Hebrews and of nineteenth-century humanitarianism in it than, for example, the Tome of Leo'.[17]

This sermon in turn, with its reference to God as the sufferer, recalls that famous Anglican sermon of Newman's in which, as David Newsome has said, he described 'in graphic detail the barbarities and indignities inflicted upon the dying figure on the Cross'. Newsome was recalling James Anthony Froude's memory of the occasion and Newman's words: '"Now I bid you recollect that He to whom these things were done was—Almighty God."'[18] Yet what Newman had said, according to the published text, whether early or late, was, 'Now I bid you consider that that Face, so ruthlessly smitten, was the Face of God Himself',[19] a

[15] *Mix.*, pp. 332–4.

[16] *Mix.*, p. 331.

[17] H. Davies, *Worship and Theology in England*, iv *From Newman to Martineau* (Oxford, 1962), 295.

[18] Newsome, Commemoration Sermon, p. 17, See J. A. Froude, 'The Oxford Counter-Reformation', *Short Studies on Great Subjects*, iv (London, 1899), 286.

[19] *PS* vi. 74.

much more subtle expression. Froude's memory may suggest Monophysitism, but Newman's teaching is Chalcedonian. His vivid illustration has been echoed more recently by Herbert McCabe: 'If, in accordance with the doctrine of Chalcedon, we say that the one person, Jesus, is truly human and truly divine, we can say quite literally that God suffered hunger and thirst and torture and death. We can say these things because the Son of God assumed a human nature in which it makes sense to predicate these things of him.'[20]

When every allowance has been made, however, and acknowledgement paid to the positive aspects of Newman's presentation of the humanity of Christ, the sense of dissatisfaction may linger still. To be human is to be at the mercy of events, but Newman's Christ retains a control which seems to compromise his involvement in the human condition. Nevertheless, while this Christ's humanity may be notional and abstract, rather than real and concrete, it is also true that in these matters Newman's primary interest lay elsewhere, namely, with mystery.

IV

At the beginning of his sermon on the 'Tears of Christ', there is a warning as soon as the question about why Jeus wept is raised: 'In attempting any answer to this inquiry, we should ever remember that the thoughts of our Saviour's mind are far beyond our comprehension.' And a little later the point is made explicitly: 'We know, indeed, there are insuperable mysteries involved in the union of His divine with His human attributes, which seem incompatible with each other; for instance, how He should be ever-blessed, and yet weep—all-knowing, yet partially [which he changed later to 'apparently'] ignorant'.[21] It is not an isolated example. Five weeks earlier, he had described the Incarnation as 'a more overwhelming mystery even than that which is involved in the doctrine of the Trinity'.[22] He explained that, while it is hardly surprising that human language should fail to convey, and the human intellect be unable to receive, the truth about God's essence, the meeting of God and man in Christ, the

[20] H. McCabe, 'The Involvement of God', in id., *God Matters* (London, 1987), 46.

[21] *PS* iii. 128, 129.

[22] *PS* iii. 156.

one quite beyond human reason, the other more on a level with it, was still more perplexing.

The concern with mystery came to the surface again the following year, 1836, in a series of sermons as yet unpublished. He preached them between 17 April and 15 May and they are noteworthy as the one place in Newman's writings in which he gave a more extended account of teaching on Christ. In them he observed, for example, that 'the humble Christian will find great comfort and a devout pleasure in contemplating the Gospel mysteries—especially that about which most is told, the Incarnation'.[23] He remarked upon 'the tendency of reasoning minds to get rid of mysteries'[24] and he criticized the way people bring conflicting scriptural statements together, 'to mingle them with each other, to view them as modifying each other, and as neutralizing each other's force and exactness, and so at length to bring out from both together some vague and general doctrine neither the one nor the other'.[25] The concern with mystery is unquestionable. How was it to be handled?

On 14 June 1829 Newman preached a sermon called 'The Christian Mysteries' and, in speaking of both the Incarnation and the Trinity, made use of the image of light and darkness: 'religious light is intellectual darkness'. Revelation casts shadows. He imagined Christ saying:

> Scripture does not *aim* at making mysteries, but they are as shadows brought out by the Sun of Truth. When you knew nothing of revealed light, you knew not revealed darkness. Religious truth requires you should be told *something*, your own imperfect nature prevents your knowing *all*; and to know *something*, and *not all*,—*partial knowledge*,—must of course perplex; doctrines imperfectly revealed must be mysterious.[26]

At about the time he was composing his sermons on Christ in 1836, he developed this imagery in his Tract Seventy-Three 'On the Introduction of Rationalist Principles in Revealed Religion':

> A Revelation is religious doctrine viewed on its illuminated side; a Mystery is the selfsame doctrine viewed on the side unilluminated. Thus Religious Truth is neither light nor darkness, but both together; it

[23] MS sermon no. 405, p. 2.
[24] Ibid., no. 407, p. 5.
[25] Ibid., no. 404, p. 15.
[26] *PS* i. 211.

is like the dim view of a country seen in the twilight, with forms half extricated from the darkness, with broken lines, and isolated masses.[27]

So how is mystery to be grasped?

V

Newman raised this question himself in *A Grammar of Assent*. He observed that, as mysteries are propositions which convey incompatible notions or are statements of the inconceivable, the very discerning of the mystery makes assent possible; at the same time, however, as the propositions cannot be conceived, they do not follow from experience, and so the assent must be notional, and not real: 'the assent which we give to mysteries, as such, is notional assent'.[28] He returned to this point later, asking 'whether a real assent to the mystery, as such, is possible'. He answered negatively: 'I say it is not possible, because, though we can image the separate propositions, we cannot image them altogether'.[29] So much is clear. As the mystery transcends all human experience, it cannot be grasped as a whole, it cannot be the object of real assent. But then he continued: 'what *is* in some degree a matter of experience, what *is* presented for the imagination, the affections, the devotion, the spiritual life of the Christian to repose upon with a real assent, what stands for things, not for notions only, is each of those propositions taken one by one, and that, not in the case of intellectual and thoughtful minds only, but of all religious minds whatever, in the case of a child or a peasant, as well as of a philosopher'.[30] So while the mystery as such can be the object of a notional assent only, its separate parts can be grasped with an assent which is real by educated and uneducated alike. This statement summarized what had been his practice for decades.

The concern for mystery and the wish for it to be received vividly and really by congregations and readers characterized the way he wrote. In his sermon 'The Humiliation of the Eternal Son', the one in which he had called the mystery of the Incarnation more overwhelming than that of the Trinity, he asked: 'What do we gain from words, however correct and

[27] *Ess*. i. 41–2.
[28] See *GA*, p. 36.
[29] *GA*, p. 88.
[30] *GA*, pp. 88–9.

abundant, if they end with themselves, instead of lighting up the image of the Incarnate Son in our hearts?'[31] He was hoping to stir up a real apprehension of the mystery. For Newman, 'a Sermon to be effective must be imperfect'.[32] He would fasten on one aspect and then on another. His unpublished sermons considered week by week the unity, the divinity, and the humanity of Christ. Sometimes he intensified the approach by presenting the mystery in stark antithesis: 'He [Christ] was as entirely man as if He had ceased to be God, as fully God as if He had never become man, as fully both at once as He was in being at all.'[33] Again, 'The Son of God most High, who created the worlds, became flesh, though remaining what He was before. He became flesh as truly as if He had ceased to be what He was, and had actually been changed into flesh.'[34] And again, 'He is as simply God as if He were not man, as simply man as if He were not God.'[35] Yet again, 'When our Blessed Lord, the Son of God, became man, He took on Him our created nature so perfectly that He was as much man as if He had ceased to be God.'[36] Writing on these matters some years ago, I remarked: 'For Newman there could be no more total affirmation of the reality of Christ's manhood than to equate it with his Godhead.'[37]

That still seems to me to be true. Bearing in mind Newman's care for the divinity of Christ, the emphasis he placed upon it, there could be no affirmation which he could make more compelling or complete of Christ's humanity than to say that it was as if that divinity had ceased to be. At the same time, Gabriel Daly's comment on these words, 'therein lies our problem today. The abstractions "humanity" and "divinity" lend themselves to considerable conceptual manœuvring while leaving the concrete situation unaffected',[38] is well judged. None the less, the problems posed by the abstractions need not undermine Newman's method in principle. It is all too easy to dismiss his teaching on Christ as inadequate, as static and positivistic. He made bald abstract statements and scarcely elaborated their significance or implications. From one point of view that is simply to acknowledge that he was writing more than a century ago; he could not

[31] *PS* iii. 169–70. [32] *LD* v. 38. [33] *PS* vi. 66.
[34] *PS* viii. 251–2. [35] *Ath*. ii. 326. [36] MS sermon no. 407, p. 1.
[37] Strange, *Newman and the Gospel of Christ*, p. 56.
[38] Daly, review, p. 290.

have presented the more tormented Jesus familiar today; in this area, it can be agreed, he was not a pioneer. So while it is important not to disguise the weaknesses which have appeared today in what he wrote then on this subject, it is also important not to overlook what is of value. His approach to mystery may be a lesson worth learning.

VI

Newman was a consistent champion of mystery, and so he was alert to the ambiguities which it raised. He once said: 'Surely it is *as* true that the Word is God as if Jesus Christ were not the Word; and it is as true that Jesus Christ is the Word, as if the Word were not God.' And he commented: 'The impossibility of our reconciling the two truths together, does not at all affect the intrinsic, independent, unchangeable reality of both the one doctrine and the other.'[39] The study of ambiguity in theological writing has become prominent more recently in the work of Stephen Prickett and it will be instructive to pause briefly to consider it.

Prickett's book *Words and 'The Word'*, was prompted in part by his amazement at the confidence displayed by the translators of the Good News Bible who declared in their preface that they were producing a version of the Scriptures in language that was 'natural, clear, simple, and unambiguous'. The book which follows can be seen as a chapter on the history of language. It probes the complexities of interpretation and argues consistently for patience with ambiguity and obscurity. There is much on poetry and its place in religious language, much on the different ways the poetic has been perceived and used, much on the Romantic tradition, much on the paradoxes of disconfirmation. In the final chapter certain conclusions are indicated and one of them is relevant here. Prickett writes:

> It was suggested in the first Chapter that the reason why it was not possible to use unambiguous language in translating the Bible was that the Bible was not about things that were unambiguous. We are now, perhaps, in a position to extend that observation and suggest that such a language of disconfirmation and ambiguity is not merely a concomitant

[39] MS sermon no. 404, p. 14.

of religious experience, but is actually characteristic of, and historically central to, man's experience of God. Elijah on Horeb, Moses and the Burning Bush, the Incarnation itself present events so baffling as to imply quite new ways of seeing the world.[40]

This conclusion is relevant, because this book is itself the sequel to *Romanticism and Religion*, in which Prickett studied the connexions between nineteenth-century theological writing in England and a literary tradition which was aware of ambiguity in human experience and saw language as expressing this ambiguity; furthermore, it recognized that the struggle to express the ambiguity is creative and stimulates development.[41] At the heart of this tradition was an understanding of religious language as no different from language of any other kind. As human words are limited, never expressing fully the truths they wish to communicate, there exists a tension between the words used and the truth in view. Both are focal points and, held in tension, they bring about what has come to be called stereoscopic vision. From the tension a deeper perception of the truth becomes available, because the words express not only their own meaning, but are symbolic of the truth in view as well. This understanding of language as symbolical and, as such, participating in the reality it symbolized, stemmed from Coleridge, but came to fruition, in Prickett's judgement, in 'the writing of Newman, the old Roman Catholic theologian', more than any other thinker.[42]

Prickett develops the same approach in *Words and 'The Word'*. He argues that

> translation, where there is no effective equivalent, is one of the major sources of change and enrichment in a living language. A language develops in range and subtlety of expression *not* by means of receptivity to translation, but through its *resistance* to new words and concepts. It is not equivalencies, but *dissimilarities* that force the modification and change necessary to accommodate new associative patterns of thought.[43]

Once again, Newman is regarded as one of the principal exponents of this tradition. He understood both the power and the limitations of language and, by recognizing in the very organic life of the Catholic Church itself that quality which is

[40] S. Prickett, *Words and 'The Word'* (Cambridge, 1986), 224.

[41] Id., *Romanticism and Religion* (Cambridge, 1976), 7.

[42] Ibid. 191.

[43] Id., *Words and 'The Word'*, p. 32.

best described as poetical, produced a solution to the problem of the relationship of the religious to the poetic which Prickett has hailed as 'the most subtle, the most satisfying, and the most comprehensive' that the nineteenth century was to see.[44]

What Prickett has drawn out with regard to biblical translation, then, emerges in Newman's writings, applied to mystery. There it was not so much the tension between the words used and the truth in view which was creative as the tension between the separate parts of the mystery. These, Newman affirmed, can be grasped with a real assent. He had no wish to reconcile the divine and the human in Christ by force. On the contrary, his patience with ambiguity and desire to live deeply within the organic life of the Church gave him the confidence to respect their distinctiveness as the threshold of mystery. No one can grasp a mystery as such, but, in his view, 'a child or a village old woman' may take in singly such beliefs as 'Jesus Christ is God' and 'Jesus Christ is man',[45] and the parts may then give way to the disclosure of the whole.

VII

Sensitivity to mystery is indispensable for theologians. Whatever defects there may now appear to be in Newman's teaching on Christ, these features of his thought—stereoscopic vision, patience with ambiguity, and a sense of the organic life of the Catholic Church—gave him an instinctive respect for mystery. There is a lesson to be learnt. One example can serve as a conclusion.

In his fine work on the modernist crisis, Gabriel Daly has shown how the terms transcendence and immanence were central to that controversy. They were used 'as a means of bringing Roman Catholic theology into alignment with developments in contemporary critical thought'.[46] However, one reviewer, Robert Butterworth, has expressed surprise that the doctrine of the Incarnation 'plays no role in this area of modernist debate'. These issues are complex, yet the question raised is intriguing. Butterworth asks: 'Were the Catholic modernists, in looking towards a philosophical method of coping with the problem, in fact denying themselves the benefit of the central mystery of the

[44] Ibid. 68; see *Ess.* ii. 442–3.
[45] *LD* xxiii. 51.
[46] See G. Daly, *Transcendence and Immanence* (Oxford, 1980), 2.

religion about which they were so rightly concerned?'[47] It may be that that question is at cross-purposes with any modernist concern with transcendence and immanence; it may be that the issue was never seen by them as a further version of the Christological problem; but the question asks whether it should have been. And if it should, I wonder whether something about the way to approach that problem, that mystery, could have been learnt from Newman, a struggling for solutions less and an acceptance of ambiguity more. People discuss regularly Newman's influence on the modernists.[48] Had it been greater, the outcome might have been more instructive.

[47] R. Butterworth, review of Daly, *Transcendence and Immanence* in *Heythrop Journal*, 22 (1981), 466.

[48] See M. J. Weaver (ed.), *Newman and the Modernists* (London, 1985).

17

Newman's Seven Notes
The Case of the Resurrection

GERALD O'COLLINS, SJ

In *An Essay on the Development of Christian Doctrine*,[1] when expounding seven notes or tests for distinguishing between faithful development and corruption, John Henry Newman illustrates his argument by using such examples as the divinity of the Holy Spirit, Christ's real presence in the Eucharist, original sin, purgatory, and papal supremacy (for example, pp. 18, 20–7). Newman refers only in passing to the crucified Jesus's resurrection (pp. 402–3) which is classically handled by him elsewhere—in the context of justification, not in that of the development of doctrine as such.[2]

At the origin of Christianity, the appearances of the risen Lord and the discovery of his empty tomb were the two dramatic causes which first triggered Easter faith. The appearances were the primary way the disciples came to know that Jesus had been raised to new life. The discovery of the empty tomb served as a secondary, negative sign confirming his resurrection. Two books, both originally published in 1974, raise doubts about those original triggers of resurrection faith.

In *Jesus*[3] Edward Schillebeeckx explains the Easter experiences of Peter and the other disciples this way. Through the real but invisible influence of the risen Lord, they experienced a deep forgiveness and conversion which they then expressed in the model of 'appearances'. But their talk of appearances was only a means for articulating what the invisible Jesus had done for them after his death and resurrection, and did not refer to genuinely

[1] This chapter uses the second edition of Newman's *Essay* (London, 1878) rather than the first edition of 1845. All page references inserted in my text itself are to the 1878 edition of the *Essay*.

[2] See *Jfc.*, pp. 202–22.

[3] E. Schillebeeckx, *Jesus* (London, 1979).

historical events.[4] In his *Interim Report on the Books 'Jesus' and 'Christ'*[5] Schillebeeckx concedes that when the first Christians spoke of appearances, this 'need not be a pure model; it can also imply a historical event'.[6] Nevertheless, he continues to play down the role of such appearances—and, for that matter, of the discovery of the empty tomb—in generating Easter faith:

> belief in the Jesus who is risen and lives with God and among us cannot be founded on an empty tomb as such, nor as such on the visual elements which there may have been in 'appearances' of Jesus.[7]

In his *On being a Christian*[8] Hans Küng clearly maintains the personal resurrection of Jesus, while throwing doubt on the historical reliability of the empty tomb story.[9] He explains:

> There can be identity of the person even without continuity between the earthly and the 'heavenly', 'spiritual' body . . . The corporality of the resurrection does not require the tomb to be empty.[10]

Here Küng defends a corporeal resurrection, but dispenses with the need for any *bodily* continuity between the earthly and risen existence of Jesus. The totally new 'spiritual' body can come into existence without involving the former, earthly body, and yet without imperilling the continuing personal identity of the crucified Jesus. In his risen state he is identical with, and no mere substitute for, the person who died on the cross and was buried. Küng seems to locate Jesus's continuity simply at the level of soul or spirit. The new, 'heavenly' body totally replaces the one which ended in the tomb.

In this chapter I wish to apply Newman's seven notes to the proposals about the risen Lord's appearances and empty tomb made respectively by Schillebeeckx and Küng. Do their interpretations represent faithful and healthy developments, or 'corruptions' which in some way 'pervert' the truth and threaten to break up Christian life (pp. 169–71)? My argument here has to presuppose the general validity of Newman's seven notes for the genuine 'development of an idea': preservation of its type, continuity of its principles, power of assimilation, logical sequence, anticipation

[4] Ibid. 346–97.

[5] Id., *Interim Report on the Books 'Jesus' and 'Christ'* (New York, 1982).

[6] Ibid. 147 n. 43; see p. 148 n. 46.

[7] Ibid. 75.

[8] H. Küng, *On being a Christian* (London, 1976).

[9] Ibid. 363–6.

[10] Ibid. 366.

of its future, conservative action upon its past, and chronic vigour (pp. 171–206).[11] Schillebeeckx's and Küng's proposals have often been commented on and criticized from a biblical, exegetical point of view.[12] Here I want to examine whether, when seen in the light of Newman's criteria, those proposals represent developments or corruptions for the doctrine of Christ's resurrection.

SCHILLEBEECKX AND THE APPEARANCES

Towards the end of his *Essay* Newman recognized that 'the one great topic of preaching with Apostles and Evangelists was the Resurrection of Christ and of all mankind after Him' (p. 402). Is that great 'idea' properly 'preserved' (p. 178) in Schillebeeckx's account of the resurrection? Despite some variations and novelty, this version of the first Easter maintains the 'personal-cum-bodily resurrection' of Jesus.[13] The core doctrine remains substantially identical and faithful to 'type' (p. 173).

What of Newman's second criterion for true development, 'continuity of principles' (p. 178)? Does Schillebeeckx maintain or alter the principles on which the doctrine of the resurrection has developed (p. 185)? Newman admits that a real difference between principles and doctrines is not always clear (p. 179). Nevertheless, he employs the distinction, arguing that 'the life of doctrines may be said to consist in the law or principle which they embody' (p. 178). Are there principles embodied in the normal doctrine about the Easter appearances which Schillebeeckx's reductive interpretation tampers with? It seems that this may

[11] In *From Bossuet to Newman: The Idea of Doctrinal Development* (Cambridge, 1957) Owen Chadwick contends that Newman's tests 'convinced no one' and were 'rather pegs on which to hang a historical thesis than solid supports for a doctrinal explanation' (pp. 143, 155); on p. 236 Chadwick provides a list of the first Anglican criticisms of Newman's *Essay*. Nicholas Lash interprets Newman's notes more benignly; see his *Newman on Development* (London, 1975), esp. pp. 114–45. See also J. H. Walgrave, *Newman: Le développement du dogme* (Paris, 1957), 285–96; id., *Unfolding Revelation: The Nature of Doctrinal Development* (London and Phil., 1972), 293–314, esp. pp. 312–14.

[12] Among the exegetes who criticized Schillebeeckx's *Jesus* see e.g. R. E. Brown, *Catholic Biblical Quarterly*, 42 (1980), 420–3; A. L. Descamps, *Revue théologique de Louvain*, 6 (1975), 212–23; R. H. Fuller, *Interpretation*, 34 (1980), 293–6.

[13] Schillebeeckx, *Jesus*, p. 645.

happen with one or even two important principles: the role of visible signs in generating faith and—possibly—God's freedom to make unusual interventions in the regular order of things. Let me explain.

Those who affirm that the risen Christ genuinely appeared to various individuals and groups find themselves criticized by Schillebeeckx for grounding Easter faith in a pseudo-empirical way:

> Faith is emasculated if we insist on grounding it in pseudo-empiricism, thereby raising all sorts of false problems: whether, for instance, this 'Christological mode of seeing' was a sensory seeing of Jesus, whether it was 'objective' or 'subjective' seeing, a 'manifestation' or a 'vision', and things of that sort.[14]

Behind this strong language about 'emasculating' faith lies the whole question about the function of visible signs and empirical evidence as (partial) grounds for initiating and legitimating faith. If God provided appearances of the risen Christ to communicate the fact of the resurrection and invite the witnesses to a new form of faith, can and should we disdain those who accept all that as catering to a 'pseudo-empiricism' which threatens to deprive faith of its integral and virile purity? There is much to discuss and debate here. I simply want to state my concern about one principle. Schillebeeckx seems bent on denying real appearances of the risen Christ, because he is uneasy about admitting empirical grounds for the disciples' Easter faith. It leaves me with the question: Does a faulty principle (a reluctance to accept the role of visible signs and evidence in the genesis of faith) control Schillebeeckx's interpretation of the New Testament texts which report the Easter appearances?[15]

The other enduring principle which Schillebeeckx's position may also threaten is the freedom of divine interventions in the course of saving history, the appearances of the risen Christ being a major example of such interventions. Schillebeeckx asserts that 'there are always intermediary historical factors in occurrences of divine grace. The [so-called] appearances form no exception to this scheme of grace.'[16] (One must add here

[14] Schillebeeckx, *Jesus*, p. 710 n. 119.

[15] On the appearances as 'very evident signs' of Jesus's resurrection see Aquinas, *Summa Theologiae*, III q. 55 a. 5.

[16] Schillebeeckx, *Jesus*, p. 710 n. 119.

'so-called', since—as we have seen—in *Jesus* Schillebeeckx denies that the risen Lord really appeared to the disciples, the appearances being merely a way of expressing the conversion they had undergone.) In Schillebeeckx's assertion that 'there are always intermediary historical factors in occurrences of divine grace', the key word is 'always'. Beyond question, there are always such intermediary historical factors. In those occurrences of divine grace which were the appearances of the risen Christ many such factors entered in: the spiritual crisis of the disciples, the places they found themselves in, the company they were keeping, and so on. Since the risen Christ encountered human beings in history, such intermediary historical factors were necessarily present. But were there *only* such factors? Schillebeeckx's doctrine of grace may be slipping from rightly affirming that intermediary historical factors are *always* present to implying that, at least in the realm of visible history, *nothing but* such factors are present. And that is a very different matter. It would rule out in principle the possibility of a transhistorical factor—the special intervention in history of the risen Christ who now transcends the normal limits of history but freely appears to certain people within history. Thus in one or two ways the test of principle raises difficulties against Schillebeeckx's interpretation of the Easter appearances.

We can move to Newman's third note for faithful development, the 'power of assimilation' (pp. 185–9). According to this criterion, doctrines develop by absorbing and incorporating fresh elements. Since he views development as a 'process of incorporation' (p. 187), Newman can suggest as his third test, 'the *unitive power* of faithful developments' (p. 189).

In support of Schillebeeckx's interpretation of the Easter appearances, it might be argued that he succeeds in assimilating and incorporating new material by highlighting the themes of forgiveness and conversion. At the same time, however, he trims the normal teaching on Jesus's resurrection by denying or doubting the factual status of the appearances. Newman's third criterion does not seem to tell decisively either for or against Schillebeeckx's position.

What then of the fourth note, 'logical sequence' (pp. 189–95)? Newman describes it not as 'a conscious reasoning from premisses to conclusion' (p. 189) but as follows:

A doctrine . . . professed in its mature years by a philosophy or religion, is likely to be a true development, not a corruption, in proportion as it seems to be the *logical issue* of its original teaching. (p. 195)

Could Schillebeeckx claim that there is a logical, 'natural succession of views' (p. 193) from the original testimony to the appearances of the risen Christ and his own explanation of what the New Testament really meant and means by them?

Rather than offering something which seems the natural, 'logical issue' of what Paul (1 Cor. 15: 5–8) and the evangelists (for example, Luke 24: 34; Matt. 28: 16–20) proclaim and teach about the appearances, Schillebeeckx turns them into a set of extraordinarily incompetent and confusing writers. They really intended to say that Peter and other disciples were converted under the impact of grace and they had the words to say just that (*μετανοέω, χάρις*). Instead they verbalized their conversion and mission by talking about appearances of the risen Christ which never actually happened.

Schillebeeckx is well aware that his hypothesis about the disciples' conversion-experiences being later expressed in the form of visions 'constitutes a break with a centuries-old hermeneutical tradition'.[17] More than that, the hypothesis hardly seems to be what Newman calls 'the logical issue of the original teaching'. The ordinary conventions governing the use of language indicate that the New Testament originally meant to say that the risen Lord's appearances effected the conversion (and call) of Peter, Paul, and others. Schillebeeckx has the disciples first believing in the risen Christ and then later articulating this experience 'in the form of an appearance vision'.[18] In Newman's terms, one cannot claim here a 'natural succession of views' from the New Testament through to Schillebeeckx. There is no 'evident naturalness' which could show the process to have been 'a true development' rather than 'a perversion or corruption' (p. 191).

'Anticipation of its future' (pp. 195–9) forms Newman's fifth test. He puts it this way:

Since developments are in great measure only aspects of the idea from which they proceed, and all of them are natural consequences of it, . . . it is in no wise strange that here and there definite specimens of

[17] Schillebeeckx, *Jesus*, p. 710 n. 119.

[18] Ibid. 390.

advanced teaching should very early occur, which in the historical course are not found till a late day.

Newman draws a reasonable conclusion from this note of faithful development:

The fact, then, of such early or recurring intimations of tendencies which afterwards are fully realized, is a sort of evidence that those later or more systematic fulfilments are only in accordance with the original idea. (pp. 195–6)

In short, 'another evidence' of 'the faithfulness of an ultimate development is its *definite anticipation* at an early period in the history of the idea to which it belongs' (p. 199).

When tested in this way, Schillebeeckx's thesis about the genesis and articulation of Easter faith could come off reasonably well. Admittedly, his 'advanced teaching' cannot claim an 'early intimation' in the sense that we find any ancient Christian writers suggesting that the New Testament's talk of appearances was only a way of summarizing what the risen but invisible Jesus had done for the disciples and did not refer to genuinely historical events. Nevertheless, the New Testament does play down the appearances in a way which Schillebeeckx might claim as an 'early intimation' of his own approach. In early Christianity we have a shift from a situation in which certain individuals and groups testify to the appearances of the risen Lord (for example, 1 Cor. 15: 5–8; Luke 24: 34) to the situation in which the Church directly professes her faith in his resurrection (Rom. 1: 4, 10: 9).[19]

That becomes the standard practice in the post-New Testament creeds which, without mentioning any appearances of the risen Christ, simply confess that 'he rose again on the third day' or that 'on the third day he rose again in accordance with the Scriptures'.[20]

Apropos of the appearances, Schillebeeckx observes that as such they are 'not an *object* of Christian faith'.[21] This is to ignore

[19] Yet one should not ignore here the Gospels which come later and, at least in the case of Matthew, Luke, and John, include appearance stories. Moreover, it is understandable that (brief) kerygmatic, credal, or liturgical material like Rom. 1: 4 and 10: 9 normally would not make reference to post-resurrection appearances.

[20] See J. N. D. Kelly, *Early Christian Creeds* (1950; 3rd edn., London, 1976).

[21] Schillebeeckx, *Jesus*, p. 710 n. 119.

two kerygmatic/credal passages where the appearances form (a secondary) part of the confession of faith (1 Cor. 15: 5; Luke 24: 34). Schillebeeckx also slips over the fact that even if—normally—the appearances do not figure as an object in New Testament confessions of faith, nevertheless, those appearances were the primary way the disciples came to know that Jesus had been raised from the dead. In that sense the appearances were essential means for first triggering knowledge of the resurrection and faith in the risen Lord. Any adequate discussion of the Easter appearances would be usefully enriched by distinguishing between the (normal) object of New Testament faith and the (primary) means for generating the original Easter faith.

All the same, in terms of Newman's fifth test Schillebeeckx could allege an 'early intimation' for his downplaying the appearances. Pontius Pilate got into the creeds as a kind of witness to the historical reality of Jesus's death. But Peter, Paul, Mary Magdalene, 'the Twelve', and others to whom the risen Lord appeared have no place in the Church's ancient creeds which simply confess the resurrection without naming those witnesses.

Schillebeeckx's reductive interpretation of the appearances does not show up too well when confronted with Newman's sixth test for a true development (pp. 199–203), 'a *tendency conservative* of what has gone before it' (p. 203). Such a development positively illustrates, corroborates, and protects its 'antecedents' (pp. 200, 202), whereas those developments 'which do but contradict and reverse the course of doctrine which has been developed before them . . . are certainly corrupt' (p. 199).

It is the normative role of the apostles which Schillebeeckx's view fails to illustrate, corroborate, and protect sufficiently. He recognizes *only one* special aspect of the *first* apostles' experience: the fact that they had known Jesus before his death.[22] For the rest they 'have no [other] advantage over us than that they were there at the time'.[23] Their Easter experience of forgiveness, conversion, a renewed life, and Jesus's 'spiritual presence' in 'the gathered community'[24] can be shared by any of his followers anywhere and at any time. There is no very significant difference

[22] Schillebeeckx, *Jesus*, p. 647.
[23] Id., *Interim Report*, p. 7.
[24] Ibid. 78, 80.

between the disciples' Easter experience and subsequent experiences of the risen Lord.

Once the special nature of their Easter experience gets left behind, it is hard to see why the apostolic witnesses should be regarded as normative interpreters of the risen Jesus and authoritative (rather than simply *de facto*) founders of the Christian Church. It is difficult to understand why their experience of him should remain a lasting criterion for believers and why their conversion should be the norm for Christian conversion. Schillebeeckx himself seems to draw this conclusion by remarking that it is only 'for the knowledge [but not for any normative interpretation?] of Jesus in whom we believe' that we depend on those witnesses. They 'have no [other] advantage over us than that they were there at the time'.[25]

Newman gives his seventh and final note the name of 'chronic vigour' (pp. 203–6). 'Corruption', he argues, 'cannot . . . be of long standing; and thus duration is another test of a faithful development' (p. 203). The '*transitory character*' of corruption distinguishes it from true development (p. 205).

With this, as with his other note, Newman normally has in mind movements rather than the ideas of individuals which might be tested during their lifetime. However, he occasionally cites particular persons like Luther (p. 198) and Mahomet (p. 201). It seems appropriate then to raise the question: Has Schillebeeckx's interpretation of the disciples' Easter experience shown 'chronic vigour' or has it looked rather 'transitory'? He has not been winning adherents so as to guarantee the lasting 'duration' of his interpretation. Such substantial recent works on the resurrection as Pheme Perkins's *Resurrection*[26] and Hans Kessler's *Sucht den Lebenden nicht bei den Toten*[27] fail to endorse Schillebeeckx's version of the appearances. Soon after first publishing *Jesus* in 1974, Schillebeeckx himself began modifying what he had said about the appearances not referring to genuinely historical events and being only a way of expressing what the risen but invisible Jesus had done for the disciples. In *Christ* Schillebeeckx explained that he did want to deny that the disciples to whom Jesus appeared had enjoyed some kind of

[25] Ibid. 7.
[26] P. Perkins, *Resurrection* (London, 1985).
[27] H. Kessler, *Sucht den Lebenden nicht bei den Toten* (Düsseldorf, 1985).

sense-experience.[28] Then in *Interim Report* he admitted that when they experienced the living presence of the risen Lord, they may have seen him alive. The 'resurrection visions' may have been 'a historical reality'.[29] In other words, when the early Christians spoke of 'appearances' of Jesus, this 'need not be a pure model; it can also imply a historical event'.[30] Such modifications on the part of the author himself scarcely encourage one to acknowledge 'chronic vigour' in his original proposal about the Easter appearances.

To sum up the whole examination of Schillebeeckx's proposal. It comes off reasonably well when tested by Newman's first and (perhaps) fifth notes. The third note does not seem to tell either one way or another. Newman's second, fourth, sixth, and seventh test would not encourage us to admit Schillebeeckx's proposal as a genuinely faithful development. Let me turn next to Küng's doubts about the historical reliability of the empty tomb story.

KÜNG AND THE EMPTY TOMB

As in the case of Schillebeeckx, by applying the seven 'notes' to Küng's view of the empty tomb story, I am going beyond Newman's primary intention. He originally wrote the *Essay on Development* 'to explain certain difficulties in its [the Catholic Religion's] history' (p. vii). In particular, Newman felt the need to 'account for that apparent variation and growth of doctrine, which embarrasses us when we would consult history for the true idea of Christianity' (p. 29). Nevertheless, his analogical method of arguments and the fact that he sometimes points to particular writers to exemplify his theory of development has encouraged me to try out his hypothesis (p. 30) on two contemporary writers. I take up now Küng's view that Jesus's empty tomb was unlikely and, indeed, unnecessary.

One should agree that Küng's version of the resurrection, at least substantially, meets Newman's first test. It 'preserves' the 'original idea'. 'Easter is an event primarily for Jesus himself: Jesus lives again *through God—for their* [the disciples'] *faith*'.[31]

[28] Schillebeeckx, *Christ* (New York, 1980), 529.
[29] Id., *Interim Report*, p. 75. [30] Ibid. 147 n. 43.
[31] Küng, *On being a Christian*, p. 352.

Whatever his doubts about the empty tomb, Küng refuses to merge Jesus's resurrection with the rise of faith after his crucifixion. In the first instance the resurrection personally affected Jesus himself by bringing him to new life. Secondarily, this event (made known through the Easter appearances),[32] triggered off a fresh relationship of faith for the disciples. Küng maintains the core doctrine of Jesus's personal and bodily[33] resurrection.

It is doubtful whether Küng's dismissal of the empty tomb stands up so well when confronted with Newman's second criterion for faithful development, 'continuity of principles' (p. 178). Are there principles embodied in or implied by the normal teaching about the discovery of the empty tomb that Küng's position tampers with? This may be happening in two ways which concern, respectively, the divine identity and the saving role of the man whom Joseph of Arimathea buried.

First, the matter of identity. From the time of the Book of Acts the emptiness of Jesus's grave has been understood to reflect the holiness of what it once held, the corpse of him who was 'exalted at the right hand of God' and known to be both 'Lord and Christ' (Acts 2: 33, 36). This 'Holy One' could not 'see corruption' (Acts 2: 27). Küng's view means that this 'Holy One' could and did 'see corruption'.

Second, the empty tomb expresses something vital about the nature of redemption which Jesus effected—namely that redemption is much more than a mere escape from our scene of suffering and death. Rather it means the transformation of this material, bodily world with its whole history of sin and suffering. The first Easter began the work of finally bringing our universe home to its ultimate destiny. God did not discard Jesus's earthly corpse but mysteriously raised and transfigured it so as to reveal what lies ahead for human beings and their world. In short, that empty tomb in Jerusalem is God's radical sign that redemption is not an escape to a better world but a wonderful transformation of our world. Seen that way, the open and empty grave of Jesus is highly significant for our appreciation of what redemption means.

The nature of redemption is then a second principle expressed by Jesus's empty tomb. Küng's dissent from this normal doctrine

[32] Ibid. 348–9, 373–9. [33] Ibid. 366.

threatens a highly significant sign of redemption as transformation, and risks turning redemption into an escape to another and better situation of totally new heavenly and spiritual bodies.

As was the case with Schillebeeckx, it is hard to decide whether Newman's third note for faithful development, the 'power of assimilation' speaks for or against Küng's downplaying the empty tomb. On the one hand, it can look as if he incorporates new material from biblical exegesis and modern science: 'Historical criticism', he concludes, 'has made the empty tomb a dubious factor and the conclusions of natural science have rendered it suspect'.[34] On the other hand, however, Küng himself knows that contemporary biblical criticism is by no means unanimous in rejecting the fact of the empty tomb: 'There are . . . a number of influential exegetes even today who hold that the empty tomb is historically probable'.[35] He might have added also that 'natural science' does not necessarily render the empty tomb suspect. Wolfhart Pannenberg and Xavier Léon-Dufour, for example, respect the findings of modern science and maintain the fact of Jesus's empty tomb.[36] All the same, it remains difficult to judge whether or not Küng's view on the empty tomb successfully exemplifies Newman's third note, 'the unitive power of faithful development'.

Could Küng claim that he satisfies Newman's fourth criterion of 'logical sequence' and presents 'a faithful development of the original idea' (p. 194) of Christ's resurrection? Newman puts the test in these terms:

> There is a certain continuous advance and determinate path which belong to the history of a doctrine, policy or institution, and which impress upon the common sense of mankind, that what it ultimately becomes is the issue of what it was at first. (p. 195)

Küng doubts the historical reliability of the empty tomb story. Is that the natural 'issue' of what the doctrine of Christ's resurrection 'was at first'?

As regards the fate of Jesus's body, both the tradition behind the Synoptic Gospels and that which entered John's Gospel

[34] Küng, *On being a Christian*, p. 366.

[35] Ibid. 365. For a long list of such exegetes see my *Jesus Risen* (London and Mahwah, 1987), 123.

[36] See W. Pannenberg, *Jesus: God and Man* (Phil.,1968), pp. 100–8; Xavier Léon-Dufour, *Resurrection and the Message of Easter* (London, 1974), 105–24.

testified to one (Mary Magdalene) or more women finding Jesus's grave to be open and empty. Early polemic against the message of his resurrection supposed that the tomb was known to be empty. Naturally the opponents of the Christian movement explained away the missing body as a plain case of theft (Matt. 28: 11–15). But we have no early evidence that anyone, either Christian or non-Christian, ever alleged that Jesus's tomb still contained his remains.

During the succeeding centuries it was only such outsiders as Celsus in the second century or Reimarus in the eighteenth who either denied the empty tomb or explained it away on merely natural grounds (as, for example, a case of body-snatching). Küng would argue that the historical and natural sciences require us to modify radically two thousand years of thinking about Jesus's empty tomb'. It should now be seen not as a fact but as a 'legendary' elaboration of the message about Jesus's resurrection, a pictorial embellishment of the Easter kerygma and the statements about appearances that we find in places like 1 Corinthians 15: 3b–5, 7–8.[37]

However, Perkins among others shows the flimsiness of the hypothesis that kerygmatic traditions about the risen Jesus's appearances produced empty tomb stories.[38] Careful exegesis indicates that the two traditions have independent origins. The differences are such that it is hard to interpret Mark 16: 1–8 as embodying some legendary elaboration of the statements about Jesus's resurrection and appearances found in 1 Corinthians 15: 3–5, 7–8. Further, as we have seen, there are those like Pannenberg and Léon-Dufour who do not agree that modern science necessarily casts doubt on the empty tomb story. In brief, neither contemporary exegesis nor the natural sciences compel us to alter radically the original teaching about Jesus's empty tomb and flout the logical sequence which Newman's fourth test expects to find in the faithful development of an idea.

Could Küng find some early anticipation for his reductive interpretation of the empty tomb story, thus satisfying Newman's fifth criterion? He might note two 'tendencies' that 'show themselves early' (p. 195) and lend some support to his case. First of all, with one exception, Küng's assertion is true: 'Even according

[37] Küng, *On being a Christian*, pp. 364–5.
[38] *Perkins, Resurrection*, pp. 84, 90, 94.

to the New Testament, the empty tomb never led anyone to faith in the risen Christ.'[39] The one exception comes in John 20: 8 where the beloved disciple sees only the sign of the empty tomb and yet believes.[40] Elsewhere the Gospels never report that the mere discovery of the empty tomb leads anyone to Easter faith. Second, unlike the burial of Jesus (1 Cor. 15: 4), the discovery of the empty tomb as such never entered any kerygmatic/credal passages preserved in the New Testament. Likewise it did not find a place in the Apostles' Creed and Nicene Creed, which confess Jesus's resurrection from the dead without explicit reference to the women finding his tomb to be empty. In this way two early 'tendencies' might be alleged in support of Küng's minimalizing approach to the empty tomb tradition.

Newman's sixth note, 'a *tendency conservative* of what has gone before it', is not verified in Küng's view. The main antecedent to be illustrated and corroborated here is surely the common Easter faith of Christians. Does Küng manage to do this? He argues that 'even if the narrative of the empty tomb had a historical core, faith in the risen Christ would not be made any easier and for some people today it would even become more difficult'.[41] It is interesting that Küng speaks only of 'some people'. I doubt whether this would be so for the vast majority. For them to deny the historicity of the empty tomb is to deny the resurrection itself. To judge from what I have heard over and over again in different parts of the world, ordinary believers' faith in Jesus's resurrection does involve his grave being empty. They would not believe in his resurrection from the dead unless his tomb had been found open and the corpse gone. For very many people today faith in the risen Christ would be made difficult and even impossible if the narrative of the empty tomb did not have a historical core. In that sense Küng's doubts about the empty tomb do not exemplify Newman's '*tendency conservative* of what has gone before'.

Küng might do better when tested by the seventh note, 'chronic vigour'. Both before and after the publication of *On being a Christian*, some have doubted or denied the empty tomb, while

[39] Küng, *On being a Christian*, p. 365.

[40] One should add that for the beloved disciple in John's story the sign included the grave cloths which had been tidily separated (John 20: 5–7).

[41] Küng, *On being a Christian*, p. 365.

maintaining the true personal resurrection of Jesus himself.[42] Küng's reductive interpretation of the empty tomb story, while not 'vigorous' in the sense of commanding great support among Christian theologians and exegetes,[43] does not look 'transitory'. My guess is that it will continue to prove 'chronic', inasmuch as a small group will continue to uphold Jesus's personal resurrection while dispensing with the fact of the empty tomb. The seventh and last note does not appear to tell decisively against Küng.

Testing Küng's position on the basis of Newman's seven notes yields the following results. Küng's view of Jesus' tomb could show up fairly well in the light of the first and fifth criteria. The third and the seventh fail to tell clearly for or against his view, whereas the second, fourth, and sixth notes point to a 'corruption' rather than a truly faithful development.

If one were allowed to enlarge and improve Newman's seven tests for distinguishing real development from corruption, one new test could well be worship—what Newman himself calls the 'development of doctrine into worship' (p. 48). Do the views of Schillebeeckx and Küng on, respectively, the appearances of the risen Christ and his empty tomb help believers to worship better? This chapter, however, has not pressed that question but has simply applied to the two cases the seven tests as Newman presented them.

Newman's central purpose in his *Essay on Development* was to scrutinize eighteen hundred years of history and to explain 'certain apparent variations' in the teaching of Catholic Christianity (p. 7). If he succeeded in so dealing with a sufficient number 'of the reputed corruptions, doctrinal and practical, of Rome', that might 'serve as a fair ground for trusting her in parallel cases where the investigation had not been pursued' (p. 32). But the fact that he also exemplified his argument from the good and bad practice of individuals has encouraged me to try out his seven tests on two contemporary writers. In any case, unless and until Newman's notes prove themselves to be serviceable today, they

[42] See e.g. Kessler, *Sucht den Lebenden*, pp. 121, 322.

[43] See J. A. Fitzmyer, *A Christological Catechism: New Testament Answers* (Ramsey, 1982), 76, 77, 79. R. E. Brown rightly concludes that 'while there may be debate about the nature of the transformed resurrected body, Catholic teaching does not permit one to maintain that the body of Jesus corrupted in the tomb' (Brown, *Biblical Exegesis and Church Doctrine* (London, 1986), 38).

will remain a matter for historical study and have no enduring value for the living doctrine and worship of the Church.

This chapter aimed at illustrating the enduring value of Newman's seven criteria by taking up two modern cases. Tested in that way, Küng's interpretation of the empty tomb tradition and, even more clearly, Schillebeeckx's original proposal about the risen Jesus's appearances look like 'corruptions' rather than faithful developments of the 'idea' of the resurrection.

18

Newman, Anglicanism, and the Fundamentals

S. W. SYKES

I

The near conjunction of two centenaries, those of John Henry Newman's death (1890) and of the Chicago–Lambeth Quadrilateral (1888), both celebrated with respect, though in one case with something less than fervour, provokes the following questions: Does the hypothesis of the development of doctrine, in Newman's Catholic formulation, put to an end Anglicanism's apologia for the fundamentals of Christianity? Does the modern Church have to live again the years 1834–1845 in order make sense of Catholic–Anglican ecumenism?

To be sure, the Anglican–Roman Catholic International Commission's *Final Report* (1982) seems to have revived both the language of fundamentals and of development, though in different places. Thus we read, on the one hand, of 'substantial agreement', and 'essential points of doctrine', 'the essentials', 'essential matters where doctrine admits of no divergence' (a remarkable phrase!), 'unity on essentials'—and on the other hand, of 'the Church's growing understanding of Christian truth', 'unfolding the riches of the original revelation'. The *Malta Report* (1968) of the Preparatory Commission, indeed, had already suggested the possibility of convergence between the Anglican distinction of fundamentals from non-fundamentals and the distinction implied by the Second Vatican Council's references to a 'hierarchy of truths',[1] on the face of it an implausible conjunction of a tradition long domesticated within Protestantism,[2] and a proposal wholly consistent with Catholicism's equally

[1] Text reprinted in *The Final Report*, (London, 1982), 110.

[2] On this history see W. Joest, 'Fundamentalartikel' in *Theologische Realenzyklopaedie*, (Berlin and New York, 1983), 727–32 and U. Valeske, *Hierarchia Veritatum*, esp. ch. 3, 'Das Problem der Fundamentalartikel in der Theologiegeschichte der Nichtromischen Kirchen' (Munich, 1968).

traditional antagonism to the notion of fundamentals.[3] The possibility that these are not in fact alternatives has had to be taken seriously since the argument of Nicholas Lash (against a number of powerful voices) that the doctrine of fundamentals is still substantially present in the *Essay on Development*.[4] On the precise exegesis of Newman this essay will be able to cast no more than a side light, in illustration of the patent fact that in Anglican history there is no one doctrine of fundamentals, nor was there in Newman's day, as he well knew. The focus of interest here will be, rather, the substantive question, namely what weight can be given today to the appeal to fundamentals from whatever quarter? And to that end we shall trade on the coincidence of centenaries in search of illumination.

In 1888, the Bishops of the Anglican Communion, assembled at Lambeth, considered the matter of what they termed 'Home Reunion'. The resolution which they passed picked up and amended an earlier formulation of the same theme by the General Convention of the Protestant Episcopal Church of the United States at Chicago in 1886. In its Lambeth form, the text is as follows:

That, in the opinion of this Conference, the following Articles supply a basis on which approach may be by God's blessing made towards Home Renunion:

(a) The Holy Scriptures of the Old and New Testaments, as 'containing all things necessary to salvation', and as being the rule and ultimate standard of faith.
(b) The Apostles' Creed, as the Baptismal Symbol; and the Nicene Creed, as the sufficient statement of the Christian faith.
(c) the two Sacraments ordained by Christ Himself—Baptism and the Supper of the Lord—ministered with unfailing use of Christ's words of Institution, and of the elements ordained by Him.
(d) The Historic Episcopate, locally adapted in the methods of its administration to the varying needs of the nations and peoples called of God into the Unity of His Church.[5]

[3] On which see A. Tanqueray, 'Articles fondamentaux (système de)' in *Dictionnaire de théologie catholique*, i/2 (Paris, 1923), cols. 2025–35.

[4] N. Lash, *Newman on Development* (London, 1979), 130–4.

[5] The texts of both the Chicago and Lambeth versions of the Quadrilateral are contained in the centenary volume of essays edited by J. R. Wright, *Quadrilateral at One Hundred* (Cincinnati, Ohio, and London, 1983) pp. vii–ix.

Thus began the chequered and remarkable history of the Lambeth Quadrilateral. Of this resolution the Director of the World Council of Churches' Commission on Faith and Order has recently remarked:

> For the first time one of the great traditions within Christianity adopted for its own ecumenical orientation and for the orientation of the endeavours toward Church unity in general a short, definite formula. No other Christian tradition has been able to do something similar up to this day.[6]

This is a generous judgement. Other individual theologians, notably Karl Rahner, have spoken of the need for a short formula.[7] But Anglicans alone, it seems, have dared, albeit cautiously and a little ambiguously, to lend such a formula a certain institutional authority.

The Quadrilateral contains a somewhat indirect endorsement of the tradition of fundamentals. Though the word itself is not present, by speaking of the Articles as a 'basis' for ecumenical approach, the statement at once hints that what is detailed in the Articles is fundamental to, but not necessarily sufficient for, its purpose. A more solid indication of the continuity between the tradition of fundamentals and the Quadrilateral lies in the conjunction of the first two Articles on Scripture and the Creeds. For it was characteristic of especially that part of the tradition which emphasized the fundamental *articles of belief* (and, as we shall see, there is a distinction to be made between fundamentals and fundamental articles of belief) to refer to the Creeds (often including the Athanasian Creed, endorsed in Article VIII of the Thirty-Nine Articles) as 'the sufficient statement of the Christian faith'. This was the view which Newman had defended in his dispute with Abbé Jager in 1834–5 and some part at least of which he subsequently abandoned on writing his book on the development of doctrine. Newman's Anglican contemporaries responded variously to what on any analysis is a complex and multi-layered book, containing enough confusion, perversity, and sheer prejudice, along with profound originality and brilliance,

[6] G. Gassman, 'Quadrilateral, Organic Unity and the W. C. C. Faith and Order Movement', in Wright (ed.), *Quadrilateral at One Hundred*, p. 179.

[7] K. Rahner, *Theological Investigations*, ix (London, 1972), 117–27, id., op. cit., xi (London, 1974), 230–44; id., *Foundations of Christian Faith* (1978), 448–59.

to keep controversialists occupied for decades. The edition of 1878 evidently contains a few signs of responses to his Anglican critics.[8] But the promulgation of the Quadrilateral in 1888 was in certain respects an institutional response to Newman's argument. Whether it is a reply which simply ignores Newman is what we shall be at pains to elucidate.

II

The first task is to comment on the relationship between the tradition of fundamentals or fundamental articles and the Quadrilateral. Here a number of points arise. In the first place it has been well observed that the word 'Articles' in 'the following Articles supply a basis . . .' is somewhat misleading. Dr Gillian Evans has rightly pointed out that the four items in the list are not propositional in form.[9] Their relationship with the Thirty-Nine Articles is thus obscure, despite the fact that in the first of the items an Article is in fact quoted (namely Article VI, to the effect that the Scriptures contain all things necessary to salvation). The Anglican Articles are an instance of the long medieval tradition of disputation in which a *conclusio* or *thesis* would be stated in summary form with a view to encapsulating the particular doctrinal point in contention. Thus of each of the Thirty-Nine Articles it would be possible to say 'I believe that . . .'. But this is not the case with the text of the Quadrilateral, in which the so-called Articles are, on the face of it, a list of 'things'.

None the less it is necessary, I believe, to insist that there is a relationship between the Articles and the Quadrilateral. In the first place some at least of the Lambeth Fathers would have been aware that the American originator of the whole discussion, William Reed Huntingdon (1839–90), an Episcopalian priest and ecumenist, had argued, and in 1885 was still arguing, that the Thirty-Nine Articles were not an adequate expression of what he called 'the Anglican principle'. In the very book in which what he called 'the Quadrilateral' of pure Anglicanism had been

[8] Lash regards J. B. Mozley as the only exception to Newman's ignoring of his critics (Lash, *Newman on Development*, p. 119). Louis Allen has made a good case for regarding Christopher Wordworth's criticism as eliciting a response (Allen, 'Newman and Christopher Wordsworth', id., *Essays presented to C. M. Girdlestone* (Newcastle, 1960), 11–26).

[9] G. Evans, 'Permanence in the Revealed Truth and Continuous Exploration of its Meaning', in Wright (ed.) *Quadrilateral at One Hundred*, pp. 113–16.

first defined, *The Church-Idea: An Essay Towards Unity* (1870), he had expressely denied that the Thirty-Nine Articles should still be considered to be 'one of the essentials of the Anglican position'.[10] Huntingdon's motivation was at least in part a desire to divest Anglicanism of some of its inessential Englishness, and make it more easily acceptable in North America. But the programme to detach Anglicanism confessionally from its reference to the Thirty-Nine Articles had much wider support. In 1865 the Form of Assent for clergy of the Church of England had been changed, specifically in order to accommodate affirmation of the Articles in less specific terms; and the closing decades of the nineteenth century witnessed the height of the anti-Protestant movement in Anglicanism during which the patently Reformed character of the Articles received both critical scrutiny and catholicising reinterpretation.[11] It was in this atmosphere that the Lambeth Fathers approved their Articles, and one cannot seriously doubt that in doing so they were giving further impetus to the movement of historical relativization of the Articles, which reached full term at the Conference of 1968.[12]

In what sense, then, are the Articles of the Quadrilateral to be understood as Articles? Here, I believe that we must answer that they are a *hierarchy of usages* in the Church, to be understood neither as inert objects, nor in the first instance as propositions (though their use plainly entails propositions of belief), but as well-known practices.

The interpretation of the Quadrilateral as usages received decisive support from the consideration of the first item of the list, namely Holy Scripture. Plainly the bishops assumed by their reference to the terms of Article VI ('containing all things necessary to salvation') that the ascribed status of the Scriptures should be maintained by the normal Anglican practice of reading them publicly in a language understood by the people. A Church

[10] See J. R. Wright's essay, 'Heritage and Vision: The Chicago–Lambeth Quadrilateral', in id. (ed.), *Quadrilateral at One Hundred*, p. 12.

[11] e.g. by Bishop Forbes in his *Exposition of the Thirty-Nine Articles* (Oxford, 1867).

[12] See *The Lambeth Conference 1968: Resolutions and Reports* (London and New York, 1968), 40–1, and the Addendum, 'The Thirty-Nine Articles and the Anglican Tradition', pp. 82–3. Behind both of these documents lies a report of the Archbishop's Commission on Christian Doctrine, *Subscription and Assent to the Thirty-Nine Articles* (London, 1968).

which affirmed the Scriptures to be a 'rule and ultimate standard of faith', but which failed to provide the whole people of God access to such a rule, would be one which denied a role to the people in the preservation of the faith. The reunited Church which the Quadrilateral has in mind would be one which gave effect to the status of the Scriptures by using them in such a way that the faith of the whole people of God would be guided and nourished by them.

It is as usages that the other items on the list are likewise to be understood, but, in the light of the first Article, necessarily in relation to the ultimacy of the Scriptures as the standard of faith. Thus the use of the Creeds, with the Nicene Creed as the 'sufficient statement of the Christian faith', the use of the two sacraments ordained by Christ himself, and the use of episcopal leadership could not be separated from the rule-character of the Scripture, either as usages—thus in the sacraments we are to use only the elements ordained by him—or as entailing beliefs. One could not celebrate the sacraments nor justify episcopacy without stating what one believed about them; and such beliefs would be subject to the rule of the Scriptures.

When, therefore, we compare the Articles of the Quadrilateral with the Thirty-Nine Articles, it is apparent that the Quadrilateral is more comprehensive than the Thirty-Nine Articles, in that it specifies not only propositions, but also points to practices. These practices amount to a selection of elements in Anglicanism for special mention, as being in the bishops' minds the sort of 'performance' of Christian faith which best perpetuates the identity of Christianity. The practices have been chosen from the Prayer Book, the Ordinal, and the Thirty-Nine Articles. Thus the use of the Scriptures is required by both Prayer Book and Thirty-Nine Articles and strongly reinforced in the Ordinal. The status of the Creeds and their use is prescribed in the Prayer Book and the Articles. The use of the sacraments and their meaning are illustrated in Prayer Book and Articles, and their significance underlined in the Ordinal. The historical episcopate is identified as requisite in the Ordinal and spoken of in the Articles. At the same time the very act of creating such a hierarchy of usages serves to diminish the importance of other facets of those documents, for example, the other 'commonly called Sacraments' in the Prayer Book or the Articles on predestination or Church and State relations. Furthermore, the ultimacy of the Scriptures as the rule of faith serves to relativize the theological interpretation of the two dominical sacraments and of historical episcopate to be found in the Prayer Book and Ordinal. This may provide us with one of the reasons why the Quadrilateral has continued to provide a very useful stimulus to ecumenism, even after 100 years of critical enquiry and emendation. Precisely by not stating the propositions to be believed about the usages contained in the list, but by specifying the rule to be applied in elucidating such propositions it has a flexibility which enabled it to survive the very severe crisis of biblical criticism, an issue far from resolved for Anglicans in 1888.

III

The place accorded to Scripture in the first Article of the Quadrilateral is precisely that which Newman asserted in his first letter to the Abbé Jager in 1834. 'The main principle which we of the Anglican Church maintain', he wrote, 'is this: that Scripture is the ultimate basis of proof, the place of final appeal, in respect of all fundamental doctrine.'[13] Invited by his friend, Benjamin Harrison to assume advocacy of the Anglican cause with the Abbé, Newman had been obliged to write to Durham to enquire of Hugh James Rose 'which of our divines treats the Popish question best'. Rose had earlier recommended the reading of two major seventeenth-century Anglicans, Archbishop William Laud (1573–1645) and Bishop Edward Stillingfleet (1635–99).[14] Newman responded immediately and engaged in a hurried immersion in the literature during the first part of the Hilary term 1834. He would quickly have discovered that the tradition was anything but homogeneous. This had already been observed by the astute Daniel Waterland (1683–1740) in his *Discourse of Fundamentals* of 1735, where the more than one hundred year history of the discussion is reviewed and alternatives discussed. Waterland's own proposal, advanced as a deliberate effort to improve on previous suggestions, is still of interest and will be discussed below. But Newman, whose attention to Waterland had

[13] The correspondence has been edited by Louis Allen in *John Henry Newman and the Abbé Jager*, (Oxford, 1975), see p. 35. It will be apparent how indebted I am to this fine piece of research.

[14] *LD* iv. 326.

been drawn by Harrison in a letter of November 1835, had already explicitly committed himself to the line taken by Stillingfleet.[15]

In preferring the earlier Stillingfleet to the later Waterland, Newman manifestly knew what he was doing. On 22 December 1835 he replied to Harrison that he had considered Waterland's objections to making the Apostles' Creed the content of the fundamentals, 'but having already taken Stillingfleet's basis with the Abbé, I could not take Waterland's without the chance of slipping between two stools'. There is more to this preference than meets the eye. The oracular tone which Newman adopted ('We of the Anglican Church') was an unconscious, but none the less decisive, opting against the admission of pluralism in the matter of fundamentals. In four central paragraphs of his first letter to Jager, Newman undertakes to expound the Anglican position on fundamentals. Beginning 'We consider the Gospel Faith to be the foundation on which the Church is built', Newman argues that in this faith, the doctrine of Christ is the foundation together with the doctrine of the Trinity—he calls them 'the fountain heads of all doctrines'—and the articles of the 'primitive Antenicene Creed' the additional content.[16] This is the content of the fundamentals in teaching which, Newman explicitly adds, following what he takes to be Stillingfleet's lead, the Church is itself infallible, a proposition likewise introduced by the magisterial 'we believe'. He then allows separate branches of the Church the power to develop (he crosses out the words 'add to') their fundamentals into articles of religion according to circumstances and not as terms of communion. Thus the Thirty-Nine Articles are said to have less authority than the Creed, because later in time, they are concerned only with one part of the truth, and more obviously embroiled with external influences. And he finally admits, as Richard Hooker had done earlier, that it is possible for Churches truly holding the fundamentals none the

[15] Allen, *Newman and Jager*, pp. 154–6.

[16] The passage expresses clearly a hierarchy of truths: 'We consider that in the first instance the doctrine of Christ is the foundation, according to the Apostle's words, "Other foundation can no man lay than that is laid, which is Jesus Christ;" or again the doctrine of the Trinity, as confessed in the baptismal form. These are certainly fundamentals, and the fountain heads of all doctrines; but they are not all the fundamentals, for we are accustomed by the guidance of Scripture to add to them, or rather to develop them into, the Articles of the primitive Antenicene Creed. Such then are the doctrines which we consider to have been revealed as the basis of the Church, the condition of baptism, the profession of Churchmen': ibid. 39.

less to overlay them with corruptions, as had the Roman Communion.

Jager's reply, published in three separate editions of *L'Univers* in late 1834 and the spring of 1835, contains, among some detailed objections of varying weight, one argument to which Newman never formally replied. This concerned precisely Newman's contention that the Church was infallible in fundamentals, a proposition plainly designed to assure the believer of the absolute security of his or her faith.[17] But, Jager points out, this is at once undermined by the admission that Churches may err, even if only in subordinate and supplementary matters. To be consistent, a Church which claims infallibly to teach the fundamentals of the faith must also be in a position infallibly to determine what those truths are. Jager asks:

> What is more fundamental in religion than the dogma of infallibility, since on this dogma depends the certainty of or uncertainty of our faith? If therefore the Church cannot be deceived on fundamental points, she cannot have been deceived in believing herself to be infallible. The dogma of infallibility is therefore supported by your own assertion.[18]

At no point subsequently does Newman undertake further to defend the phrase 'infallible in fundamentals' *expressis verbis*. But it is important to note that Newman's justification for the assertion that only some scriptural doctrines are in the Creeds and not others is historical. 'Historical proof is quite sufficient',[19] he asserts—presumably to account for the presence in the Creed of a limited number of doctrines. For proof of the infallibility of the doctrines so proposed one assumes, for lack of explicit statement, that Newman relied upon the doctrine of the infallibility of the

[17] Louis Allen notes that in the following year Newman added a manuscript comment on the phrase, 'infallible in fundamentals'. He wrote '(awkward expression) . . . yet Stillingfleet seems to use it'. The passage which Allen cites from Stillingfleet refers to General Councils as infallible in fundamentals, but not of themselves, rather in the judgement of those who receive their decisions. Newman's necessarily hurried reading of Stillingfleet at this point is problematic. In his substantive treatment of the 'Protestant Doctrine of Fundamentals', in ch. 4, Stillingfleet argues that moral certainty is a sufficient foundation for faith, and that mathematical or physical proof is not relevant to it. In general Stillingfleet's position is closer to Chillingworth than Newman would have found comfortable. See R. T. Carroll, *The Common Sense Philosophy of Bishop Edward Stillingfleet* (The Hague, 1975), 57–67.

[18] Allen, *Newman and Jager*, p. 67.

[19] Ibid. 83.

Scriptures.[20] This at least would be wholly consistent with an apologist committed to defend the position believed to have been inherited from Laud and Stillingfleet.

Newman's further treatment of the question, once he had explained to Jager the importance of Stillingfleet's distinction between 'necessary for salvation' and 'necessary for Church communion', consisted in the development of the idea of the 'prophetical tradition' in the Church, the flesh on the bones of the infallible 'Apostolical tradition', and unlike the latter capable of being corrupted in details. But the degree to which he was, in fact dependent on maintaining what he took to be Stillingfleet's doctrine of the infallibility of Scripture emerged only in the final unpublished part of his reply. Here, to the horror of his friend Harrison, Newman advanced a very strong doctrine of the ultimacy of the appeal to Scripture and a defence of the terms of Article VI. When Harrison read in Newman's manuscript that 'Scripture and Scripture only is the rule and canon of faith', he denounced Newman for 'Ultra-Protestantism' and for imposing a theory of his own upon the controversy. [21] Harrison was both right and wrong. He was right to see originality in Newman's work, though it lay elsewhere; he was wrong to think that Newman was not defending a traditionally Anglican view of Scripture as Newman quite justly replied. Laud, for example, had explicitly taught that Scripture is the infallible Word of God, to be affirmed as the prime principle of faith. Here Harrison was simply blinded by anti-Protestant prejudice. The discussion of fundamentals, as he knew from reading the footnotes to Waterland's essay, had an embarrassing pedigree, 'Geneva—Holland—Lord Bacon: a thoroughly ultra Protestant result of Calvinistic dogmatism'.[22] Like Pusey, he hoped that the controversy with Rome could have been carried on, not on Genevan but on Catholic principles.[23] Like Bishop John Jebb, whose superficial little tract, *The Character of the Church of England as distinguished both from other Branches of the Reformation and*

[20] Note e.g. the reference to the infallibility of Scripture in *Dev*. 2. 2. 7, a passage unchanged between 1845 and 1878. Taken literally the text only commits itself unequivocally to the infallibility of the Apostles.

[21] Allen, *Newman and Jager*, pp. 157–63.

[22] Ibid. 154–5.

[23] Ibid. 7, citing a letter from Pusey in H. P. Liddon, *Life of Edward Bouverie Pusey* ii (London, 1893), 4–5.

from the Modern Church of Rome (1815; 2nd edn., 1816, repr. 1839), had been the initial focus of the controversy, Harrison believed that the uniqueness of Anglicanism lay in its obedience to the so-called Canon of St Vincent.

Newman defended St Vincent's rule, indeed, but found himself also defending the doctrine of St Vincent, 'who after all, you cannot deny, does make Scripture the Canon of Faith, and Tradition but interpretation'.[24] If the unspoken but crucial issue between Jager and Newman was infallibility, then Newman's vigorous commitment to the unique authority of Scripture is intelligible. In future Newman would be somewhat condescending about how the religion of England (including doubtless that of many, even most Anglicans) depended on belief in 'the Bible and the whole Bible'. He wrote in 1861 that what he now called the 'plenary inspiration of Scripture' was 'a peculiarly Protestant question'. On the limits of inspiration, he held, the Catholic Church has had little to say; it would turn out, he prophesied, that in the great battle between the Holy Catholic Roman Church and Antichrist all the forces of Protestantism would prove to be no more effective than children's toys.[25] None the less the infallibility of the Apostles remained a datum. The Apostles knew by divine inspiration the whole *depositum*, which was not a list of articles which could be numbered, but 'a large philosophy'. What the Apostles had by inspiration, part explicitly and part latently, the Church has from the gift of infallibility. Thus the infallibility of the Apostles and that of the Church are inseparable. 'The Creed . . . [by this he means the 'large philosophy'] was delivered to the Church with the gift of knowing its true and full meaning'.[26]

In 1835–6, however, Newman was defending a thoroughly Protestant-sounding doctrine of the unique authority of the Scripture, to which even the Creed is but 'a concurrent and second witness to certain truths'.[27] The irony of the dispute between him and Harrison does not escape the modern reader; two Catholic-minded Anglicans embarrassed, puzzled, and at odds with each other at the blatant Protestantism of classic Anglicanism. History was to have another shock for this tradition

[24] Allen, *Newman and Jager*, p. 133.
[25] *LD* xix. 488.
[26] Letter of 15 February 1868 to J. S. Flanagan, repr. in *TP* ii. 158–9.
[27] Allen, *Newman and Jager*, p. 119.

when it discovered that the principles of historical criticism could not consistently be held to be inapplicable to the scriptural miracles mentioned in the Creeds, those of the virginal conception of Jesus and of his bodily ressurrection. The attempt by such liberal Anglo–Catholics as Charles Gore to throw a *cordon sanitaire* around the articles of the Creeds, was quite speedily abandoned as artificial,[28] but the position so defended has remained deeply instinctive to Anglicanism, and fuels the recurrent public rows about 'challenges to the fundamentals'.

But what are the fundamentals? The tradition from Stillingfleet seemed to suggest that the Apostles' Creed was, if not a comprehensive list of articles—which Stillingfleet himself declined to give—none the less a standard example of the fundamentals. The same argument insisted that the authority of the Creed rested on the prior authority of Scripture. Stillingfleet, however, had been wise enough to see that faith in God's Word is faith in the doctrine, not in the instruments of its conveyance; and that the writing of Scripture, though infallible, is only the condition by which the revelation is made known.[29] Behind both Creed and Scripture lay something else, which Newman in 1835, and again in 1878, was to identify as the doctrine of the Incarnation. But he already knew of a development of that thought which he had chosen to ignore, namely Waterland's essay on fundamentals, to which we now turn.

IV

The reason for this reprise to the neglected Waterland needs some further explanation. The terms of Article VI of the Thirty-Nine Articles to the effect that Scripture contains all things necessary to salvation, and the way in which Anglicans have persisted in using Scripture in the worship of the Church, are not matters of which contemporary Anglicans have any reason to be ashamed. Nor has their importance diminished in any way under the impact of biblical criticism. On the contrary, the recent expansion of interest in hermeneutics has revealed with great clarity the complexity of the act of reading a text and the fruitfulness of the

[28] The story of the subsequent challenge to Gore's view of authority is well told in A. M. Ramsey, *From Gore to Temple* (London, 1960), ch. 7.

[29] E. Stillingfleet, *A Rational Account of the Grounds of Protestant Religion* (1664; new edn, Oxford, 1844) i. 330–2.

idea of performing a text. The realization that the reader is of importance in constructing what happens when a text is 'understood' has tended to restore the text to a plurality of readers, instructed and uninstructed alike, and to rescue it from a Protestant prelacy of biblical critics. The context provided by liturgy, art, music, and architecture has simultaneously confirmed the importance of the Church as an element in the act of understanding. Finally the modern capacity for greater critical scrutiny of the limitations imposed by our immediate circumstances has helped the Church rediscover the importance of the practice of liberation as a pre-condition of the authentic understanding of the good news for the poor. None of those developments present major obstacles for the Anglican use of the Scripture. If they are embarrassed by the poverty, blindness, or selective partiality of their attention to the Scripture, they find themselves in distinguished company.

Newman's departure from Anglicanism was by no means a leave-taking from the Scriptures, but he discarded (with evident relief) to such Anglicans as were willing to defend it, that impossibly static version of the fundamental articles tradition, according to which God had communicated to humanity a certain number of unique truths selected from the Scriptures by the unanimous voice of the Primitive Church. When Newman abandoned the defence of the Vincentian canon, some Anglicans like F. D. Maurice agreed with him, others most emphatically did not. W. J. Irons was of the view that Anglican writers 'cling to the rule with an increasing tenancity', and called for a volume in which it would receive the full vindication it deserved.[30] Whatever currency such views and the feeble chauvinism of Jebb had among English Anglicans—and England was, we must recall, at its most isolated in the late eighteenth century—static, quantitative, and propositional theories of revelation were already being thoroughly challenged and discarded in Protestant Europe from the days of Semler. The pious reproduction of the works of the Caroline divines in the Library of Anglo-Catholic Theology from 1841 onwards was a deliberate attempt to revive and give renewed currency to an apologia for English Christianity, which the editors of the series knew was under attack in Protestant

[30] W. J. Irons, *The Theory of Development examined with reference especially to Mr Newman's Essay and to the Rule of St Vincent of Lerins* (London, 1846), 48–53.

Germany, the home, so far as they were concerned, of ruinous infidelity. What they were not so willing to admit was the fact that seventeenth- and eighteenth-century Anglicans had shared their views of the fundamentals with a variety of Continental precursors, including unorthodox Catholics and highly orthodox Protestants. The myth of a unique 'Anglicanism', a term traced first to the pen of John Henry Newman, was being created.

Modern Anglicanism has had, somewhat painfully, to reappraise its commitment to the idea of fundamentals, especially to the proposal that the Church is infallible in regard to fundamentals. The documents of the modern Anglican communion no longer formally defend the doctrine of the infallibility of the Scriptures; and Anglicans have never professed the infallibility of their own authoritative councils. What account, then, does Anglicanism give of the source of its authority? If it continues to answer with the Thirty-Nine Articles, the Anglican Newman, and the Chicago–Lambeth Quadrilateral, that the Scriptures are the rule and ultimate standard of faith, then modern voices are bound to enquire whether this reply is intelligible. Are all the Scriptures equally normative? Is there a *de facto* canon within a canon? Does not historical criticism destroy the confidence of faith in the events of the gospel, and so forth?

A modern reformulation of the doctrine of fundamentals, which Anglicans have characteristically pillaged from Protestant sources, Continental and North American, is to refer to story or narrative as the raw material of revelation. The endorsement of this modern apologetic occurred most strikingly in the Report of the Church of England's Doctrine Commission entitled *Believing in the Church* (1981). This report was the successor, one might almost say antidote, to the earlier document *Christian Believing* (1976) which had administered the most devastating blow any official Anglican document has ever formulated to the authority of the Creeds on historical and exegetical grounds. If *Christian Believing* represented a critical assault on the fundamental articles tradition, *Believing in the Church* contained the reformulation of an apologia for the *via media* on the basis of appeal to story or narrative.[31]

[31] See *Christian Believing: The Nature of the Christian Faith and its Expression in Holy Scriptures and the Creeds* (London, 1976), and *Believing in the Church: The Corporate Nature of Faith* (London, 1981).

It is in this context that Waterland's brief writing on the fundamentals deserves to be investigated.[32] Its main contention is that Christianity constitutes a covenant between God and humanity; and for the central importance of this idea he refers his readers throughout the argument to a distinguished German Lutheran political philosopher and lay theologian, a disciple of Hugo Grotius, Samuel Pufendorf (1632–94).[33] The thought is that God and humanity are involved in an exchange of a quasi-legal kind. The idea is, of course, not new; Anselm had, after all, extensively theorized upon the concept of debt. On the premise that Christianity is the name for a covenantal relationship, then it follows, reasoned Waterland, that what is essential to Christianity is everything that belongs to the covenant; the parties, and their relative status, the agreement, the person of the mediator, and the conditions, means, and sanctions attached to the covenant.

There is a pedantic literalism about Waterland's careful analysis and exposition which strikes the modern reader unfavourably. At the same time one notes certain advantages of his proposal over its contemporary rivals. Chief among these is the fact that covenantal language sets God and humanity in a unique relationship of exchange, which Pufendorf had spoken of as a friendship and union. The precise terms of the covenant are determined by the particular situation of both parties and what is to be achieved. The making of the covenant is the central episode of personal and communal histories. Within the somewhat artificial framework of covenant-making Waterland is seeking to respond to the story of God's dealings with humanity, a story which has a grammar of setting, theme, plot or plots, and resolution.

A second advantage to Waterland's proposal is the fact that the fundamentals so formulated cannot be reduced to fundamental articles of belief, but must include fundamentals of worship and

[32] Waterland, *A Discourse of Fundamentals* (1735) in *The Works of Daniel Waterland*, viii (Oxford, 1823), 85–125.

[33] Pufendorf, *Ius feciale Divinum sive de consensu et dissensu Protestantium: exercitatio postuma*, trans. Theophilus Dorrington (rector of Wittresham, Kent), as *The Divine Feudal Law; or Covenants with Mankind represented: Together with Means for the Uniting of Protestants* (London, 1703). As an ecumenical work it is in the line of Pareus and Calixtus, except that it does not adopt Calixtus's quinquesecularism. It is an attempt to provide a basis for inner Protestant reunion, unusual for a Lutheran in deploying the idea of covenant. It is fully orthodox in incarnational and Trinitarian theology. See H. Rabe, *Schriften zur Kirchen und Rechtsgeschichte*, v *Naturrecht und Kirche bei Samuel von Pufendorf* (Tübingen 1958).

of conduct. A multidimensional view of Christianity is therefore implicitly promoted above the artificial reductionism implicit in concentration solely upon doctrine, and the relegation of matters of structure, ritual, or behaviour to secondary status.

Thirdly, and as a corollary to the previously named feature, was the advantage that Waterland explicitly declined to specify a complete list of fundamentals. One might, he asserted, give examples of fundamentals and specify a rule for establishing whether a given feature of Christianity was fundamental or not, but the idea of a catalogue of fundamentals, even of fundamental truths, was not feasible. This denial had featured in an earlier significant contributor to the discussion, namely William Chillingworth (1604–44), who had argued in *The Religion of Protestants: A Safe Way to Salvation* (1638) the necessity of 'honest endeavour' in the obedience of faith and the pursuit of truth.[34] At this stage of the discussion, of course, Stillingfleet's important distinction between fundamentals necessary for salvation and fundamentals necessary for Church communion had not been drawn. Chillingworth's reticence in specifying fundamentals arose as a consequence of his insistence on the moral character of personal faith. Christian believers, he held, were responsible for doing their best to respond to the Church's direction of its members, to the Scriptures as containing all things necessary to salvation (Article VI). Chillingworth's argument was of importance inasmuch as lists of fundamentals had regularly figured in early attempts at ecumenical agreements; it was plainly of major importance to insist, with Waterland, that no such lists could be drawn up. The route was barred to the realization of one aspiration, namely that when disputes erupted in Christianity, they could be immediately resolved, or shelved as unnecessary to resolve, by reference to an already agreed list of fundamentals.

Waterland undertook to support the case he had outlined by a brief critical discussion of the plethora of proposals offered by various writers on the fundamentals. Among these are the following: articles of belief defined by the Church, he held, could not supply us with the fundamentals, since they do not identify the reasons for the declaration; nor could the assertion

[34] See R. R. Orr, *Reason and Authority: The Thought of William Chillingworth* (Oxford, 1967), 92–102.

of the infallibility of the Church itself be unchallengeable. The Scriptures themselves are not the fundamentals since they plainly contain matter of different weight and significance, and lack their own principle of canonicity. The proposal that every doctrine expressly taught in the Scriptures is fundamental fails to guide, in being unable to identify true consequences of Scriptural teaching. The invoking of the Creed as the rule of fundamentals is inadequate in its omission of fundamentals of worship and morality, and its failure to deal with later sophisticated heresy; and Waterland expressed his uncertainty about the meaning and status of the doctrine of the descent into hell. Waterland also dismissed Locke's recent proposals about the simple confession of the Messiahship of Jesus; such general professions he argued, may suffice at initiation but are not adequate for later life. Universality of agreement is, he held, another chimera—what article of faith has ever gone undisputed? Nor does abandonment of belief in favour of a moral criterion deliver us from the difficulty of discordant moralities.[35]

When Harrison read, or reread this discussion in November 1835 he told Newman that he thought Waterland had demonstrated 'solid objections to the plan of putting forward the Apostles Creed as a complete catalogue of fundamentals'. Newman wrote on the letter, 'I have never said, at least intentionally, "complete"'.[36] It is true that his mentor Stillingfleet, like Chillingworth though less prominently, refused to give a complete list of fundamentals. But the more strictly it was argued, with Jebb, that the rule of St Vincent precluded either additions or subtractions, the more the impression was given that the Apostles' Creed was complete, but for a few minor verbal variations. Stillingfleet as a matter of fact was notably more sophisticated than Jebb about the Vincentian canon, remarking that it was a rule easier to use negatively, so as to determine what was not considered as a necessary article of faith, than positively.[37] Waterland's objections were much more far reaching and incisive, and eventually reappear in altered form in the writing of the Catholic Newman. For the latter, too, Christianity was to be seen as a phenomenon with a multiplicity

[35] Waterland, *Discourse of Fundamentals*, in *Works*, viii. 105–121.
[36] Allen, *Newman and the Abbé Jager*, p. 154.
[37] Stillingfleet, *Grounds of Protestant Religion*. i. 89.

of aspects, whose centre was Christ and his redemption, and whose dynamic implied a capacity to resist new and sophisticated heresy by the eludication of the consequences of God's act. Newman's decision, doubtless made in considerable haste, to fortify Jebb's Vincentian citadel with what he took to be Stillingfleet's and Laud's orthodoxy, and thereby to conceal from view the pluralism over which Waterland had puzzled, was an error of some consequence. It was an error of which William Palmer (of Worcester College) left him in no doubt, when he roundly declared in 1835 that the term fundamentals was 'unqualified to be of any practical utility in questions of controversy'.[38]

Palmer's challenge, however, is as pertinent to Waterland's position as it is to Laud's or Stillingfleet's. It is a reasonable question, which has to be faced if it is claimed that there are advantages in a view of fundamentals which declines to specify what they are, whether that refusal destroys any claim for the practical authority of the proposal. If the point of appealing to fundamentals is to enable a Church to make decisions in disputed cases, is the comparative imprecision of the notion of covenant, or, in modern terms, of narrative, fatal to its usefulness? We can answer this question by pursuing the implications of Waterland's denial of the possibility of a comprehensive list of features. It follows that when a dispute occurs, there is only a possibility of immediate solution if the proposition or practice advanced is the explicit negation of one of those examples of what is involved in the covenant which Waterland undertakes to supply. For example, there is no question that the terms of the covenant involves the death of Jesus. If it is said that Jesus did not die, as the Gnostics asserted, then a fundamental of Christianity has been breached, and an immediate decision is possible. It cannot therefore, be maintained that the fundamentals so conceived are incapable of providing authoritative guidance.

The difficulty is, however, that disputes arise from the nature of the case in much less unequivocal instances. Can it be known, for example, from the fundamentals of Christianity, conceived as covenant or narrative, that the manufacture, deployment, and threat to use nuclear weapons is inconsistent with Christian faith? Or that one may use in certain circumstances techniques

[38] W. Palmer, *Treatise on the Church of Christ*, i (London, 1838), 122.

for the control of conception? Or that women may be ordained as deacons, priests, or bishops? Or that belief in the story of the empty tomb should not be considered a necessary entailment of belief in Christ's resurrection?

None of these examples involve matters which on principle could not be consistent with the fabric of the Christian religion. In each case, before a state of dispute could be said to have arisen, the novel proposal in question would have to be shown in some sense or another to have been developed in a Christianly appropriate argument. The authority of the arguments on both sides would then derive from the cogency of the case which could be made for the connections between the disputed contentions and the less disputed or generally agreed beliefs or practices of the faith. The usefulness of Waterland's proposal is, therefore, not destroyed. Examples can be given of fundamentals. The fact that some issues may generate dispute does not mean that there are no undisputed issues. Boundaries may exist even when their precise location is difficult to specify.

More difficult than the examples of arguments we have mentioned is the moral pre-condition for the resolution of disputes, the recognition of the authority of the Church to make binding decisions. Here again, however, Waterland's proposal is not without force. The argument that God is the kind of God who would take care not to leave his people bereft of guidance, having taken such pains to establish the terms of his covenant with humanity, is an argument of weight and substance, deriving from the consistency of God's character. The argument that the history of the people of God has included episodes of infidelity, betrayal, and disaster, even while embodying an overarching purpose, is likewise considerable, deriving from the observable consistency of the knowledge of the 'chosen people'. Arguments about the nature of the authority of the Church are not of necessity irresolvable, even if a church whose nature is in dispute is unable to issue an indisputable declaration of its own infallibility. It seems that 'Church' like 'Christianity' is an essentially contested concept, but that does not make arguments about the Church a waste of time.[39] Moreover, all such arguments must refer to those decision-making competencies of which all institutions

[39] For a discussion of this proposal see S. W. Sykes, *The Identity of Christianity* (London, 1984), esp. ch. 10.

have to be possessed. Sociologically speaking it is what one would expect that decisions at different levels would be accorded different degrees of authority. Waterland's proposal, therefore, by no means destroys the authority of the Church, though it makes living with disputes a necessity, including dispute about levels and degrees of authoritativeness. Such disputes have to be conducted by means of Christian arguments, some of which may be of a less final and immediate character than others. But that, I submit, is the actual condition of Christendom.

V

The notion of fundamentals, then, is capable of significant formulation in terms of narrative, a modern way of rendering Waterland's proposal concerning covenant. It remains finally to relate this less familiar construal of the fundamental articles tradition to the Lambeth Quadrilateral.

As we set out by observing, the Quadrilateral evokes the Anglican tradition of reference to fundamentals by speaking of its Articles as 'a basis' for ecumenism. But the Quadrilateral is not a set of propositional beliefs; its Articles are, we argued, a hierarchy of usages inclusive of, but not restricted to beliefs. As such the Quadrilateral offers, as does Waterland's proposal, a multi-dimensional model of Christianity.

Furthermore, the Quadrilateral does not purport to be exhaustive; it is 'a basis upon which approach may be by God's blessing made towards Home Reunion', rather than a sufficient basis for reunion itself. If the Article on the Scriptures is understood as referring to the public use of the Scriptures in the life of the church, in preaching, public reading, and catechesis, then interpretative activity and the adjudication of disputes are necessities. The Article on the Scriptures and those on the Creeds and the episcopate are interrelated. The Creeds in particular, provide the basis for the baptismal reception of new members and the catechesis of adult participants. In themselves they constitute a brief narrative summary of the contents of the Scriptures. They are a series of prompt lines inviting further inquiry or, in Newman's phrase, the 'heads and memoranda of the Church's teaching'.[40] They are 'sufficient' because they are

[40] 'The Brothers Controversy: Apostolical Tradition' in the *British Critic, Quarterly Theological Review, and Ecclesiastical Record*, 20 (1836), 187; cited in Lash, *Newman on Development*, p. 130.

capable of being learnt by repetition and remembered, in a way in which longer and more discursive or argumentative statements are not. They are not sufficient in the sense of being omni-competent to prevent disputes or to resolve them, or to satisfy all the theological questions which may be addressed to the narrative outline.

The episcopate is an integral part of the Quadrilateral, and related essentially to the first two articles, precisely because many disputes arising from Christian questions or arguments are not resolvable by reference to the Creeds or directly to the Scriptures. The episcopate is a provision for the preservation of unity, which is in principle and in practice never to allow itself to be separated from the use of the Scriptures, by which the life of the whole Church is nourished.

If nothing in the Quadrilateral is strictly irreconcilable with Waterland's proposal, none the less its deficiencies when judged by the same criterion become immediately apparent. One is at once struck by the formalism of its proposals. There is nothing which evokes the sense that with the Church we are dealing with a community of persons drawn into relationship with God by his own gracious action. The normal life of the Church and its sense of purpose is wholly absent from explicit mention, perhaps, we may guess, because it is simply assumed by the Lambeth Fathers. We can less confidently, suppose, however, that the omission of any ethical content, least of all of the kind characteristic of the community described in Acts 2, which sold its possessions and distributed to all who were in need, was based on a similar presupposition. The idea that humanity is engaged in a covenant with God through Jesus Christ involving the integrity before God of the whole of the created order is not the least of the possibilities in Waterland's proposal. That there might be an extensive blasphemy involved in betrayal of the environment could be Christianly argued on the basis of the covenant, which makes the lack of any sense of *coram deo* in the Quadrilateral all the more striking and regrettable.

But this criticism amounts to saying that the Quadrilateral's list might well be extended to include further provisions, which is not in doubt. Moreover it has formulated the rule upon which the extension would be justified, namely by its coherence with the contents of the Holy Scriptures as used and effective in the life of the Church as a whole. What the Quadrilateral lacks is the sense that the Scriptures provide above all a sort of portraiture of Christianity, a showing that it is a phenomenon of a particular kind. To speak of it as narrative of a peculiar people engaged in a determinative friendship with God is to give what Newman would have called 'a distinct and significant description of Christianity'.[41] If the identity of Christianity is to persist, there has to be a preliminary view of the kind of thing the Christian movement was in its origins. The preservation of type in Newman's *Essay on Development* is of original type, and the methods he deploys in the description of early Christianity are comparative, sociological, and historical, a fusion of vision from outside and inside. It is for this task of inside portraiture that the Scriptures are indispensable, giving an irreplaceable idea of what it might mean to be the covenanted people of God.

VI

My conclusion, therefore, is that the events of 1834–45 during which time Newman wrestled with the tradition of fundamentals as he inherited it in the Church of England are still of interest and importance. The weaknesses and strengths of the Chicago–Lambeth Quadrilateral as an instrument of ecumenism become clearer when they are confronted again both by what Newman rejected in the tradition he received, and what he chose to ignore. But it is also apparent that the requirement for a credible modern form of ecumenism between Anglicans and Roman Catholics is a willingness on both sides to appreciate that Lutheran and Reformed Churches have made massive contributions to the discussion of fundamentals without which Anglicanism is itself unintelligible.

[41] *Dev.*, 6. 1. 3. The phrase was retained from 1845.

19

The Threefold Office in Newman's Ecclesiology

AVERY DULLES, SJ

John Henry Newman is perhaps the most seminal Roman Catholic theologian of modern times. He did not shape his theological agenda according to the problems traditionally debated in the schools but rather in the light of new questions arising out of the British empirical and liberal tradition. Content to ignore many themes of continental thought, he remained surprisingly insular. He was, of course, well grounded in the biblical and patristic sources, and he had a passing acquaintance with medieval and post-Tridentine scholasticism, but he adopted a highly personal approach, even to the extent of fashioning somewhat novel terminology. Because his thought was so largely determined by his own quest for religious truth, his work is difficult to fit into the history of nineteenth-century Catholic theology. His greatest merit is to have directed attention to many neglected areas in the relationship between faith and reason, the theory of apologetics, the development of doctrine, the theology of the laity, and the doctrine of infallibility. On each of these questions Newman gathered such a wealth of relevant material, achieved such profound insights, and expressed himself with such literary elegance, that his contribution remains to this day unsurpassed.

Newman was a generalist in religious knowledge rather than a specialist in the theology of the Church.[1] But nearly all the questions that engaged his interest have an ecclesial dimension. This is evident in the cases of the theology of the laity and of infallibility and in the field of the development of doctrine. A pervasive theme in his work is the role of authority in religion.

[1] Besides the well-known works of W. H. Van de Pol (1936) and Norbert Schiffers (1956) there are today several new monographs on Newman's ecclesiology: G. Lease, *Witness to the Faith: Cardinal Newman on the Teaching Authority of the Church* (Pittsburgh, Pa., 1971) and E. J. Miller, *John Henry Newman on the Idea of the Church* (Shepherdstown, W. Va., 1987).

For him a Church that did not claim to speak with divine authority could not credibly present itself as the legitimate heir of the Church of the New Testament. Newman was vehemently opposed to liberalism, which he saw as substituting the private exercise of reason for the traditionary faith of the Church. Against the liberals he passionately defended the authority of Scripture, the Fathers, and the ecclesiastical magisterium. 'The essence of all religion', he maintained, 'is authority and obedience.'[2] Yet Newman also wished to make ample room for sincere inquiry and conscience in the Christian life. Thus he cannot fairly be characterized as an authoritarian. Both critical reason and authority were for Newman held in check by religious devotion. Without an attitude of loving reverence, he believed, one could not find religious truth by the interpretation of evidence nor could one recognize the genuine voice of authority.

I

The interplay between critical scholarship, piety, and ecclesiastical authority is basic to the topic of the present essay—Newman's theory of the threefold office of the Church. The threefold division, of course, did not originate with him. The depiction of Christ as prophet, priest, and king was a patristic theme that Newman would have known from Eusebius of Caesarea among others.[3] Since Calvin the threefold office had been standard in much Protestant theology, most notably in the field of Christology. Already in his sermons as an Anglican, Newman made extensive use of the triad both in Christology and in ecclesiology.[4]

Newman's fullest and most mature treatment of the three offices of the Church is to be found in his last major work, his 1877 Preface to the third edition of *The Via Media of the Anglican Church*,[5] a republication with new footnotes of his 1837 work

[2] *Dev.*, p. 86.

[3] The history of the theology of the triple office is traced in L. Schick, *Das dreifache Amt Christi und der Kirche: Zur Entstehung und Entwicklung der Trilogien* (Frankfurt and Berne, 1982) and in greater detail in A. Fernandez, *Munera Christi et Munera Ecclesiae: Historia de una teoría* (Pamplona, 1982). For a briefer survey see Y. Congar, 'Sur la trilogie: prophète—roi—prêtre', *Revue des sciences philosophiques et théologiques*, 67 (1983), 97–115.

[4] See *SD*, esp. sermon 5, 'The Three Offices of Christ', pp. 52–62.

[5] *VM* i. In the present article small Roman numerals in parentheses in the text will be used to designate page references.

Lectures on the Prophetical Office of the Church viewed relatively to Romanism and Popular Protestantism. In the original lectures Newman had limited himself to treating the prophetic office, almost to the exclusion of the priestly and the regal. He did, however, make a distinction between two forms of tradition—the episcopal and the prophetic.[6] The episcopal tradition preserves and hands down, in stable form, the apostolic deposit of faith. The prophetic tradition is the living and dynamic reception of the apostolic faith as it pulsates through the Church with the assistance of the Holy Spirit. Against popular Protestantism, which had allegedly eroded the apostolic heritage, and Rome, which had allegedly added to that heritage, Newman took his stand on the rule of faith set forth by Vincent of Lerins: what had been believed everywhere, always, and by all. Newman's charges against Rome were essentially two: that it had departed from the religion of the early Church by unauthorized additions and that its popular and political manifestations were discordant with its formal teaching.

In 1877, forty years after the original publication, Newman reissued these lectures. In his new Preface he explained that he had already answered the charge of innovation in his *Essay on the Development of Christian Doctrine*, published in 1845, but that the second charge still required a full response. Newman the Catholic apologist now took up the pen to refute the earlier Anglican Newman. Primarily the Preface is a work of apologetics, directed especially to 'those, not a few, who would be Catholics, if their conscience would let them' (p. xxxvi). Among works of apologetics the Preface stands out for its frank acknowledgement that there are conflicts and abuses in the Church.

Newman in this work takes his departure from the notion of the Church as sacrament. It is, he maintains, a visible representation of Christ, an organ of the Paraclete. In the words of his Anglican friend, the theologian and poet John Keble, it is Christ's 'very self below' (p. xxxix). The Church, then, is not just a reminder of, or pointer to, Christ; it is a locus where he makes himself present and active in the world today.

From this Christological perspective Newman embarks on his study of the Church's mission: our Lord, he declares, combined

[6] *VM* i. 249–52. See also G. Biemer, *Newman on Tradition* (New York, 1967), 46–8.

in himself the offices of prophet, priest, and king, which in the Old Testament had been held by distinct figures. His celestial anointing eminently fulfilled what was prefigured in the anointings given to each of these religious leaders. As Newman had said in one of his Anglican sermons,[7] Christ exercised his prophetic office in teaching and in foretelling the future; he performed his priestly ministry in his sacrificial death on the cross and when he consecrated the bread and cup to be the sacramental representation of that sacrifice; he showed himself a king and conqueror in his glorious resurrection and ascension, and in sending forth the Spirit of Truth to convert the nations and to rule them by means of the Church.

Newman gave the threefold office a particular modality in line with his epistemology. Ever the opponent of rationalism, he was shy of definitions and abstract concepts. Reality, he believed, is concrete, complex, and impervious to systematization. The Church, like other historical realities, is most successfully apprehended not by clear concepts but by what Newman, like Coleridge and others, called ideas.[8] Ideas are global representations that bring opposite characteristics into a harmony perceived in a preconceptual and supraconceptual way.

In his *Essay on Development* Newman contended that the Christian idea was complex and consisted of a variety of aspects that could seem at first sight incompatible. 'But one aspect of Revelation', he added, 'must not be allowed to exclude or obscure another; and Christianity is dogmatical, devotional, practical all at once'.[9] It is precisely these three aspects of the Christian idea that now appear as the three offices of the Church. All three of them enter into the idea of the Church, standing in a dialectical relationship of mutual tension and mutual support. Using the analogy of a harmony of sounds, Newman can say that the unity of the various offices of the Church is 'musical'.

In one of his Anglican sermons Newman had insisted that every member of the Church shares in all three offices.[10] Every

[7] *SD*, p. 53.

[8] Newman's similarities with and differences from Coleridge on the concept of 'idea' are examined by J. Coulson, *Newman and the Common Tradition* (Oxford, 1970), 58–63 and *passim*.

[9] *Dev.*, p. 36.

[10] *SD*, p. 62.

Christian, he maintained, is bound to bear witness to the truth and thereby engage in the prophetic task. All are likewise called to suffer for the sake of the Kingdom of God, and thus to take part in the priestly function. All, finally, are obliged to obey the word of revelation, because Christ is our king. The Christian's participation in the royal office of Christ would, in this sermon, appear to be a matter of submitting to authority rather than exercising it.

In the 1877 Preface the offices are attributed not so much to individual Christians as to the Church as a body. Instead of emphasizing the participation of each Christian in all three offices, Newman holds that different elements in the Church embody one or another of the offices. As a result Newman here depicts the offices in sharp contrast, if not in mutual separation. Having received the three offices of Christ "after his pattern, and in a human measure" (p. xl), the Church is a philosophy (presumably meaning a system of truth); it is a religious rite (that is to say, an organ of worship), and it is a political power (Newman's expression for ecclesiastical polity). Newman then connects the three offices—rather tenuously, it would seem—with the four classical notes or attributes of the Church set forth in the Niceno-Constantinopolitan Creed. As a religion, he says, it is holy; as a philosophy, it is apostolic; and as a political power, it is one and catholic.

Newman also remarks on a certain temporal sequence in the development of the three offices. In the primitive period the Church appeared primarily as a community of worship, spreading among the lower ranks of society, whom Newman seems to regard as particularly devout. Then it spread among the learned, giving rise to schools and to theology. Finally it took root among the holders of political power and established Rome as its centre.

One of the most interesting features of Newman's analysis is his apportionment of the three offices among different classes in the Church. He links the teaching function not with the official magisterium of popes and bishops but rather with the theological schools. In the Preface the bishops are not identified as official teachers. As the essay proceeds, Newman attributes to the official rulers a certain indirect exercise of the teaching function in view of their responsibilities to protect the unity and welfare of the community. But this function, as we shall later see, can hardly be called directly doctrinal.

The priestly function in Newman's schematization is not particularly assigned to the ordained, as one might have expected. Initially he attributes this office to the 'pastor and flock', but in the main body of the Preface he focuses almost entirely on popular religion and on the beliefs of the simple faithful.

The ruling office in Newman's analysis is ascribed to 'the Papacy and its Curia' (p. xl). On the same page he remarks in passing that he has not forgotten that the pope 'as Vicar of Christ' inherits all three offices, but this, he says, 'is another matter'. The papacy in the Preface appears almost exclusively as a centre of regiminal power. Rather surprisingly, the other bishops do not figure prominently in the discussion of the ruling office, and their relationship to the pope is left unclear.

Newman speaks also of the guiding principles and instruments of the three functions. The principles are, for theology, truth; for worship, devotion and edification; and for government, expedience. The instruments correlated with these three principles are: for theology, reasoning; for worship, emotion; and for rule, command and coercion.

Each of these three offices, Newman contends, suffers from a characteristic temptation to excess. For theology the dangers are rationalism and scepticism; for worship, superstition and enthusiasm; and for the ruling power, ambition and tyranny. These temptations are offset in so far as each of the three offices is held in check, to some degree, by the other two. Newman's operative model, therefore, seems to be a system of checks and balances.

II

In the early part of his exposition Newman gives a definite priority to the prophetic office. He states:

> Theology is the fundamental and regulating principle of the whole Church system. It is commensurate with Revelation, and Revelation is the initial and essential idea of Christianity. It is the subject-matter, the formal cause, the expression of the Prophetical Office, and, as being such, has created both the Regal Office and the Sacerdotal. (p. xlvii)

Newman then goes on to explain that the prophetic office exercises a certain 'power of jurisdiction' over the other two, which are in his judgement more liable to excess and corruption. Alluding to a variety of papal errors in the past (namely, those of Liberius, Vigilius, Boniface VIII, and Sixtus V), he traces these to an effort on their part to 'venture beyond the lines of theology' (p. xlviii).

When Newman here characterizes theology as the regulating principle in the Church there can be little doubt that he means the work of theologians, the discipline practised in the schools. In a letter of 5 February 1876 to Lord Blachford he used very similar phraseology: 'The Schola Theologorum is (in the Divine Purpose *I* should say) the regulating principle of the Church.'[11] In this letter he explained that the Catholic Church, like Great Britain, has a constitutional form of government that protects it against the excesses of individuals. Just as the courts and lawyers preserve the body politic from the absolutistic tendencies of monarchs, so, Newman argued, the theological school protects the Church from the wilful encroachments of popes and councils.

Because he attributed this crucially important role to the theological schools, Newman frequently lamented their virtual destruction by the French Revolution and other calamities of recent centuries. In a well-known letter of 19 May 1863 to Emily Bowles, he observed mournfully that 'there are no schools now, no private judgment (in the religious sense of the phrase), no freedom, that is, of opinion'.[12] In the present situation, he complained, theological schools, Newman longer subjected to intellectual examination by theological faculties before judgement was pronounced upon them by the Roman authorities. Extreme centralization was the order of the day.

These claims for the supremacy of theology are not easy to reconcile with what Newman elsewhere has to say about the subordinate status of theology in relation to other fonts of truth. To gather up Newman's full thinking on the subject one would have to weigh the passages just quoted against what he says in the twelfth of his *Oxford University Sermons*, in which he calls attention to the need for a regulative or corrective principle to

[11] Quoted in Ward, ii. 374; and quoted more briefly in P. Misner, *Papacy and Development: Newman and the Primacy of the Pope* (Leiden, 1976), 166.

[12] Quoted in Ward, i. 588. See in the same sense Newman's letter to Lord Acton of 18 March 1864, ibid. 560–1.

keep faith from falling into credulity or superstition. The discriminating principle, he concludes, cannot be reason, for reason depends upon antecedent presuppositions and attitudes. Love, rather, is the principle that keeps faith from fastening upon unworthy objects and from degenerating into enthusiasm or superstition.[13]

The subordinate status of theology is indicated even more expressly in other works. In his *Essay on Development* Newman insists that faith, 'being an act of the intellect, opens the way for inquiry, comparison and inference, that is, for science in religion, in subservience to itself,' and these subservient operations he designates by the name of theology.[14] The main burden of this section of the *Essay* is to establish the inferiority of theology to faith, dogma, and the mystical sense of Scripture. 'The contempt of mystery, of reverence, of devoutness, of sanctity', he concludes, are 'notes of the heretical spirit.'[15]

In his article *On Consulting the Faithful in Matters of Doctrine* Newman once more assigns a rather modest place to theology. He exalts the consensus of the whole body of the faithful as 'the voice of the Infallible Church'.[16] He freely admits that many points of defined dogma cannot be found in the ecclesiastical writers, but this absence is not fatal, he remarks, provided that the faithful accept the doctrines in question by a kind of Christian instinct implanted in their hearts by the Holy Spirit. The apostolic testimony, according to Newman, can manifest itself through a great variety of means other than the *doctores*; for instance, the people, liturgies, rites, ceremonies, and customs. All of these channels must be treated with respect 'granting at the same time fully, that the gift of discerning, discriminating, defining, promulgating, and enforcing any portion of that tradition resides solely in the *Ecclesia docens*.'[17] The absence of any reference to the *ecclesia docens* is one of the most puzzling features of the Preface of 1877.

In the *Grammar of Assent* Newman's general position about the secondary role of theology appears in different form. Faith, he asserts, is a real apprehension, whereas theology is merely notional. Theological science is nothing more than 'the exercise

[13] *US*, pp. 236–8, sermon 12, 'Love the Safeguard of Faith against Superstition'.
[14] *Dev.*, p. 325. [15] *Dev.*, p. 354. [16] *Cons.*, p. 63.
[17] Ibid.

of the intellect upon the *credenda* of revelation'.[18] The dogmatic statements of the Church, in Newman's opinion, are often phrased in poetic and imaginative forms, so as to act 'as a check upon our reasonings, lest they rush on in one direction beyond the limits of the truth'.[19] In his discussion of the dogmatic statements about the Holy Trinity Newman demonstrates how they illustrate the maxim *lex orandi lex credendi*. It must be reckoned a limitation of the 1877 Preface that it contains no reference to this maxim.

Newman's praise for the record of the schools in the 1877 Preface may be seen as an effort to respond to the charges he had made in the 1837 text of the *Prophetical Office*. Perhaps his response claims too much for the schools. At many points in history they have tended to be overbearing; they have engaged in hate-filled rivalries and have attempted to manœuvre the ecclesiastical magisterium into giving dogmatic status to their own theories. At their best, however, the schools did and do perform a useful service in sifting through the evidence about disputed points and thus in some sense preparing for doctrinal developments. They have also served to give exact interpretations to papal and synodal utterances, as Newman emphasized in his 1874 *Letter to the Duke of Norfolk*. Newman's 1877 Preface is surely correct in holding that the Church must not let emotion or practical expediency override the concern for truth.

III

In the remainder of the Preface Newman offsets his previous exaltation of theology. The second major section deals with the priestly office, which Newman introduces with the remark that theology is 'too hard, too intellectual, too exact' to have the final say (p. xlviii). The theme of the priestly office provides Newman with an occasion to answer his earlier complaint, in the 1837 edition, that the popular religiosity of Catholics was not in keeping with the official teaching of their Church.

In several earlier works Newman had insisted on the importance of distinguishing between faith and devotion. For instance, in his 1865 response to Pusey's *Eirenicon*, he aligned theology with the intellectual element and worship with the emotional element in religion. In Catholicism, Newman there declared, 'the faith is

[18] *GA*, pp. 98–9. [19] *GA*, p. 90.

everywhere one and the same, but a large liberty is accorded to private judgment and inclination in matters of devotion'.[20] In that connection Newman frankly confessed that 'the religion of the multitude is ever vulgar and abnormal; it ever will be tinctured with fanaticism and superstition, while men are what they are. A people's religion is ever a corrupt religion, in spite of the provisions of Holy Church.'[21] Logic, Newman wrote to Pusey, is no remedy, for, as in the case of Arius, it can easily carry the theologian into heresy.

In his 1877 Preface Newman shows the same ambivalent attitude toward popular religion. The Church, he says, is precise in the enunciation of its doctrine but tolerant in sanctioning devotions, except in so far as they imply doctrines (p. lxxv). Theology has no dominion over worship because 'theology did not create it, but found it in our hearts' (p. lxix). The religious instinct, as Newman sees it, is connatural with humanity and antecedent to positive revelation.

The natural religious sentiment is respected in the Catholic cult of saints and angels. Polytheism is but a corruption of this natural tendency. We are intended to glorify God not only in himself but in his creatures, especially the holiest of them. The possible abuses of superstition and idolatry should not be allowed to prevent the proper indulgence of this instinct.

Devotion, then, serves to temper the rigidity of theological principles, including the principle of monotheism. In Catholic thinkers such as Robert Bellarmine, devout reliance on God's mercy has served to prevent the Tridentine doctrine of merit from leading to complacency or anxiety (pp. xlix–l).

Yet in many cases, Newman admits, popular religion stands in tension with correct theology. For example, the veneration of relics may rest on unfounded beliefs, and even so be the occasion of true devotion. The cult of saints and martyrs can sometimes detract from the pure worship of God. To deal with cases such as this Newman proposes what we may call a theology of compromise. Church authorities, while seeking to purify devotion, should be careful not to crush it. Error should not be uprooted, Newman believes, where its removal will do more harm than its toleration. In the concrete, the admission of some measure of

[20] *Diff.*, ii. 28. [21] Ibid. 81.

superstition may be the price of a living and heartfelt faith. On the same ground, Newman contends that it is permissible to leave certain points of faith undefined for the moment in the interests of charity and religious peace. In this connection he alludes to the principle of economy advocated by many of the Greek Fathers (pp. l, lxi).

Newman proposes a number of biblical arguments for his theology of compromise (as I have called it). For millennia, he notes, God suffered the nations to walk according to their own lights, without biblical revelation. Under the Old Dispensation God permitted polygamy, concubinage, and divorce. Jesus himself, though he relentlessly attacked ambition, avarice, and pride, made concessions in favour of superstition. Where does Jesus in the Gospels 'insist on the danger of superstition, an infirmity which, taking human nature as it is, is the sure companion of faith, when vivid and earnest?' (p. lxviii.) The woman with a haemorrhage in the Gospels seems to have relied upon some kind of magic power in Jesus's garments, but he, instead of rebuking her, praised her faith and rewarded it (pp. lxvi–lxviii). The Evangelists warn against quenching the smoking flax and against uprooting the wheat in an attempt to rid it of weeds. These principles seem to have been observed by Paul, who repeatedly admonishes mature and sophisticated Christians to take care not to scandalize the weak by their own freedom of action (pp. lvi–lviii; cf. Rom. 14: 13–23).

Popular piety, Newman observes, tends to resist novelty. As an example he mentions the widespread opposition to Jerome's improvement upon his own previous version of the Psalms. In this respect there is a contrast between the religious and the scientific mentality. Scientists readily embrace new hypotheses on the chance that they may be correct, whereas religious people have a holy fear of forsaking ideas and institutions that have sustained the community of faith. This tendency sometimes brings the simple faithful into conflict with theologians and scholars, who partake of the scientific mentality. Church authority frequently supports the hesitations of the devout. On this ground Newman attempts to explain, if not to excuse, the opposition to Galileo in official Church circles. Charity toward unsophisticated believers, he holds, made it necessary at the time to delay the new interpretation of Scripture implied in Galileo's theory until the popular imagination could become accustomed to heliocentrism.[22]

In concluding his discussion of the sacerdotal office Newman touches on yet another sensitive issue between Catholics and Protestants, the problem of missionary accommodation. Newman clearly opts for a Church that adapts to the cultures of various peoples in so far as these cultures are not incompatible with Christianity itself. He points out how Paul became a Jew to Jews and a Greek to Greeks in order that he might save all (p. lxxvi; cf. 1 Cor. 9: 22). Newman also thinks it likely that the Fourth Evangelist took over a concept of the Logos current in Greek philosophy in order to capture the interest of Platonizing Jews. In the same connection Newman defends the seventeenth-century Jesuits for their efforts to present Catholicism in a form palatable to Asian audiences.

Newman's treatment of the priestly office, even from this brief survey, may be judged original and impressive. It forthrightly addresses some of the most serious objections raised by the *Prophetical Office* and still pressed against Catholicism in our own day. On the other hand it must be recognized that Newman did not present a full and balanced theology of the priestly office. Such a theology would have to include a more ample consideration of topics such as the holiness of the Church, the sacraments, the liturgy, and the ministry.

If the devotional corresponds, as Newman maintains, to worship, it is surprising that the Preface concentrates on private devotions almost to the exclusion of the liturgy and the sacraments, in which the priestly ministry of Christ is most palpably perpetuated in the Church. If Newman had dwelt more on this aspect of worship, he could have established a more positive relationship between devotion and theology. He would have had occasion to discuss the principle *lex orandi lex credendi*, showing

[22] The intellectual élite of any generation will be scandalized by the apology for censorship and for suppression of new ideas countenanced by Newman. Typically, James Gaffney, in his recent article, 'Newman's Criticism of the Church: Lessons and Object Lessons' (*Heythrop Journal*, 29 (1988), 1–20), finds Newman's 'dubious and digressive' argument in this section of his Preface 'a spontaneous intrusion of his antiliberal convictions at their most prejudiced' (p. 13). But Gaffney's objection manifestly presupposes that theology is not 'different in kind from any secular discipline' (ibid.). If he held, as Newman did, that the sacred sciences rest upon a once-for-all revelation mediated by living tradition, Gaffney might have to modify his strictures.

how the sense of the faithful, shaped by participation in liturgical worship, is equipped to detect and repel heresy, as occurred in the Arian crisis. In his 'Letter to Pusey' Newman had complained that the *Eirenicon* took as sources for the allegedly abusive practices not the approved liturgy of the Church but popular and merely local devotions. He argued also that Catholics were restrained from falling into idolatry by their devotion to Christ in the Eucharist.[23]

The *Prophetical Office* unfortunately took much the same line of approach as Pusey's *Eirenicon*. In adhering rather closely to the charges he was answering, Newman in his Preface missed the opportunity to develop a positive and comprehensive theology of the priestly office in the Church.

IV

Many theologians, such as Paul Tillich in the twentieth century, have dwelt on the dialectical tension between the priestly and the prophetic elements in the Church. A special feature of Newman's system is that he recognizes a third component, the regal, and depicts it as standing in a dialectical relationship with each of the other two.

Already in his Anglican days Newman had declared with great emphasis that the Church is on earth a visible kingdom having as its rulers the successors of Peter and the Twelve, who are to sit upon thrones 'judging the twelve tribes of Israel' (Luke 22: 29–30).[24] As Christ's viceregents, the holders of ecclesiastical power have full authority to bind and to loose, exercising the power of the keys. It is not enough, Newman holds, to call the Church a kingdom. Rather, it should be called an imperial power, for it extends beyond the borders of every state and aspires to worldwide dominion on behalf of Christ. Nations as well as individuals are subject to it.

Neither in the Preface of 1877 nor in the earlier Anglican *Sermons bearing on Subjects of the Day* is Newman very specific as to the persons who wield this imperial power. In the Preface, as we have seen, he speaks of the 'Papacy and its Curia' and of the 'sovereign pontiff' as holding kingly rule. He refers likewise

[23] *Diff.*, ii. 94–6.

[24] *SD*, Sermon 16, 'The Christian Church an Imperial Power', pp. 222–3.

to the 'the imperial see of Peter' (p. lxxxix). But in his examples of regal authority in the Church, he mentions, besides the actions of popes, those of various bishops and of the Emperor Constantine. Regarding the type of rule they exercise, Newman asserts that the Church has always had 'a hierarchy and a head, with a strict unity of polity, the claim of an exclusive divine authority and blessing, the trusteeship of the gospel gifts, and the exercise over her members of an absolute and almost despotic rule' (p. lxxx).

This conclusion, difficult though it be to reconcile with Newman's remarks cited earlier on the Church's constitutional form of government, is a central element of his ecclesiology. In a letter to Pusey of 23 March 1867, Newman contended that 'the Pope must have universal jurisdiction' and reasoned: 'Now the Church is a Church Militant, and, as the commander of an army is despotic, so must the visible head of the Church be; and therefore in its idea the Pope's jurisdiction can hardly be limited.'[25] Similar statements occur in the section on 'The Papal Supremacy' in the *Essay on Development*.[26]

Some recent theologians have striven to show that the pope's sovereignty is inherently limited either by the principle of collegiality or by the priestly and vicarious character of his rule. Yves Congar, for example, maintains that the three offices intrinsically qualify one another through a kind of perichoresis.[27] Newman, in his 1877 Preface, recognizes no such restraints. The principle of the regal power, for him, is expediency. By this he does not mean the self-interest of individual rulers but rather what is dictated by the finality of the Church, which is divinely commissioned to extend its dominion and to consolidate itself. Whatever is truly necessary for the survival and mission of the Church, Newman contends, cannot be contrary to God's will. Conversely, whatever is harmful to the unity, sanctity, and expansion of the Church must also be theologically wrong.

It does not follow, however, that theological reflection will always be able to validate the concerns of the regal office. Newman gives a whole series of examples to prove just the opposite. He speaks first of the adoption of certain pagan festivals, invested with a new Christian meaning, such as the

[25] Quoted in Ward, ii. 223. Ward gives the full text of this letter.

[26] *Dev.*, pp. 148–65.

[27] Congar, 'Sur la trilogie', p. 112.

banquets and sporting events organized by Gregory Thaumaturgus in the third century to honour the martyrs—a practice roundly disapproved by graver teachers such as Peter Chrysologus in the fifth century. Newman speaks next of the use of force for the maintenance of religion, contrary to the convictions of Athanasius and even of the young Augustine. Newman apparently has in mind occurrences such as the forced conversions of the Saxons under Charlemagne.[28]

As additional instances Newman then mentions the recognition of heretical and schismatical baptisms and ordinations. After quoting a whole series of Fathers as witnesses to the invalidity of heretical baptisms, Newman concludes that the decision of Pope Stephen to acknowledge their validity was so solidly founded in expediency that it ultimately prevailed. On the question of simoniacal ordinations in the Middle Ages, Newman shows how Pope Leo IX was compelled by practical considerations to reverse his decree of invalidity. Here again the regal prevailed over the prophetic.

In some cases the theological reasoning has supported the argument from expediency. Newman is able to cite Prosper Lambertini (who in turn appeals to Thomas Aquinas) as upholding the infallibility of the pope in solemn canonizations on the ground that if the pope could err in so designating the saints the indefectibility of the Church in its prayer and worship would be compromised. Similarly, Newman argues that Catholics may be confident, notwithstanding the lack of complete historical evidence, that the apostolic succession in the ordination of bishops has been maintained without a break, for such a break would defeat the very purpose of the Church's existence. Newman is here constructing what I would call an indirectly theological argument. He establishes theological conclusions by reasoning from practical expediency.

In this section of his Preface Newman is so taken up with the relationship between the regal and prophetic offices that he almost ignores the devotional. Toward the end, however, he does supply one example of tension between the regal and the priestly.

[28] The reference to Charlemagne is from the original manuscript. It was deleted from the printed text. See R. Bergeron, *Les Abus de l'Église d'après Newman: étude de la Préface à la troisième édition de la 'Via Media'* (Montreal and Tournai, 1971), 181. Bergeron's is the fullest study known to me of the Preface of 1877.

Constantine, with the sanction of Church authorities, took the sign of the Cross, previously a symbol of non-resistance, and placed it on his military standard, the *labarum*, to make it into a symbol of victory by the sword.

This concluding section of the Preface stands in marked tension with the statement, early on in the Preface, that the prophetic office, embodied in the theological school, is 'the regulating principle of the whole Church system'. This might seem to imply that any infringement of the regal or the priestly on the prophetic could only be considered an abuse. Newman, however, does not draw this conclusion. Religious sentiment and ecclesiastical interests, for him, have their rights, which must act as a restraint upon theology itself.

Essential to Newman's argument is the principle 'that no act could be theologically an error, which was absolutely and undeniably necessary for the unity, sanctity, and peace of the Church' (p. lxxxiii). In asserting this principle Newman is quite aware of shocking the liberal mentality of his day. Some contemporary Catholics hold that Newman is here attempting to placate the ultramontane party[29] or inconsistently giving way to his anti-liberal prejudices.[30] Is he not making an unscrupulous transfer to the Church of the discredited doctrine of *raison d'état*? Perhaps, however, Newman's principle is basically sound. There can never be a true conflict between the spiritual goals of the Church and its fidelity to the gospel. A policy that is right will be recognizable by its salutary fruits. The proper use of any charism serves not for destruction but for edification—for the upbuilding of the Church.

Newman recognizes that his pragmatic principle is not easy to apply. The holders of regal power, notwithstanding the divine assistance granted to them, have not been able to avoid all mistakes.

This aid, however, great as it is, does not secure her [the Church] from all dangers as regards the problem which she has to solve; nothing but

[29] John Coulson in his essay, 'Newman on the Church: His Final View, Its Origins and Influence', in id. and A. M. Allchin (eds.), *The Rediscovery of Newman: An Oxford Symposium* (London, 1967), 167, explains that Newman's language 'is chosen deliberately to conciliate the Ultramontane party'.

[30] James Gaffney speaks of this as 'probably [the] least satisfactory portion' of the Preface, inasmuch as it 'betrays at times a tendentiousness that suggests strong undercurrent prejudices'; see Gaffney, 'Newman's Criticism of the Church', p. 16.

the gift of impeccability granted to her authorities would secure them from all liability to mistake in their conduct, policy, words and decisions, in her legislative and her executive, in ecclesiastical and disciplinarian details; and such a gift they have not received. (p. xliii)

At times, Newman grants, there may be a temporary suspense of one or another of the Church's functions due to the deficiency of the rulers, the theologians, or the people.

Newman, therefore, has no intention of justifying everything. But he does seek to excuse, so far as possible, the failures of the popes. He admits, as every Catholic must, that Liberius and Honorius fell into doctrinal errors, but adds that their want of firmness or clear-sightedness may have arisen out of their keen sense of obligation to work for the consolidation of the Church. Without approving their errors, Newman holds up their concern for the unity and peace of the Church for admiration.

The most questionable element in Newman's theology of the regal office, I would suggest, is his apparent separation of it from the other two. In spite of his initial observation that he is not forgetting that Christ gave all three offices to the papacy, Newman discusses the papacy in the body of his Preface as though it possessed the regal office alone. For this reason he falls into a kind of papal absolutism that is not only offensive to liberals but theologically unwarranted. He overlooks the mutual coinherence of the three offices and the inner qualification of each by the other two.

Another weakness of the Preface is that it treats the regal office almost though it were the responsibility of the pope alone. This surely was not Newman's full thought on the matter. In his 1842 sermon 'The Church an Imperial Power', he had argued at length that imperial power in the Church could not have been vested in Peter alone, nor only in the Twelve:

We must conclude that the power was vested in others also from the size of the empire; for a few persons, though inspired, cannot be supposed to have been equal to the care of all the Church. As Moses found his charge too great for him, and was permitted to have associates in his office, so doubtless would it be with the Apostles.[31]

Here we find a hint, lacking in the Preface, of the solidarity of the whole body of bishops. If the Preface had been composed as

[31] *SD*, p. 225.

a positive exposition of office in the Church, rather than as a response to his own Anglican objections, Newman might have given us a less centralized presentation of the regal office. This is not to say that he would have anticipated the Vatican II doctrine of episcopal collegiality, which was at the time just beginning to surface.

V

Newman's new Preface to the *Via Media* made little impression on the general public of the day.[32] It was, however, reviewed in a number of journals. The Catholic reviews—with certain exceptions, such as William G. Ward's—were generally favourable. Some praised the apologetical dexterity whereby Newman absolved himself of having to defend the whole record of the Church's past. The Anglican reviews were, at best, reserved. Some even contended that in admitting conflicts among the three offices, Newman disproved his own contention that the Church had received these three offices from Christ.[33]

The Preface to the *Via Media* did not enter into the mainstream of Catholic writing on the Church. It has been shown, however, that Friedrich von Hügel was considerably influenced by it.[34] In his major work *The Mystical Element of Religion*,[35] von Hügel understands religion as a composite of three elements corresponding to the three offices of Christ. Von Hügel designates the three elements as the institutional (or historical), the rational, and the mystical, and connects them respectively with the Petrine, Pauline, and Johannine tendencies in New Testament theology.

Von Hügel differs from Newman in that he grounds the threefold distinction primarily in his analysis of the human psyche, whereas in Newman's analysis the ecclesiological predominates. For von Hügel the Church scarcely figures except in connection with the first element—the institutional or historical. When he describes the other two elements—the rational and the mystical

[32] On the reception given to the Preface, including its influence on von Hügel, see Bergeron, *Les Abus*, pp. 195–219.

[33] This, according to Bergeron, was the thesis of the critique in the *Contemporary Review*, 30 (1877), 1097; cf. Bergeron, *Les Abus*, pp. 203–4.

[34] See J. Coulson, *Newman and the Common Tradition*, pp. 175–6; Bergeron, *Les Abus*, 207–9.

[35] F. von Hügel, *The Mystical Element of Religion as studied in Saint Catherine of Genoa and her Friends*, i (London, 1909), 53.

—he moves into a generalized psychology of religion. He applies the triadic model in his typological comparisons between Judaism, Brahmanism, Buddhism, and Islam.

In many of von Hügel's shorter writings the influence of Newman's triadic theology of office seems to be detectable. For instance, in a published letter to Charles A. Briggs on *The Papal Commission and the Pentateuch* von Hügel maintains that Catholicism as a religion is simultaneously historical and institutional, critical and speculative, mystical and operative.[36] It calls the whole person into play. In various essays von Hügel comments that Catholicism, as a strongly institutional religion, tends to breed an imperial mentality in its leaders, so that they expect prompt and visible conformity to their decrees. For this reason the official Church commonly neglects the work of pioneers in the historical and natural sciences, and at times oppresses scholars. Not infrequently, high ecclesiastics have succumbed to greed and political ambition. At its best, however, Catholicism displays a rich inclusiveness. Its very complexity leads to a patient acceptance of tensions.[37]

VI

The phenomenological treatment of the triple office, which von Hügel developed in continuity with Newman, contrasts markedly with the more juridical type of thinking characteristic of continental Catholicism. The doctrine of the threefold office, though extensively used in the Christology of the Roman Catechism published after the Council of Trent (1566), was generally neglected until the nineteenth century, when it became prominent in ecclesiology thanks to the influence of several canon lawyers. The German canonist Ferdinand Walter in his *Lehrbuch des Kirchenrechts* (1829) defended the threefold division of powers in preference to the twofold distinction of the power of order and the power of jurisdiction, which had been common since the Middle Ages. The threefold division was even more vigorously promoted by the Austrian canonist George Phillips (1804–72), a convert from Protestantism, particularly in his

[36] C. A. Briggs and F. von Hügel, *The Papal Commission and the Pentateuch* (New York, 1906), 46.

[37] F. von Hügel, 'The Catholic Contribution to Religion', in *Essays and Addresses in the Philosophy of Religion*[2] (London and New York, 1926), 245–51.

seven-volume *Kirchenrecht* (1845–72). Combining Calvin's threefold partition of the functions of Christ with a 'body of Christ' ecclesiology derived from Johann Sebastian Drey and Johann Adam Möhler, Phillips set the pattern for many works on ecclesiology.

Paralleling the work of these canonists, the theologian Heinrich Klee in his *Katholische Dogmatik* (1834–5; 4th edn., 1861), analysed the functions of the Church under the headings 'magisterium', 'ministerium', and 'regimen'. To this day it remains disputed whether it is necessary to choose between the twofold and the threefold division of powers. Some theologians maintain that the power of jurisdiction may be taken in a broad sense, as including both teaching and ruling, and thus that the two powers of order and jurisdiction include the three functions of sanctifying, ruling, and teaching.[38] Others object to the reduction of teaching to jurisdiction on the ground that the two are specifically distinct.[39]

The threefold division of office has come into increasing prominence in official Catholic teaching on ecclesiology. In each of the two schemas on the Church prepared for Vatican I (drafted by Clemens Schrader and Joseph Kleutgen respectively) the threefold division, formulated in language reminiscent of Phillips and Klee, is juxtaposed to the classical twofold division of power of order and power of jurisdiction. Both schemas insist that Christ bestowed the ecclesiastical office and its powers on the hierarchy alone. A generation later, Leo XIII in his encyclical *Satis cognitum* (1896) taught that the three powers of teaching, sanctifying, and ruling were given by Christ to the apostles and their successors. Pius XII in his encyclicals *Mystici corporis* (1943) and *Mediator Dei* (1947) likewise restricted the triple office to members of the hierarchy.

The increasing tendency to limit the three offices to the pope and the bishops gave rise to some misgivings on the part of theologians. Toward the middle of the twentieth century several progressive thinkers began to raise the question whether the

[38] J. B. Franzelin in his *Theses de Ecclesia* (Rome, 1887), thesis 5, pp. 46–64, attempted in this way to reconcile the bipartite and tripartite divisions of powers. See also L. Billot, *De Ecclesia Christi*, i (5th edn., Rome, 1927), 335–53.

[39] On the debate whether the power of teaching and of ruling are specifically distinct, see I. Salaverri, 'De Ecclesia Christi' in *Sacrae Theologiae Summa* (1950; 2nd edn., Madrid, 1952), nos. 1304–27, pp. 939–46.

threefold office was not in some way shared by the Church as a whole and thus by all its members. Paul Dabin, in his pioneering studies of the biblical and patristic sources, came to the conclusion that all Christians, by virtue of their baptism or confirmation, possess a certain priesthood (*sacerdoce*), a certain prophetic power (*prophétisme*), and a certain regal dignity (*royauté*), provided that these terms be understood in a broad, though not merely metaphorical, sense.[40]

Yves Congar in his *Jalons pour une théologie du laïcat*[41] sought to spell out in greater detail the manner in which the laity participate in the threefold office of Christ, while at the same time distinguishing this from the functions proper to the hierarchy. Baptism, he maintained, conferred a certain cultic power enabling all the baptized to share in Christ's priesthood but not, of course, to celebrate the sacrifice of Christ liturgically for the ecclesial community. All Christians, moreover, could share in Christ's prophetic office by living up to the grace of their baptism and confirmation, bearing witness to the faith that was in them, even though without ordination they were not qualified to perform public authoritative teaching. Finally, the laity could share in Christ's kingship as this is exercised in the Church by way of energy and dignity, but unlike the hierarchy the laity do not have authority over the Church as a body.

Thanks to the pioneering studies of Dabin, Congar, and many others, Vatican II (1962–5) was able to set forth a more comprehensive theory of the threefold office than can be found in earlier official documents. Vatican II adopted the threefold division of functions for its Christology, its ecclesiology, its theology of the episcopacy, its theology of the presbyterate, and its theology of the laity. The entire Church, and each class of persons in the Church, are seen as participating in the threefold ministry of Christ. In this way the council develops a very dynamic theology of mission.

The basis of this entire theology is the role of Christ as teacher, priest, and king. Although Vatican II did not deal

[40] P. Dabin, *Le Sacerdoce royal des fidèles dans la tradition ancienne et moderne* (Brussels, 1950), 52. See also his earlier study, *Le Sacerdoce royal des fidèles dans les livres saints* (Paris, 1941).

[41] Y. Congar, *Jalons pour une théologie du laïcat* (Paris, 1953), trans. D. Attwater as *Lay People in the Church* (Westminster, Md., 1957).

thematically with Christology, it did on several occasions speak of the three offices of Christ.[42]

The Constitution on the Church in its second chapter (entitled 'The People of God') asserts that the three offices of Christ are perpetuated in the Church as a whole. Pursuing holiness, the Church presents itself as a living sacrifice; in word and action it bears witness to Christ; and in transforming society and individual lives it exercises a spiritual kingship.[43]

The three offices of the Church are specified in different ways in the council's teaching on bishops, presbyters, and laity. According to the third chapter of *Lumen gentium* episcopal consecration confers the three offices of sanctifying, teaching, and governing, but the latter two of these offices cannot be exercised except in hierarchical communion with the head and members of the episcopal college.[44] In subsequent articles the three offices of the bishop are dealt with in succession.[45] In its Decree on the Pastoral Ministry of Bishops Vatican II repeated these same points with fuller elaboration. Each bishop in the college is declared to possess the offices of teaching, sanctifying, and governing[46]—offices spelled out in greater detail in the following articles.[47]

The Decree on the Ministry and Life of Priests begins with the assertion that presbyters by ordination and canonical mission are called to the service of Christ the teacher, priest, and king.[48] The duties of presbyters as ministers of the word and of the sacraments and as leaders of the community are described in relation to the threefold ministry of Christ.[49] The Decree on Priestly Formation sets forth the model of Christ the teacher, priest, and shepherd as normative for seminary training.[50]

Vatican II's theology of the laity is likewise structured according to the triple office. After an initial affirmation that the laity are by baptism made sharers in the priestly, prophetic, and kingly functions of Christ,[51] the fourth chapter of *Lumen gentium* explains each of these functions in some detail as they pertain to

[42] *Lumen gentium*, paras. 13 and 31; *Optatam totius*, para. 4; *Presbyterorum ordinis*, para 1; *Apostolicam actuositatem*, para. 10.

[43] *Lumen gentium*, paras. 10–13, cf. 17.

[44] Ibid., para. 21.

[45] Ibid., paras. 25–7.

[46] *Christus Dominus*, para. 11.

[47] Ibid., paras. 12–16.

[48] *Presbyterorum ordinis*, para. 1.

[49] Ibid., paras. 4–6.

[50] *Optatam totius*, para 4.

[51] *Lumen gentium*, para. 31.

the laity.[52] The Decree on the Apostolate of the Laity makes use of a similar schematization.[53] In the council's theology of the laity it is not difficult to recognize the influence of theologians such as Congar.

VII

How is Newman's study of the threefold office related to the development we have traced from the early nineteenth century to the present day? In the first place we must say that it is regrettable that Newman seems not to have been aware of the theology of the three offices as it was being formulated by Catholics of his day in Germany, Austria, and Italy. He never refers to Walter, Phillips, Klee, Passaglia, Franzelin, Schrader, or Kleutgen on this subject. Nor does he clarify his own position with reference to the view, increasingly prevalent in his lifetime, that the three offices are conferred upon the pope and the bishops by ordination and canonical mission. His own apportionment of the offices among different classes (theologians, devout laity, and popes) seems difficult to reconcile with the outlook of the continental theologians just named.

Conversely, Newman's Preface to the *Via Media* does not seem to have significantly influenced the developments that led from Vatican I to Vatican II. Catholic ecclesiologists of the period were accustomed to quote from other works by Newman, such as *On Consulting the Faithful*, the *Letter to the Duke of Norfolk*, and even his *Sermons bearing on Subjects of the Day*, but the Preface to the *Via Media* was almost totally ignored by Catholics outside the English-speaking world until after Vatican II. It is surprising that two major post-Vatican II studies of the history of the theology of the threefold office both omit to make any mention of Newman's Preface.[54]

John Coulson, at the beginning of his chapter on the Preface to the *Via Media*, calls it Newman's 'final and explicit formulation of his idea of the Church'. This formulation, Coulson maintains, 'both supplements the incomplete definitions of Vatican I and anticipates the Constitution *On the Church* (*Lumen Gentium*)

52 Ibid., paras. 34–6.

53 *Apostolicam actuositatem*, paras. 2, 10.

54 I refer here to Schick, *Das dreifache Amt Christi*, and Fernandez, *Munera Christi*.

of Vatican II'.[55] That Newman supplemented the fragmentary statements of Vatican I on the Church cannot be doubted, but the extent to which he anticipated the achievements of Vatican II in this particular work is a more difficult question.

Certain resemblances between the Preface and *Lumen gentium* can be discerned. Both depict the Church as a sacrament, emphasizing the presence and activity of Christ in the Church.[56] Vatican II's portrayal of the Church as 'showing forth in the world the mystery of the Lord in a faithful though shadowed way'[57] resonates with Newman's description of the Church as indefectible but not impeccable. Like Newman, also, Vatican II makes use of the threefold office of Christ as the basis for its understanding of the mission and activity of the Church as a whole. Like Newman again, *Lumen gentium* is unwilling to restrict the three offices to the hierarchy or to the ordained; it teaches that all members of the Church, in varying modes and degrees, partake of the three offices.

Vatican II's theology of the threefold office is both more sacramental and more hierarchical than that of Newman in the work we have examined. Whereas Newman seems to make the distribution of the offices depend largely on the temperament and training of individuals, Vatican II asserts that the threefold office is conferred to lay Christians by baptism and confirmation, and that a deeper incorporation into Christ's threefold mission is given by ordination, especially episcopal ordination.

Although the council allows that non-ordained Christians have a real and important mission from God, it does not set up the same kind of dialectical opposition that Newman describes in his Preface. While encouraging the laity to make their views known, Vatican II does not seem to envision, as Newman does, a clash between representatives of different offices. It contents itself with projecting the ideal of a harmonious dialogue between groups having complementary functions.

Newman can be regarded as in some ways ahead of Vatican II, at least in the sense that he grappled with certain questions that the council did not explicitly face. Through personal experience and historical study Newman had learned that devotion sometimes stands in tension with the requirements of ecclesiastical policy,

[55] Coulson, *Newman and the Common Tradition*, p. 165.

[56] *Lumen gentium*, paras. 1, 48.

[57] Ibid., para. 8.

and that either or both of these factors may have to be balanced against the demands of theological precision. Even at the price of certain apparent inconsistencies Newman allowed his sympathies to be carried from one side to another as he considered each office in turn. At different points he warns against letting this or that office dominate over the others. Thus he strongly urges office holders to listen to the theological *schola* and then admonishes theologians that they cannot always have the last word. They must sometimes defer to the devout feelings of the multitude or to the dictates of practical expediency, which are the special concern of those who rule. Unlike ecclesiologists who deal in abstract conceptions, Newman realistically admits that abuses and failures have occurred; he recognizes that compromises are sometimes necessary.

By leaving the conflicting claims of the three offices theoretically unresolved, Newman's Preface shows a proper regard for the limitations of speculative thought. It also sets an important agenda for the theology of future generations. Like many of Newman's earlier works, his final contribution to ecclesiology is not a finished product. As a theoretical treatise on the three offices it leaves much to be desired. But it gives new and valuable input into the question and is a truly seminal work that can always be reread with profit.

20

Conscience in the *Letter to the Duke of Norfolk*

JOHN FINNIS

Gladstone's *Expostulation* made little use of the word 'conscience'. But others besides Newman saw that conscience was the pamphlet's theme. Bismarck wrote personally to Gladstone to express his 'deep and hopeful gratification to see the two nations, which in Europe are the champions of the liberty of conscience encountering the same foe, stand henceforth shoulder to shoulder in defending the highest interests of the human race'.[1] The Reich Chancellor's expression of favour for 'liberty of conscience' recalls for us the ambiguity of that phrase, and the experiences which now stand between us and the Gladstone–Newman debate.

Newman's *Letter*[2] does not concern the freedom of religious

[1] Letter dated 1 Mar. 1875: see V. Conzemius, 'Acton, Döllinger and Gladstone: A Strange Variety of Anti-Infallibilists', in J. D. Bastable (ed.), *Newman and Gladstone: Centennial Essays* (Dublin, 1978), 51. Bismarck's own circular-despatch of 18 May 1872, claiming that Vatican I established a papal totalitarianism, had been first made public on 29 Dec. 1874. The response of the German bishops, written in Jan. 1875, had been signed by them all by Feb., and includes the sentence 'es ist wahrlich nicht die katholische Kirche, in welcher der unsittliche und despotische Grundsatz, der Befehl des Obern entbinde unbedingte von der eigenen Verantwortlichkeit, Aufnahme gefunden hat' ('it is not the Catholic Church that has accepted the immoral and despotic principle that superior orders release one unconditionally from personal responsibility'): Denzinger-Schönmetzer, *Enchiridion Symbolorum Definitionum et Declarationum de rebus fidei et morum* (Barcelona, 1967), 3115; *Irenikon*, 29 (1956), 143–8, quotation from p. 146. Some chronology: Gladstone's *The Vatican Decrees in their Bearing on Civil Allegiance: A Political Expostulation* was published on 5 Nov. 1874; Newman's reply was signed by him on 27 Dec. 1874, finally corrected on 8 Jan. and published on 14 Jan. 1875. Gladstone's response, *Vaticanism: An Answer to Replies and Reproofs*, appeared on 24 Feb. 1875, and Newman's rejoinder appeared, by way of postscript to the fourth edition of the *Letter*, on 5 Apr. 1875. The written exchanges between Bismarck and the German bishops and between Gladstone and Newman thus will have proceeded entirely independently.

[2] Cited from *Diff*. ii. 175–378; page numbers are given in parenthesis in the text.

conscience from state coercion,[3] the freedom which, within due limits of public order, respect for others' rights, and public morality, is defended by the Second Vatican Council.[4] Nor does the *Letter* restate Newman's argument that the experience of conscience justifies belief in God's existence, power, and providence.[5] Another lifelong theme of Newman's which is likewise helpfully absent from the *Letter* is the contrast he often drew between conscience and reason.[6] Indeed, the *Letter* has its peculiar power from its celebration of conscience precisely as an 'intellectual endowment' (p. 248) enabling the 'rational creature' (p. 246) to share in 'the Divine Light' (p. 247), the Divine Law, 'Divine Reason or Will of God' (p. 246)—as against the theories of 'the great world of philosophy now', which dethrone conscience as 'but a twist in primitive and untutored man', a 'simply irrational' product or manifestation of 'imagination' (p. 249).

I

How does this high philosophical theme emerge?

Newman saw two charges to be met: (1) Catholics cannot now be trustworthy subjects, since the council has given the

[3] *Pace* E. D'Arcy (in an otherwise valuable article), 'Conscience and Meta-Ethics: Newman vis-à-vis Anglo-American Philosophy Today', in *John Henry Newman, Theologian and Cardinal* (Studia Urbaniana, 10; Brescia and Rome, 1981), 181.

[4] *Dignitatis Humanae*, Declaration on Religious Freedom, 7 Dec. 1965, esp. paras. 1–8. For Newman's apparent indifference to this political freedom, see *Diff.* ii. 204, 267, 271, 274; these pages also express his antipathy to the modern liberal ideal of a morally 'neutral' state which will allow 'free love' and even 'infanticide', which for Newman are 'atrocities' which 'the good sense of the nation would stifle and extinguish' even when they are practised in the name of conscience (p. 274).

[5] *Diff.* ii. 248 states in passing that non-Catholic Christians, like Catholics, consider conscience 'to be the internal witness of both the existence and the law of God'. The argument to God from conscience had been most recently stated by Newman in *GA*, pp. 47, 72–7, 251–2.

[6] In the word 'felt' there is just a hint (*Diff.* ii. 349) of that distinction between reason and conscience which, in relation to the same decision (to join 'that Catholic Church, which in my own conscience I felt to be divine'), is drawn in Newman's letter of 30 Mar. 1845 to Maria Giberne: 'My own convictions are as strong as I suppose they can become: only it is so difficult to know whether it is the call of *reason* or of conscience. I cannot make out, if I am impelled by what seems *clear*, or by a sense of *duty* . . . Then I am waiting, because friends are most considerately . . . asking guidance for me: and, I trust, I should attend to any new feelings which came upon me, should that be the effect of their kindness.' *Apo.*, p. 208. For Newman's contrast between reason (i.e. reasoning) and everything concerned with the 'antecedents' of an act of reason(ing) (moral sense, intuitions, *νοῦς*, the dictates of conscience, the inspired Word, the decisions of the Church, etc.), see e.g. 'Revelation in its Relation to Faith' (1885–6) in *TP* i. 141–2, 152–5.

pope a hold over their consciences such that he can interfere with their civil duties and allegiance (pp. 179, 180, 181, 195, 349); (2) the same dogma of papal infallibility equally requires Catholics to renounce their mental and moral freedom and uprightness (pp. 179, 180, 350). Already, in the ground-clearing polemics about the Irish bishops' opposition to the Irish University Bill of 1873, and about the eighteenth- and early nineteenth-century assurances of Irish and English bishops that papal infallibility was no dogma, Newman reminds his readers, with lightest touch, that popes and bishops, too, have claims of conscience, duty, principle (pp. 183, 185). And he artfully recalls, in passing, a case where every reader would reject the claims of civil allegiance: 'a heathen State might bid me throw incense upon the altar of Jupiter, and the Pope would bid me not to do so' (p. 187).

Similarly, the chapter on the 'Ancient Church' presents the whole history of the Church as 'the very embodiment of that tradition of Apostolical independence and freedom of speech which in the eyes of man is her great offence now' (p. 197). While Anglican and Oriental Churches are ashamed before kings, or lie under their bondage, 'Rome is now the one faithful representative, and is thereby heir and successor, of that free-spoken dauntless Church of old' (p. 198), fulfilling 'the very mission of Christianity to bear witness to the Creed and Ten Commandments' (p. 197). The chapter on 'The Papal Church' reinforces the point: Gladstone's objection cannot be merely to 'the Pope's special power' (p. 209). 'It is not the existence of a Pope, but of a Church, which is his aversion. It is the powers themselves, and not their distribution and allocation in the ecclesiastical body which he writes against' (pp. 209–10). Whenever Christians act in the political realm, they are responsible to God and conscience (p. 211); when the pope acts as supreme judge of Christendom, the 'basis and rule' of his sentence must 'appeal to the supreme standard of right and wrong, the moral law' (p. 221).

The chapter on 'Divided Allegiance', which immediately precedes the central chapter on 'Conscience', is announced as the beginning of 'a long explanation, and, in a certain sense, limitation' (p. 223) of what Newman has been saying about the sovereignty of the Church and of the pope as its head. The explanation will extend to the end of the *Letter* (p. 224). It will show why

Newman can reject Gladstone's conclusions (the charges of allegiance to a foreign power, and moral slavery) while accepting his premisses: that the pope claims infallibility in morals, and that there are no departments of human life which fall outside the domain of morals (p. 224).

Newman says he will 'put aside for the present and at first the Pope's prerogative of infallibility in general enunciations, whether of faith or morals', and confine himself to considering the pope's 'authority (in respect to which he is not infallible) in matters of conduct' (p. 224). The implications of the pope's prerogative of infallibility are not formally taken up, I believe, until the last substantive chapter, chapter 9 'The Vatican Definition'. But, as we shall see, the questionable thesis there developed is aired in the fifth chapter, on conscience.

Meanwhile, the long fourth chapter on 'Divided Allegiance' proceeds to make two broad points: that the pope's interpositions into 'our private affairs, . . . our routine of personal duties' (p. 228) are so rare as to be 'absolutely unappreciable' (p. 229); and that, while there are cases (particularly involving the performance of religious duties) in which 'we should obey the Pope and disobey the State' (p. 240), there are cases, hypothetical, in a sense 'impossible' (pp. 241, 244), but imaginable, in which 'I should side, not with the Pope, but with the Civil Power' (p. 241). In relation to each point, Newman's argument is clouded by unclarities about the logic of the Church's *moral* teachings, unclarities which will later cloud his discussions of conscience's relation to the Church's infallibility *de moribus*.

For, in his treatment of the first point we find Newman bundling together papal directives on 'matters sacramental, ritual, ecclesiastical, monastic, and disciplinarian' (p. 230) with papal teachings on matters moral. The whole discussion sets morality firmly within a framework in which moral truth and positive law, though distinguished in principle, are commingled in the practice of moral formation.[7] In our 'ordinary duties', Newman says, we are guided by books of moral theology and casuistry, 'based on the three foundations of Faith, Hope, and Charity, on the Ten Commandments, and on the six Precepts of the Church, which relate to the observance of

[7] On legalism in the moral theology and casuistry to which Newman is referring, see G. Grisez, *Christian Moral Principles* (Chicago, Ill., 1983), 13, 15, 292–5, 304–6.

Sunday, of fast days, of confession and communion, and . . . to paying tithes' (p. 229). The books give 'directions' which are 'little more than reflexions and memoranda of our moral sense', though sometimes their answers, like those of 'private conscience itself', may be 'difficult to us or painful to accept'. Our 'private judgment' need not in every case give way to the books, which after all 'are no utterance of Papal authority' (p. 229). And when that authority has intervened in moral matters it has been by condemnations which 'relate for the most part to mere occasional details of duty, and are in reprobation of the lax or wild notions of speculative casuists, so that they are rather restraints upon theologians than upon laymen' (p. 230).

Newman here instances 'at random' two of the sixty-five laxist propositions condemned by the Holy Office in 1679 under Innocent XI: that domestics who think themselves underpaid may compensate themselves by stealing from their employers,[8] and that public persons may head off otherwise unavoidable calumny by killing the intending calumniator (p. 230).[9] Are even these so wild, so speculative, so removed from the passions of lay people? In any event, today's reader will think instead of the moral teachings on which twentieth-century popes and council have had to insist, not against a few 'speculative casuists' but against many priests, some bishops, very many influential clerical moralists and numerous 'private Catholics' (cf. p. 231) who wish to feel justified in accepting what is accepted in their affluent cultures: intentional abortion, contraception, euthanasia, baby-making, adultery, remarriage after divorce, and the area-bombing of enemy cities.

Newman does not deny or overlook, of course, the authority of the pope 'to speak definitively on ethical subjects', and he affirms that what the pope thus propounds 'must relate to things good and bad in themselves, not to things accidental, changeable, and of mere expedience' (p. 231; similarly p. 331). But by casting his discussion in the terms (common to virtually all the moral

[8] Proposition 37: see Denzinger-Schönmetzer, *Enchiridion*, 2137, which editorially identifies Leonard Lessius, SJ, Antoninus Diana, and Matthaeus de Moya, SJ as proponents of the condemned proposition.

[9] Proposition 30: see ibid. 2130 which editorially identifies Martinus Becanus, SJ as affirming the proposition, and implicates also the Jesuits Vasquez, Filliucci, and Escobar, 'and many others' including Jesuits and non-Jesuits of high theological standing.

theology of his age) of law and obedience, and by granting (if not conceding) that moral teachings are a weight on conscience, Newman here encourages rather than dissipates the confusion of teaching with law-*making*, a confusion he would have deplored had he confronted its modern manifestations. This is a passage where we feel, again, our distance from his age.[10]

What of Newman's other broad point in this chapter, that one can imagine cases where Catholics should 'act with the Civil Power, and not with the Pope' (p. 241)? The theological authorities he cites (pre-Reformation, Counter-Reformation, and nineteenth-century) establish convincingly that papal orders *ought* to be disregarded and disobeyed when they contradict 'Holy Scripture, or the articles of faith, or the truth of the Sacraments, or the commands of the natural or divine law' (p. 242).[11] But Newman's two examples scarcely instantiate a clear-cut contradiction between papal orders and faith or morals, and today seem problematical.

The first example supposes that a member of Parliament or privy councillor has sworn not to acknowledge the right of a Catholic to succeed to the throne, and that a pope has purported to release him from that oath and commanded him to acknowledge a Catholic succession. As Newman himself observes, the Catholic councillor can avoid the clash between Church and State by resigning his office, thereby ridding himself of the binding force of his oath.

The other example is more interesting. A member of the armed forces, serving in a war which he cannot in conscience see to be unjust, is with all his fellow Catholic servicemen 'suddenly'

[10] Only twenty years before, Newman had written, 'never was the Church less troubled with false teachers, never more united'. He had treated as distant (though not necessarily merely in the past) the miserable times 'when a man's Catholic profession is no voucher for his orthodoxy, and when a teacher of religion may be within the Church's pale, yet external to her faith': 'A Form of Infidelity of the Day' (1854) in *Idea*, p. 318. In 1874 there possibly are slight, but certainly only the slightest, intimations of a return of those times: see *Diff*. ii. 208–9.

[11] Newman here cites Cardinal Turrecremata, '*Summ. de Eccl.*, pp. 47, 48'; see Ioannis de Turrecremata (Juan de Torquemada, OP (1388–1468), named *Defensor fidei* by Eugenius IV in 1436 for his theological defence of papal authority), *Summa de Ecclesia*, (1448–9; Venice, 1561), lib. II, cap. 49, p. 163^{v}. (In this edition, at least, the phrase translated or emended by Newman 'truth of the Sacraments' is 'veritati sanctorum'; cf. e.g. Gregory IX's letter of 7 July 1228: theologians ought to expound theology 'secundum approbatas traditiones Sanctorum' i.e. of the Fathers ('sanctorum Patrum'): Denzinger-Schönmetzer, *Enchiridion*, 824.)

ordered by the pope 'to retire from the service' (p. 242). Here all turns on Newman's word 'suddenly'; we must read it as excluding the case which is rather easier to imagine: the pope judges that the war, though just in its cause and objectives, is being prosecuted by an immoral strategy of taking and killing non-combatant hostages and destroying and threatening to destroy whole cities and their inhabitants in the manner denounced by Vatican II as a crime against God and man; and the pope, having stated his judgement, and his further judgement that combatant service in a State campaigning under the protection of a counter-civilian terror strategy amounts to participation in the immoral acts of terrorism, 'bids' (p. 242) all Catholic servicemen to retire from the service unless their government immediately renounces the immoral strategy. The question is not whether this is a likely contingency, but whether, confronted by the pope's (or a council's) moral judgement about the immorality of any combatant service under the umbrella of a terrorist strategy, one should follow that judgement even if one's own moral assessment were that only those who personally authorize or execute the terrorist acts are participants in terrorism.

You will say: that is not the sort of case Newman was considering, and his 'suddenly' shows that he had another case in mind. All he needed was *some* case in which a Catholic might rightly disobey a papal injunction. I agree, and wish only to note that Newman's example raises for us certain questions which he and his readers felt unreal, but which later events and our own predicament make real.

The chapter on divided allegiance thus concludes with a proposition which Newman, in effect, formulates in two different ways: (1) One should disobey papal orders *which are contrary to morality*; (2) One should disobey papal orders *which are contrary to one's conscience*. The first is the more fundamental formulation, the second derivative. Their propositional equivalence consists in this: When judgements differ on the question whether a papal order is contrary to morality, the judgement one must follow (after testing it as best one can against the arguments and opinions of others) is one's own; so (1) and (2) are each equivalent to: (3) One should disobey papal orders *which one judges to be contrary to morality*.

In short: Talk of following one's own conscience has a distinct point only when there is *disagreement* about whether the moral norm to which one is appealing has indeed the truth or the application which one judges it to have:

I should look to see what theologians could do for me, what the Bishops and clergy around me, what my confessor; what friends whom I have revered: and if, after all, I could not take their view of the matter, then I mûst rule myself by my own judgment and my own conscience. (pp. 243–4)

But throughout, the object of one's inquiry is not to discover one's own conscience, but to discover what (as best one can see) is the *truth* of the matter. That my judgement is *mine* adds not a jot to my grounds for thinking that it is true. Hence the priority of formulation (1). Newman would be the first to agree that his preference for formulation (2), in ending the chapter on divided allegiance and in opening that on conscience (p. 246), arises not from any doubt about the priority of (1), but from concern to show that Catholics are not mental and moral slaves, since they make their own judgements.

II

In the depths of conscience, man discerns a law which he does not dictate to himself but which he ought to obey. Always summoning him to love and do the good and to avoid evil, the voice of this law[12] sounds when necessary in the ears of his heart as 'Do this, shun that'. For man has in his heart a law written by God; to obey that law is his very dignity, and according to it he will be judged [Rom. 2: 15–16]. Conscience is the most secret core and sanctuary of man, in which he is alone with God, whose voice resounds in his inwardness [citation to Pius XII, 23 March 1952]. Conscience, in a wonderful manner, makes known that law which is fulfilled by love of God and neighbour. . . . [T]o the extent that a correct conscience holds sway, persons and groups turn away from blind choice and seek to conform to the objective norms of morality.[13]

This teaching of Vatican II 'on the dignity of the moral conscience' is, of course, the teaching proposed by Newman in the powerful opening pages of his chapter on conscience. Not that the council

[12] Not 'the voice of conscience', as mistranslated in *The Documents of Vatican II*, ed. W. M. Abbott, SJ (London, 1966), 213.

[13] *Gaudium et Spes*, Pastoral Constitution on the Church in the Modern World, 7 Dec. 1965, para. 16.

takes the teaching from Newman; Mgr. Delhaye's book on conscience in Christian thought, published shortly before he became involved in the drafting of this part of the council's work, refers to well over a hundred classic Christian sources, in which virtually every element and phrase of this passage can be found.[14] Newman is not among them. This is no surprise; these pages of the *Letter* are what they profess to be: a statement of what is 'acknowledged by all Catholics' (p. 246).

With rhetorical economy and power, Newman begins by showing that Catholics acknowledge 'the prerogatives and the supreme authority of conscience' (p. 246) precisely because they acknowledge the 'sovereign, irreversible, absolute authority' of 'the Divine Law [which] is the rule of ethical truth, the standard of right and wrong' (p. 246), the eternal law of which Augustine wrote, the natural law which Thomas Aquinas called 'an impression of the Divine Light in us, a participation of the eternal law in the rational creature' (p. 247).[15] For:

> This law, as apprehended in the minds of individual men, is called 'conscience;' and though it may suffer refraction in passing into the intellectual medium of each, it is not therefore so affected as to lose its character of being the Divine Law, but still has, as such, the prerogative of commanding obedience. (p. 247)

At this stage of his exposition, Newman is discussing what many theologians since Aquinas have called the 'habitual conscience'. One's understanding of the fundamental principles of practical reasonableness, like one's understanding of fundamental non-practical principles (e.g. of logic), is not so much a special power (as Newman sometimes seems to suggest (e.g. p. 248)) as, rather, a state of mind, a disposition or *habitus*, whereby one is in a position to proceed to other, derivative, and more particular acts

[14] P. Delhaye, *La Conscience morale du chrétien* (Tournai, 1964), trans. C. Underhill Quinn as *The Christian Conscience* (New York, 1968); see esp. ch. 3 'Patristic Signposts'.

[15] Here Newman vaguely cites 'Gousset, *Theol. Moral.*, t. i. pp. 24, &c.', namely T. M. J. Gousset (Archbishop of Reims), *Théologie morale à l'usage des curés et des confesseurs* (Paris, 1845), where the passages from Augustine and Aquinas which Newman quotes both appear on p. 48, in the chapter on 'Divine Laws' (which, as in the treatise of Gousset's master St Alphonsus Liguori, follows rather than precedes the chapter on 'Conscience' from which (p. 24) the other passages quoted by Newman are taken). (Cardinal Gousset, 1792–1866, was a notable defender of papal infallibility, and opponent of Gallicanism and Jansenism.)

of understanding and of reasoning to particular conclusions. The theological tradition has been inclined to reserve the term 'conscience' for one's last, best judgement, whereby the principles which one 'habitually' knows are brought to bear in a fully specified act of judgement that a particular practical proposal is good or bad, right or wrong. But Christian tradition has from the outset used the term 'conscience' (*συνείδησις*, *conscientia*) to refer to our grasp of natural and divine law in all its universality and immutability *as well as* to our grasp of a particular option's rightness or wrongness or eligibility here and now. So theologians came to call the former the 'habitual conscience', while the latter they called the 'actual conscience', i.e. conscience *qua* one's last best act of practical judgement. (The scholastic jargon does not matter, but the distinction it signifies is real and important in any explanation of how conscience can both illumine and deceive.) Later in the chapter, as we shall see, Newman will abruptly switch to speaking of the actual conscience. At the outset, however, his magnificent portrayal of the conscience which philosophers condemn and 'the popular mind' (p. 249) counterfeits is a portrayal of the habitual conscience.

To speak of conscience, in this sense, is to speak of *principles*, the principles one's understanding of which simply *is* one's having a (habitual) conscience. Hence Newman's defence of conscience against Enlightenment reductions is centred on his rejection of the moral principles proposed by the Renaissance and the Enlightenment:

> The rule and measure of duty is not utility, nor expedience, nor the happiness of the greatest number, nor State convenience, nor fitness, order, and the *pulchrum*. Conscience is not a long-sighted selfishness, nor a desire to be consistent with oneself; but it is a messenger from Him, who, both in nature and in grace, speaks to us behind a veil, and teaches and rules us by His representatives. (p. 248)

And these representatives are two: nature and grace, conscience and revelation. For by 'conscience . . . we mean, the voice of God in the nature and heart of man, as distinct from the voice of Revelation' (p. 247). So:

> Conscience is the aboriginal Vicar of Christ, a prophet in its informations, a monarch in its peremptoriness, a priest in its blessings and anathemas, and, even though the eternal priesthood throughout the Church could

cease to be, in it the sacerdotal principle would remain and would have a sway. (p. 248–9)

That is, if the voice and vehicle of revelation were stilled (*per impossibile*: Matt. 28: 20), the Word would still be heard, inasmuch as habitual conscience could still grasp what the Creator intended as the rule and measure of the rational creature's choices and actions—could still be aware of the 'truths which the Lawgiver has sown in our very nature' (p. 253), the 'Natural Law' (p. 254), and 'the rights of the Creator, . . . the duty to Him, in thought and deed, of the creature' (p. 250).

Still, 'Natural Religion, certain as are its grounds and its doctrines as addressed to thoughtful, serious minds, needs, in order that it may speak to mankind with effect and subdue the world, to be sustained and completed by Revelation' (p. 254).[16] In the 'insufficiency of the natural light' (p. 253) is the justification of the pope's 'very mission . . . to proclaim the moral law, and to protect and strengthen that "Light which enlighteneth every man that cometh into the world"' (p. 252). For conscience is weak:

the sense of right and wrong . . . is so delicate, so fitful, so easily puzzled, obscured, perverted, so subtle in its argumentative methods, so impressible by education, so biassed by pride and passion, so unsteady in its course, that, in the struggle for existence amid the various exercises and triumphs of the human intellect, this sense is at once the highest of all teachers, yet the least luminous; and the Church, the Pope, the Hierarchy are, in the Divine purpose, the supply of an urgent demand. (pp. 253–4)

But revelation, though going beyond 'a mere republication of the Natural Law' (p. 254), has its point not by being independent of, or without relation to, the natural law known to the (habitual) conscience, but rather by being the 'complement, reassertion, issue, embodiment, and interpretation' of that natural law (p. 254). Thus, if the pope were to speak against conscience in the true, 'high sense' (p. 255) of the word, 'he would commit a suicidal act

[16] Cf. Vatican I, *Dei Filius*, Dogmatic Constitution on the Catholic Faith, 24 Apr. 1870, ch. 2: 'It is by virtue of this divine revelation that those things which *in rebus divinis* are in themselves not inaccessible to human reason can, even in the present condition of the human race, be known by all with ease, with firm certainty, and without contamination of error': Denzinger-Schönmetzer, *Enchiridion*, 3005; Vatican II, *Dei Verbum*, Dogmatic Constitution on Divine Revelation, 18 Nov. 1965, para. 6.

. . . cutting the ground from under his feet', denying his mission and undercutting 'both his authority in theory and his power in fact' (p. 252). When popes such as Gregory XVI and Pius IX have scoffed at 'liberty of conscience', enclosing the phrase in their own quotation marks, they have been speaking against conscience only 'in the various false senses, philosophical or popular, which in this day are put upon the word' (p. 251) and which Newman has just sketched with memorable animus and force:

> Conscience has rights because it has duties; but in this age, with a large portion of the public, it is the very right and freedom of conscience to dispense with conscience. . . . Conscience is a stern monitor, but in this century it has been superseded by a counterfeit, which the eighteen centuries prior to it never heard of, and could not have mistaken for it, if they had. It is the right of self-will. (p. 250)

III

Newman's direct and 'distinct' (p. 255) answer to the charge of mental and moral slavery employs two arguments for its correct conclusion. Of these, the first and most prominent has premisses which, I shall argue, are mistaken:

> conscience is not a judgment upon any speculative truth, any abstract doctrine, but bears immediately on conduct, on something to be done or not done. 'Conscience,' says St. Thomas, 'is the practical judgment or dictate of reason, by which we judge what *hic et nunc* is to be done as being good, or to be avoided as evil.' Hence conscience cannot come into direct collision with the Church's or the Pope's infallibility; which is engaged on general propositions and in the condemnation of particular and given errors. (p. 256)[17]

Both the premisses of this argument are mistaken. (1) Conscience is 'engaged on' and makes 'judgment upon' propositions more general than that *this* particular option is not to be made *now* by *me*. (2) And the general propositions which are the proper object of the Church's infallibility include negative universals which,

[17] This or a very similar argument seems to be recalled prominently in the concluding chapter: since the 'prerogative of infallibility lies in matters speculative . . . infallibility bears upon the domain of thought, not directly of action, and while it may fairly exercise the theologian, philosopher, or man of science, it scarcely concerns the politician' (pp. 342–3).

by absolutely excluding all actions of a specified type, exclude *this* particular option which could be made by *me now*.

(1) Newman's discourse at this point has shifted, without warning, from the 'habitual' to the 'actual' conscience. There can be no objection to that; both are legitimate senses of 'conscience' and there is no incompatibility between them. But his argument here forgets that the actual conscience, being a rational (even if mistaken) judgement about a particular option, is an *application* of rational (even if mistaken) norms and principles of judgement —at the highest level, the principles understood and affirmed in the habitual conscience.

The quotation which Newman ascribes (p. 256) to St Thomas does indeed represent Aquinas's opinion. But the words are those not of Aquinas but of St Alphonsus Liguori;[18] reading page 24 of Gousset's *Théologie morale*, Newman's eye has slipped from footnote 2 to footnote 3.[19] The passage to which the latter footnote is attached gives the relevant teaching of St Thomas: 'Conscience is simply the *application* of knowledge to a particular act.'[20] The whole point of the Church's teaching about conscience, as recalled by Newman in the early pages of the chapter, is that in obeying one's conscience one is unconscious of any

[18] Gousset's citation is 'S. Alphonse de Liguori, Theol. Moral., *de Conscientia*, n. 2'; see Alphonsi de Ligorio, *Theologia Moralis*, lib. I, cap. 1, par. 2 (9th edn., 1785) (ed. L. Gaudé (Rome, 1905), p. 3); it is Alphonsus's primary definition of (actual) conscience.

[19] See Gousset, *Théologie morale*, p. 24. It is amusing to see the US bishops, in the section on conscience in their joint pastoral letter *Human Life in Our Day* dated 15 Nov. 1968, saying (just before quoting from Newman's *Letter*) that 'Thomas Aquinas describes conscience as the practical judgment or dictate of reason, by which we judge what here and now is to be done as being good, or to be avoided as evil'; they give no citation to Aquinas; they are unwittingly quoting Alphonsus via Newman. More serious is the inappropriateness of the US bishops' extended quotation from the *Letter*; the passage (pp. 257–8) concerns the pre-conditions for conscience 'to prevail against the voice of the Pope' (p. 257) in his 'laws', 'commands', 'acts of state', 'administration', and 'public policy' (pp. 256, 258), not in his enunciation of 'general propositions' or his 'condemnation of particular and given errors' (p. 256), still less in his restatement of truths which, like the central propositions in Paul VI's encyclical *Humanae Vitae*, 25 July 1968 (on which the US bishops were then commenting), had already been infallibly taught by the Church's ordinary magisterium even though they were not formally defined *ex cathedra* by the encyclical itself.

[20] Gousset correctly cites *Quaestiones Disputatae de Veritate*, q. 17 a. 3. Aquinas first states this clearly in the preceding article, where he adds that, when we say that conscience is the application of *knowledge*, we do not imply that the 'knowledge' is always really knowledge, i.e. *true* belief; in mistaken conscience it is only *seeming* knowledge: *de Veritate*, q. 17 a. 2c & ad 2.

mistake one may in fact be making[21] and so considers oneself to be obeying the divine *law*, i.e. the natural and/or revealed *general* and *universal* rule and measure of human acts.[22] One's reasons (right or wrong) for judgement are necessarily general propositions, and are present to one's conscience in one's conscientious final judgement, which therefore can 'come into direct collision' with a general proposition which in fact has been infallibly proposed.

(2) This is particularly evident when the general proposition infallibly proposed by the Church is a negative universal of the form 'Acts of type X [e.g. directly killing an innocent human being] are always wrong, whatever the circumstances'. As Karl Rahner rightly put the point:

it goes without saying that a man must obey his conscience. . . . It is right that the Christian conscience should be mature. But this maturity of the Christian conscience is not an emancipation from and casting off of the universal norms preached by the Gospel and the Church . . . it is the ability to apply these norms oneself to a concrete situation without needing help in every case. . . . When the whole Church in her everyday teaching does in fact teach a moral rule everywhere in the world *as* a commandment of God, she is preserved from error by the assistance of the Holy Ghost, and this rule is therefore the will of God and is binding on the faithful in conscience, even before it is expressly confirmed by a solemn definition. A moral norm is by nature universal but, precisely as a universal law, is intended to be the rule for the individual case. And so when it is fully grasped and rightly understood and interpreted (that is, understood as the magisterium means it, not just as an individual thinks fit to interpret it), and bears on an individual case, then this unique

[21] As Aquinas says, *de Veritate*, q. 17 a. 4c: 'one who has a mistaken conscience, and believes that it is correct (*otherwise he would not be mistaken*), clings to his mistaken conscience because of the correctness he believes is there; indeed, speaking *per se*, he is clinging to a correct conscience, but one which is as it were mistaken *per accidens*, insofar as this conscience which he believes to be correct happens to be mistaken'. (Emphasis added.)

[22] 'A precept does not bind save by force of [one's] knowledge [of it], nor does [that] knowledge bind save [by mediating] the force of the precept. So, since conscience is simply the application of knowledge to an action, it is obvious that conscience is said to bind by the force of divine law': *de Veritate*, q. 17 a. 2c. Or again: "The binding force of conscience, even mistaken conscience, is the same thing as the binding force of the law of God ('idem est ligamen conscientiae etiam erroneae et legis Dei'). For conscience does not say that X is to be done or Y avoided unless it believes that Y is contrary to, or X in accordance with, the law of God': Aquinas, *In ad Romanos*, cap. 14 lect. 2 ad v. 15.

individual concrete case is bound by the norm and obliged to abide by it. When, for example, the Church teaches that *every* directly induced abortion is morally wrong . . . then this applies to every individual case quite regardless of the circumstances.[23]

The only clarification that need be added to Rahner's lucid statement is that there are many universal norms and principles which cannot by themselves supply sufficient premisses for a secure application to the particular case, but must be supplemented by additional premisses which one's conscience will find in one's own prior commitments, in the responsibilities of one's special roles (such as parenthood), in the applicable civil or ecclesiastical laws and directives, and, quite generally, in one's own chosen vocation. This is true of all the norms and principles which specify *affirmative* responsibilities—to do such and such (honour parents, educate children, serve the community, etc.).

Still, the same cannot be said of the few but vital norms which specify the *negative* responsibilities common to all human beings. To these negative moral norms there are no true exceptions. In their application, they are the exception to the 'rule' (generalization), reiterated throughout the *Letter*,[24] that to every rule (generalization) there are exceptions. An example? In Vatican II's words: '*Every* warlike act aimed indiscriminately at whole cities . . . is a crime against God and man.'[25]

From (1) and (2) together it follows that Newman's conclusion that 'conscience cannot come into direct collision with the Church's or the Pope's infallibility' (p. 256) is mistaken. His statement can be made true only by taking 'conscience' here to

[23] K. Rahner, 'Dangers in Catholicism Today: The Appeal to Conscience', in id., *Nature and Grace* (London and New York, 1963), 96–100. Later writings of Karl Rahner, SJ seem to overlook this position, but offer no reasons for departing from it.

[24] See *Diff*. ii. 243, 261, 338, 342, 359. There can be no doubt that Newman, in reiterating this generalization and in other aspects of his argument in the *Letter*, had no thought of questioning the Church's teaching of negative moral absolutes, or of proposing that they are subject to the exceptions alleged by modern theologians who do not share Newman's conviction that the pope is 'appointed by his Divine Master to determine in the detail of faith and morals what is true and what is false', with 'dogmatic authority' (p. 278).

[25] *Gaudium et Spes*, para. 80: 'Omnis actio bellica . . .'. For the distinction between affirmative moral norms, which bind 'semper sed non ad semper', and negative moral norms which bind 'semper et ad semper', see e.g. Aquinas, *In ad Romanos*, cap. 13 lect. 2 ad v. 9; id., *De Malo*, q. 7 a.1 ad 8; id., *Summa Theologiae* II–II q. 33, a. 2c, etc.; Alphonsus Liguori, *Theologia Moralis*, lib. I, tract. 2, cap. 1, dub. 1, para. 101 (ed. Gaudé, p. 82).

mean exclusively a conscience which correctly acknowledges all the infallible moral teachings of the Church. (There are hints on pages 255 and 257 that this is what Newman may here have had in mind;[26] and Newman will later say that the Church's infallible moral teachings are 'such as in fact will be found to command the assent of most men, as soon as heard' (p. 332)—another sign of his distance from our age.) But, if 'conscience' be taken thus, his argument distinguishing general from particular becomes redundant, irrelevant. And his denial of the possibility of collision between (such a) conscience and the Church's *de fide* teaching *de moribus* becomes tautologous, scarcely an answer to those who regard acceptance of the Church's infallible teaching authority as slavery.

The primary true reply to that accusation is that the Church's irreformable teachings are not a burden but an enlightenment.

A secondary reply is the one developed by Newman in parallel with his mistaken argument about general and particular:

> a Pope is not infallible in his laws, nor in his commands, nor in his acts of state, nor in his administration, nor in his public policy. (p. 256)

In relation to these, one's conscience has (i.e. one has) the responsibility of identifying the bearing of one's affirmative responsibilities (vocation) in one's own circumstances—something which no moral teaching, infallible or otherwise, could fully settle. Moreover, in these matters one is not merely *bound* to follow one's conscience; one's conscience can even be said to have, on certain conditions, 'the *right* of opposing the supreme, though not infallible Authority of the Pope' (p. 257, emphasis added). In the practical matters which are the primary subject-matter of the Church's infallible teachings *de moribus*, i.e. as to 'things in themselves good or evil' and 'necessary for salvation' (p. 331), the whole theological school from Aquinas and before (p. 259) to Newman and after will willingly say that one has a *duty* to follow one's conscience[27]—for though one may indeed

[26] See below, n. 28.

[27] The solidity of this theological teaching is not affected by the fact that the striking dictum 'Quidquid fit contra conscientiam, aedificat ad gehennam' which Gousset ((*Théologie morale*, p. 24); the sentences quoted from him in *Diff*. ii. 247 are an amalgamation of passages from paras. 55 and 57) and Newman (p. 259: 'He who acts against his conscience loses his soul"') ascribe to the Fourth Lateran Council is taken not from that council but from a letter of 1201 by Innocent III touching the

be culpable for erroneously rejecting what the Church has taught (p. 259), and though one has a duty to correct one's conscience by conforming to that teaching, still one is certainly culpable if one fails to do what one's *conscience* (not mere self-will) bids one do. But this *duty* is not a *right* of opposing papal authority, such as Newman speaks of in relation to the many matters in which the pope does not act infallibly.[28] That 'right', manifesting an aspect of conscience's autonomy overlooked in the allegation of mental and moral slavery, is simply an entailment of the fact the magisterium's divine mission is to hand on the deposit of revelation and faith, not to co-ordinate the political communities and other lesser groups to which each of us belongs, nor to supersede personal discernment (and choice) of vocation.

IV

I add one remark. Certainly, if I am obliged to bring religion into after-dinner toasts, (which indeed does not seem quite the thing) I shall drink—to the Pope, if you please,—still, to Conscience first, and to the Pope afterwards.' (p. 261)

'difficultas quasi perplexa' of a wife who is ordered by an ecclesiastical court to return to a marriage bed which she believes ('habet notitiam') incestuous: 'propter sententiam oporteret eam reddere debitum, et propter conscientiam debitum reddere non deberet'. The pope's canonical solution is prefaced by the reflection that she ought not to disobey God by obeying the judgement, but ought humbly to accept the excommunication which will follow disobedience to the court: 'quoniam omne, quod non est ex fide, peccatum est, et quicquid fit contra conscientiam aedificat ad gehennam'. See *Corpus Iuris Canonici*, ed. Richter (1881), ii. 287 (Decretales Gregorii IX, lib. II, tit. xiii de restitutione spoliatorum, cap. 13). Theologians of the 13th cent. treated Innocent III's dictum as of quite general significance, 'generaliter verum', as Bonaventure says in his *Commentary on the Sentences* (*c.* 1250), II, d. 39, a. 1, q.3 ad 4.

[28] The distinction I am drawing seems to be implied in what Newman says on p. 257: 'infallibility alone could block the exercise of conscience, and the Pope is not infallible in that subject-matter in which conscience is of supreme authority'. This passage makes best sense if 'conscience' is taken here to mean 'well-instructed Catholic conscience'. Otherwise, the statement is another version, even more questionable, of the failed argument that general cannot collide with particular. See also p. 345, where Newman reaffirms that, for the Catholic, 'private judgment' is liked, possessed and maintained 'just so far as the Church does not, by the authority of Revelation, *supersede* it' (emphasis added). See, likewise, *Dev.*, p. 86: 'Revelation consists in . . . the substitution of the voice of a Lawgiver for the voice of conscience. The supremacy of conscience is the essence of natural religion; the supremacy of Apostle, or Pope, or Church, or Bishop, is the essence of revealed . . . Thus, what conscience is in the system of nature, such is the voice of Scripture, or of the Church, or of the Holy See, as we may determine it, in the system of Revelation.'

These closing words of the chapter on conscience seem to have been intended to anticipate the remark, three pages later, about 'what Bentham calls Church-of-Englandism, its cry being the dinner toast, "Church and king"' (p. 264). But Newman's toast has made its way in the world quite divorced from its context—not merely the now unimportant context just mentioned, but the essential context established by the whole *Letter*: reverence for the truth of divine law disclosed by conscience; 'generous loyalty towards ecclesiastical authority' which 'a true Catholic . . . must have', 'accept[ing] what is taught him with what is called the *pietas fidei*' (p. 339; similarly p. 258); the horror of false consciousness, that 'miserable counterfeit' (p. 257) masking self-will.

At the end of a penetrating exposition of the Christian philosophy of conscience, and of this century's philosophical explorations of the corrupt consciousness engendered by corrupt societies, the Episcopalian philosopher Alan Donagan recalls Newman's toast, and drily adds:

> Were we obliged to bring morality into toasts, we should not refuse to drink to conscience; but we should beg to drink to a truthful consciousness first.[29]

For our generation, Donagan's toast expresses better than Newman's the essential premiss, and something of the spirit, of the *Letter*.

[29] A. Donagan, *The Theory of Morality* (Chicago, Ill., and London, 1977), 142.

21

Newman on Infallibility

FRANCIS A. SULLIVAN, SJ

The First Vatican Council defined that when the pope speaks *ex cathedra*, he enjoys the same infallibility which the Church has in defining doctrine of faith and morals. In this solemn definition, the infallibility of the Church was taken for granted as so undisputed a fact that it did not need to be directly defined, but could serve as the pattern for the infallibility of the pope. The infallibility of the Church was assumed as a dogma of faith (even though it had never been explicitly defined); it was the infallibility of the pope that became a dogma of faith in 1870 by being defined as such.

For John Henry Newman, the difference between the infallibility of the Church and that of the pope, and between the claim of the one and the other on his act of faith, was no merely academic question. It was a very real issue that affected a great part of his life. Even as an Anglican, as we shall see, he believed that the Church enjoyed something akin to infallibility; but it was only some months after the definition by Vatican I that he could give his full assent to papal infallibility as a dogma of his faith.

In the light of the foregoing, our treatment of 'Newman on Infallibility' falls into two parts, presenting first his views on the infallibility of the Church, and second his views on papal infallibility.

1. NEWMAN ON THE INFALLIBILITY OF THE CHURCH

His views as an Anglican. As we have already suggested, our treatment of this question must begin with what Newman believed concerning the infallibility of the Church while still an Anglican. He expressed his mind on this most explicitly in the eighth of his

Lectures on the Prophetical Office of the Church, entitled 'The Indefectibility of the Church Catholic'.[1]

The main purpose Newman had in these lectures was to describe Anglicanism—in what he saw as its most authentic tradition, if not in actuality—as the *via media* between the deficiencies of Protestantism, and the excesses of Roman Catholicism. The defect of Protestantism was its failure to recognize the need of a visible Church equipped with a 'prophetical office' to safeguard the purity of the apostolic faith against the errors inevitable in the exercise of private judgement on Scripture as a sole rule of faith. The excess of Romanism was its claim to possess an abiding and pervasive infallibility that would allow it to create new dogmas practically at will.

Against Protestantism, which exalts Scripture as the sole rule of faith, Newman argued from Scripture itself, which describes the Church as 'the pillar and ground of truth' (1 Tim. 3: 15), and tells us how Christ gave to the Church pastors and teachers so that all could come to unity and not be carried about by every wind of doctrine (cf. Eph. 4: 11–14). He concluded from these and other passages that Scripture presents the Church as the great and special support of truth, and assures us that a divine promise has been given that the word of truth given her shall never be lost.[2] The following passages of his lecture show how 'high' a view he had of the role of the Church as guardian and teacher of revealed truth.

Not only is the Church Catholic bound to teach the Truth, but she is ever divinely guided to teach it; her witness of the Christian faith is a matter of promise as well as of duty; her discernment of it is secured by a heavenly as well as by a human rule. She is indefectible in it, and therefore not only has authority to enforce, but is of authority in declaring it. . . . The Church not only transmits the faith by human means, but has a supernatural gift for that purpose; that doctrine, which is true, considered as an historical fact, is true also because she teaches it.[3]

Our reception of the Athanasian Creed is another proof of our holding the infallibility of the Church, as some of our Divines express it, in matters of saving faith. In that Creed it is unhesitatingly said, that

[1] These lectures were originally published in 1837. As a Catholic, Newman re-edited them, adding a preface and footnotes, and published them in *VM* i. In the 1877 edition used here, lecture 8 is on pp. 189–213.

[2] *VM* i. 193.

[3] *VM* i. 190.

certain doctrines are necessary to be believed in order to salvation; they are minutely and precisely described; no room is left for Private Judgement; none for any examination into Scripture, with the view of discovering them. Next, if we inquire the *ground* of this authority in the Church, the Creed answers; that she speaks merely as the organ of the *Catholic* voice, and that the faith thus witnessed, is, as being thus witnessed, such, that whoso does not believe it faithfully, cannot be saved. "Catholic," then, and "saving" are taken as synonymous terms; in other words, the Church Catholic is pronounced to have been all along, and by implication as destined ever to be, the guardian of the pure and undefiled faith, or to be indefectible in that faith.[4]

If, as is obvious, there is not a word in what we have just quoted that Newman would have to repudiate as a Catholic, one has to ask how it is possible that about half of these lectures consist in a polemic against the belief of Roman Catholics in the infallibility of their Church. Towards the end of this same eighth lecture, he summed up the difference by saying: 'Both we and Roman Catholics hold that the Church Catholic is unerring in its declarations of faith, or saving doctrine; but we differ from each other as to what is the faith, and what is the Church Catholic.'[5]

What Newman meant by 'the Church Catholic' here, was the 'undivided Church' of Christian antiquity, which he believed continued to exist, although imperfectly united, in the three 'branches' (Eastern, Roman, and Anglican) which had maintained the apostolic faith and apostolic succession in ministry. He distinguished between two ways in which the 'Church Catholic' was 'unerring in its declarations of faith'. In antiquity, while it still enjoyed full unity, it could be described as infallible in such declarations of faith as it made in its creeds, and its conciliar definitions of the basic Trinitarian and Christological dogmas. However, when, during the course of the first millennium, the Church lost its unity, it also lost its prerogative of infallibility, and hence also its warrant to formulate new creeds or define new dogmas. But, since the apostolic faith, in its essentials, has a divine guarantee of being preserved through the 'prophetical office' of the Church, the Church Catholic must be indefectible in maintaining the apostolic faith. In other words, it must have a divine guarantee of remaining faithful to the essential dogmas already determined by the undivided Church of antiquity. For

[4] *VM* i. 192. [5] *VM* i. 212.

Newman as an Anglican, then, the true norm of faith is Scripture as interpreted by Christian antiquity.

Furthermore, he was convinced that the 'Church Catholic is unerring in its declarations of faith' in the sense that those Christian doctrines which all its branches teach as necessary to be believed for salvation are bound to be true, and that such agreement actually has always been had, and will always be had, but only in the essential dogmas that were already determined in Christian antiquity.

In the light of the above, it is not difficult to understand Newman's polemic against the claim of the Roman Church to infallibility. First, it arrogantly makes an exclusive claim to be the 'Church Catholic', denying the claim of the Eastern and Anglican Churches to belong to it as integral branches. Then it attributes to itself the unique prerogatives of the undivided Church, including infallibility in formulating new creeds and defining new dogmas. But most grievous of all, in defining new dogmas, it does not see itself as limited to declaring what is already to be found in the faith of the ancient Christian Church, but rather introduces such novelties as its doctrines about the Blessed Virgin Mary, indulgences, purgatory, and the like. He saw this as evident proof that it has given up the only true norm of apostolic faith, and has come to rely on its own beliefs and practices as sufficient basis for defining new dogmas.

Before proceeding to consider the changes that took place in Newman's thinking when he became a Catholic, it would be useful to recall some of the basic convictions he had as an Anglican, which would continue to characterize his religious thinking as a Catholic. First of all, there was his absolute faith in Divine Providence, which grounded his confidence that as God could not have created the world and then left it to its own devices, neither could he have given mankind the Christian revelation, and not provided an effective organ by which this revelation would be propagated and maintained in its purity. He was convinced that the visible Christian Church was this divinely established organ of revealed truth for the world, and that it must have a 'prophetic' or teaching office, capable of maintaining the whole body in the unity of the true faith. He further saw that since this organ was human and therefore fallible, it could only perform its task effectively if it were given supernatural help that would secure it from error when it proclaimed the truths that must be believed for salvation.

Having seen how Newman, as an Anglican, understood the indefectibility in faith which this supernatural help guaranteed to the 'Church Catholic', we must now see what new elements entered into his understanding of the Church's infallibility during the process that led to his becoming a Roman Catholic.

Newman's view as a Catholic. As we have seen, Newman as an Anglican looked to Christian antiquity as the norm of Christian faith. In the event, it was his further study of and reflection on Christian antiquity that led him to the Catholic Church. The story of his conversion is well known, and need not be retold here. Suffice it to say that the more deeply he came to understand the process by which the early church rejected Arianism, Nestorianism, and Monophysitism as heresies, and hammered out the great Trinitarian and Christological dogmas of the creed, the more convinced he became that it must be God's plan that the Christian revelation should undergo development, whereby what was at first only obscurely or implicitly contained in the deposit of faith would come to be recognized as contained therein and thus become an object of explicit faith. It was while he was spelling out the implications and consequences of this insight in his *Essay on the Development of Christian Doctrine* that he reached his definitive conviction that he must become a Roman Catholic. At the risk of over-simplification, I would summarize the process of his thought in the following way.

If the truths that are arrived at by a process of legitimate development of doctrine are really implicitly contained in the original revelation, it follows that they are really part of that revelation. Then Divine Providence, which safeguards the original revelation from being corrupted in its transmission in the faith of the Church, must also preserve the Church from error in its acceptance of such developments as articles of its faith. Such developments were already taking place in the ancient church, as we see in the definition of the Trinitarian and Christological dogmas, and in the writings of the Fathers, who both prepared and subsequently defended and explained the conciliar decisions. If such development can rightly be seen as part of God's plan for the Church, there is no reason to restrict such development to a limited period of history. Actually such development has continued in the Roman Catholic Church, and the doctrines that are the fruit of such development can be shown to be homogeneous with the faith of Christian antiquity, and none can be shown to be a corruption of it. Of the three branches of what Anglicans call the Church Catholic, only the Roman Catholic Church truly corresponds to the Church of the first centuries; it is the only one that can invoke St Augustine's dictum: 'Securus judicat orbis terrarum.' What the whole Roman Catholic Church believes and teaches as an article of apostolic faith must then be truly contained in the original revelation; indeed this Church must be infallible in its profession of faith and in the solemn definitions by which its teaching body has proposed articles of faith to be professed.

Having briefly indicated how Newman arrived at his belief that the Roman Catholic Church alone was the legitimate successor to the Church of Christian antiquity, and the infallible teacher of Christian faith, we shall now mention some particular aspects of his understanding of the infallibility of the Catholic Church. I would first observe that among the aspects that we shall speak of here, questions about the *limits* and the *seat* of infallibility will not be included. These questions came to the fore only in the controversy about papal infallibility. Writing to a friend in July 1867, Newman said: 'For myself, I have never taken any great interest in the question of the limits and seat of infallibility.'[6] These, however, became crucial questions, in which he had to take interest, when it became likely that papal infallibility would come up for discussion and possible definition at Vatican I. We shall consider these aspects of his thought in the second part of this paper.

Belief in the infallibility of the Church: essential to Catholic faith. We get an insight into Newman's own Catholic faith when we read how emphatically he declared: 'That the Church is the infallible oracle of truth is the fundamental dogma of Catholic faith.'[7] Indeed, in his opinion, a person who did not believe in the Church's infallibility 'never had the indispensable and elementary faith of a Catholic'.[8] To become a Catholic, it was not enough to believe all that she had up to that time proposed for belief; one must believe her infallible also in future definitions

[6] *LD* xxiii. 275. [7] *GA*, p. 102. [8] *GA*, p. 162.

and have an implicit faith in all that she has defined or will ever define as divinely revealed. Undoubtedly, this was Newman's own act of faith when he became a Catholic, at a time, it may be noted, when he could hardly have foreseen that the Immaculate Conception and papal infallibility would become dogmas of Catholic faith during his own lifetime.

'*Securus judicat orbis terrarum.*' In his *Apologia pro Vita Sua*, Newman describes the powerful impact this phrase of St Augustine had upon him, and the role it played in the process of his conversion, comparing it with the 'tolle lege, tolle lege' of St Augustine's *Confessions*.[9] As a Catholic, Newman came back to this dictum again and again, insisting that the *orbis terrarum* could only be identified with the Roman Catholic Church, since this was the only Christian body that was both spread over the whole world and at the same time united in faith and communion. The meaning of *securus judicat*, as he explained it, was 'that the deliberate judgment, in which the whole Church at length rests and acquiesces, is an infallible prescription, and a final sentence against such portions of it as protest and secede'.[10] He could put the same idea either negatively: 'What is not taught universally, what is not believed universally, has no claim on me,'[11] or positively: 'As to faith, my great principle was: "Securus judicat orbis terrarum."'[12] 'What bishops and people say all over the earth, that is the truth.'[13] He spoke of a 'passive infallibility' of the Catholic people, explaining this to mean that 'the body of the faithful can never misunderstand what the Church determines by the gift of active infallibility.'[14]

In a letter written just a few days after the definition of papal infallibility at Vatican I, at a time when he was still not sure that all the necessary conditions for a valid conciliar definition had been fulfilled, Newman wrote to a friend:

> If the definition is eventually received by the whole body of the faithful, as valid or as the expression of a truth, then too it will claim our assent by the force of the great dictum, "Securus judicat orbis terrarum." This indeed is the broad principle by which all acts of the rulers of the Church are ratified. But for it, we might reasonably question some of the past Councils or their acts.[15]

[9] *Apo.*, p. 110.
[10] Ibid.
[11] *LD* xxiii. 275.
[12] *LD* xxiii. 275.
[13] *LD* xxv. 235.
[14] *LD* xxvii. 338.
[15] *LD* xxv. 165.

Having quoted this passage of his private letter in his published *Letter to the Duke of Norfolk*,[16] Newman clarified what he had meant by the term 'ratified' in the Postscript which he added to the second edition of his *Letter to the Duke of Norfolk*. He there explained:

> Nor have I spoken of a subsequent reception by the Church as entering into the necessary conditions of a *de fide* decision. I said that by the 'Securus judicat orbis terrarum' all acts of the rulers of the Church are ratified. In this passage of my private letter I meant by 'ratified' brought home to us as authentic. At this very moment it is certainly the handy, obvious, and serviceable argument for our accepting the Vatican definition of the Pope's Infallibility.[17]

I take this to mean that an authentic definition needs no such 'ratification', but if there were some doubt whether a doctrine had been defined or not, its universal reception would assure us that it had really been defined. This was undoubtedly Newman's attitude in the months after the definition of papal infallibility, until it became clear that the decision was being universally received.

Infallibility a supernatural gift. We have already seen that, as an Anglican, Newman was convinced that the Church could be assured of indefectibility in faith only by a supernatural gift. This conviction remained with him all his life, and was even stronger when applied to the abiding infallibility of the Catholic Church which he had denied as an Anglican. Another of his lifelong convictions was that 'the very essence of religion is protection from error, for a revelation that could stultify itself would be no revelation at all'.[18] Given the propensity of the human mind to go astray, of which Newman was particularly conscious, he saw no possibility of such protection from error in religious matters except by supernatural help. Hence he saw it as a necessary inference from the nature of the role which God had entrusted to his Church, that he would provide the help needed to keep the gift of divine revelation from being corrupted by human error in its transmission. One among many passages in his writings that express his mind on this is the following from his *Letter to the Duke of Norfolk*:

[16] *Diff*. ii. 303. [17] *Diff*. ii. 372. [18] *LD* xxv. 259.

For, if the Church, initiated in the Apostles and continued in their successors, has been set up for the direct object of protecting, preserving, and declaring the Revelation, and that, by means of the Guardianship and Providence of its Divine Author, we are led on to perceive that, in asserting this, we are in other words asserting, that, so far as the message entrusted to it is concerned, the Church is infallible; for what is meant by infallibility in teaching but that the teacher in his teaching is secured from error? and how can fallible man be thus secured except by a supernatural infallible guidance?[19]

Infallibility not positive inspiration, but negative protection from error. While Newman was convinced that the infallibility of the Church could only be understood as a supernatural gift, he also insisted that it did not involve a positive gift of inspiration, but that it was rather negative in character. In a letter to a friend, written almost a year after Vatican I, he explained how he conceived this negative aspect of infallibility.

I have always thought, and think still, that the infallibility of the Church is an *inference* (a necessary inference) from her prerogative that she is the divinely appointed Teacher of her children and of the world. She cannot fulfil this office *without* divine help—that is, she never can be *permitted to go wrong* in the truths of revelation—This is a negative proposition—the very idea of infallibility is a negative. She teaches by human means, she ascertains the truth by human means—of course assisted by grace, but so is every inquirer, and she has *in kind* no promise of invincible grace, which a Father or a divine, or an inquirer has not—but she has this security, that, in order to fulfil her office, her *out come* is always true in the matter of revelation. She is not inspired—the word has sometimes been used, and in Councils especially,—but, properly speaking, inspiration is positive, and infallibility is negative; and a definition may be absolute truth, though the grounds suggested for it in the definition, the texts, the patristic authorities, the historical passages, are all mistakes.[20]

Precisely because infallibility is not inspiration, Newman insisted that it did not dispense the pope or bishops from the task of consultation and deliberation when they undertook the weighty responsibility of defining a dogma of faith. The preparatory work of the *schola theologorum* had an indispensable role to play

[19] *Diff.* ii. 323.

[20] *LD* xxv. 309. In *Letter to the Duke* he compares this to the help a man's good angel might give him to keep him from falling into a pit: *Diff.* ii. 328.

in the process leading up to making final decisions on matters of faith. Nor could those enjoying the supernatural help assured to the church's official teachers neglect the gift of reason possessed perhaps in extraordinary measure by individuals who did not share the bishops' gifts. From his intimate knowledge of the history of the early councils, Newman could affirm that

> Ecumenical Councils . . . have been guided in their decisions by the commanding genius of individuals, sometimes young and of inferior rank. Not that uninspired intellect overruled the superhuman gift which was committed to the Council, which would be a self-contradictory assertion, but that in that process of inquiry and deliberation, which ended in an infallible enunciation, individual reason was paramount.[21]

Infallibility differs from certitude. Newman treated this aspect of the nature of infallibility at some length, as one might have expected, in his *Essay in Aid of a Grammar of Assent*. Rather than trying to summarize his thought, I shall let him explain it in his own inimitable style.

> It is very common, doubtless, especially in religious controversy, to confuse infallibility with certitude, and to argue that, since we have not the one, we have not the other, for that no one can claim to be certain on any point, who is not infallible about all; but the two words stand for things quite distinct from each other. . . . A certitude is directed to this or that particular proposition; it is not a faculty or gift, but a disposition of mind relatively to a definite case which is before me. Infallibility, on the contrary, is just that which certitude is not; it *is* a faculty or gift, and relates, not to some one truth in particular, but to all possible propositions in a given subject-matter. We ought in strict propriety, to speak, not of infallible acts, but of acts of infallibility. A belief or opinion as little admits of being called infallible, as a deed can correctly be called immortal, so a belief, opinion or certitude is true or false, but never infallible. . . . It is persons and rules that are infallible, not what is brought out into act, or committed to paper. A man is infallible, whose words are always true; a rule is infallible, if it is unerring in all possible applications. An infallible authority is certain in every particular case that may arise; but a man who is certain in some one definite case, is not on that account infallible. . . . as I may do a virtuous action, without being impeccable, I may be certain that the Church is infallible, while I am myself a fallible mortal; otherwise, I cannot be certain that the Supreme Being is infallible, until I am

[21] *Apo.*, pp. 237–8.

infallible myself. It is a strange objection, then, which is sometimes urged against Catholics, that they cannot prove and assent to the Church's infallibility, unless they first believe in their own. . . . Therefore we may be certain of the infallibility of the Church, while we admit that in many things we are not, and cannot be, certain at all.[22]

It would perhaps not be out of place to remark in this context that what Newman says here about beliefs, opinions, and certitudes being true or false, but never infallible, applies equally well to propositions: a point that was frequently mentioned by critics of the book *Infallible: An Inquiry*, in which Hans Küng based one of his arguments against the Catholic doctrine of infallibility on the impossibility of infallible propositions.

2. NEWMAN ON PAPAL INFALLIBILITY

Prior to Vatican I: an opinion, not a certitude. In the passage quoted just above from the *Grammar of Assent*, we have seen Newman defend the reasonableness of Catholic certitude about the infallibility of the Church. We know that he not only shared this certitude, but considered it to be 'the fundamental dogma of Catholic faith',[23] even though it had never been explicitly defined as such. We have also seen above that he spoke of the infallibility of the Church as a 'necessary inference' from her role as divinely appointed teacher of her children and the world.[24] Obviously, when he described this inference as 'necessary', he meant one that led him to an unconditional assent. As we know from the *Grammar of Assent*, he was convinced that such an assent, involving a state of certitude, must be founded on sufficient reasons, but the reasons could consist in a convergence of probabilities, no one of which, by itself, would justify certitude. As a matter of fact, he could and did say that his certitude about the infallibility of the Church was based on 'an accumulation of probabilities'.[25] At the same time, it was for Newman a matter of the most absolute certitude.

Strikingly different from this was his state of mind about the infallibility of the pope. He arrived at certitude about this only some months after it had been defined at Vatican I, and only

[22] *GA*, p. 146–8.
[23] *GA*, pp. 146–8.
[24] *LD* xxv. 309.
[25] *VM* i. 122 n. 2.

when he was satisfied that the bishops of the minority and the Catholic faithful at large were accepting it. In other words, it was his certitude about the infallibility of the Catholic Church that finally brought him to certitude about papal infallibility, when it became clear that the Church had committed herself to this as a dogma of her faith.

How, then, did Newman describe his state of mind about the doctrine of papal infallibility during the previous twenty-five years since he became a Catholic? He answered this question quite often in his letters. The following are some examples of the way he expressed his mind about this between 1866 and 1868. 'I have ever thought it likely to be true, never thought it was certain.'[26] 'On the whole, then, I hold it, but I should account it no sin if, on grounds of reason, I doubted it.'[27] 'I hold the Pope's Infallibility, not as a dogma, but as a theological opinion; that is, not as a certainty, but as a probability.'[28] 'I have only an opinion (not faith) that the Pope is infallible.'[29]

Even though, during all this period, papal infallibility was not a matter of personal faith for Newman, he could say honestly that he 'held' it, and he did not hesitate to present it as Catholic doctrine and defend it against Protestant misrepresentations, as he did, for instance, in one of his *Lectures on the Present Position of Catholics in England*.[30] After Vatican I he indignantly responded to the published calumny that he was only pretending to accept a dogma that 'in his heart he could not and did not believe'. He refuted this charge by referring to passages in his earlier writings in which he had spoken positively of this doctrine.[31]

Grounds sufficient for an opinion, but not for certitude. As we have seen above, it was one of the basic theses of the *Grammar of Assent* that genuine certitude could be based on a convergence of probabilities. One way to describe Newman's state of mind about papal infallibility prior to his acceptance of it as a dogma in the aftermath of Vatican I, would be to say that the reasons that justified his holding it as a theological opinion did not amount to the kind of convergence or accumulation of probabilities that would have satisfied his mind in giving it his unconditional assent.

[26] *LD* xxiii. 157.
[27] *LD* xxiii. 105.
[28] *LD* xxiv. 92.
[29] *LD* xxiii. 275.
[30] *Pre. Pos.*, pp. 334–5, 338.
[31] *LD* xxvi. 167–8.

Two questions arise, then: what were the reasons that led him to hold it as a theological opinion? and why did he not find them sufficient grounds for certitude?

The following are some of the reasons that he gave, mostly in his private correspondence, to explain why he had held papal infallibility as a theological opinion. 'I think there is a good deal of evidence, on the very surface of history and the Fathers, in its favour.'[32] 'The fact that all along for so many centuries, the head of the Church and the teacher of the faithful and the Vicar of Christ has been allowed by God to assert virtually his infallibility, is a great argument in favour of the validity of his claim.'[33] 'I consider the self-assertion, the ipse dixit of the Pope for 1800 years, a great and imposing argument for the validity of their claims.'[34] 'The Popes acted as if they were infallible in doctrine—with a very high hand, peremptorily, magisterially, fiercely . . . *They acted in a way that needed infallibility as its explanation*.'[35] In a letter of 1875 he explained in greater detail how he understood this argument from history.

I should say that the word 'infallibility' has never been ascribed to the *Church* in any authoritative document till the Vatican Council. . . . Yet the Church acted *as* infallible and was accepted as infallible from the first. What was the case with the Church was the case with the Pope. The most *real* expression of the doctrine is, not that he is infallible, but that his decisions are 'irreformabilia' and true. So that the question did not arise in the mind of Christians in any formal shape 'is he infallible, and in what and how far?' for all they felt was that what he said was 'the Voice of the Church', 'for he spoke for the Church', 'the Church spoke in him', and what the Church spoke was *true*. . . . Honorius then or any other Pope of those times, when he chose, *acted* as infallible and was *obeyed* as infallible, without having a clear perception that his ipse dixit arose from a *gift* of infallibility. . . . *Practically* the Pope has taught dogmatically from the first, e.g. it is not at all clear that Leo's famous Tome against Eutyches is an act of infallibility; but what *is* clear is that it had the effect of turning a great mass of Bishops right round, as if he were infallible, and making them with him in the Council of Chalcedon use the words definitive of the two natures in One Person, which he had in his Tome forced upon them.[36]

[32] *LD* xxiii. 105.
[33] *LD* xxv. 168.
[34] *LD* xxv. 186.
[35] *LD* xxv. 299.
[36] *LD* xxvii. 286–7.

As far as I have been able to ascertain, it is this argument from the historical exercise of papal doctrinal authority that Newman consistently offered when he set out to explain why he had held papal infallibility as a theological opinion ever since he became a Catholic. It is obvious that he did not judge this argument sufficiently cogent to justify an assent of certitude. One has to ask: was he not aware of other arguments in favour of papal infallibility, such as those given by his friend the Roman theologian Giovanni Perrone, SJ?[37] Would not those other reasons, added to his own, have produced a convergence of probabilities that would be sufficient for certitude in the matter?

There can be no doubt about Newman's familiarity with the arguments that Perrone and other Catholic theologians had offered in favour of papal infallibility. In fact, there are some references to such arguments in his letters and private notes, which, while brief and sometimes enigmatic, do suggest that he did not find them adequate to form the kind of convergence of probabilities that he required for certitude. This is all the more interesting, in view of the fact that he did find in those same arguments a convergence of probabilities sufficient for certitude about the doctrine of papal supremacy. We know this from chapter 4 in his *Essay on Development* which he devoted to an exposition of the traditional arguments from the 'primacy texts' and from patristic tradition in favour of the supreme pastoral authority of the pope.[38] Perrone and other Catholic theologians used these same texts to prove the doctrine of papal infallibility: drawing their arguments either directly from the scriptural texts and the sayings of the Fathers, or indirectly, as a necessary consequence of papal supremacy, on the grounds that the supreme *munus pascendi* necessarily required infallibility in teaching as well. While Newman recognized the cogency of those arguments for papal supremacy, he evidently did not find them convincing for papal infallibility.

First of all, with regard to the 'primacy texts' (Matt. 16: 16–18; Luke 22: 31–2; John 21: 15–17): there is a significant passage in a letter which he wrote to his closest friend in the oratory, Fr. Ambrose St John in July 1870, while he was not yet convinced

[37] G. Perrone, *De Locis Theologicis*, in id., *Praelectiones Theologicae*, i (25th edn., Milan and Genoa, 1857), 550–74.

[38] *Dev.*, see esp. pp. 156–65.

that the dogma of papal infallibility had been validly defined. In this letter he explained various grounds on which a person with his doubts about the conciliar definition might already be obliged in conscience to accept the doctrine as a dogma of faith.

But there are other means by which I can be brought under the obligation of receiving a doctrine as a dogma, that is, as part of the faith necessary to salvation.

For instance, if I am clear that it is in Scripture, as that Baptism is the initiatory rite of Christian Discipleship—or again that it is in primitive and uninterrupted tradition, as the Divinity of Our Lord. Or when a high probability, drawn from Scripture or tradition, is partially or probably confirmed by the Church. Thus a particular Catholic might be so nearly sure that the promises to Peter in Scripture proved that the Infallibility of Peter is a necessary dogma, as only to be kept from holding it as such, by the absence of any judgment on the part of the Church—so that the present unanimity between Pope and 500 Bishops, even though not sufficient to constitute a formal synodal act, would at once put him in the position, and lay him under the obligation of receiving the dogma, as a dogma, i.e. with its anathema.[39]

From the fact that Newman at that time did not feel under such an obligation, we have to conclude that he was *not* 'nearly sure that the promises to Peter in Scripture proved that the infallibility of Peter is a necessary dogma', nor even that there was a 'high probability' for this doctrine to be drawn from Scripture or tradition. The probability that led him to hold it as a theological opinion was evidently not 'high' enough to satisfy the conditions he was laying down here for accepting it as a dogma of faith.

The only other reference I have found to the 'primacy texts' as providing a scriptural basis for the doctrine of papal infallibility is in the *Letter to the Duke of Norfolk*, where Newman defends the council's use of those texts as witnesses to the doctrine of its decree. He does not attempt to show how the doctrine can be drawn out of these texts, but describes papal infallibility as the fruit of 'a growing insight' into their meaning: 'What has the long history of the contest for and against the Pope's infallibility been, but a growing insight through the centuries into the meaning of those three texts, to which I just now referred, ending at length by the Church's definitive recognition of the doctrine thus gradually manifested to her?'[40]

[39] *LD* xxv. 167. [40] *Diff*. ii. 328.

As has been mentioned, Perrone and others also argued for papal infallibility on the grounds that it was a necessary consequence of papal supremacy, since the pope's office as supreme pastor, his *munus pascendi*, involved his role as teacher of all the faithful. While I have found no discussion of this argument in Newman's published works, there are several references to it in the private notes which he wrote on the question of infallibility between 1865 and 1867.[41]

I never have been against the doctrine of the Pope's Infallibility—certainly strong acts from the beginning but I don't see that the munus pascendi requires infallibility.[42]

The munus pascendi does not require infallibility in the Pastor, but somewhere—i.e. in the Ecumenical Council.[43]

Some writers argue as if the munus pascendi involved infallibility. I do not see that at all. It involves a sort of infallibility in teaching somewhere, and that he is the ordinary enforcer of its teaching. But to enforce a point is not to rule it. . . . The ordinary pastio or pascendi actio of the Pope is enforcing old and known truths. This does not require infallibility, any more than a Bishop's enforcing them. The Bishop is the doctor of his diocese—the Pope of the Universal Church.

The Pope's munus pascendi consists very much more in directing conduct than in any dogmatic determination of points of faith and morals—and by aiming at the latter he may miss the former.[44]

During the month of March 1870 Newman received a letter from Bishop Moriarty of Kerry, who was then at the First Vatican Council, in which he quoted one of the cardinals there as having said: 'We must give up the first ten centuries, but the infallibility is an obvious development of the supremacy.' In his reply to Moriarty, Newman remarked: 'Nor do I think with your friend that infallibility follows on Supremacy—yet I hold the principle of development.'[45]

While Newman was not convinced of the cogency of some of the arguments being put forward in favour of papal infallibility, neither was he convinced by the arguments brought against it by Döllinger and others, who claimed that it was contradicted by the serious doctrinal errors that various popes, such as Honorius,

[41] *TP* ii. 99–160. [42] *TP* ii. 102. [43] *TP* ii. 104.

[44] *TP* ii. 117. In this passage, I venture to surmise that the phrase '*sort* of infallibility' is a misreading for '*seat* of infallibility'. My italics.

[45] *LD* xxv. 58.

had made in their official pronouncements. In commenting on a pamphlet published in 1868 with the title 'The Condemnation of Pope Honorius', Newman wrote to its author Peter Le Page Renouf:

I certainly did not know how strong a case could be made out against Pope Honorius. But with all its power, I do not find it seriously interferes with my own view of Papal Infallibility. . . . You have brought out a grave difficulty in the way of the doctrine; that is, you have diminished its probability, but you have only diminished it. To my mind the balance of probabilities is still in favour of it.[46]

Seven years later, when defending the Vatican dogma against Gladstone's attack, Newman devoted several pages of his *Letter to the Duke of Norfolk* to showing that the letters of Honorius that were condemned as heretical by the Sixth Ecumenical Council, were certainly not the kind of *ex cathedra* definitions which Vatican I had declared to enjoy infallibility.[47]

Newman's position on controversial issues prior to Vatican I. We know what Newman's position was on these issues before the council, from his correspondence and from his private notes, not from his published writings. This is because he deliberately chose not to enter publicly into controversy with his fellow-Catholics, who included Archbishop Henry Edward Manning and the editor of the Dublin Review William G. Ward. It was for this reason also that he decided not to publish the second part of his reply to Edward Pusey's *Eirenicon*, in which he would have answered Pusey's objections to the doctrine of infallibility. The problem was that at that time there was no one Catholic doctrine on several important issues concerning infallibility, and if Newman put forward only his own opinion, he would have either to criticize or to ignore opinions held by other Catholics. As he put it in his notes: 'I should not be writing against Pusey, but making a case against Ward, and every one would say so.'[48]

However, for a time he did contemplate writing a second reply to Pusey, on the question of infallibility, and with that in view he compiled a fairly extensive volume of notes, which have only recently been edited for publication by J. Derek Holmes.[49] These notes give us valuable information not only about his

[46] *LD* xxiv. 90, 92.
[47] *Diff*. ii. 315–17.
[48] *TP* ii. 112.
[49] *TP* ii. 99–160.

thoughts, but also about the sources he was using. They also tell us which were the issues that he felt most needed to be clarified: namely, the extent of the subject matter about which the Church and the pope can speak infallibly, and the kind of utterances which enjoy the prerogative of infallibility. On both of these issues Newman maintained a position that his opponents called 'minimizing' and 'half-Catholic', but which he himself would eventually describe as 'legitimate minimizing'[50] in contrast to what he strongly felt was unjustifiable maximizing on the part of Ward and Manning. To anticipate my conclusions, I will say that Newman's position was solidly based on the traditional doctrine of such 'approved authors' as Perrone of the Roman College, and was subsequently vindicated by the careful terms in which papal infallibility was actually defined by Vatican I. Let us briefly consider Newman's position on these two controversial issues.

The question of the extent of the subject-matter for infallibility. Newman believed strongly that the Church had a guarantee of infallibility only with regard to the divine revelation that had been entrusted to her. Of course, in the light of his *Essay on the Development of Doctrine*, which had led him into the Catholic Church, he fully admitted legitimate developments as belonging to the deposit of revelation. In his view, the gift of infallibility guaranteed that the Church would define as dogma only such developments as were legitimate. In addition to such developments, he also recognized certain kinds of 'dogmatic facts' as belonging to revelation, and hence possible matters for infallible decision, provided that they were merely 'concrete expressions' or 'concrete exhibitions' of what was revealed. For example, in order effectively to reject the heresy of Jansenism, the Church had to be able to say definitively whether certain of the writings of Jansenius were heretical or not. The Church would not be able to speak infallibly at all if it could not determine with infallibility whether particular expressions were orthodox or heretical; this was merely the 'concrete exhibition' of the revealed truth.[51]

On the other hand, Newman was aware that it was not easy to draw the line between facts that were truly 'dogmatic' in this

[51] *TP* ii. 119–20. [50] *Diff.* ii. 334.

sense, and those that were not. One example he gives of something he would not allow as such a 'concrete exhibition' of revealed truth was the absolute necessity of the pope's temporal power as required for the exercise of his spiritual authority. The temporal power was a historical fact, but he did not see that it belonged in any sense to revelation.[52]

Questions of morality also belonged within the scope of infallibility; here Newman insisted that this does not apply to mere precepts, but only to 'general categorical enunciations' of moral doctrine; and only to such doctrine as is based on divine law and has to do with things necessary for salvation.[53]

Newman also recognized that, in order to be able to safeguard revelation itself, the Church needed to be able to speak with infallibility about certain matters which, while not in themselves revealed, were necessarily connected with revelation. Of these he used the Latin word *pomoeria*, which literally referred to the boundary zone which the ancient Romans left free of buildings inside and outside their city walls. Modern theologians generally speak of such matters as constituting a 'secondary object' of infallibility. With regard to such a 'boundary zone' of the subject-matter for infallible teaching, Newman's basic principle was: 'No declaration or proposition of the church is infallible except those which relate to the res revelata.'[54] But he saw that some propositions that were not in themselves part of the *res revelata* could be variously related to it. He distinguished between two kinds of such propositions, in the following way.

Though the Church cannot increase the depositum fidei, there are two ways in which it can make positive enunciations beyond it, (viz by stating the *relations* of other propositions to it). In the first place, it can affirm that certain propositions are injurious to it. It does not affirm or deny their predicates of their subjects—but it affirms that the propositions, as they stand, are inconsistent with or injurious to the depositum. That is, it can condemn propositions.

And next she can enunciate that certain other propositions are more or less connected with or congenial to the depositum; necessarily connected, or probably so, or morally, and therefore absolutely true, or certain, or probable, as the case may be.[55]

[52] *TP* ii. 131.
[53] *LD* xxvii. 214; see also *Diff*. ii. 331.
[54] *TP* ii. 115.
[55] *TP* ii. 142.

While he does not say so explicitly in this context, it is safe to presume, from his general approach to the question of infallibility, that Newman would consider as subject-matter for infallibility only such propositions as were so necessarily connected with the depositum that they could be declared to be absolutely true. What he did explicitly state, in notes that he wrote for his friend Fr. Stanislas Flanagan, is that it is not easy to determine the exact boundary between *pomoeria* that admit of infallible definition, and those that do not. In his *Apologia* he had spoken of the *pomoeria* in the following way.

I enlarged just now upon the concrete shape and circumstances, under which pure infallible authority presents itself to the Catholic. That authority has the prerogative of an indirect jurisdiction on subject-matters which lie beyond its own proper limits, and it most reasonably has such a jurisdiction. It could not act in its own province, unless it had a right to act out of it. It could not properly defend religious truth, without claiming for that truth what may be called its *pomoeria*; or, to take another illustration, without acting as we act, as a nation, in claiming as our own, not only the land on which we live, but what are called British waters. The Catholic Church claims, not only to judge infallibly on religious questions, but to animadvert on opinions in secular matters which bear upon religion, on matters of philosophy, of science, or literature, or history, and it demands our submission to her claim. It claims to censure books, to silence authors, and to forbid discussions. In this province, taken as a whole, it does not so much speak doctrinally, as enforce measures of discipline.[56]

The reader will have noticed that in this passage, Newman does not speak of the possibility that the church could speak of any such *pomoeria* with its prerogative of infallibility. Four years later, in his notes for Fr. Flanagan, Newman explains the reason for this.

As to the Apologia, it must be recollected that it was not a didactic work—nor did it contain a statement of my own personal views about infallibility, but was addressed to Protestants *in order to show* them what it was that a Catholic fairly undertook in the way of theological profession, when he became a Catholic. . . . It was for this reason that I spoke so vaguely about the Pomoeria. I myself hold that the doctrines which may be considered as belonging to it are in some cases of obligation and in others not; but which are such and which not, is

[56] *Apo.*, p. 230.

decided by theological opinion and it varies. Such, for instance, would be the infallibility of canonization—to him who thinks it infallible, it is such. . . . It was for the same reason, that, in speaking of condemned propositions, I did not expressly say, whether the condemnation was infallible or not, because a distinct assertion could not be made without turning a statement of twenty pages into a volume. All I did, was to say that such condemnations from their general character constituted no great burden for our faith to bear.[57]

In all of this complex question concerning the limits of the subject-matter of infallibility, what most deeply concerned Newman was the way that Ward and other Catholics, during the years leading up to Vatican I, were extending these limits so as to include matters that were neither revealed nor necessarily connected with revelation. Their line of argument ran as follows. The infallible teaching authority determines the limits of its own infallibility. Whenever the pope speaks with his authority as supreme teacher in the Church, he speaks infallibly. Since he exercises his supreme teaching authority in his bulls, encyclicals, and allocutions, he also speaks with infallibility in such pronouncements. Therefore, whatever is the subject-matter of such authoritative statements, is also subject-matter of infallibility. It does not have to be contained in or necessarily related to the deposit of faith; all we have to know is that the pope has spoken with his supreme authority, and therefore with infallibility about it.

One of the reasons Newman was so deeply disturbed by this point of view was that he himself agreed with the first premiss: he also believed that 'the Oracle of infallibility' determined the limits of his own infallibility. But he vigorously rejected the further premiss that whenever, and about whatever matter, the pope spoke with authority, he also spoke with infallibility. This brings us to the second of the controversial issues on which Newman argued for 'legitimate minimizing' against the 'maximizing' of Ward and Manning.

The question of the kind of papal statements that enjoy the prerogative of infallibility. Newman came back again and again to this question in the theological notes that he wrote between 1865 and 1867. We have already quoted his remark that if he

[57] *TP* ii. 155.

wrote in answer to Pusey on the question of infallibility, everyone would know he was writing against Ward. Indeed it was Ward who, at least in the English-speaking world, was most vociferously claiming infallibility for every document issued with papal authority. As we know, Newman did not want to enter into public controversy with Ward, but he did give his advice and encouragement to a younger priest of the Oratory, Fr. Ignatius Ryder, who in 1867 published a work critical of Ward's extravagant views.[58] Some of the notes we are referring to were written for Ryder's use in his controversy with Ward. However, in the earlier part of the notes (which are all dated), Newman twice describes the opinion which he objects to, without mentioning the names of its proponents. He says: 'Some have thought that the *words* of their Bulls etc. prove (1) that they were *infallible* (2) that the *province* of their infallibility was larger than revelation.'[59] 'Some have thought that the authoritative tone and wording of the Bulls and Briefs showed that they were infallible enunciations —but I cannot admit this argument at all.'[60]

Newman then gives the reasons why he cannot admit this argument from authoritative language to infallibility.

> Every one who teaches, must by the fact that he is teacher, 'lay down the law', as it is called. Every schoolmaster speaks as if he is infallible. . . . Every Bishop in his Pastoral speaks as if he were infallible, for he is the teacher of his flock; he speaks, from the nature of the case, as if no one could answer him. . . . and as such strong expressions used of or by a Bishop do not prove him infallible, neither do the like expressions used of or by a Pope. . . . But if, all this being considered, the authoritative language of the Briefs does not prove the Pope's Infallibility, neither (still less) does the matter of them imply that he has the power of enlarging the bounds of the revealed dogma.[61]

Later on, in the notes which he wrote for Fr. Ryder's use, he is referring explicitly to Ward when he says: 'In other words, he does not allow that the Church can speak *solemnly* without speaking with her *infallible* voice. *This then is the main proposition* to which I shall direct my attention—viz, to show that there is a department of teaching, in which the Church speaks, authoritatively indeed, but not infallibly.'[62]

[58] H. I. D. Ryder, *Idealism in Theology* (London, 1867).
[59] *TP* ii. 110.
[60] *TP* ii. 118.
[61] *TP* ii. 118.
[62] *TP* ii. 147.

Newman then indicates, rather schematically, how he would go about showing this. He recalls that the two instances which he would give of teaching that is authoritative, but not infallible, are papal encyclicals, and statements in which erroneous opinions are proscribed with 'minor censures', that is, less than condemning them as heretical. He continues:

> Thus I am led to the more accurate discussion of the *Principle*—the Church has whatever infallibility she claims—the point being this, *what* is the token or evidence of her claiming it, viz
> (1) either her saying a proposition is de fide
> (2) or marking it with an anathema, taking anathema in a vague sense as including censures (or some censures) under it. (Do the minor censures come under the word 'anathema' is a question to be decided).
> If, however, other tests *besides* de fide or anathema are to be admitted, this must be done on the authority of the *Schola*; which determines BOTH *the proof* that a pronouncement is infallible or not, *and also* what the meaning of the pronouncement is. Thus I am brought to discuss the justice of an objection made to me that, instead of letting the Pope interpret his own words, I put the Schola as a sort of Pope over him. I answer that my opponents put *their own private judgment as a Pope over* him—and that the question is, whether he shall be supposed to speak by theological rule, by the rule of traditional phraseology, of the Schola and of the Bishops as interpreters, or by such interpretation which the rude intelligence of the lay mind gives to his words.[63]

This passage reflects Newman's confidence that it was he, and not Ward, whose position on this question was backed by the authority of the 'Schola', that is, of the great majority of approved Catholic theologians. This, in fact, was the strength of Newman's claim that his 'minimizing' was legitimate, because he knew from his wide reading of theological manuals that his position was solidly based on the doctrine being taught at the Roman College by Perrone, and elsewhere by other reputable Catholic theologians. What he knew was that they restricted the exercise of papal infallibility to *ex cathedra* pronouncements. The following is one of several passages in his notes in which Newman appeals to the authority of his friend Fr. Perrone. After noting that even the ecumenical councils use the formula with anathema to mark their infallible dogmatic definitions, he goes on to say:

[63] *TP* ii. 147–8.

But, if even the enunciations of General Councils require some formula, rare as such Councils are, how much more do the Pope's pronouncements which are made at his pleasure every day of the year . . . One should think that at the very least they require the anathema of contrary doctrine, in order to mark their dogmatic importance.

And accordingly we find divines laying down this condition broadly —Perrone says '*Dogmaticae* definitionis nomine, seu . . . definitionis editae *ex cathedra* significatur Rom. Pontificis decretum quo proponit aliquid universae ecclesiae *de fide tenendum*, aut respuendum veluti fidei contrarium *sub censurae aut anathematis* poena'. In the first clause, Fr. Perrone lays down the condition which I first stated, viz that there should be a declaration that a doctrine is *de fide*—and in the second its equivalent, viz the *anathema*. . . . That a proposition should be formally censured, it is not enough that the Pope should denounce it in the fluent sentences of an Encyclical.[64]

In further notes for Fr. Ryder, Newman says that he has no objection to Ward's holding the infallibility of encyclicals as his own private opinion, but he insists that he cannot declare this to be a matter of obligation for all Catholics, as he was in fact doing, unless he can prove it to be so; and he cannot prove 'it from the consensus of theologians, since it is an opinion that was 'unheard of till late centuries. . . . We can trace the authors in whose writings it arose, etc. etc. It is not generally received now.'[65] The many references in these notes to the writings of Catholic theologians show the firm grounds on which Newman based his confidence that his view of the limits of papal infallibility was shared by the most numerous and respected Catholic theologians.

In passing, it should be noted that while he rejected Ward's arguments for the infallibility of papal encyclicals, Newman agreed that their authoritative teaching called for a response of silence and acquiescence, motivated by what he called the *pietas fidei*, and the Catholic's duty of obedience to papal authority.[66]

Newman's acceptance and interpretation of the Vatican dogma. It does not fall within the scope of this article to go into detail concerning Newman's objections to the way the council was conducted, and the way it arrived at its definition of papal infallibility. What he most feared might happen: that the council would promulgate a decree that would allow Ward and Manning

[64] *TP* ii. 105–6. [65] *TP* ii. 149–50. [66] *TP* ii. 155.

to claim that their opinion was now defined dogma, did not take place. Newman's reaction, when he saw the wording of the decree, was one of relief at its contents, although he was not happy that the dogma had been defined, nor was he yet convinced that it had the force of a conciliar decision, since it had not been approved with the moral unanimity he believed to be required. However, as far as the doctrine itself of the decree was concerned, he was satisfied that it imposed no more on him that what he had always held. While he refrained from publishing his views on the Vatican dogma for several years after it had been defined, he did express his mind freely in his private letters to friends. The following are some of the comments he made during the year after the council was adjourned.

I saw the new Definition yesterday, and am pleased at its moderation, that is, if the doctrine in question is to be defined at all. The terms used are vague and comprehensive, and, personally, I have no difficulty in admitting it.[67]

The definition is what the Church has acted on for some centuries, and a very large body of Catholics have long held.[68]

You must not fancy that any very stringent definition has passed—on the contrary it is very mild in its tenor, and has been acted on by the Pope at least for the last 300 years.[69]

I agree with you that the wording of the Dogma has nothing very difficult in it. It expresses what, as an opinion, I have ever held myself with a host of other Catholics.[70]

Very little has been passed indeed—and they *know* this, and are disappointed who have been the means of passing it—but they use big words just now to conceal their disappointment, and they hope by speaking big and breaking down opposition, to open the way to passing something more. From what I heard at Rome, while the matter was going on, from almost the first authority, they hoped to get a decree which would cover the Syllabus, and they *have not* got it. They have only got *authoritatively* pronounced *that* which Fr. Ryder maintained against Mr. Ward.[71]

As to your friend's question, certainly the Pope is not infallible beyond the Deposit of Faith originally given—though there is a party of Catholics who, I suppose to frighten away converts, wish to make out that he is giving forth infallible utterances every day. . . . I have no hesitation in

[67] *LD* xxv. 164. [68] *LD* xxv. 170. [69] *LD* xxv. 173.
[70] *LD* xxv. 174–5. [71] *LD* xxv. 224.

saying that, to all appearances, Pius IX wished to say a great deal more, (that is, that the Council should say a great deal more) than it did, but a greater Power hindered it.[72]

As the foregoing quotations attest, Newman was confident that the dogma as defined by the council could be correctly interpreted to put the same limits on the exercise and the subject-matter of papal infallibility which he had been expressing in his private notes. However, as some of his personal remarks also show, he knew that others (no doubt he had Ward and Manning in mind) had not abandoned their 'maximizing' views. Newman's concern in this regard was confirmed when Archbishop Manning on 13 October 1870 published his pastoral letter setting forth his interpretation of the Vatican decrees.[73] The passage in it that most disturbed Newman was the following:

In like manner all censures, whether for heresy or with a note less than heresy, are doctrinal definitions in faith and morals, and are included in the words *in doctrina de fide vel moribus definienda*. In a word, the whole *magisterium* or doctrinal authority of the Pontiff as the supreme Doctor of all Christians, is included in this definition of his infallibility. And also all legislative or judicial acts, so far as they are inseparably connected with his doctrinal authority; as, for instance, all judgments, sentences, and decisions, which contain the motives of such acts as derived from faith and morals. Under this will come laws of discipline, canonisation of Saints, approbation of religious Orders, of devotions, and the like; all of which intrinsically contain the truths and principles of faith, morals, and piety.

The Definition, then, limits the infallibility of the Pontiff to his supreme acts *ex cathedra* in faith and morals, but extends his infallibility to all acts in the fullest exercise of his supreme *magisterium* or doctrinal authority.[74]

While this final sentence, if standing alone, would be susceptible of a moderate interpretation, in its context it can only mean that all the instances mentioned in the previous paragraph must be taken to be examples of the 'supreme acts *ex cathedra*' in which the pontiff exercises his infallibility. And this is put forward not as a theological opinion which one may hold or not, but as the

[72] *LD* xxv. 297, 299.

[73] Archbishop Manning, *The Vatican Council and its Definitions: A Pastoral Letter to the Clergy* (London, 1870). This was subsequently published, together with two previous pastoral letters by Manning, in one volume, with the title *Petri Privilegium* (London, 1871).

[74] Manning, *Vatican Council*, pp. 89–90.

official interpretation of the Vatican decree, to be accepted as dogma of faith by all Catholics under pain of excommunication.

About a month after this pastoral appeared, Newman received a letter from a prominent member of Manning's archdiocese, Lady Simeon, who spoke of her distress at the contents of her Archbishop's letter. Newman's reply contained the following very frank remarks on that subject.

> The Archbishop only does what he has done all along—he ever has exaggerated things, and ever has acted towards individuals in a way which they felt to be unfeeling. . . . And now, as I think most cruelly, he is fearfully exaggerating what has been done at the Council. The Pope is not infallible in such things as you instance. I enclose a letter of our own Bishop, which I think will show you this. . . . Therefore, I say confidently, you may dismiss all such exaggerations from your mind, though it is a cruel penance to know that the Bishop where you are, puts them forth. It is an enormous tyranny.[75]

Although Newman expressed his mind so freely in private correspondence, he remained firm in his resolve not to enter into public controversy with Catholics, least of all with the Archbishop of Westminster. For the next four years he busied himself with other projects, such as preparing new editions of previous works. But in November 1874 a challenge presented itself that he felt he could not ignore, in the form of a pamphlet by the Prime Minister William Gladstone, entitled 'The Vatican Decrees in their Bearing on Civil Allegiance: A Political Expostulation'. Gladstone's attack on the civil allegiance and personal freedom of Catholics was based on a gross 'maximizing' of the meaning and consequences of the Vatican definition of papal infallibility. Thus Newman saw a golden opportunity presented him not only to defend his fellow-Catholics against Gladstone's charges, but to put forth and to justify a moderate interpretation of the Vatican dogma, thus indirectly refuting Ward and Manning at the same time.

Toward the end of 1874, Newman had reason for added confidence that his 'minimizing' was legitimate, because during that year he had come to know of a work written by Bishop Joseph Fessler, entitled *The True and the False Infallibility of the*

[75] *LD* xxiv. 230. The 'letter of our own Bishop' to which Newman refers is probably the letter of Bishop Ullathorne of Birmingham that was published in the *Birmingham Daily Post* of 14 Nov. 1870.

Popes: A Controversial Reply to Dr. Schulte.[76] The latter was a leader of the 'Old Catholics' who rejected the Vatican dogmas; Fessler had been the Secretary-General of Vatican I, and had voted with the majority for the decree; but in answering Schulte had given a very moderate interpretation of the limits of papal infallibility. He had sent a copy of his work to Pius IX, who had it immediately translated into Italian, read it, and wrote to Bishop Fessler giving it his full approval. Newman set his close friend Ambrose St John to work preparing an English translation, which he was able to make use of while writing his reply to Gladstone; at the same time he had the use of a French translation published in 1873.[77] Thus, at the very outset of chapter 9 of his *Letter to the Duke of Norfolk*, in which he gave his interpretation of the Vatican decree, he was able to appeal to the uncontrovertible authority of Bishop Fessler's work in support of his own lifelong conviction that 'a moderation of doctrine, dictated by charity, is not inconsistent with soundness in the faith'.[78]

The twenty pages of this chapter on 'The Vatican Definition' present, in Newman's limpid style, his 'wise and cautious theology'[79] of infallibility. I see no need to go into detail here about the contents of this chapter of his reply to Gladstone. Newman himself declared, when he had seen the wording of the Vatican decree: 'It expresses what, as an opinion, I have ever held myself with a host of other Catholics.'[80] If the present article has made a contribution to the study of Newman's thought, it will be to have demonstrated the truth of the statement we have just quoted, by illustrating, from his previous writings, and largely from his private letters and notes, that his interpretation of the Vatican dogma in 1874 was in fact what, as a Catholic, he had always believed with unshakeable faith about the infallibility of the Catholic Church, and what he had held as a personal opinion, about the nature and limits of the infallibility of the pope.

[76] English translation from the German by A. St John (London, 1875).

[77] Fessler, *La Vraie et la Fausse Infaillibilité des papes*, trans. and introd. E. Cosquin (Paris, 1873). There is a reference to this French version in *Diff*. ii. 325. In the first edition of the *Letter to the Duke* (London, 1875), 115, the footnote incorrectly attributes to Fessler what the latter edition correctly attributes to the letter of the Swiss bishops that was quoted by Cosquin in the introduction to his French translation.

[78] *Diff*. ii. 321. [79] *Diff*. ii. 332. [80] *LD* xxv. 174–5.

22

Tides and Twilight
Newman since Vatican II

NICHOLAS LASH

1. THE TURNING TIDE

It was, said Nicholas Theis, time to bring Newman home.[1] And so in March 1966 the first Oxford Newman Symposium was held at Oriel. The Second Vatican Council had ended just three months before, and it was spring. 'Now after a hundred years', said Bishop Christopher Butler, 'we have had another Council, marked like the first by the emergence of two broadly contrasting wings of opinion and aim. But this time, it is those who can be considered the heirs of the neo-Ultramontanes who have constituted the minority, and have been forced back on their defences . . . The tide has been turned, and a first, immensely important, step has been taken towards the vindication of all the main theological, religious, and cultural positions of the former Fellow of Oriel'.[2] Had Newman been able to address the symposium himself, he might have reminded the participants that tides which flow inexorably ebb again and that the English, of all people, have reason to know that spring can be an 'anxious time of hope and fear, of joy and suffering,—of bright promise and budding hopes, yet withal, of keen blasts, and cold showers, and sudden storms'.[3]

Because that Oxford symposium affords such excellent evidence of what, as Vatican II ended, it seemed that Newman had to offer to Christian (especially Catholic) theology and spirituality in a post-conciliar age, I shall take my bearings from it in attempting one man's view of Newman's standing in our now

[1] J. Coulson and A. M. Allchin (eds.), *The Rediscovery of Newman: An Oxford Symposium* (London, 1967), eds., introd., p. vii.

[2] B. C. Butler, 'Newman and the Second Vatican Council', in Coulson and Allchin (eds.), *Rediscovery of Newman*, pp. 244–5.

[3] *OS*, p. 180.

very different world and Church.[4] For the identification of three of the four themes that I have chosen, however, I turn not to *The Rediscovery of Newman* but to a more recent study by James Cameron.

'We cannot say he was a fine poet, or a distinguished historian, or a first-rate theologian; but it was the one man who was in all these things and who was great in the ensemble of these roles'. And if, continues Cameron, 'we ask what, apart from the gift of his own mind and sensibility, Newman has left to the world of religious thought, the common answer is bound to be: the theory of development', to which he adds 'two other possible answers': Newman is 'the theologian of Grace, as this is expressed through all his sermons of the Anglican period . . . and he is the man who attempted to construct, out of the difficult materials inherited through the British philosophical tradition, a theory of belief'.[5]

To these three themes, development, the philosophy of belief, and the doctrine of grace, I shall briefly add a fourth: Newman's increasing recognition, the fruit of often bitter experience, of the importance of constitutional issues for the health and integrity of the Christian community. But, first, it may be useful to recall how slight, in fact, was Newman's presence at the council which was deemed to vindicate his work.

2. NEWMAN AND VATICAN II

If you are not a pope, the only way to win yourself a place in the footnotes to conciliar decrees was, it seems, to have died before the fourteenth century (rare exceptions include Robert Bellarmine and Mgr. Pio Paschini, the author of a work on Galileo).[6] We would not, therefore, expect to find evidence of Newman's influence on the council in this form. Perhaps, since not a few *periti* knew their Newman well, we might detect his influence on speeches in the *aula* drafted with their aid. There is, quite possibly, a useful study to be undertaken here but, at least so far as Xavier

[4] This is my brief and, in trying to meet it, I unavoidably touch lightly on a range of topics treated in greater depth by other contributors to this volume.

[5] J. M. Cameron, 'John Henry Newman and the Tractarian Movement', in N. Smart, J. Clayton, S. T. Katz, and P. Sherry (eds.), *Nineteenth Century Religious Thought in the West*, ii (Cambridge, 1985), 90, 93.

[6] See *The Documents of Vatican II*, ed. W. M. Abbott, SJ (London, 1966), pp. 48, 234.

Rynne's indications of explicit mention of him are concerned, the catch is very small.

In the fourth session, Cardinal Heenan reminded the Fathers that we should toast conscience before we toast the pope and, in the third, the Archbishop of Baltimore suggested that the *Essay on Development* be mentioned in the Constitution on the Church in the Modern World (*Gaudium et Spes*), although Rynne's summary of his speech gives the impression that the American supposed development to mean progress.[7] In the second session, the *Essay on Development* was mentioned twice; by Cardinal Gracias of Bombay on 7 October 1963, who thought it was the text 'whereby the Council should proceed', and on 28 November by the Rector of the Institut Catholique de Paris Bishop Blanchet, who deemed it 'still most useful after one hundred years'.[8]

It was, however, on the margins of the council, and on the coat-tails of a friend, that Newman came nearest centre-stage. In his address at the beatification of Dominic Barberi on 27 October 1963, Paul VI took occasion to praise the contribution of the English to the well-being of Christianity down the centuries, referring to Newman ('quel singolarissimo spirito') as one who 'traced an itinerary, the most toilsome, but also the greatest, the most meaningful, the most conclusive, that human thought ever traveled during the last century'.[9]

There are two things worth underlining about this slight and anecdotal evidence, which bears out Bishop Butler's impression that Newman's influence on the council was not 'deep or determinative'.[10] First, if we allow that 'the Council was the means by which the Church as a whole was at last brought to accept the demands of historical development',[11] then it is not so surprising

[7] See X. Rynne, *The Fourth Session: The Debates and Decrees of Vatican Council II, September 14 to December 8, 1965* (London, 1966), 36; id., *The Third Session: The Debates and Decrees of Vatican Council II, September 14 to November 21, 1964* (London, 1965), 126.

[8] Quoted from M. Novak, *The Open Church: Vatican II, Act II* (London, 1964), 111; B. and B. Wall, *Thaw at the Vatican: An Account of Session Two of Vatican II* (London, 1964), 140.

[9] See X. Rynne, *Second Session: The Debates and Decrees of Vatican Council II, September 29 to December 4, 1963* (London, 1964), 126; Wall and Wall, *Thaw at the Vatican*, p. 76; Novak, *Open Church*, pp. 113–14. Paul VI was, we remember, a friend of Jean Guitton, whose translation of *On Consulting the Faithful* 'appeared just as the second session opened' (Novak, *Open Church*, p. 164).

[10] Butler, 'Newman and the Second Vatican Council', p. 245.

[11] Coulson and Allchin (eds.), *Rediscovery of Newman*, eds., introd., p. xx.

that it should have been as the author of the *Essay on Development* that mention of Newman was most often made.

In the second place, if 'it is not until the study of theology is seen to require a diversity of approaches and disciplines that Newman is valued in his own right as a theologian',[12] then it may be more fruitful to consider the council's influence on Newman's accessibility to the Catholic imagination than to pursue the quest for traces of Newman's (exceedingly limited) influence upon the council. To 'think historically' is to think not only of different times but also different places, different modes of speech and action; it is to begin to learn to take the conceptual and imaginative *weight* of finitude: to think particularly of particularity, not eschewing the general or the universal but acknowledging that generalization, like all abstraction, follows fact. It is only in recent decades that Catholic theology, at least in its approved and erudite forms, has begun to learn in this sense to think historically, after three centuries of captivity to more 'classicist' and rationalist modes of procedure. It is, accordingly, only in recent decades that Newman has come to seem less like a stranger and more like a doctor of the Church.

From a technical point of view of course, the steady stream of first-rate editions of Newman's published and unpublished writings, appearing since the council, has contributed enormously to raising the standard of Newman studies.[13] It is, happily, no longer true that Newman's only influence 'in any province . . . of British theology . . . [is] that of a certain dated Church of England ecclesiology'.[14] And, thanks to the tireless efforts of (amongst others) Louis Bouyer, Bernard Dupuy, and Maurice Nédoncelle in France, and Johannes Artz, Werner Becker, Heinrich Fries, and Matthias Laros in Germany, the provision of

[12] Coulson and Allchin (eds.), *Rediscovery of Newman*, eds., introd., p.xvii.

[13] The dates speak for themselves: Coulson's edition of *On Consulting the Faithful* first appeared in 1961 (and has recently been reissued); Svaglic's edition of the *Apologia* in 1967, Ker's of *The Idea of a University* in 1976 and of the *Grammar of Assent* in 1985. The *Letters and Diaries* began to appear in 1961, *On the Inspiration of Scripture* in 1967, the *Philosophical Notebook* in 1970, and two volumes of *Theological Papers* in 1976 and 1979 (details in *An Essay in Aid of a Grammar of Assent*, ed. I. T. Ker (Oxford, 1985), pp. ix–x).

[14] H. F. Davis, 'Newman's Influence in England', in Coulson and Allchin (eds.), *Rediscovery of Newman*, p. 216. There is no need to document here the contribution made by (to risk a random sample) J. Cameron, J. Coulson, D. Holmes, J. Kent, D. MacKinnon, D. Pailin, G. Rupp, S. Prickett, R. Strange, and S. Sykes.

good translations and editions has proceeded steadily, during this period, elsewhere in Europe.[15] A glance through the bibliographies in the volumes of *Newman-Studien* (which lay no claim to comprehensiveness or often to accuracy!) is enough to indicate the extraordinary flourishing of Newman studies in the last thirty years—from Luxemburg to Los Angeles and from Cracow to Tokyo.

At which point, some sobriety is in order. That Newman is read widely is, in itself, no evidence that he is read well. Thus, Werner Becker once celebrated the fact that, 'in his great work on dogmatics begun in 1937, but not concluded until 1958, Michael Schmaus dealt with Newman as a classic theologian comparable to the Fathers of the Church'.[16] Yet, some years later, Hans Küng selected Schmaus's *Dogmatik* as 'typical' of the tendency of Catholic theology to go on 'in a good neo-Scholastic way, while of course insights of theological outsiders at the time—such as Romano Guardini and John Henry Newman—were cleverly incorporated into the neo-Scholastic system'. The illustration is pre-conciliar, and the neo-scholastic edifice has collapsed, but the warning is still in order.[17]

More generally, I would hazard the remark that Newman's influence is extraordinarily difficult to chart because that very *closeness* of speech to speaker, of text to thinker, which is a hallmark of his genius ('it was the one man who was in all these

[15] Thus e.g. 1964 saw the appearance of both Gérard's and Lacroix's translations of the *Essay on Development*, while Robillard and Labelle's translation of *The Idea of a University* appeared in 1968. In German, Becker and Laros's edition of *The Idea of a University* was published in 1960, Artz's painstaking edition of the *Essay on Development* in 1969, while in 1962 Artz's translation of the *Grammar of Assent* appeared, on which Werner Becker remarked: 'The German public has so far not yet realised what an exact German edition of the *Essay in Aid of a Grammar of Assent* will mean for the appreciation of Newman' ('Newman's Influence in Germany', in Coulson and Allchin (eds.), *Rediscovery of Newman*, p. 188).

[16] Ibid. 182.

[17] H. Küng, *Does God Exist? An Answer for Today*, trans. E. Quinn (London, 1980), 518, 771. 'Cleverly', however, may polemically impute bad faith where none need be suspected. The problem lies deeper, in the resistance of Newman's rich, allusive prose to conceptual or linguistic translation. It is e.g. a continual source of astonishment that even Newman scholars can miss the irony in the portrait of the 'gentleman' as one whose 'benefits may be considered as parallel to what are called comforts or conveniences in arrangements of a personal nature: like an easy chair or a good fire', and, in so doing, miss the point of Newman's marvellous description of 'the lineaments of the ethical character, which the cultivated intellect will form, apart from religious principle' (*Idea*, pp. 179, 180–1).

things') means that it is *Newman* who makes a difference to those touched by his spell, far more deeply than his arguments or ideas considered in abstraction from the man. It therefore follows that explicit acknowledgement of particular lessons learned[18] is a poor guide to the impact he has had. Thus, for instance, we should not be misled by the lack of references to Newman in Schillebeeckx's two massive volumes on *Jesus* and on *Christ*, or by the mere half-dozen references in twenty volumes of Rahner's *Theological Investigations*, into underestimating how much both men learned from him.[19]

3. THE END OF 'DEVELOPMENT'?

None of the papers delivered to a Roman congress on development of doctrine in 1951 considered Newman's *Essay*.[20] Four years later, in his Birkbeck Lectures (which Cameron still deems 'the best general study of the topic of development of doctrine') Owen Chadwick sought to set the *Essay* 'in the context of intellectual history'. In 1969 Jaroslav Pelikan judged it 'the almost inevitable starting point for an investigation of development of doctrine'. Two years earlier, however, Maurice Wiles had included the *Essay* under the general judgement that 'the debates of the eighteenth and nineteenth centuries must not be expected to

[18] I have in mind e.g. the discussion of the *Lectures on Justification*—'though too little known . . . one of the best treatments of the Catholic theology of justification'—in Hans Küng, *Justification: the Doctrine of Karl Barth and a Catholic Reflection* (London, 1964), 203, and Bernard Lonergan's well-documented acknowlegement of his debt to the *Grammar of Assent*, the 'main parts' of which he read, as a student at Heythrop, 'six times' (B. J. F. Lonergan, *A Second Collection*, ed. W. F. J. Ryan and B. J. Tyrrell (London, 1974), 38).

[19] In 1964 Schillebeeckx lamented the 'remarkable fact that, although Newman is frequently quoted by modern authors, the recent attempts to solve the problem of the development of dogma are not supported by a sufficient knowledge of Newman's ideas' (E. Schillebeeckx, *Revelation and Theology*, trans. N. D. Smith (London, 1967), 75–6). Schillebeeckx's reading of Newman owed much to J. H. Walgrave (esp. to his *Newman the Theologian* (London, 1960)), not always, on the *Essay on Development*, the most reliable of guides: see N. Lash, 'Second Thoughts on Walgrave's "Newman"', *Downside Review*, 87 (1969), 339–50. In Rahner's case, we should remember his long friendship and frequent collaboration with Heinrich Fries. For a rare instance of direct discussion, see K. Rahner, 'Reflections on a New Task for Fundamental Theology', *Theological Investigations*, xvi, trans. D. Morland (London, 1979), 156–66 (essay first published in 1972).

[20] The papers were published in *Gregorianum* in 1952 and 1953. For details, see N. Lash, *Newman on Development: The Search for an Explanation in History* (London, 1975), 153.

throw any great light on the road we have to tread in pursuit of [the study of doctrinal development] at the present time'.[21]

So far, I have mentioned two Anglicans and a Lutheran. But the Catholics were not idle. The Second International Newman Conference, meeting in Luxemburg in 1961, took Newman's writings on development as its theme, and the Dogmatic Constitution *Dei Verbum*, promulgated in 1965, was widely welcomed as liberating from neo-scholastic confinement that cluster of fundamental questions concerning the life of God's Word in history for which 'development' of doctrine had become, in part under Newman's influence, the dominant motif.[22]

By the 1960s, then, 'development' was the buzzword and was widely seen as Newman's gift.[23] John Courtney Murray's observation that 'the question underlying all other questions treated at the Council was doctrinal development'[24] may thus throw light on the myth of 'Newman's council'. And yet, as Paul Misner remarked in 1973, in a most perceptive essay, 'just as the greater part of practising theologians of the Roman Catholic persuasion are rejoicing that the notion of development has at last opened the door to a thoroughgoing confrontation with the historical aspects of Church teaching and tradition, some others, as yet few in number, are expressing doubts about the whole paradigm of development'.[25] Misner especially commended Jean-Pierre Jossua's fine study, 'Immutabilité, progrès ou structurations multiples des doctrines chrétiennes?', the importance of which I also urged in lectures which were (I think) among the first

[21] O. Chadwick, *From Bossuet to Newman: The Idea of Doctrinal Development* (Cambridge, 1957), p. ix; Cameron, 'Newman and the Tractarian Movement', p. 106; J. Pelikan, *Development of Christian Doctrine: Some Historical Prolegomena* (London, 1969), 3; M. Wiles, *The Making of Christian Doctrine* (Cambridge, 1967), 2.

[22] The proceedings of the Luxemburg Conference were published as *Newman-Studien*, vi, ed. H. Fries and W. Becker (Nuremberg, 1964).

[23] Catholic thought in the 1960s had, we might say, caught up with Mark Pattison who in 1878, acknowledging Newman's gift of a copy of the third edition of the *Essay*, wrote: 'Is it not a remarkable thing that you should have first started the idea—and the word—Development, as the key to the history of church doctrine, and since then it has gradually become the dominant idea of all history, biology, physics, and in short has metamorphosed our view of every science, and of all knowledge' (*LD* xxviii. 339; Owen Chadwick quoted the passage in *From Bossuet to Newman*, p. x).

[24] Quoted from E. MacKinnon, '*Humanae Vitae* and Doctrinal Development', *Continuum*, 6 (1968), 269.

[25] P. Misner, 'Note on the Critique of Dogmas', *Theological Studies*, 34 (1973), 690–1.

attempts by a theologian to learn lessons from the debate initiated in 1962 amongst historians and philosophers of science, by Thomas Kuhn's *The Structure of Scientific Revolutions*.[26] And when Maurice Wiles returned to the topic in his 1973 Hulsean Lectures, he commented that, if my reading of Newman's 'notes' or 'tests', as apologetic rather than criteriological in function, were correct, then 'many of the criticisms often raised against the essay would fall to the ground, but only at the cost of drastically reducing the usefulness and applicability of the book's approach outside its own very specific and personal terms of reference'.[27]

Let me spell out a little the story I have tried to tell. Between (about) 1960 and 1975 two rather different issues came to be intertwined. On the one hand, there was the question of Newman's stature and reliability. Before the council, still an occasionally suspect stranger, an outsider to the neo-scholastic world. After the council, its godfather and our guide into the strange territory that now lay before us. On the other hand, there was the question of the most appropriate paradigm, or motif, in terms of which to tackle the twofold task of acknowledging the diversity and contingency of doctrinal history (as of all other history) while yet coherently confessing the maintained identity of the gospel: of human witness borne to God's unswerving faithfulness, unchanging truth.

Newman wrote an essay on development. If we decide that 'development' is not the answer, then, so the story goes, we close his book and place it on the shelf marked 'nineteenth century', for it does not throw great light on the road we have to tread. If 'development' goes, in other words, then Newman (or, at least, his *Essay*) may be pensioned off as not the guide we any longer need. Now, there is no doubt, to my mind, that 'development' has had its day. It is not the solution to a problem, but simply a name for it; a name invented to come between immutability and change, the latter betokening corruption. There is, however, no such space for it to occupy. What we have to learn is that acknowledging the comprehensiveness of change, in doctrine as

[26] J.-P. Jossua, 'Immutabilité, progrès ou structurations multiples des doctrines chrétiennes?', *Revue des Sciences philosophiques et théologiques*, 52 (1968), 173–200; N. Lash, *Change in Focus: A Study of Doctrinal Change and Continuity* (London, 1973).

[27] M. Wiles, *The Remaking of Christian Doctrine* (London, 1974), 6.

elsewhere, does not entail (as earlier generations feared) denying the maintained identity and continuity of Christian tradition, nor does it necessarily make 'modernists' or 'liberal Protestants' of us all. These larger issues, however, are not here my concern. I only wish to register, once again, my own belief that those who lose interest in 'theories of development' may still have much to learn from Newman's *Essay*.

In the first place, there is surely something unreal, and itself suspiciously non-historical, in the suggestion that texts, and the problems which they tackle, can be readily divided into those which speak only to their time and those which are of permanent significance? (Ironically, we show ourselves to be much *more* 'old-fashioned' than Newman was if we are still obsessed by Lessing's little ditch!)

In the second place, if interest in Newman's *Essay* fades with diminishing interest in theories of development, then this is not because it is a nineteenth-century text, whose time is passed, but, on the contrary, because for too long it was taken to embody that very *twentieth*-century thing, an explanatory or theoretical account of how doctrine develops. It is when the *Essay* is properly embedded in the context of its origin (as all good hermeneutical advice would surely encourage us to do) that it is, in fact, most likely to shed light upon our very different problems in what is now a very different world.

Thus, for example (and I offer this example because it touches on a general issue to which I shall return) theologians are slowly learning that they need the skills of the literary critic at least as much as they require those of the metaphysician. Newman's technique, in the *Essay*, of fugal argument and the complex interweaving of metaphorical allusion, still seems to me well suited to the pedagogy required by practical reason in its negotiation of a history in whose bewildering variety and conflictual complexity faith seeks to discern the presence and activity of the mystery of God; far better suited, perhaps, than more abstract and theoretical explanations which always risk giving us illusory clarity and security in a dark, and dangerous, and most confusing world.[28]

[28] For some argument in support of these contentions, see Lash, *Newman on Development*; also id., 'Literature and Theory: Did Newman Have a "Theory" of Development?, in J. D. Bastable (ed.) *Newman and Gladstone: Centennial Essays*

4. EXPLORATION AND ASSENT

'Newman', said Bernard Dupuy, 'reminds theologians that belief, to be living, must always be linked with personal experience. For this reason faith is in some way related to art and to the creative imagination . . . the *Grammar of Assent* is thus the grammar of a personalism that is both required and assumed by contemporary theological investigation'. Assisted by the fact that, 'for the first time in a conciliar text', the Dogmatic Constitution *Dei Verbum* made mention of the role of personal experience in the appropriation of revealed truth, the time (he went on) may now be ripe for the development of such a philosophy 'which might prove the most fruitful of all Newman's work in the Catholic Church'.[29]

This seems an almost prophetic passage, especially in view of the fact that it was as true in 1966 as it had been in 1960 that Newman's 'philosophical originality' was still generally 'underestimated'.[30] Since then, where the relationship between belief and imagination is concerned, one has only to think of the rich vein exlored, in so many studies, by John Coulson (whose admiration for the work of Hans Urs von Balthasar is, in this context, unsurprising).[31] The vitality, today, of hermeneutical currents in philosophy and theology, and the (not unconnected) growth of interest in metaphor, combine to create a climate of philosophical activity singularly congenial, it seems to me, to an

(Dublin, 1978), 161–75. The most powerful illustration that I know of the use to which lessons learned here from Newman might now be put is A. MacIntyre, *Whose Justice? Which Rationality?* (London, 1988), in which MacIntyre acknowledges his 'massive debt' to the *Essay on Development* (see p. 354).

[29] B.-D. Dupuy, 'Newman's Influence in France', in Coulson and Allchin (eds.), *Rediscovery of Newman*, p. 173.

[30] See J. Cameron, 'Newman and Empiricism', *The Night Battle* (London, 1962), 223. For a similar judgement, see *GA*, ed.'s introd., p. lv. And I see no reason to revise the opinion I expressed ten years ago that W. Ward, *Last Lectures* (London, 1918) and M. Nédoncelle, *La Philosophie religieuse de John Henry Newman* (Strasburg, 1946) are rare exceptions to the rule that studies of Newman's philosophy of religion produced before 1950 have little in them of enduring interest: see *An Essay in Aid of a Grammar of Assent* (Notre Dame, 1979), introd. N. Lash, pp. 19–20. Dupuy, in the passage just quoted, noted that his hope for the development of a 'personalist' philosophy under Newman's influence had been expressed by Nédoncelle as early as 1938.

[31] See e.g. J. Coulson, *Newman and the Common Tradition* (Oxford, 1970); id. 'Belief and Imagination', *Downside Review*, 90 (1972), 1–14; id. *Religion and Imagination* (Oxford, 1981).

appreciation of Newman's originality along the lines indicated by Coulson's work.[32]

'Personalism' is not, I think, a term much favoured these days by English-speaking philosophers. In Dupuy's hands, as in Nédoncelle's, however, it had to do with the place of personal experience in the conquest of truth.[33] Surprising as it may seem, fascination with what we may then call the 'personal' and particular, a taste for induction as both matter and method of philosophy, is one of the strands connecting Newman and Hume and, through him and Joseph Butler, to the main tradition of British empiricism.[34] It is from the heirs of that tradition, construed not in terms of a repertory of philosophical doctrines but rather as a 'temper of mind that acknowledges the authority of a vast number of very different sorts of intellectual procedure, of methods of moving from premises to conclusion, as appropriate in one field as they are inappropriate in another', that some of the most interesting and appreciative recent work on Newman has been done.[35]

It is worth pointing out that, quite apart from studies directly engaged in discussion of Newman's texts,[36] his philosophical influence is increasingly apparent either (as with Bernard Lonergan and Basil Mitchell, for example) in the manner of a thinker's

[32] On hermeneutics the literature is now too vast to make selection sensible. On metaphor, see P. Ricœur, *The Rule of Metaphor* (London, 1978); J. M. Soskice, *Metaphor and Religious Language* (Oxford, 1985).

[33] I choose the phrase in order to acknowledge the enduring interest of A. J. Boekraad, *The Personal Conquest of Truth according to J. H. Newman* (Louvain, 1955).

[34] James Cameron has been arguing this case for thirty years. As I mentioned in my introduction to the *Grammar of Assent* (p. 10), failure to appreciate it is a major weakness in Edward Sillem's excellent and indispensable study of Newman's philosophy: *Phil. N.* i. *General Introduction to the Study of Newman's Philosophy*.

[35] D. M. MacKinnon, 'Introduction', *Newman's University Sermons* (London, 1970), 11. In that introduction, MacKinnon too emphasized the influence of Hume and insisted that 'what Newman found in Butler . . . was another manifestation of that same subtle empiricist temper which he found so congenial' (p. 14).

[36] The range of which runs from H. H. Price's 1960 Gifford Lectures, *Belief* (London, 1969), and D. A. Pailin's *The Way to Faith: An Examination of Newman's Grammar of Assent as a Response to the Search for Certainty in Faith* (London, 1969), to M. J. Ferreira, *Doubt and Religious Commitment: The Role of the Will in Newman's Thought* (Oxford, 1980) and G. Casey, *Natural Reason: A Study of the Notions of Inference, Assent, Intuition, and First Principles in the Philosophy of John Henry Cardinal Newman* (New York, 1984). The first three of these, and several other studies, are discussed in Ian Ker's introd. to his edition of the *Grammar*, for some comments on which see my review in *Heythrop Journal*, 28 (1987), 340–2.

treatment of the relationship between knowledge and belief or, more diffusely, in the extent to which the vocabulary of the *Grammar* (for instance, the distinction between notional and real assent) is now common coinage far beyond the small world of Newman studies.

Once again, however, it is important not to exaggerate. Not only do Newman's terms and distinctions tend, the more widely they are used, to be (unsurprisingly) used in ways that would have astonished him, but his philosophical impact is still, for the most part, limited to the territory of philosophy of religion. And this is ironic, in view of his conviction, displayed in the very architecture of the *Grammar*, that 'When faith is said to be a religious principle, it is . . . the things believed, not the act of believing them, which is peculiar to religion'.[37] Moreover, one of the most powerful features of his argument: namely, the analysis of certitude as matter for retrospective acknowledgement rather than prospective achievement, is still often overlooked or misunderstood even by philosophers of religion who take his work quite seriously.

The views expressed in the *Grammar* 'on such matters as the status of propositions, truth, images, are confused and indefensible'.[38] If this is so, then how are we to account for the abiding fascination exercised by this text and for the increasing respect shown to it by philosophers of religion? The answer is, in part, that technical soundness is a poor measure of intellectual power. In his 'feeling for the right direction', says Cameron, Newman 'is superior even to so acute a contemporary as John Stuart Mill. He is close to the Wittgenstein of *On Certainty*'.[39] But there is also a deeper reason, having to do with what Bernard Lonergan called 'the dethronement of speculative intellect or of pure reason'.[40] Dethronement is not murder, but a matter of putting something in its place (not that Lonergan could be suspected of anti-intellectualism or a weakness for irrationality!).

[37] *PS* i. 191.

[38] Cameron, 'Newman and the Tractarian Movement', p. 99.

[39] Ibid. 101.

[40] Lonergan, 'Revolution in Catholic theology', *Second Collection*, p. 236. This essay dates from 1974. Here, as in many other places, Lonergan refers, as pioneers and engineers of this dethronement, to Newman—along with Kierkegaard, Schopenhauer, Dilthey, Blondel, and Paul Ricœur. To which list the names of Heidegger and Wittgenstein should surely be added.

And somewhere near the centre of the Second Vatican Council's achievement was the impetus which it gave to the healing, within Catholicism, of that dissociation of mind and heart, of argument and experience, of structure and feeling, which is our negative legacy from the Enlightenment's achievement.

If the consequences for theology of this dethronement will, as Lonergan supposed, be 'a lot less metaphysics . . . far less talk about proofs, and . . . far more about conversion',[41] then we should not be surprised if Newman's writings on the philosophy of belief enhance their claim to classic status.

The 'temper of mind' of which MacKinnon spoke is one which knows not only the power of disciplined exploration, but also the patient and endlessly painstaking attention to detail, the tolerance of incompleteness, that are required if exploration is to bear fruit. Thus, in the last of the *Oxford University Sermons* as in the first, 'Newman shows himself still the same essentially subtle exploratory intelligence'. And Coulson, who speaks of the 'note of interrogation, so characteristic of his epistolary style', sees 'this note of interrogative subtlety as the true characteristic of Newman's method as a philosopher of religion'.[42] There is far more at issue here, however, than matters of intellectual style. We are, once again, near the centre of the conciliar vision: a vision of a pilgrim people. Pilgrims are people in quest, explorers, moving ever into the unknown. In order to develop this hint, however, we now need to change the subject, and to speak of matters which fall under Cameron's third head of Newman's legacy: the theologian of grace.

5. LIBERALISM AND GRACE

Where is Newman to be located in relation to those 'two broadly contrasting wings of opinion and aim' which, according to Christopher Butler, existed at the time of the Second Vatican Council, as of the First?[43] In this section, I propose to treat this question from the standpoint of the ethos, spirituality, or style

[41] Ibid. 237.

[42] MacKinnon, 'Introduction', *Newman's University Sermons*, p. 22; Coulson, *Religion and Imagination*, p. 50.

[43] Butler, 'Newman and the Second Vatican Council', in Coulson and Allchin (eds.), *Rediscovery of Newman* p. 245.

of Newman as 'theologian of Grace'. Then, in the next section, I shall consider the same question from the standpoint of his doctrine of the Church.

Stephen Dessain, Newman's most tireless and erudite archivist, died in 1976, a week before he was due to preach a retreat to the Oratory of France. In the materials for that retreat, he left us in no doubt as to his opinion on the question I have raised:

> at the Second Vatican Council the tides of clericalism, over-centralisation, creeping infallibility, narrow unhistorical theology and exaggerated mariology were thrown back, while the things Newman stood for were brought forward—freedom, the supremacy of conscience, the Church as a communion, a return to Scripture and the fathers, the rightful place of the laity, work for unity, and all the efforts to meet the needs of the age, and for the Church to take its place in the modern world. Any disarray or confusion there may now be in the Church is the measure of how necessary this renewal was.[44]

At Vatican II, the standard labels for the two wings were 'conservative' and 'progressive'. It would be difficult to find a less appropriate description for Newman than 'progressive'! Moreover, those called 'conservative' in our time, as also their predecessors at Vatican I, strive energetically to conserve their power and present intellectual possessions, both of which (as Newman knew) are, in fact, of very recent origin. Newman was, undoubtedly, a most conservative man, but to describe him so, at present, would be to associate him with attitudes and policies which he deplored.

If, in order to avoid misunderstanding, we were to try the terminology of Newman's own day, we would soon find ourselves in a similar dilemma. 'The fact is', says Owen Chadwick, that 'what Newman denounced as liberalism, no one else regarded as liberalism. And this led to misunderstanding. Men supposed that Newman was illiberal because he kept saying so'.[45] Nicely said but not, I think, *quite* true: it exaggerates, by implication, the homogeneity of nineteenth-century uses of the concept of 'liberalism'. Nevertheless, there was, I think, some idiosyncracy in Newman's use of the concept, even if it was not so marked as to make his meaning quite unclear. Then, as today, there were

[44] C. S. Dessain, *Newman's Spiritual Themes* (Dublin, 1977), p. 30.

[45] O. Chadwick, *Newman* (Oxford, 1983), 74.

strong currents of religious liberalism which operated on the assumption that religious symbols were not only human products but also our property and plaything, to be used, or altered, or discarded, according to our tastes and preferences. And against *this* liberalism, which knows nothing of the otherness of God or of obedience to his will (or, if it does, supposes these things to cramp and thwart our freedom) Newman campaigned quite tirelessly.

'That truth and falsehood in religion are but matter of opinion; that one doctrine is as good as another . . . that it is enough if we sincerely hold what we profess . . . that we may take up and lay down opinions at pleasure . . . that we may safely trust to ourselves in matters of Faith, and need no other guide'; these are the elements of the liberalism which he contested. Against it, he set what he called 'the dogmatical principle, which has strength': 'That there is a truth then; that there is one truth . . . that the mind is below truth, not above it, and is bound, not to descant upon it, but to venerate it', and so on.[46] The theme of these passages is considered elsewhere in this volume. Concerning them, there are just two points that I wish to make. The first is that 'dogmatism', in Newman's hands (or what might otherwise be thought of as religious 'realism') is the formal expression of that 'intense awareness of God and the "unseen world"',[47] that overriding conviction of the presence and prevenience of God's grace, which is the heart and centre of Newman's religion. But the second point would be that, just because this was the religious basis of his antipathy to liberalism, its trustfulness enabled him to entertain in tranquillity all manner of complexity, uncertainty, diversity, and darkness.

That 'wing' of Catholicism now usually called 'conservative' was the target of Lonergan's invective against 'classicism'.[48] But

[46] *Dev.*, pp. 357–8.

[47] H. Graef, *God and Myself: The Spirituality of John Henry Newman* (London, 1967), 182.

[48] Lonergan, who regarded 'classicism' as 'never more than the shabby shell of Catholicism', described it as follows: 'On classicist assumptions, there is just one culture. That one culture is not attained by the simple faithful, the people, the natives, the barbarians. None the less, career is always open to talent. One enters upon such a career by diligent study of the ancient Latin and Greek authors. One pursues such a career by learning scholastic philosophy and theology. One aims at high office by becoming proficient in canon law. One succeeds by winning the approbation and favor of the right personages. Within this set-up the unity of faith is

classicism, the ideology of clericalism, is religiously neurotic, seeking *self*-assurance. It is liberalism's antithesis, rather than its cure. And this, especially as a result of his experience as a Catholic, Newman came to know.

6. EMPIRES AND CONSTITUTIONS

There are two strands or currents in what we might call Newman's ecclesial polity. 'As an old Tory, he saw nothing wrong in personal and societal relations of the feudal type, the essence of which is loyalty.' It is, therefore, not surprising that there came 'flooding out' in his writings, especially at the height of Tractarian resistance to Erastianism, what Misner calls an 'imperial image of the Church'.[49]

'Given Newman's temperament and background, it was probably necessary that the malfunction of the ecclesiastical machinery be keenly felt, before he would critically deal with it.'[50] But deal with it he eventually did, and his letters, especially during the period before and after Vatican I, document with a wealth of always fascinating and sometimes surprising detail the development in his thinking of an alternative view of the Church in less romantic and more constitutional terms: that is, as fundamentally a system of checks and balances.[51]

Nevertheless, according to Misner, the imperial vision remained to the end 'a factor in his ecclesiology, the more disconcerting

a matter of everyone subscribing to the correct formulae' (B. J. F. Lonergan, *Method in Theology* (London, 1972), 326–7). See N. Lash, 'Catholic Theology and the Crisis of Classicism', *Ratzinger on the Faith: A Response*, (*New Blackfriars*, 66; 1985), 279–87.

[49] P. Misner, *Papacy and Development: Newman and the Primacy of the Pope* (Leiden, 1976), 141, 51, 57.

[50] Ibid. 141.

[51] At a time when Catholics are becoming newly conscious not only of the need for checks and balances in the ecclesial system but also (as Vatican II helped to demonstrate) of their availability in the Catholic tradition, it is not surprising that so much attention should now be paid to that great Preface to the third edition (1877) of the *Via Media* (pp. xv–xciv). See e.g. R. Bergeron, *Les Abus de l'Église d'après Newman* (Tournai, 1971), a study prepared under Nédoncelle's guidance; Coulson, *Newman and the Common Tradition*; J. Gaffney, 'Newman's Criticism of the Church: Lessons and Object Lessons', *Heythrop Journal*, 29 (1988), 1–20; Lash, 'Life, Language and Organization: Aspects of the Theological Ministry', *Theology on Dover Beach* (London, 1979), 89–108; S. W. Sykes, *The Identity of Christianity* (London, 1984).

because it is presupposed rather than defended'.[52] If he is right in this (and, though I would take issue on some points of detail, I find the account on the whole persuasive), what are we to make of this apparently quite serious inconsistency in Newman's thought? There are, I suggest, three possible answers. First, one could simply accept it as inconsistency, as unresolved dilemma in his mind: not even Newman thought all things clearly through! Secondly, one could see here some evidence for the kind of temperamental weakness, exacerbated by the pathologies of ultramontane Catholicism, which Egner made the substance of his study.[53] But, thirdly, without discarding the elements of truth in either of these suggestions, it could be said that, in the tension between his two visions of the Church, Newman embodied, in one exceptionally intelligent and sensitive individual, strains running so deep as almost to be *constitutive* of Catholicism in his time, and our own.

But this is not to say that we can doubt where he would now have thought it proper to place the emphasis. He would not, I think, have been unsympathetic to that impatience with self-indulgence and indiscipline which characterizes the present pope. Newman did, after all, write in 1869: 'in the present state of the world, the Catholic body may require to be like an army in the field, under strict and immediate discipline'.[54] But is there not an uncomfortably contemporary ring to the remark (made in 1861): 'I cannot help feeling that, in high circles, the Church is sometimes looked upon as if made up of the hierarchy and the poor, and that the educated portion, men and women, are viewed as a difficulty, an incumbrance, as the seat and source of heresy; as almost alien to the Catholic body, whom it would be a great gain, if possible, to annihilate'?[55]

More generally, the invention of air travel and television, making possible a much more absolute short-circuiting of intermediate instances and institutions than that against which he campaigned so tirelessly in his letters, gives to what Newman had to say about the necessity of checks and balances fresh and

[52] Misner, *Papacy and Development*, p. 57.

[53] See G. Egner, *Apologia pro Charles Kingsley* (London, 1969). Egner describes the *Apologia* as, in part, 'a symptom of the damage done to Newman by the system under which he had to work' (p. 197).

[54] *LD* xxiv. 325.

[55] *TP* i. 35.

compelling urgency. Even when all allowance has been made for the bleakness of his mood in the autumn of 1870, it is still startling to find one so loyal to the papacy saying: 'We have come to a climax of tyranny. It is not good for a Pope to live 20 years. It is anomaly and bears no good fruit; he becomes a god, has no one to contradict him'.[56]

7. TWILIGHT

The exuberance, the sense of spring, of fresh things in the air, with which both Butler and Dessain celebrated the achievement of Vatican II, seems strangely dated now. The tide has turned. And if, in the years immediately following the council, the reforming energies which it unleashed could be seen as vindication of so much that Newman stood for, his significance today will be a little different.

At least where Western society is concerned, we live, ecclesiastically and politically, in twilight times. Not that this would have come as much of a surprise to Newman, who perceived, as deeply as did Nietzsche, the comprehensive *cultural* significance of what Buber called the 'eclipse' of God. But Newman and Buber knew, as Nietzsche, I rather think, did not, that there is no depth of darkness which affords licence for despair.[57]

Newman had little direct influence on what took place at Vatican II. He is now both much more widely and, on the whole, much better read. And this is just as well, for we have need of him.

[56] *LD* xxv. 231.

[57] On Newman and Nietzsche, see M. J. Buckley, *At the Origins of Modern Atheism* (New Haven, Conn., 1987), 28–9; see also C. Geffré and J.-P. Jossua (eds.), *Nietzsche and Christianity* (*Concilium*, 145; 1981); and on Buber see N. Lash, *Easter in Ordinary: Reflections on Human Experience and the Knowledge of God* (Charlottesville, Va., and London, 1988), 199–218.

Index